W9-ACX-037

Twentieth-Century Views of Music History

Twentieth-Century Views
of Music History

Edited by
WILLIAM HAYS

With an Introduction by
RICHARD F. FRENCH

CHARLES SCRIBNER'S SONS / *New York*

√ ML
55
.H29

Copyright © 1972 Charles Scribner's Sons
"The Why and How of Our New Music"
copyright © 1972 Kurt Stone
"Electronic Music: Synthesizers and Computers"
copyright © 1972 Gerald Wakefield.

This book published simultaneously in the
United States of America and in Canada —
Copyright under the Berne Convention

All rights reserved. No part of this book
may be reproduced in any form without the
permission of Charles Scribner's Sons.

1 3 5 7 9 11 13 15 17 19 B/C 20 18 16 14 12 10 8 6 4 2

Printed in the United States of America
Library of Congress Catalog Card Number 77-76822
ISBN 0-684-15149-9

Contents

Contents

Preface

THE contents of this anthology have been chosen to provide a collection of modern writings covering some of the major points in the development of Western art music from medieval to modern times, and at the same time giving variety in style and approach among the individual contributions. Most of the articles first appeared elsewhere and are reprinted here. Two, however, "The Why and How of Our New Music" by Kurt Stone and "Electronic Music: Synthesizers and Computers" by Gerald Warfield, have been commissioned especially for this volume and appear here in print for the first time, along with Mr. Warfield's notes on Milton Babbitt's important article on serial music. Sources for the reprinted articles range from reference works to periodicals and papers delivered at music congresses, from general works to those devoted exclusively to music, and include some works long out of print and almost unobtainable — all hopefully making the reader aware of the great variety of sources containing not only scholarly but frequently charming writing about music.

An attempt has been made to provide material comprehensible to those unfamiliar with the technical language of music. Those readers unfamiliar with some of the musical terminology that does appear should consult one of the standard musical dictionaries such as the *Harvard Dictionary of Music*, 2nd ed. (1969), or the *Harvard Brief Dictionary of Music* (1960), the latter written particularly for the non-specialist.

Insofar as possible the material is arranged in chronological order. Some selections, however, such as the one on oratorio, cover lengthy periods of history and cut across the chronological limits normally given to style periods. Such selections have been placed according to the earlier dates in their subject matter.

The introductions attempt to serve sometimes one, sometimes several purposes. Some seek to place the succeeding entry within its historical

*Available in paperback edition.

context; others to provide information the editor thought helpful for better understanding of the subject; still others to underline the author's point (although hopefully not overshadowing him). The bibliographies have been prepared by the editor to serve as suggestions to the reader for pursuing additional, more detailed, and sometimes differing treatments of each subject. These suggestions are, of course, highly selective and make no pretense at being definitive; with few exceptions they are limited to items either written in English or available in English translation. Titles preceded by an asterisk are available in a paperback edition.

It has been said that before talking about music, one should hear some. One might even improve on this by adding, "better still, one should perform some." In any case the point is an excellent one; reading is of little value if the reader has never heard, or possibly performed, the music about which he is reading. For those who have performance abilities the bibliographies provide minimal information about editions of music pertinent to the subject of each selection. Those unable to perform and to whom live performance is unavailable must, of course, rely on recordings; but because of the proliferation of recorded music since the invention of the long-playing record, any discography prepared by the editor would very likely be out-of-date before it reached the reader. Readers desiring information about available recordings should consult a current issue of the *Schwann Tape and Record Guide,* issued monthly and available at most record shops.

An anthology such as this is never the work of one person. Many have assisted directly and indirectly in the preparation of this volume and their help is gratefully acknowledged: librarians who have aided in bibliographical matters; students who have been assigned potential selections and who have chosen some and rejected others; friends who have gone through earlier drafts of the material and made suggestions for improvement; and especially Professor Richard F. French of Union Theological Seminary, and Mr. Kurt Stone and Mrs. Elsie Kearns of Scribners, whose kind criticism, patient assistance, and valuable contributions have helped make this anthology possible.

WILLIAM HAYS

Introduction

RICHARD F. FRENCH

WORDS about music have a limited but distinctive usefulness. This collection of essays provides an unusual view of historical matters deemed interesting and important to leading musicians of our modern era. It brings together musicians who have written in quite different decades of this century, who have worked in different countries under differing circumstances and traditions, composers and scholars, listeners and critics and performers, all of whom have felt impelled to give some part of their attention to verbal statements about an art which, as you will see from reading the essays, has had over the centuries a very ambivalent relationship to words. Music owes, and recognizes that it owes, a great debt to words. It was the words of the liturgy in the early Middle Ages that sustained the Gregorian chant and provided the impetus for new chant composition; two great and widely known musical forms, the madrigal and the opera, are inconceivable without words; it is through words that the great polemicists of music history—Martin Luther and Richard Wagner, for instance—have sought to propagandize their views. But words have never quite succeeded in seducing music; she has always managed to wriggle herself free, and indeed some of her finest progeny—the instrumental sonata, symphony, and concerto, to name three—are, with respect to words, immaculately conceived.

But to say that words have not succeeded is not to say that they have not tried. Indeed they continue to try, and one of the ironies of the present volume is that whereas most of it has been selected from the writings of scholars, critics, and teachers, the final portion of it, dealing with music composed largely since the Second World War, is mostly made up of essays written by composers. Do not reach too quickly for conclusions. The best composers are not necessarily the best qualified or most articulate advocates or critics (though they may be, and they may rank with the best performers and scholars as well). It is wiser to infer that even composers recognize the usefulness of words: words can never be substitutes for the immediate experience of music, but they do have an important function as adjuncts to music and to musical life. Words are not music, but through them we may approach music and try to reach out to touch its essential nature.

There are many things, of course, that the essays in this volume cannot do. Most importantly, for instance, they cannot teach you how to play a guitar, how to sing a madrigal, or how to know what key a piece is in. They are not designed to do these things, and they could not do them even if they were so designed. Playing a musical instrument (or making any musical activity) has one important thing in common with carpentry and baseball: it has to be learned by practice, by doing it — going through the physical motions — under the tutelage of a master. If you want to learn to sing, join a chorus and learn to sing by singing in the chorus. If you want to learn to play the guitar, buy a guitar and learn to play it by playing it. In either case you won't get very far by yourself, but you won't get anywhere at all if you confine yourself to watching, listening, or reading instruction books.

Following this line of thought one step further, we come upon two interesting possibilities, one of which is the obverse of the other. Let me put them in the form of questions: (1) if you could play the piano as well as Van Cliburn, wouldn't you know everything you needed to know about music? (2) If you can't play the piano as well as Van Cliburn, is there any value in trying to know anything about music at all? Or, to put them in a slightly different way: (1) if you can make music, does not this activity suffice for your musical understanding? (2) If you cannot make music, can you through other means — through reading about music, for instance — come to know anything of value about it?

The answers to these questions, and the arguments leading to the answers, could serve as a basis for the history of music in higher education in the United States during the first seven decades of the twentieth century. Music-making is the elemental musical experience, for which there is no conceivable surrogate. Any musical performer, therefore — amateur or professional, beginner or advanced — lives an experience that is unique; he knows something about music through making it that no other approach can provide and that no verbal enthusiasm can even faintly convey, let alone equal. But just as sex is not all of love, neither is music-making all of music. In Cliburn's case, the instrument which is the vehicle for his musical personality, the pianoforte, was perfected in its present form scarcely a hundred years ago, and there is hardly any music composed for it that is more than two centuries old. Piano music, furthermore, is only a small fragment of all the music composed since the middle of the eighteenth century, even if one were to include all the music written for piano and voice or piano and another instrument or instruments. Were Cliburn to confine himself to playing the music composed for his solo instrument, he would box himself into performing a small number of pieces written, as music history goes, only during a recent and very short span of time.

It is true, as I have said, that by being able to play these pieces, a pianist (or any performer) knows something about music-making that he cannot learn by any other means. But such a performer is still fatally undernourished. The sonority of the piano as we know it, the depth, brilliance, and glitter of its sound, can only be produced by strings stretched very tightly over a resonant frame, a frame whose resonating material — wood — cannot by itself bear the strain of the tension needed to produce such sonority; hence the development of the piano was intimately tied to nineteenth-century developments in metallurgy that produced a metal skeleton light enough and strong enough to be incorporated into the piano frame. Similarly, the popularity of piano music in the nineteenth century was due in important measure to the wide distribution of such instruments from a relatively small number of manufacturers; such manufacture and distribution was unthinkable before the development of roads, canals, and railroads, which not only made possible the transportation of the instruments but encouraged the development of related international standards — of pitch measurement, for instance, without which the wide use of the piano with other instruments in the orchestra would have been impossible. Musicians did not produce iron and steel or build railroads, but musicians who remain ignorant of their debt to such developments — and thus remain ignorant of the qualities of the instrument they use and love — are condemned to cultural starvation.

I have said that this book will not teach you to play an instrument. (I hope it may now impel you to try, but for that you will have to look elsewhere.) Neither will it teach you how to read musical notation, which can be read by musicians, of course, as easily and fluently as you are able to read these pages. If you could not read them, you would be technically classified as illiterate (that is, unlettered); and if you cannot read music, you are (in a corresponding sense) musically illiterate. Though there is a lot of confusion nowadays about its meaning and definition, we have been accustomed to think of the overcoming of illiteracy (however defined) as a valid educational objective, and the attainment of literacy (however measured) as evidence of superior intelligence. Put simply, we believe that a person who can read and write knows more than one who can't. A simple proposition like this is hazy but deceptive. Literacy is not necessarily an index of intelligence, private or public, but it does have two quite practical advantages. First, it enables a person to develop his intelligence without having to depend on information obtained aurally from other people (which makes it necessary for him to be within earshot of such people); and second, it opens up to him the whole field of information learned and disseminated by other people through reading and writing. This is not the whole of knowledge, by any means, but it is a very respectable and very useful portion of it. The ability to read music, for instance, means that a musician can read a piece of music silently or play it by himself, without having to hear it performed or to learn it by rote. He is thus freed, liberated from dependence on the presence and actions of other people. If he can read words about music as well, he can feed his curiosity even faster and can be to a very much greater degree the master of his own development.

Thus, though this book cannot teach you how to read musical notation, it may impel you to learn, to try to become musically literate. The prolongation of any kind of illiteracy today, voluntary or involuntary, is quite clearly a prolongation of servitude, a barrier to freedom. It is also, in the field of music, a barrier to wisdom. Musical invention—the writing of melodies and the working up of them into longer musical pieces—has for the last thousand years been conditioned by the ways in which music could be written down to be read and sung or played by other people. To see the history of music merely as the record of man's musical imagination, as the tracings of free flights of musical fancy, is to indulge in rhetoric at the expense of truth. At every point, and never more critically than at this present moment, musical imagination and invention have been constrained by the severe and imperious demands of musical notation. A musical idea is not only audible; it must be legible as well.

The essays in this book, then, have a limited usefulness, as I have tried to demonstrate. But if we now see more clearly what they cannot do, that leads us inexorably toward what they can do, to their distinctive worth. That usefulness, as I see it, lies over and beyond the scope of the individual topics, into that area where the total impression of the essays as a group invites us to contemplate the nature of our musical artifacts, the uses of our past, and their relation to us now.

All the essays in this book are retrospective, that is, they focus their attention on some aspect of the music of the past thousand years, music which has already been composed and which thus exists in some form. Had it not been for the invention and development of musical notation, of some means of making and preserving a graphic record of aural phenomena, we should have no music as we now know it. Our entire musical heritage has survived by virtue of its notation, that small set of simple symbols by which men have been able to conceive, set down, and transmit to each other and to posterity the products of their musical imaginations. Musicians tend to take the existence of this notation very much for granted, but it has for our music a significance and importance comparable to that of the Roman alphabet for our spoken and written languages and of the Arabic numeral for the language of mathematics. We think of music as an aural art, an art of sound, but only a tiny portion of all the music we have is at any time in an active state, sounding, setting air waves in motion. All the rest of it is inert, without life, but not therefore irrecoverable—as it would be without a system of musical notation. Notation provides the data of a memory bank for our music, a storage system for the musical heritage of the past which by some miracle lends itself to retrieval and resurrection, just as the Roman alphabet miraculously enables us to retrieve the wisdom of Augustine and the humor of Molière, and the Arabic numeral to read the thoughts of Isaac Newton and Albert Einstein. Most of the time—most of the time for all time—music has existed not as active sound but as inert notation. Thus the basic substance of our musical legacy is graphic, not aural; and our music is in a very fundamental sense a graphic, not an aural, art.

This may seem odd to you, but knowing it does help to explain a lot of musical activity that might otherwise appear nonsensical and irrational. To a musician, for instance, a piece of music notated six hundred years ago is just as intriguing as one notated two months ago. It is just as natural for him to be interested in the former as in the latter piece; anything else, indeed, would be a perversion of his musical curiosity. It may also seem strange to you that the essays in this book cover a period of as much as a thousand years; but if we had adequate musical records stretching back one or two thousand years earlier, and if we could read them, the scope of this book would necessarily be that much larger.

The written aspect of music also helps to explain the character of musical scholarship—why it exists, why it must necessarily foster disagreements, but why it continues from discovery to discovery. Musical scholarship—the systematic investigation of musical matters—exists because the music exists, first of all, and because the musical curiosities of some people are disposed to be satisfied not merely by performing and listening to pieces, but by deciphering, analyzing, and comparing them with one another. To musical scholars, a discovery of musical archives is just as exciting as the unearthing of the Dead Sea Scrolls was to Biblical scholars or as the capture and return of moon rocks has been to geologists. Note that no one has hurled the epithets of "antiquarianism" and "irrelevance" at geologists of the moon, who are now privileged to make a study of objects far older than any human artifacts we now know. Note also that though our understanding of the earth may be radically altered by geological investigation, and our knowledge of the early history of the Judeo-Christian era widened or even contradicted by the evidence of the Dead Sea Scrolls, we feel instinctively in both cases that by learning about our past in the present we are learning something about ourselves. The excitement of musical scholarship is exactly comparable: new discoveries lead to the confirmation or destruction of currently held views, views that, reconfirmed or reconstituted, enrich our common knowledge. Every essay in this book is characterized by its author's desire to test and assimilate the significance of new musical or historical evidence, to set forth the facts as they are newly comprehended, regardless of conflict with conventional wisdom. No fortress is secure, no enclave safe; indeed the more conventional the wisdom, or monumental the musical personality, the more engagingly it lends itself to scholarly re-examination.

Thus there must be conflicts and contradictions: the best evidence of lively scholarship is that its practitioners often disagree. But if this collection is a record of current dissatisfactions and disagreements, it is also something more. It is also a record of a tradition and of an attitude toward tradition, and it is to these that I want finally to call attention.

We have all read and heard a great deal about things "Western"— Western Civilization, Western Culture, Western Art. One of the most comprehensive and widely used textbooks on the history of music is Donald Grout's *"A History of Western Music,"* which summarizes the important facts about the development of our music (many of which were originally announced as discoveries in essays like these) and arranges them into a chronological narrative. But does the adjective "Western" mean anything? Does the notion, vague or precise, that attaches to its use have any substance, or is it merely a convenient way of being able to avoid talking about lots of other music? The essays in this book, I think, help to confirm the authenticity of the view that the study of things Western refers not just to an artifical separation of one package of conveniently related ideas from all the rest, but to a stream of cultural development whose traditions have been handed down by contact from generation to generation from at least the beginning of the Christian era to the present time. The fact that we are Western has no necessary link to virtue. But how we think and play, our moral sensitivities, and our views of ourselves, others, the world, and the universe are the end products of contacts between people that began more than two thousand years ago in the eastern Mediterranean, spread gradually northwestward into Italy, Southern France, and Spain, up through Central and Western Europe to the British Isles and Scandinavia, and then leaped across the Atlantic Ocean to North and South America. This is not to say that we have not made contactwith people from other traditions or that our culture has been unaffected by cultural developments outside our own (consider the Arabic numeral), but it does mean that the people who have lived and died throughout this geo-chronology have shared more with one another and learned more from one another than they have shared with or learned from cultures outside their own.

Western music forms a part of this geo-chronology as typical and as important as Western art, science, literature, or politics. By this fact it is also distinctively different from the musics of other cultures—not better or worse, but different. Ethnomusicology, for instance, which is the name we now give in the West to the study of musics other than our own, has taught us a lot in the last few decades about cultural traditions often coinciding chronologically and geographically with ours but remaining nonetheless apart. *The Bay Psalm Book,* whether we like it or not, belongs to the tradition of Western music in a sense in which the music of the American Indian does not; jazz and rock are ours, contemporary Chinese music is not. The bulk of these essays, for instance, deals with music composed in a very small area of Western Europe, and it is not until the end of the book, where our twentieth-century music is treated, that American music and American musicians make their appearance. This arrangement reflects a heretofore conventional view of the history and significance of musical development in the United States that is currently being challenged and revised, but it is less untruthful than an equally parochial American view that inflates American values by minimizing or denying the valuable contact with the European tradition made by a large number of important American composers in the early twentieth century. Charles Ives has become as much of our Western music as Arnold Schönberg, but they did not paddle down the same musical current together.

They do, however, with all their colleagues of the West, living and dead, typify Western culture in yet another way. No one can read these essays without coming away with the very strong and consistent impression that a fundamental characteristic of our culture is that it has always looked to the record of its own experience as a guide to the future. What it has known of the record, of course, has varied from generation to generation, and how it has used what it has known as a guide toward its ends has been largely unpredictable, so that the reading of our history is much less exciting for the patterns it reveals than for its startling and everlasting surprises. But at every moment in this history, including our own, the study of the past has been a contemporary activity, made relevant to its own time in its own way. Indeed, were it not for the continuingly vital awareness of the past, our future would be unimaginable.

1

ALL too frequently the student beginning the study of music history approaches his subject with the mistaken idea that, apart from a few yet undiscovered facts, the recording and interpretation of the history of the music of the past has been accomplished. Thus, all that remains for the student to do is to find a work which covers the subject adequately and digest it; then he may turn his attention to other things. That such is not the case may be seen from the following selection, which gives a brief and necessarily selective history of music histories. Views of music history, including the division of the subject into period headings, have varied considerably in the past and will continue to do so, because a definitive view of music history is impossible. One must approach the subject ready to do his own thinking, solve his own puzzles, have some of his own opinions, and make his own mistakes. Only then will he begin to have a valid concept of what constitutes the history of music.

Sir Jack Allan Westrup is editor of *Music and Letters* and was, until his recent retirement, Heather Professor of Music at Oxford University. His writings include *An Introduction to Musical History* (London, Hutchinson & Co., 1955) and contributions to *Grove's Dictionary of Music and Musicians, The New Oxford History of Music, Die Musik in Geschichte und Gegenwart, Music and Letters, The Musical Quarterly,* and others.

The Historians and the Periods

JACK ALLAN WESTRUP

So long as musicians were primarily interested in the music of their own time there was no question of writing a history of the art. The English attitude in the late sixteenth century can be seen very clearly in the pages of Thomas Morley, who regards most music before his time as old-fashioned or impossibly remote. On the Continent, however, there were signs of an awakening interest in the music of past ages. Speculation about Greek music was one of the strongest factors which went to the creation of the first operas about 1600; and significantly enough it was in 1600 that Sethus Calvisius (Seth Kallwitz), cantor of St. Thomas's, Leipzig, included in his *Exercitationes Musicae* a substantial outline of the history of music, entitled *De origine et progressu musices*. The purpose of this section was to show how music, through the devoted labours of the great men of the past, had "progressed" up to the end of the sixteenth century; but in developing this point of view the author did not hesitate to express his admiration for the earlier masters of the century, such as Josquin des Prés, Clemens non Papa and Lassus. The whole section might be described as a historical essay rather than history, and the same is true of the historical discussion to be found in Praetorius's *Syntagma Musicum*.

It was not until the end of the seventeenth century that a serious attempt was made to write an independent history of music. Wolfgang Caspar Printz's *Historische Beschreibung der edlen Sing- und Klingkunst* appeared in Dresden in 1690. Five years later an Italian, Giovanni Andrea Angelini Bontempi, published at Perugia his *Historia musica*. This was followed in 1715 by a French work, the *Histoire de la musique, et de ses effets depuis son origine*, compiled by the Abbé Bourdelot and completed by his nephews Pierre and Jacques Bonnet. It is characteristic of the early histories that they devote much attention to speculation about the

FROM Jack Allan Westrup, *An Introduction to Musical History* (London, Hutchinson & Co., 1955), pp. 49–64. Reprinted by permission of The Hutchinson Publishing Group, Ltd.

origins of music, regardless of the fact that this is a subject about which no certain information is possible. Greek mythology and the Bible are both regarded as sources which call for serious discussion. This old-fashioned and basically unscientific attitude is still to be found in Padre Martini's *Storia della musica,* which began to appear in 1757: the first volume deals systematically with successive periods of Biblical history, beginning with "Music from the Creation of Adam to the Flood," continuing with "Music from the Flood to the Birth of Moses," and eventually reaching the time from the reign of King Solomon to the destruction and rebuilding of the temple.

Though these speculations survived till the end of the eighteenth century and even later, there was also a growing realization that history depends on evidence and that no adequate account of the music of the past can be attempted without extensive research. Martin Gerbert's *De cantu et musica sacra* (1774)—a history of church music—is the work of a man who was assiduous in collecting materials, and who ten years later published the first collection of medieval treatises. But the most substantial and elaborate histories of music in the late eighteenth century were the work of Englishmen. Sir John Hawkin's *General History of the Science and Practice of Music,* in four volumes, appeared in 1776.[1] In the same year Charles Burney published the first volume of his *General History of Music,* which was finally completed by the issue of the fourth volume in 1789.[2] Comparison between the two works is inevitable, and was freely made at the time. The result is strongly in Burney's favour. There is no doubt that in his later volumes he utilized Hawkin's researches; but the conception of the work as a whole is original, and much of the illustrative material had been collected by himself during his travels on the Continent. Hawkins, however much he may have enjoyed music, was not a musician. The principal value of his work lies in the industry it displays. An enormous amount of material is presented to the reader: there are substantial translations from theoretical works, many complete musical examples, extracts from original documents, letters and so on. But all this is thrown together without any discrimination or any fear of irrelevance. Chronological treatment is constantly abandoned in the desire to explore some side issue, and even with an index the reader is hard put to it to construct a coherent narrative from what is in fact a well-intentioned jumble. Unfortunately the nineteenth-century reprint made it available to a much wider circle, and it was too often accepted as an authority without any reasonable justification. Burney's work is very different. It is by modern standards ill-balanced, spending far too much time on the ancient world and devoting a dis-

---

[1] A second edition, in two volumes, was published in 1875.

[2] A second edition, in two volumes, edited by Frank Mercer, was published in 1935.

11

proportionate amount of space to eighteenth-century opera. But the arrangement is clear and logical, the style is distinguished, and throughout the reader is aware that he is following in the steps of someone to whom music was a living art. Modern critics have sometimes taken Burney to task for his prejudices, but the censure is misapplied: a historian without prejudices would make very dull reading, and Burney's are sufficiently obvious to be innocent. Though he was quite ready to believe that eighteenth-century music was a model of correctness and purity, he was not wholly blind to the merits of older music. He did much to revive interest in the music of Josquin des Prés and drew attention to the work of Robert White 150 years before the publication of *Tudor Church Music*.

The industry shown by eighteenth-century authors in collecting materials made it increasingly obvious that the writing of musical history was a gigantic undertaking. It is not surprising that more than one writer since that time has failed to complete a projected work. Forkel, the first biographer of Bach, published an *Allgemeine Geschichte der Musik* in two volumes (1788-1801) which did not get beyond the sixteenth century. A similar fate attended the *Geschichte der Musik* by August Wilhelm Ambros, which first began to appear in 1862. When he died in 1876 only three volumes had been published, and the account of the sixteenth century was still incomplete. A fourth volume, prepared from his notes and dealing with Palestrina and his Roman contemporaries, was published posthumously, and this was later supplemented by a fifth volume consisting of musical examples from the fifteenth and sixteenth centuries which Ambros himself had collected. Incomplete as it is, Ambros's history is still a work of unusual distinction, based on the most thorough research into original sources and reflecting the wide culture of its author. Ambros's career answers effectively the popular view that musicologists are not musicians, since he was accomplished both as a pianist and as a composer; and it also exhibits a triumph of tenacity of purpose over obstacles, since for a considerable part of his life he was employed in the Austrian Civil Service and could devote only his leisure to research.

The nineteenth century saw the production of a large number of histories of music, as well as dictionaries and biographies. It was a time when writers were acutely conscious of the significance of great men and tended to see the history of music as a progress from one eminence to another. The theory of evolution, uncritically transferred from its proper sphere to the history of art, encouraged them also to see this progress, or at any rate a substantial part of it, as an upward march from lowly beginnings to splendid heights. The application of the theory of evolution is perhaps seen in its most extravagant form in the three-volume *History of Music to the Time of the Troubadours* by John Frederick Rowbotham

(1885-87).[3] His attempt to show that primitive man was originally content with one note (which was G) and subsequently progressed to two and
three notes is the purest fantasy; so is the assertion that in instrumental
music a "drum stage" was followed by a "pipe stage" and that in turn
by a "lyre stage." The main principles of evolutionary theory were also
accepted by Sir Hubert Parry in *The Art of Music* (1893, later published
as *The Evolution of the Art of Music)* but with a sanity and balanced
judgement that remove his arguments from the realm of mere invention
and make possible a critical examination of their validity.

The danger of regarding the history of music as a sequence of great
men is that we easily fall into the error of using their names to describe
a period or a style without any clear idea of the implications. Thus
people who are ill-informed about the late eighteenth century often use
the adjective "Mozartian" to describe characteristics of style which are
in fact common both to Mozart and to his contemporaries. It is no
doubt convenient to speak of the "Bach-Handel period," but the term may
easily create confusion of thought unless we know from the first exactly
what it implies. If we use it with any pretension to accuracy we mean two
things: first, a period of which Bach and Handel are now seen to have
been the most eminent men; and second, a period in which certain processes
of thought, certain forms and so on were common to a large number
of composers, including Bach and Handel. The pursuit of this definition will
lead us to consider how far Bach and Handel were different from other
composers, and how far they were different from each other.

A period has therefore a significance quite apart from the great men
who lived in it. We may define a period in general as a time when composers tend to be inspired by ideals materially different from those of an
earlier time, or when old processes of thought have had their day. These
changes in style have sometimes been deplored by sentimental historians.
They speak, for example, of the "decline of the madrigal" — as though
composers might have been expected to continue writing madrigals from
the early seventeenth century down to the present day. Such changes are
inevitable and healthy: if they did not occur composition would become
(as it sometimes has become) merely an imitation of the letter without
the spirit — a form of art to which the Germans have given the expressive
name *Kapellmeistermusik*. With this proviso our definition of a period
is simple and obvious enough. On the other hand there is no absolute
unanimity about specific periods, nor can we exactly determine where
they begin or where they end: if we could we should make nonsense of
the principle of continuity. In general we may say that a term which in-

---

[3]An extract is quoted in Warren Dwight Allen, *Philosophies of Music History* (New York, 1939), pp. 111-12.

dicates a style is preferable to one that merely describes a particular technique. Thus, provided we know what we mean by "baroque" it is preferable to speak of the "baroque period" than to follow Hugo Rieman and speak of the "figured bass period." The difficulties, in any case, are considerable; but some form of periodization is essential, if only for the purpose of dividing the material into manageable sections and clarifying our own minds.

Unfortunately this simple, practical necessity has often been confused with a desire to interpret the facts in accordance with particular doctrines. The application of evolutionary theory has induced authors to regard a period as a time of steady progress from small, or even insignificant, beginnings to heights of supreme mastery. The method is seen in its most grotesque form in the *History of Music* by Sir Charles Stanford and Cecil Forsyth. The chapter on the fifteenth and early sixteenth centuries (the work of Forsyth, who wrote the greater part of the book) contains an extraordinary passage on the pupils of Josquin des Prés:

> The characteristic of this whole group is an aversion from the frightful mechanical ingenuities of Josquin and his fellow-workers. This aversion becomes more noticeable in the group of men that immediately succeeded them. And we may be thankful that it was so. For these men cleared away the choking masses of blind-weed that lay on the foot-hills leading upwards to the heights of Palestrina.[4]

This is extraordinary for three reasons. First of all, it is historically inaccurate. The work of Josquin is not marked by "frightful mechanical ingenuities," and no one who had given even a casual glance at his music could imagine that it was. Secondly, it is a pure assumption that Palestrina was immeasurably superior to all his predecessors. Thirdly, the metaphor is nonsensical and appears to be designed merely to give verisimilitude to an untenable proposition. In fact Forsyth becomes intoxicated by metaphor to the extent of abandoning both reason and probability. The chapter ends by warning us not to imagine

> that the muddy stream of misplaced ingenuity dried up suddenly with Josquin's death. On the contrary, it continued to flow for many years. But it was not the main stream. And its impurities were only a fleck on the surface when it met the big tidal-wave that brought Palestrina's galleon up to her anchorage.[5]

The mechanical ingenuity has now become a muddy stream, and Palestrina has exchanged a mountain top for a ship. By the next chapter he has acquired a new means of locomotion:

[4]Charles Villiers Stanford and Cecil Forsyth, *A History of Music* (London, 1916), p. 155.
[5]Ibid., p. 157.

It is true that the two pairs of brothers Nanini and Anerio rode in Palestrina's chariot. But, when Palestrina dropped the reins, it was at the top of a hill. The new drivers thought, no doubt, that there was a long stretch of level road in front of them. But certain cunning eyes in Italy saw even then that the grade was imperceptibly downhill and was likely to end in a quagmire.[6]

Absurdity could go no further.

EQUALLY misguided is the attempt to establish an artificial sequence of the arts. Cecil Gray, in his book *Predicaments, or Music and the Future* (London, 1936), sees the centuries dominated respectively by architecture, sculpture, painting, literature and music. The argument is advanced that "during the period of the ascendancy of one particular art, the other arts aspire towards the aesthetic ideals embodied in that leading art."[7] The language is clumsy but the meaning is clear. It follows that Dante's *Divina Commedia* is architectural, "like a vast Gothic cathedral," Chaucer's *Canterbury Tales* are pictorial, the operas of Monteverdi and Gluck are literary, while even Mozart, "pure musician though he was in a sense, lives for us today primarily by virtue of his operas."[8] We might be tempted to ask in what sense Mozart was a pure musician, or to question whether we should ignore him if he had not written operas. We might suggest that operatic libretti are not the same thing as literature. We might go so far as to suggest that when the author tells us that "the central date" of the Gothic style "is round about 1100" he is talking nonsense. But these are minor criticisms. The principal objection is simply that the facts of history have been manipulated to fit a preconceived pattern. It is no justification of the pattern to say that it is neatly arranged: it is the very neatness which inspires suspicion. And when we find that every century bristles with individual examples which reduce the theory to mere woolgathering, it is time to call a halt.

A near relative of the theory of the sequence of the arts is the doctrine of cycles. According to Alfred Lorenz[9] a pendulum swings at regular intervals from homophony, rational rhythm, subjectivity and emotion on the one hand to polyphony, irrational rhythm, objectivity and reason on the other. In its motion it naturally passes through periods of transition. The decisive points of change occur at intervals of 300 years, beginning about A.D. 400. According to Lorenz's diagram we should now be in the middle of a transition period from homophony to polyphony. If the theory were sound, it would be convenient, since one could then safely

[6]Ibid., p. 173.
[7]*Predicaments*, p. 58.
[8]Ibid., pp. 58-61.
[9]*Abendländische Musikgeschichte im Rhythmus der Generationen* (Berlin, 1928).

predict the future of music until at least A.D. 2200, if not further. But like most symmetrical patterns it can only be constructed at the cost of ignoring everything that goes to prove it false. It makes nonsense, for instance, to say that 1510 was one of the furthest points of the swing to polyphony, since this was a time when homophonic part-songs enjoyed a great vogue: just as 300 years later plenty of polyphonic music was being written by Beethoven and his contemporaries. The theory, like most theories of this kind, is a product of wishful thinking. It is quite possible to survey past history in this way, but it can be done only by imitating Nelson and putting the telescope to one's blind eye.

Though the division of musical history into periods is convenient for the purposes of a continuous narrative, it is not the only method. Hermann Kretzschmar, for instance, edited a series of ten volumes entitled *Kleine Handbücher der Musikgeschichte nach Gattungen* (Leipzig, 1905-22) in which the division is by forms: one volume deals with the oratorio, another with the concerto, another with the motet, and so on. The advantages of this method are obvious. The continuity of musical forms may be obscure unless we can study all the stages in their development. Bach's motets may seem, to a superficial eye, to have nothing to do with the motet in the thirteenth century: Elgar's oratorios may appear to have only a slender connexion with Handel's. By examining the intermediate stages we discover the imperceptible process by which forms change—a process depending not merely on the individuality of composers but on the environment in which they grow up. The disadvantages of the method are equally obvious. The separation of opera from the symphony, for instance, is purely artificial: each nourished the other. The study of a form in isolation may easily foster the illusion that its growth was a spontaneous development, remote from the circumstances in which other departments of the art were rooted and flourished.

The ten volumes of the *Handbuch der Musikwissenschaft* edited by Ernst Bücken (Potsdam, 1928-31) make the best of both worlds. Six volumes are devoted to periods—ancient and oriental music, the Middle Ages and the Renaissance, baroque music, and so on—while a further two deal with Catholic and Protestant church music respectively. In addition there is a volume devoted to aesthetics and form and another on methods of performance *(Aufführungspraxis)*, and the first volume also includes a substantial section on instruments. The only objection to this scheme is that there is a considerable amount of overlapping. This would not matter if additional volumes had been devoted to other specific branches of music (which may well have been the editor's original intention). But as it stands the work pays a disproportionate amount of attention to church music.

Another, less serious, objection is that the excellent volume on the Middle Ages and the Renaissance (the work of Heinrich Besseler) compresses more into the space than is desirable in a work of this scope. If the baroque period is to have a volume to itself, it is equally important that the Middle Ages should receive a similar treatment. The problems raised by the titles of the volumes are another matter, which is necessarily more controversial. When, for instance, did the Renaissance begin? What, if any, are its boundaries? There is no absolute unanimity on this point, and in the last resort we are driven to read the volume to see what interpretation the editor, or the author, has adopted. There is less difference of opinion about the terms "baroque" and "rococo," both of which figure in the titles of Bücken's publication. The terms are borrowed from architecture and were first used in a disparaging sense, just as "Gothic" was once assumed to mean "barbarous." The application of these terms to music is recent and is based on the assumption that at any period there are certain basic similarities between the arts, not because practitioners of different arts necessarily copy each other but because all arts are a product of the same environment and exist in the same society. The pompous splendour of baroque architecture has its counterpart in much of the music of Lully, Purcell, Handel and Bach, just as the delicacy of rococo painting can be related to the late eighteenth-century minuet or *divertimento.* The parallel must not be pushed too far. The expressive recitative of seventeenth-century opera, for example, can be matched in literature, but hardly in architecture. But so long as the terms are used in the broadest and most general sense, they do no harm; and for most musicians today they certainly have a far more definite sense than such vague expressions as "pre-classical" or "classical."

The subdivisions of the *Oxford History of Music* also call for some comment. This work, which began to appear in 1901, was the first history of music to be produced by a team of contributors. The first two volumes, by H. Ellis Wooldridge, cover roughly the same ground as Besseler's volume on the Middle Ages and the Renaissance, though the treatment is entirely different and, naturally enough, the later work was able to profit by the intensive research devoted to medieval music during the intervening years. Wooldridge's volumes bear the title "The Polyphonic Period." It is at first sight not an unreasonable title, since the development of polyphony as a means of artistic expression figures prominently in the history of the period. But as a description of the period it is obviously inadequate, since other periods also cultivated polyphony; in fact the conception of musical texture as a combination of independent lines has never been abandoned and is still accepted today. The centuries before 1600 could only be described as *the* polyphonic period if a limited and arbitrary interpretation were given to the word "polyphony." Furthermore, a great deal of the music before 1600 is not "polyphonic" in this sense. Quite apart from the songs of the troubadours, Minnesinger and Meistersinger, and the lute-songs of the sixteenth century, there is plenty of secular music which is homophonic in treatment; and even in the field of church music—for example, in the Old Hall manuscript of the fifteenth century—we find pieces which are little more than harmonizations of plainsong melodies. The idea that sixteenth-century music was wholly polyphonic in conception can be refuted by looking at the bass parts of almost any collection of madrigals: over and over again one finds a bass with no more significant function than to act as a harmonic support to the other voices.

The fourth volume of the *Oxford History of Music*, published in 1902, is called "The Age of Bach and Handel." We have already discussed (p. 13) the implications of this title. Even if we are aware of those implications it is still open to criticism. The period corresponding to the lives of Bach and Handel is not necessarily a decisive one, and also there is a good deal of music composed within that period which differs radically from the traditions accepted by Bach and Handel respectively. The most notable example is Bach's second son, Carl Philipp Emanuel, who was thirty-six years old when his father died and already by that time a fully-fledged composer. Within his lifetime, as Hadow points out,[10] fall both Bach's cantata *Ich hatte viel Bekümmernis* (1714) and Mozart's "Jupiter" symphony (1788). There is more justification for speaking of "The Age of Beethoven"—the title of the eighth volume of the *New Oxford History of Music* (now in course of publication)—since Beethoven was not only the dominating figure of his time but was accepted as such by nineteenth-century composers. It is not extravagant to say that he towered so high that he threw a shadow over the work of many of his successors. Yet even here we may lose a sense of proportion. Schubert's career coincides with the latter part of Beethoven's; but there is nothing in his work to suggest that he was ever dominated by the older man's example, much as he admired him. And there is plenty of music of this period by French and Italian composers which owes nothing to Beethoven. If anything, the influence is the other way round: there is no mistaking the impression made on Beethoven by the music of Cherubini.

More important than the titles of volumes are the divisions between them. Both the *Oxford History of Music* and Bücken's series divide roughly at 1600. This is in many ways a convenient date. It coincides with the appearance of opera—a new form which rapidly conquered Europe and had a decisive influence on the development of music in general. It marks the time when composers began systematically to use a harmonized bass to supply the lower parts of a vocal or instrumental ensemble or to support a solo voice or instrument. It marks also the growth of a passion for virtuosity which invaded all fields of musical

[10]*The Viennese Period* (Oxford, 1904), p. 68.

performance. At the same time it is easy to exaggerate the nature of the change and to attach too much importance to a single date. In England, for example, the year 1600 has no special significance. Most of the English madrigals and lute-songs were published after that date, and the new style did not appear in church music until the Restoration. For this reason the division adopted in the *New Oxford History* is more satisfactory: the fourth volume of that work covers roughly the period from 1530 to 1640. The first date corresponds with the beginning of the Italian madrigal; the second with the opening of public opera houses in Venice and the outbreak of the Civil War in England, both of which, for different reasons, were decisive events. The title of the volume is "The Age of Humanism"—a title which places music in its proper relation to the art, literature and scholarship of the time.

Wherever we draw lines across the history of music, we are faced with problems. The first appearance of harmonized music is obviously of great importance, but it is very difficult to say precisely when it occurred. We know that the first written records date from the ninth century. But the fact that simple harmony, the use of a drone bass and even canon are found in the music of primitive peoples today suggests very strongly that these practices are not necessarily the product of Western civilization—that there may, in fact, be an ancient tradition of popular music-making behind the first appearance of systematic polyphony in the music of the Western church. Again, it would be convenient if we could fix a time at which the modern conception of harmony as a sequence of related chords could be said to have invaded the tradition of independent part-writing. It is conventional to say that this happened in the course of the sixteenth century; but English music of about 1300 shows plenty of examples in which there is the simplest possible harmonic sequence. It is impossible to suppose that musicians wrote a series of what we now call first inversions without being aware of the chords as such or of their relation to each other. More complex but equally convincing examples are to be found in the music of the fifteenth century. Again, one of the decisive changes in musical style is the supersession of baroque polyphony in the eighteenth century by the *style galant,* where the emphasis was on pointed rhythms and clearly defined melodies heard above a simple and symmetrical accompaniment. But it is not too easy to say when this change occurred. Certainly it had begun long before the death of Bach, who was regarded by some at least of his contemporaries as a turgid and old-fashioned composer.

In every change of style old fashions persist for a long time beside the new. This is very evident in twentieth-century music. There is little in common between Strauss's *Der Rosenkavalier,* Sibelius's fourth symphony, Stravinsky's *Petrouchka* and Ravel's *L'Heure espagnole;* yet all these works appeared in the year 1911, not to mention Elgar's second symphony,

Scriabin's *Prometheus*, Mahler's *Das Lied von der Erde* (posthumously) and Wolf-Ferrari's *Jewels of the Madonna*. And a year later Schönberg's *Five Orchestral Pieces* had their first performance. Opera in the early seventeenth century was far less an innovation than is commonly supposed. The style of declamatory song—its melodic pathos, its abrupt changes of harmony—owed much to the madrigal. In Monteverdi's *Orfeo* (1607), the most distinguished example of the form, not only the madrigal but also the motet and the instrumental ensemble music of the sixteenth century have clearly been a powerful influence. A revolution in music is in fact impossible, since previous experience cannot at one stroke be obliterated from our consciousness.

The difficulty of defining exactly the characteristics of any period is seen most clearly if we try to establish the outstanding features of our own time. It is true that a later age will probably see distinct resemblances where we see wholly independent styles, and it is also true that twentieth-century composers are much less inclined than their predecessors in the eighteenth century to accept a common idiom. But even if we make allowances for these considerations, we shall still be acutely aware of the difficulty of establishing a coherent pattern. The exact relationship of the twentieth century to the nineteenth is often a matter for dispute. Is impressionism, for example, an independent growth or is it merely a development of romanticism? Future historians may be able to be more dogmatic about these matters when they see the picture of the complete century. But it is equally possible that the passage of time will blur for them some of the sharp outlines of which we are conscious today.

The differences between the music of one age and the next are not simple. There are differences in technique, in approach, in environment. Music is affected by the circles for which it is intended: it may be written for a cultured aristocracy, for the great public of music-lovers, or for a mutual admiration society. Though its appeal is the same for every age, there is always a difference in the terms in which emotion is expressed. In consequence, though it may continue to give delight to music-lovers of succeeding ages, it can never mean exactly the same to them as it did to those who first heard it. Our environment, our reactions, our first impressions are different from those of our forefathers. The music which comes to us from the past has to pass through the veil of our own experience; and that experience includes our consciousness of many other kinds of music. We have to deal with an elusive, intangible art. We might be tempted to cry, with Shelley, "Rarely, rarely comest thou, spirit of delight." The miracle is that it comes so often.

20

Bibliography

The history of musical historiography is not a subject that has attracted many authors. Most important is the work of Warren Dwight Allen, *Philosophies of Music History* (New York, American Book, 1939; reprinted with a new preface by the author, New York, Dover, 1962). Other works by Allen are "Baroque Histories of Music," in *The Musical Quarterly*, 25 (1939), and "Histories of Music," in *The International Cyclopedia of Music and Musicians*, Oscar Thompson, ed., 9th ed. (New York, Dodd, Mead, 1964). Also valuable is the essay by Frank Harrison, "American Musicology and the European Tradition," in Frank L. Harrison, Mantle Hood, and Claude V. Palisca, *Musicology* (Englewood Cliffs, N.J., Prentice-Hall, 1965). Simon Towneley Worsthorne has assembled an extensive list of both general and specialized histories of music under "Histories" in *Grove's Dictionary of Music and Musicians*, 5th ed. (1954), vol. 4, pp. 296-306.

2

GREGORIAN chant forms the earliest large corpus of Western music of which we have any record. For centuries it has remained in widespread use in the Roman church, and some of it has been adapted for use in the churches of the Anglican and Lutheran communions, as well as in those of other non-Roman faiths. It appears in introits, graduals, responses, and canticles, to mention only a few, and it is a rare modern hymnal that does not contain at least one item having a Gregorian ancestry. Gregorian chant served as the stimulus for the composition of early sacred song, such as the sequence and the hymn, and it is possible that its style influenced secular medieval monophonic song. With the invention of polyphony the chant served as the source of the thematic material that formed the basis of much early polyphonic composition, and, by means of the *cantus firmus* technique, the chant has served as the impetus for much musical composition throughout the history of Western music. Even today it is still being drawn upon by composers for thematic material for new compositions. Thus, by reason of its great influence in the history of Western music, Gregorian chant is the subject with which one is often introduced to music history.

A study of Gregorian chant is complicated by at least three factors: legends, accepted as historical fact, that assert that the chant was written or at least codified by Pope Gregory I (reigned 590-604) or even that the chant was dictated to him by the Holy Spirit; a lack of chant manuscripts dating earlier than the ninth century; and a lack of any precise system of musical notation at the time the chant was written down, thus making it difficult to decipher those manuscripts we do have. Current scholarship, aided by the development of techniques of stylistic analysis, is finally beginning to invalidate the legends, date the manuscripts, and decipher the notation. The following selection serves as a good introduction to Gregorian chant and its problems, as well as to the history and present status of Gregorian research.

The Most Rev. Rembert G. Weakland, OSB, is Abbot Primate of the worldwide Benedictine Federation, Rome. He served as the music editor and contributed many of the music entries to *The New Catholic Encyclopedia* (New York, McGraw-Hill, 1967).

Gregorian Chant

R. G. WEAKLAND

The revival of monasticism in the 19th century by Dom P. Gueranger of Solesmes Abbey and the concomitant revival in liturgical studies brought about a renewed interest in the history of Gregorian chant. This chant was seen as belonging to the golden age of the formation of Roman liturgy and thus as holding priority of place in the history of sacred music. Although terms such as plainsong or plainchant (*cantus planus,* unmeasured chant, in contradistinction to *cantus mensuratus* or rhythmically organized song) also are used, Gergorian chant has become the most popular term because it can be easily differentiated from Ambrosian, Mozarabic, Gallican, and Byzantine chant. Gregorian chant was first written down in the 9th century and has continued in unbroken use in the Roman rite to the present day. In each period of music history it has been influenced by the contemporary musical idiom, and constant attempts to find out what its original character was like have been made during the centuries. Present scholarship has unearthed many problems that remain unsolved. The Solesmes school has continued its paleographic work through Dom E. Cardine and Dom J. Hourlier and its analytic work through Dom M. Claire and Dom J. Gajard. More important historical persepctives have been opened up by: M. Huglo, H. Hucke, J. Handschin, and B. Stäblein. Valuable contributions have been made by E. Wellesz, Dom L. Brou, and O. Strunk on the relationship between Gregorian chant and other Eastern and Western chants. Scholars such as E. Jammers, J. Vollaerts, S. Corbin, and H. Husmann have continued to probe specific areas such as paleography, rhythm, rhymed Offices, drama, Sequence, and trope. Work on the medieval theorists has not ceased, and valuable reediting and interpreting of texts has been done by J. Smits van Waesberghe, H. Oesch, and H. Hüschen. The most comprehensive and complete study on Gregorian chant to date, bringing together all of the information thus

FROM *The New Catholic Encyclopedia,* vol. 6, pp. 756-761. Copyright © 1967 by The Catholic University of America, Washington, D.C. Reprinted by permission of the McGraw-Hill Book Company.

far arrived at by scholars and offering a balanced judgment on recent theories, has been made by Willi Apel (*Gregorian Chant*, Bloomington, Ind. 1958). This present brief survey of mid-20th-century scholarship indicates the renewed interest in the field and the areas that are the subject of most concern.

Problem of Origin.

General histories of music had too easily assumed that Gregorian chant dates back to at least the 6th century and was put in its present form by Pope Gregory the Great (590-604). Although this theory was often seriously challenged (see F. Gevaert, *Les Origines du chant liturgique de l'église latine,* Ghent 1890), it persisted in vogue, carried along by centuries of tradition. It must, however, be recalled that the first MSS containing Gregorian chant came from the 9th century from the Frankish empire. Many of these MSS, especially the *Graduales,* contain a famous introductory trope, *Gregorius praesul.* It is a kind of Carolingian publicity technique to advertise the fact that the new chants were in the Roman style, the *cantilena romana.* It cannot be proved that Gregory the Great is the Gregory here alluded to, and the possibility that it refers to Gregory II (715-731) must also be considered. Even if one accepts the assumption that Gregory the Great is referred to, it remains dubious how much of the music that is first written down in the 9th century goes back to Gregory's time in an oral tradition.

Gregory's Role. What can be said with certitude concerning the activity of Gregory the Great is that he sought to bring order into the liturgical texts by compiling from various sources the *antiphonarius cento.* This could not have been done without reference to the music accompanying the texts, but about this nothing is known. His concern for music can be seen also in the founding of monastic groups to serve the basilicas and in the impetus he gave to the *schola cantorum.* The general principles of music-making that lead to Gregorian chant and especially the principles of formulae that form its psalmodic structure must have existed in his day, but there is no way of proving that any given piece of Gregorian chant goes back to that date. In the lists of popes in the Liber pontificalis, other pontiffs also are included as contributing to the history of the annual liturgical cycle (*annalis cantus omnis*), but the lack of accurate musical examples from the period makes its impossible to assess the contribution of any particular individual to the formation of the chant corpus.

The Role of Rome. The problem of the origin of Gregorian chant is complicated by the difficulty of ascertaining the nature of chant at the Roman basilicas until the 11th century. It can be accurately documented that Roman chant from the 11th to the 13th century was not the same as Gregorian chant. Five MSS dating from that time contain a tradition that is unique. They are: Vat. lat. 5319, a *Graduale* from the last quarter of the 11th century; a *Graduale* dated 1071 and written for Santa Cecilia in Trastevere, now in the M. Bodner collection, Cologny-Genève, Switzerland; Vat. Bas. F22, a *Graduale* from the first half of the 13th century; Vat. Bas. B79, an antiphonary, 12th century; and British Museum, Add. 29,988, an antiphonary from the 12th century. The theory that the tradition contained in these MSS dates back to the Carolingian period and beyond and is thus the "Old-Roman" repertoire has had strong support among scholars ever since the theory was seriously proposed by Bruno Stäblein (see *Die Musik in Geschichte und Gegenwart* 2:1265-1303). In general, Old-Roman chant is more ornate than Gregorian chant, but the melodic contours and formulae are too close to deny some original relationship between the two. That the Gregorian was simply derivative from the Old Roman without other influences seems impossible. It is also impossible to assert that the Old-Roman is simply an ornamented version of the Gregorian. Other solutions proposed make both chants of Roman origin, the Gregorian being the "monastic" practice that was carried northward by the monks into England and France. Such a solution does not explain the relationship between the two chants, however. The best solution still seems to be that proposed by M. Huglo and arrived at also by W. Apel, that the Old-Roman version comes closest to the Roman practice at the time of Charlemagne and that it combined with the Gallican usage to give birth during the 8th century to the version now called Gregorian. The testimony of Amalarius of Metz (early 9th century) certainly supports this view. The role of Gregory in the formation of the Old-Roman repertoire remains just as dubious. A solution to the problem, without the unexpected discovery of yet-unknown documents containing the Old-Roman version and dated before the 11th century, will have to rely on internal evidence and comparative studies not yet completed.

Repertoire.

When Gregorian chant was first written down in the 9th century, the type of notation employed merely indicated the direction the melody was to take, up or down, without accurate pitch differences. Until that time the repertoire had to be retained by memory without such an aid. It is remarkable, nevertheless, that the oral tradition, written down almost simultaneously throughout the vast area of present-day France, Germany, and Italy, showed such great uniformity. The retention of this repertoire by memory must have been an ever-increasing burden to the choirmaster, and the necessity of teaching it to the monks and succeeding cantors gave added impetus to the search for a system of notation. The repertoire for Mass and Office at the beginning of the 9th century must have comprised well over 2,000 pieces. These pieces were not all different one from another, and the early cantors and chant theorists exploited such similarities in inventing didactic processes.

The Recitative and Psalmody. Since the texts for most of the liturgical services are taken from the Old and New Testaments, musical systems for their proclamation had to be devised that could be altered to suit prose texts of various lengths. Simple formulas for the Epistle and Gospel at Mass and for the Lessons at Matins consisted of a single recitation pitch with variants from the pitch to indicate inner and final pauses in the texts. More solemn tones were devised for the greater solemnities. Special tones were reserved for the Lamentations on Good Friday and the reading of the Passion. The tones for the orations of the Mass and the Prefaces followed the same general principles of a recitation tone with cadential figures but respected the nature of the text by having two types of inner cadences. This simple principle served also for the frequent singing of Psalms at Mass and Office, where the antithetical structure of the text was clearly outlined by the musical cadences. There is some indication that the second half of the verse was not always sung on the same pitch as the first and that the text structure was delineated more clearly by a second reciting tone.

Responsorial and Antiphonal Chants. Although Gregorian chant may have arisen out of the recitation system just described, individual pieces—at first derived almost exclusively from the Psalter—became a part of the entire system. The greatest body of these pieces are the antiphons of the Mass and Office. Their counterpart are the responsories. The antiphons may originally have been sung as a kind of refrain after two groups alternated verses of the Psalter; but this practice had disappeared before the 9th century, and the antiphons that are found in Gregorian chant are larger and more elaborate and were sung only before and after the Psalm. At Mass the Introit and Communion were sung in this fashion: at the Office the many Psalms of all the hours had antiphons to be sung with them. The tonary of Regino of Prüm (d. 915) contained 1,235 such Office antiphons. It was evident to the Carolingian cantors that these antiphons could be catalogued according to certain melodic characteristics. From this one can surmise that the preceding oral tradition for the antiphons must have had a kind of repertoire of melodic formulae to which new texts were adapted. These formulae, it can be seen, often have a kind of psalmodic structure to them, consisting of a recitation tone with cadential figures. If such was the primitive state of the music of the antiphons, with the passing of time they tended to become independent pieces in their own right.

In origin the responsory too consisted of a refrain sung after verses of a Psalm, but this time the verses were sung by a solo cantor. By the time Gregorian chant was written down, this form had lost much of its primitive shape, except that its soloistic nature had tended to make the responsory more elaborate, especially the psalmodic verses. At Mass the Gradual and Alleluia are responsorial in nature. The Offertory seems to have passed from being antiphonal to responsorial in character shortly before the chant repertoire was written down. Even in the responds, especially in the substructure of the elaborate verses, one can see the original psalmodic principle of reciting tone and cadential figures. At Matins the responsory follows the reading of the Lessons as a kind of musical commentary on the Scriptures. Their original improvisational nature had been lost before the 9th century.

Other Pieces. The chant repertory included other specific pieces that were needed to complete the Mass and Office services. Some of these chants may originally have been quite simple in nature, somewhat in the style of a litany, but later developed into full-blown, ornate pieces. This had become true of the Ordinary of the Mass by the late Carolingian period. Elaborate Kyrie's, Gloria's, Sanctus's, and Agnus Dei's can be found in all *Graduales* and form one of the most complicated groups of the chant repertoire. Only the Ordinary and the Alleluia cycle seem to have remained areas for new compositions after the 9th century. They were the last pieces of the standard repertory to be fixed; the composition of new chant Ordinaries continued even after the high Middle Ages. All of these items were affected by the new forms of the trope and Sequence.

Sources.

Various claims have been made periodically by scholars that they have found fragments of musical notation that go back to the 8th century. But each of these items, such as the *Orationale* of Verona, when subjected to closer scrutiny, has been declared as non-musical in nature or as additions by later hands. The first verified fragments are still from the mid-9th century with the first full MS from the end of the century. The fragments are usually of isolated pieces that do not belong to the standard repertoire or are newly composed—evidence that these first attempts at mnemonic notation had a practical, didactic purpose. The treatise of Aurelian of Réomé (written about 850) has several passages that imply a knowledge on his part of a primitive notation. Of special interest are the paleofrankish fragments from the end of the 9th century that show a different system from that which became standard throughout the West. A treatise such as Hucbald's *De institutione harmonica* (written about 900) shows the growing concern on the part of cantors for a more precise notation than that of the mnemonic neumes then in use. (A list of full MSS from about 900 can be found in Suñol, *Introduction à la paléographie musicale grégorienne* [Tournai, 1935], P. 32.) Not until a century later (about 1000) was the staff invented, and then it required another half century before it was perfected to the point where melodic accuracy could be perfectly ascertained. For this reason chant scholars must search for the pieces of the earlier MSS in later 11th- and 12th-century MSS to transcribe with accuracy. In sum, the first MSS containing Gregorian chant in an accurate unequivocal melodic notation came from shortly after the year 1000; the repertory can be traced back to 900 in a mnemonic notation, but only in fragments and descriptions before that.

Theorists.

In addition to the MSS containing the chant repertory, there exist the chant theorists, who furnish invaluable information on the repertory and how it was performed. The first such theorist is Aurelian of Réomé, who wrote his *Musicà disciplina* about 850. A fragment of this treatise has been erroneously attributed to Alcuin. Aurelian in the first eight chapters of his work gives a résumé of the theory of music inherited from the ancient Greeks through Boethius and Cassiodorus. He makes no attempt to reconcile this theory with the chant practice of his day. Boethius in particular was used in the Carolingian schools as the *auctoritas* in music. From ch. 9 to 20, however, Aurelian makes a first attempt of cataloguing the chant repertory according to the *toni*. For the first time he speaks of the Byzantine octoechos, or eight modes, and of the manner in which the Psalms sung in these modes are to be joined to the antiphons and responds. Subsequent chant theorists, such as Regino of Prüm (d. 915), Hucbald of St. Armand (d. 930), and Remy of Auxerre (end of 9th century), began the arduous task of trying to combine these two divergent theoretical systems and to use them for an explanation of Gregorian chant. The octoechos became identified for the first time with the eight-mode Boethian system in the treatise *De alia musica* (late 9th century). It is not until the 11th century that the amalgamation is completed in the treatises of Guido of Arezzo, Berno of Reichenau, and Hermannus Contractus. There is evidence that the inherited Boethian theory had an effect on the chant that may have been altered at times to fit the *auctoritas*. Boethius continued to be taught as the authority in the schools and universities of the Middle Ages, while Guido became the infallible guide to the cantor.

Gregorian Chant Style.

To the 20th-century ear, accustomed to the gigantic sounds of the orchestra of the romanticist period and the striking contrasts of dynamics and timbre inherent in the romanticist style, Gregorian chant seems unemotional and less expressive. To the man of the Middle Ages, however, this was not true. The Gregorian style was broad in its expressive content, even though more austere than the music of recent centuries. Since it had to accommodate so many prose texts, it ranged from formulalike patterns such as psalmody and antiphon types to highly expressive melismatic passages such as the *jubilus* of the Alleluia. These extremes in the style have often been labeled syllabic and melismatic, or *accentus* and *concentus*. Such terms, however, are not synonymous. Syllabic chant refers to those pieces in which each syllable has predominantly one note, seldom more; melismatic chant has expressive vocalises on important syllables. In between these two lie most of the chant pieces. The Sequence, for example, is syllabic; the Alleluia is melismatic. Most of the Introits, Offertories, and Communions lie in between. *Accentus* refers to the recitative formulas used for orations and the readings—the heightened speech patterns, while the *concentus* refers to true melody. In the latter the laws of music itself have their role.

Chant Rhythm. Perhaps no other aspect of Gregorian chant has been so feverishly debated by scholars as that of the original rhythm of the chant. The following facts are accepted by all: The earliest chant MSS (from *c.* 900) show various ways of writing the same neume and these variants imply rhythmic differences. Many of these MSS reinforce this notational difference with letters (called Romanian letters) to signify rhythmic alteration. Other differences in notation involve vocal phenomena (such as the liquescents and the quilisma) that also have rhythmic implications. The basic difference in interpretation of these signs among scholars centers around the length of the altered notes in relationship to a given pulse. Further dispute arises as to the rhythmic organization of the given pulse. It was in answer to this latter question that Dom Mocquereau developed the theory of rhythm, usually called the Solesmes theory, in which the basic pulses are related by groups of two or three and with the unifying factor being called the ictus. This ictus is conceived as the end of rhythmic motion in its fundamental state of movement—repose. Mocquereau attempted to show at great length that this is the natural rhythm of the Latin word, which gave its rhythm to the

30

chant. Such a theory has much merit in dealing with psalmody and other pieces belonging to the *accentus* group; it proves more difficult to maintain in dealing with the *concentus*. Here the ictus, or rhythmic subdivision, corresponds at times with the end or repose of the Latin word, at times with accent or force (as when it corresponds in larger phrases with the accent of the text), at times with length, or even at times with melodic contour. There is no doubt that Mocquereau's theory grew out of the accentualist or oratorical theory of Dom Pothier, where the textual accent of the Latin word was the organizing principle, and that he broadened the concept so that it could serve also for the melismatic passages. To introduce it into present books, an elaborate system of vertical and horizontal bars was invented.

The Solesmes theory was rejected at the turn of the 19th century by most German scholars who ranked themselves among the mensuralists, i.e., those favoring various time values with accent as the chief unifying factor. The former mensuralist theories of Dechevrens, Peter Wagner, Dom Jeannin, and Bonvin have all but been forgotten. Chief exponents of mensuralism today are E. Jammers and J. Vollaerts, although their theories admit of only two or three time values and are a kind of free rhythm with irregularly occurring accents. It can be said that the weakness of the Solesmes theory lies in its historical justification in the nature of the Latin word since it presupposes that this rhythm was established for chant in the 5th and 6th centuries during its formative period, a supposition that is hard to maintain. The historical evidence in favor of the long and short time values comes chiefly from the theorists, and it seems a less forced interpretation of the early neumes and the different ways in which they are written. More recent rhythmic studies by T. Agostoni and E. Cardine are tending to a modification of the Solesmes theory that brings it closer to the interpretation of J. Vollaerts. It is unfortunate that the introduction of polyphony and the tendency to clearer pitch indications in notation saw at the same time a less accurate rhythmic care. The notation *in campo aperto*, i.e., without lines, and thus mnemonic in character, is less accurate in pitch but more accurate in rhythm, while the later diastematic MSS, i.e., with lines, are more accurate in pitch but less so in rhythm and vocal nuances.

Formal Aspects of Gregorian Chant. All patterns found in later Western music are found also in chant. Musicologists have taken great pains to find ABA and Rondo forms in various chant pieces. All of this is true but says little about the formal structures of the chant melody. Being pure melody, the chant relies on purely melodic motives for its formal structure. In general, the high point of the line is arrived at rather rapidly and tapers off gradually. The length of the line is frequently dictated by the text and its components. There is no music where the shape of the text so affects the shape of the line. Sequential structures are found but never stressed as formative elements. The general punctuation of the text determines the inner cadences, which, as a rule, do not stress the final tone. Later melodies tend to have larger leaps in succession, while the older melodies use the leap beyond a third with great discretion. The word accent does not always receive musical development but frequently is higher in pitch than the unaccented syllables. There is some evidence that interest in the Latin rhythmic cursus may have had some influence in cadential formulas, especially of the psalm tones. The manner in which a typical pattern can be altered to fit a new text shows a keen appreciation of text declamation and a freedom within a given form that is always expressive and sensitive. The subtlety was lost or obscured by the advent of polyphony.

The Modal System. The chief unifying element in Gregorian chant is its modal structure. The oral tradition from which chant arose was undoubtedly one of a group of melodic formulae or phrases that could be adapted to various texts. These formulae were traditionally grouped into eight divisions depending on the melodic contour, the manner of beginning, and the relationship between the reciting or dominant tone and the ending formula. There is reason to believe that originally the beginning was most important in such a grouping, but certainly after the influence of the classical Greek theories inherited through Boethius the ending or final note and its relationship to the reciting or dominant note proved the vital factor in determining mode. Also from Boethius is derived the influence of range as an important element. The Byzantine theory that was inherited spoke of four authentic modes and four plagal or derivative modes. A plagal mode shared with its respective authentic mode the same final but usually had a lower dominant or reciting tone, thus throwing the whole range somewhat lower. In the authentic modes the final or cadential figure comes at the bottom of the range; in the plagal modes, it is in the middle. The accompanying table presents the standard modal theory as it was fully developed in the treatises of the 11th century. This theory cannot be applied rigidly to all chants. By the introduction of the B♭ the general favor of a mode can be altered and transpositions can be effected. There are no other accidentals possible in chant, and thus chromaticism is impossible. The tritone (interval of the augmented fourth) was avoided also in later chant, although the treatise of Hucbald *De institutione harmonica* cites this interval without prejudice and gives examples of it. Later tonaries give model modal melodies that embody the characteristics of each mode and served didactic purposes, but the repertory itself is much freer in its adherence to modal structure. Some of the more elab-

Standard 11th-Century Modal Theory

Byzantine name	Ancient Greek name	Final	Range	Dominant
1. Authenticus protus	dorian	d	d —— d'	a
2. Plagalis protus	hypodorian	d	A —— a	f
3. Authenticus deuterus	phrygian	e	e —— e'	b or c'
4. Plagalis deuterus	hypophrygian	e	B —— b	a
5. Authenticus tritus	lydian	f	f —— f'	c'
6. Plagalis tritus	hypolydian	f	c —— c'	a
7. Authenticus tetrardus	mixolydian	g	g —— g'	d'
8. Plagalis tetrardus	hypomixolydian	g	d —— d'	c'

orate verses of the soloistic responsories use both the plagal and authentic ranges of the same mode and thus exploit all of the melodic possibilities of the mode.

Subsequent History of Gregorian Chant.

After the Carolingian period the interests of the chant composer turned to tropes and Sequences and the rise of polyphony. The standard repertory remained in use, but it lost its rhythmic piquancy and became the source for polyphonic treatment. Several new Offices were written that exploited the modal theories by presenting the antiphons of the night Office in modal succession, but general interest in chant composition waned.

The Council of Trent. By the 16th century the condition of chant was truly lamentable, and a reform was badly needed. Unfortunately the Medicean edition that resulted from an attempt at reform was not founded on scholarly principles and reflected more the esthetics of the late Renaissance than the early Middle Ages. This edition, however, remained the source for all subsequent editions until the 19th century. Pioneers in musical research in the 19th century, such as Lambillotte, La Fage, D'Ortigue, and Nasard, laid the basis for the subsequent more accurate work of the Solesmes school. To this latter, under the directorship of Dom Pothier and Dom Mocquereau, belongs the lasting credit of making available the original mnemonic MSS in facsimile editions in the series *Paléographie musicale grégorienne* and of initiating a series of monographs that made scholars search out the original documents. The treatises of the theorists were gathered together by M. Gerbert and E. Coussemaker. The controversies that arose in opposition to the Solesmes theories, with P. Wagner and F. Gevaert as chief protagonists, gave rise to intensive chant studies that are still accurate sources for information.

Present Practice. As a result of chant scholarship since the mid-19th century, the present practice can be said to come closer to the original in its melodic precision than that of any previous century. However, the rhythmic controversies still continue; there are more performances in the mensuralist style, and there is less adherence to the Solesmes school. Frequently the chant is accompanied on the organ, which thus adds a third dimension never intended by the original composers. Often this accompaniment totally falsifies the underlying modal structure. True chant must be unaccompanied. Attempts at congregational use of the chant repertory in the 20th century have been limited to the simple Mass Ordinaries and have not been universally successful. It is generally found to be too alien to 20th-century aesthetic tastes. Various systems of arm and hand motions also have been invented to direct chant (called chironomy) and have been most successfully used. With the increase of the vernacular in the liturgy, less interest has been shown in Gregorian chant, although many attempts at adapting its melodies to new English texts have been made.

Bibliography

Willi Apel's *Gregorian Chant* (Bloomington, Ind., Indiana University Press, 1958) is the standard English-language study of Gregorian chant. Also by Apel is "The Central Problem of Gregorian Chant," *Journal of the American Musicological Society,* 9 (1956), which is concerned with the problems of dating the chant. Higinio Anglès, "Latin Chant before St. Gregory" and "Gregorian Chant," both from vol. 2 of *The New Oxford History of Music,* should be consulted, as well as Gustave Reese, *Music in the Middle Ages* (New York, Norton, 1940). For information about the relationship of Gregorian chant to Jewish music see Eric Werner, **The Sacred Bridge* (New York, Columbia University Press, 1956). A bibliography for Gregorian chant may be found under "Choral" in *Die Musik in Geschichte und Gegenwart.* For those who are unfamiliar with liturgical terminology, Dom Anselm Hughes's *Liturgical Terms for Music Students* (Boston, McLaughlin & Reilly, 1940) is helpful. It also contains an outline of the structure of the mass and of the offices.

One cannot gain much from a study of Gregorian chant, nor from a study of any other music for that matter, without examining and performing the music itself. Much of the chant, in a modern edition, is contained in three volumes, all published by Desclee in Tournai, Belgium. These are the *Graduale,* containing the music for mass; the *Antiphonale,* containing the music for the offices; and the *Liber Usualis,* which is a modern compendium of the first two books. It should be kept in mind, however, that these books are simply the most recent of a long line of editions of the chant. While they have been very carefully prepared, they must not be viewed as a definitive version of the chant as it might have originally existed. Photo reproductions of a number of chant manuscripts dating from the ninth century and later have been prepared and published by the Benedictine monks of Solesmes, France, under the series title *Paléographie musicale.*

3

A COMMON but dangerous approach to the study of any body of unfamiliar material is to begin by adopting a definition of terminology, either one's own or another's, and to apply this terminology to one's findings even if the two are not compatible. Such has often been the case concerning that body of accretions to the liturgy known as tropes and to their relatives the sequences. Tropes frequently have been regarded as textual additions to an already established and officially recognized liturgy of the Roman Church, and their presence has been explained by stating that, due to the lack of an accurate system of musical notation, the tropes were added to long textless sections of chant in order to serve as memory aids. This view of tropes and of their origin is considered by the author of the following article to be no more than an hypothesis that the evidence of research does not support. Rather than taking terminology from such an hypothesis, one should, instead, begin by examining the tropes themselves and only afterward make his terminology from the findings that result from such an examination. This approach will enable one to realize more from a study of tropes than such oft-quoted but dubious axioms as "all sequences are tropes but not all tropes are sequences," axioms that too frequently represent the student's entire knowledge of tropes.

Richard L. Crocker is a member of the faculty of the University of California at Berkeley. His published works include *A History of Musical Style* (New York, McGraw-Hill, 1966) and contributions to the *Journal of the American Musicological Society* and *The Musical Quarterly*.

The Troping Hypothesis

RICHARD L. CROCKER

The most valuable thing Jacques Handschin taught us was to mistrust our own systems. By instinct he dug out the exceptions, the anomalies, the cases that just did not fit. By instinct he provided each explanation with its antinomy, each potential system with an antidote. Recalcitrant fragments were what irritated his mind into activity; small wonder his thought came out as a disjunct series of footnotes. Provocative, even if provoking, to read, his writings pose questions that may not always have answers but often have important consequences.

Because of his mistrust of system, Handschin's tussle with the definition of trope is all the more fascinating. In his article *Trope, Sequence, and Conductus*,[1] he was unusually concerned with being systematic; the first two pages embody a kind of categorical definition quite unlike him. Yet his whole being must have reacted against the idea that a trope was a single, clearly definable thing, as is evident from his efforts in the rest of the article to adjust the original definition to the documentary facts.

The same tension between systematic theory and recalcitrant fact is present in three previous discussions of troping—Léon Gautier's *Histoire de la Poésie liturgique au Moyen Age* (1886), the introduction to Walter Howard Frere's *Winchester Troper* (1894), and the introduction to the 47th volume of *Analecta hymnica*, edited by Clemens Blume and Henry Bannister in 1905. To straighten out the complexities of definition embodied in these studies would require far more space than is available here, and would, furthermore, be futile because of the whole approach to defining a trope that these authors have taken.

Actually a trope, in the medieval understanding, can be easily defined. Indeed, there is no need to make up a new definition, for Bishop

---

[1] *New Oxford History of Music*, ed. J. A. Westrup, London, II (1954), 128-74.

FROM *The Musical Quarterly*, 52 (1966), 183-203. Reprinted by permission.

Durand wrote a perfectly good one in the 13th century:[2] "A trope is a kind of versicle that is sung on important feasts (for example, Christmas) immediately before the Introit, as if a prelude, and then a continuation of that Introit. Tropes include three [parts of the Introit], namely antiphon, verse, and *Gloria Patri*." This definition was dismissed out of hand by Blume, with the implication that Durand had not the foggiest idea of what he was talking about. It seems to me, however, that the good bishop was right and that everyone else has been wrong—wrong in trying to include under "trope" all sorts of things that do not belong there. The problems of definition in Gautier, Frere, Blume, and Handschin are merely those that would be encountered in trying to define under one heading oranges, elephants, and, say, meteoric dust.

Hence, the well-known definition ("a trope is an interpolation into an official, liturgical chant") has always been extensively qualified, for almost every element of it raises questions when tested against specific cases. The most immediate questions are these: does an introduction or epilogue count as an interpolation? is the interpolation a musical one, or a textual one, or both? and most important (but usually ignored), what really constitutes an official chant, or a liturgical one, and does this involve text, or melody, or both?

These and other difficulties encountered by Gautier, Frere, Blume, and Handschin seem due in the last analysis to a desire for a single, clear explanation—which I call the "troping hypothesis"—for the confusing wealth of musical forms introduced in the 9th and 10th centuries. If only there were one ruling idea to govern the medieval scene! If only that curious, little-known phenomenon, the trope, could be seen as the ruling idea of a process whereby all medieval music was necessarily and intimately tied to pre-existing materials, concerned primarily with their development or ornamentation, within the limits of respected authority imposed by a presumably all-powerful church whose grip on music was already evident in liturgy or the modal system! If all that were true, then how clear and orderly the medieval picture would be. But if the trope was to become the ruling idea, its image would have to be changed, expanded, generalized. This, I think, was the reasoning behind the inclusive definition of the trope—and the source of the difficulties.

Clarity was purchased at a price, for the troping hypothesis led easily to an evaluation: tropes seemed by nature artistically inferior to their subject. Whether or not this evaluation was made, tropes were generally supposed to be lacking in originality, since they were the products of what was considered to be a rigidly controlled environment. As a result, medieval music of the 9th to 11th centuries came to be viewed

---

[2]Quoted by Blume in *Analecta hymnica* 47: *Tropi graduales. Tropen des Missale im Mittelalter, I. Tropen zum Ordinarium Missae*, Leipzig, 1905, pp. 7-8.

not as individual works of art, consciously created, but rather as an "outgrowth of the chant," subject to laws of vegetative morphology rather than to those of original artistic creation. The troping hypothesis also produced a distorted picture of medieval polyphony by undue emphasis upon the use of a cantus firmus, or rather, upon the fact that a cantus firmus is used while neglecting the differences in the *way* it is used; but that is another story.

There has been a strong trend since the war to revise the troping hypothesis in certain respects. Ewald Jammers has insisted on an important distinction between Gregorian chant and medieval chant. Gregorian chant here refers to the Propers of Mass and Office as found in 9th-century sources, while medieval chant begins with the new forms and styles of monophonic sacred music of the 9th century or later.[3] This distinction, which opens the door to a more realistic appreciation of tropes, must be retained in any serious discussion of the problem. Bruno Stäblein, dealing indefatigably with all kinds of tropes in a wisely pragmatic manner, has often taken exception to the troping hypothesis in specific cases, as will be noted later.[4]

On the other hand, there is still a strong tendency for the troping hypothesis to direct research towards isolated examples that demonstrate the hypothesis. Exceptional items that happen to have multiple liturgical and paraliturgical connections are studied in detail, while more representative items or repertories are ignored. A striking example is the almost complete neglect of hymn melodies[5] and votive antiphons, two extensive categories of musical composition in the 9th to 12th centuries that may be stylistically more important than tropes. But hymns and antiphons have few tropic connections, and for this reason, I think, have been passed over by historians of music in favor of instances of text-underlay to pre-existing melismas, which better fit the trope image.

It would be highly desirable to abandon the whole troping hypothesis—which is, after all, only a hypothesis, not a fact, and therefore has no claim on our credulity beyond its ability to organize known facts or suggest the discovery of new, significant ones. It seems to me that the troping hypothesis is on the one hand invalidated by the real, basic differences that exist between the several things called trope; and on the other, contradicted by the fact that the great bulk of medieval musical composition, within and without the realm of tropes, shows

[3]*Das mittelalterliche Choral: Art und Herkunft*, Mainz, 1954.

[4]See especially *Die Unterlegung von Texten unter Melismen. Tropus, Sequenz und andere Formen*, in *International Musicological Society. Report of the Eighth Congress, New York 1961*. ed. Jan LaRue, Kassel, I (1961), 12-29.

[5]Except, of course, Stäblein's volume of melodies, *Hymnen; die mittelalterlichen Hymnenmelodien des Abendlandes. Monumenta monodica medii aevi*, Vol. I, Kassel, 1956.

more or less the same degrees of originality generally prevailing in Western music.

One of the most important steps towards reconstruction is to become familiar with the manuscript sources—sources that the originators of the troping hypothesis knew intimately. Here again, a desire for clear definition and classification has tended to obliterate the individuality of the various sources. The separation of 9th–10th century manuscripts into firm categories of graduals on the one hand and tropers on the other is too summary.[6] The best we can do is to retain a long-standing distinction between manuscripts whose repertories are relatively stable and manuscripts where contents vary greatly from one source to the next.

The relatively stable repertories are the Gregorian Mass Propers and the Office antiphons and responsories; in fact, the only workable definition of "Gregorian Mass Proper" seems to be one based upon the repertory held in common by the earliest manuscripts. These include, beside the six manuscripts edited by Dom Hesbert in his *Antiphonale missarum sextuplex* (Brussels, 1935) such manuscripts as St. Gall 359, Laon 239, and Chartres 47.[7] Presence of an item in a significant number of these sources seems to be a necessary—though not a sufficient—condition for its being "Gregorian."

The manuscripts with the unstable repertories, usually known as "tropers," are not so much later than those just mentioned. The earliest tropers are 10th–11th centuries rather than 9th–10th; but the tropers often present a very different appearance, being extremely varied in their make-up. Dating of the troper manuscripts has always been subject to strong differences of opinion, now more than ever.[8] The following summary is designed to reflect a consensus, with full awareness that exception can and will be taken.

I   Verona, Capit. MS XC (85): c. 900?
    H. Spanke, *Deutsche und französische Dichtung des Mittel-alters*, Stuttgart, 1943, p. 33
    Munich, Staatsbibl. Cod. lat 14843: c. 900? Toul (for the proses) Husmann TS p. 78; Von den Steinen, *Die Anfänge der Se-quenzendichtung*, in *Zeitschrift für schweizerische Kirchen-geschichte*, XL (1946), 256-63
    Paris, B.N. MS lat. 17436, fol. 24, 29-30: c. 900?
    J. Hesbert, *Antiphonale missarum sextuplex*, Brussels, 1935, p. xx. Facs. fol. 30, W. Apel, *Gregorian Chant*, Blooming-

---

[6]The separation has most recently been proposed by Heinrich Husmann, *Tropen und Sequenzenhandschriften. Répertoire International des Sources Musicales*, BV¹, 1964, p. 9 (=TS).

[7]*Paléographie musicale*, Series 2, Vol. 2, 1924; Series 1, Vol. 10, 1909; Vol. 11, 1912.

[8]Husmann, TS, includes many attempts to revise customary datings.

ton, 1958, pl. 8. J. Handschin, in *New Oxford History of Music*, II, 153

Autun, Bibl. Mun. MS 28 S, fol. 64: c. 900?

Facs. B. Stäblein, *Zur Frühgeschichte der Sequenz*, in *Archiv für Musikwissenschaft*, XVIII (1961), Abb. 1, pp. 7-8

Vienna, Nationalbibliothek, MS 1609: 10th cent.

Husmann TS p. 20; R. Weakland, *The Beginnings of Troping*, in *The Musical Quarterly*, XLIV (1958), 477-88

II Paris, B.N. MS lat. 1240: c. 935; St. Martial de Limoges.

Husmann TS p. 137

London, B.M. MS add. 19768: 10th cent., second half; Mainz.

Husmann TS p. 152

III St. Gall, Stiftsbibl. MSS 484, 381: c. 1000; St. Gall.

Husmann TS p. 47, 42

Paris, B.N. MS lat. 9448: c. 1000; Prüm.

Oxford, Bodl. lib. MS 775: c. 1000; Winchester.

Husmann TS p. 158

Cambridge, Corpus Christi College MS 473: c. 1000; Winchester.

Husmann TS p. 150

Paris, Bibl. de l'Arsenal MS 1169: 996-1024; Autun.

Husmann TS p. 110

Paris, B.N. MS lat. 1084: 10th cent., second half, with many later additions;

Aquitainian.

Husmann TS p. 120

Paris, B.N. MS lat. 1118: 987-996; Aquitainian.

Husmann TS p. 128

The more important early sources for tropes can be divided into three groups (even if more accurately located on a continuum). The first group, probably the earliest, are small collections of a dozen or so items (sometimes less) included in much larger manuscripts of often non-musical nature. These small collections may be as early as 900, in any case seem to reflect an early 10th-century stage (*pace*, Professor Husmann). A second group, consisting of two items, presents somewhat larger, more systematic collections reflecting a mid-10th-century stage. Finally, from the end of the 10th century come very large, standardized anthologies in ever-increasing numbers, of which only the first few are listed here. It should be noted that the provenance of those listed— St. Gall (484, 381), Prüm (9448), Winchester (775, 473), Autun (1169), and Limoges (1084, 1118)—represent the periphery of what we now imagine to be the primary locus of trope development, the triangle between the Seine and the Rhine.

INSTEAD of beginning with a definition, it is far better to examine singly some of the important kinds of medieval chant usually included in the notion of trope, stressing what is peculiar to each kind. Introit tropes, recently described in an excellent article by Paul Evans,[9] are of two basic types—those with text and those without. Those without text are the less important, being merely short melismas usually tacked on to ends of phrases of the Introit antiphon. These appendix-melismas are much smaller and much less frequent than tropes with words. In accord with Evans, I see no developmental connection between the two types; in fact, it is not clear to me that the melismatic tropes as a class preceded those with text.

Introit tropes with text are much larger and overwhelmingly more frequent. They consist of phrases of text set to usually neumatic melodies, placed either before the Introit as a whole, or before each of the phrases of an Introit antiphon. In both cases such tropes serve as introductions. They are usually rubricked in the plural, *tropi*. And in fact, Introit tropes occur as sets, several phrases of text and music being provided as a set of tropes for a given Introit, as in Example 1.[10]

It is important to be clear about the over-all relationship between a set of tropes and its Introit. The tropes are newly composed, in music as well as words. There is no question of texting or text-underlay to a pre-existent tune. It has been observed that trope melodies sometimes resemble their Introit antiphons, but in my experience this is by no means so frequent as sometimes claimed; rather, I find that tropes resemble each other (and other types of medieval chant) far more than they resemble their antiphon. But even when there is such a resemblance to a Gregorian original, still the trope is a new composition, deliberately referring to the Gregorian antiphon perhaps, but certainly not "growing" out of it (in the impersonal, organic way proposed by the troping hypothesis).

The set of tropes in Example 1 is in hexameters, a frequent form for Introit tropes, as can beseen in the tropes printed in *Analecta hymnica* Vol. 49.[11] The significance of the hexameter trope for us here is that the hexameter verse, unrelated in form to the text of the Gregorian antiphon, is superimposed as a totally foreign element on it. Often these hexameters come in sets of three, regardless of how many phrases the Introit antiphon itself may have. (Example 1 is a set of

[9]*Some Reflections on the Origin of the Trope*, in *Journal of the American Musicological Society*, XIV (1961), 119-30.

[10]Transcribed from Paris B.N. MSS lat. 1084, fol. 61, and 1118, fol. 33v. This and following examples are presented only as working transcriptions. See *Analecta hymnica*, Vol. 49, p. 154, for text and concordances, some of which include a trope for the psalm verse.

[11]That collection is misleading, of course, because Blume included only those tropes (or worse still, those parts of tropes) that had some kind of poetic form. Since he was editing a *hymn* series, he omitted texts in prose, that is, not in verse, as a matter of principle. Hence his collection of Introit tropes includes a higher portion of hexameters than is found in manuscript sources.

Ex. 1 Introit Tropes

TROPOS SONI VIII. NATALE SANCTI VINCENTI MARTIRIS

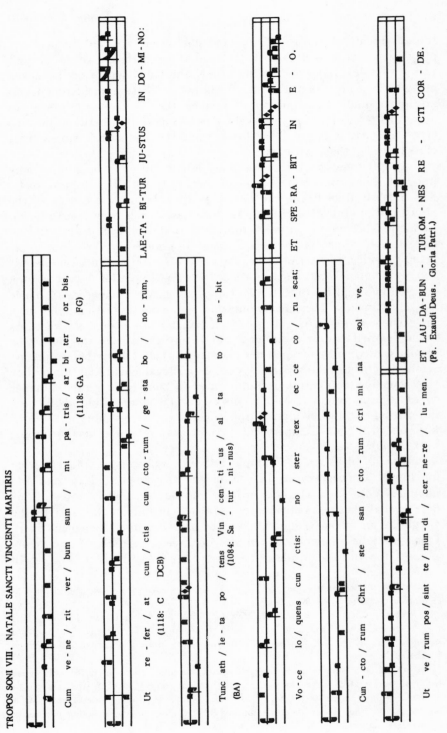

Cum ve - ne / rit ver / bum sum / mi pa - tris / ar - bi - ter / or - bis,
(1118: GA G F FG)

Ut re - fer / at cun / ctis cun / cto - rum / ge - sta bo / no - rum, LAE-TA-BI-TUR JU-STUS IN DO - MI - NO:
(1118: C DCB)

Tunc ath / ie - ta po / tens Vin / cen - ti - us / al - ta to / na - bit
(BA)

Vo - ce lo / quens cun / ctis: no / ster rex / ec - ce co / ru - scat; ET SPE - RA - BIT IN E - O.

Cun - cto / rum Chri / ste san / cto - rum / cri - mi - na / sol - ve,

Ut ve / rum pos / sint te / mun - di / cer - ne - re / lu - men. ET LAU-DA-BUN - TUR OM - NES RE - CTI COR - DE.
(Ps. Exaudi Deus. Gloria Patri.)

44

three pairs, a larger but not infrequent type.) Furthermore, even though the scheme of the hexameter is not reflected in the trope melody or its rhythm (as far as can be seen), still the hexameter lines, recurring in alternation with the lines of the prose text of the antiphon, gain a certain stylistic ascendancy over them by being the more organized element.

In bulk and form, the tropes tend to overrun the Gregorian original, swallowing it up into their own substance. Now it might seem that this was a particularly ungrateful thing for the tropes to do, if they were in essence parasites of the Introit, depending upon it for their structural and stylistic existence. But precisely that, it seems to me, is what is not clearly established. Taken in company with a Gregorian antiphon, a single set of tropes may indeed seem closely wedded to it; tropes seem "proper" in the proper context. But beyond that context the language of the tropes appears to consist of acclamatory texts of a quite general nature, set to generalized phrases of melody, in a style not to be explained as mere parasitical outgrowth.

Perhaps the greatest obstacle to seeing tropes as autonomous works of art is their seeming structural dependence upon another work, in this case, on a Gregorian Introit. How could three interpolations into a pre-existing piece be a "piece"? Without trying to answer this difficult question, it might be suggested that the whole matter of what constitutes a "piece" of Western music might bear further reflection. Aside from that, however, some sets of tropes (such as the one in Example 1) actually show a relatively clear, closed musical form when considered by themselves, apart from their Introit.

Of everything called "trope" in medieval MSS, Introit tropes are so called most consistently, as Blume long ago observed. Of all types, Introit tropes (along with less frequent but exactly analogous types provided for Offertory and Communion) best represent what tropes really were. In them the difference between Gregorian, "official" chant and Carolingian addition is most clear. And in them the meaning of trope as rhetorical ornament—the meaning I take to be the real one—is most plainly evident.[12]

Introit tropes are rivalled in quantity in the earlier sources by tropes to the *Gloria in excelsis*. While Gloria tropes are very similar to Introit tropes, they are often called *laudes* rather than *tropi*, another indication that the Middle Ages tended to keep apart what we have tried to put together.

Like Introit tropes, Gloria tropes come in two forms, with text and without. The latter are short appendix melismas, once again, sometimes

---

[12]Attempts, especially by Handschin *(Trope, Sequence, and Conductus,* p. 128), to make "trope" a strictly musical term are not convincing; such attempts are merely another expression of the contradictions inherent in the troping hypothesis.

believed to be very ancient. But that is sheer hypothesis. Far more prevalent, and important, are the tropes with text, inserted phrase by phrase into the text of the Gloria, as in Example 2.[13] The first line in Example 2 is an introductory trope used for different sets of interior tropes. Like Introit tropes, these for the Gloria are basically neumatic in style; some sets are hexameter in form. This particular set has small melismas in the tropes as well as at the ends of some of the phrases of the original text (which can happen in Introit tropes too). The most interesting feature of these melismas is the way they create a musical form among the tropes as a set, parallel to but independent of the form of the Gloria melody.

While these Gloria tropes are very interesting in themselves, even more interesting is the relationship to the original. The text of the original begins with the hymn the angels sang ("Glory be to God on high . . ."), still towards 800 reserved to the bishop and only gradually released to his representative, the priest. The rest of the text is a series of acclamations ("We praise thee, we bless thee . . ."). The whole text has a status in the liturgy quite different from that of the Roman Propers, and indeed was once used in parts of Gaul as an opening hymn at morning prayer.

None of the melodies preserved for the Gloria is Gregorian in any strictly historical or documentary sense. None of them enjoys documentary evidence for being older than the 9th century. One in particular has been alleged to be older than that, but the evidence is very tricky;[14] in any case, this Gloria melody is a simple one. All the ornate, neumatic melodies are certainly 9th-century or later, some of them being demonstrably much later.

As a matter of fact, Gloria melodies make their first appearance in the MSS in connection with their tropes, or *laudes*. This means that while we can speak of Gloria tropes being interpolations into a pre-existent *text*, we have no assurance that we can categorically describe Gloria tropes as interpolations into a pre-existent *melody*. As far as the sources tell, someone in the 9th century could have sat down with the Gloria text and set it to music adding tropes as he went.

Where several different sets of tropes are written for the same Gloria melody (or cued in a MS to the same Gloria melody), then of

[13]Transcribed from Paris B.N. MS lat. n.a. 1235, fol. 185; there beginning on G, with B♭ first appearing over *voluntatis*, as also at fol. 192, 197. But the version on fol. 188v begins on F, which seems easier here. Cf. Stäblein, *Gloria in excelsis*, in *Die Musik in Geschichte und Gegenwart*, V, 307. See *Analecta hymnica*, Vol. 47, p. 220, for concordances and first half of text. This set of tropes, found in most of the MSS in groups II and III of those listed on p. 42, goes on to the end of the Gloria, including a fine *Regnum*-trope.

[14]Gloria XV of the *Liber Usualis*, Tournai, 1959. See Willi Apel, *Gregorian Chant*, Bloomington, 1958, pp. 82, 409.

Ex. 2 Gloria Tropes

ANTIPHONA AD EPISCOPUM

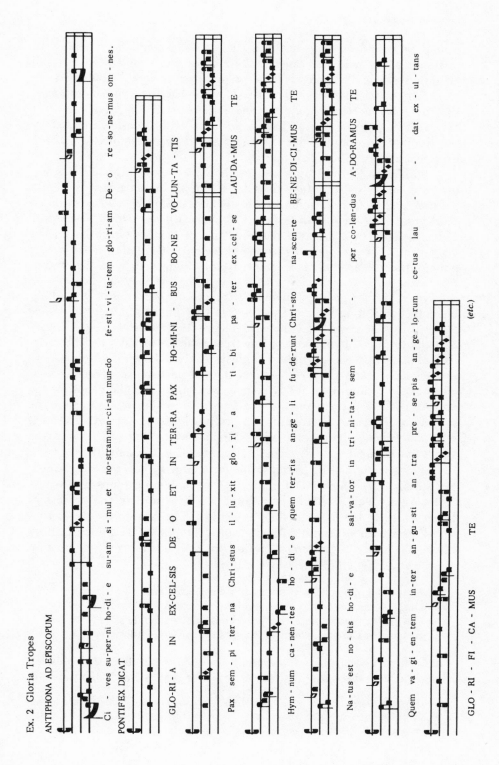

Ci - ves su-per-ni ho-di - e su-am si-mul et no-stram nun-ci-ant mun-do fe-sti-vi-ta-tem glo-ri-am De - o re-so-ne-mus om - nes.

PONTIFEX DICAT

GLO-RI-A IN EX-CEL-SIS DE - O ET IN TER-RA PAX HO-MI-NI - BUS BO-NE VO-LUN-TA - TIS

Pax sem-pi-ter-na Chri-stus il - lu-xit glo-ri - a ti - bi pa - ter ex - cel - se LAU-DA-MUS TE

Hym-num ca-nen-tes ho - di - e quem ter-ris an-ge-li fu-de-runt Chri-sto na-scen-te BE-NE-DI-CI-MUS TE

Na-tus est no - bis ho-di - e sal-va-tor in tri-ni-ta-te sem - - per co-len-dus A-DO-RAMUS TE

Quem va-gi-en-tem in-ter an-gu-sti an - tra pre - se-pis an-ge-lo-rum ce-tus lau - - dat ex - ul - tans

(etc.)

GLO - RI - FI - CA - MUS TE

47

course we would assume that only one of them could have come into existence along with that melody. The other sets would then have to be described as "composed to a pre-existing melody." But in such cases — characteristic of a wide range of what has been called troping — the thing being troped may only have pre-existed for a few years; it may still be modern music. This is not at all the situation implied by the troping hypothesis, which pictures tropes as accretions to official, liturgical chants of hoary antiquity.

Similar to Gloria tropes are the Sanctus tropes, although less frequent in earlier sources. Like the Gloria text, the Sanctus text is clearly defined, and in fact occupies a more ancient and more solid position in the liturgy than the Gloria text. But also as with the Gloria, the status of the melodies is a different matter. None of them is Gregorian in the very strict sense of appearing in one of the early Gregorian Mass books; none of them is an "official" chant. In a brilliant article on the Byzantine Sanctus,[15] Kenneth Levy has shown that it may be possible to discern in various sources (including tropers) the outlines of an old acclamatory inflection for the Sanctus text that might represent a 7th- or 8th-century congregational melody. But as it appears in 10th-century Sanctus tropes, this melodic outline seems to me to have more the nature of a reminiscence, within a sophisticated art-form, of an older congregational acclamation, rather than its real persistence. (Sanctus melodies of the 10th century are, of course, written for the choir, not for the congregation.) In other words, the melody of a Sanctus may resemble the melody of its tropes not because the tropes imitate a pre-existing melody, but because both trope and Sanctus melody are products of the very same musical style, composed at more or less the same time.

Problems of distinguishing trope from original become increasingly difficult with the Agnus Dei, and here the problem extends to the text itself. Agnus Dei, it should be pointed out, was still in the process of being added to the Mass in the 9th century. The Agnus Dei text occurs in versions both with and without tropes. Tropes to the Agnus Dei are often cued only to *miserere*, indicating the replacement of most of what we call the official text by the trope.[16]

Agnus Dei, qui tollis peccata mundi, miserere nobis!
Omnipotens, pie te precamur assidue, miserere nobis!
Qui cuncta creasti, nobis semper ad auge, miserere nobis!
Redemptor Christe, exoramus te supplices, miserere nobis!

What, then, is the official, original, liturgical text? But the question should be *was* there such a text, at least for Agnus Dei? Or was there

[15]*The Byzantine Sanctus and its Modal Tradition in East and West*, in *Annales musicologiques*, VI (1958/1963), 7-67.

[16]Paris B.N. MS lat. 1118, fol. 25v; cf. *Analecta hymnica*, Vol. 47, p. 384.

at first only a wealth of texts, whose boiled-down common denominator, fit in the 9th century only as an expedient for ferias or penitential season, has become our official text?

Such questions come to a climax in *Kyrie Eleison,* musically the richest of these acclamations, and the hardest to handle. The whole liturgical history of the Kyrie is exceedingly intricate, no safe subject for anyone but a full-time liturgist. I shall only call attention to one relevant detail. In a letter most famous for its discussion of the Alleluia, Gregory the Great says:[17]

> But we have not, nor do not, say *Kyrie eleison* as the Greeks do. For with the Greeks, all sing together, but with us the clergy sing, the people respond. And *Christe eleison* is said just as many times, which is certainly not done by the Greeks. In daily Masses, moreover, we do not say the other things usually said, but only *Kyrie eleison* and *Christe eleison,* in order that we may concern ourselves with these supplications at greater length.

This formulation can hardly be taken (as it sometimes is) as a description of what we now call the nine-fold Kyrie. Gregory mentions only that *Christe* is said as many times as *Kyrie,* which certainly does *not* describe the nine-fold Kyrie. Then, there is the intriguing reference to those "other things usually said." We should notice that, whatever they were, the saying of them was normal; it was their omission that elicited Gregory's explanatory comment. We should notice too, that elsewhere in the liturgy the acclamation *Kyrie eleison* normally appears in connection with "other things"—in the litanies, for example. One does not, in the earlier liturgies, normally stand up and say "Kyrie eleison" without accompanying it by some more prolix expression. Thus when Amalarius of Metz (around 830) illustrates the Kyrie with these words,[18]

> Kyrie eleison, Domine pater, miserere;
> Christe eleison, miserere, qui nos redemisti sanguine tuo;
> et iterum Kyrie eleison, Domine Spiritus Sancte, miserere,

we automatically look for the "other things" among Kyrie tropes, and not finding them there, assume they are a lost ancient proto-trope. Perhaps so; but I take Amalarius's *verba* to represent the normal form of Kyrie as he knew it, that is, a Greek acclamation combined with more prolix Latin ones.

For what is it that is being troped, in the case of *Kyrie eleison?* Only a liturgical position (after the Introit), to be filled by an acclamation ending *eleison.* From the Carolingian point of view, this acclama-

---

[17]Latin text in Egon Wellesz, *Gregory the Great's Letter on the Alleluia,* in *Annales musicologiques,* II (1954), 14-15.
[18]Quoted in Stäblein, *Kyrie,* MGG, VII, col. 1942

tion had only recently been fixed by convention in a nine-fold form. On simple feasts the acclamation names merely *Kyrie,* "Lord," then specifies *Christe,* "Savior." On more elaborate feasts these simple titles are replaced by longer acclamatory descriptions, such as those cited by Amalarius, and then found in elaborate Kyries of the 9th through 15th centuries. One of the earliest preserved Kyries, *Tibi Christe supplices,* is also one of the most elaborate.[19]

Kyries are almost entirely absent from the earliest sources. When eventually they do appear, it is often in two forms — once with the full acclamation (neumes being entered over the individual syllables), then again with only the two words *Kyrie eleison* (separated by a melismatic notation of the same melody. According to the troping hypothesis, this melismatic melody would be much older than the text, which would have been added as a type of trope. Recent research first corrects the terminology:[20] Text-underlay is not troping, and was not usually called troping in the early Middle Ages. Second, it is now suggested that melisma and text came into being simultaneously. This seems to me entirely justified. After all, this is what the sources themselves tell us, the melismatic notation appearing not earlier than the syllabic. If anything, the syllabic form might be a shade earlier, depending on how certain sources are dated. Here, as always, it is the troping hypothesis that asserts something contrary to the sources, and must bear the burden of proof.

There are many points to be made on the difficult subject of the Kyrie, points that I can only summarize. First, even if some of the melismas existed before their texts, it would be by only a few years. It has several times been pointed out that Kyrie melodies have little if anything in common with Gregorian melodies, being instead modern chant of the 9th century or later. Second, in the early sources melismatic Kyries come in two sizes, large and small. The small ones, with only a few notes between *Kyrie* and *eleison,* are often without any other text. The larger ones, on the other hand, always seem to have syllabic versions with the long Latin acclamations. The reasons for the double notation — melismatic and syllabic — are admittedly not clear, but do not, I think, present an insurmountable obstacle. Third, the type of Kyrie text claimed by the troping hypothesis to be the proto-type, for example

Kyrie Deus sempiterne vita vivens in te *eleison*

turns up in later sources rather than earlier ones, while the earlier ones have this type:

[19]A transcription *ibid.,* 1941. As *Te Christe rex,* Kyrie ad lib. VI, *Liber Usualis.* Concordances and an over-edited text in *Analecta hymnica,* Vol. 47, pp. 45-48.
[20]Stäblein, *Die Unterlegung . . .,* p. 17, also note 44.

Tibi Christe supplices exoramus cunctipotens ut nostri digneris eleison!
(Kyrie...eleison!)

Finally, one of the most important early Kyries, *Cunctipotens genitor*, is of course in hexameters, hence is not a very convincing example of text-underlay to an ancient, official melisma.

In summary, then, tropes to Introit, as well as analogous tropes to Offertory and Communion, are new compositions added to old, official ones—although in terms of bulk and form one might think it was the old, official compositions that had been added to the tropes. Tropes to Gloria and Sanctus are new compositions added to old texts; but we have to add that the *melodies* for these old texts were not old, being more or less the same age as the tropes. In the case of Agnus Dei and Kyrie it becomes progressively more difficult to separate "official" text, "original" melody, and "trope" from each other. What is now usually called a Kyrie trope (but what I would prefer to call simply a Kyrie) seems to me to be an integral, autonomous artistic creation.

These kinds of pieces make up the bulk of what are usually regarded as tropes of the 9th and 10th century. None of these types involves text-underlay to a pre-existent melisma in any important way. Still, text-underlay, or texting, did occur throughout the 9th and 10th centuries, in forms now to be described.

THE famous melisma mentioned by Amalarius of Metz[21] as borrowed from the Roman singers was sung in the north in the Christmas responsory *Descendit de caelis,* and provided in the 10th-century sources with abundant *Fabrice* textings. Here we know the melody to be not merely pre-existent, but Roman rather than Frankish in origin. This, however, is a special case, not to be taken as typical of a wide range of phenomena. More typical (but still not numerous) are the textings supplied for Alleluias, or just as frequently for melismas occurring at the end of the second or third verse of Offertories.[22] Alleluia and Offertory textings tend to be grouped apart from tropes in the MSS.

Texting of the Offertory verse melismas presents interesting problems of chronology. As preserved in the sources, these textings pre-suppose at least a minimum repertory by 900. The Offertory verses themselves, however, may not be much older than that. Indeed, Dr. Apel has placed their composition towards the end of the 9th century.[23] This dating, based on an oblique piece of evidence in Aurelian of Réomé,

---

[21]Handschin, *Trope, Sequence, and Conductus,* pp. 142-45

[22]The largest early collections in Paris B.N. MS lat. 1240, fol. 43v-46, 79v-80. Examples in Apel, *Gregorian Chant,* pp. 433-36.

[23]*The Central Problem of Gregorian Chant,* in *Journal of the American Musicological Society,* IX (1956), 126.

may well be subject to discussion; but in any case it is probable that these Offertory verses, with their concluding melismas, come either at or after the end of the development that produced the Gregorian Propers. As with Gloria and Sanctus tropes, it is modern, not ancient, music that is being worked over. If Dr. Apel's dating were right, the earliest textings would have been made almost before the ink was dry on the originals, which for their part would scarcely qualify as either "official" or "Gregorian."

Alleluia textings boast one of the earliest dated instances (817-834) of all medieval chant, the famous *Psalle modulamina*, a text-underlay for the Alleluia *Christus resurgens*.[24] Here the new text is added under the Alleluia, the jubilus, and the whole verse, incorporating the original text with very little change. Sometimes, however, early Alleluia textings provide text only for the Alleluia and jubilus, and for the repeat after the verse, but not for the verse itself. In either case, there is no question as to the prior existence of the melody. Surely the Alleluia textings are the castle impregnable of the troping hypothesis! Yet even here there are cracks in the wall. Alleluia textings are not so frequent, after all, nor do they multiply at a very fast rate,[25] nor can so very many be pushed back to the 9th century, in spite of *Psalle modulamina*. The Alleluias involved have a way of being those presumably later within Gregorian development (for example, *Christus resurgens)*, if not actually neo-Gregorian Frankish Alleluias of the 9th or even 10th century.[26] I have the distinct impression that here, too, we are dealing with an ongoing current of musical activity. In any case, Alleluia textings themselves involve no musical composition, therefore offer no valid measure of the new composition going on around them. We cannot, I think, take Alleluia texting as the font and origin of medieval chant.[27]

WHILE it is sometimes admitted that most if not all the Kyries, say, that we now have are new compositions (rather than textings of old melismas), still it is argued that Kyries as a type are tropes in origin, therefore as a type heir to all that the troping hypothesis asserts about lack of originality. I think this view entails a real confusion between where a thing came from and what it actually is. This confusion, it seems to me, is especially prevalent in discussion of the prose or sequence, usually classed as a trope on the grounds of its putative origin.[28]

[24]J. Smits van Waesberghe, *Zur ursprünglichen Vortragsweise der Prosulen, Sequenzen und Organa*, in *IGM Kongress Bericht*, Cologne, 1958, p. 252 and facs. Facs. also in MGG, *Notation*.

[25]In comparison, say, to proses; but cf. Stäblein, *Die Unterlegung* . . ., p. 21.

[26]The 20-odd Alleluia textings in Paris B.N. MS lat. 1118 are a revealing collection in this respect.

[27]Stäblein, *Die Unterlegung* . . ., p. 21, calls the Alleluia a "Tummelplatz."

[28]For example, by Handschin, *Trope, Sequence, and Conductus*, p. 128; not, however, by Stäblein, *Die Unterlegung* . . ., p. 12, note 1.

It is now clear from recent research[29] that there was a thing called a *sequentia* before there was a *prosa*, and that this *sequentia* (for which it is convenient to retain the Latin form of the term) was a melisma to replace the repeat of the Alleluia after the verse—or actually to be interpolated into the Alleluia as its expansion. Such a *sequentia* can be seen in Example 3b, after its Alleluia, *Beatus vir*, in 3a.[30] As it stands in Paris B.N. MS lat. 1118, the *sequentia* is incomplete, ending on A. It must be completed (as in early MSS the verse itself must be completed) by supplying the end of the jubilus, which drops neatly into place to end on the final F. Thus the *sequentia* is a real interpolation into the Alleluia, replacing a shorter jubilus, in effect, with a longer one.

Such a *sequentia*, corresponding to what is described under that name by Amalarius around 830, may be assumed to be what the sequence was before it was equipped with a prose. You can, if you want to, call such a *sequentia* a trope—a melismatic trope comparable to the short appendix-melismas we saw in Introit and Gloria tropes. But this is the only phase of the development of the sequence to which the term "trope" can be legitimately applied. It is the melisma that is the trope; at least, we would be driven to that confusing conclusion if we tried to apply a consistent definition of troping.

But discussion of terms will get us nowhere; only by looking at the things can we understand how they are related. Comparing the *sequentia* in Example 3b with the sequence-with-prose *Gloriosa dies* in Example 3c (a famous 9th-century piece), it is immediately apparent how great a difference separates the two. The old *sequentia* is of quite a different size—indeed, a different order of magnitude—than the sequence-with-prose, and quite different as well in musical construction. They are simply not the same kind of music, and no amount of emphasis on a trope origin can overcome this immense difference. A good-sized sequence-with-prose, such as is frequent in the decades after 850, can be 300-600 notes long, when sung with all the double versicles. In cases where the sequence is related to a known Alleluia (and this is less than half the time in the part of the repertory known to be of the 9th-century origin) the relationship typically involves 5-10 notes at the beginning and occasionally the same number at the end, but not anywhere in between. To describe the relationship between such a sequence and its

---

[29]Summarized by Stäblein in *Sequence*, MGG, XII, 530-31.

[30]The *sequentia*, transcribed here from Paris B.N. MS lat. 1118, fol. 133v, is found also in Paris B.N. MS lat. 1084, fol. 213 with variants and an ending. *Gloriosa dies* is transcribed from Paris B.N. MSS lat. 1240 and 1118. For concordances see *Analecta hymnica*, Vol. 53, p. 351.

This *sequentia* (Ex. 3b) would seem to be the one referred to in the 9th-century Gradual Blandinensis, where it says "Alleluia Beatus vir cum sequentia," cf. Stäblein, *Zur Frühgeschichte der Sequence*, in *Archiv für Musikwissenschaft*, XVIII (1961), 4-5, who thinks it might mean *Gloriosa dies*, given in Ex. 3c.

Ex. 3 Alleluia, sequentia, and prose

a Alleluia (V. *Beatus vir qui timet*)

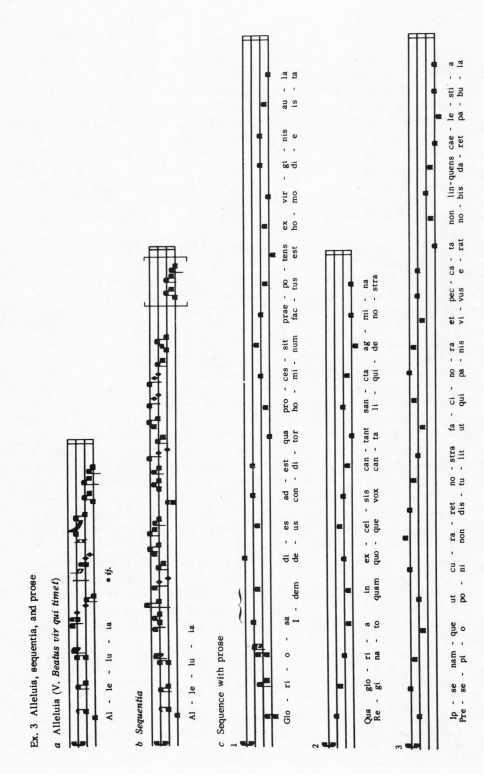

Al - le - lu - ia *ij.*

b Sequentia

Al - le - lu - ia

c Sequence with prose

1 Glo - ri - o - sa di - es ad - est qua pro - ces - sit prae - po - tens est ex vir - gi - nis au - la
   I - dem de - us con - di - tor ho - mi - num fac - tus est ho - mo di - e is - ta

2 Qua glo - ri - a in ex - cel - sis can - tant san - cta ag - mi - na
   Re - gi - na - to quam quo - que vox can - ta li - qui - de no - stra

3 Ip - se nam - que ut cu - ra - ret no - stra fa - ci - no - ra et pec - ca - ta non lin - quens cae - le - sti - a
   Pre - se - pi - o po - ni non dis - tu - lit ut qui pa - nis e - rat no - bis da - ret pa - bu - la

54

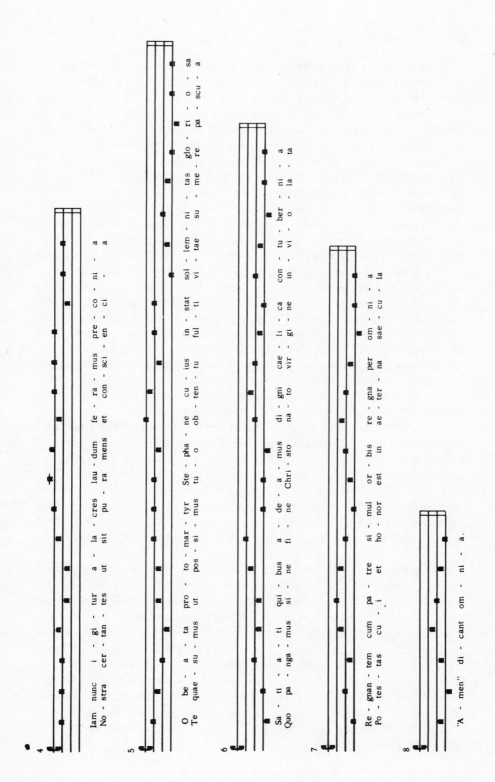

Alleluia as an example of the troping process, whereby the composer's activity is allegedly limited to servile embroidery of traditional materials, rigidly circumscribed by liturgical rule and devoid of artistic originality — is this really a fruitful kind of description? Does it really illuminate the artistic process responsible for the other 590 notes that the composer got from somewhere else — or perhaps even made up all by himself?

It may actually be possible to trace the musical development that led from the short, rhapsodic, old *sequentia* to the long, highly structured newer sequence-with-prose. If we succeed in doing so, it will only be to show a spectacular (but not unparalleled) case of stylistic growth, all the more requiring a kind of musical understanding that the troping hypothesis cannot provide. In any event, we only obscure the development from old *sequentia* to new sequence by saying that since the first is a trope, so is the second. We are accustomed to make a fundamental distinction between a Beethoven symphony and an early 18th-century opera overture, in spite of the fact that they are called by the same name *(sinfonia)* and that one came from the other. The sheer size (if nothing else) of the larger prevents us from confusing the two. Just so, it seems to me, there should be no question of confusing a full-size sequence with a *sequentia*. As in the case of the sinfonia, we might be misled at first by the terminology into identifying the two types, large and small; but the mistake is evident as soon as we gain a first-hand knowledge of how the pieces themselves actually go.

For if we say that all music built on any element of the past, no matter how slight, is a trope, then indeed most medieval music becomes tropes; but so does most other music too. We already have trouble distinguishing "tropic" from "non-tropic" motets in the 13th century; if we broaden the definition of trope we have to include cantus-firmus technique, and parody too. What about new arias composed to be inserted in old recitative? Or new recitative for an old opera-comique? Is any work that quotes another work a trope? Is the *Lyric Suite* a trope of *Tristan?*

I HAVE stated the case as forcefully as I know how, which probably means I overstated it; if so, the overstatement should be taken as, in all modesty, corrective in intent. It is true, of course, that all these forms have connections with the past. What has happened with the tropes is that their connection with the past has been emphasized all out of proportion, thus obscuring completely the ways in which tropes are different from their past, the ways they are different from each other. As in other times, composers of the 9th and 10th centuries worked in a stylistic continuum, writing music about music to a greater or lesser degree. We need to determine for each age, each composer, each piece, the measure of significant difference from its past, if we are to grasp the composer's intent, and his achievement.

Bibliography

For further study of tropes consult Willi-Apel, *Gregorian Chant* (Bloomington, Ind., Indiana University Press, 1958); Richard Crocker, "The Repertory of Proses at Saint Martial de Limoges in the 10th Century," *Journal of the American Musicological Society,* 11 (1958); Paul Evans, "Some Reflections on the Origin of the Trope," *Journal of the American Musicological Society,* 14 (1961); Hans-Jörgen Holman, "Melismatic Tropes in the Responsories for Matins," *Journal of the American Musicological Society,* 16 (1963); Rembert Weakland, "The Beginnings of Troping," *The Musical Quarterly,* 44 (1958); H. M. Bannister, "The Earliest French Troper and its Date," *Journal of Theological Studies,* 2 (1900-1901); and Jacques Handschin, "The Two Winchester Tropers," *Journal of Theological Studies,* 37 (1936). The reader should also consult the work of Handshin with which Professor Crocker takes issue, "Trope, Sequence, and Conductus" in *The New Oxford History of Music,* vol. 2 (London, Oxford University Press, 1954). Heinrich Husmann, *Tropen- und Sequenzenhandschriften* (Munich, G. Henle, 1964), which is vol. BV¹ of *Répertoire Internationale des Sources Musicales,* is a catalog containing complete bibliographical information concerning trope and sequence manuscripts. For background material on the poetry of tropes see F. J. E. Raby, *A History of Christian-Latin Poetry* (Oxford, Clarendon, 1927); and as a guide to the development of the liturgy see Dom Gregory Dix, *The Shape of the Liturgy* (London, Dacre Press, 1945).

An extensive collection of trope and sequence texts, without music, is contained in *Analecta hymnica medii aevi,* 55 vols. (Leipzig, Reisland, 1886-1922; New York, Johnson Reprint Corp., 1961). Vols. 47 and 49 contain tropes, and vols. 7-10, 37, 39-40, 42, 44, and 53-55 contain sequences. Paul Evans's *The Early Trope Repertory of Saint Martial de Limoges* (Princeton, Princeton University Press, 1970) includes both text and music of a large number of tropes for the proper of the mass.

4

GOTHIC is a term frequently used by historians of the visual arts to refer to art, and especially to architecture, as it existed in northern European countries from the twelfth to the fifteenth centuries. By extension, the term has sometimes been used by musicologists to designate the music of the same period. During this period two aspects of music developed from simple beginnings to reach a high degree of complexity, and without these developments all further art music as we know it in Western civilization would have been impossible. The first of these was the development of polyphony from the earlier organum into musical forms of which the French motet represents both the most prevalent and the most complex example. The second development was that of a systematic method of rhythmic notation that permitted the writing down, and thus the preservation, not only of polyphonic music but also of secular song and dance music.

Current fashions in terminology tend to ignore the term Gothic music in favor of such terms as *ars antiqua, ars nova,* and even "twelfth-century music," "thirteenth-century music," etc. Thus, some readers may question Professor Leichtentritt's use of the term Gothic to refer to medieval music; however, his central argument remains firm regardless of terminology. The music of the late Middle Ages represents a "peculiar combination of the strictest, coolest logic, the most rigid law, with the fantastic flight of the imagination . . . ," and modern music is greatly indebted to it.

Hugo Leichtentritt (1874-1951), scholar, critic, and composer, was Professor of Music at Harvard University. His writings on music, both books and contributions to periodicals, are too numerous to permit a complete bibliography here. Among them are *Geschichte der Motette* (Leipzig, Breitkopf & Härtel, 1908), *Musical Form* (Cambridge, Mass., Harvard University Press, 1951), and *Music, History, and Ideas* (Cambridge, Mass., Harvard University Press, 1940).

The Gothic Period

HUGO LEICHTENTRITT

The most important of all the changes experienced by music is without question the rise and growth of polyphony, which, beginning rather crudely about the year 1000, transformed the art of music, giving it an entirely new aspect and opening for it new possibilities of fantastic compass that are still effective. If we ask ourselves what kind of mind could have devised and developed these incomparably fertile and far-reaching musical ideas, we are led to an examination of the spiritual forces active from about 1100 to 1400, to a consideration of the political problems of the epoch and its achievements in theology, philosophy, literature, and art. Possibly the fundamental idea of polyphony, the idea of singing or playing several different sounds simultaneously, came from the pagan nations of northern Europe, the Scandinavians, Germans, and Britons, and the Celts of England and Ireland. But the credit for having perceived the possibilities in this primitive conception of harmony is due to the Christian scholars and artists of the Benedictine monasteries in France, England, and Germany. Polyphony as a principle of art is inseparably connected not only with the music of the Catholic Church but also with the ecclesiastic spirit in its various manifestations, artistic and otherwise.

The analogy of Romanesque architecture with Gregorian chant has been pointed out in the preceding chapter. Gregorian chant, like Romanesque architecture, represents the first phase of the great medieval art of construction. Musical polyphony in its spiritual basis corresponds to the second phase of medieval constructive art, to the Gothic style. The art of polyphony could only have been invented in an age capable of conceiving the fantastic magnificence of Gothic structure. Both Gothic art and polyphony are emanations of the scholastic spirit which dominated the theology, philosophy, and poetry of the later Middle Ages. The im-

FROM Hugo Leichtentritt, *Music, History, and Ideas* (Cambridge, Mass., Harvard University Press), pp. 51-73. Copyright 1938, 1947 by the President and Fellows of Harvard College, © 1966 by Regina Buchwald. Reprinted by permission of the publisher.

posing Gothic cathedrals of Rheims, Rouen, Amiens, Cologne, the bold polyphonic structures of the Parisian school of Leoninus and Perotinus in the thirteenth century and later of the early English and Dutch schools, the scholastic theology and philosophy of Thomas Aquinas, Albertus Magnus, Bonaventura, Duns Scotus, the German mysticism of Meister Eckhart, the magnificent poetic conception of Dante's *Divina Commedia:* all these different achievements are outgrowths of the same quality of mind. Compared with the monumental character of the Gothic cathedral, or scholastic philosophy, or Dante's profound transcendental poetry, the polyphonic music of this epoch seems immature and even crude. It could not be otherwise, for music was a new and very young art, taking its first steps on an unknown road, whereas philosophy, poetry, and architecture were old, filled with a rich inheritance from antiquity. Nevertheless, the scholastic spirit is as evident in the immature conceptions of the early French motet, the first great achievement of the new polyphonic art, as in the accomplished and ingenious music of the great Dutch masters two hundred and fifty years later.

Before discussing the musical expression of the scholastic spirit, however, it seems proper to ascertain what attitude this scholastic spirit had toward the study of music.

Medieval education and learning were comprised of the seven liberal arts. Four of these, the so-called quadrivium, were put under the head of mathematics: arithmetic, geometry, astronomy, music. Music was considered a part of mathematics, a very strange conception for us. Yet there is a certain truth in it, though ordinarily the close connection of music and mathematics is not apparent. It is revealed only after penetrating studies in acoustics, as well as in musical composition and form. Boethius is responsible for the doctrine that science is far superior to art as a mental achievement, and his great authority contributed largely to the scholastic conception of music as a mathematical science. To us this attitude seems to lessen the significance of music, but in medieval times it was a distinction that helped music to be deemed worthy of serious study. It also explains the considerable number of medieval theoretical treatises in comparison with the almost total absence of actual musical documents other than Gregorian chant and hymns. Though he considered music a part of mathematics, Boethius still attributed to it a special aim. While the other disciplines of mathematics are concerned with the search for truth, music has in addition an ethical tendency, a striving toward the Good. Boethius also teaches that the human body and human mind are shaped by nature in proportions analogous to the proportions that dominate music.

When Clovis, king of the Franks, desired to have in his service a musician who could both sing and play on the cither (a "kitharoidos") in the Italian style, he applied to the Gothic king Theodoric in Ravenna. Theodoric sent the request to the greatest musical authority in his vicinity, Boethius. The letter written to Boethius by Cassiodorus in Theodoric's name, which is to be found in Cassiodorus' writings, contains a rather complete enumeration of the moral powers of music, its exhilarating and pacifying effects, and an interesting aesthetic evaluation of the five ancient modes of music: "The Dorian mode effects chastity and pudicity. The Phrygian stirs to fighting and engenders wrath, whereas the Aeolian mode calms the tempests of the soul and lulls the calmed soul into sleep; the Iastic mode sharpens dull insight and directs the profane mind toward heavenly aspirations; the Lydian mode soothes the heavy cares of the soul and expels vexation by pleasant entertainment." Here music reaches decidedly beyond the confines of mathematics, moving in the direction of emotional impression, even though it is not yet ready for precise expression of feeling. Yet all these powerful emotional effects are due to the mathematical order in music. We perceive here that strange coupling of the fantastic with a strict, cool constructive faculty so characteristic of the later medieval, especially the Gothic, mind. These two opposing traits do not always manifest themselves in the same person. Some authors represent the scholastic type, others the mystic type. But there is hardly a theologian of rank, a philosopher, politician, historian, poet, who does not consider it his duty to speculate on the nature of music in his writings.

One of the great problems of the art of music, the emotional problem, is solved here by Cassiodorus in an elementary way by means of a readymade prescription, a certain scale being assigned to each of the varying sentiments. Later ages devised more highly differentiated systems of emotional expression. By and by, all the constituents of composition are called upon for aid. In the later Italian madrigal picturesque word-associations are sought through melodic and rhythmical means. Monteverdi looks for support of declamatory accent and colorful chromatic harmony; tempo, melodic cut, rhythm are exploited in the symbolical formulas or motives of Bach and Handel; harmony, tonal color, symphonic complication are added to the expression of the various *affetti*, till a climax of emotional expression is reached in Beethoven. Wagner and the modern romantic composers exercise their inventive ingenuity in more and more subtle and differentiated "expression," until in the twentieth century "impressionism" and "expressionism," up to that time almost identical, are evolved as separate styles.

All through the Middle Ages, as late as the fifteenth century, the great universities of Paris, Oxford, Bologna, Padua, Prague, expressly prescribe the study of music, not only for professional musicians but for every candidate for the degree of *magister artium*. Music is here considered an art in the scholastic sense (that is, a science), not an art in the modern sense.

There are, however, various trends even in scholastic speculation on music: a rationalistic tendency on a Greek basis; an emotional, irrational tendency on an Oriental basis. These two attitudes are represented musically in Christian church music by the strictly measured "closed" form, the symmetrical melody of the Ambrosian hymns, and the "open" style of the jubilant coloraturas, with their almost formless melodies. Both tendencies were later combined in a highly ingenious manner in the Dutch polyphony of the fifteenth century. But even within the rationalistic Greek theory there are distinct classifications. The Pythagorean doctrine of numbers and proportions was interpreted in two different manners in later Greek philosophy: the Platonic idealistic harmony of the spheres is denied by Aristotle's doctrine, based on a realistic empiricism. The earlier centuries of the Middle Ages rather favor the Platonic conception of music, whereas the later ones are influenced by the philosophy of Aristotle as interpreted by Arabian scholars. Through the Crusades and the Moorish domain in Spain, Arabic speculation had come into close touch with occidental philosophy. Adelard of Bath, the most celebrated English scholar before Robert Grossetest and Roger Bacon, was a pioneer in the study of Arabic science and philosophy in the twelfth century. He wrote a commentary on the Arabic *Liber ysagogarum Alchorismi in artem astronomicam,* in which, according to the medieval academic practice, music is also treated.

Roger Bacon, the founder of modern philosophy, studied in Paris at the time of the great Parisian school of Perotinus. In his *Opus majus* is included an essay on music, in which he treats not only sound but also gesture, and couples elocution with vocal music. He also studied the effect of music on the health and the temper of man and animals. Michael Scotus, the astrologer of the Emperor Frederick II in Palermo, gives in his *Physionomia sue de secretis naturae* a compendium of the occult sciences, including the music of the spheres, followed by a "notitia totius artis musice," with discussion of the doctrines of Boethius and Guido Aretinus: "The number seven rules the world . . . for seven is the number of the planets, of the metals, the arts, the colors, the tones of music, the odors."

Medieval Jewish philosophy also believes in the mysterious power of the sacred numbers seven, ten, and twelve. Neumark in his *Geschichte der jüdischen Philosophie des Mittelalters* summarizes these tendencies as follows: "The insight into this eternal principle of number and measure is also the essence of prophecy, and thus the connecting link between prophecy and music. The prophetic mood is evoked by music because the principle of number and measure is the same in both forms of utterance of human emotion: The law of proportion, valid in music and in color combinations, is the law of world-creation."

From these mysterious regions the distance is not very far to the occult conceptions of the Jewish cabala, speculations indulged in earlier in ancient China, Egypt, and Arabia. In scholastic musical theory there is a reflection of these mystic doctrines. One Elias Salomonis (1274) makes fantastic sketches of the solmization syllables of Guido of Arezzo to show their mysterious symbolism and hidden meaning. The eight church modes for him are descendants of the mystic primeval *tonus;* his "son" is the first church mode, the others are brothers, grandsons, companions, etc. Aribo Scholasticus shows in strange drawings the analogy between the various tetrachords and the life of Christ, from the lowest tetrachord (Christ's humble life in poverty) to the highest (Christ's ascension). Johannes de Muris, the great musical scholar of the University of Paris, a man of European celebrity, explains that the entire structure of music is based on the number four, in conformity with the structure of the world, the macrocosm, and of the human body, the microcosm. There are four elements: warm fire, moist air, dry earth, cold water. These elements build up the entire world, but by the varying proportions of their mixture they also produce the four temperaments: the choleric, the sanguine, the phlegmatic, and the melancholy. There are four seasons, four weeks in the month, four divisions of the day. The four final notes of the authentic modes, D, E, F, G, are built on top of each other, just as the four elements are: earth at the bottom, water above the earth, air above both, and fire still higher, in the empyrean. The relative position of the authentic and plagal modes de Muris very cleverly connects with the main and secondary properties of each element. Water, for instance, is cold, but also moist, like air; earth is dry, but sometimes also wet, like water. In his great work *Speculum musices* Jacobus of Liège describes a whole cosmology of music, one of the most fantastic and grandiose attempts of this kind, akin in smaller proportions to Dante's *Divina Commedia;* the Church, Heaven, human life, the virtues, the Last Judgment, and many more ideas are here brought into direct relation with the laws of music. And the great Dante himself thought much about music, observed its effects, formulated its laws. In his poetry he is mainly concerned with the beautiful and touching effect of singing; in his prose writings, however, the scholastic spirit induces him to systematic investigations of the nature of music. It would not be difficult to collect from Dante's poetry a little musical anthology, and from his prose-writings a very professional-looking extract of a thoughtful and speculative character.

After such glances into the extensive medieval theory of music we shall be better prepared to understand and to appreciate the mental attitude of the famous Parisian school which in the twelfth and thirteenth centuries created the strange Gothic form of the French motet, with its scholastic traits. This rather complicated form is surprisingly bold and fantastic. Its idea consists in building two entirely different and independent melodies on top of a third one, whose theme is a *cantus firmus* from Gregorian chant. The scholastic trait is found in the peculiar treatment of this *cantus firmus*. It is not plainly stated, according to the common practice in similar cases, but is subjected to an academic prescription. The form demands that this *cantus firmus* should be arranged, in one of half a dozen different modes, in a rhythmical order conforming to one of the ancient classical prosodic systems. The *cantus* had to follow from beginning to end either iambic, spondaic, trochaic, dactylic, or anapestic meter, with rests between the sections, without any regard to the natural rhythm of the melody. Here one sees scholastic law and orderly system enforced. It is immaterial whether the system suits the melody or not; the *cantus firmus* has to conform and is forcibly cut up accordingly. Along with this rigid, dry scholastic system, however, the bold Gothic spirit of complication comes into play. Against the strict order and regularity of the *cantus* in the lowest part are written two higher voices, or counterparts, without any apparent connection with each other or with the *cantus*. Three totally different melodies are forcibly welded together; in general, also, three different texts are sung simultaneously, very often in different languages: dance melody and amorous song against solemn Gregorian chant, 3/4 against 6/8 time, French words against Latin words. This fantastic play of the imagination delighted the people who reveled in those grotesque heads of animals and demons, in those curiously distorted human faces carved in stone which are so strange an ornament of the Gothic cathedrals. The boldness and novelty of the musical conception is apparent at once, but its immaturity is equally apparent, for in the thirteenth century music was far from having acquired sufficient technical mastery to cope with constructive problems of such great complexity and difficulty.

Yet at times this music of the Parisian *ars antiqua* rose to high summits. When the now nonexistent International Society of Music celebrated its last festival in Paris in June 1914, shortly before the outbreak of the World War, a sensational impression was produced by French motets of the thirteenth century, heard for the first time, probably, since the Middle Ages. The Sainte-Chapelle, a gem of Gothic architecture, was exactly the right place for this memorable performance; seven hundred years ago Leoninus and Perotinus, the two far-famed heads of the Parisian school of composition, may have performed their motets in this very same chapel. Some of Perotinus' most powerful works have recently been published both in books and in records, and it is now possible to get a clear impression of this remarkable music. Its almost barbaric strength, its utter disregard of beauty of sound, its constant use of piercing dissonances, and its ingenious polyphonic structure give it a curious resemblance to some of the ultramodern music of the Schönberg type.

It is in the music of the great Dutch masters, however, that the

Gothic spirit, with its grandeur and with its scholastic subtlety of speculation, finds its finest and most adequate expression. To reach this summit nearly three hundred years were needed, and in order to understand the nature of such a progressive development it is necessary now to turn to some of the other roads pointing toward the still distant summits. So far we have dealt exclusively with ecclesiastical music, inspired by Christian religious feeling, written for the needs of the church service by composers who were almost always priests. The motet of the *ars antiqua* is an attempt to combine the old ecclesiastic severity with an entirely new feature, the charm of the love songs and dance melodies of chivalry.

Toward the year 1200 a new kind of music made its appearance, a secular music which did not originate in the convents and did not enjoy the protection of the Church: the songs of the troubadours in France and Italy, of the minnesingers in Germany. We possess many thousands of these melodies, often very attractive and even beautiful, full of a lyric charm, a youthful freshness altogether different from the solemn strains of Gregorian chant. This new lyrical amorous music is the product of a new culture, a new class of society; it is the music of the age of chivalry. Until about the eleventh century higher education and learning were a monopoly of the clerical orders; slowly, however, the privileged nobles acquired some intellectual culture. After centuries of barbaric warfare they gained an interest in the gentler arts of peace. About 1200 poetry sprang up in profusion in all the European countries; a rich literature of romance and song was accumulated, and at the same time a new style of music made its appearance.

The easiest access to the spirit of medieval chivalric society and culture is to be found, however, not in the parchment manuscripts of the twelfth century and in the vast modern literature devoted to them, but in the music-dramas of Richard Wagner: *Tannhäuser* and *Lohengrin, Tristan und Isolde,* and *Parsifal.* With the insight of genius Wagner knows how to animate the soul of this distant epoch, even without the aid of an antiquarian spirit in his music. Though as a dramatist he does not aim at historical exactness, though he always speaks of myth as the proper subject matter for music-drama, yet myth can reveal historical truth by reviving the atmosphere and spiritual attitude of a certain epoch, and it is through this visionary power of revival that Wagner aids the student of the history of culture and of music.

This chivalric society is quite distinct from the Church. It represents the worldly power and the splendor of the imperial court. The entire history of the years 900 to 1200 is filled with one recurring theme in a hundred variations: the unceasing struggle for supremacy between Pope and Emperor. The Roman Church had evolved its music, the Gregorian chant; the imperial state likewise produced its poetry and music, very different from the music of the church in style and spirit. This new music of the troubadours, with its delight in melody, may be characterized as ennobled folk song. So far the music of the people had been considered too vulgar and insignificant to be worthy of recording; we do not, in fact, possess a single collection of popular tunes prior to 1200. This does not mean that such tunes did not exist earlier. The people had always had some sort of popular music, but the Church had no desire to encourage or propagate it, and it was entirely ignored in the centers of learning and education, the famous convent schools. When, however, the constant struggle between the papal power and the imperial power made the knights more and more antagonistic toward the Church, more and more independent of it, they ceased to go to it for the satisfaction of all their cultural needs, and turned to the people, whose popular style of singing they adapted to their more refined taste. The result is a great treasure of lyric poetry and music from about 1200 to nearly 1400. Thibaut, king of Navarre, Le Châtelain de Coucy, Wizlaw, prince of Rügen, Walther von der Vogelweide, Gottfried von Strassburg, Wolfram von Eschenbach — these are some of the outstanding names of men who were noblemen, knights, poets, and composers at the same time. In this literature we cherish the earliest blossom of lyric love song, and one of the most precious products of early music. The songs of the troubadours have lost almost none of their fragrance and freshness, their melodic charm, even after seven hundred years. The high perfection of lyric style in this literature cannot, of course, have sprung into existence suddenly; the troubadours must have had a long chain of predecessors, of whom nothing is recorded as yet in the annals of history.

In the culture and literature of chivalry we see for the first time since antiquity the rise of a romantic spirit, as opposed to the classical spirit of the Gregorian art. It is a common — but erroneous — notion that romanticism is a modern trait which first appears in the nineteenth century. Classical and romantic tendencies are as old as art, and even ancient art has its romantic features. The history of art shows a constant swing from the classical to the romantic and back again, with all varieties of intermediate stages. The classical and the romantic are like the north and south poles, certain sections of art being for generations under the influence of one and then for generations under the influence of the other. The romantic spirit is one of the chief elements of Gothic architecture, with its play of light and shade, its fantastic lines, its mystic qualities, its high-soaring pillars and spires leading the eye and the spirit upwards, heavenwards, away from the dullness of everyday life. It also animates the great epic poetry of the Middle Ages, the romance of Tristan and Isolde, the mystic piety of the Parsifal legend, great parts of the *Nibelungenlied;* and in lesser degree it permeates the songs of the troubadours, whose lyric poetry has as its central point the erotic theme, the glorification of the beloved mistress by the young knight. For the first time since antiquity woman makes her appearance in lyric song and music, and the eternal mystery of the two sexes comes within the confines of art. Imagination is set in play; profound instincts are excited and let loose; in short, the romantic element is introduced. One may even go as far as to say that the erotic problem in art is perhaps the central point of all romanticism.

Even the realm of medieval religious spirit is not free from this romantic atmosphere. The austere piety of early Christianity, the sublime severity of Byzantine art, the unfriendly, almost repulsive looks of the images of Christ and the Apostles, so characteristic of early mosaic work and Byzantine art—all these are changed in the twelfth century. It is the age of the Crusades. That all Christianity should unite in a vast campaign against the infidels and make great expeditions overseas into unknown foreign countries in order to liberate the holy seats of Jerusalem, expel the Moslems, and make Jerusalem the capital of Christianity is an idea so fantastic that it could have originated and been realized only in a romantic age. The old fanatical religious austerity is now softened, too, by the introduction of the feminine ideal. It was in these ages of the Crusades that the Marianic cult sprang up. Mary, the mother of Christ, the immaculate virgin queen of heaven, the mild, compassionate, forgiving, consoling spirit, the bright evening star, is the idealization of all womanly virtues. If anything is romantic, this new passionate cult of the Virgin Mary is romantic, and Mary herself is altogether different from the austere Christ, the stern judge of the world, depicted in Byzantine art. Marianic poetry is lyric and romantic and musical at the same time. It was St. Francis of Assisi who discovered this bright new light of humanity, and if he had accomplished no more than this it would suffice to make his name immortal. One of the most cherished themes of spiritual poetry, painting, and music all through the ages, down to our own time, originates in this Franciscan conception: the queen of heaven, soaring above the heavenly hosts, surrounded by the choir of the angels, and, below, unfortunate mortals yearning for peace of soul and praying to her with deeply felt, passionate outcry. A reflection of this new idealization of womanhood animates even the erotic poetry and music of the troubadours, minstrels, and minnesingers.

Thus far music had been serious, fervent, austere, even ecstatic. Now a new quality is added of sweetness, grace, tenderness, delicacy; in short, a womanly note. Music, until now exclusively masculine in character, is transformed by the addition of new lyric, romantic, and erotic tones. A new world of expressiveness is discovered. Though these troubadours' songs, taken singly, are brief and unpretentious in bearing, the new possibilities opened up by their fresh spirit are immense; they have not yet been exhausted, and the art of music is immensely indebted to them even now.

This new lyric music is a reaction against contrapuntal church music; it asserts the right of the individual against the control, frequently tyrannical, exercised by the Church. Supremacy and universality were the aspirations of the Church; it demanded obedience and complete subjugation from the people and stood firm against manifestations of individualism.

The youthful romantic spirit of the twelfth century marks the dawn of the Italian Renaissance. It is the immediate precursor of this great movement. The Franciscan spirit rejuvenates the Church, brings it closer to man, gives a friendlier, more humane aspect to religion, and reconciles to a certain extent the ecclesiastical and worldly interests so hostile to each other in these ages. Music, too, gains from this new lyric and romantic spirit its first springtime, full of budding blossoms, of fresh young green, of mild air and bright sunshine. Secular art has now gained a place; it has asserted its power and remains as a force in art forever. The history of music henceforth has to deal with a new problem of prime importance: ecclesiastical music and secular music in their antagonism and their mutual relations.

By and by this new romantic and lyric spirit in music goes beyond its original confines of solo song with a very primitive instrumental accompaniment. Polyphony, or counterpoint, so far almost exclusively the domain of church music, is gradually adapted to the new lyric style. This combination proved very fertile indeed, and its descendants may be traced down to the twentieth century. The first remarkable results of the mixture of polyphony and secular melody appear in what is known as the *ars nova* in the fourteenth century. This "new art" fills the gap between the older Gothic style of the great school of Paris in the twelfth century and the beginning of the Dutch school early in the fifteenth century. An immensely interesting literature of this music, mainly Italian, between 1300 and 1450 has been explored only recently and constitutes one of the chief discoveries in the field of musicology.

In its aesthetic tendency the Florentine *ars nova* is closely in touch with the rise of poetry and fiction in the early Italian Renaissance, with the beginning of humanistic studies. The rapid rise of culture in the numerous Italian city-republics and princely courts had as a consequence a growing demand for a more refined and elegant type of music, fit for the social entertainment of artistically minded people. Musicians were not slow in recognizing the possibilities for musical treatment that were offered by the new poetry, starting with Dante's *La Vita nuova* and continued by the many minor poets around Dante, whose sonnets Dante Gabriel Rossetti has translated into English so beautifully. Petrarch's famous sonnets and *canzone* to his adored Laura were for centuries favorite texts for musical settings. In Boccacio's *Decameron* and other collections of amusing, though not always very chaste and moral stories, music is frequently mentioned and musical scenes are occasionally described. The peculiar slender grace and refined elegance of the new Italian madrigals, *ballate,* and *caccie* (for one or two solo voices with instrumental accompaniment) is perfectly in keeping with the painting of Botticelli and other early masters. Reading the poetry chosen by these Italian madrigal composers we find ourselves in the atmosphere of cultivated Italian society between 1300 and 1400; through the music we catch glimpses of the delightful scenes that appear in so many of the frescoes painted on the walls of Italian palaces, city houses, and cathedrals in the fourteenth century. As an example we may take a *caccia* (i.e., a catch, a canon) for two voices, with a free third part for an accompanying instrument, by Nicolaus Praepositus de Perugia, who lived in the fourteenth century.[1] The poem describes a company of girls walking in the blooming meadows and woods of spring, gathering flowers and herbs, chatting with each other. One of them exclaims with pleasure as she perceives an especially pretty flower; another suddenly cries aloud, having wounded her finger by touching a thorn. A grasshopper is admired; mushrooms are picked. Then the vesper bell sounds. The sky darkens; there are distant thunder and threatening clouds, but the nightingale begins singing beautifully. Suddenly torrents of rain come down, and everybody hastens home as quickly as possible. One might search the entire art of music back to antiquity without finding anywhere a single piece of music that attempts to describe a scene of this character.

With these innovations entirely new problems spring up in music. Looking at the style of composition in these early Italian madrigals we perceive that at first they continue the style of the French motet, with a *cantus firmus* as basis and two independent parts above it. But there is a very remarkable progress in harmonic feeling. The powerful but almost barbaric ground-tone of the old French motet is changed to a graceful play of rhythms and melodic phrases. A little later, about 1350-1400, the Italian masters advance a step further. Solo singing, as found in the troubadours' songs, is used again, but instead of the former improvised instrumental accompaniment, which was never written out, we find an elaborate polyphonic accompaniment. The voices of solo instruments, flutes, little violas, lutes, harps, little organs or psalteriums, most artistically intertwined, provide an elaborate, graceful, and fantastic figuration, especially in the interludes between the single vocal phrases.

One of the most impressive creations of early Renaissance art is that striking wall painting in the famous *campo santo,* the cemetery at Pisa, representing the Triumph of Death. This monumental painting, generally ascribed to the master Orcagna, includes in its tragic scenes one delight-

---

[1]This charming piece is accessible in Professor Johannes Wolf's valuable collection of old masterpieces, *Sing- und Spielmusik aus älterer Zeit.*

ful and touching little episode, a musical scene. We see a gathering of young ladies and gentlemen, fastidiously dressed in the newest, most splendid fashion, playing and singing, while grim Death, waiting in a corner, is just raising his huge scythe to fell his victims. Here is a very realistic representation of the practice of the *ars nova:* one gentleman is playing the viola; a young lady has in her lap a little psaltery, a tiny clavier, such as we often see in old pictures, worn on a silk ribbon around the neck by elegant ladies.

This new madrigal style with florid instrumental accompaniment spread from Italy to France, to the Netherlands, and to England. A representative northern composer in this style is Guillaume de Machault (1300-1377), the leading master of the French *ars nova.*[2] A fine example of Machault's art is to be found in the three-part motet, "De souspirant cuer," remarkable for its rhythmical freedom as well as for its surprisingly advanced harmony.[3] The satirical "Roman de Fauvel," well known in early French literature, contains (at least in the splendidly illustrated Parisian manuscript, fonds français 146, published in facsimile by Pierre Aubry) many motets, ballads, rondeaux, and lais, in a style similar to Machault's, as musical illustrations. These pieces have a special significance for the connection of music with literature and with miniature painting, all three arts being combined in this precious manuscript, which is dated about 1310.

Quick tempo, lively rhythms, elaborate instrumental figuration are especially characteristic marks of many of these Italian and French pieces of the fourteenth century. In Italy this extremely original, vivid, and picturesque art comes to a surprisingly abrupt end at the beginning of the quattrocento, about 1425. The cause probably lies in political changes, which brought with them corresponding changes in art. The most flourishing period of the Italian madrigal, *ballata,* and *caccia* coincides almost exactly with the removal of the papal residence from Rome to Avignon, in southern France. During the years of this Avignon residence Rome lost a good deal of its ecclesiastic power, and Italian music in this period was much less occupied with church music than with secular song.

As early as 1324 Pope Johannes XXII sent forth from Avignon a famous decree against figurated music in the Church, anticipating the charges brought against contrapuntal music at the Council of Trent more than two hundred years later, in the time of Palestrina. Pope Johannes attacks the abuse of polyphony in church music, aiming mainly at the

[2]A complete edition of his music (edited by Professor F. Ludwig) is in course of publication in Germany.

[3]Included in Johannes Wolf's *Sing- und Spielmusik aus älterer Zeit.*

artificial motets of the *ars antiqua*. Composers, writes the Pope, "cut the melody into pieces with *hoquet* (an effect of sobbing, sighing), enervate it by descant and *tripla* (counterpoints), and sometimes even add secular motets. Thus they show a lack of respect for the basis of church music, are ignorant of its laws, do not know the church modes, and do not distinguish them from each other, but rather confuse them . . . . Thus their tones run about restlessly, intoxicate the ear without calming it, falsify expression, and disturb the worship of the congregation instead of awakening it; they favor lasciviousness instead of dispelling it."

The scandalous state of the papacy in the fourteenth century could hardly have a good effect on church music. In 1378, one year after Pope Urban VI had returned to Rome, one of the most shameful episodes of papal history had its beginning. An anti-pope, Clement VII, was elected by an opposing party of cardinals, and while Urban, just returned from Avignon, took up his residence in the Lateran Palace in Rome, his adversary, Pope Clement, took possession of the newly vacated papal palace in Avignon. This Great Schism, the simultaneous rule of two hostile popes, divided Christianity into two opposed camps. This miserable state lasted from 1378 to 1417, and its influence on music is seen in the fact that the period is barren of good church music, while the secular Italian *ars nova* continues to flourish. The old ecclesiastic motet had been debased more and more through the use of erotic songs and dance melodies, and during the period of papal depression and schism Italian composers lost all taste in church music. It was not until 1417 that the Schism was brought to a definite close by the exciting Council of Constance, when the papal power showed all nations that it had regained its strength. The Dominican Inquisition, begun in the thirteenth century, was let loose against reformers of faith, like the already deceased Wycliffe, translator of the Bible into English, whose bones were burnt, and John Huss, the Bohemian reformer, who was burnt alive at Constance.

The immediate consequence of the restored power of the papacy under Martin V is soon perceived in a new rise of ecclesiastic music in the period starting about 1425. After two hundred and fifty years the famous old Paris school of counterpoint and the French motet had lost their vitality. The successor of the French school in leadership is the school of Cambrai, in the Netherlands, which dominated the entire musical world for more than a century. The age of the great Dutch music now has its beginning.

At the time of the *ars nova*, in the fourteenth century, a new and simpler style of polyphony began in England and later spread to France and the Netherlands. French contrapuntal complexity is replaced by a more harmonic style of writing; euphonious triads are preferred to the former fierce discords. Three great names represent this transition to the new Dutch style of Cambrai, those of John Dunstable, the greatest English composer of his age, and the Dutch masters, Binchois and Dufay. The three are contemporaries. Dunstable, famous both as musician and astronomer, died in 1453 in London, where one can still see his tomb in St. Stephen's Church; Dufay lived in Cambrai after 1450 and died there in 1474; Binchois died in 1460. The reorganized papal power in Rome soon made use of this rising Dutch music, for which the Avignon popes had a marked predilection. During its sojourn in Avignon the papal see had come into closer contact with French and Dutch music, at that time nearly identical, and, native talent for ecclesiastic music being scarcely available in Italy after a hundred years of erotic madrigals and ballads, the papal chapel now turned to Dutch singers and composers. Thus from about 1450 there was an invasion of Dutch musicians into Italy which for a hundred and fifty years to come established the predominance of Dutch music throughout Europe. We have come to the start of a most important new chapter in the history of music.

Everybody speaks of Dutch music and Dutch painting. Few people, however, are aware of the fact that in the fifteenth century, at least, Dutch music and painting were at home in Burgundy. This once rich and powerful country disappeared from the map of Europe completely four hundred years ago, and for most people the famous Burgundy wine is the only reminder of the existence of one of the most flourishing of European countries. The territory of Burgundy, now divided between Belgium, France, Luxembourg, Switzerland, and Germany, comprised a broad corridor starting at the Dutch seacoast at the entrance of the English Channel and extending southward as far as the Lake of Geneva. It reached the height of its power and wealth under the rule of its dukes Philippe le Beau and, especially, Charles the Bold, who came to the throne in 1467. The court of Philippe and of Charles in Brussels was one of the most luxurious of the European courts. Both dukes were extremely cultivated and great lovers of art. Their immense wealth, the general prosperity of the country, the great commerce of cities like Brussels, Antwerp, Bruges, and Ghent, and the natural talent of the Flemish for music, painting, and architecture all helped to make this country the most cultivated region of Europe, the only rival of Italy, which was just entering on the artistically rich period of the Renaissance.

Charles the Bold was a liberal protector of artists. Great painters like Jan and Hubert van Eyck of Ghent, Rogier van der Weyden, and Hans Memlinck were in his service, and a whole galaxy of great Dutch masters of music embellished with their unrivaled art the splendor of the brilliant and luxurious Burgundian court. Gilles Binchois, Anton Busnois, Pierre de la Rue, Alexander Agricola, shining lights of the first Dutch school, were active for many years at the Brussels court, and their new style of music, their brilliant achievements in performance carried the fame of Dutch music all over Europe. Charles was himself an accomplished musician, a composer of motets and chansons. The splendor of the tournaments and festivities at his court was unparalleled, save here and there in Italy, and his court chapel at that time hardly found an equal anywhere in Europe. In the incomparably charming old town of Bruges the magnificent bronze monument erected over the tomb of this warrior and lover of the arts is still one of the great sights.

The town of Cambrai in Burgundy was the seat of the most celebrated school of music of the fifteenth century, and in Cambrai most of the great Dutch masters of music were educated. It was to the school of Cambrai cathedral that the papal court and the royal courts of Europe turned to secure able musicians for their chapels. Nowhere could one find composers, conductors, singers, and players comparable to these Dutch-Burgundian artists. We shall meet them everywhere in our rapid survey of the artistic state, in Italy, France, Germany, Spain, and even such smaller countries as Poland.

While the music of Burgundy and the Netherlands filled all Europe with its fame, history is singularly silent as regards great musical accomplishments in France during the fifteenth century. A glance at French history will explain why Paris, for centuries the greatest metropolis of music, enjoying absolute supremacy and authority over all Europe, should have sunk into insignificance toward 1400. France had reached one of the most unfortunate eras of her history. What is known as the Hundred Years' War with England raged, with a few intermissions, from 1337 to 1453. This long-drawn-out struggle has gained a romantic glamour through the heroic and marvelous feat of the peasant girl, Joan of Arc, who brought about the defeat of the English army besieging Orléans in 1430. These hundred years of warfare utterly exhausted France, and it was fifty years before the country recovered sufficiently to show results of weight in art and science. Scarcely had peace been established between France and England when the new king of France, Louis XI (1461-1483), filled out another quarter of a century fighting his most powerful neighbor and adversary, Charles the Bold of Burgundy, and a number of other powerful French princes, with the final result of a transition from feudalism to monarchy in France to the royal power of the Valois dynasty, but the price paid for this victory was the poverty and cultural ruin of the French people, who had to endure a rule of terror under a despotic, cruel, almost insane king.

One of the most remarkable and interesting historical documents we possess is a description of the state of Europe about 1450 written by the papal legate, Aeneas Sylvius, later Pope Pius II, who in those years traveled about on diplomatic missions in many countries. This cool, shrewd, and highly cultivated observer tells us of the low state of culture and prosperity in France as compared with the great artistic accomplishments of the wealthy and flourishing cities of Burgundy. Charles of Burgundy had great political plans. He aspired to erect a great Rhenish empire, to add to his countries the rich Rhenish provinces, so that the great river Rhine, from its source high up in the Swiss Alps, on its course through Switzerland and Germany to its mouth in the Netherlands, should be entirely controlled by Burgundy, adding immensely to the wealth of the country by its incomparable commercial utility. But the jealousy of France and the independent spirit of Switzerland frustrated this great Rhenish enterprise. In murderous battles with the Swiss and the French Charles was defeated; he fell in battle near Nancy on the fourth of January, 1477. Louis of France had got rid of his most formidable rival. His aim now was to get as much as possible of the immensely rich Burgundian country. Charles's daughter and heiress, Mary of Burgundy, the richest princess of Europe, he planned to make the wife of his son, Charles VIII, hoping thus to secure Burgundy to France by inheritance, without long wars and endless troubles. But Mary of Burgundy, we need not be surprised to find, had no less than seven suitors from the princely families of many countries, and she finally chose young Maximilian of Habsburg, later the German emperor Maximilian I, of whom we shall have more to say as one of the greatest patrons of music. Louis of France, enraged at Mary's refusal to become his daughter-in-law, did not give up his desire of possessing the Burgundian countries. A war with Maximilian was the consequence. Finally in 1482 peace was made, and Burgundy was divided between Germany and France. In this same year Mary of Burgundy, wife of Maximilian, lost her life by an accident, and a year later her relentless enemy, Louis of France, died after a vicious life full of cruelty, destruction, and war. At the time of his death France was still the real lowland of Europe in cultural respects, much inferior to the Burgundian Netherlands, to Italy, and even to Germany. This state of affairs explains why we hear next to nothing of music in France during the entire fifteenth century, when Dutch music had begun to win renown throughout Europe.

The Dutch music of the fifteenth century represents the final expression of the Gothic spirit in terms of musical composition. Extending from about 1450 to nearly 1600, from Dufay to Orlando di Lasso and Jan Pieterzon Sweelinck, it is not uniform in style throughout the course of its vigorous life of a hundred and fifty years. Only its first half, from about 1450 to 1530, belongs to Gothic art proper; its later productions add features that are more or less in the spirit of the Italian Renaissance. Most of the great Dutch musicians—Dufay, Okeghem, Josquin de Près, Heinrich Isaak, Pierre de la Rue, Obrecht, Alexander Agricola, Adrian Willaert—were internationally famous artists, traveling constantly from one country to another, in eager demand at the imperial court at Vienna or Innsbruck and at the French royal court at Paris, sought by the kings of Bohemia and Poland, by numerous dukes and princes in Italy, and especially by the papal chapel in Rome. Dutch music, with its peculiar complication, joined to an ecclesiastic character of great impressiveness, appealed to all the European countries as the perfect musical expression of the dominant spirit of their age. As Gothic architecture spread throughout Europe and reached to England and the Scandinavian countries, the complex Netherlandish art of music followed. And just as Gothic architecture was modified more in Italy than in any other country, so the Netherlandish art of music, practiced by the great Dutch masters themselves, was not fully assimilated by Italian artists. It is extremely interesting to observe the way in which, after about 1530, Italian composers who were pupils of the Dutch masters asserted their national traits against the powerful influence of the imported Dutch art. The final outcome of this struggle we see in Palestrina and his school, in the two Gabrielis in Venice, in the Italian madrigal, where the spirit of the Italian Renaissance asserts itself victoriously. More detailed treatment of this phase of development, however, belongs in the chapter on the Renaissance.

A closer inspection of Dutch music at its climax, with Josquin de Près as the dominating figure, reveals the traits which justify us in calling it closely akin in spirit to Gothic architecture. The art of counterpoint had attained a virtuosity of treatment, a mastery of complication, an organic, logical development hardly ever paralleled in later styles, except by Bach in certain aspects of his art, which revives the Gothic spirit to some extent. In the Dutch motets and masses the piling up of several voices on top of each other, the complex subtleties of canonic treatment, the fantastically curved melodic lines running parallel, obliquely, contrary to each other, intermixed with pauses, with strange, adventurous coloratura—these are like a reflection of the pointed Gothic arches, the slender spires, the lofty pillars, the complex play of lines in the Gothic cathedrals. An ecstatic piety and the play of a fantastic imagination are combined in a unique manner with the strictest, most severe, and most complex plan of construction, a union of apparently irreconcilable elements that characterizes the Gothic style of architecture as well. The *conditio sine qua non* of this music is polyphony. A strictly linear style of writing is here carried to its final consequences.

Thus the Gothic spirit, that peculiar combination of the strictest, coolest logic, the most rigid law, with the fantastic flight of the imagination, led to the discovery of possibilities in music undreamt of before— to the rise of lyric and romantic music as we find it in the songs of the troubadours and in the fascinating amorous music of the Italian *ars nova* in the fourteenth century, and to the marvelous structure of Dutch polyphony, the application of architectural ideas to music on the grandest scale, full of daring feats of musical engineering, yet of the most strictly logical development. Both these accomplishments, polyphonic construction and the introduction of the romantic spirit, are like new continents discovered in music, comparable in their artistic importance to the discovery of America by Christopher Columbus. They have not had a merely local and temporary importance; they have become the lasting property of the art of music. They have been varied a thousandfold, changing their proportions, their mutual relations, in every age, but since their first appearance, they have never been absent from music, and they have enriched it beyond measure. Modern music owes an immense debt to the Gothic spirit, for its characteristic traits, transposed into music, are the very elements and foundations of symphonic music. No later influence is comparable in lastingness and vitality, and all later artistic revolutions and innovations, fascinating as they may be, dwindle into comparative insignificance beside the enormous sustaining power of these Gothic contributions to the art of music.

Bibliography

The standard work in English on medieval music still remains that of Gustave Reese, *Music in the Middle Ages* (New York, Norton, 1940), Of considerably less ambitious scope but extremely readable is Albert Seay's *Music in the Medieval World* (Englewood Cliffs, N.J., Prentice-Hall, 1965). The period of medieval music is also treated in vols. 2 and 3 of *The New Oxford History of Music* (London, Oxford University Press, 1954-   ). Excerpts, in English translation, from the writings of several of the medieval theorists mentioned by Professor Leichtentritt may be found in Oliver Strunk, ed., *Source Readings in Music History* (New York, Norton, 1950). For general background material on late medieval life, thought, and art, *The Waning of the Middle Ages* by Johan Huizinga is highly recommended (first published in 1924; reprinted Garden City, N.Y., Doubleday, 1954).

   Examples of medieval music may be found in Archibald T. Davison and Willi Apel, eds., *Historical Anthology of Music*, vol. 1 (Cambridge, Mass., Harvard University Press, 1946) and in Arnold Schering, ed., *Geschichte der Musik in Beispielen* (Leipzig, Breitkopf & Härtel, 1931).

5

IF a study of sacred music must begin with Gregorian chant, then a study of secular song must begin with medieval secular monophony. As with Gregorian chant, our knowledge of early medieval song is hindered by the lack of an accurate system of musical notation during the period. Even when such a system had come into use, its rhythmic elements may not have been used in secular song with any consistency. Furthermore, it is thought that much of the music of early secular songs was improvised by the performers or else learned by rote and thus never written down, and that many of the performers were illiterate anyway and incapable of reading and writing musical notation. Then, too, since the medieval view of life emphasized preparation for the afterlife as the goal of this life, things of the secular world were considered transitory and unworthy of the effort and attention necessary for preservation, so that there was no reason to leave any permanent record of secular music. The wonder is that as much of this music has been preserved for us as has been the case.

The contributions of the composers of secular song lie in the forms which they developed and in their feeling for lyricism. While the origins of these songs may very well have come from a Gregorian stimulus, by the thirteenth century they were entering into polyphonic music, both sacred and secular, with considerable force. Not only are there numerous examples of polyphonic motets containing phrases and refrains taken from secular song, but some scholars believe that the shaping of the individual lines of medieval polyphony shows considerable evidence of influence from secular lyricism. As for the forms of medieval secular monophony, three of them, the rondeau, the virelai, and the ballade (these three usually referred to as the *formes fixes*), came to have polyphonic counterparts which were of great importance in the fourteenth and fifteenth centuries. The following selection provides a survey of secular monophonic music in the medieval world.

Albert Seay is a member of the faculty of Colorado College. He has written *Music in the Medieval World* (Englewood Cliffs, N.J., Prentice-Hall, 1965), and edited a number of works from the medieval and Renaissance periods including: *French Chansons* (Evanston, Ill., Summy-Birchard, 1957); Jean Tinctoris, *The Art of Counterpoint* (Rome, American Institute of Musicology, 1961); and Jacob Arcadelt, *Opera Omnia* (n.p., American Institute of Musicology, 1965-1969).

Secular Monophony

ALBERT SEAY

The study of non-liturgical monophony to the twelfth and thirteenth centuries contains many problems and complications that cannot allow final answers. That there must have been a great quantity of non-religious music during these ages is a truism, for we have intimations of its importance in the history of the hymn; the adaptation of popular melodies to new poetry of sacred character implies the existence of a large stock of music without relation to liturgical purposes. Enough mention of music in connection with purely secular activities is made that we can be sure that it played an important role in the everyday life of the time. Nevertheless, our knowledge is both skimpy and uncertain.

A major reason for our difficulties is the almost complete failure of transmission. If music (and its allied poetry) were to exist for future generations, it needed to be copied into manuscripts and then preserved in some kind of library. In view of the laborious processes required, the expense of materials, and the length of time needed, there was the natural tendency of those who directed the scribes to emphasize that which was most essential in their eyes. Since the preparation of manuscripts was the exclusive province of the trained cleric, working either within a monastery or a royal court, the end result was an almost complete neglect of all that did not contribute to the functioning of the one or the other establishment. Within the monastery, the emphasis fell on the copying of material for the liturgy, religious tracts of various kinds, and instructional works in all those areas needed for religious training. Within the courts, major effort was spent on correspondence and items directly tied to the process of government, with passing attention to chronologies, history, and laudatory poems. In view of what was to men of the period their lack of seriousness and meaning, secular productions received scant attention and were not normally considered worthy of preservation.

FROM Albert Seay, *Music in the Medieval World* (Englewood Cliffs, N.J., Prentice-Hall, Inc.), pp. 58-75. Copyright © 1965. Reprinted by permission of the publisher.

A second factor is the background of what was preserved, for it reflects principally one social group, the clerical circles that had sufficient education to write down their achievements. If we remember that the skills of reading and writing were restricted to a comparative handful, and that this handful was part of the religious segment of society, then it can be understood that those works we do have are, in the main, representative of that class and no other. Only when social conditions had begun to change and the non-religious had begun to have something of the same education as the cleric could there be any preservation of great numbers of compositions from men not of monastic background.

Finally, there is the question of musical notation, often a secondary matter in the minds of the scribes and therefore omitted. Even when included, because of the slow development of accurate methods, many of our earlier sources cannot be accurately deciphered and, in all too many cases, we can only be sure that there was music to accompany certain texts; from the indefinite character of the notation used it is impossible to define the melody. In certain cases, there is even the implication that the melody to be sung was so familiar that it did not need to be indicated, a familiarity that does not exist for us today.

With all these factors at work, the secular music preserved from these early centuries is certainly not a complete representation, for it is far too fragmentary and inadequate. The poetry is in Latin, the language of but one class; the music is indefinite, although implied. In most cases, we can only infer and suggest; we cannot be certain.

Latin Secular Music

In the beginning, sacred and secular monophony are exceedingly difficult to separate. Those men whom we know to have been the major representatives of secular creation, men such as Venantius Fortunatus (530?-609), are part of both worlds, reflecting both the religious and the laic; their poetic and musical forms indicate that they were highly influenced by those developed within the liturgy. While much of the poetico-musical activity took place in Southern France, in Provence and Aquitaine, important centers also existed in Northern Italy, in Bobbio and Verona. The two latter monasteries, founded by the Irish monk, St. Columban, were extremely productive in the seventh through ninth centuries. Perhaps their most important achievement was the development of refrain forms, to be taken over later by works in the vernacular.

With the period of Charlemagne, the ninth century, a certain rebirth of interest in the Latin classic made its appearance. From this time come musical settings of such works as Boethius' *Consolation of Philosophy,* certain of the Horatian *Odes* and parts of Vergil's *Aeneid;* because of the notation used, they are indecipherable. With this looking backward, there also came an enlargement of subjects treated, including now love songs, songs of praise, and laments. There is within all these an implied necessity for music even when music does not appear with the text. There are also included within these texts descriptions of instruments of the time, suggesting the growth of instrumental accompaniment to vocal pieces.

The most important secular Latin products of a slightly later time are those found within the compositions produced by the Goliards or wandering scholars. These men, all clerics who roamed from one university to another as they pleased, show in their works the naturalism of the young, their subjects ranging from the most chaste of love lyrics to the most obscene of drinking songs. Preserved principally in a Cambridge manuscript of the twelfth century and a thirteenth-century manuscript from Benedictbeuern known as the *Carmina Burana,* these poems show the mixture of sacred and secular forms and rhythms to be expected from those whose training has been religious but whose lives were spent outside religious establishments. While musical notation appears in both sources, it is of an early type that will not allow transcription. Certain melodies can be supplied from later sources, where the notation is more advanced, but not sufficient in number to give a complete picture.

There is, however, a strong suggestion that many of the melodies used by the Goliards were of sacred origin, a not implausible source in view of the custom of troping. We have one secular piece, "O admirabile Veneris idolum" ("O lovely image of Venus"), which uses as its melody that of a processional hymn, "O Roma nobilis" ("O noble Rome"). It is probable that many others have been arrived at by the same process, termed *contrafactum,* by which new texts are supplied as replacements for the old; this technique is well within the medieval tradition of building on the pre-existent.

Troubadours and Trouvères

Under the onslaught of successive waves of barbarians and the varieties of languages brought with them, Latin as a means of communication at all levels of society began to weaken. While it remained the language of the Church and of educated men, it steadily assumed less and less importance for those outside clerical circles, for secular society turned to those variations brought about by the impact of the invaders. While this process was going on all over Europe, the first evidences of an effort to elevate the new languages to carriers of artistic intent were seen in France, where two strong movements can be discerned.

The first of these, found in Southern France from around the middle of the eleventh century, is that associated with the language now known as Provençal or the *langue d'oc* and whose musician-poets are known as troubadours. The second, in Northern France and rising from the middle of the twelfth century, used the language variation at the root of modern French or the *langue d'oïl;* artists working in this tongue are called trouvères, In both cases, the names suggest connection with the older process of troping.

The major center for the growth of early troubadour art was around Poitiers, the seat of the Duke of Aquitaine; one may recall that this area is that from which came both Hilary and Venantius Fortunatus. As a part of that duchy and with a chateau for the Duke, Limoges in Limousin also acted as a secondary center, with much cross influence between the ducal establishment and the monastery of St. Martial. In time, the influence spread through most of southern France, covering the basin of the Garonne to Toulouse and Narbonne. These areas were generally unified by their political outlook as well as their language; a certain kind of civilization arose there that was conducive to the production of art of all kinds.

This new civilization was one of leisure, without the necessity of continual combat to protect itself. Influenced by the Church and its desire to keep peace, except against the Church's own enemies, the knights of Provence found themselves attached to their castles in a life of comparative ease. With this new leisure for men came leisure for women and a change in the relations between the sexes to an exaltation of the place of the lady in noble society. As a way of showing greatness, a lavish scale of living became the custom, demonstrated by attention to display in clothing, furniture, housing, food, drink, and in all other pursuits of enjoyment. Among these pastimes, the art of the troubadour soon took a high place, for, within this new framework, the achievements of a noble musician-poet could give him the same high reputation that a preëminence in battle could have given in previous times.

The first important representative of the new spirit was William IX, Duke of Aquitaine (1071-1127), of whom eleven works are preserved, with a fragmentary melody for one. These pieces show the broad characteristics of those to follow, among them the understanding that these songs are intended for an aristocratic audience and that the poetry is to be expressive of the feelings of the author, subjective reactions to the topic involved. In later generations this subjectiveness became a deliberate obscurity of expression, even to the use of coined words; the best representative of this tendency is Arnaut Daniel (1180?-1210?), much praised by Dante.

The principal subject of troubadour pieces is love in all its various aspects; indeed, the forty poems we have of Bernart de Ventadour (after

1150) are built on nothing else. In addition, there are dialogues in the manner of debates, wherein a subject is proposed and two viewpoints are exposed in alternation; this poetic contest, perhaps modeled on real ones, is the *tenso, partimen* or *joc partit.* A third broad category is the *sirventes,* taking up almost any subject except that of love. Among its subtypes are the Crusade song, the political satire, and the *planh* on the death of a protector or friend. These songs were not normally performed by the creator but by a special class of musicians known as the *jongleur.* The jongleur was not a composer or poet, but merely a performer who made his living by going from place to place and displaying his talent for any social level that would pay him. While the great mass of jongleurs remained the servants of the lower classes, some few were lucky enough to be received into the castles, where their talents were at the service of the nobility; these men were known as minstrels. They were expected to please their various audiences and therefore had large repertoires of almost every type of musical entertainment. Not only did they sing the short creations of their betters, but also gave much attention to the long epic poems of the time, the *chansons de geste* of which the "Song of Roland" is the best known example; these were sung to short melodic formulae that fitted the rhythmic patterns of the poem. In addition to accompanying themselves instrumentally, they were also expected to provide music for dancing, with acrobatics and juggling as supplementary diversions.

The art of the troubadour disappeared at the beginning of the thirteenth century, with the destruction of Provençal civilization in the Albigensian Crusades that began in 1209 and ended twenty years later. With the conquest of Southern France by men of the North and the consequent political and social upheavals, the class that had brought forth the troubadour vanished. By the end of the thirteenth century the last troubadour, Guiraut Requier (1235?-1292), had brought the story to an end; even he spent the last years of life in Spain, under the protection of Alfonso X.

Contact between Northern and Southern France had been constant for many centuries and many troubadours, Ventadour and others, are known to have visited Northern courts during the twelfth century. The Crusades too caused many meetings between the nobles of both areas, occasions on which the troubadour art was demonstrated. By the mid-twelfth century the exchange had become sufficiently effective that certain Northerners began to imitate in their own language the work of their Southern masters. These first productions are little more than changes of language, following southern technique and content almost slavishly. Indeed, admiration for troubadour models was so great that many of the most highly esteemed were later quoted in trouvère works.

While the original trouvère productions were imitative, as with the songs of Conon de Béthune (1150?-1219) and Guy de Coucy (1186-1203), later creations moved toward an individuality based on dance forms and the refrain. Certain troubadour forms did have imitators, but these gradually disappeared before the popularity of the rondeau, the virelai and the ballade, forms of minor importance within the troubadour repertoire. All three of these forms are organized by a refrain, suggesting the possibility of responsorial performance, using a leader and a choral group. In its classic form, the rondeau began with a refrain of a full strophe, followed by a half-strophe and a half-refrain; after a succeeding full strophe there was a return to the full refrain to close the work. Musically, there were but two fragments, one for each half-strophe and repeated in accord with the poetic text; the full diagram is ABAAABAB. The ballade was normally of three strophes of seven or eight lines each; the last one or two lines of each strophe are identical and act as a refrain. The musical form is AAB, each A standing for two lines and the closing B the remaining ones; this form is much like the *canzo* of the troubadours. The third form, the virelai, begins with a refrain of a full strophe, followed by two half-strophes (the *ouvert* and the *clos*), a *full strophe (the tierce)* and closes with the full refrain. Musically, the form is ABBAA, with each A representing a full strophe, each B a half. All three of these forms remained important well into the Renaissance.

Preservation of poetry and music of both troubadours and trouvères has been comparatively plentiful, for we have about 2500 troubadour poems and 250 melodies, with over 4000 trouvère texts and some 1400 musical accompaniments. In view of the high social distinction accorded to gifted nobles, it was felt appropriate that collections (*chansonniers*) be subsidized by them for presentation purposes or for simple glory. It may be presumed that the copyists were clerics attached to the household.

The music for troubadour and trouvère songs is generally simple, frequently emphasizing the syllabic and with normally short melisma, again much like the hymn. The influence of the modes is apparent, although there is a tendency to introduce accidentals in such a way as to suggest more of our modern major and minor. The range is usually limited, seldom going to the octave. As to rhythm, most authorities today agree that the notes of these songs were not of equal length and were organized into rhythmic patterns much like those seen in the polyphonic works of the thirteenth century. The agreement ends here, for there is often much dispute over the application of these patterns to the individual composition. As a sample of both the melodic appearance and the possible rhythmic interpretation that may be used, we give here a short troubadour work in honor of the Virgin Mary, taken from a twelfth-century manuscript originating at St. Martial in Limoges:

O Ma - ri - a deu mai - re, Deu tes e fils e
pai re, Dom-na pre - ia per nos, To fil lo glo - ri - os.

Secular Monophony in Italy

With the Albigensian Crusade and the consequent confusion, many troubadours fled to other parts of Europe. One of the preferred refuges was
Northern Italy, an area already visited by many Provençal artists during the late twelfth century; particularly important was the court of the
Marquis of Montferrat, who had received Peire Vidal (1175?-1205?) and
Raimbaut de Vaqueiras (1155?-1207?). Raimbaut's works show the international character of the troubadour, for he is the author of a *descort*
that has its first five strophes successively in Provençal, Italian, French,
Gascon, and Galician-Portuguese; the sixth, of ten lines, repeats the order of languages in its five paired lines. He is the writer of the earliest
known poetry in Italian (1202).

The Italian *trovatori* of the North generally followed their troubadour masters closely, not only taking over their techniques but also their
subject matter. Some few Italian poems are almost literal translations
of Provençal models, although the more usual derivation is that of a
transfer of imagery. More originality is found in the output of the South,
for, under Frederick II (1211-1250), Sicily became a major center of
development. The climax of the process of development of an individual
Italian approach came only at the end of the thirteenth century and in
Central Italy, with Dante (1265-1321) as the real founder of Italian
literature.

No music for any of these Italian courtly songs has survived, but
a great number of hymns in the vernacular have remained. These hymns,
known as *laudi spirituali,* were the result of a spiritual revival climaxed
by the work of St. Francis of Assisi (1182-1226) and were designed
for performance by the lower classes. Written in a popular Italian, the
laudi show the influence of chant, but there are other secular elements
apparent. In form, the Italian equivalent of the virelai, the ballata (not
to be confused with the ballade) is normal, although the music may not

be as simple as its French counterpart; there are often fresh melodies in each section.

Secular Monophony in Spain and Portugal

The situation in Spain and Portugal was almost exactly that seen in Italy, for the various courts of the Iberian peninsula had long held close connections with those of Southern France. Peire Vidal was one of the close friends of Alfonso II of Aragon, and other troubadours had become well known in Castille and in Portugal. As in Italy, the earliest productions were extremely close to their sources in all facets, with the rise of peculiarly Iberian manifestations coming in the thirteenth century; even here, there were some reproaches for failure not to follow the Provençal models closely enough.

Preservation of a Spanish-Portuguese repertoire of purely secular music has been poor, for only six songs in Galician-Portuguese have survived with their music. What has come down to us is a collection of Marian songs, the *Cantigas de Santa Maria,* settings of poems relating miracles performed by Her. Although the *Cantigas* are all anonymous, it is probable that certain ones are by Alfonso X (1221-1284) of Castille and Leon, for the collection was put together at his court. Many of these songs reflect French influence, the whole group recalling the *Miracles de Notre Dame* by Gautier de Coinci (1177-1236). In form, the majority follow the outlines of the virelai, while the music harks back to the chant.

Secular Monophony in England

In spite of a close connection between England and the continent, there seems to have been little growth of a purely native response to troubadour influence. During the late twelfth century, parts of Southern France were possessions of the English crown through the marriage of Eleanor of Aquitaine to Henry II, and the presence of troubadours at the English court was common; Bernart de Ventadour visited there. Indeed, Eleanor's son, Richard the Lion-Hearted, became a practicing trouvère; his death in 1199 was mourned by Gaucelm Faidit (1180?-1220) in a moving *planh,* the only one whose music has come down to us.

The failure of troubadour art to call forth extensive English reaction lies in the great gulf between the Norman nobility, speaking a variation of French, and the rest of the country. Not until England could develop an individual language of literary capability could there be great progress, a stage that did not occur until Chaucer's time. Nevertheless, a few simple melodies with English text have remained, generally syllabic and with scale-wise motion as a major characteristic; there is much repetition of similar fragments, suggesting an approach to melody through formulae.

Minnesingers and Meistersingers

As in the other parts of Europe, Germany underwent the influence of the troubadours early, during the late twelfth century. Exchanges were facilitated principally by the Crusades, but there were frequent visits by troubadours and trouvères into Northern Europe; these visits extended quite far, for Peire Vidal is found at the Hungarian court of Emeric around 1200. Intermarriage was also of importance in furthering cultural exchange, with an outstanding example in the wedding of Beatrice of Burgundy to Frederic Barbarossa in 1156.

On the whole, as descendants from the troubadour-trouvère tradition, the Minnesingers remained closer to their masters. Recent research has indicated that the early development of Minnesinger poetry is almost completely imitative, with few individual touches; themes, techniques, forms, and imagery are all closely tied to French originals. It may be that this will explain the comparative poverty of musical sources, for it is probable that the first Minnesingers not only took over all the poetic characteristics of their teachers but their melodies as well. We do have the story from one Minnesinger that his lady had sent him an untexted French melody to which he should supply a German text.

Whether or not there was originally a direct taking over of French melodies, it is certain that German forms followed closely those developed in the South. Of particular importance was the German equivalent of the ballade, the *Barform*, with its *Stollen-Stollen-Abgesang*, so eloquently described by Hans Sachs in Richard Wagner's "Die Meistersinger" of over five centuries later. Other forms included imitations of the troubadour patterns, the *Spruch* following the *sirventes*, the *Geteiltezspil*, the *joc partit*, and the *Leich* the *descort* or *lai*.

Later Minnesingers show a greater individuality, although there is always a reliance upon French models in the background. The peak of the movement comes somewhat late in comparison to other areas, the closing thirteenth and early fourteenth centuries marking the high point. After this time the Minnesinger art declined rapidly, passing over into bourgeois society as imitation of upper-class customs. This movement within the middle class was undertaken by the group known as the Meistersingers, a guild-like organization that survived into the early nineteenth century. Although the Meistersingers were theoretically both poets and composers, the accent fell most strongly on the poetic side, for the major efforts were devoted to the provision of new poetry for a stock of traditional melodies. Musically, there was little viable in the Meistersinger movement, for it represented an effort to take over an activity of an upper social level by a middle class to whom it was artificial and at a time when it no longer held artistic possibilities.

It is significant that the full flowering of secular monophony comes at a time when monophony was no longer of great concern to musicians within the Church. With the steady development of polyphony, the attention of professional church composers and performers turned to the new technique, for it made a greater appeal to their artistic talents. As a result, the provision of new monophonic works within the Church was left more and more to the less trained, the amateur, a man not able to work with the new complications. The task of providing the liturgy with a new polyphonic adornment, replacing or supplementing older monophony, was sufficiently challenging and intriguing to cause a comparative neglect of further expansion of the sacred monophonic repertoire by the professional; he turned to polyphony.

The amateur status of monophony in the twelfth and thirteenth centuries is reflected by the taking over of this area by the secular musician-poet working in the vernacular, a man with little of the musical background common to the church-trained. A musical novice, he perforce fell back on what he had heard—chant and popular melodies—without going further. For him, the area of greatest interest was not the music but the poetry. The very notion of a stock of melodies, a group of formulae, to which many poems could be set implies this lowered place of music, as does the failure to preserve melodies and poems in equal quantity. Even in those cases where the music is of some artistic significance, and there are many, there is still a sense of reliance upon an already developed artistic foundation, one carried to a peak by church musicians of the past.

Together with the failure of monophony to maintain its previously high artistic position goes its consequent drop in philosophical importance. In treatises of the time, the place of monophony becomes more and more a demonstration of certain fundamentals whose philosophical meaning is intensified when absorbed into polyphony. In a nutshell, polyphony demonstrates the meanings of speculative music better than does monophony and thus stands on a higher level. Where Guido had spent time giving directions on how to compose simple monophony, thirteenth-century theorists take the same space on how to compose simple polyphony.

With the failure of sacred monophony to continue its expansion in the face of the rise of polyphony, it is no surprise to see the Church turning to secular productions when it needed monophony for particular

purposes. Stylistically in accord with the already existing repertoire because of their background, secular monophonic works could be and were
provided with new texts to fit a new function. Many thirteenth-century
monophonic conductus were so derived and numerous other works were
given Latin religious *contrafacta,* for the continuation of monophonic
composition in secular circumstances gave ample stocks of melodies to
satisfy the Church's requirements. In time, many of these were made
part of later polyphonic compositions, for the custom of providing *contrafacta,* in both directions, from sacred to secular and vice versa, gradually destroyed any feeling on the composer's part that any melody necessarily carried connotations from the text to which it had been originally fitted. It became to him but a musical element, to be used in a
musical construction and handled in the same fashion, regardless
of whether its origin be sacred or secular. All of this is but one facet of
the increasing secularization of the Middle Ages, to which we will return
later, in our discussion of the polyphony of the thirteenth century.

Like the decline of monophony in the Church, the disappearance
of secular monophony may be tied to the rise of polyphony. As the new
technique showed its higher artistic possibilities, the secular musician
became more and more aware of its increased opportunities for expression. Just as monophony fell to a second place in the Church, so did it
drop in secular circles. With an appreciation and understanding of the
superiority of polyphony, the secular composer endeavored to carry over
the new technique into secular areas; the growth of secular polyphony
can be directly tied to the gradual disappearance of secular monophony.
In those areas such as France, where polyphony made its first gains,
secular monophonic works on the upper levels disappeared first; in Germany, where polyphony developed late, it remained long after it had
vanished almost everywhere else.

Of course, secular monophony never completely vanished. Perhaps
a better phrase would be that it lost its artistic significance for the social class that had originally fostered it. As of lower artistic import it
remained a manner of musical expression to lower levels of society, either as imitation of their betters or as an artless expression in musical
terms. The folk song survived, as it always had and always will, but
it was no longer taken as worthy of professional attention and elevation.
Art music henceforth was to be polyphony, something not capable of
composition by anyone without thorough grounding in its techniques. In
monophony, the amateur might compete, but in polyphony he could not.

Instruments and Instrumental Music

As we have seen, the early Church Fathers were deeply opposed to the use of instruments within the liturgy, regarding them as too much a part of pagan culture. As such, they had no place within a Christian life and were to be shunned by every believer. Some exceptions were made from time to time, such as a certain acceptance for the lute and kithara because of their relation to King David, but these were always understood to be special cases. In spite of Biblical reference to the trumpet, cymbals, and other instruments, their relation to Greek and Roman society was such as to inspire mistrust.

With the split of East and West and the continual influx of barbarians careless of the artistic agreements of the past, the problem of forbidding instruments became simpler; most of those under suspicion had disappeared and those in use had no connotational problems. In the course of time, there was a general movement to forget many of the attitudes of the past and to accept as part of the musical scene the use of instruments. While many were indigenous products, coming from various parts of Europe and especially from the outer edges, some were importations from Asia via the many contacts that we have already noticed. By the tenth century, instruments were an acknowledged part of musical practice and, to judge from our sources, with standard symbolic meanings.

So far as the Church was concerned, the most useful of all instruments was the organ. Although the Romans had developed a form of organ called the *hydraulis,* from its reliance on water pressure, the medieval organ or *positive* was supplied with air from a bellows, worked by either hands or feet. The choice of tones was not governed by a keyboard in the earlier examples but by a series of slides that opened and closed the appropriate pipe. A true keyboard as we know it was not developed until the twelfth century, but even then mechanical friction made the action so hard that it required a full-fisted blow on the key to cause the sound. In spite of the primitive state of engineering, attempts were made to enlarge the organ's possibilities, one instrument of the twelfth century at Winchester being built with two manuals, 26 sets of bellows and 400 pipes. Early organs were loud and not in tune; nevertheless, the positive became an important part of the Church's music, so much so that all other instruments were eventually banned from the services. By the fourteenth century, it had assumed a place in the symbolism of the time as "the king of instruments," a term used even today and derived from both its sound and its place in worship.

As a form of easily transported organ, the *portative* became part of the music at court. Small and capable of being worked by one man without assistance, it carried none of the religious overtones associated with its larger brother. Since one hand of the executant was occupied in building up the air pressure, its position was not that of a polyphonic instrument but one used in group performance, as a member of chamber combinations.

Together with the portative were associated many other monophonic instruments of varying types and methods of sound production; these include the harp, the psaltery, and the lute (plucked stringed instruments) and the vielle and the rebec (bowed instruments). Although the harp had a long history, the one used by the Middle Ages was brought from Ireland where it had the connotations of a royal instrument; it appears even today in the Irish coat-of-arms. By the late twelfth century it had lost something of its position, for it was then the instrument favored by jongleurs and wandering actors. Both psaltery and lute were originally brought to Europe by the Moors in Spain and slowly spread to the rest of the continent; curiously, both were not normally plucked by the bare finger but by a quill or rod. The goal seems to have been a certain impersonality of tone.

The vielle, like the harp, was primarily an instrument used by the jongleur to accompany the *chanson de geste* or to provide music for dancing. One of the more celebrated secular works of the twelfth century, the "Kalenda Maya" by Raimbaut de Vaqueiras, was the result of the troping of an *estampida* played for him on the vielle. While usually played with the bow, it could be plucked. The rebec, an instrument of Arabian origin, is the distant ancestor of our violin, although its original shape suggests a relation to the lute; in the thirteenth century, it had but two strings, tuned to C and G.

Two groups of instruments, the brass and percussion, were the particular property of the nobility. Of the highest significance was the oliphant, a horn most often made of an elephant's tusk, although sometimes found in gold; its Eastern origin is obvious. As a symbol of nobility, it was carried by a knight as part of his standard equipment; it could not belong to any other class. It was an oliphant that the dying Roland sounded at Roncesvalles, and certain medieval miniatures show it as being used by the Archangel Gabriel at the Day of Judgment. The trumpet, in wood or brass, also served as a military instrument, used on all grand occasions. Together with the timpani, brought to Europe in the Crusades period, it was symbolic of the royal presence and its players were given precedence over other instrumentalists of the court. Its functions in war were similar to those in later periods.

There is sufficient evidence to prove that instruments were a normal part of almost all musical performances, but the music itself gives no clue as to how instruments took part. Modern performances of medieval music have attempted to reconstruct as well as possible the original conditions, but there can be no final guarantee of authenticity. About all that we can be certain of is that medieval audiences liked varieties of instruments, not homogeneous choirs. In Guillaume de Machaut's description of a concert from the fourteenth century, 31 different instruments are listed as part of the orchestra and a total of more than fifty players in the ensemble is implied. The music as we find it in the sources suggests none of this. Indeed, we have no firm ideas of how monophonic music was accompanied, although we are sure that it was; in all likelihood, the accompanying line essentially duplicated that of the singer, with occasional added ornamentation, in what is called heterophony.

The earliest independent instrumental pieces in our sources come from late thirteenth-century English manuscripts and are dances for one instrument. The most interesting of these is the *stantipes*, formally organized in the double cursus of the sequence. Derivations from this form can be found until the early Renaissance, in both French and Italian sources. That even the few examples we find have survived is surprising, for the place of the dance in the Middle Ages was such that copying of these works into a permanent shape was not to be expected; in the manuscripts where they appear, they are obvious afterthoughts.

Some polyphonic music for instruments has been preserved, the most important being two codices of keyboard music from the fourteenth century, the *Robertsbridge Codex* of English provenance and the Italian *Faenza Codex*. Both contain sacred and secular works in idiomatic arrangements and show an effort to add figurations and ornaments to give the work a more instrumental cast. From inspection of the contents of both sources, it is evident that truly independent instrumental music was only at its beginnings and that vocal music was the center of creative activity.

Bibliography

Though written in 1910, Pierre Aubry's *Trouvères and Troubadors* (New York, Cooper Square Publishers, 1969) still has much to offer concerning secular monophony. Jack Westrup, "Medieval Song," in *The New Oxford History of Music*, vol. 2, should be consulted, as should Gilbert Reaney, "The Middle Ages," in Dennis Stevens, ed., *A History of Song (London, Hutchinson, 1960; New York, Norton, 1961), and, of course, Gustave Reese, *Music in the Middle Ages* (New York, Norton, 1940). Works of a more general nature and not devoted specifically to music are E. K. Chambers, *The Mediaeval Stage*, 2 vols. (Oxford, Clarendon, 1903), and Helen Waddell, *The Wandering Scholars* (Garden City, N. Y., Doubleday, 1955). Some periodical articles of value are Willi Apel, "Rondeaux, Virelais, and Ballades in French 13th-century Song," *Journal of the American Musicological Society*, 7 (1954); Robert Perrin, "Some Notes on Troubadour Melodic Types," *Journal of the American Musicological Society*, 9 (1956); Gilbert Reaney, "Concerning the Origins of the Rondeau, Virelai, and Ballade Forms," *Musica Disciplina*, 6 (1952); and L. M. Wright, "Misconceptions Concerning the Troubadours, Trouvères, and Minstrels," *Music and Letters*, 48 (1967).

Several examples of medieval monophonic song may be found in *Historical Anthology of Music*, vol. 1. More extensive collections are those edited by Friedrich Gennrich, *Troubadours, Trouvères, Minne- und Meistersinger* (Cologne, Arno Volk Verlag, 1960) which also contains a brief historical preface, and *Rondeaux, Virelais, und Balladen*, 2 vols. (Dresden, Gesellschaft für romanische Literatur, 1921-1927). For information concerning medieval insturments see Curt Sachs, *The History of Musical Instruments* (New York, Norton, 1940).

6

THE invention of polyphony was the event that was to turn Western music down a path of development different from that of other cultures. Other music concentrated on subtle shadings of melodic intervals, complex rhythms, and the improvisation of polyphony by the performer. Western music, while perhaps beginning its polyphonic stage with such performer improvisation, soon came to have both the melodic lines (at first there were only two) conceived by a single composer and written down. This step is significant because it brings into consideration for the first time the concept of the composer as one who has produced music; in which improvisation, though perhaps not eliminated, has been lessened. By being able to notate his composition the composer controlled not only its shape but also repetitions of it in the same basic shape. Seen from this viewpoint, electronic music in which today's composer has total control of his composition is but a logical continuation of a principle which had its beginnings in polyphony, as Albert Seay has pointed out (*Music in the Medieval World,* p. 79).

Musical notation developed alongside polyphony, not coincidentally. Accurate notation had not been devised previously because it had not been thought necessary. Now accurate systems of pitch and rhythmic notation were essential if performers were to reproduce the composer's work rather than create their own. First, pitch was made more precise with the invention of the staff; rhythmic standardization soon followed with the invention of the rhythmic modes.

Early polyphony has been considered by some to be a form of troping applied to music. This argument may have some substance in that it appears that polyphony and troping did come into being at about the same time. The first polyphony was created by a compositional technique known as the layer technique: first a melody was either composed or selected from another source, and then a second melody was composed to be performed simultaneously with the first. If one defines troping as the addition of text to an already existing text, then the basic principle of creation is the same. The troping principle was carried even further when the second melody of polyphony was provided with its own separate text, not only in different words from that of the first melody but frequently in a different language as well. When this point was reached the motet was born.

A motet in its earliest definition was merely a polyphonic composition in which each voice sang a different text. A third voice, also with its own text, came to be added to the first two, and sometimes even a fourth voice also, although three-voice composition was the usual texture during the Middle Ages. These three-voice medieval motets, growing out of the music of the Notre Dame composers in Paris, became the principal form of church composition during the thirteenth and fourteenth centuries. Secular motets existed, however, in considerable number, and it is thought that many of those motets using a fragment of Gregorian chant in the tenor but having secular texts in the upper voices were intended as much for secular as for sacred use. Only in the early fifteenth century was the medieval motet replaced in popularity by the cyclic mass and by a newer type of motet composed by the Renaissance technique of simultaneous composition rather than by the medieval layer technique.

Medieval polyphony is presently arousing new interest in many who, although they may not be aware of the reason, are possibly attracted to it because of its construction. The upper voices of medieval polyphony functioned as duets with the tenor, at that time the lowest pitched voice of the composition, rather than as equal members of a three- or, occasionally, four-voice texture; also, this music was a soloistic art, or one which employed only a few singers on each part at most. These points are sometimes overlooked in performances that work too much from an ensemble point of view and therefore do not capture the element of chance that results from two performers singing two different duets with a third performer while more or less ignoring each other. Medieval music thus combines in fine balance two elements that play a great part in twentieth-century music, control by the composer and chance. There may not be as much difference in spirit between a thirteenth-century French motet and the music of our own time as might first appear. The beginnings of medieval polyphony, some of the things which gave it impetus, and some of the forms it took are the subjects of the following selection.

Romain Goldron is the pseudonym of A. Louis Burkhalter, Swiss musicologist. His writings include *Johannes Brahms "le vagabond"* (Paris, Flammarion, 1956) and the first twelve volumes of a twenty-volume series, *Histoire de la musique* (Lausanne, Editions Rencontre, 1966).

The Birth of Polyphony

ROMAIN GOLDRON

Let us suppose that some new and very powerful barbarian invasion or some natural cataclysm had put an end to Christianity around the year 1000. How might its music have been distinguished from that of other civilizations? On the surface, the marks would appear indistinct. Moreover, it would be outdone by even ancient Mesopotamia or China in view of their instrumental and orchestral development. If we regard Gregorian music as superior in quality to other forms of music, this is because we are much closer to it in history and all our music is based on it; there is the additional reason that we have nothing with which we can accurately compare it. Neither Egypt nor Greece left any similar collection, though future discoveries are not outside the bounds of possibility.

On the face of it, the only element that might suggest a new trend is the fact that musicians were very much concerned with finding a new and more exact system of notation. When one thinks of what music became in the interval between Perotinus, choirmaster and organist at Notre Dame de Paris at the end of the 12th century, and J. S. Bach—a mere few centuries—one is bound to ponder the why's of such a transformation. This was a short span of time compared with the thousands of years of musical culture that preceded it without any major break or any significant innovation.

Was the change due to a new awareness in man himself, as Ernest Ansermet (a conductor born at Vevey in 1883) would have it? To man's dawning realization of himself as a complete, individual entity, possessing his own means of self-determination? Ansermet thinks this was so, and that this was a feature of the West's entry onto the stage of history.

FROM Romain Goldron, *Byzantine and Medieval Music* (New York, H. S. Stuttman and Company, Inc., 1968), pp. 99–118. Reprinted by permission of the publisher.

He says further that this new awareness had a direct bearing on the rules and principles governing musical creation. This is why, he maintains, music is the most Western of all Western arts, just as the culture that resulted from it is specifically Western, though open to all.[1]

Or was the transformation, as Max Weber thinks, consequent upon the development of a spirit of rationalism? As a result of some inexplicable inner foresight, was it, in fact, that man wanted to create for himself an ideal world of sound, a virtual "reservoir" of spirituality from which he could draw when mere reason palled? For he stood at the threshold of an age that was to rob life of the piquancy which society had hitherto known and deliver it up to the cold genius of science.

These problems must perforce be left to philosophers.

As for the parallel often drawn between the development of polyphony and the birth of Gothic, what significance has it, even assuming that it was not merely by chance that polyphony and Gothic appeared together? No movement of ideas ever has the same meaning throughout all the arts, for the simple reason that each considers a different aspect to be the most valuable.

At all events, music, which had up to now been transmitted orally and remained more or less homophonic, was to take on a visual form, which would render it objective—the score; and the demands of accuracy would become more and more exacting. Other voices came to join the main melody in obedience to certain laws. The simultaneous sound that resulted from polyphony fostered in musicians a completely new idea, that of *harmony*, which in its turn generated its own grammar and syntax. The role of the performer, which till now had been paramount, would be diminished for the benefit of the composer, whose importance and whose demands increased more and more as it became possible to write down everything.

Music had hitherto been created on the basis of certain systems, and although these were sometimes improved upon, there was always a certain amount of improvisation. From now on, *works* would be produced in which the creator could express himself with the same facility and the same versatility as the sculptor or the painter.

The consequences of this development were as far-reaching for civilization as had been, some four thousand years before, the discovery that the spoken word could be committed to writing. The credit for this acheivement belongs to Western cilization. It was unique and without precedent. Outside Europe, there has been no one like J. S. Bach or Mozart.

It is curious that none of the great Eastern civilizations thought, before the end of the 19th century, of using polyphonic notation, not

[1] Ernest Ansermet, *Foundations of Music;* Baconniere, 1961.

even the civilization of the Arabs, which had remained in contact with ours, on Spanish soil, right up to the time of the Renaissance.

Organum

Briefly, organum is the term used for the duplication of melody at a different pitch. It is described in *Musica enchiriadis* (Manual of Music), a 9th-century treatise which dealt with the problem of polyphony. For a long time the work was attributed to Hucbald, a monk of Saint-Amand, but today the author is thought to have been Ogier, possibly a native of Laon.[2] Its true significance is its detailed description of a song for two voices, written in combination, in what was still a very elementary method, called organum or diaphony.

"Harmony is the suitable combination of two different voices," says the author of the treatise. "In the same way that if one joins letters together in any haphazard fashion one does not achieve syllables or words, in music, too, one can only join certain intervals."[3] There we have, at the very beginning, a clear statement of basic principles, which were, it would seem, not the invention of the author of the work in question, but which seem rather to confirm something that had been in practice for a long time. As luck would have it, the text is decorated with examples of diaphony, showing a double melody in octave at lower fourth and fifth and following it closely in parallel movement.

In the choice of intervals, one can detect again Greek influence. Pythagoras (he owed his knowledge perhaps to Egypt) used to teach that according to mathematics the fifth and its opposite number, the fourth, are, after the octave, the first concords. (The third was not used for a long time, since it was considered to be a discord.)

But the author did not stop here. In another chapter, he recommends in some cases that the organal voice be made more flexible. After starting in unison, he suggests it should gradually leave the melody and wait for the fourth before relinquishing the initial note, in order to follow the tune in diaphony. The end part of the singing was again performed in unison. Organum is the word used to describe this procedure.

One question remains. Does the use of diaphony and organum date from the treatise *Musica enchiriadis*? If not, what is the date of its origin? Einstein points out that the Nordic peoples have an innate liking for harmony, and he wonders if the great S-shaped bronze wind instru-

[2] *Gallimard Encyclopedia.*
[3] Quoted from Jacques Chailley, *The Musical History of the Middle Ages,* P.U.F.

ments, from the Bronze Age, which were dug out in pairs, were used for signals performed by two voices.[4]

The Irish philosopher, Scot Erigen, in the 9th century, was acquainted with two-part singing. According to Giraldus Cambrensis (12th century), polyphonic singing had ancient roots in northern England and Wales, whence it had, perhaps, been imported from Denmark and Norway.[5] The texts are too vague to permit any categoric conclusions. All that one can say is that England, together with France, is the country whose attempts at polyphony are the most interesting. The first great collections of organa (more than 150) come from the Gothic Cathedral of Winchester, in Hampshire. Winchester was an important musical center.

It seems, on the other hand, unlikely—though this cannot be proved either—that those numerous ancient and Oriental peoples who practiced heterophony and possessed great musical ensembles were never at any time instinctively drawn to the use of diaphony. Let us cast our minds back to the Gagaku of Japan, to the Javanese Gamelan and to the great orchestras of Babylon. The great Roman orchestras and the gigantic hydraulic organs, which were to be heard in the Roman circus, under the Empire, must have been a throwback to these ancient customs, which were thus handed on to the Christian West. It is probable that the tradition was maintained right up to the time of the instrumentalists at Reichenau, thanks to wandering musicians about whom history can tell us nothing since nothing concrete has survived. This much, however, we do know. Their activities were very much appreciated by the rank and file of society, as is evidenced (negatively from the Church's point of view!) by the frequency of the warnings issued against them by Church leaders.

Finally, certain wind instruments, together with other stringed instruments, often supported by harps, bells, viols and a number of other instruments, must by their very nature have led instinctively to the use of simple forms of harmony and polyphony or mixed melody. We must not forget that some of these instruments had been in use for thousands of years.

Marc Pincherle reminds us that although today *organum* is not considered a derivation of "organ," the fact remains that "medieval organs sounded the same successions of parallel notes in the same way as modern organs do in some works." He adds: "Each level—the equivalent of our stop—controlled not just one note, but several, arranged in fifths and in octaves. In the great organ at Winchester, England, built around 950 (it had four hundred pipes, twenty-six bellows worked by seventy men and two organists strapped to a keyboard with twenty stops, according to the monk Wulstan), a single lever set in vibration ten pipes

---

[4]Alfred Einstein, *History of Music*.
[5]*Ibid*.

all sounding fifths and octaves at once, echoing each other and super-imposed on each other. This was an exceptional instrument, powerful, barbaric. . . ."[6] The organ could be heard in every corner of the city, The first time it was played women fainted at the sound.[7]

The real importance of *Musica enchiriadis* is, then, as follows: For the first time a method that was in all probability instinctive, and per-haps very old indeed, enters upon the sphere of reasoning awareness and for the first time will be subjected to notation. Let us remember that the treatise included examples with notation. As a result, this instinctive and ancient practice was to become the object of critical thought.

Throughout the whole of Mediterranean and Oriental Antiquity mu-sic gave rise to wonderful meditations, which benefited its theory rather than its performance. The Western spirit, however, was not much given to metaphysics; the bent in the West was essentially toward organization and dogmatics, and it was to busy itself with techniques. Music would prove one of the spheres in which this turn of mind would find much to do. And the treatise we have spoken of was the first evidence of this.

It can be safely said that no present-day historian of music would omit to mention this work. Yet its appearance was not hailed as a rev-olutionary event. Neither those who were alive at the time, nor those who followed, felt very deeply about it, and there was no further devel-opment for two hundred years!

Guido d'Arezzo, in the 9th century, had to be born before we find any further mention of organum, and even then we see that the process had not evolved in the slightest degree. Guido himself was not particu-larly enthusiastic about *Musica enchiriadis* either, any more than was his contemporary, John Cotton, although Cotton in one of his works does condescend to make a "brief" reference to it.

This reference, Cotton wrote, was "to satisfy the reader's curiosity," but he refrained from giving any examples for fear of boring the reader. His conclusions on the subject of diaphony—"Some do it this way, others do it another way"—are vague and almost contemptuous.[8] This lack of interest (Chailley calls it "this obvious disfavor") is usually ascribed to the fact that diaphony was not understood. Could it not, however, have been due to that repugnance which scholars and theorists felt toward the introduction of instruments into religious vocal music, something they associated with common minstrels? In other words, was it not the humble origin of diaphony that shocked them, rather than its novelty? The question is worth examination—all the more so since after a slow pe-riod of preparation and "conditioning," we shall find that when polyph-ony began in earnest, it was St. Martial at Limoges, Fleury, Tours and Fécamp that were the active and decisive centers. "Now it was at Fé-

[6]M. Pincherle, *Illustrated History of Music,* N.R.F., 1959.
[7]G. Nestler, *History of Music;* Bertelsman, 1962.
[8]Jacques Chailley, *op. cit.*

camp that Abbot William of Dijon had founded the first confraternity of musicians and singers, and it is precisely in the Manuscripts from St. Martial that we find the earliest drawings of these musicians."[9]

One must mention, too, the recent research of the German musicologist Walter Krüger into the subject of the performance of primitive organum. His research upset all traditional ideas on the matter.[10] According to him—and this is his most revolutionary statement—organum was not performed note against note, uniformly and without rhythmic differences, as was generally thought. The notation fixed only the general structure, which was "completed, according to certain rules, by a miscellaneous collection of instruments." In other words, the notation was merely a guide to remind the players of the line of a melody on which they were to execute their embellishments. The "play of bells" and the organ in particular could be used. It is worthwhile to pursue Krüger's research further and to examine it more closely.

The Descant

About the end of the 9th century, Fleury and Chartres saw the development of a principle that really was to liberate polyphony and to rescue it from the simple heterophony which had held it captive. This principle of "contrary movement" would enable polyphony to take a decisive lead, by rejecting the idea of parallelism which had so far enslaved it.

Contrary movement allows one voice to rise while the other goes down, or vice versa. In addition, the organal voice is placed above the principal voice and is called a descant. The interval was, at first, still fourths, fifths, or octaves, but between the supporting chords they developed freely. Quite soon, moreover, this procedure was codified into movements that were permissible and those that were not. As early as the beginning of the 13th century these rules can be found set out in a tract called *Discantus positio vulgaris*. The rules enabled choristers to improvise descant without reference to a score.

The Drone or Faux-Bourdon

One kind of descant that probably goes back to the 12th century is generally thought to have been developed in England. This is known as the drone or faux-bourdon, or false bass. It was written at the lower third of the melody, but was actually played an octave higher, which explains, incidentally, the origin of its name. It was characterized by its

---

[9]*Ibid.*
[10]Walter Krüger, *Primitive Organum: Its True Sound Pattern;* Bärenreiter.

use of a succession of parallel thirds. Since it was usually performed in three parts, an upper parallel third was added to the melody.

It would seem, then, that it is to England that music owes the introduction of the third as a chord. From remote times, moreover, that country had known a particular kind of two-part singing (*cantus gemellus* or "twin-song"), which progressed through parallel thirds. This is believed by some people to have come from Scandinavia. The Vikings, who were established in Scotland and England in the 9th century, would have taught the local population this kind of singing.[11]

Vocalized Organum

There was to be one more development at the beginning of the 9th century at St. Martial de Limoges, which had continued to be one of the most prolific centers of many-voiced music. This was the *organum fleuri* or vocalized organum, wherein the second voice embroidered and graced each note of the main tune. To allow time for this, the principal voice had to be extended, and it became the *cantus firmus,* or fixed melody or tenor, in other words, the *support* of the descant. With this development, we shall now see as we come to Leoninus and Perotinus, the way is clear for everything to be put to great effect.

The Conductus

After two-part sound, the descant and the organum fleuri, it was the conductus that opened up wide perspectives for musical invention and helped it to a fuller independence.

The conductus, which might be termed "passage work," was sung during the moments when the celebrants moved about from one place to another in the chancel. The term tells us nothing about its musical form, any more than the word "passage" in literature describes a particular part.

The essential difference between the conductus and organum fleuri lies in the origin of the main voice or cantus firmus, which was always, in organum, a Gregorian chant. This was not the case with the conductus, which used a hymn or a sacred verse, that is, a piece of free verse, in verses and lines. Moreover, the tenor did not need to be extended. The conductus therefore did not constitute an opposition with long or short notes; both voices were equal in this respect.

We must emphasize one point. The conductus was not obliged to use a given liturgical text. It was then a composition-for-many-voices,

[11]V. Lederer, cf. Karl Nef, *History of Music.*

in which all parts were *freely* written. It is not difficult to imagine the potentialities of such an innovation.

The conductus developed independently, as we shall see, creating its own structures, and it was not long before it took to imitating and borrowing, for the tenor part, pieces of many different origins, even popular rounds in the common tongue.

The School of Notre Dame

Polyphony, or many-voiced music, was, then, a French invention. Central France especially was its cradle. The memorable innovations at St. Martial (called the "Conservatory of the Middle Ages"), at Chartres, and at Fleury were to find their ultimate expansion in the works of the first great names in polyphonic music: Leoninus and Perotinus.

Already, in advance of these two masters, musical history had recorded the name of one "Master Albert of Paris." And the one piece of his that we have, a conductus for three voices, links the name of this same capital, Paris, with "A quest for the enrichment of polyphony, just as later the name of Perotinus would be linked with the writing of music for four voices."[12] All other manuscripts that mention Master Albert are for one or two voices only.

The author concluded: "There is in existence a volume containing four-part works like *Viderunt* and *Sederunt*, composed by Perotinus, which are full of color [by which he meant ornament] and beauty . . . and another of three-part works which are indeed greater than great, like the *Alleluia, Dies Sanctificatus*, in which we have color and beauty in abundance; and no matter who would celebrate Divine Service, if he celebrated in this way he would be using the best book we have concerning this art."

It was only at the end of the 19th century that this book from Notre Dame was identified at Florence *(Magnus liber organi, 1898).*

Other choir manuals of the French school were found in Spain, in Germany and in Scotland. None stayed in France.

All the two-part organa of the *Magnus liber* are now attributed to Leoninus, but only by supposition.[13] The organa for three and four voices in the same volume are ascribed to Perotinus, several of them with certainty. There are several hundred of these works (organa and conductus) from the Perotinus school, and we are not able to determine exactly the share which the master himself took in these.

We know nothing about Leoninus. He would have been gathered to the ranks of the great anonymous had not a writer at the end of the

[12]Jacques Chailley, *op. cit.*
[13]*Ibid.*

106

13th century by chance mentioned him. "Take note, too, that Master Leoninus was a composer of organa of great excellence, who produced a great book of organa for Gradual and Antiphonary in order to extend the service of God. This book was in use up to the time of the great Perotinus, who abridged it and wrote many cadenzas and phrases which were more beautiful; he was very clever at descant, better than Leoninus."

That is the sum total of our knowledge of Leoninus.

The rest deals with Perotinus. "Now this master himself, Perotinus, wrote some very lovely four-part pieces, such as *Viderunt* and *Sederunt,* full of colorful harmony. There was an even greater number of three-part works, full of dignity, like his *Alleluia posui adjutorium* and *Nativitas.* The book, or books, composed by Perotinus were in use up to the time of Robert de Sabilon in the choir of B.V.M. in Paris (Notre Dame)."

Those manuscripts that have been identified reveal Perotinus as the inventor of rhythmic notation, from which our own system has been developed.

What do we know of the man himself? Not much more, to be sure, than we know of Leoninus. Indeed, scholars have discovered some five people who *could* have been the master, with no iota of proof in favor of one or the other.

Leoninus and Perotinus were both organists; they wrote organa; and that is all the texts tell us. The term organist corresponded to no specific function. It applied as much to those who wrote organa as to those who sang them. It could also mean one who played the organ, but at the time in question that instrument was still a rarity in churches.

In spite of our ignorance about Leoninus and Perotinus, however, there is no doubt at all about the strong influence of the Notre Dame school. Musicians from every corner of the known world came to Paris to drink in the genius of Perotinus and to take its lessons back with them to their own countries. At that time, Notre Dame was truly the musical center of the West.

Organum had developed enormously since the first tentative efforts at St. Martial, and now it was composition with majesty and proportions of greatness. It was sung mainly during the great feasts at Christmas and Easter and at solemn ceremonies. The singers, wearing beautifully colored copes, performed in the choir. Chailley writes, "Since, as was generally the case, the texts thus set to music were *graduals* or *alleluias,* they were inserted into the Solemn Mass, and when one calculates that an organum by Perotinus lasted no less than twenty minutes, one can well believe that it was a veritable spiritual concert at which the faithful of the Cathedral were present."

Nothing could be more in keeping with the Gothic architecture of Notre Dame, still quite new at this time, than this unearthly counterpoint of Perotinus, whose pure, marvelously free lines unfurled their fanciful forms upon the slow syllables of the main melody; nothing could merge more happily with the light from the great windows, or the sinewy lightness of the columns, rearing upwards to the great vault, defying, as it were, all laws of weight.

Still greater freedom in the conductus allowed Perotinus to achieve in them a transparency and freedom of voices that made them masterpieces of pure counterpoint, all the more so because as yet there was no restraining harmony to confine his imagination. Each voice, by itself—not only the tenor—had its own beauty, its own meaning, its own feeling.

Considerable tribute must be paid to present-day musicology. One of its glories is that by methodical research in medieval music, into its principles of rhythm, into its rules of performance, into its notation, it has restored to us these works from the Notre Dame school. Listening to records, everyone can travel again along the road that led to polyphony. Everyone can get to know a language and a writing from which all subsequent music sprang—and on which it still feeds, like a flower drawing life from roots deep in the earth.

There is no better illustration of the way in which a taste for this music has evolved than the verdicts pronounced not long ago on Perotinus by some of the more enlightened spirits: "We know for certain that these strange compositions were played in church . . . but it is difficult for us to assess the musical value of an art like this . . . its content is so hard!" Thus writes a famous historian.

Such an opinion was by no means isolated and was in accordance with the general view. Its author (Combarieu, *History of Music*, 1920) was a man of culture and enlightenment, with great breadth of vision. He would have been mightily surprised had he been able to foresee that forty years later Perotinus would be a neighbor of Heinrich Schütz and J. S. Bach in the displays of record stores!

Perotinus' works were almost certainly written in the early years of the 13th century, perhaps even in the closing years of the 12th. He was, therefore, a contemporary of Bernard de Ventadour, of Villehardouin, and of St. Francis of Assisi. Poets and romanticists were bringing to life some of the great figures of our European literature: Tristan, Percival (the Parsifal of Wagner), El Cid. Those who built cathedrals were going on with their grandiose plans; beneath their scaffolding, Laon and Chartres, the dome at Siena and the Tower of Pisa were launching into space the silhouettes which for centuries to come were to symbolize the very spirit of the West.

The efforts of St. Ambrose and St. Gregory, the inventions at Jumièges, St. Gall, Reichenau and St. Martial, the genius of countless anonymous musicians who preceded Leoninus and Perotinus—all these secured for music a position that is no longer in question. All the resistance of old has been vanquished. The art of sound has achieved full status.

The admirable text of St. Thomas Aquinas, who was a child when

Perotinus was an old man, defines the role of music. It is evidence of the position that music was to enjoy and the fundamental importance that society would attach to it from that time on. In *Arte Musicae*, the philosopher writes:

"Music holds first place in the seven liberal arts. It is with music that the Church celebrates her struggles and her victories for God. It is music that the Saints use in their devotions and it is with music that sinners beg pardon. Music is solace to the sorrowful and courage to the brave. As Isidore, Archbishop of Seville (*ca.* 600) says in his book of Etymologies, it is a disgrace not to be able to sing; it is almost as shameful as not being able to read; for the Saints, with angels and archangels, with Thrones and Dominations and with all the heavenly hosts, fill the heavens each day with a never-ending song of glory: *Sanctus, Sanctus, Sanctus.*

"It is then clear that music is the most noble of human sciences, and each person must study it in preference to all others, for apart from music, no science has ever been bold enough to enter the portals of the Church."

Bibliography

Comprehensive coverage of early polyphony is contained in Gustave Reese, *Music in the Middle Ages* (New York, Norton, 1940). For those, however, who may have no background in the subject, Reese may not be the best place to begin. A less formidable introduction to polyphony is that of Albert Seay, *Music in the Medieval World* (Englewood Cliffs, N.J., Prentice-Hall, 1965). Vol. 2 of *The New Oxford History of Music* also covers the subject of early polyphony. Specialized aspects of polyphony are treated in the following: Willi Apel, "From St. Martial to Notre Dame," *Journal of the American Musicological Society*, 2 (1949); Willi Apel, "The Earliest Polyphonic Composition," *Revue Belge de Musicologie*, 10 (1955); Amédée Gastoué, "Three Centuries of French Medieval Music," *The Musical Quarterly*, 3 (1917); Dom Anselm Hughes, "The Origins of Harmony," *The Musical Quarterly*, 24 (1938); Finn Mathiassen, *The Style of the Early Motet* (Copenhagen, Dan Fog Musikforlag, 1966), of which pp. 32-42 are recommended for their treatment of the cultural function of the early motet; Norman Smith, "Tenor Repetition in the Notre Dame Organa," *Journal of the American Musicological Society*, 19 (1966); and William Waite, "Discantus, Copula, Organum," *Journal of the American Musicological Society*, 5 (1952). Many articles on aspects of early polyphony have appeared and will continue to appear not only in the periodicals already mentioned but also in *Speculum*, which is devoted to medieval studies of all kinds, and in *Musica Disciplina*, devoted to medieval and Renaissance music.

Transcriptions of early polyphonic music may be found in *Historical Anthology of Music*, vol. 1, and in *Geschichte der Musik in Beispielen*. More extensive collections of music are contained in the following editions: Pierre Aubry, *Cent motets du XIIIᵉ siècle*, (Paris, A. Rouart, Lerolle & Co., 1908); Yvonne Rokseth, *Polyphonies du XIIIᵉ siècle*, 4 vols. (Paris, l'Oiseau Lyre, 1935-1939); William Waite, *The Rhythm of Twelfth Century Polyphony* (New Haven, Conn., Yale University Press, 1954), which contains the presumed compositions of Leonin and Perotin; and Harry Wooldridge, *Early English Harmony*, 2 vols. (London, B. Quaritch, 1897-1913).

7

THE men of the fifteenth century considered the creations of their time to be vastly superior to those of the centuries immediately preceding. Not since the days of ancient Greece and Rome, they thought, had civilization experienced such brilliance as was theirs; their age represented a rebirth which came after centuries of darkness and barbarian crudity. Thus much of the inspiration for the art of the Renaissance came from an earlier classic period, but this could not be the case for music. No example of Grecian music was known to Renaissance composers. Only a few philosophical and theoretical writings on music had survived, and while these were at times cited as authority to justify the style and theory of Renaissance music, they were probably as often misunderstood as understood. Professor Schrade, in the following selection, discusses the attitude of the men of the Renaissance toward the art and music of their own time. Let us then, as an introduction, outline briefly some of the points which made Renaissance music different—and different it was—from the music of the late Middle Ages.[1]

The fifteenth century saw a reorganization of the institutions that sponsored music. While the churches and the court chapels continued to require Latin liturgical music, this was no longer the dominating force in the creation of music. The free cities and towns were now requiring ceremonial music for state occasions. And perhaps most important, the rise of an aristocratic middle class initiated a need for more secular music in the vernacular and for instrumental and dance music. This gave impetus not only to the emergence of a class of musical amateurs but also to a class of professional and virtuoso musicians. Increasingly, the composer signed his compositions, and anonymous compositions became less and less the norm.

---

[1] In the following remarks I am much indebted to the works of Professors Blume and Lowinsky, both of whose writings are listed in the bibliography at the end of the selection.

As for the style of fifteenth-century music, two items came to dominate as the generating factors of music, the text and musical sonority. Since there was a great interest in literature in the Renaissance, it was only logical that composers began to pay greater attention to their choice and setting of texts. No longer were phrases and words broken in two for purely musical reasons; phrases were now respected as units, requiring that the composer conceive his composition as a whole, not as a patchwork series of prefabricated parts. As discussed in the introduction to the preceding selection, medieval compositions had been assembled by what might be termed a layer or stencil technique. A polyphonic composition was written one polyphonic line at a time, and the lines were then laid one atop the other. Even the individual lines were frequently assembled by putting together a series of pre-existing rhythmic patterns. Renaissance technique, on the other hand, was one of simultaneous composition. All parts of the polyphonic texture were written at the same time, and the general outlines of the composition were conceived as a whole in the mind of the composer before work was begun. The composer now became an individual free to form a creative work according to his own imagination, stimulated by the text he had chosen to set. This was a giant step in the history of musical creativity.

If music now sprang from the word, it also sprang from sonority. The composers of the Renaissance tended more and more to control dissonance in their compositions. Conventions began to be accepted and followed in approaching and resolving dissonant harmonies. Consonance became the foundation of musical composition; dissonance was an ornament to that foundation, and what determined dissonance was no longer speculative philosophy but, instead, the human ear. The common triad became the basis of musical sonority, and the path toward a tonal system determined by triad progression was begun, although it was to be almost three centuries before such a system was reached.

Fifteenth-century music does represent a considerable accomplishment. It is still the earliest polyphonic music to which many modern ears can relate.[2] Admittedly this music has a certain ring of archaism in some passages, but it does not sound completely foreign to us, as earlier music does sometimes. Because of this, we run the risk of being caught up in the vanity of the Renaissance and dismissing all earlier music as crude, worthy only of the attention of those who are so peculiar as to be attracted to medievalism. It must be emphasized that the changes that differentiate medieval from Renaissance music did not come about abruptly. There was no sudden, clean break between the two

[2]Recent trends in twentieth-century music may be changing this, however. Many today are of the opinion that modern man, in Western civilization, is developing an affinity for music of an earlier date than that of the Renaissance.

styles. Those things which characterize fifteenth-century music may be seen developing in the music of the fourteenth century. Only gradually did they rise to govern musical style. Despite the pride of the Renaissance in its accomplishments, fifteenth-century music would have been impossible without there first having been fourteenth-century music.

Leo Schrade (1903-1964) was a member of the faculties of the Universities of Königsberg, Bonn, Basel, and Yale. His works include *Monteverdi: Creator of Modern Music* (New York, Norton, 1950) and his edition of *Polyphonic Music of the 14th Century*, 4 vols. (Monaco, L'Oiseau Lyre, 1956-1958), as well as periodical contributions. The following selection was delivered as a paper at the meeting of the International Musicological Society held in Utrecht in 1952.

Renaissance: The Historical Conception of an Epoch

LEO SCHRADE

"In this our age, the arts once more have revealed themselves; they have turned to the light again; they have been refined and perfected by many masters." Thus, the 15th century humanist Matteo Palmieri briefly, but comprehensively and exactly, indicated the problems which will be our business to discuss. Despite all well-known efforts of many a student the Renaissance still calls for clarification as an epoch of the history of music; it still presents the old vitality of challenge to the erudition and ingenuity of scholars in every province of human endeavor and artistic achievement. For the Renaissance shares company with the singular phenomena that keep changing their meaning with every generation of historians. Beset on two sides, by the Middle Ages on one end, by the Baroque on the other, the Renaissance has suffered considerably from all-too perplexing ambiguities.

Three factors, I believe, have been chiefly instrumental in preventing the historian of music from clarifying the Renaissance as an epoch: his frequent attempt prematurely to define the musical Renaissance in totally abstract terms, his appropriation of stylistic patterns and criteria taken from the visual arts, and a falsely constructed relationship to Greek music. Since I shall completely ignore the avenue of an abstract approach, I shall give no additional definition: still, I think a clarification of the Renaissance on strictly historical grounds to be within reach.

An historical interpretation must, above all, find the answer to certain basic, even simple questions which, strangely enough, have been either overlooked or forgotten. When has the term "Renaissance" been introduced into musical literature? What meaning did it carry when it first came into usage? Did it embody characteristic connotations at the time of its coinage? Did it refer to an epoch or to chronological cycles? Were musicians aware of a rebirth? And what was it that the Renaissance has

FROM the *Compte rendu* of the Fifth Congress of the International Society of Musicology (Ryswick, Netherlands, Vereniging voor Nederlandse Muziekgeschiedenis, 1952), pp. 19-32. Reprinted by permission of the publisher and the Estate of Leo Schrade.

reborn: a style, a frame of mind, or a set of ideas? Did it embrace uniformity of thought and stability of character? To continue: did the term Renaissance disappear from the musical literature, or else remain even after the consummation of rebirth? And if the latter, did it retain its original meaning, or else become subject to change with the passage of time? However primitive these questions might appear, the answer will surely unburden the term Renaissance from views, beliefs, prejudices put upon it by modern historiography; it grants what, in the very sense of the word, is a historically objective interpretation.

When searching through literature on as full a scale as possible, that is: on the basis of the Liberal Arts, the litterae bonae, we constantly fall upon terms which can quickly be recognized as idiomatic vocabulary common to the representatives of all the bonae litterae. Not restricted to any special discipline, the standardized terms range through musical, rhetorical, grammatical, artistic literature. Some of the terms are plainly objective, others are descriptive metaphors. They should be listed first: restitutio, restauratio, renovatio, revocatio, renasci, rinascimento, rinascità; renaître, renaissance des lettres, des beaux arts, restitution des bonnes lettres, and as the translation of Vasari by Sandrart shows, Wiedergeburth in German. The meaning of rebirth, common to all, is of course inherent also in such kindred terms as renascentes Musae or reflorescentes artes.

The long period prior to the moment of rebirth also obtained an official term commonly used; it was named intervallum immensum, lacuna, or metaphorically exilium, abyssus, ignoratio tenebris, while "tempestas media," apparently coined in the 15th century, but rarely used, gave rise to medium aevum, the Middle Ages.

A fairly extensive terminology has been introduced to designate the very act of rebirth; we find such words or phrases as origo, initium, fons, or fontes, the awakening—ex somnio, ex tenebris ad lumen, ad lucem, e tenebris in lucem revocare, in lucem prodire, remis au jour.

The growth that followed the rebirth extended the period in which simultaneously the activities of several generations unfolded; and this process of growth was most frequently termed accretio, accrescere, accrescimento. But this accrescimento, looked upon as an organic growth, stimulated the assumption of the biologic process of passing through the phases of infancy or youth, mature manhood and old age. It seems but natural that the biologic idea of an organic growth toward fullest ripeness suggested the principles of progressiveness and perfection. Thus, in logical succession, all these terms fall in place jointly to represent a universal vocabulary upon which all men of letters, of music, of the visual arts, have freely drawn within the limits of an epoch. We must lay open what all these terms enclosed at the time when they were used.

An issue of Italian humanists, the idea of recovery from impotence took shape within the political historiography of the 15th century. Since according to all competent accounts Italy greatly suffered from an extreme economic depression during that time, the idea of recuperation obviously did not have its roots in material conditions. The histories of Leonardo Bruni and Flavio Biondi were, nevertheless, eminently successful in establishing the doctrine of restoration. Their exposition was guided by certain conceptions worthy of mention. 1. They understood the process of history to possess no continuity. 2. They saw after the downfall of the Roman Empire the diluvium of the barbarians to have caused total destruction, the effects of which lasted for centuries. 3. They discovered that in their own time the process of historical evolution at long last made the turn to a new rise: denique quotcumque ex variis barbarorum diluviis superfuerunt urbes per Italiam, crescere atque florere et in *pristinam auctoritates sese attollere* [coeperunt] (Bruni, Hist, Flor. pop. libri XII, 23.) 4. Fascinated by the new rise in Italy, they were disproportionately preoccupied with the history of their own time, for the sake of which their historiography came into being. Biondi took steps accordingly; he employed his attention first upon the all-important years 1412-1442 before writing the long history of all the centuries prior to his day.

When discussing the evolution of culture in Italy, both Bruni and Biondi discovered in the history of letters the same turning point which they had fixed for political history. Since neither wrote a continuous history of culture, their thought unfortunately remained fragmentary. But the biography of prominent men appeared to offer ideal opportunities to elucidate the evolution of arts and letters; in this literary category Filippo Villani set the pattern with his Liber de civitatis Florentiae famosis civibus, completed shortly before 1400.

The phases of the artistic development followed closely the periods of political history. Antiquity, the first phase, represented the climax of human culture; its complete breakdown, in the eyes of most of the writers, coincided with the fall of the Roman Empire. A complete cessation of all cultural activities characterized the second phase. But then a new ascent started off the third period, and by the middle of the 15th century it reached such a vantage-point on the up-grade toward a new climax as to allow both a retrospective search after the very first indications of the rise and a comparison with the culture of antiquity. The search after the earliest signs of an improvement of culture gave Petrarch the distinction of having been the first "che riconobbe e *rivoco in luce* l'antica leggiadria delle *stile perduto e spento*" (Bruni); it discovered Dante had put poetry on its feet again, *"quasi ex abysso tenebrarum eruptam revocavit in lucem,* dataque manu, iacentem erexit in pedes" (Villani); it proved that Cimabue and Giotto had set the art of painting into motion again. Once the bonae litterae started to move they rapidly rose to the height they reached by the middle of the 15th century: "i quali dapoi crescendo montati sono nella presente altezza."

The rebirth, the Renaissance of culture, gave the men of the 15th century an exhilarating feeling of pride and enthusiasm. The awareness of being reborn to civilization furnished sufficient reason to glorify the new achievements in arts and letters. Moreover, of reasons to justify any measure of enthusiasm, there were many. The escape from the dark prison of ignorance called forth a universal joy over the new light shed by the renaissance of culture. But this metaphor "ex tenebris ad lumen" soon effected a habit of looking back with utter contempt upon the long years of imprisonment. A further reason to rejoice in the restoration resulted from the understanding that once again man could liken the nobility of his regained culture to that of his ancient ancestor. And finally the completeness of the renaissance stimulated additional enthusiasm. All provinces of culture shared in the blessing of renovation; all arts and letters were reborn. Even if one discipline alone was chosen to assert the resurgence of the stile perduto e spento, the revival of one was thought to be to the benefit of all. Hence, the "Musae renascentes" advanced all together, not severally, although Marsilio Ficino once recorded the renaissance of the liberal arts all together, and, probably under the impression of Gaffori, of music specifically. Of one thing, however, there seems to have been a firm conviction which asserted itself the more forcibly the more the 15th century advanced: that the benefits of restoration issued from the arts and letters, rather than from any political strength. Not Rome, but the Roman language granted the renaissance of a universal culture: linguam romanam plus quam urbem cum ea disciplinas omnes iri restitutum, to quote the magnificent dictum of Lorenzo Valla whose Neapolitan activities still resounded at the time when Tinctoris came to Naples.

When presenting the conception of the renaissance of culture at the beginning of the 15th century, the humanists hardly ever failed to point, even somewhat ostentatiously, to the previous intervallum, lacuna, abyss from which they had arisen. For the change from the complete darkness of infamous illiteracy to the light of civilization would certainly render the advent of rebirth all the more striking. But the various authors estimated differently the width of the gap that had swallowed all achievement of note and dignity. Although the majority of writers determined the interval to have lasted from the 5th century to the beginning of the 15th, the variety of measures seems to suggest that the inception of the Renaissance had always had a characteristic flexibility. But many authors frequently dated the inauguration under conditions that were locally colored, as they also often drew from personalities of their own situation to eulogize those who prompted the rise to the new climax of culture. Above all: no matter how far back into the 14th century they might reach when looking for the first symptoms of a rebirth, it is always their own time and environment that filled them with pride, enthusiasm, and the feeling of superiority. Dante, Petrarch, Cimabue, Giotto, all were laudable initiators, but no more than precursors of the glorious 15th century; still far remote from the new culmination, all predecessors were subject to criticism. Hence it is only at the beginning of the 15th century that for the first time man was shown to have reached a stage admitting comparison with the previous climax of human civilization, with antiquity.

When speaking of such a comparison, it is to be stressed that only the rank to be attributed to the standards of culture became subject to comparison. The heights of the two civilizations were measured and found to be very nearly equal. But it was not the imitation or copy of ancient models that produced the Renaissance. To be sure, the Ciceronian eloquentia was taken as a guide; but none of the early humanists ever stated that the rebirth came about because of imitating the ancients. Hence their awareness of living in an age that had risen to new heights of culture did not derive from any faithfully copied model. When observing the rise of the visual arts in the work of Brunelleschi, Donatello, Ghiberti, and Luca della Robbia, Leone Battista Alberti was most outspoken in claiming independence for the renaissance; according to him the work of his contemporaries came about *"senza praeceptori, senza exemplo alchuni";* all the more was it worthy of admiration.

One further element deserves our special attention. The idea of rebirth possessed the power of continuance. For without any essential change it lasted through the 15th and 16th centuries. Certain additional aspects entered the discussion on account of the passing of time, but nothing basic changed. Authors of the latter part of the 16th century used exactly the same expressions and images of the renaissance that the humanist had introduced at the beginning of the 15th century; the first climax of culture in antiquity, the great interval during which culture lay at the bottom of the abyss, the new rise to light. In view of the extraordinary adherence to an idea together with its terminology, it is evident that from the very outset the humanists thought of the rebirth of culture, not in terms of a fleeting moment or a historical event that comes and goes, but in terms of a lasting epoch.

When this theory passed from Italy to the North, the northern scholars proved themselves to be the faithful and enthusiastic disciples of Italian humanists. Guillaume Budé, Robert Gaguin were quick in adopting the whole terminology of the decline and new rise of the liberal arts. Probably the most detailed presentation came from Johannes Trithemius. But the most beautiful, and, surely, the profoundest, work is the famous *Antibarbarorum Liber* of Erasmus, written about 1490, but published in 1520, a work that, apart from all its high qualities of individuality, testifies to the international renown of Lorenzo Valla and other Italian humanists. The northern authors, and Erasmus among them, added a feature of their own which was to play a significant role in the Reformation; within the first phase of the history of culture, that is: within the epoch of antiquity, they placed the early Church fathers at the side of the classics of the pagan world. Perhaps, they also laid greater emphasis on the renaissance of the bonae litterae and paid little attention to the rise of the visual arts. In every other respect, however, did the theory of the order of cultural phases, of the historical cycles of culture, remain untouched, as did the sum total of terms and imagery.

As a member of the liberal arts music shared all the benefits of their renaissance. While for obvious reasons the pictorial arts required a disquisition of their own, music needed no special discussion. Hence, many authors treated the bonae litterae with an all-embracing understanding, though Rabelais, for instance, paid special attention to the resurgence of music when he adopted the theory of rebirth, and others did likewise. But the professional authors of music did not permit themselves to be excluded from inquiring, on their own, into the properties of the evolution of music. Seized by the universal enthusiasm about the arrival of a new age, they were quick in discovering a renaissance of music within their own epoch. By taking over all the paraphernalia of the terminology, they expounded the idea of rebirth most faithfully.

Elsewhere, and in a different context, I assumed Tinctoris to have been the first in making himself the partner of the humanistic school of thought. After having come upon an earlier witness, I welcome the opportunity to correct the statement. Once, moreover, all documents have been canvassed, further changes and corrections may well be expected. Not Tinctoris, then, but Johannes Gallicus seems to have given the first indications of a musician's familiarity with the doctrine of the 15th century renaissance. That a northerner started off a long list of humanists, should, of course, be no surprise in any case. For the music itself with which to associate the rebirth actually came from the North. And furthermore, though born in Namur, the theorist Jean came fairly early in his life to one of the centers of Italian humanism, to Mantua. There he was a Carthusian monk, but also a disciple of the most admirable Vittorino da Feltre, whose humanistic school included the teaching of music. Jean himself recorded having received his training in music directly from Vittorino. Completed probably not much after the middle of the century, the treatise carried a characteristic title: *Ritus Canendi vetustissimus et novus,* showing old and new in direct opposition. Although his comments are parceled out all over his large treatise, hence without aiming at coherence in discussing the Renaissance, Jean revealed himself as a genuine humanist when setting old and new over against each other. But his music of old was not that of pagan antiquity; he rather thought of the early Christian period, or of those standards of music which, according to him, the fathers of the Church established. Taking Marchettus of Padua mercilessly to task as the epitome of ignorance, he hardly recognized anything of merit within the lacuna of well over 800 years. When speaking of a certain subject, he had but two recom-

119

mendations to make; the study of Boethius and the reading of the 10th chapter in his own treatise as though nothing of note had been done in between. With no intention of introducing any new music (quam quidem non dici novam introducere volens), he wanted to renew the true practice of the ancient fathers (renovare veram antiquorum patrum practicam). The true practice sprang from the church of the first Christian centuries—ab illo fonte procedit. But the fountain must be made to spout again, which he set out to accomplish "si possim renovare." The stress placed by Jean, the northerner, upon the musical culture of Christian antiquity might well appear to have been effected by the North where such an accent was to be the custom. But since Vittorino da Feltre made his doctrine of education embrace the culture of both pagan and Christian antiquity, the influence of the Italian humanist upon Jean has more in its favor. For the humanist's task of renovatio, of rebirth, was present with Vittorino as much as with Jean, the musician.

Johannes Gallicus displayed a good deal of learnedness which apparently attracted many a pupil. He continued the school of Vittorino. Among his own most loyal disciples he was to count Nicolaus Burtius, who, in devotion to his teacher, copied manu propria the large treatise *Ritus canendi*. The school was transferred to Parma where Jean died in 1473. This school which must be traced back to Vittorino da Feltre as the original founder gained a most powerful influence. At the side of Burtius appeared Gaffori who verified his intimate acquaintance with Jean. All those who in the controversy around Ramis de Pareja took opposite sides were diligent students of Jean's theory. Ramis de Pareja himself and Spartaro, his companion-in-arms, knew the treatise inside out. Next to Burtius, Gaffori, Ramis, and Spataro, Pietro Aron had an indirect relation to the school of Mantova/Parma. A further lead points to Tinctoris whom Gaffori joined in Naples for a short time. Thus the leading figures of musical theory that appear on the scene in the 15th century seem all to be grouped around Vittorino da Feltre, the great philosopher of humanistic education.

Although each of these men maintained remarkable differences in their theories, they all were bound together in the belief that a new epoch had been born, that a renaissance had taken place. They may not all present their belief with the same energy or elaborateness; in fact, we find considerable shades of opinion; and in some of the literature the polemics were so much in the foreground that they threatened to overshadow any other matter. Yet even amidst the most heated controversy the authors seek an opportunity to allude to the rise that they had witnessed in their own time: "Omittam . . . quoscunque etiam nostris temporibus in Italia claruerint viros et *sensim emergunt*. Hi sunt gemmae, hi uniones, saphiri lapidesque preciosi, quos Italia pullulat et producit." (Burtius, *Florum libellus*).

Some of the theorists seemed to associate the beginning of the new epoch directly with their own work, or at least with the theory of music. Although principally they subordinated the musica prattica to the musica theorica, as did Ramis de Pareja, they all drew heavily upon compositions of the time in support of their theories. Conscious of the novelty of contemporary music, Ramis was aware that as a result of the renovation "nostri cantores" follow their own imagination (quod imaginationi seu fantasiae suae placet); when turning to music, ad harmoniam novam, they no longer accept a model, an example, as was the case in olden times. "Senza preceptori, senza exemplo," such was the claim Alberti raised for the achievements in the visual arts. Such is the judgment Ramis passed on the reborn music. Having discussed the position of music in the ancient world, he immediately gave his attention to the music of his time; and he had this to say: "If those highly esteemed musicians (of antiquity) whom we mentioned would be recalled to life, they would deny that the music of our time is the same they had invented." (Si enim illi, quorum supra meminimus, probatissimi musici ad vitam revocarentur, musicam nostri temporis a se inventam negarent). Surely, that denial that the harmonia nova resulted from imitating ancient music could hardly be more outspoken. Though an offspring of the artist's imagination, the harmonia nova could still compare with ancient music when appraised as a manifestation of culture.

All direct members of the school of Mantua-Parma were soon excelled by Gaffori and above all by Tinctoris who gave the doctrine of rebirth the classic formulation of the 15th century. I need not recall all the details of Tinctoris' theory; but certain aspects should be singled out. Like Johannes Gallicus before him, Tinctoris placed the early Christian fathers at the side of the classic writers to represent antiquity. On the side of his own period, he surveyed the work of two generations and grouped the composers accordingly; he named the generation of the founders, that is: the "fons et origo," and the generation of their younger successors, that is: the moderni. Enthusiastic about the universal renovation, he welcomed the renaissance of music, the resurgence of musical culture. He did not say that imitation of ancients prompted the rebirth; nor did he have in mind any special technical aspect of music when speaking of the ars nova reborn to rise toward the new climax. He recognized the process of history and drew the picture of the first climax of antiquity, of the drop to the bottom of the abyss, of the lacuna of centuries, and finally of the fons et origo that produced the Renaissance.

It matters little, whether or not Gaffori presented his humanistic understanding of the restoration of music under the influence of Tinctoris, since the ideas had become common property by the end of the century. Gaffori made his contribution in both the Practica Musica and the Theoricum opus; but nowhere does the interpretation appear as coherent or systematic as in the work of Tinctoris. He adopted the conception of the novelty of his epoch; he assessed the achievement of the musicians as did Tinctoris; but he had no clear approach to the idea of fons et origo. Many a time a polemical trait affected the integrity of thought. But it is worthy of mention that a good many of his contemporaries made use of the humanistic theory of rebirth in order to praise Gaffori as the founder of the Renaissance. "Necesse est confiteri artem musicam ab Antiquis quidem inchóatam, sed ab eo absolutam fuisse." Thus Malegolo attributed the restoration, even the completion, of music to his friend Gaffori. The idea that the culture of music had suffered in darkness for centuries past to arise to new light once again was often and in various ways expressed by Gaffori's friends and followers, each taking Gaffori himself to be the bringer of light. Giovanni Cornago, Gaffori's Neapolitan colleague, whose musical work is preserved as a fragment in Trent 88 and f.frçs. 15.123, voiced the idea in verse: "Prodiit et stygia per te de sede revulsa/ Musica, nec notos attulit ipsa modos." Still more to the point did Johannes Jacobus Bilia use the metaphor to specify the suffering of culture in darkness: "Music in obscuro fuerat"; the horrifying labyrinth kept her there: "Labyrinthus habebat Horridus hanc." Now due to the monumental work of Gaffori, however, music stepped forward from darkness: "non est amplius in tenebris." And with cultural standards in mind Aemylius Merula extolled Gaffori for having restored music to its old appearance: "Musicam in antiquam restituit faciem." Of course, such a eulogy, or rather flattery, has a dubious value. Nevertheless, what we must recognize to be of value is the terminology, the manner of expression and imagery, the very idea of rebirth.

From then on musicians discussed the doctrine of rebirth regularly. They gave their lists of composers whom they regarded as founders or participants of the Renaissance. With the passage of time the original founders gradually disappeared from the lists. Pietro Aron (in his *Toscanello*, 1523) called men such as Orto, Agricola, Isaac, Pierre de la Rue, Compere, Obrecht, the "antichi," although, according to his own statement (in *Institutio*) he knew personally Isaac, Agricola, Josquin. He held them to be antichi, because he understood them to have been responsible for the rebirth of music. Vanneo, on the other hand (*Recanetum*, 1531) who drew upon Lorenzo Valla for his distinction between musicus and cantor, extended the list of renowned composers close to his own day, without concerning himself with the founders.

A most interesting version of the humanistic view appears in Lanfranco's *Scintille di Musica* (1533). He ranged over all the provinces of culture to find the proper men whom he named examples, on both ends of the wide lacuna, of the cultural climax in antiquity and the culture reborn in modern times. Thus he placed Virgil as the last of the ancients on the one side of the abyss, while Petrarch, Bocaccio, Bembo, Sannazaro appeared on the opposite side; in the pictorial arts he set Praxiteles and Apelles against Michelangelo, Raphael, and Titian, and in music "el Divino Boetio Romano" opposite Gaffori, Giorgio Valla,

Burtius, Aron, Spataro, Josquin, La Rue, Agricola, Mouton, Richafort, Willaert, Costanzo Festa, Jachet, Hesdin.

In contrast to the other bonae litterae and to the visual arts as well, the rebirth of music came to pass as an achievement of northern composers, a fact which Italians themselves did not hesitate to recognize since their lists of musicians showed the northerners by far in the majority. As the generations grew, adding their accomplishments one by one to the advancement of the rising evolution, a further order seemed to be required. While most of the writers remained satisfied [with the] distinction between the antichi as the founders of the reborn culture and the moderni as the younger followers, Glareanus, previous to Vasari, introduced the idea of an organic growth which put the evolution of the epoch into the order of youth, manhood, and old age. The idea of an organic growth which he gained from viewing the achievements of the past in retrospect, enabled him to clarify the work of many generations. But inherent in this idea from the very start is the conception that the period of "new music" is an epoch of the total history of music. The term "ars nova" Tinctoris introduced was not intended to be discarded after it had fulfilled a specific purpose. It embodied the belief in a lasting epoch. In contrast to any previous use of such a term, the Ars nova of Tinctoris was meant to stay, and so it did.

The phases of the epoch in conformity with an organic, biological growth stimulated another positive idea; that of perfection reached at the time of mature manhood; but also a negative idea which when thought through to the end of all its implications was fraught with calamity; that of the biologic decline which should be expected to come with old age. The idea of perfection, an idea of classic virtus, is bound to enter whenever progressiveness is recognized as the driving force of evolution. The biologic process from infancy to manhood unfolds the growth to the best, to the summit of potentialities. Manhood being reached, perfection has come into its own which allowed the 16th century authors to speak of a golden age. But this idea of perfection in music did not result from any intention to imitate the Greeks. The meaning of perfection, relative to the rediscovered nature of music, has been clarified, without a shadow of doubt, by Zarlino. Together with his thesis of organic perfection, he summarized once again the theory of the rebirth of an epoch; he saw the somma altezza in ancient times; he saw the downfall of musical culture to the infima bassezza, the abyss, the lacuna; he saw the moment of redemption, rebirth, restoration, of music which at last by gradual accrescimento rose to the new somma altezza. Tinctoris gave the classic formulation for the century past, Glareanus and Zarlino for the 16th century. But we should also mention the greatly interesting "Raggionamenti accademici" of 1567 from which I quote: "Josquin, the disciple of Ockeghem, can well be said to have been in music what our Michelangelo Buonarotti was in architecture, painting and sculpture; for just as Josquin had none who reached him in composition, so is Michelangelo alone and without companion among all who practice these arts; but both opened the eyes of all those who now take pleasure in these arts and shall find delight in the future." But Ockeghem must be regarded as the restorer, the very man whose art produced the rebirth of music, just as Donatello brought about the rebirth of sculpture; "Ocghem fu quasi il primo che in questi tempi *ritrovasse la musica quasi che spenta del tutto;* non altrementi che Donatello *ne suoi ritrovo la sculture.*" Is this not the echo of words used by the 15th century humanist when speaking of the stile perduto e spento, lost and extinguished?

The end of the epoch brought one more complete survey of the generations, undertaken by Lodovico Zacconi, who as author of the first part of his Musica Prattica was still a member of that epoch which possessed "la musica ristorata." Writing at the end of the century he enjoyed the advantages of complete retrospection. At great length did he discuss the relation between theory and practice; he defined the functions of the theoretical and practical musicians most carefully and in a verbose manner in order to drive home the contrast between antiquity and renaissance. He used the term "antichi" in the double sense of the ancients proper, and of the founders of the reborn music. Josquin, Mouton, Ockeghem, Brumel, Senfl are the antichi of the Renaissance. Whenever he speaks of the antichi in general, it is to them that he refers. If he has in mind the authors of antiquity proper, he calls them by name — Boethius, Plato, Pythagoras. Next to the antichi stand the vecchi, the old ones; they are Willaert, Morales, Rore, Zarlino, Palestrina. And then there are the moderni; they still live, young or old; and he is one of them, for he belongs to that epoch in which our music flourished (a quel tempo che la Musica nostra fioriva). As at the beginning Tinctoris had seen the fons et origo to be a phenomenon independent of antiquity, so at the end did Zacconi declare the rinascimento to be free from ancient models of music. Thus, the idea of the Renaissance, without a change in its conceptions, terms, or images, embraces a whole period in the history of music ranging from about 1430 or 1440 to 1600. All men living within the limits of that period were conscious of the momentous restoration, of the rebirth.

Despite all modern disputes, the Renaissance retains its validity as a conception of history. Renaissance means the act of rebirth effected spontaneously; in the minds of the musicians it also means an epoch well-defined within the history as a whole. It does not mean the imitation of antiquity; nor does it mean the renaissance of antiquity. It means the renaissance of the standards of culture in music. After having its cultural function restored, music moves into all branches of a society that holds the art in esteem again; hence a large variety of stylistic manifestations, an abundance of compositions without which culture would be unthinkable. Zarlino recorded these ramifications of music in society as an indication of the return of musical culture; Tinctoris took the new wealth of musical activities at all the courts of Christian princes to be the evidence of Renaissance. Renaissance does not mean a single stylistic or technical feature; it is not a one-sided aspect of music. It means an historical conception by which the humanists established their epoch as a cultural entity.

Bibliography

Gustave Reese's *Music in the Renaissance* (New York, Norton, 1954; rev. ed. 1959) is unsurpassed as a comprehensive treatment of the music and musicians of the Renaissance. Because of its encyclopedic scope, however, it is more valuable as a reference work than as one to be read for an introduction to its subject. Shorter works which are essential as survey introductions to the Renaissance are Friedrich Blume, **Renaissance and Baroque Music* (New York, Norton, 1967), and Edward Lowinsky, "Music in the Culture of the Renaissance," *Journal of the History of Ideas*, 15 (1954). Other periodical selections of value are Manfred Bukofzer, "Changing Aspects of Medieval and Renaissance Music," *The Musical Quarterly*, 44 (1958), and Hugo Leichtentritt, "The Renaissance Attitude towards Music," *The Musical Quarterly*, 1 (1915). A brief but useful summary of the change from fourteenth- to fifteenth-century musical style is that of Brian Trowell, "The Transition to the Renaissance," which is chapter 1 of vol. 2 of **The Pelican History of Music*, 3 vols. (Baltimore, Md., Penguin, 1963). Renaissance music is also covered in vols. 3 and 4 of *The New Oxford History of Music*.

That there is a much greater amount of music available from the Renaissance than from earlier periods is partially due to the fact that music printing began during the Renaissance. A sampling of Renaissance music is contained in the *Historical Anthology of Music*, vol. 1. *Music in the Renaissance* contains in its footnotes and bibliography many references to and information about modern editions of Renaissance music. Also consult the bibliographies following the selections on the mass and the madrigal (see pages 135 and 161) in this anthology.

8

THE idea of a single composition consisting of several movements and conceived by a single composer as a complete musical unit is taken for granted by the musician today. His earliest musical experiences frequently include such compositions in the forms of opera, sonata, symphony, suite, and mass. Therefore, it is sometimes startling to consider that such compositions have not always existed and that it was necessary for them to be invented. The cyclic mass, that is a mass consisting of Kyrie, Gloria, Credo, Sanctus-Benedictus, and Agnus Dei, all written by one composer and unified by the use of common material, was the first musical manifestation of such an idea. Arising about the turn of the fifteenth century and propagated if not even originated by the English, the cyclic mass was quickly taken up by the continental composers. Through them, from Dufay to Palestrina, the mass was firmly established and remained the most important large musical form of the Renaissance. The earliest examples of the cyclic mass and the thought that there once was a time when these compositions represented a new and innovative musical idea are the subjects of the following selection.

Manfred F. Bukofzer (1910-1955) was a lecturer and teacher at the universities of Basel, Oxford, Cambridge, Western Reserve University, and finally at the University of California at Berkeley. Among his best-known works are *Music in the Baroque Era* (New York, Norton, 1947), his edition of the *Complete Works* of John Dunstable (*Musica Britannica*, vol. 8), and *Studies in Medieval and Renaissance Music* (New York, Norton, 1950). A complete bibliography of his writings compiled by David D. Boyden, "In Memoriam: Manfred F. Bukofzer," may be found in *The Musical Quarterly*, 42 (July, 1956).

The Origins of the Cyclic Mass

MANFRED F. BUKOFZER

Since the early days of musical research Mass cycles of the fifteenth century have attracted special attention of scholars and musicians alike for reasons that are still valid today. The cyclic Mass holds a central place in the music of the period because it embodies the most representative and extended form of Renaissance music. Not without justification have early historians like Ambros molded their conception of the period after this form. Very little would be left of the chapters on the fifteenth and sixteenth centuries in his *Geschichte der Musik* if the sections on the Mass were omitted. It is no exaggeration to assert that the cycle of the Ordinary of the Mass was the focal point on which all the artistic aspirations and technical achievements of the composer converged. It held as dominating and prominent a place in the hierarchy of musical values as the symphony did in the eighteenth and nineteenth centuries.

The idea of combining the five parts of the Ordinary of the Mass into one cycle is not as old as is generally believed. From the liturgical point of view there was no need to unify the unchangeable items of the Ordinary, because they are not sung in direct succession during the celebration of the Mass, except for the Kyrie and Gloria. Even if there were unity it would be made immaterial by the intervening prayers and chants. It is for this reason that in medieval music only individual movements were set to music just as they were used in the liturgy. The first suggestions of the cyclic Mass are to be found in the fourteenth century. The so-called Mass of Tournai, which has for a long time been regarded as the first cyclic Mass,[1] cannot strictly be regarded as a Mass cycle. Its constituent parts were composed separately and were only later arbitrarily combined. No musical relations exist between the single move-

---

[1] Coussemaker, *Messe du XIIIe siècle,* 1861. The editor placed the work by mistake in the thirteenth rather than the fourteenth century.

FROM Manfred F. Bukofzer, *Studies in Medieval and Renaissance Music* (New York, W. W. Norton & Company, pp. 217-226. Copyright 1950 by W. W. Norton & Company, Inc. Reprinted by permission of the publisher.

ments. They are, moreover, composed in different styles. The first cycle known to have been composed as a unit comes from the pen of the French composer-poet Guillaume de Machaut. There can be no question that in this work the Ordinary is in a certain sense a six-section cycle (the sixth part is the *Ite missa est*, which Machaut has included in the musical setting).[2] It has sometimes been claimed that Machaut's Mass is unified musically by recurrent motives, but this claim is open to question because the motives seem to be figures and formulae that are not characteristic enough and are not placed conspicuously enough to serve a really unifying function. Actually some of the movements are composed freely in conductus style without use of plainchant, while others are written like isorhythmic motets with the proper plainchants in the tenor. The unity displayed by this Mass is primarily that of the liturgy, not of musical material.

The distinction between musical and liturgical unity is a crucial point, the importance of which has not been sufficiently stressed in past discussions.[3] Without it the significance and spiritual background of the Mass cycle cannot possibly be understood. It takes a very bold and independent mind to conceive the idea that the invariable parts of the Mass should be composed not as separate liturgical items, but as a set of five musically coherent compositions. In the latter case the means of unification are provided by the composer, not the liturgy. This idea, which is the historical premise of the cyclic Ordinary, betrays the weakening of purely liturgical consideration and the strengthening of essentially aesthetic concepts. The "absolute" work of art begins to encroach on liturgical function. We discover here the typical Renaissance attitude — and it is indeed the Renaissance philosophy of art that furnishes the spiritual background to the cyclic Mass. The beginnings of the Mass cycle coincide with the beginnings of the musical Renaissance.

It is therefore hardly surprising that the decisive turn in the development of the cyclic Mass occurred only in the early fifteenth century. At this time the first attempts are made to unify the movements of the Ordinary by means of the same musical material. We must distinguish here between two methods. First, the composer may use a brief characteristic motive in one or more voices which recurs at the beginning of each movement in the same or only slightly varied form and thus serves as a motto for the entire cycle. These motto beginnings, however, affect only the first few measures and have no influence on the further course and structure of the composition. Secondly, the composer may employ a borrowed cantus firmus in the tenor which underlies all movements as a structural voice and thus serves as a much more powerful and consistent

[2]Editions by Machabey and de Van.

[3]Peter Wagner's *Geschichte der Messe* (1913), though out of date in many details, is still the best book on the subject.

unifying factor than the motto.[4] Both the motto and cantus may be used in conjunction.

The two methods of unification arose independently but developed, interestingly enough, in exactly parallel stages. The first stage, the incipient cycle, comprises only two paired movements, either the Gloria and Credo, or the Sanctus and Agnus. The coupling of just these movements was probably prompted by the text, since each group has a similar text structure in common; Gloria and Credo are built in alternating lines in the manner of a psalmody, Sanctus and Agnus have a tripartite structure. The latter is true also of the Kyrie, and it is significant that in certain early cycles the Kyrie is indeed more closely related to the Sanctus-Agnus group than to the other.

According to all evidence available at present, it may be stated that incipient cycles with motto beginning originated a little earlier than those with cantus firmus. The former will therefore be discussed first. The pairing of movements by means of a motto is clearly documented by a number of sources. The first intimations are found in the Turin MS (TuB) of c. 1410-20. It records five Gloria-Credo pairs[5] which obviously belong together stylistically, although only a few of them give indications of a motto, and even these are slight. The earliest source to carry out the pairing on a large scale is the Bologna MS (BL), written originally for Piacenza, a considerable part of which is organized exclusively in Gloria-Credo pairs.[6] Many of these stem from the same composer and have a very clear motto connection, for example those by Hugo de Lantins (fol. 84v-86) and Dufay (fol. 33v-38); others by the same composer do not have a clear motto, e.g. Antonius de Civitato (fol. 81-84); still others consist of compositions written by different composers and have been combined more or less arbitrarily by the scribe in analogy to the genuine pairs. In the last case, obviously, there cannot be a motto. It should be noted that BL contains only Gloria-Credo pairs. Pairing of Mass fragments (Gloria-Credo as well as Sanctus-Agnus) is vaguely suggested in certain compositions by Leonel in the Old Hall MS,[7] although the scribe did not yet actually group them together. In the Aosta and Trent MSS the pairing of Gloria-Credo and Sanctus-Agnus has become a recognized

[4]A third possibility, unrelated to the other two, is the polyphonic plainsong Mass, which paraphrases the chants of the Ordinary. Since the musical material differs in each movement, we cannot speak here of musical unification in the strict sense, for it is really an extension and intensification of the liturgical unity which was known in medieval music. However, the plainsong Mass of the Renaissance is modeled after the unified tenor Mass and achieves artistic coherence through musical style.

[5]The MS presents at another place (fol. 139v-141v) an almost complete cycle (only the Agnus is lacking). The four movements are based on various sections of the same (secular?) tune in the tenor. This unusual and interesting piece is a later addition to TuB and would bear further investigation.

[6]See de Van's list in *Musica Disciplina*, II, 231.

[7]See *Studies in Medieval and Renaissance Music*, pp. 44 and 60.

practice. The scribe of Tr has sometimes pointed out the connection between the pairs by written remarks. We may infer from the manuscripts that the Gloria-Credo pair was the first one to be joined together, and that it was soon complemented by the corresponding Sanctus-Agnus pair.

The next step of the motto Mass is the combination of two separate pairs in one composite cycle, a process that repeats on a higher level the pairing of two unrelated single compositions. BL contains several such cycles by Zacharia-Dufay, Ciconia-Arnold de Lantins, and others. The cycle by Ciconia-Lantins deserves special mention, as it consists of three pairs— (1) the introit *Salve sancta parens* and Kyrie by Lantins, (2) Gloria and Credo by Ciconia, and (3) Sanctus and Agnus by Lantins again. The settings by Lantins use the plainsongs of the *Missa de B.M.V. (Grad. Rom. IX)* in the tenor and thus represent a partial plainsong Mass (the introit, too, is similarly treated in the tenor). Ciconia's pair, however, is not unified by a motto and is freely composed. The disparate pairs have nevertheless been grouped together to a composite cycle. The same manuscript contains, on the other hand, a few complete cycles written as a unit by one and the same composer (Lymburgia, Arnold de Lantins,[8] and Dufay[9]) which are more or less unified by means of motto beginnings. Dufay's *Missa Sancti Jacobi* includes not only the complete Ordinary but also the pieces of the Proper based on the "proper" plainsongs. This is a special Office and takes an unusual position among the early cycles in BL. The Mass cycles by Lymburgia and Lantins are clearly held together by the same motto. It is significant that the Gloria-Credo pair on the one hand and the Sanctus-Agnus pair on the other begin almost identically and form two closely related pairs within the larger cycle. In both cases the Kyrie stands somewhat apart. Thus the original pairing is still reflected in the first known examples of the unified Mass cycle with motto beginning. Since this type of cycle is associated primarily with Lymburgia, Lantins, and Dufay, we may safely assume that it was developed by the composers of the Franco-Flemish school around 1425.

The first manifestations of the tenor Mass or cantus-firmus cycle appear only slightly later, in the second quarter of the century, and are associated primarily with composers of the English school, notably Leonel Power and Dunstable. As to the date, it is characteristic that TuB, OH, and BL, while they give evidence of the incipient, and even of the complete, cycle with motto, do not show a trace of the cantus-firmus cycle, except for the above-noted addition to TuB. Mass cycles on a cantus firmus are to be found only in such later sources as the Aosta and Trent MSS and a newly discovered fragment in the Bodleian Library.[10]

[8]Published in *Polyphonia Sacra* (ed. van den Borren), 1932, Nos. 1-5.

[9]*Missa Sine Nomine,* printed in *Opera omnia* (ed. de Van), Vol. 3.

[10]Add. MS C 87 with music by Benet, Bedingham, Plomer, and anonymous composers. I have dealt with this important fragment in "English Church Music of the XVth Century," in *The New Oxford History of Music.*

The idea of writing a Mass setting on a tenor not borrowed from plainsongs of the Ordinary was prompted by a medieval form, the isorhythmic motet. The fountainhead of the development is the transfer of the isorhythmic technique to the Mass, to which many single isorhythmic Mass sections in OH and LoF attest. So far as the cyclic idea is concerned, it is important to keep in mind that the setting of the complete Ordinary is unified by an independent tenor whose liturgical function does not relate to the Ordinary. It has been pointed out above that Machaut did not take this step; his isorhythmic tenors are still chants from the Ordinary and change from movement to movement, as they do also in a paired Gloria and Credo by Leonel (Ao 169-170). This pair is historically important, as it is intermediate between the traditional and the new practice which Leonel himself adopted toward the end of his career. In the Mass sections under consideration here the tenors may still be liturgical, but they have as a rule nothing to do with the Mass. Significantly, these tenors continue to be isorhythmic even though the upper voices gradually abandon that device. There are, in addition, settings with non-isorhythmic tenors drawn from sources foreign to the Ordinary. These settings, too, are mostly of English origin.[11]

The decisive step toward the cycle is again the pairing of two movements on the basis of the same tenor which establishes an unequivocal element of unity and, unlike the motto, conditions the entire musical structure. Dunstable's Gloria and Credo on *Jesu Christe fili*[12] illustrates the incipient Mass cycle with cantus firmus. The two movements are built on the same isorhythmic tenor, and neither has a motto, which the English composers seem to have cultivated less extensively than their Continental colleagues, since there was no need for it if a common tenor was used. Once the idea of joining two movements by means of a cantus firmus had been established, its extension to all movements of the Ordinary lay close at hand. The first known complete cycles[13] are transmitted in the old layer of the Trent codices and the Aosta MS and include the *Missa Alma redemptoris* by Leonel Power[14] and the *Missa Rex seculorum*, ascribed in Tr to Power and in Ao to Dunstable. The former work is based on an isorhythmically repeated tenor, the latter on a tenor

[11]See the Credo on *Alma redemptoris* by Anglicanus (DTOe, Vol. 61, 92) and an anonymous Gloria on *Virgo flagellatur* in Pemb. One of the rare Continental settings of the type is a Credo on *Alma redemptoris* by Johannes de Gemblaco (BL, Tr, Ao), which may have been prompted by English models. There seems to be no other Mass section on a foreign tenor in BL, and this one has been paired (incorrectly?) with a Gloria by the same composer in free treble style.

[12]DTOe, Vol. 61, 114 and 117. The editor has obscured the isorhythmic structure of the tenor by irregular barring.

[13]According to English custom the Kyrie was chanted; its omission from the polyphonic setting does not make the cycles incomplete.

[14]Published in *Documenta Polyphoniae Liturgicae* (ed. Feininger). Ser. 1, No. 2.

that presents the chant in free rhythm and varying melodic elaboration. We thus have evidence that the two types of tenor treatment, the rigid and the flexible, are as old as the form itself. The Bodleian fragment contains the remnants of Gloria, Credo, and Sanctus from a *Missa Requiem eternam,* built likewise on an isorhythmic tenor. It is not a Requiem Mass (which contains no Gloria) but a Mass cycle on the introit from the Mass for the Dead. Other cycles by English composers have come down to us in incomplete form. A case in point is Dunstable's Credo and Sanctus on *Da gaudiorum premia.*[15] Here again the tenor is isorhythmic. The two movements found in Ao probably belong to a complete cycle, now lost, because the pairing of Credo and Sanctus is rather anomalous. The earliest English Mass cycles are all based on liturgical tenors and do not particularly stress the motto beginning. Leonel Power's *Missa Alma redemptoris* has at best a slight suggestion of a motto; other works have none at all. Only later in the century does the motto become a regular feature of the English Mass cycles, doubtless in imitation of Franco-Flemish practice. That the paired arrangement of movements persisted even in the complete Mass cycle (where it was no longer necessary) can be seen in the *Rex seculorum* Mass.

What proof do we have that the above-mentioned works are actually early examples of the type? No theorist of the time tells us anything about the development of the cyclic Mass, and none of the compositions is precisely dated. All we have by way of historical data are the scant biographical facts about Power and Dunstable. If it is correct that Leonel Power died in 1445—the date has not yet been verified—he can have composed his Mass cycles only in the second quarter of the century, probably in the last decade of his life. Aside from that, we are reduced to inference—but rather conclusive inference from the repertory of the sources themselves. It is revealing that a major part of Ao groups the movements of the Mass still in the medieval manner according to classes (all Kyries together, etc.), whereas they are grouped in another part, at times incorrectly, in pairs. Leonel's *Missa Alma redemptoris* is the only complete cantus-firmus cycle of the entire manuscript, and the same cycle appears also in the oldest part of Tr (Codex 87). The partial or complete cycles with borrowed tenor are attributed in the earliest sources (Ao, Tr 87 and 92) almost exclusively to English composers, and there remains no doubt as to their essential contribution to the creation of the form.[16] The cyclic tenor Mass is the most influential achievement of the English school of Renaissance music.

Once established, the form was soon generally adopted in European music. It cannot be doubted that Dufay's leadership was decisive also in

[15]The Sanctus has been transcribed in *Musica Disciplina* II, 70.

[16]This bears out an old thesis of von Ficker *(Studien zur Musikwissenshaft,* VII [1920], 30), even though his claims rested on shaky foundations and the particulars of his position were untenable.

this respect. Since his late Masses always employ a cantus firmus, he must have recognized at this stage of his development that the tenor cantus firmus was the safest means of cyclic unity. His cycles draw on sacred melodies (*Caput, Ecce ancilia, Ave regina*), but also on secular ones (*L'homme armé, Se la face*[17]). Not only does Dufay extend the source of the cantus firmus to the secular field (he is perhaps the first composer to do so), but he invariably opens with a motto beginning before he permits the tenor to come in. Thus he combines the two means of unification and merges the two streams leading to the cyclic Mass in one great tradition which was to dominate the second half of the century and which was to form our idea of a typical cyclic Mass.

Cycles with motto but without cantus firmus do not disappear completely—they survive in certain works of Okeghem, e.g. *Missa Quinti toni*—but they hold a subordinate place.

These are, in rough outline, the origins of the Mass cycle, a musical form that took tremendous strides within a very short time. Two points relating to the form have not yet been touched upon: how the cyclic idea manifested itself in the Gregorian Ordinary, and what criteria determined the choice of cantus firmus. The first point has been briefly discussed by Peter Wagner[18] but would deserve a more thorough study. It is well known that the medieval collections of plainchant group the melodies of the Ordinary by classes, and this arrangement persisted well into the sixteenth century. The same classification prevails in many medieval sources of polyphonic music, as may be seen in OH and as late as Ao. The arrangement of plainsongs in single Ordinaries for certain feasts or liturgical occasions, found in the current reference books, is only a recent development; indeed, even the term *Ordinarium Missae* is foreign to medieval practice. The unified classification was prompted, in the opinion of Peter Wagner, by the polyphonic Mass cycle. In the second half of the century polyphonic manuscripts generally adopt the grouping by Mass cycles, as found for example in Modena, Est. lat. 456, and this order may be called the typical arrangement of a Renaissance manuscript. However, Wagner's idea that polyphonic sacred music may have set the model for plainsong collections is rather startling in view of the fact that the reverse is generally true in medieval music. While most Gregorian collections of the fifteenth century do continue to lump the chants of one class together, certain sources group them in closed Ordinaries, composed probably for special occasions. It is significant that TuB, which gives the first indications of the incipient cycle in polyphonic music, contains also no less than five Gregorian Mass cycles, two *Missae breves* and three complete Ordinaries.[19] This isolated example suggests that the idea of cyclic order was in the air at the beginning of the fifteenth century. The plainsong

[17]DTOe, Vol. 14/15, 120 ff.
[18]*Gregorianische Formenlehre (Einführung,* III), 1921, 438.
[19]See the list of contents published by Besseler in AMW VII (1925), 212.

Ordinaries do not antedate Machaut's Mass, but they do appear sooner than the musically unified Mass cycle of the Renaissance.

Let us consider, finally, the principles underlying the selection of the cantus firmus. While the recurring music of the motto beginning was as a rule freely composed, the opposite is true of the cantus firmus, which was borrowed from plainchant or a *res facta*, either sacred or secular. In certain cases the cantus firmus could also be contrived by the composer (*soggetto cavato dalle vocali*, solmization syllables, etc.). It has frequently been commented upon that Renaissance composers were apparently indiscriminate in choosing their structural voice. Many pious souls have found it shocking that love songs appear as cantus firmi of Mass cycles. This certainly is indicative of the weakening of liturgical observance, but at the same time it bespeaks the interpenetration of the secular and sacred spheres which prevailed in the Middle Ages even more strongly than in the Renaissance. Secular tenors in sacred compositions are in fact a heritage of the medieval motet. Furthermore, it should be considered that the selection of a sacred cantus firmus, for example the Marian antiphon *Ave regina*, is perhaps even more startling from the liturgical point of view. Such an antiphon was sung in the Office, not in the Mass, and, moreover, serving as cantus firmus, it was relegated to a mere scaffolding voice without liturgical function. The mixture of Ordinary and Office and the non-liturgical use of a liturgical melody betrays, perhaps, a more serious lack of liturgical propriety than the choice of a secular cantus firmus, which, at any rate, could not create liturgical confusion. The Renaissance musicians recognized the cyclic Mass as the most dignified form of composition and thus indirectly also recognized its liturgical dignity, but in their essentially artistic approach to the problem, which put musical unity above all, they were no longer guided by the strictly liturgical attitude of medieval musicians. It may seem paradoxical that the Mass cycle, the most extended composition before the advent of the opera and the symphony, and regarded today as liturgical music *par excellence*, was actually the result of the weakening of liturgical ties at the oncoming of the Renaissance.

Bibliography

A study in English of the polyphonic mass of the fifteenth and sixteenth centuries has yet to be written. Though out of date in some respects, the work of Peter Wagner, *Geschichte der Messe* (Leipzig, Breitkopf & Härtel, 1913), is still the best book on the subject. Much valuable information may be found in Gustave Reese, *Music in the Renaissance* (New York, Norton, 1954; rev. ed. 1959) as well as in vols. 3 and 4 of *The New Oxford History of Music*. Of interest also are the remarks by

Heinrich Besseler in the preface to Guillaume Dufay, *Opera Omnia,* vol. 3 (Rome, American Institute of Musicology, 1951), which discuss the influence of the English composers of cyclic masses on Dufay. Edgar H. Sparks, *Cantus Firmus in Mass and Motet* (Berkeley, Calif., University of California Press, 1963), is especially useful for the music of Dufay, Ockeghem, Obrecht, and Josquin. Of more specialized interest is Phillip Gossett, "Techniques of Unification in Early Cyclic Masses and Mass Pairs," *Journal of the American Musicological Society,* 19 (Summer, 1966). Paul Henry Lang, "The So-called Netherlands School," *The Musical Quarterly,* 25 (1939), contains information about national stylistic influences on the composers of masses in the Renaissance.

For musical editions of complete cyclic masses consult the complete works of Dufay (Rome, American Institute of Musicology, 1947-); Ockeghem (Leipzig, 1927; New York, American Institute of Musicology, 1947-); Josquin (Amsterdam, Alsbach, 1925-); and Palestrina (Leipzig, Breitkopf & Härtel, 1862-1907), to mention only a few of the most important composers. An anthology of ten masses all based on the tune *L'homme armé* is published in *Monumenta Polyphoniae Liturgicae,* series 1, vol. 1 (Rome, 1947), edited by Laurence Feininger. The music of the Old Hall Manuscript, containing mass movements from the early fifteenth century by English composers, has been transcribed and edited by A. Ramsbotham in *The Old Hall Manuscript,* 3 vols. (Nashdom Abbey, The Plainsong and Medieval Music Society, 1933-1938). The complete works of John Dunstable have been edited by Manfred Bukofzer and published in *Musica Britannica,* vol. 8 (London, Stainer & Bell, 1953).

9

THE music of the sixteenth century has sufficient traits in common with that of the fifteenth century that both may be considered as music of the Renaissance. However, there are between the two centuries differences obvious and distinct enough so that historians frequently divide the period into Early Renaissance and Late or High Renaissance, corresponding roughly to the fifteenth and sixteenth centuries respectively. But even the music of the sixteenth century does not stand as an unbroken unit; within it there may be seen at least two apparently opposite trends. One, a conservative trend, is exemplified, but not uniquely, by the music of the Roman school, culminating with Palestrina. It manifests itself largely in Latin liturgical music, although it may also be seen in the madrigals of this group. The second trend, much less conservative, appears to influence Latin liturgical music slightly, such as that of the Venetian school, but is most obvious in secular music, especially the Italian madrigal. It is to this second, less conservative trend that the authors of the following selection have applied the name "Mannerism."

Mannerism is a term which has been in use for some time by art historians. Reference works devoted to the visual arts usually contain lengthy entries on the subject and an extensive bibliography may be assembled easily. Music historians, on the other hand, seem to have avoided the term almost entirely. None of the standard English-language reference works devoted to music contains an entry for Mannerism. Reese lists only two brief references to Mannerism in the index to *Music in the Renaissance*, and a number of music histories, such as Lang's *Music in Western Civilization*, Grout's *A History of Western Music*, and *The New Oxford History of Music*, contain no index references to Mannerism. It is only with the greatest searching that references to Mannerism in music may be found. Thus some may question the use of this term to apply to that style of sixteenth-century music that leads on to the seventeenth, but it is not the purpose here to enter into a debate on the definition of the term Mannerism as applied to music or to defend its use. Rather, my point is to emphasize that there was in the sixteenth century a style that was developing and moving in a direction different from that of the sacred polyphonic style; that this style is most obvious in the music of the Italian madrigal; and, finally, that it leads rather directly to the Baroque style of the seventeenth century.

The music of Mannerism, and I shall use that term here for the sake of convenience, has two principal characteristics, both of which arise from Grecian philosophy as certain sixteenth-century composers interpreted it and related it to their music. First, there is an ever-greater attempt to imitate and portray the sense of the text in its accompanying music, resulting in extreme cases in the fragmentation of the text to the point that any sense of a literary phrase is almost completely lost. Second, there is an increasing use of chromaticism to the point that all final remnants of the medieval system of modes are destroyed. As has happened so frequently with new trends in musical style, these tendencies began slowly and developed gradually. Their beginnings may be seen in some of the motets and secular music of Josquin (though not sufficiently to mark him as a mannerist composer), yet it was not until a century later that these two characteristics came to rule certain compositions completely, as in the madrigals of Gesualdo. Nevertheless, Mannerism's influence was enormous, and if one carefully traces its course through the Italian madrigals of the sixteenth century, the monodies and early operas of the turn of the seventeenth century can be seen only as a highly logical continuation of the style.

Beekman Cox Cannon and William Gilman Waite are members of the faculty of Yale University; Alvin H. Johnson is on the faculty at the University of Pennsylvania. Cannon is the author of *Johann Mattheson, Spectator in Music* (New Haven, Conn., Yale University Press, 1947), and Waite has written *The Rhythm of Twelfth Century Polyphony* (New Haven, Conn., Yale University Press, 1954).

Mannerism: 1520-1600

BEEKMAN CANNON, ALVIN JOHNSON,
AND WILLIAM WAITE

"I acknowledge two masters, Christ and literature." With these bold words the humanist Ermolao Barbaro (1480) epitomized the transcendent status of literary studies in the Renaissance. From the beginning the humanistic preoccupation with linguistics had been intimately associated with the problems of human society. Language, as the means whereby men communicate with and influence one another, was seen to be a key to the problems of human knowledge and conduct. Through language, through grammar and rhetoric, which are the product of the human spirit and belong to man alone, the humanists sought to justify and explain the moral and spiritual behavior of mankind.

Thus the kingdom of letters began to encroach upon areas of knowledge which had once been the exclusive property of philosophy. Forced to yield before the onslaught of a horde of literary humanists, traditional Aristotelian philosophy withdrew to the outer fringes of the scholarly world where it contented itself with tedious disputations and the splitting of dialectical hairs. The grammarian and rhetorician now installed themselves upon the thrones of the philosophers. In the pride of newly won authority, the Florentine humanist Angelo Poliziano, author of books in medicine, ethics and philosophy, could state: "I do not claim the title of philosopher, but demand no other name for myself than that of grammarian."

The world that the humanist claimed for himself is not the realm of the absolute, as it was for the mediaeval philosopher, but the domain of human activity. Where the aim of the Aristotelians had been to attain knowledge of eternal verities through the use of dialectics, the humanists sought to establish the relative truths of human affairs from models of

FROM Beekman C. Cannon, Alvin H. Johnson, and William G. Waite, *The Art of Music* (New York, Thomas Y. Crowell Company, Inc.), pp. 174-182. Copyright © 1960 by Thomas Y. Crowell Company, Inc. Reprinted by permission of the publisher.

behavior provided by literature. The arts of language are to be used to effect specific results: the poet and orator with all the means at their disposal are to persuade and move men to proper actions, leading them to virtue and away from evil. The rhetoric of the poet and orator, not the frigid argumentation of the logician, is the moving force in society, stirring the hearts of men and persuading them to right conduct. "Hail to thee, Oh Poetry! fertile mother of every doctrine!" wrote Giovanni Pontano. "You have come with the immortality of your authors to succor humanity condemned to die. You have drawn men out from caves and forests. Through you we have knowledge, through you we have before our eyes the things of the past; through you we understand God, through you we have religion and its ritual."

Poetry and philosophy, rhetoric and humanity: these are all for the humanist one and the same thing. The danger inherent in such a view is that the value of literature may be exaggerated and that literary studies may become an end in themselves. Problems of literary style may come to outweigh all other considerations. Just such an overemphasis began to manifest itself in the latter part of the fifteenth century and in the early years of the sixteenth. Arguments arose about which language was the most perfect, Latin, Greek, or the vernacular. Should Ciceronian Latin be taken as an idealized model to be imitated slavishly or should it only serve as a point of departure for a contemporary, living language?

In the case of the Italian vernacular the problem of literary style was settled for the sixteenth century by canonizing the poetic idiom of Petrarch. Not only the poetic forms and the turns of speech of Petrarch, even his subject matter was adopted by the poets of this new era. They sing of sighing lovers in language encrusted with metaphor and glittering with paradox. An enamored youth, losing his soul in the raptures of love, exclaims:

> The white and winsome swan
> While singing dies, and I,
> Complaining, near the end of my existence.
> Strange and different fates,
> That he should die disconsolate
> And I should die in bliss.
> Death that e'en in dying
> Filleth me with joy replete and with desiring.
> If no other pain I feel in dying,
> A thousand times a day I gladly would expire.

These are not the accents of true emotion, but the polished conceits of the litterateur. In this poem of Alfonso d'Avalos, which when set to music by Jacques Arcadelt became the most famous madrigal of the sixteenth century, it is style and manner which is of paramount importance. Love's passion is transmuted into rhetoric.

Into this world where a problem of correct literary usage could touch off a war of polemics there was introduced at the very end of the fifteenth century a book destined to dominate artistic theory for nearly three centuries. In 1498 Giorgio Valla published a Latin translation of the *Poetics* of Aristotle, a work which had been unknown to the Middle Ages. In a society intensely preoccupied with art and its relationship to life, the *Poetics* was received as though it were divine revelation; for this treatise, though incomplete, presents a consistent theory of art which may be integrated with the whole philosophical system of Aristotle.

One should not assume from the title of this work that Aristotle is here concerned only with poetry. Though his discussion is centered around dramatic and epic poetry, his use of the term "poetics" has a much broader connotation. For Aristotle all knowledge is divided into three branches: theoretical, practical, and poetic. The first deals with speculative thought, the investigation and contemplation of the eternal laws of the universe, while the second is devoted to the realization of these laws by man in his activities as a member of society. Poetics on the other hand is that branch of knowledge concerned with man the creator, and its name means literally the art of "making." The wheelwright, the architect, and the dramatist are all in a sense "makers," since all are engaged in applying certain types of knowledge in order to create some material object.

Some of these arts are utilitarian, while others serve no such practical end. The latter are what we call the fine arts, and it is for the men who work in these fields, the dramatist, the musician, the choreographer, that the title of poet, "maker," is reserved. Though these arts may differ in substance, they are related by common principles. For this reason the doctrine expounded by Aristotle primarily in terms of poetry is applicable to the other arts as well.

The central tenet of the *Poetics* is that art imitates nature. Aristotle maintains that imitation is a basic element of human nature and that imitative art is therefore one of the most natural forms of expression in man. "The instinct of imitation is implanted in man from childhood, one difference between him and other animals being that he is the most imitative of living creatures, and through imitation learns his earliest lessons; and no less universal is the pleasure felt in things imitated. . . . Objects which in themselves we view with pain, we delight to contemplate when reproduced with minute fidelity: such as the forms of the most ignoble animals and of dead bodies. The cause of this again is, that to learn gives the liveliest pleasure. . . . Thus the reason why men enjoy seeing a likeness is, that in contemplating it they find themselves learning or inferring, and saying perhaps, 'Ah, that is he.' For if you happen not to have seen the original, the pleasure will be due not to the imitation as such, but to the execution, the colouring, or some such other cause."[1]

[1] This and the following quotations are from S. H. Butcher's translation of the *Poetics*.

When Aristotle says that art imitates nature, he does not mean that art copies natural objects such as scenery. Nature for Aristotle is in this case specifically the world of man. "The objects of imitation," he states, "are men in action," the moral character of the soul revealing itself in terms of specific events. "Tragedy is the imitation of an action; and an action implies personal agents, who necessarily possess certain distinctive qualities both of character and thought; for it is by these that we qualify actions themselves, and these—thought and character—are the two natural causes from which actions spring, and on actions again all success or failure depends." What art imitates are states of the soul, either permanent characteristics such as courage and magnanimity or transient emotions such as pity and anger. In thus depicting emotional states through events the poet arouses in his audience reciprocal emotions which are pleasing and at the same time instructive and edifying.

The world of nature of which Aristotle speaks is not static, but full of motion and action. It is a world in which everything is the product of form realizing itself in matter. Since this is a dynamic process constantly renewing itself, those arts which are able to represent the flux and motion of things coming into being are more to be esteemed than those which can only represent a single, fixed moment of an action. Painting and sculpture can portray the outward appearance of an emotional state, but it is an emotion forever frozen in time. Poetry, music, and the dance, however, are by their very nature arts in which motion is an essential element. Thus they are able to imitate an action from its inception to its completion.

In the arts of motion

> the imitation is produced by rhythm, language, or 'harmony' [melody], either singly or combined. Thus in the music of the flute and of the lyre 'harmony' and rhythm alone are employed; also in other arts, such as that of the shepherd's pipe, which are essentially similar to these. In dancing, rhythm alone is used without 'harmony' for even dancing imitates character, emotion and action, by rhythmical movement. There is another art which imitates by means of language alone, and that either in prose or verse—which verse, again, may either combine different metres or consist of but one kind. . . . There are, again, some arts which employ all the means above mentioned,—namely, rhythm, tune, and metre. Such are Dithyrambic and Nomic poetry, and also Tragedy and Comedy; but between them the difference is, that in the first two cases these means are all employed in combination, in the latter, now one means is employed, now another.

If art imitates nature, the task of the artist is to abstract the form from an action of man and to impose this form upon the particular material of his art. The poet orders his words to conform to the event that he has chosen to imitate, and the musician orders his melody and rhythm for the same purpose. In such a theory the value of the artwork lies not in the subject matter being imitated but rather in the appropriateness of the manner of imitation. It is therefore on questions of style that the artwork is to be judged. Through style the artist will make the meaning of his subject matter apparent to his audience; through style he may ennoble or demean the actions of his narrative; through style he will depict and arouse the appropriate emotions and sentiments.

To imitate successfully the artist must utilize all the resources of his art, choosing whatever is appropriate to the subject at hand. In the *Art of Rhetoric* (III,vii) Aristotle states that

> propriety of style will be obtained by the expression of emotion and character, and by proportion to the subject matter. Style is proportionate to the subject matter when neither weighty matters are treated offhand, nor trifling matters with dignity, and no embellishment is attached to an ordinary word; otherwise there is an appearance of comedy. . . . Style expresses emotion, when a man speaks with anger of wanton outrage; with indignation and reserve, even in mentioning them, of things foul or impious; with admiration of things praiseworthy; with lowliness of things pitiable; and so in all other cases. Appropriate style also makes the fact appear credible; for the mind of the hearer is imposed upon under the impression that the speaker is speaking the truth, because, in such circumstances, his feelings are the same, so that he thinks (even if it is not the case as the speaker puts it) that things are as he represents them. . . . [2]

The influence of Aristotle's theories began to make itself felt in all fields of artistic endeavor in the third decade of the sixteenth century. This intrusion of Aristotelian dogma precipitated an artistic crisis. The problem confronting the artist of the sixteenth century was to reconcile the precepts of Aristotle with the idealized art that had emerged from Florentine Platonism: to imitate man in action while preserving the formal unity and symmetry of the Platonic Idea. In the paintings of this new generation, the figures turn and twist as if caught in the middle of some action that will be completed as soon as we take our eyes from them. The tension and sense of motion in their gestures are at variance with the formal scheme in which they have been disposed. Where the figures of a Raphael seem forever at peace within their pyramidal and spherical arrangements, the formal structures of the mannerist painters seem as impermanent as the gesticulations of the figures of which they are composed. The eye is attracted everywhere by flickering motions of hands and limbs and arrested by countenances frozen in the distorted grimaces of emotion. These paintings, in comparison with those of the preceding generations, are richly ornamental, crowded with figures and adorned with the rhetoric of gesture.

A similar transformation is to be discerned in the music of the six-

[2]tr. J. H. Freese. *The Loeb Classical Library.*

teenth century. Perhaps the best formulation of the new attitude is to be found in the *Istituzioni armoniche* published in 1558 by the theorist Gioseffe Zarlino. In agreement with classical authority, he maintains that the function of the poet and musician are one and the same. "The proper aim of the musician, like that of the poet, is to please and delight with singing or instrumental music according to the rules of musical art." The pleasure that we derive from music must not, however, be superficial or unworthy. It must be used to inculcate good habits and virtuous character. "The proper office of music is to delight; and we must use it not dishonestly, but honestly."

Since music is an imitative art, the musician, like the poet, must first choose a subject to be imitated. "Just as the builder, in all his operations, looks always toward the end and founds his work upon some matter which he calls the subject, so the musician in his operations, looking toward the end which prompts him to work, discovers the matter or subject upon which he founds his composition. Thus he perfects his work in conformity with his chosen end. Or again, just as the poet, prompted by such an end to improve or to delight . . . . takes as the subject of his poem some history or fable, discovered by himself or borrowed from others, which he adorns and polishes with various manners, as he may prefer, leaving out nothing that might be fit or worthy to delight the minds of his hearers, in such a way that he takes on something of the magnificent and marvelous; so the musician, apart from being prompted by the same end to improve or to delight the minds of his listeners with harmonious accents, takes the subject and founds upon it his composition, which he adorns with various modulations and various harmonies in such a way that he offers welcome pleasure to his hearers."[3]

While Zarlino accepts without reservation the Aristotelian thesis that art is a process of imitation and adornment of a chosen subject, he carries this theory beyond the limits imposed by Aristotle. Where the philosopher had limited the subject matter to men in action, the musician broadens it to include purely musical material. Rationalizing existing musical techniques, Zarlino transforms all of them into modes of imitation. According to Zarlino, counterpoint, in which one part is derived from another because of its harmonic relationships to it, and successive imitation, in which all the voices state the given subject, are forms of imitation.

> Beginning with the first, then I say that, in every musical composition, what we call the subject is that part from which the composer derives the invention to make the other parts of the work, however many they may be. Such a subject may take many forms, as the composer may prefer and in accordance with the loftiness of his imagination: it may be his own invention, that is, it may be that he has discovered it of him-

[3]Oliver Strunk, *Source Readings in Music History*, p. 219.

self; again, it may be that he has borrowed it from the works of others, adapting it to his work and adorning it with various parts and various modulations. And such a subject may be several kinds; it may be a tenor or some other part of any composition you please, whether of plainsong or of figured music; again, it may be two or more parts of which one follows another in consequence or in some other way, for the various forms of such subjects are innumerable.

When the composer has discovered his subject, he will write the other parts in the way which we shall see later on. When this is done, our practical musicians call the manner of composing "making counterpoint."

But when the composer has not first discovered his subject, that part which he first puts into execution or with which he begins his work, whatever it may be or however it may begin, whether high, low, or intermediate, will always be the subject to which he will then adapt the other parts in consequence or in some other way, as he prefers, adapting the harmony to the word as the matter they contain demands. And when the composer goes on to derive the subject from the parts of the work, that is, when he derives one part from another and goes on to write the work all at once, as we shall see elsewhere, that small part which he derives without the others and upon which he then composes the parts of his composition will always be called the subject.

By reinterpreting the musical practices of the past in the light of Aristotle, Zarlino sanctified and safeguarded them for his own time. Nevertheless the position of these old techniques was not secure, for the doctrine of imitation imposed still other demands upon music, demands which were soon to undermine and then destroy the centuries old polyphonic tradition. If music was to be a truly imitative art, it must imitate men in action; it must, in other words, endeavor to imitate the text which embodies the emotions and actions of men. Musical equivalents must be found for the meanings of the words; melodic progressions, rhythmic motions, and harmonies must all conform to the text.

In this treatise Zarlino described the numerous means which practicing composers had devised to express the content of their text. In melodies grief, sadness and other "feminine" emotions were to be depicted through small melodic intervals, while larger intervals would be chosen to represent harshness, anger, and other "masculine" emotions. The melodic line would also be colored by the use of accidentals for grief and languishing. Slow and fast notes would be chosen to represent sorrowful and happy emotions. At the same time the rhythmic progression must be made to conform to the metrical rhythm of the text, matching long notes with accented syllables and shorter notes with unaccented ones. The harmonies too must be obedient to the text: minor intervals were to be applied to words of grief, while major intervals were equated with the more aggressive emotions. For bitter, harsh words it was fitting to introduce dissonances and harmonic clashes.

A vocabulary of imitative musical devices was created in this manner, a vocabulary rooted in metaphor and onomatopoeia. For such words as hill, climb, and heaven the melody must ascend; similarly it must descend for such words as valley and hell. Laughter was transformed into a passage of rapid, purling notes, and sighs became rests interpolated within the melodic phrase. Composers even resorted to what has been called "eye-music," sharping a note when the text refers to a pointed arrow or introducing two blackened notes into a passage written in white notes because the text is describing a pair of black eyes. There is scarcely an aspect of the text which did not determine in some way the musical setting chosen for it. Even punctuation was brought to bear upon the musical structure and cadences were formed when the sense of the words was closed by a comma or period.

In this theory it is assumed that music moves the emotions through the imitation of the text. The desire to create an emotional response was whetted by the testimony of classical literature that ancient Greek music could modify the souls of men, heal the sick, tame wild beasts, and even move the rocks and trees. If music's power was such in ancient times, why was its efficacy no longer the same? One theory was that music had lost its ability to achieve such results because it had neglected the words. Had not Plato said in the *Republic* that music and rhythm must follow speech? Therefore if music is made subservient to the text, its power to stir the emotions will be restored.

Another theory held that modern music used only diatonic scales, whereas Greek music had also employed the chromatic and enharmonic genera. If modern music was to achieve its ends, then it must revive these other scales. The most ardent advocate of this theory was Nicolo Vicentino (1511-1572). He composed madrigals employing chromatic and enharmonic intervals, constructed instruments capable of performing these finely gradated tones, and wrote theoretical works explaining and defending his practices. Vicentino, it goes without saying, failed in his attempt to rehabilitate these long-forgotten scales, but his theories had some effect upon later composers. Many musicians used chromaticism in their works, and in so doing they introduced an element contributing to the downfall of the old modal system.

The musical theories introduced in the sixteenth century are a notable departure from those of the past. Music, in accepting its literary yoke, had abdicated its lofty position within the quadrivium. It is now the servant of poetry, and the laws which govern it are no longer drawn from its own nature but are derived from another tradition. Though the composer of the sixteenth century still clings to imitative polyphony as his medium of expression, slow and rapid passages, polyphony and homophony are now juxtaposed in a logic derived not from music but from the text. Each significant word evokes a musical image which passes hastily from voice to voice, creating a nervous, brilliant mosaic of short, graphic motifs. The composer does not strive to attain a uniform musical texture or to create a single emotional atmosphere. He chooses instead to reveal his subject and to create his effects through musical rhetoric. Piling musical figure upon figure, he sways his audience as an orator would, by technical brilliance and luxuriant imagery. This is indeed a "mannered" music.

The role that Josquin played in preparing the ground for this reorientation of musical art has already been observed in his motets. But it was not within the motet that succeeding generations of composers worked out the new style. In that category of composition Josquin's successors preferred to maintain the more conservative, traditional approach to musical composition. Similarly, the French chanson was already too steeped in its own tradition to allow the full development of new musical ideals. It is an axiom of art that new ideas are usually worked out in forms least encumbered by convention. So it came about that the vehicle chosen for the expression of the new aesthetic aims of the sixteenth century was not one of the forms assiduously cultivated by the northerners but the Italian madrigal.

Bibliography

The bibliography on Mannerism in music is meager but growing. A good introduction to the general subject of Mannerism in the visual arts is Luisa Becherucci, "Mannerism," in *Encyclopedia of World Art,* vol. 9, 443-478 (New York, McGraw-Hill, 1964). Somewhat more specialized is Nikolaus Pevsner, "The Architecture of Mannerism," *The Mint,* 1 (1946), which is reprinted in vol. 2 of Harold Spencer, ed., *Readings in Art History,* 2 vols. (New York, Scribners, 1969). An excellent article on Mannerism in music is that of Robert Erich Wolf, "The Aesthetic Problem of the 'Renaissance,'" *Revue Belge de Musicologie,* 9 (1955). Other articles are those of Don Harran, "'Mannerism' in the Cinquecento Madrigal?" *The Musical Quarterly,* 55 (1969), and Maria Rika Maniates, "Musical Mannerism: Effeteness or Virility?" *The Musical Quarterly,* 57 (1971). Professor Maniates is reported to have a work in preparation, *Mannerism in Italian Musical Culture, 1530-1630.* Daniel B. Rowland's *Mannerism — Style and Mood* (New Haven, Conn., Yale University Press, 1964), though narrow in its definition of Mannerism, attempts to relate Mannerism in literature, music, and painting, and contains an interesting chapter devoted to Gesualdo.

The music of Mannerism is best exemplified in the Italian madrigal, for which a bibliography is given at the conclusion of the following selection (see page 162).

10

THE great quantity of sacred polyphonic music of the sixteenth century, as well as its high artistic level, has sometimes been a stumbling block to scholars. The coincidence that Palestrina died at the very end of the century, just when the opera with its new monodic style was becoming established, has even further confused the situation. This has led some to hold the view that the development of the sacred polyphonic style represents the mainstream, and possibly even the only important stream, of sixteenth-century music. Palestrina is assumed to have carried this style to its highest possible development, while the new monodic style, apparently arising so soon after his death, is taken to represent a sudden and complete break with sixteenth-century music, a search for a new means of musical expression caused by the realization that the technique and style of Palestrinian counterpoint could be developed no further. To the contrary, the contrapuntal style of the mass and motet was not the only style developing during the sixteenth century, nor was it the style that was to prepare the way for the operatic and instrumental styles of the seventeenth century. It is in the secular music, especially in the madrigal, that the germs of the music of the future are to be found, as is pointed out in the following selection. The madrigal, arising early in the sixteenth century from such ancestors as the frottola, the chanson, and the Florentine carnival songs, flourished throughout the century as the medium of expression containing the most advanced musical ideas. Then, after almost a century of development, the madrigal gave way at the turn of the seventeenth century to its issue, the opera.

Edward Joseph Dent (1876-1957) was Professor of Music at Cambridge University. In addition he served as president of the International Society for Contemporary Music and of the International Society of Musicology. Among his writings are *Mozart's Operas* (London, Oxford University Press, 1947, 2d ed.), *Foundations of English Opera* (London, Cambridge University Press, 1928), *Handel* (London, Duckworth, 1947), as well as contributions to *Encyclopaedia Britannica, Grove's Dictionary of Music and Musicians, The Oxford History of Music, The Musical Quarterly,*

Acta Musicologica, and *Music and Letters.* A bibliography of his writings prepared by L. Haward, "E. J. Dent: Bibliography," may be found in *The Music Review,* 7 (Nov., 1946).

The Musical Form of the Madrigal

EDWARD J. DENT

It is only within recent years that we have been able to form an adequate conception of the musical history of the sixteenth century; indeed, we are still only in the stage of beginning to understand it. Much research still remains to be done, especially in the department of instrumental music, and even when that has been made more accessible to us, there still remains the important problem of summing up the whole century and surveying its music as a whole. The historians of the age of Ambros were interested chiefly in church music and regarded Palestrina as the one great outstanding figure of the period. The general idea was that Palestrina represented the climax of Gothic art in music, and that the Renaissance, as far as music was concerned, did not begin until the days of Peri, Caccini and Monteverdi. If we reflect for a moment that Palestrina composed his Masses for performance in a chapel decorated with frescoes by Michelangelo, which must have been perpetually before his eyes, it is inconceivable that his music should have represented a Gothic conception of the art. The Renaissance, in fact, was already past history in the days of Palestrina, and his music belongs to the days of the Catholic reaction and to the spirit which caused Michelangelo's nude figures to be painted over with decent drapery. Musical historians have for some reason been quietly content to suppose that music is an art which is always behind the times and that it does not attempt to express the characteristic emotions of any period until the other arts, such as architecture, painting and poetry, have long finished with them.

This attitude towards music is obviously absurd and is equally obviously based on ignorance of facts. As far as the sixteenth century was concerned the ignorance was for a long time justifiable enough; the bulk of the music of the period was inaccessible. Thanks to Sandberger, Einstein, Fellowes and others too numerous to mention, the secular music

FROM *Music and Letters*, 11 (1930), 230-240. Reprinted by permission of the Trustees for the Estate of Edward J. Dent.

of the sixteenth century has been to a large extent reprinted, and better still, a great deal of it is at the present day being constantly performed, so that we are now much better able to form a judgment on it and see the truth with our own eyes. We can see now that it is the madrigal and not the Mass or motet which can really explain that century to us. Jeppesen has shown clearly that Palestrina, despite his wonderful accomplishment of technique, is for musical history simply a *cul-de-sac*.

The word "madrigal" has generally been used, as I confess to having used it in the previous paragraph, to cover all types of secular music for more than one voice, but such usage is improper, and we ought clearly to distinguish the different forms employed in vocal music in various countries. We ought not only to distinguish the obviously different forms, such as madrigal, ballet, frottola, etc., but we ought to study all this music from the point of view of musical form in the more scientific sense. It is curious that theorists have hitherto paid little attention to musical form before 1600, and even during the seventeenth century the varieties of form have been little analysed. Text-books of form generally take the classical sonata as their starting point; they go back to Corelli or a little earlier in order to show the formal ancestry of C. P. E. Bach and Haydn, but they seldom even tackle the formal problems of Handel and J. S. Bach. It has been tacitly assumed that "form" is a quality of "classical" music only, and that it is almost exclusively a quality of instrumental music. Perhaps it is a relic of the romantic tradition that vocal music should be supposed to have no form of its own, and that form in vocal music is entirely dependent on the words to which music is set.

Historians who have dealt with the sixteenth century have either been interested primarily in the ecclesiastical modes, especially when they were concerned chiefly with sacred music, or in the early suggestions of modern harmonic progressions. In both cases they have exhibited what a German professor once called *Kurzhörigkeit*, "short-hearingness" as analogous to short-sightedness—the characteristic of the pianist who can understand only the one bar which he is playing and has no vision of the movement as a whole. It is a dangerous thing to pick out single progressions which are harmonically interesting; it tempts us to find the rest of the work dull, and prevents us from seeing the broad outlines, which are of far greater importance. We can never rightly understand any piece of music unless we understand its general rhythmical shape; and most readers will probably agree with me in saying that the general rhythmical shapes of sixteenth century vocal music are singularly hard to grasp.

Form in the days of the classical sonata generally means the grouping of melodic subjects in various keys, tonic, dominant and others. But we cannot apply this system to the sixteenth century, because the classical key-system had not yet been evolved. Yet it would be absurd to say that sixteenth century music had no form; one might as well say that sixteenth century English had no grammar or syntax. All music has form of some kind, for without some kind of form it would not be music at all in an artistic sense. Our problem is to find out what actually was the formal basis of music in the days before classical tonality had become established. How and when classical tonality first began to be suggested and then gradually established will naturally be a very important problem to be investigated.

The first step towards classical tonality is the discovery of the dominant cadence. In mediaeval music the natural cadence is the melodic cadence, the fall by a whole tone to the "final" of the mode—E to D in the Dorian, A to G in the Mixolydian. If the falling part is sung by the lowest voice, the harmony above it will naturally be a suspended 7 6. Later comes a moment when the composers began basing their cadence on a rising fourth—A to D or D to G. In the earlier stages this was not done openly or directly, but it was arrived at in practice by the crossing of parts. The dominant cadence is not written in any one part, but it is heard when the parts are sung together.

It is not my purpose to pursue the history of the dominant cadence here in detail; what I want to point out is that the development of the dominant principle coincides with the development of stress-accent as the controlling force in musical form. Throughout the sixteenth century we shall find that the incipient sense of classical tonality is always most strongly to be felt in the music which is most vigorously accented. Form, rhythm and tonality are in fact inseparably bound up with one another, and they ought to be studied as inseparable things. If this principle were adopted in ordinary theoretical teaching, pupils would have far less difficulty in understanding the problems of modern music as well as those of the past.

Practically all the music of the sixteenth century is based on the form of the mediaeval song, the *Lied* or *chanson*. It is convenient to call it by the name of *chanson*, as that is the term generally accepted by historians for the Netherlandish type which towards the middle and end of the fifteenth century was harmonised in simple imitative counterpoint. It is originally a simple strophic song like any of the Latin hymns or such things as are called folk-songs because the names of their composers do not happen to be known. The metrical scheme of the verse varied in different countries and in different languages, but the simplest type is that consisting of four strains, and, generally speaking, it is the four-strain type which can be traced most easily throughout the centuries.

There are three aspects of the *chanson* and if it is to be developed into something else the composer may concentrate his attention on any one of these three. It may be considered as a song, that is, as a setting

EDWARD J. DENT

of words. When composers concentrate on the words and on the emotional expression of them the *chanson* develops into the Italian madrigal; later on the madrigal develops into recitative and opera. Secondly, the *chanson* may be considered as to harmony and rhythm. When harmony and rhythm are made to take the most important place, and the harmony is considered vertically rather than horizontally, we get the dance form, which in many of the sixteenth century lute tablatures reduces itself to the most commonplace type of "vamping." Thirdly, we may consider the *chanson* as a piece of imitative counterpoint; this leads us naturally to the *canzona* and to the *fugue* of the seventeenth century.

Further, we shall find in the course of the sixteenth and seventeenth centuries that these three types of composition interact on one another; they interact even in the eighteenth century and indeed interaction of formal principles must be an eternal and ever increasing phenomenon throughout the history of artistic music. For instance, the dance and the fugue interact; I am not here alluding to complete fugues in dance rhythms or to dances which are constructed on the lines of fugue. The examples in J. S. Bach's suites are too obvious to need pointing out; the neatest example of all is the comic fugal variation in the "Goldberg" variations. The interaction of dance and fugue to which I wish to draw attention for the moment is of a less conspicuous nature just because it is so common to all the music of Bach's period. Most of the instrumental music of the seventeenth century is either definitely dance music, that is, dance music composed to be danced to, not as "artistic music," or else it is written in contrapuntal forms. The imitative opening was so habitual a device that later on it became a fixed habit, and composers, when writing for a single voice or instrument, seem to want that voice or instrument to work out a fugue all by itself; it sings the subject, and then immediately proceeds to sing the answer. This habit explains many of the very curious forms that we find in the vocal music of the seventeenth century, as for example in the cantatas and operas of Stradella and in the early church music of Alessandro Scarlatti. But at the same time the dance forms, with their regular rhythmical accents, were establishing classical tonality and the primitive type of what is generally called sonata form—the binary form of Corelli's dances and Domenico Scarlatti's sonatas. In these latter the "subject and answer" type of theme is very common.

I have made this long digression from the music of the madrigals because it is easier to illustrate principles of composition from music which is well known. The reader will no doubt be well accustomed to the analysis of eighteenth century music and will easily recall plenty of familiar examples, so that he will have no difficulty in grasping the underlying principles involved. The music of the sixteenth century is less familiar and it has not been subjected to analysis in the ordinary text-

154

books of form, so that at first sight it may be difficult to see the underlying principles and to regard this music from a formal point of view.

I do not propose in this paper to say much about the development of the dance or of the fugue out of the *chanson;* I am here concerned mainly with the madrigal, and the dance and fugue will interest us only in so far as they interact with the madrigal. The creators of the madrigal were almost all of them Netherlanders, not Italians. Italy was overrun with Netherlandish composers attached to the various small courts; the Italian aristocracy preferred foreign musicians to natives just as the English and German aristocracy of the eighteenth century preferred Italian composers to those of their own nationality. The first music printed by Petrucci in 1500 was Netherlandish. The madrigal arose, as Cesari has well pointed out, from the contact of the Netherlandish composers with the Italian poets. Madrigals were composed for the pleasure of a highly cultivated literary society. Literary expression was the dominating feature of the madrigal and we can watch it becoming more and more literary from the days of Arcadelt to those of Marenzio and Monteverdi, until with Gesualdo it almost falls to pieces from the exaggeration of literary expression and in the hands of Monteverdi it becomes opera.

The *chanson* form is always the underlying skeleton of it. The various types may be very conveniently studied in the two volumes of *Ausgewählte Madrigale* edited by William Barclay Squire and published by Breitkopf and Härtel. One volume contains English madrigals, the other foreign. A glimpse at the technical method may be easily obtained by reading first Arcadelt's madrigal "Il bianco e dolce cigno" and then Orazio Vecchi's free transcription of it. Arcadelt sets the words expressively, but with great simplicity. The *chanson* form is perfectly clear throughout. Counterpoint is kept in the background, and is used mainly to provide a *coda.* The one essential feature of the madrigal as a verse form was that it should end with two rhyming lines of equal length; the other lines might be of what length the poet pleases and might rhyme irregularly. The two rhyming lines at the end, like the rhymed couplet at the end of any scene in a play of Shakespeare, brought the poem to a firm conclusion; we see the same principle adopted in many other cases—in the Ariosto stanza and in the Shakespearean sonnet. The composers generally made a practice of elaborating their music to these concluding lines and very often repeat them entirely. Singers of English madrigals will remember that in the repeat the first and second sopranos generally exchange parts; this was no doubt directed for the pleasure and amusement of the singers.

The relative positions of vertical and horizontal writing in a madrigal vary considerably, and are often dependent on the expression of the words. The most obvious principle is to make the first two lines of the poem vertical, the third contrapuntal and the last vertical again. This appears often in such simple and elementary compositions as the "Laudi Spirituali." It is a natural thing in a four-line melody for the first two strains to establish the key, or for the second line to modulate to a related key; the third line then often suggests a more distant modulation and the fourth re-establishes the tonic firmly. The same principle is apparent in the sonatas of Domenico Scarlatti; first subject in the tonic, second subject in the dominant, development section with free modulations and return to the second subject in the tonic. But there is not always so sharp a distinction between the vertical and horizontal style. Sometimes the whole movement is contrapuntal; the suitable contrast can then be made by rhythmical devices—the third line may have shorter themes for imitation, more energetic in character and introduced at distances of time.

An example of this type may be seen in Giaches de Vert's madrigal in the same collection "Chi salirà per me." This is an easy madrigal to grasp as a whole, provided that the reader can pick out the main melody from the contrapuntal imitations. This is in most cases the chief difficulty of understanding a madrigal as a whole; owing to the imitations the cadences do not seem to come at the expected distances of time, and it is always the cadences which determine the musical form of a piece of music. We are normally accustomed to cadences at distances of four (sometimes eight) bars; when a phrase starts in a series of imitations the number is thereby lengthened. Further, the start of a new series of imitations sometimes takes place before the previous cadence appears to be completely finished, and this produces an additional complication. In analysing a madrigal we must, therefore, work backwards from the cadences, and if we have any difficulty in discovering which are the main cadences we must look out for conspicuous suspensions. As a general rule main cadences are always brought into prominence by a suspension—4 3 or 7 6. This principle applies to sacred music just as it does to secular. Students of counterpoint who are learning to write in the style of Palestrina do not always realize this; this rule will not be found in the ordinary textbooks of counterpoint, and the practice of exercises in fourth species easily leads the student to imagine that suspensions can be put in wherever convenient. But the real function of the suspension is to mark the cadence by creating a stress accent through its dissonance. In earlier sixteenth century music, especially in sacred music where there is no strongly marked accentual rhythm, the suspension at the cadence is very important. Later on, when the feeling for classical tonality was becoming more apparent, suspensions are more freely used and sometimes a composer will make a suspension in each bar (as the modern reader would say) in order to obtain regular stress accents and create the impression of a regular series of bars in music which as originally written or printed had no bar-lines at all.

Having found the suspension, it is generally easy to find the voice which carries the main rhythmical line; as a rule it is the voice which enters last in the imitations. Here again we see that the student of counterpoint often goes about his work in exactly the wrong way. When we first learn to write imitations our inevitable tendency is to regard the first voice as the most important one; the voices which follow carry on the imitations as far as our humble skill will permit, and the result is that each successive voice is less accurate in its imitation than the preceding one and less interesting in its line, until the last voice to enter becomes the least important and the least effective of all. This is exactly contrary to the practice of the old composers. The practice of Bach in his chorale preludes is just the same as that of Palestrina in his hymns and of plenty of secular composers too; the final entry, not the first, in each strain is the really important one, and the preceding imitations are merely introductory to it. It is easy enough to see this in Bach's organ music where the chorale may be in minims and the introductory imitations in quavers; it is often very difficult to understand the design in some old church composer who writes a plainsong *canto fermo* in double breves against a counterpoint in semibreves and minims. But in the secular music of the sixteenth century we can make ourselves more easily at home; the madrigalists are not hampered by traditions of ritual and they write music from purely artistic motives. They have poetry instead of prose to set and consequently their musical form is much more clearly designed.

A further stage of Italian madrigal composition is illustrated in Barclay Squire's collection by Orazio Vecchi's transcription of Arcadelt's "Il bianco e dolce cigno." Here we have an early example of what journalists call "hyphenated music"; they are familiar with Bach-Tausig and Schubert-Liszt, but perhaps not so familiar with Arcadelt-Vecchi. Vecchi's madrigal would be very puzzling if we were unacquainted with Arcadelt's. But sing Arcadelt through and then Vecchi, and the process of composition is clear enough. Vecchi takes Arcadelt's music, rearranges it for a lower group of voices, and elaborates it with poetical illustrations. Notice the difference of procedure between Vecchi and Liszt. Liszt may put in a cadenza here and there, but roughly speaking he will not alter the lengths of Schubert's phrases; the extra decoration has to be simultaneous with the original. Vecchi works horizontally, not vertically, so that he has to prolong the original phrases, as well as adding counterpoints on the top of them. It is this prolongation of the phrases which makes such a madrigal difficult for the modern reader to take in as a whole. The Italian madrigal becomes in the course of time more and more literary in its expression; Vecchi's comments on Arcadelt are literary and illustrative; his transcription reminds one of some old edition of Petrarch where the text of Petrarch is printed in large type and surrounded by a margin of commentary in small type. One might say the same thing about Bach's chorale preludes.

With such composers as Marenzio, Monteverdi and Gesualdo the literary expression becomes so complicated and so intense in its detail that it becomes more and more difficult to follow the musical shape of the whole madrigal. Here we must act on the principle laid down by many modern teachers of song singing. The first thing to do is to read the words and if possible learn the poem by heart before looking at the music at all. When we have completely grasped the form and the emotion of the poem, we may turn to the music and look for its expression of this emotion. We shall find in Marenzio two distracting tendencies. Marenzio is an accomplished musician, who loves to develop a musical idea in a purely musical way, and he is at the same time a pictorial composer who loves to paint a musical landscape. "Scaldava il sol" is all landscape painting. But while we are appreciating the detail with which each line of the poem is "painted" separately, we must never for a moment forget that Tasso's words are a formal stanza with a shape of its own; the words have a rhythmical form, and those words would have no particular beauty or interest if they were not arranged by the poet in a metrical form. We have to see these two forms simultaneously as we sing the madrigal; if we forget that Tasso's stanza is a whole in itself our interpretation of Marenzio's madrigal will be choppy and incoherent.

The other Marenzio madrigal in Squire's collection, "Scendi dal Paradiso," is to some extent descriptive, but more essentially musical in its construction. The descriptive passages arise out of momentary literary allusions of a rather conventional character; the madrigal was evidently composed for a wedding in some noble family, and might perhaps have been sung by a group of professional singers, perhaps in fantastic costume and placed in a gallery of the hall which the bridal procession would enter. The modern reader is at once struck by the beauty of the initial phrase, and may perhaps be disappointed to find that this phrase is never used again in the course of the work. The madrigal appears, as indeed most madrigals of the later and complex type do, to be a string of disconnected ideas. The way to arrive at an understanding of the whole is to take the phrases one after another, just as they are set to the words, disregarding rests and imitations—repetitions of words will then be found to be fewer than one might expect—and look at the result as a continuous setting of the whole stanza. It may not make a very satisfactory musical composition, but it will give us a reasonably firm outline.

With Monteverdi and Gesualdo the difficulty of understanding is in some ways greater and in some ways less. We must begin by concentrating on the words, and on their emotional expression. The musical phrases of the composer are often intelligible only when they are sung with intensely passionate feeling; they require, in fact, an intensity of passionate expression which most English madrigal singers cannot possibly imagine, much less realise. Even English people who speak Italian fluently can seldom bring themselves up to the necessary temperature. On the other hand, the tendency of Monteverdi and Gesualdo is to compose madrigals as if they were solo songs with accompaniment; some of Monteverdi's do in fact exist in both versions. This means that the expressive line is easier to see, if not to interpret. The harmonies which to us are so strange are really subsidiary. Thus Gesualdo often ends a sentence with a sudden rise of the voice in the soprano part; we shall find exactly the same rise of pitch in many phrases of Verdi's "Falstaff." It is a musical representation of normal passionate Italian speech. Under the harmonic system of about 1600 this melodic rise, when accompanied by chords, produces what to us may be a most startling modulation; but the modern reader must never forget that what Gesualdo is aiming at is passionate literary expression, not musical modulation. The harmony, however strange it may be, is subsidiary.

Let us now turn to a complete contrast in Byrd's "I thought that Love had been a boy." This will show us how remote Byrd is from the Italian type of madrigal. Dr. Fellowes tells us that Italian madrigals were known in England as early as 1564, but although Byrd's *Psalmes, Sonets and Songs of Sadnes and Pietie* were published in the same year as *Musica Transalpina,* they show not the slightest trace of Italian influence. The Italian madrigals are above all things literary; Byrd's inspiration is never literary at all, but purely musical. I state this merely as a historical fact; I do not mean to imply that Byrd is a better or a worse composer than, say, Marenzio. Neither Dr. Fellowes nor Mr. Howes, in their biographies of Byrd, draw any attention to Byrd's preface, in which he clearly states that the songs were "originally made for instruments to expresse the harmonie and one voyce to sing the same." Dr. Fellowes certainly notes in his introduction that "in several instances of this set the composer has labelled one of the voices (not always the top part) as *the first singing part"* and goes on to observe that this part "is, as a rule, somewhat more melodious and also more regular in rhythmic outline than the other parts."

These psalms and songs are in fact songs for a solo voice accompanied by a quartet of viols. In the psalms the "first singing part" is indicated as such for every psalm except the first, in which it is obviously the treble part. In the others it is sometimes the second or third voice. In the secular songs the solo part is not always indicated, but can always be recognised at once; as a general rule it is the last to enter in the series of imitations, and it never repeats the words, whereas the other parts often repeat words where the counterpoint makes repetition inevitable. If there are exceptions to this rule of not repeating the words, they are due either to special emphasis, or to the practice (common in the opera songs of Alessandro Scarlatti) of anticipating the initial phrase of the main melody. (The most obvious example that the reader will recall is Handel's "Angels! . . . Angels ever bright and fair," etc.) Sometimes the last line of a stanza is repeated entirely to form a *coda;* further small final repetitions are most probably due to Byrd's wishing to utilise all five voices at the end, whereas in the original setting the solo voice might have rested while the instruments played the *coda*.

Here we have the original Netherlandish *chanson* form, each strain of the *chanson* being treated in imitations. What holds the entire composition together is the shape of the primitive song itself. In some of Byrd's examples the song melody is very long; the first psalm of 1588 has a melody covering 16 lines of verse; it forms one continuous composition and shows Byrd's remarkable power of pure melodic invention, a gift in which Byrd is always far superior to Palestrina—superior even to the greater Continental composers of that day.

It is not necessary here to analyse all Byrd's secular vocal music in detail. All I need point out is that the *chanson* principle remains Byrd's standard form. The three-part compositions do not conform to it; here the main melody stands out less prominently. It may also be observed here that even in the three-part compositions the style is never at all Italian. Another difference to be noticed is that in very many cases the songs in the manner of solos with quartet are songs with several stanzas sung to the same music; in the three-part songs there is no more than the one stanza, which therefore can be treated with more musical elaboration. The standard form of solo voice with four subsidiary voices appears even in Byrd's Italian composition "La verginella"; the Italian words are treated in a purely English fashion quite unlike the style of Italian madrigals. The collection of 1589 shows the same system elaborated; some songs have a four-part choral refrain added on. In some cases the main melody is divided between two chief singers. This is to be seen in "Penelope" and in the psalm "Behold how good a thing." Even in "Christ rising," where the words are in prose, Byrd contrives to make something like a *chanson* out of them, dividing the first singing part between the two upper voices and accompanying them with a quartet of viols. The whole musical conception is on the same lines as the secular works.

Byrd's final volume of 1611 probably includes pieces composed at various times. They show more the influence of the madrigal style. But Byrd never really absorbed the Italian style which the younger composers Weelkes and Wilbye so quickly adopted and made their own. They were still in their twenties when *Musica Transalpina* was published; Byrd was a man of middle age. The most interesting madrigal in the collection of 1611 is "Come woful Orpheus," the words of which speak of "strange chromatic notes," of "sourest sharps" and "uncouth flats." Byrd represents them all in his music with masterly skill, but they have none of the expressive power of the new devices as handled by the Italians and the young English school. Byrd had no sympathy with them; as in Stanford's "Ode to Discord" and the similar scene in D'Indy's "Saint Christophe" he is satirising the younger generation with all the gusto of elderly facetiousness.

Byrd's style is old-fashioned, but it is marvellously accomplished, and it shows purely musical inspiration together with astonishing wealth of melody. A study of these songs is very illuminating, for they not only show us the clear principles of musical construction, but they are also a recognisable link in the chain of English composers which unites Fayrfax and Cornysshe with the lutenists, Dowland, Ford and the rest. Conductors who have time to try experiments might well ask their choruses to try through "I thought that Love" or others of the type with one part singing the first singing part with the words, while the rest sing their parts with closed lips. This will give a rough and ready imitation of a quartet of viols, and the chorus (and conductor, too) may then obtain a clearer idea of the general form—and therefore of the general musical intention—of the composition.

Bibliography

The most extensive work on the madrigal is Alfred Einstein's *The Italian Madrigal*, 3 vols. (Princeton, N.J., Princeton University Press, 1949). Vol. 3 of this work is devoted to musical examples. Also by Einstein are "The Madrigal," *The Musical Quarterly*, 10 (1924), and "The Elizabethan Madrigal and 'Musica Transalpina'," *Music and Letters*, 25 (1944). An article taking issue with some of Einstein's ideas is Dean T. Mace's "Pietro Bembo and the Literary Origins of the Italian Madrigal," *The Musical Quarterly*, 55 (1969). A volume that contains three essays on the musical beginnings of the madrigal and its development from the frottola and chanson and includes several musical examples is J. Haar, ed., *Chanson and Madrigal, 1480-1530* (Cambridge, Mass., Harvard University Press, 1964). Works on the English madrigal include J. Kerman, *The Elizabethan Madrigal* (New York, American Musicological Society, 1962; distributed by Galaxy Music Corp.), and two works by E. H. Fellowes, *The English Madrigal Composers* (Oxford, Clarendon, 1921) and *The English Madrigal* (London, Oxford University Press, 1925).

Selected musical examples of madrigals may be found in the *Historical Anthology of Music,* vol. 1. Larger and more important collections are contained in Einstein, *The Golden Age of the Madrigal* (New York, G. Schirmer, 1942), and Fellowes, *The English Madrigal School,* 36 vols. (London, Stainer & Bell, 1921-1924), which has been revised and re-edited by Thurston Dart and reissued under the title *The English Madrigalists* (London, Stainer & Bell, 1956-1961).

11

THE music of the Baroque has enjoyed great popularity during the past quarter of a century. Concerts and even series of concerts have been devoted exclusively to its performance; much emphasis has been placed on performing Baroque music on instruments that were known and used during the Baroque period, resulting in a revival of popularity of such instruments as the harpsichord and the recorder; and emotions on the subject of Baroque music have at times become so intense that friendships have been made or broken over such a small detail as the proper performance of a Baroque ornament. Yet it has often been overlooked that much of the music which has enjoyed such recent popularity comes from the last third of that period which is known as Baroque and that there is an equal if not greater amount of music representing the earlier phases of the Baroque. While the Baroque had an end, and a glorious one, it also had a beginning which was in its own way just as exciting. But what and when was this beginning? The year 1600 is a convenient date and one easy to remember; thus it has usually been the one assigned by textbooks as the beginning of the Baroque. Scholars, however, are not necessarily of the opinion that 1600 is the proper date to assign, nor do they agree on any other date. Professor Wellesz, in the following article, has wisely avoided assigning dates to limit the Baroque. Instead, he has concentrated on determining those stylistic elements that differentiate the music of the Baroque from the music of the preceding period and on how these elements came to be established and to grow into a Baroque style, all of which is far more important for the understanding of Baroque music than dates. Many elements found in sixteenth-century music lead quite naturally into the music of the seventeenth century—there is no sudden and dramatic break between the two. The Baroque did indeed have a beginning, and a fascinating one, but in no way was it sudden or mystical. And certainly the year 1600 must not be viewed as a sort of witching hour when Renaissance music became Baroque.

Egon Joseph Wellesz has been a professor at the University of Vienna and at Oxford University. In addition he has lectured at such American universities as Columbia, Yale, California, and Princeton. He is best known for his research in Byzantine music, exemplified by works such as *A History of Byzantine Music and Hymnography* (Oxford, Clarendon, 1949; 2d ed., 1961) and *Eastern Elements in Western Chant* (Boston, Oxford University Press for the Byzantine Institute, 1947), and for numerous periodical contributions as well as his editorship of vol. 1 of *The New Oxford History of Music*. For a bibliography of his writings see R. Reti, "Egon Wellesz, Musician and Scholar," *The Musical Quarterly,* 42 (Jan., 1956).

The Beginning of Baroque in Music

EGON WELLESZ

Translated by Patricia Kean

To divide up a period of artistic development by means of dates is always an arbitrary proceeding. It is to assume a final point, a place of rest, where everything is in a constant state of flux and motion. And yet limitation is necessary if we are to orientate ourselves in the immense variety of the phenomena which make up the history of art, and for this reason sections must be marked off in time, the periods of art history.

In order to obtain more easily a general view of the separate periods, we are accustomed to refer to them by names which are intended to sum up and to distinguish them accurately from each other. These names have been handed down and accepted without criticism for a long time now, though they are by no means fitted for the use to which they are put. They are not the result of critical reflection, but have been thrown up by chance and crystallized into formulae. They are either entirely misapplied, like "Gothic" in the derogatory sense of "barbaric art" in which it was used by Vasari, or they only fit a single one among a variety of movements to which they are applied, like "Renaissance" which applies to the rebirth of Classicism. Or else they express an adverse judgement like "Baroque" which, though its etymology is still uncertain, was very early connected with *barocco*, a term applied to painting meaning an excessive emotionalism, as in the case of some of the followers of Michelangelo.

These terms were first employed for systematic classification in the Romantic period. If we wish to use them nowadays as aids to the study of the history of art we must not expect them to provide an explanation of the phenomena but must consider them only as conventional fictions, coined to aid our understanding.

Since they belonged to a period in which the study of history was

FROM Egon Wellesz, *Essays on Opera*, translated by Patricia Kean (London, Dennis Dobson, 1950) pp. 13-32. Reprinted by permission of the publisher.

still essentially concerned with the description of facts, these terms could hardly be adequate to a period in which it had advanced to the idea of a continuous development in the realm of cultural activity.

But it was only when the individual work of art was no longer considered in isolation, when its relationship to the other works of its time was investigated, its antecedents explored, and all the tangled threads followed out until every connection was laid bare, that it was possible to form a fair judgement of the works of the past. It then became necessary to subject the ideas which were associated with the terms Gothic, Renaissance, Baroque, and Rococo to a revision, because the limits of the periods designated by them had shifted.

This modification is particularly striking in the case of the terms Baroque and Renaissance. Before Jacob Burckhardt wrote, Gothic had to lend its name to part of what we now call the art of the Renaissance, and it is to a great extent his achievement to have set the beginning of the Renaissance further back. But Burckhardt went too far in his conclusions, with the result that he valued this period too highly and too one-sidedly, while his judgement of the preceding Gothic and the following Baroque period suffered.

Once the prevailing idea of a period of outstanding achievement, complete and isolated, had been overcome it was possible to rediscover the Renaissance. It is an outstanding period, in so far as it solves all the problems of an earlier age and gives them a new impulse through its re-orientation to the ancient world. But from the point of view of the hidden forces which determined the development, the Renaissance is a period of transition, standing between Gothic, which still belongs to the Middle Ages, and Baroque which already belongs to the modern period. The germ of a new art had already begun to stir in it, and it was to lead to entirely new artistic problems. In painting, for example, to the problem of the treatment of light and space; in architecture to the problem of the unification of space in a design, to the use of light and shade to produce illusion, to the invasion of plastic art by painting. In music it is the final overthrow of the *cantus firmus* and, connected with this, the emergence of the highest part to bear the melody; the organized use of successions of chords, which are subjected to the laws of tension and relaxation, through which the evolution of new forms was first made possible; the penetration of the melodic line by *fiorituri;* the emergence of a characteristic way of writing for the instruments, and with it the beginnings of the use of orchestral colour. If we take all these phenomena together, they mean nothing else but the beginning of the subjective in music.

Events of far-reaching importance in the political, religious, and economic spheres mark the beginning of the new period which we call Baroque, and which has been an active influence, creative in the highest degree up to the present day. We may place the beginning of the new Baroque feeling in art in the fifteen-twenties. As the result of the discoveries and experiences of the preceding period, and of the economic developments which were bound up with them, many new values had arisen in the world of ideas, which, in art, led to new forms and new problems.

The home of the new movement was the centre of what was then the cultivated world, Rome, and the towns of central Italy.

Born in a violent and eventful age, the new art took as its subject the titanic — the Italians speak of *"il stile colossale"* — the eternally moved which presses outward beyond its own boundaries, and it held to this principle throughout the greater part of two centuries. It was only gradually, as the aspirations of the cultured world changed and turned to the ideal of the return to nature, that the external form of this style altered, and that, in place of the heroic and the dynamic of Baroque emerged the grace and delicacy of Rococo. This did not mean a break with the essential ideas of the preceding period, only an emotional change.

Recently it has become the custom to apply the terms Gothic, Renaissance, Baroque, Rococo and Classical not only to the periods with which they were originally associated but wherever similar phenomena are to be found. Thus we speak of a "classical Rococo," a "classical Baroque" and a "Carolingian Renaissance." It seems to me that there is a certain danger in this; that terms like these which, as we have seen, are only to be used by necessity and in full recognition of their inadequacy, should not become part of the general terminology of the history of art.

But perhaps the following remarks may be of use to point the antithesis between Renaissance and Baroque.

From the Ancient World onwards two streams can be traced which have persisted without intermission; an individualizing and a generalizing tendency. The individualizing tendency, in which the individual will is predominant, is subjective. The generalizing, in which the collective experience comes into play, is objective. For the individualizing tendency content is more important than form. For the generalizing, form is more important than content. In the former all is in a state of evolution and movement; in the latter all is fixed and at rest. In the individualizing tendency content shatters old forms and creates new; in the generalizing, forms harden and compel the content to adapt itself to them. The individualizing tendency confuses the means proper to the separate arts. The generalizing stands for clarity and unity.

The continued co-existence of these two which only seem to follow each other in time, can easily be overlooked if the attention is only directed to the masterpieces of the art of any period. But from an adequate investigation of the whole artistic activity it will always be found that where one tendency emerges as the main stream of the period the other will always be there as the secondary stream. In transitional periods both flow, either equally strong, side by side, or, coming to the surface in rapid succession, they imitate in miniature the successions which constitute the longer periods. Whichever tendency was the ruling one in a given period will in the next be carried on eclectically, as the secondary stream until, in a new altered form, it again takes the lead.

THE creation of larger forms in music, up to the Baroque period, was bound up with the existence of constructive means. But from the moment when the leading part became also the upper part—melody in our sense—the great revolution in music began. The melody came to express emotion with embellishments and coloratura, and therefore gained such importance that all other parts had to subordinate themselves to it. From this it follows that it was still necessary to compose these subordinate parts with as much care as before, but it is no longer the progression of parts which is important, but the accord of the accompanying parts with the melody. The harmonic element which had arisen from the variety of the ecclesiastical modes through the introduction of accidentals comes into the foreground, and it tended more and more towards the clear contrasts of major and minor. The chords are carefully chosen and linked together. Dissonance becomes a means of heightening the harmonic effect. Now for the first time music is freed from the restriction of a form imposed from outside. The first stage was passed in the development of polyphony, and now it was equally necessary to begin again from the beginning. In its turn the instrumental music written at the beginning of the sixteenth century appeared primitive and crude in comparison with works in the old style. But it is the beginning of a new way of writing based on the qualities of the instruments, tne beginning of an instrumental structure and a thematic treatment distinct from that of vocal music. If for example we glance at the music of the lutenists we will be struck by the incoherence of the progression of parts, but if we hear it we will realize that the method of composition is conditioned by the technical and sonorous possibilities of the instrument.

The advance, or rather the development of music is dearly bought, for under the influence of this new development in style, the splendid achievement of the *a capella* singing lost ground during the sixteenth century and in the course of the seventeenth gradually vanished. A similar process is to be observed in the eighteenth century: here it is the highly developed contrapuntal style which is sacrificed to the growing power of symphonic writing. And at the present day we ourselves can see how, in its turn, this style, which was brought to such perfection by the orchestral composers of the nineteenth century, is in process of being displaced by a new tendency which renounces the high achievement of the orchestral style for a new primitive mode of expression, just as monody renounced the riches of the *a capella* style.

In histories of music the revolutionary change which was brought about by the replacement of polyphonic choral singing by one-part, monodic singing was not until recently given due weight. To an understanding of art which was biased by the so-called "classical" idea of beauty this movement was entirely foreign. The real beginning of Baroque in music was, therefore, overlooked, and the appearance of music-drama was considered to be the decisive point of the development. Goldschmidt in the *Lehre von der vokalen Ornamentik*, Leichtentritt in the revised edition of the fourth volume of Ambros's *Geschichte der Musik*, Riemann in the *Handbuch der Musikgeschichte* II, 2, and Adler in the *Stil der Musik*, were the first to form an historically objective judgement of the monodic style. But a comprehensive account of the period is still lacking. It ought not to restrict itself to the music alone, but to take into account all the factors which brought about this radical change in the sphere of aesthetics. It must in fact be put upon the broad basis of the history of civilization.

The history of music itself has not fully utilized the primary sources at its disposal. For, besides the actual musical works which have been preserved either in manuscript or in print, the prefaces of composers to their works, and the treatises of the theorists must be taken into consideration, for they have for the most part in this period lost their earlier more theoretical character and are concerned with the philosophy of art. The time has come for a systematic explanation of these sources, so that a complete picture may be obtained of this exceptionally important period.

THE struggle for the supremacy of the new tendency lasted throughout almost the whole of the sixteenth century. It is not only the new forms which are filled with its spirit; the old ones, too, were affected by the impulse towards greater expressiveness. In polyphony also, the free ornamentation of the separate parts was usual, with the result that each singer tried to outdo the rest and orderly singing degenerated into a wild confusion of parts. This destruction of choral singing by the use of the new methods did not, however, discredit the new movement, but was used as proof of the imperfection of singing in the old contrapuntal style.

The development of monodic singing was carried through in a systematic and interesting way. Monody begins when, in a polyphonic work, the highest part, and the highest part only, is ornamented. It is thus distinguished technically and aesthetically from the other parts, which become less important and are no longer performed by singers but by instruments. Here two courses are open. Each part may be taken by separate instruments or they may all be rendered together in the manner of a piano arrangement, by organ, clavichord, or lute. The arrangement was particularly popular at this period. It made it possible for an amateur, alone and unrestricted, to perform works which, up to now, had needed four or five musicians. When this method of adaptation had been in use for a time works began to be written for such settings without recourse to the intermediate stage of the arrangement. In these compositions the independence of the accompanying parts became more and more reduced. The whole attention was now concentrated on the development of the solo-voice part. The emergence of the *basso generale*, or *basso continuo*, provided the most important technical means to the construction of monody. It used to be thought that it was discovered by Lodovico Grossi da Viadana after 1600, but this view has been long ago abandoned since a number of works with *basso continuo* existed as early as the end of the sixteenth century.

Here, an innovation in notation must be mentioned, which later had a great influence on the essential structure of the work. When the parts which accompanied the leading vocal part had lost their independent life to such an extent that we can no longer speak of parts, but only of accompanying chords, the composer simplified the writing out of his score by only putting down the vocal part and the instrumental bass, leaving it to the instrumentalist to fill in the harmonies of the middle parts. In this, however, he was guided as to the intentions of the composer by figures set under the bass part.

The monodic style was, then, towards the end of the seventeenth century capable, with its expressive melodic technique, of embodying passionate feeling and was ready to join itself to a new kind of lyric as it later actually did in the cantata when the appearance of the music drama gave it another direction.

The drama had been prepared for music by the *intermedii* and by the religious drama. It was given the final impulses through the endeavor of a circle of learned men to revive Greek tragedy with singing and acting.

The oldest example of music inserted in a spoken drama is the pieces of music in Poliziano's *Orfeo* of 1471, and it is noteworthy that they were placed where the dramatic tension was highest. It is not without interest to recall that even when the *dramma per musica* with its complete musical setting had evolved, theorists like Doni held that it was better only to set the crises of the action to music, not the whole drama.

From 1480, when a *Conversione di S. Paolo* was performed, it became the established custom to accompany the entrance of important characters with music. But these musical parts only became of importance when they were moved to the end of the act.

These *entr'actes*, called *intermedii*, were, in the beginning, purely instrumental. Their music is for the most part lost, but we possess instructions in the text books which give an adequate idea of the relation of the music to the drama.

But gradually the *intermedii* were enlarged to such an extent that Antonio Francesco Grazzini could write in 1582, "Formerly the *intermedio* was an appendage of the comedy; nowadays the comedy is an appendage of the *intermedio*."

Besides purely instrumental music, songs in madrigal form also made their appearance, linked together in such a way that it is possible to speak of a madrigal drama. The *Amfiparnasso* of Orazio Vecchi represents their highest achievement. From this it was a natural step to the monodic drama, as is evident when we consider that the desire for convincing characterization could not be satisfied for long with the expression of the feelings of an individual by a company of singers.

The second source, the liturgical drama with music led in the Middle Ages to Complaints of the Virgin and Passion Plays, which later gave way to the Italian *rappresentazione* of the sixteenth century in Florence and other towns of central Italy.

The true origin of the religious semi-dramatic form of the Oratorio, which appears about 1600, is to be found in the *Laudi* which already contained elements of dialogue. Through them it became possible to develop a religious art, independent of the liturgy, which finally led to the Oratorio. But this gradual development was cut short, and given a fixed form by the intervention of a circle of cultured amateurs who met, as has been said, towards the end of the sixteenth century, at the house of Count Bardi in Florence, to revive Greek tragedy.

Here, as in other spheres, the precepts of the Greek and Roman writers were the point of departure for all discussion of art, and the decisions of Plato and Aristotle were of absolute authority to the Florentine *camerata*.

Starting from the knowledge that Greek tragedy was not spoken but sung, Count Bardi and his friends tried to call this lost dramatic style back to life. As has been said, the stage was well prepared, and the musicians of the circle, Caccini and Peri, were inspired by these discussions, whose importance they fully acknowledged, to a change of style, or, it would be better to say, to the consistent use of a style which already existed in embryo.

The real manifesto against the old style, the "Declaration of War

171

against Counterpoint," as Ambros called it, came from the originator of the whole movement, Count Bardi. He wrote a long treatise, addressed to Caccini, on Greek music and the art of *bel canto*. As evidence of the effect of ancient music on the hearer he adduced a number of well-known myths and stories which he, the enlightened scholar, treats, surprisingly enough, as incontrovertible facts.

"But now-a-days," he wrote, "music falls into two main divisions; one belongs to counterpoint. The other should be called *arte di ben cantare*." He criticizes the artificial style of the madrigal, and finds fault, for example, with the fact that the bass moves in sustained notes while the higher parts have a quicker movement. "Our composers," he says, "would consider it a deadly sin if they happened to hear the voices at the same moment on the same syllable of the text and on notes of the same rhythmical value. The more they bring the parts into motion the more gifted they consider themselves. . . . And since we now find ourselves in such impenetrable darkness, we want at least to try to make a little light for poor Music, for, since her decline up to the present day she has not found, in so many centuries, one composer who thinks about her needs, who does not rather force her into the ways of her mortal enemy, Counterpoint."

The most important means, he says, of improving music is to pay attention to the verse rhythm and not to imitate the musicians of the present day who, to flatter their own inclinations, destroy the verse and tear it to pieces. Thus, Bardi demands what Wagner was to call "the birth of *melos* from the rhythm of speech."

The first attempt in the recitative style was made by Vicenzo Galilei, the father of the famous astronomer. He had written a dialogue in the style of Plato on the old and new music. He had also discovered the ancient Greek hymn of Mesomedes, which was only deciphered in the nineteenth century. Yet this discovery seems to have given him a strong impulse to revive the lost art, and, if it could not be done by deciphering the document, to replace it by a fitting new composition. He therefore set to music the words of Count Ugolino in Dante's *Divina Commedia*. He himself sang the work, accompanied by several viols. This seems still to have been in the style of those madrigals already mentioned, in which a polyphonic work was so performed that only the highest part was sung. The novelty seems to have been the dramatic character of the recitative voice part.

The real development to drama, however, first occurred when Bardi had already left Florence, called to Rome by Pope Clement XIII. Now the circle met at the house of Jacopo Corsi. Here Peri took the lead. He was the pupil of Cristoforo Malvezzi, and had had a better training than his rival Caccini. His extraordinary virtuosity on the organ and the other keyboard instruments was of importance for the technique of his compositions. He also possessed a good soprano voice, which gave him the *entrée* to all the aristocratic salons of Florence. The Duke, too, had made him Director of Music, and he felt that this position placed him above all other musicians.

Besides Peri, Rinuccini the librettist must be mentioned as influential. He was the poet of most of the opera texts of the period, and he influenced their style for a full century. He too was filled with the idea of the supremacy of Greek tragedy, and he tried to realize this ideal, believing that through a well constructed plot, elevated diction, and concise expression, it provided an excellent basis for the musical setting.

Thus the prerequisites were established out of which the new form of the *dramma per musica* could develop.

FROM what has been said it is clear that those who were contemporary with the change felt that they were faced with an evolution in music, not a sudden break with the past as was assumed in the early days of the study of the history of music, even if some composers had no small opinion of the part they played in the movement. The numerous treatises and opera-prologues which contain the programme of the new movement prove this. In most of the treatises we can see the effort of the musicians to compare the old with the new and to bring into prominence one or the other, according to the party to which they belong. In most cases, of course, the treatises end with the praises of the New Art. It is not clear who was pre-eminent in the development of the monodic style to real recitative. Three men were cited in the various treatises as *Inventori:* Giulio Caccini, Jacopo Peri, and Marco da Gagliano. Nowadays it is generally agreed that the true pioneer of the modern movement was Don Carlo Gesualdo, Principe di Venosa, whose vocal style, in his madrigals, had shown the way to his successors. It is, too, a most remarkable fact that his madrigals survived through several editions, an unusual circumstance and a sign that they must have been eagerly studied by musicians.

In the treatise *Discorsi e Regole sovra la musica* of Severo Bonini the privilege of discovering the new style is attributed to Giulio Caccini detto Romano alone, and Jacopo Peri and Marco da Gagliano are only mentioned in the second place. But the author relies mainly for his account on Caccini's own Preface to the *Nuove Musiche*, since the *Discorsi* is concerned with the same subject.

Marco da Gagliano, on the other hand, in the preface to his opera *Dafne* gives another version of the facts and brings forward Jacopo Peri as the discoverer of the new style: "It was Jacopo Peri who discovered that ingenious manner of speech-song which the whole of Italy admires.

I shall never be weary of praising him, since everyone must praise him unceasingly, and every music-lover has the songs from the *Orfeo* constantly before him. But I must also say that no one can fully appreciate the beauty and power of his songs who has not heard them performed by him."

Caccini, a most self-conscious artist, speaks specifically of his own merits in the preface to the *Nuove Musiche,* which was Bonini's main source. Certain expressions from this preface have gained general currency and form the kernel of most accounts of the origins of monody. It is therefore necessary to point out that Caccini's statements need to be treated with caution. The beginning of the preface shows Caccini's opinion of himself: "If I have finished my studies in the art of singing with the famous Scipione del Palla, my teacher, and have not published my madrigals and arias, written over a period of years, it is because I did not think them worth publication, and believed that they had met with honour enough, and even beyond their deserts, when I knew my music to be continually performed by the most famous singers of Italy and by the most distinguished amateurs."

Caccini's modest opening is, it is clear, only a rhetorical trick to throw into stronger contrast the wide circulation of his music. Of great importance, however, is his emphatic insistence on "a certain noble subordination of singing" (*una certa nobile sprezzatura del canto*), for music "should be speech and rhythm in the first place, sound only in the second, and not the other way round." This is the central point of his teaching, and it is in conformity with Gluck's remark, that when he began to compose he tried to forget that he was a musician.

Caccini demanded of the singer a perfect understanding of the sense and the emotional content of what he sang. It was not enough merely to have behind one a long experience of singing. One must also, by virtue of intelligence, be able to master the whole material. "This talent," he says, "is incompatible with any half-measures, and the more brilliant characteristics are contained in it, the greater effort and care must the teacher expend, industriously and lovingly to draw them out."

As has already been said, the battle against counterpoint was a central part of the movement. Counterpoint was regarded as the principal evil, because it had become associated with repetition and lengthening of the text to the destruction of the sense. Its opponents set themselves against the *Laceramento della Poesia* and opposed the idea that in the madrigal different words should be sung at the same time. This revolt against the ruling tendency is to be explained as the reaction of the Italians against the complicated contrapuntal style of the Netherlands, which was practised in Venice. In the sixteenth century famous Northern masters had been brought there as teachers, but their art, apparently, never became really popular. It was too foreign to the Italian character in feeling and technique for it ever to mean to them more than a temporary excursion into a strange world.

But now the revolt against counterpoint was reinforced by a style of composition which originated in Spain and spread over South Italy. With its clearly organized simple structure of chords it soon gained a large following. That it was due to Spanish influence was not known until the most recent period of research. It was only when interest was aroused in Spanish vocal music that problems which had seemed obscure and insoluble took on a new aspect.

Through Spain and Italy the East made its last bid to influence the West, and even if it could no longer offer the plenitude of those times when an unbroken stream of caravans from the great metropolises of Asia made their way to the coasts of the Mediterranean bringing gifts and treasure to the West, when monks, artists, and craftsmen from Persia, Armenia, and Syria brought their native culture to the ports of Italy and France, and workmen and musicians penetrated as far as the Rhine, yet even this last effort of a culture which was continually losing ground before the increasing power of the West, must be accounted of great importance. It is the last wave in the great backwards and forwards ebb which was responsible for the whole relationship of the Greeks and the Persians, ending, with the temporary victory of the Greeks, in Hellenism, against which a proportionately violent reaction from the East set in.

The Spaniards used the favourite instrument of the Arabs, the lute, and a considerable literature arose for voice and lute accompaniment. The fact that the instrument was so well adapted to play chords sharpened the Spanish ear for harmony.

In the few pieces of music which survive, a strong feeling for harmonic progressions is evident and a concentration on the highest part at a time when, in Italy, the *cantus* was still in the middle part. One document proves that the importance of the highest part was already appreciated: the prohibition in the *Libro primo de la declaracion de instrumentos musicales* by Juan Bermudo (1549) of the introduction of melodic ornament by the performers where it is not expressly required by the composer. This prohibition of the weakening of the melodic line means that a very strong feeling existed for developed *cantilena*, complete in itself and needing no ornament.

Caccini's complaint of the singers who ignore his instructions and make an abuse of ornament corresponds to the prohibition of Juan Bermudo, and indeed, if we examine the works of the Italian theorists on the art of singing we shall be struck by the excessive richness of the art of ornamentation in the second half of the sixteenth century.

The Florentine Reformers did not, however, as is always assumed, abolish ornament: they systematized it. They themselves wrote very important ornaments. In the new style for solo voice accompanied by the *basso continuo,* on the other hand, the ornaments could no longer cause such confusion.

Caccini occupied the most extreme position among the theorists. He considered that passages were only the invention of those who did not know how to express real emotion. If one was capable of this, he said, passages would without doubt be cast aside, for nothing could be in greater opposition to truth than they are. He himself only used them at tranquil moments, and in final cadences. This new style, therefore (and it must be strongly stressed), was not concerned with recitative singing in the sense in which Monteverdi developed it in his late operas, but with expressive solo singing. The innovation was the complete predominance of the highest part, and, in order to carry through this principle, the whole art and achievement of polyphonic singing was sacrificed. Even though there was a last flowering of the madrigal in the seventeenth century it was only important for its harmonic subtleties, not for the art of its polyphony.

The means by which the new style was systematically developed was, as has been said, the introduction of the figured bass. It is evident that the result of this was to make the performer concentrate on correct, and later on interesting harmonies rather than on a beautiful and smooth progression of parts. A feeling for harmonic sequences, for intensification and relaxation in the harmony, for extension of cadences was however also developed. The aim was always to develop these even further, increasingly to expand the melodic curve and to group the chords within this curve with ever increasing effectiveness.

Two other harmonic processes mark the beginning of monody: the loss of chromatics, and the introduction of freely placed dissonances.

In the last years of the sixteenth century chromaticism had developed to an extraordinary degree of subtlety. But with the end of polyphonic vocal music it became restricted mainly to the upper part and one of the most important methods of composition, chromaticism in the middle part, was gradually lost through the uncertainty of the notation. But even in the highest and lowest parts it gradually vanished during the course of the seventeenth century and was maintained only in a few cases. It still played a very important part in a few standard *bassi ostinati* until late in the eighteenth century.

The process of freeing dissonance began with the introduction of the unprepared dominant seventh chord. It was this which helped to build up our modern cadence. This tendency to use the dominant structure is older than is generally assumed. Even in the most flourishing period of the church modes a similar effect was attempted with the chord of the fifth. But the systematic fixing of the cadences by means of the dominant seventh chord and the decrease in importance of all the intervals before the fifth which took place from the seventeenth century onwards, was new. The freeing of dissonance from the rules of counterpoint, its use according to the impulse of the composer is, again, a sign of awakening subjectivity.

Monteverdi dared to introduce an unprepared ninth followed by an equally unprepared seventh and to make the resolution only after these chords. This was, for the period, an unheard-of boldness and it called forth opposition. A theorist, the Canon Giovanni Maria Artusi of Bologna opposed such harmonic freedoms in a work which appeared in 1600, *L'Artusi overo delle imperfezione della moderna musica*. He maintained that these madrigals were aberrations and would lead to barbarism. People tried to excuse violations of the rules as the "new style" but it was not practicable to overthrow the soundly based rules of the theorists. "The new composers only want to satisfy the ear and to deceive it through the rapidity of the movement. But they forget that their cantilenas must also be judged by the understanding. They are ignoramuses who only want to make a noise and do not know what one ought to write and what one ought not."

Here the academic line of argument is easily recognizable. Since Monteverdi did not write in accordance with the rules of the classical theorist, his music, even if it sounds well, is to be blamed. Monteverdi defended himself from this criticism. He accused Artusi of only judging the notes without the text, which, alone, could reveal the meaning of his work. Here we find once more Caccini's demand that the music must adapt itself to the sense of the words.

The conflict between music and words has never ceased from this time onwards and in periods of the predominance of music over words it has led to the great reforms which are associated with the names of Gluck and Wagner.

IF we take together all these features which mark the new style in contrast to earlier music — predominance of a highest part with coloratura used for sound painting and declamation following the sense of the text with reduced importance of all other parts in contrast to the highest, which tries to unite and render in itself the content of all the parts; the beginning of a harmonic logic, a careful consideration of the harmonic structure and, in connection with this, the gradual freeing of dissonance; the beginning of a characteristic instrumental style utilizing the special qualities of the instruments to enliven the melody as such (orchestral colour), the growth of new forms whose development continues up to the present day and whose chief characteristics can be regarded as thematic structure using a crescendo based on the repetition of a motive—then all these features, which are paralleled in the other arts, point to the desire for personal expression, for larger proportions, greater emotional range, a necessity to give expression to every emotion. If for example we make a brief comparison with architecture it is clear that the ambition of the Baroque architect to bring together all parts in a self-contained whole in order to achieve an impression of completeness corresponds to the form of an ever bolder melodic curve. Just as in architecture in order to achieve this end by visual means the centre of the façade was emphasized and certain parts of the wall brought forward from it while the parts at the side were pushed back, so in music an attempt was made to concentrate on a few important points by an enhanced harmonic structure at the climaxes. Just as those parts of the façade which are to be focal points are emphasized by doors with elaborate portals, by pillars or windows with ornamented pediments, so those parts of a musical composition which are to be emphasized are brought out by the scoring. In architecture great use is made of optical illusion brought about by the intensification of shadow. Corresponding to this, Baroque music developed to an increasing degree the contrast between *piano* and *forte, solo* and *tutti*. The architects favoured pillars placed in a flat surface and intended to give the impression of support, though they are built in such a way that their only use is to break up the surface. In music middle parts began to be written which simulate a contrapuntal movement while in reality they fulfil a definite rhythmical function. As Baroque architecture tries to break through or to dissolve a closed line, for example in the breaking up of the contour of the gable, the interruption of the cornice by jutting moulding, backward or forward projections which throw shadows, the modification of the outline with ornament, so in music the corresponding tendency is to be found to keep the melodic line as much in motion as possible, to ornament it with more sustained notes and to introduce coloratura at important points. To the splendour of the late Baroque façades, the richly gilded interiors of churches, corresponds in music the growth of orchestral colour, the conscious use of single instruments or groups of instruments to capture the listener by the charm of the sound. Just as the interiors of many churches seem not to be covered by a solid roof but, through the painter's continuation of the architect's work, to extend into the open space of heaven, filled with troops of angels and with clouds, so in music a similar feeling of boundless space is produced when in a Mass several vocal and instrumental choirs of different range seem to sound from a mysterious distance. In music the association of certain ideas with corresponding sounds was so highly developed that the emotional content of the music can be determined from the use of the instruments. Tone-symbols arose which form the basis of the modern art of scoring.

The first period of Baroque music, the period of conflict and of the first creations, lasted up to the middle of the seventeenth century, up to the time when the architectonic forms of opera, oratorio, and cantata, fluid to begin with, hardened into rigid formulae. Now emotion becomes conventional, the fresh dramatic impulse weakened to a sentimental lyricism.

The music drama has outgrown its youth and entered on its period of maturity. From now on dramatic proportion between words and music is at an end. The aria becomes predominant—from the musical point of view an event of the greatest importance since almost all problems of form were solved by the tripartite form of the aria, but from the point of view of the text, it meant the end of a truly dramatic plot. For, to provide for the lyrical development of the aria the whole action was forced into *recitativo secco* which became musically less and less important. This state of affairs only ended when a reforming movement set in with the same principles and archaizing tendencies as the Florentines had had, and was given form and expression by Gluck.

But instrumental music had already, at an earlier period, developed in an increasingly elaborate way, and it finally became an important factor at the moment when the symphony of the opera, separated from the music drama, was performed in the concert hall, and when true symphonies were composed without any connection with an opera. These concert symphonies were most common in Austria and South Germany, and they are the first sign of emancipation from the Italian taste. A fourth movement, the minuet, was added to the usual three and thus the form was reached in which Haydn, Mozart, and Beethoven expressed their most profound feelings and ideas, and which, up to the present day, even if in an altered and extended form, remains the most important medium of musical expression.

Bibliography

Manfred Bukofzer's *Music in the Baroque Era* (New York, Norton, 1947) is the standard English language study of the music of the Baroque. Other works by Bukofzer on the subject are "Allegory in Baroque Music," *Journal of the Warburg Institute*, 3 (1939-1940), and "The Baroque in Music History," *Journal of Aesthetics and Art*

Criticism, 14 (1955). A viewpoint taking issue with chapter 1 in *Music in the Baroque Era* is expressed by Arnold Salop in "On Stylistic Unity in Renaissance-Baroque Distinctions," found in *Essays in Musicology: A Birthday Offering for Willi Apel*, Hans Tischler, ed. (Bloomington, Ind., Indiana University Press, 1968). Friedrich Blume's article "Barock," in *Die Musik in Geschichte und Gegenwart*, is essential reading for a study of the Baroque and is available in English translation in Friedrich Blume, **Renaissance and Baroque Music: A Comprehensive Survey* (New York, Norton, 1967). Also useful is Claude V. Palisca, **Baroque Music* (Englewood Cliffs, N.J., Prentice-Hall, 1968). Chapter 10 of Paul Henry Lang, *Music in Western Civilization* (New York, Norton, 1941) treats early Baroque music within the context of the general culture and history of the period. For information on the beginnings of opera see Donald J. Grout, *A Short History of Opera*, 2 vols. (New York, Columbia University Press, 2d ed., 1965).

Selected examples of Baroque music are contained in the *Historical Anthology of Music*, vol. 2, and in *Die Geschichte der Musik in Beispielen*. Much valuable and detailed information about modern editions of Baroque music is contained in the footnotes and bibliographies of Bukofzer, *Music in the Baroque Era*, and in the bibliographies of Palisca, **Baroque Music*. These should be consulted if the reader is seeking information about editions of a specific composer, country, form, or medium.

12

THE following selection on oratorio differs in many respects from the other selections in this anthology. Its subject is a musical form, oratorio, which is surveyed from its beginnings to the early twentieth century; its approach is at the same time explanatory and critical; its source is a standard, scholarly, general encyclopedia commonly found in many homes. Its uniqueness lies, however, not so much in these things as in its insight, its wit, and most of all in the completely disarming charm of its style and expression. Because of these qualities it seems not only unnecessary but out of place to give here an introduction like those given to other selections in this anthology. But an explanation of the reasons for the choice of such an article for inclusion here may be interesting to the reader. These reasons are two: first, as has already been mentioned, the charming manner in which the selection is written, and second, the fact that it first appeared in a general encyclopedia. It is often overlooked that the entries on music in many of the standard reference works are written, and sometimes delightfully so, by musicians of the first rank. Sir Donald Francis Tovey serves as an excellent example. Not only did he contribute to the eleventh and later editions of *Encyclopaedia Britannica*, he also served as musical editor for the fourteenth edition. Unfortunately, Tovey's entries no longer appear in the *Britannica*, having been removed in favor of newer, updated entries. And so, while even the smallest library usually has the earlier editions of the *Britannica*, the reader assumes that the latest edition is the best, not stopping to realize that when an edition is updated it does not mean that the earlier edition was inferior or incorrect in its information, although this may be the case, but that it was probably merely out of date. Thus the work of those such as Tovey can become completely forgotten. To remind the reader that fine writing about music may be hidden away in seemingly unlikely places, and because it is an excellent example of its type, the following selection is included here.

Donald Francis Tovey (1875-1940), pianist, composer, author, and lecturer, was Reid Professor of Music at the University of Edinburgh.

181

His writings on music were mostly in the form of essays, and he is best known for *Essays in Musical Analysis*, 7 vols. (London, Oxford University Press, 1935-1944), and *The Mainstream of Music and Other Essays* (New York, Oxford University Press, 1949).

Oratorio

DONALD F. TOVEY

Oratorio is the name given to a form of religious music with chorus, solo voices and orchestra, independent of, or at least separable from the liturgy, and on a larger scale than the cantata. Its history is involved in that of opera, but its antecedents are more definite. The term is almost certainly (but see Schütz's "stilo Oratorio" on p. 184) derived from fact that St. Filippo Neri's Oratory was the place for which Animuccia's settings of the *Laudi Spirituali* were written; and the custom of interspersing these hymns among liturgical or other forms of the recitation of a Biblical story is one of several origins of modern oratorio. A more ancient source is the use of incidental music in miracle plays and in such dramatic processions as the 12th century *Prose de l'Âne*, which on Jan. 1, celebrated at Beauvais the Flight into Egypt. But the most ancient origin of all is the Roman Catholic rite of reciting, during Holy Week, the story of the Passion according to the Four Gospels, assigning the words of the Evangelist to a tenor, distributing all *ipsissima verba* among appropriate voices, and giving the *responsa turbae,* or utterances of the whole body of disciples (e.g., "Lord, is it I?") and of crowds, to a chorus. The only portion of this scheme that concerned composers was the *responsa turbae,* to which it was permitted to add polyphonic settings of the Seven Last Words or the eucharistic utterances of the Saviour. The narrative and the parts of single speakers were sung in the Gregorian tones appointed in the liturgy. Thus the settings of the Passion by Victoria and Soriano represent a perfect solution of the art-problem of oratorio. "Very tame Jews" is Mendelssohn's comment on the 16th century settings of "Crucify Him"; and it has been argued that Soriano's and Victoria's aim was not to imitate the infuriated Jews, but to express the contrition of devout Christians telling the story. On the other hand, ancient tradition ordained a noisy scraping of feet on the stone floor to indicate the departure from the place of the judgment

FROM *Musical Articles from the Encyclopaedia Britannica* by Donald Francis Tovey (London, Oxford University Press). Reprinted by permission of the publisher.

seat! And so we owe the central forms of Bach's Lutheran Passion-oratorios to the Roman Catholic ritual for Holy Week.

With the monodic revolution at the outset of the 17th century the history of oratorio as an art-form wholly controlled by composers begins. There is nothing but its religious subject to distinguish the first oratorio, Emilio del Cavalieri's *Rappresentazione di anima e di corpo*, from the first opera, Peri's *Euridice*, both produced in 1600. Differentiation was brought about primarily by the fact that oratorios without stage-presentation gave opportunity for a revival of choral music. And oratorios on the stage discouraged, by reason of their sacred subjects, whatever vestiges of dramatic realism could survive the ascendancy of the aria. For lesser composers than Bach and Handel this ubiquitous form represented almost the only possibility of keeping music alive, or at least embalmed, until the advent of the dramatic and sonata styles. The efforts of Carissimi (d. 1674) in oratorio clearly show how limited a divergence from the method of opera was possible when music was first emancipated from the stage. Yet his art shows the corruption of Church music by a secular style rather than the rise of Biblical music-drama to the dignity of Church music. Normal Italian oratorio remains indistinguishable from serious Italian opera as late as *La Betulia liberata*, which Mozart wrote at the age of 15. Handel's *La Resurrezzione* and *Il Trionfo del Tempo* contain many pieces simultaneously used in his operas, and they contain no chorus beyond a perfunctory operatic final tune. *Il Trionfo del Tempo* was a typical morality play, and it became a masque, like *Acis and Galatea* and *Semele*, when Handel at the close of his life adapted it to an English translation with several choral and solo interpolations from other works. Yet between these two versions of the same work lies half the history of classical oratorio. The rest lies in the German Passion-oratorios that culminate in Bach; after which the greatest music avoids every form of oratorio until the two main streams, sadly silted up, and never afterwards quite pure, unite in Mendelssohn.

Luther was so musical that while the German Reformation was far from conservative of ancient liturgy, it retained almost everything which makes for musical coherence in a Church service; unlike the English Church, which with all its insistence on historic continuity, so rearranged the liturgy that no possible music for an English Church service can ever form a coherent whole. The four *Passions* and the *Historia der Auferstehung Christi* of H. Schütz (who was born in 1585, exactly a century before Bach) are as truly the descendants of Victoria's Passions as they are the ancestors of Bach's. They are Protestant in their use of the vulgar tongue, and narrative and dialogue are set to free composition instead of Gregorian chant, although written in Gregorian notation. The *Marcus Passion* is in a weaker and more modern style and stereotyped in its recitative. It may be spurious. But in the other Passions, and most of all in the *Auferstehung*, the recitative is a unique and wonderful language. It may have been accompanied by the organ, though the Passions contain no hint of accompaniment at all. In the *Auferstehung* the Evangelist is accompanied by four viole da gamba in preference to the organ. The players are requested to "execute appropriate runs or passages" during the sustained chords. A final non-scriptural short chorus on a chorale-tune is Schütz's only foreshadowing of the contemplative and hymnal element of later Passion oratorios.

The *Auferstehung*, the richest and most advanced of all Schütz's works, has one strange convention, in that single persons, other than the Evangelist, are frequently represented by more than one voice. If this were confined to the part of the Saviour, it would have shown a reverent avoidance of impersonation, as in Roman Catholic polyphonic settings of the Seven Words. But Schütz writes thus only in *Die Auferstehung* and there on no particular plan. While the three holy women and the two angels on the scene at the tomb are represented naturally by three and two imitative voices, Mary Magdalene is elsewhere always represented by two sopranos.

Shortly before Bach, Passion oratorios were represented by several remarkable works of art, most notably by R. Keiser (1673-1739). Chorale-tunes, mostly in plain harmony, were freely interspersed in order that the congregation might take part in what was, after all, a church service for Holy Week. The meditations of Christendom on each incident of the story were expressed in accompanied recitatives (*arioso*) leading to arias or choruses, and the scriptural narrative was sung to dramatic recitative and ejaculatory chorus on the ancient Roman plan. On slightly different lines was Graun's beautiful *Tod Jesu*, which was famous when the contemporary works of Bach were ignored.

The difference between Bach's Passions and all others is simply the measure of his greatness. Where his chorus represents the whole body of Christendom it has as peculiar an epic power as it is dramatic where it represents tersely the *responsa turbae* of the narrative.

In the Matthew Passion the part of Christ has a special accompaniment of sustained strings, generally at a high pitch, though deepening at the most solemn moments. And at the words "Eli, Eli, lama sabacthani" this musical halo has vanished. In power of declamation Bach was anticipated by Keiser; but no one approached him in sustained inspiration and architectonic greatness. The forms of Passion music may be found in many of Bach's Church cantatas; a favourite type being the *Dialogue;* as, for instance, a dispute between a fearing and a trusting soul with, perhaps, the voice of the Saviour heard from a distance; or a dialogue between Christ and the Church, on the lines of the Song of Solomon. The Christmas Oratorio, a set of six Church cantatas for performance on separate days, treats the Bible story in the same way as the Passions, with a larger proportion of non-dramatic numbers. Many of the single Church cantatas are called oratorios, a term which by Bach's time seems definitely to have implied dialogue, possibly on the strength of a false etymology. Thus Schütz inscribes a monodic sacred piece "in stilo Oratorio," meaning "in the style of recitative." The further history of oratorio radiates from the heterogeneous works of Handel.

There are various types and several mixtures of style in Handelian oratorio. The German forms of Passion music evidently interested Handel, and it was after he came to England, and before his first English oratorio, that he set to music the famous poetic version of the Passion by Brockes, which had been adopted by all the German composers of the time, and which, with very necessary improvements of taste, was largely drawn upon by Bach for the text of his Johannes-Passion. Handel's Brockes Passion does not appear ever to have been performed, though Bach found access to it and made a careful copy; so Handel must have composed it for his own edification. He soon discovered that many kinds of oratorio were possible. The emancipation from the stage admitted of subjects ranging from semi-dramatic histories, like those of *Saul, Esther* and *Belshazzar,* to cosmic schemes expressed entirely in the words of the Bible, such as *Israel in Egypt* and *The Messiah.* Between these types there is every gradation of form and subject, besides an abrupt contrast of literary merit between the mutilated Milton of *Samson* and the amazing absurdities of *Susannah.*

The very name of Handel's first English oratorio, *Esther,* and the facts of its primary purpose as a masque and the origin of its libretto in Racine, show the transition from the stage to the Church; and, on the other hand, Haman's lamentation on his downfall is scandalously adapted from the most sacred part of the Brockes Passion.

We may roughly distinguish three main types of Handelian oratorio, not always maintained singly in whole works, but always available as methods. First, there is the operatic method, in which the arias and recitatives are the utterances of characters in the story, while the chorus is a crowd of Israelites, Babylonians or Romans (*e.g., Athalia, Belshazzar, Saul,* etc.). The second method retains the dramatic rôles both in solos and in choruses, but (as, for instance, in "Envy, eldest born of Hell," in *Saul)* also uses the chorus as the voice of universal Christendom. Handel's audience demanded plenty of arias, most of which are accounted for by futile, when not apocryphal, love affairs. The haughty Merab and the gentle Michal are characterized with fatal ease, and make parts of *Saul* almost as impossible as most of *Susannah.* The third Handelian method is a series of choruses and numbers on a subject altogether beyond the scope of drama, as, for instance, the greater part of *Solomon* and, in the case of *The Messiah* and *Israel in Egypt,* treated entirely in the words of Scripture, and those not in narrative but in prophecy and psalm.

After Bach and Handel, oratorio fell upon evil days. The rise of the sonata style, which brought life to opera, was bad for oratorio; since not only did it accentuate the fashionable dislike of that polyphony which is essential even to mere euphony in choral writing, but its dramatic power became more and more disturbing to the epic treatment that oratorio naturally demands.

Philip Emanuel Bach's oratorios, though cloying in their softness and sweetness, achieved a true balance of style in the earlier days of the conflict; indeed, a judicious selection from *Die Israeliten in der Wüste* (1769) would perhaps bear revival almost as well as Haydn's *Tobias* (1774).

The Creation (Die Schöpfung) and The Seasons *(Die Jahreszeiten)* will always convey to unspoilt music-lovers the profound message of the veteran Haydn, who could not help "worshipping God with a cheerful heart." This spirit was well known to Bach, the composer of *"Mein glaubiges Herze,"* and it is compatible with the romantic sound-pictures and Handelian sublimity of the opening Representation of Chaos and the great chord of C major at the words "and there was light." The childlike gaiety of much of the rest ought not to blind us to its fundamental greatness which brings the naïvely realistic birds and beasts of *The Creation* into line with even the wine-chorus in the mainly secular *Seasons*, and removes Haydn from the influence of the vile taste which henceforth pervaded oratorios, until Mendelssohn effected a partial improvement. Haydn strenuously resisted the persuasion to undertake *The Seasons* which had a close connection with Thomson's poem, as *The Creation* had a distant connection with *Paradise Lost*. He thought the whole scheme "Philistine" (his own word) and, both before he yielded to persuasion and after he had finished the work, said all the hard things about it that have ever been said since.

Roman Catholic oratorio was under the disadvantage that it was not permitted to take Biblical texts except in the Latin language. Jomelli's *Passione* for once had the benefit of a meditative text with some distinction of style; and in closing the first part with a dominant seventh on the word *"pensaci"* he achieved a stroke of genius which at the present day would still startle the listener and leave his mind in the desired frame of meditative astonishment.

But words fail to characterize the libretto of Beethoven's unfortunate *Christus am Oelberge (c.* 1800). The texts of Lutheran church-music had often been grotesque and even disgusting; but their barbarity was pathetic in comparison with the sleek vulgarity of a libretto in which not only is the agony of the garden of Gethsemane represented by an aria (as in Handel's lamentation of Haman), but Christ sings a brilliant duet with the ministering angel. In after years Beethoven had not a good word for this work, which, nevertheless, contains some beautiful music exquisitely scored. And justice demands praise for the idea of making a Hallelujah chorus conclude the work as soon as the betrayal of Christ has been accomplished, thus compensating for the irreverent opening by avoiding all temptation to treat the rest of the passion-story with the same crassness. A well-meant effort was made to provide the *Mount of Olives* with an inoffensive subject in English, but the stupidity of *Engedi: or David in the Wilderness* passes belief.

Schubert's interesting fragment *Lazarus* is strangely prophetic of Wagnerian continuity and has a morbid beauty that transcends its sickly text. There are signs that the despair of the Sadducee was going to be treated with some power. The result might have been a masterpiece; but fate ruled that the next advance should again be Protestant.

Bach's Passions were rediscovered by the boy Mendelssohn after a century of ignorance of their very existence; and in *St. Paul (Paulus)* and *Elijah (Elias)* rose upon the early middle 19th century like the sunrise of a new Handel.

Today *St. Paul* has almost sunk below the horizon; and *Elijah*, which still shares with *The Messiah* the Christmas repertoire of every British urban choral society, is in many points an easy target for criticism. Yet the ascendancy of Mendelssohn is the one redeeming feature in the history of oratorio during the first three quarters of the 19th century. Let us admit the defects of *Elijah;* the all too lifelike tiresomeness of the widow (achieved after strenuous revision), the parochial softness of the double quartet, the Jewishness of the Jews (but is this a defect?), and the snorts of the trombones whose third summons causes the Almighty to capitulate: when all these unconscious profanities are discounted, there remains a vivid and coherent oratorio that, musically and dramatically, towers above later works by many accomplished composers who despise it. Spohr is the only contemporary of Mendelssohn whose sacred music is still known. So tremendous a subject as that of *The Last Judgment*, ought, indeed, to be treated with reserve; but the softness and slowness which pervades nine-tenths of Spohr's work is not reserve but self-indulgence. Spohr has moments of vision; but an almost random glance at the pages of *St. Paul* shows that even in eclipse Mendelssohn has characterization, movement and the capacity for dramatic moments.

In England, the influence of Mendelssohn completed the devastation begun by our inveterate habit of praising the inspired literary skill of the sacred narrative, as a preface to our restatement of it in 40 times as many words of our own. Deans and chapters listened in graceful official pride and imperfectly secret glee to the strains in which the cathedral organist celebrated with equal realism the destruction of Sennacherib's hosts and his own octuply-contrapuntal doctorate of music. Before 1880 our composers had, as Dr. Walker says, "set with almost complete indiscrimination well-nigh every word of the Bible." Had they confined themselves to the second chapter of Ezra they would have escaped dangers of unconscious humour that lurk in the opportunities for "naturalness" in declaiming the dialogues and illustrating the wonders of scriptural narrative.

Neither Sterndale Bennet nor Macfarren improved matters; but Parry and Stanford, towards the end of the century, completely changed the situation. Stanford's *Eden* has a libretto by Robert Bridges. The disgruntled professional librettists, who were also musical critics, had the effrontery to say that this magnificent poem would be the better for extensive cuts. The real truth is that Stanford's music, especially in its orchestral introductions, is diffuse. But it has many beautiful features, and achieves a coherent scheme on exactly such lines of Wagnerian continuity as can be applied to oratorio. Parry preferred to be his own librettist, and by this means he achieved more significant results. The lapses of the amateur poet are less distressing than the *clichés* of the ordinary professional librettist; and the works of Parry and Stanford permanently raised English oratorio from squalor and made it once more an art-form which educated people could enjoy. Some of Parry's architectonic and dramatic ideas will never lose the power to thrill, if only the works as wholes can live in spite of a certain dryness of melody and heaviness of texture. For example, the exploit of Judith is shown with a total avoidance of the cheap and salacious opportunity for a scene between her and Holofernes. Instead, we listen to the watchmen anxiously making their circuit of the city walls in darkness. The music of their march is at a low pitch. It is reaching a normal close when, high above the tonic chord, the cry of Judith bids the watchmen open the gates to her. If this moment cannot thrill, there is no meaning in art. In *King Saul* Parry made a significant discovery as to the emancipation of dramatic oratorio from the stage conditions of time and space. The Witch of Endor prophesies the battle of Gilboa. Her tale becomes real in the telling and is immediately followed by the final dirge.

As with opera, so, but more easily, with oratorio, the method of Wagnerian continuity at last enabled composers to take extant poems and set them to music in their entirety. Thus the fragrant mysticism of Roman Catholic oratorio, dimly adumbrated in Schubert's *Lazarus*, at last came to fruition in Elgar's wonderful setting of Newman's *Dream of Gerontius*, while the old miracle play *Everyman* was very successfully composed by Walford Davies. In his later works, *The Apostles* and *The Kingdom*, Elgar pursues a comprehensive religious design on texts arranged by himself. Oratorio on the basis of Wagnerian continuity and *Leit-motif* is unquestionably a living art-form. Its greatest difficulty is its fatal facility. The oratorio-composer is lost who omits to transcend the limits of the stage; yet when these are transcended only the steadfastness of genius can prevent the composer from sinking to the fashion-storming eclecticism of Honegger's *Le Roi David* which, with the aid of a reciter to read the Bible, takes up the arts of all periods from Handel on and drops each of them before anything like an art-problem arises.

Why not follow more often the method of *The Messiah* and of *Israel in Egypt;* and deal with the religious subjects in terms of prophecy and psalm? Brahms's *Deutsches Requiem* is really an oratorio; and since its production (all but one later movement) in 1866 it continues year by year to tower over all other choral music since Beethoven's Mass in D. Form, disciplined form, is not the only thing needed to save future oratorios from the limbo of vanity; but it is their first need.

Bibliography

As is the case with so many of the subjects covered in this anthology, a comprehensive English-language study of the oratorio does not exist. The best survey in English is that of Ernest Walker, "Oratorio," in *Grove's Dictionary of Music and Musicians,* 5th ed. (1954), vol. 6, pp. 247-262. The current entry on oratorio in *Encyclopaedia Britannica* is by Winton Dean and should be consulted especially for information on oratorio in the twentieth century. Also by Dean is *Handel's Dramatic Oratorios and Masques* (London, Oxford University Press, 1959), an essential reference for the excellent survey of the pre-Handelian oratorio presented in its first chapter as well as for the subject of its title. Detailed analyses of the oratorios of Heinrich Schütz may be found in Hans Joachim Moser, *Heinrich Schütz, His Life and Work,* translated from the 2d rev. ed. (St. Louis, Mo., Concordia, 1959).

A few selected excerpts from seventeenth-century oratorios may be found in vol. 2 of the *Historical Anthology of Music* and in *Die Geschichte der Musik in Beispielen.* Many of the oratorios dating from the time of Handel or later are easily available in one or several modern editions published by G. Schirmer, Kalmus, Peters, and others.

13

THE doctrine of affections, we are frequently told, was one of the principle elements common to all Baroque music. Its appearance may be used to help cite the beginning of the period, and its wane signals the decline of Baroque style. According to the simplistic explanation sometimes given to this complex aesthetic philosophy, any musical motive evokes an emotional response in man, usually a rather well-defined response such as joy, love, or fear. Therefore, if a musical composition is to have unity it must represent only one affect or emotion, which means that it must have only one musical idea or theme. This, then, would seem to indicate that monothematicism is a main characteristic in all Baroque music; it would also explain one of the principal Baroque-Classic distinctions, monothematicism versus polythematicism.

Armed with this apparent truth, one approaches optimistically a toccata of Frescobaldi, for example, to see just how it is representative of Baroque music and to determine what emotion one should try to evoke in the listener when performing it. But, alas, things don't seem to fit very well. Not only are there clearly marked sections within the toccata, each with its different musical theme or motive, but Frescobaldi tells us in his preface that the sections are to be played in different manners, some gay, some languid. As if that were not enough, the composer also tells us that if we wish a shorter piece, we may conclude the toccata at any cadence. What kind of unity of affection is this that permits omission of part of the composition? Retiring somewhat bruised from our first skirmish with Baroque music and the affections, we turn to a fugue of Bach. Surely he must have followed the rules, since his works are the prime examples of Baroque style. In Bach's fugue we can easily find the main theme or subject, although it may not be so easy to determine whether the affect is to be joy, faith, or whatever. But a closer analysis of this fugue may reveal a second theme or countersubject and possibly even a third. By their presence do these additional themes evoke additional affects? What then has happened to the trusted equation that one composition equals one affect equals one motive or musical idea?

In the following selection the author puts the doctrine of the affections and its relation to Baroque music into proper focus. Although a philosophy of affections had been professed by some, perhaps even many, composers since at least the sixteenth century, it was not until the late seventeenth century that it began to be codified into something resembling a system. Thus it does not apply to earlier Baroque music, such as a Frescobaldi toccata of 1637, in the same way that it does to the late Baroque. Furthermore, the doctrine of the affections was only a philosophy which, even though accepted by many, did not dictate to all. Finally, the doctrine of the affections was not a system of composition nor a substitute for musical imagination, nor did it alone govern the achievement of musical form in the Baroque. A late Baroque composition does normally use only one principal theme, and the composer may have had a certain affect in mind to be represented by this theme, but these facts do not preclude the use of additional complementary, rather than contrasting, thematic material. If the composer is competent (and we must not overlook the fact that music has survived that brings the competence of its composers into question), then the thematic material and the way in which it is shaped into a musical composition comes not from some compositional bag of tricks, as the affections are sometimes represented to be, but from the composer's own musical imagination.

Paul Henry Lang is editor of *The Musical Quarterly* and was a faculty member of Columbia University for many years until his retirement in 1970. His writings include a number of periodical contributions and several books, among them *George Frideric Handel* (New York, Norton, 1966), *Music in Western Civilization* (New York, Norton, 1941), and *The Symphony, 1800-1900* (New York, Norton, 1969).

Musical Thought of the Baroque: The Doctrine of Temperaments and Affections

PAUL HENRY LANG

As far as a phenomenon can be reduced to elements which permit quantitative measuring, it can be analyzed objectively and its physical nature explained. For such a procedure empiricism offers a suitable approach, but it is evident that it cannot lead to a full comprehension of an artistic phenomenon. Although rhythm and proportion, converted into optical and acoustical symbols, offer measurable components of every art, the quality, that is, the essentially aesthetic moment, remains irrational. The criterion of the beautiful sees in rhythm and proportion only the means of presentation of an idea. The realization of such ideas is brought about in the several arts in different ways. Most arts present their general ideas in a concrete example: they represent "something." But while this "something" serves as the first act for the realization of a work of art, the essentially aesthetic moment is the "how" of the presentation; the symbolic is manifested in the concrete. It is quite common, however, that the nature of the representation, the primarily aesthetic element, is overshadowed by the object represented. Unlike the other arts, music presents the symbols as pure abstraction not bound by any concrete content. It can embody the "how" without expressing the "something." It does not present content, as the representation is its very content. This absolute music—defined by no elements outside of musical ones—should, then, be conceived as pure contemplation. It is possible, however, to substitute for these purely musically expressed symbols concrete realities. In its urge to achieve a most objective realization of things, rationalism

FROM Paul Henry Lang, *Music in Western Civilization* (New York, W. W. Norton & Company), pp. 434-444. Copyright 1941 by W. W. Norton & Company, Inc. Reprinted by permission of W. W. Norton & Company, Inc., and J. M. Dent & Sons Ltd.

introduced into music the expression of the realities of life. The Renaissance in its *musica reservata*, in its careful observance of the rights of the text, and in its attempted musical representations of comprehensible actions began to demonstrate an interest in a musical art that was not "free." In the subsequent era, music was increasingly dominated by the spoken word, comprehensible ideas, and concrete actions.

The spirit of the Renaissance eschewed medieval longing for the beyond and reinstated love of life as cherished by the ancients. Man and his natural circumstances became the center of interest. The baroque contributed to this new conception a keener sense for the comprehension of characters, passions, and "affections." The subject of arts and letters was man, the conditions of his mental life, the power of his affections, the divergent character of individuals and nations. This was, of course, fully expressed in philosophy, but it was not less plainly evident in the arts. The musical authors of the baroque are fairly well known to the students of music history, for the number of tracts on composition, figured bass, ornamentation, etc., is considerable; but theories of music based on the technical abilities and limitations of musicians and musical instruments do not properly fit under either of the reigning philosophical processes. Beyond this technical apparatus, offered for practical purposes, there were theories concerning style and aesthetics of music, buttressed with profound philosophical contemplations. Unlike the legion of nineteenth- and twentieth-century theoreticians and historians, the musicographers of the baroque did not define music and its style by objective-technical precepts, but saw it conditioned by nationality, time, place; briefly, in the diversity of man's bent of mind. Rationalism sought in music as in other arts the "imitation of nature," the cherished dogma and foundation of its musical thought. We should not, however, expect this to mean tone-painting or program music, or the imitation of sounds that can be found in nature, such as the rippling of a stream, the buzzing of insects, or the chirping of birds. While such things sometimes occupied composers, literal imitations form a very small part of the musical aesthetics of the baroque, the musical thought of which was first and foremost concerned with rendering and translating into music the temper, disposition or frame of mind, passions, and mental reactions characteristic of man. The "doctrine of temperaments and affections" which had already appeared in the anthropological-philosophical literature of the sixteenth century became the nerve center of baroque music. On previous occasions we used the term "affect" as a technical term accepted by modern psychology. In the seventeenth century, however, the Italian *affeti* and the German *Affekte* had a counterpart in the English "affections," a word which today is applied to mild feelings, but which formerly stood for the strongest emotional expressions, distinct from "passions." This can be ascertained from the very title of an *Essay on the Nature and Conduct of the Passions and Affections* (1728), by Francis Hutcheson, Irish metaphysician (1694-1746). The same distinction is encountered in writings on music. "Musick hath 2 ends, first to pleas the sence, & that is done by the pure Dulcor of Harmony, which is found chiefly in ye elder musick, of wᶜʰ much hath been sayd, & more is to come, & secondly to move ye affections or excite passion."[1] It was found advisable to employ the original English word in spite of the strange impression it makes on the modern reader when used in this sense, because the foregoing quotation indicates clearly that to the musician of the seventeenth and eighteenth centuries "affections" and "affective" expressions were definite notions associated with the baroque style, and cannot be replaced by "emotions" or "passions" as modern usage would require.

Athanasius Kircher (1602-1680), the celebrated German polyhistorian, one of the most learned men of the century and the author of treatises on every conceivable subject, is our best witness for the scientific formulation of the doctrine of temperaments and affections in the seventeenth century. In his monumental *Musurgia Universalis*, this eminent Jesuit attempted to give an explanation for the existence of different styles of music:

> Melancholy people like grave, solid, and sad harmony; sanguine persons prefer the *hyporchematic* style (dance music) because it agitates the blood; choleric people like agitated harmonies because of the vehemence of their swollen gall; martially inclined men are partial to trumpets and drums and reject all delicate and pure music; phlegmatic persons lean toward women's voices because their high pitched voice has a benevolent effect on phlegmatic humour.[2]

These were the *constitutio temperamenti* of the individual man, who is conceived as largely passive, exhibiting a leaning or preference for a certain style. To the *constitutio temperamenti* was added an active agent of style, the *constitutio regionis*, with which we are virtually in the neighborhood of Taine's philosophy of art. The *constitutio regionis* stood for the influence of the environment on the creative musical activity of the population, professing that the combination of temperament and environment will result in a national style.

Toward the third quarter of the seventeenth century the rather vague organization of genres and styles gave way to a classification which was to be followed even by the first generations of the eighteenth. In general the writers distinguished between three styles: the *stylus*

---

[1] *The Musicall Grammarian*, by Roger North (c. 1728), edited by Hilda Andrews, London, 1925, p. 15.

[2] Athanasius Kircher, *Musurgia Universalis sive Ars Magna Consoni et Dissoni*, Rome, 1650, VII, 545.

ecclesiasticus, the *stylus cubicularis* (chamber), and the *stylus scenicus seu theatralis*. While composers and writers agreed on this classification, musical thought showed two currents in their interpretation, converging occasionally to produce curious combinations. One of these currents, reactionary in content and nature, summarized once more the classic-medieval elements, the other tendency was progressive and seems remarkably advanced even in this forward-looking period. While the first school of thought offered the professional-formal side of the musician's craft in a naïve and uncritical fashion, the rationalism of the Enlightenment invited reflection and reasoning in the second. Although seemingly irreconcilable, both schools had certain things in common.

Among the leading exponents of the first school we find Agostino Steffani (1654-1728), one of the greatest composers of the late baroque, and Andreas Werckmeister (1645-1708), musician and mathematician, better known for his work in furthering the cause of correct tuning. Werckmeister's musical conceptions still rest, to a considerable extent, on purely medieval precepts; hence his extensive mathematical-musical speculations. To him music is *scientia mathematica*, and in his writings we again meet with the Boethian leitmotives: *ratio* and *sensus*. Allegorical, mystical, and astrological discussions and theses, rather strange in this period, abound.

The second school was headed by the Saxon court conductor Johann David Heinichen (1683-1729), whose writings, highly esteemed in his time, remain sound and useful reading in our day and are one of the chief sources of the doctrine of the affections.[3] The picture that confronts us on these lively pages differs sharply from the one painted by the exponents of the other school. Heinichen's tirades against the ancients sound like the radical diatribes of the modernists. He berates their "so-called sense and judgments," and their "overwhelming and exaggerated metaphysical contemplations"; all that matters is "how the listeners like it," and it is immaterial how it looks on paper. With this we encounter a new criterion, the taste and approval of the public, and, indeed, the French term *goût* now makes its first appearance in musical literature. There is mention of French and Italian *goût*, *goût der Welt*, or "universal taste," which would be a "happy mixture" of all styles, unmistakably an idea of the rationalistic Enlightment.

The Alsatian Sébastien de Brossard (c. 1654-1730), learned priest, church composer, and conductor, whose remarkable library, offered to Louis XV, furnished the groundstock for the collection of old music of the Bibliothèque Nationale, is another important representative of baroque musical thought. He was the author of one of the oldest musical

---

[3]Johann David Heinichen, *Neu erfundene und gründliche Anweisung*, Hamburg, 1711.

encyclopedias,[4] an excellent work rich in documents and information concerning the musical life of his times.[5] A fact of great interest is Brossard's emphasis on the origin of styles, which he places in Italy. His enumeration shows the wide dissemination of the doctrine of the affections and temperaments:

> Style means, in general, the particular manner or fashion of expressing ideas, of writing, or of doing some other thing. In music, it signifies the manner in which every individual composes, plays or teaches, and all this is very diversified according to the genius of the authors, the country and the nation: as well as according to the materials, the places, the times, the subjects, the expressions, etc. Thus one is wont to say the style of Carissimi, of Lully, of Lambert, etc; the style of the Italians, of the French, of the Spaniards, etc. The style of gay and joyful music is very different from the style of grave and serious music . . . therefore we have different epithets in order to distinguish among all these different characters, such as ancient and modern style, Italian, French, and German style, ecclesiastic, dramatic, and chamber style, etc. . . . The Italians have expressions for all that we have mentioned, and we shall explain them in the order of their importance.

The last sentence is of great significance, for *à leur rang*, "in the order of their importance," is meant to apply to the degree of affective communication in the various styles and genres. Consequently we are dealing here with the conception and classification of music which is neither mathematical-symbolical, like that of the Middle Ages or of such baroque theoreticians as Kircher and Werckmeister, nor formal-empirical, like that of the Italians, but an aesthetic conception which attempts to range the musical phenomena according to established laws of evaluation and appraisal. The measure was supplied by the doctrine of the affections being identified with the content, and their provocation being considered the sole aim and purpose of music.

The music of the baroque sprang from the background furnished by the affections and temperaments; and from its very beginnings preference was accorded to music connected with words and action. While the importance of the literary element was recognized by Zarlino and other earlier musician-thinkers, it is only natural that it was the rising opera which contributed the decisive opportunity for a development of the new principles of musical aesthetics and composition. The literary element dominated this new musical style at the outset so completely that, in the recitative, it dissolved the musical structure. Musical composition lost some of its absolute-musical traits; on the other hand it was en-

---

[4]Brossard, *Dictionnaire de Musique*, Paris, 1703.
[5]Cf. Michel Brenet, *Sébastien de Brossard d'après des Papiers Inédits*, Paris, 1896.

riched by new characteristics and means of expression of a dramatic nature. The danger of delivering music to drama altogether by abandoning its purely musical qualities was a real one. Fortunately the sheer musical genius of such men as Monteverdi was able to retain the intrinsic values of music and place it in the service of new ideals, unscathed and even enhanced, at the very time when the literary amateurs were about to submerge music completely. But the aesthetic interest of his contemporaries was concentrated primarily on the dramatic; they wanted to gain insight through aesthetic sensation, thereby relegating the essential in art to a secondary place. Like philosophical rationalism, this rationalistic aesthetics found its most radical and uncompromising representatives in France. Lamotte-Houdar, the Abbé Pluche,[6] the Abbé Dubos,[7] Batteux,[8] and Voltaire advocated a conception of the beautiful which was independent of sentiments. Boileau's maxim *Rien n'est beau que le vrai* became the guiding principle and soon took the form of "imitation of nature," finding immediate application in music.

This aesthetic orientation viewed art solely from an intellectual angle, Lamotte-Houdar going so far as to deny any merit and necessity for versification in poetry and declaring the essence of poetry to lie in the boldness of the ideas, the truth of the pictures, and the power of expression. As a logical consequence of his beliefs, Lamotte-Houdar wrote his odes and tragedies in prose. It is easy to see in what way music would suffer from such tenets, and while Fontenelle's famous saying, "Sonate, que me veux tu?" may be considered an extreme attitude, valid only in France, it is undeniable that pure instrumental music was placed at a level considerably below that of vocal music. The main objection to instrumental music was that it was not able clearly to express the affections. Since the prevailing aesthetic conception considered the affections the only content of music, this limited affective expressiveness was a serious shortcoming in their eyes. "An instrumental player or composer must observe the rules which lead to good melody and harmony much more clearly and assiduously than a singer or a choral composer, because when singing, the singer or composer is aided by the great clarity of the words, while the latter are always missing in instrumental music."[9] At the same time the old ethical and symbolic connotations attached to musical instruments were transformed and their erstwhile sociological ties disappeared. With Mattheson, the most important theoretical writer of the late baroque, the instruments became integral parts of the general *Affektenlehre,* the doctrine of the affections. He speaks of the "most magnificently sounding trombones, the lovely pompous horns, the proud

[6]L'Abbé Pluche, *Spectacle de la Nature,* Paris, 1732.
[7]L'Abbé Dubos, *Réflexions Critiques,* Paris, 1719.
[8]Charles Batteux, *Les Beaux Arts, Réduits à un Même Principe,* Paris, 1743.
[9]Johann Mattheson, *Der Vollkommene Capellmeister,* Hamburg, 1739, p. 82.

bassoons, the harsh cornets, the modest flutes, the heroic kettledrums, the flattering lutes, the solid *viole da braccio*, the grumbling bass fiddles," etc.[10] All this should not be confused, however, with the purely extraneous, sensualistic, tone-color characterization of the nineteenth century, although the starting point of the romantic orchestral color palette undoubtedly lies in the affective expression of the late baroque.

Beginning with Mattheson the philosophical conceptions and empirical leanings of the Enlightenment began to displace entirely the many medieval survivals still extant in earlier baroque musical thought. In his very first work, *Das Neu-Eröffnete Orchestre* (1713), the tendency to turn to the educated music lover instead of to the professional musician is apparent. The ideal of the Enlightenment, the universally cultured man, the *homme galant*, becomes the addressee of dissertations. The aim is no longer to justify new theoretical findings by reconciling them with ancient musical doctrines or to introduce musicians into the art and science of musical composition, but to enable the educated person to "form his tastes, understand the technical terms, so that he can discuss this noble science with understanding." With this begins an entirely new era of musical thought.

Rationalism — Irrationalism — Symbolism

The rationalistic tendency in baroque thinking cannot, however, be applied to music with the exclusiveness and simplicity demonstrated by such exponents of musical symbolism as Albert Schweitzer, the distinguished biographer of Johann Sebastian Bach. What seems to be a hard and fast system in the writings of the theoreticians, in the manuals of composition, and in the recorded statements of composers, is not borne out completely by the compositions themselves. The intuitively creating musician remained "irrational" to a considerable degree even though he was a true child of the baroque, and it is only our unfamiliarity with the baroque style and with the overwhelming majority of its musicians that makes us take the naïve and often puerile "realism" and "symbolism" apparent in the works of even the greatest of baroque musicians for the essential stylistic feature of this art. Music that would reflect, weigh, and reason at every turn would abandon the most precious of its possessions: the immediate, elementally musical invention.

The empirical process of discovering laws of nature is rooted in observation to the exclusion of preconceived theoretical doctrines, while the scientific process follows a planned route. In the course of musical his-

[10]Johann Mattheson, *Das Neu-Eröffnete Orchestre*, Hamburg, 1713, I, 266.

tory it was demonstrated that practitioners of either of the two methods could not avoid instinctive application of both precepts. The Pythagorean interval doctrines of medieval theorists, making the third into a dissonance, did not prevent the gradual rise of a new conception of consonance based precisely on the proscribed third, and when Zarlino offered his harmonic system he only codified and equipped with a scientific apparatus a doctrine long in universal use. The empiric origin of such procedures is even more strikingly illustrated by the next phase of harmonic thought. The eighteenth century undertook a scientific investigation of the whole tonal system, emphasizing the physical aspects of the interval doctrine rather than its mathematical aspects. In Rameau's *Traité de l'Harmonie Réduite à Ses Principes Naturels* (1722), the laws of chordal associations were formulated into a system which is recognized today as the basis of modern musical composition. Yet the system was effectively prepared by the practical figuring of the thorough bass, providing a statistical list of the chords in actual use. The most commonly used chords soon became so stereotyped that their arbitrarily established graphical measurements (from the bass) stood henceforth for constant notions such as the sixth chord, the seventh chord, etc. It was not long before the laws of harmony and harmonic progressions, hidden behind the graphic symbols, were recognized and brought into a logical system. Empiricism was able, then, to establish the musical physiognomy of harmony by laws of nature as manifested in the harmonic overtones.

Thus the problem confronting us in the musical thought of the baroque is not so much the attitude of theoreticians and composers, admittedly derived from philosophical sources: it is, rather, whether music developed within its province, by its own powers, and without the conscious application of scientific theories, an artistic will and tendency which was in sympathy with the general trend of culture and civilization.

Viewed from the premises of general aesthetics, it is evident that ever since the late Renaissance music was gradually leaving the sphere of "absolute music," absorbing poetic and pictorial characteristics. While this is instantly discernible in vocal music, it is not less unmistakably present in instrumental music, supposedly least susceptible to extramusical stimuli. The early instrumental paraphrases of songs as well as canzoni and ricercari carried with them the lyric mood of the vocal models. In the simpler examples the periodic construction still showed the formal structure of the original piece of poetry. The dance pieces of the instrumental suites also carried with them a lyric atmosphere recalling the poetic origin of dance songs. But perhaps the most influential agent in shaping the future of free music was the music drama. The music drama impressed itself so firmly on the whole field of musical composition that we can safely say that all important innovations, from the early seventeenth century to our day, can be attributed to operatic influences. The overture shows this clearly, as does the modern symphonic poem, its first cousin, but the seemingly independent forms of instrumental music exhibit it with equal certitude, although more subtly.

The student trying to find his way in this labyrinth is likely to forget a fact of the utmost importance: namely, that the arts, especially music, were struggling for equality with the sciences, for to be classified with the sciences meant to be accorded a higher intellectual rank. Hence we have the many rationalistic codifications of simple musical practice, codifications and summaries which freeze the elastic spirit of living art into inexorable rules and definitions. The formal-structural importance of the affections found, of course, a scientific formulation in musical literature. Manuals containing musical "figures" which corresponded to certain affections began to appear with Mauritius Vogt's *Conclave Thesauri Magnae Artis Musicae* (Prague, 1711), and toward the middle of the century there was offered a thorough exposition of "the doctrine of the musical figures" in Johann Adolf Scheibe's *Der Critische Musicus*. Using Gottsched's *Critische Dichtkunst* as his model, Scheibe expounds the importance of the figures, emphasizing that, far from being mannerisms, they are the components of musical form, decisive factors, and therefore not casual or arbitrary but essential parts of musical composition itself. While these figures seem naïve and are cloaked in a formidable scientific garb—Vogt employs terms like *polyptoton, polysyntheton, schematoides,* etc.—there can be no question that the theoreticians merely tried to express in the current rational-scientific manner what was widely practiced by the musical composers. Wherever we look in contemporary literature we shall find the same anxiety to warn the reader of the presence of the affections for fear he will not notice them. Georg Muffat, in the preface of his *Florilegium,* found it advisable to warn his "friendly reader" that if he finds in these compositions "rough and strange" things he should not ascribe them to a "dry and coarse style"; such flaws are rather due to the fact that "to elucidate certain words, manners, or gestures, one has to compromise occasionally."[11]

All this was taken too literally by a number of authors, chief among them Schweitzer, who attempted to explain the whole art and style of Bach on the basis of symbolism and the doctrine of the musical figures. While his contentions are often true, especially in relation to vocal music, the essence of baroque form lies in far less concrete formulae. Form in baroque music, especially in instrumental music, is to be understood as the consequence of the elevation and exaltation of soul and mood, a circumstance which is not an aesthetic, but a real, psychological elevation and exaltation. That is the reason why the authors standing at the opposite pole from Schweitzer are even more at a loss when

---

[11]Cf. *DDT,* II, 19.

they attempt to approach the music of this period by the time-honored methods of nineteenth-century musical theory. The counting of measures and the enumeration of modulations are as meaningless in this era as in the music of Schönberg. The specific formal principle of the baroque is the statement of the "basic affection" and its subsequent exploitation by continuous expansion. This means that the basic affection (which) does not necessarily express any concrete idea or notion must be stated in the most pregnant and concentrated manner—the fugue theme—for the rest of the musical composition depends on it. The baroque sonata does not have contrasting themes as used by the symphonists of the classic era, for it is concerned with the exploitation of *one* affection which would be weakened and disturbed by additional material, introducing a different state of mind, idea, or affection. The robust directness, the magnificent pathos, the sharp delineation of the opening measures in Buxtehude's or Handel's compositions testify to the affective concentration at the beginning of baroque musical form. Once a fugue or a concerto gets under way, it brooks no obstacles, ignores challenges, refuses to pause until it reaches its destination, which is the end; the material is exhausted. Thus baroque form gives free rein to the artist's imagination, and nothing can illustrate more clearly the profound misunderstanding of the essence of this art than the statement found in most counterpoint treatises and histories of music that the fugue is "the strictest form of polyphonic writing," with hard and fast rules governing its construction. Ebenezer Prout in the preface to his *Fugue* (1891) actually mentions the instance of a counterpoint teacher in his time who forbade the study of Bach's fugues because they are "contrary to the rules." It would be difficult, indeed, to find many among Bach's fugues that are built on the same plan. Modern writers have recognized that the fugal form—most representative and highest of baroque forms—may be said to be "a question of texture rather than of design" (Tovey), a conception which comes near to the essence of freely unfolding baroque form. Viewed from the conventional angle of formal theories (usually labeled "classical," although with little justification), this baroque unfolding of music seems essentially formless, always reaching out for wider expanses and never ending; but history teaches us how quickly the understanding of the art of even a recent period vanishes.

If we do not understand the music of the baroque, the latter was not less estranged from the Renaissance, and it is astounding to observe how remote was the second half of the seventeenth century from the great art of the late Renaissance. Italian writers between about 1660 and 1670 speak of Palestrina and Lassus as *gli antichi*, considering their music archaic, written in the *stylus gravis* to the exclusion of any other style. These ancient composers had "but one style and one manner," while the *moderni* have three. Brossard distinguished three musical eras, the *musica antiqua, the musica antiquo-moderna,* which is "modern when compared to the Greeks but ancient when compared to ours," and, finally, music that is *veritablement moderne.* The first era lasted until Guido d'Arezzo; the second, "a sort of grave and serious music for many voices," reigned from Guido's time "until the beginning of the past [seventeenth] century," the third being that "which started about fifty or sixty years ago [Brossard writing in 1703] when musicians started to improve music and make it more gay and expressive and better suited to the text."

There was, then, a fundamental metamorphosis in musical thought already in full swing in the early baroque, shifting the ideal-symbolic toward the concrete-illustrative. The temper of the baroque, the dominating musico-dramatic style, explains the preponderance of operatic aesthetics. The field of action of music was undoubtedly immensely enriched by the tendency toward truth of expression and experience, but, by forgetting that music was originally pure tonal effect free of descriptive or delineative elements forced on it from without, composers and writers came very near to abandoning the fundamental principles of musical aesthetics. Fortunately, the transition period between baroque and classicism was weathered, and when, toward the middle of the eighteenth century, rationalism arrived at the crossroads it admitted that imagination is a thing by itself, and conceded to it laws and properties that were different from those of reason. The new philosophical orientation freed music once more from reflection and reasoning and restored its immanent, absolute-musical powers, launching it into another glorious period of flowering.

Bibliography

Most of the works pertaining to the doctrine of the affections are in German. Bibliographies listing these German language works may be found under "Affections, doctrine of" in the *Harvard Dictionary of Music,* 2d ed. (1969) and "Affektenlehre" in *Die Musik in Geschichte und Gegenwart,* vol. 1, pp. 113–121. Several of the items listed in the bibliography following "The Beginning of the Baroque in Music" (see page 179) treat the subject of the affections, especially the work of Blume and two of those of Bukofzer, *Music in the Baroque Era* and "Allegory in Baroque Music."

14

IT has already been pointed out several times in this anthology that the Baroque period is far from an indivisible unit. The latter third of the seventeenth century is considered the dividing point between an Early Baroque and a Late or High Baroque. Music written after this date no longer sounds strange to the modern ear. Certainly there are obvious stylistic differences between the music of the Late Baroque and that of Classicism or Romanticism, but the Late Baroque no longer contains those traces of archaism which may still be sensed in the Early Baroque. The phenomenon which erases any such archaism and makes the style completely acceptable to the modern ear is the subject of the following selection, tonality.

Strictly speaking, tonality is not the proper term to identify this phenomenon. Tonality actually means the state of having a tonal center, of there being one tone or pitch around which all the other tones tend to be subordinated, a tone which is obviously sensed as a final resting point for a composition. When one speaks of the rise of tonality this implies that there was a time when music had no tonality or tonal center, and this is not exactly true. All the music which has been discussed thus far in this anthology, from Gregorian chant on, had tonal centers in this general sense. What actually arose near the end of the seventeenth century was not the presence of a tonal center but a new means of establishing and maintaining that tonal center. This new means was in the form of a harmonic system which has come to be identified as "functional harmony."

Harmonic progressions had occurred at cadences in music since the beginning of polyphony, but they resulted from melodic formulae commonly used at cadences rather than from an intentional harmonic plan. Gradually, during the fifteenth, sixteenth, and seventeenth centuries, more attention came to be paid to harmonic progressions as ends in themselves until by the time of the late seventeenth century a harmonic system had been established into which all chords then in use had been absorbed and under which they progressed according to convention. These conventional harmonic progressions were so convincing to the ear that it seemed as if they alone established tonal centers and that by means of harmonic progressions one could change the tonal center of a composition, denying the old tonal center and establishing a new one. Melodic structure now dictated or at least implied a harmonic progression which established tonality. This system of traditional harmony, which remained essentially unchanged for two centuries, most clearly identifies the style of Western music from the late seventeenth to the late nineteenth century.

For biographical information concerning Manfred Bukofzer see page 127

The Rise of Tonality

MANFRED F. BUKOFZER

It is a strange though incontestable fact that of the immense treasure of baroque music only certain compositions in late baroque style have succeeded in finding a permanent, if subordinate, place in the present-day musical repertory and that, as a consequence, the characteristics of late baroque style are commonly mistaken for those of the baroque as a whole. It would be wrong to explain this preference by contending that the late baroque masters were "greater" than their predecessors; this interpretation would only confirm the lack of familiarity with the previous periods of baroque music. The reason lies deeper than that. Late baroque music does indeed differ from that of the earlier phases of baroque style in one important respect: it is written in the idiom of fully established tonality. After the pre-tonal experimentations of the early baroque and the use of a rudimentary tonality in the middle baroque period, the definitive realization of tonality in Italy about 1680 marks the decisive turning point in the history of harmony which coincides with the beginning of the late baroque period. It is precisely the use of tonality in the late baroque that connects this period more closely than any other with the living musical repertory of today.

TONALITY was not "invented" by a single composer or a single school. It emerged at approximately the same time in the Neapolitan opera and in the instrumental music of the Bologna school and was codified by Rameau more than a generation after its first appearance in music. Tonality established a graduated system of chordal relations between a tonal center (the tonic triad in major or minor) and the other triads (or seventh chords) of the diatonic scale. None of these chords was in itself new, but they now served a new function, namely that of circumscribing

FROM Manfred F. Bukofzer, *Music in the Baroque Era: From Monteverdi to Bach* (New York, W. W. Norton & Company, Inc.), pp. 219-222. Copyright 1947 by W. W. Norton & Company, Inc. Reprinted by permission of W. W. Norton & Company, Inc., and J. M. Dent & Sons Ltd.

the key. While in middle baroque harmony this function had been performed chiefly by the two dominants, it was now extended to all chords.
Significantly, this inclusive system of chordal functions is known as functional harmony.

The functional or tonal chord progressions are governed by the drive
to the cadence which releases the tension that the movement away from
the tonic produces. The technical means of achieving key-feeling were,
aside from the cadence itself, diatonic sequences of chords that gravi-
tated toward the tonal center. The degree of attraction depended on the
distance of the chords from the tonic, and this distance was measured
and determined by the circle of fifths. The sequence in fifths crystallized
as the most common and conspicuous harmonic formula that underlay
the harmonic structure of an extended piece. The diatonic circle always
included a diminished fifth and precisely this irregularity gave it its defining power with regard to key. The logic of chord progressions was
heightened by melodic means, such as dovetailing suspensions of the
seventh. Seventh chords on every degree of the scale, one of the most
characteristic earmarks of late baroque music, were uncommon in early
and middle baroque harmony. Also the seventh chord on the leading
tone in minor (diminished-seventh chord) became an important resource
of tonality. It was considered not as a chromatically altered chord but
as a member of the diatonic family. It had already occurred in early
baroque harmony, though only sporadically and not in the strictly tonal
function it acquired now. Its dissonant quality made it the favorite chord
at climactic points placed directly before the release of the accumulated
tension in the final cadence.

Among the various harmonic formulas and sequences that tonality
employed, the descending series of sixth chords stands out as another
important resource. Tonally less conclusive than the circle of fifths and
still subservient to contrapuntal part-writing, it harmonized the steps of
the scale in diatonic fashion and thus also served as a means of circumscribing the key. This formula occurred in its barest form with Corelli
(see the example on page 209) who was the first to put the tonal formulas to systematic use.

Both formulas appear so often in late baroque style that it can be
categorically stated that there is hardly a composition in late baroque
style in which they are not present. The formulas presented the tones of
the diatonic scale in systematic form, preferably in descending order, and
defined the key; however, since they could be interrupted at any point
they served at the same time as the main means of modulation. Simple
as they may seem today, they were elaborated time and again with
astonishing resourcefulness.

The establishment of tonality naturally affected all aspects of composition. Above all, it permeated the contrapuntal writing. The absorp-

66. Corelli: Excerpt from violin sonata op. 5, 7.

tion of tonality into counterpoint gave the melodic design and the contrapuntal texture unprecedented harmonic support. The poignant melodic dissonances or "false" intervals could not be integrated into the tonal system. The interpenetration of harmony and counterpoint resulted in the harmonically saturated or "luxuriant" counterpoint of the late baroque period, which began with Corelli and cluminated in the works of Bach. Tonality provided also a framework of harmony able to sustain large forms. It set up harmonic goals without which the extended forms of late baroque music would not have been possible. It gave a new perspective to the two structural voices of the composition. In the relation between melody and chord progression the consideration of the latter began to weigh more heavily than the former. The melodies were increasingly conditioned by and dependent on the harmonic accompaniment—a process that led finally to the homophony of the Mannheim school. However, in late baroque music the homophony was held in check by the continuo which preserved the dualistic conception of musical structure. The harmonic orientation was thus counterbalanced by the melodic orientation of the bass. This most characteristic idiom may be designated as continuo-homophony after its two constituent elements. Luxuriant counterpoint and continuo-homophony represent opposite poles in the texture of late baroque music. Continuo-homophony differed from the plain homophony of the Mannheim school in its fast harmonic rhythm and its energetic and sweeping rhythmic patterns that prevailed in both melody and bass.

Continuo-homophony originated in the concerto style which must be regarded as the most significant stylistic innovation of the late baroque period because it pervaded not only the concerto but also all other forms of music, both instrumental and vocal. The concerto style realized a strictly instrumental ideal of abstract or "absolute" music. It was characterized by its consistent adoption of continuo-homophony, frequent unison passages in all voices, fast harmonic rhythm, and themes that emphatically circumscribed the key by stressing the fundamental triads and the diatonic scale. Contrapuntal writing disintegrated in the concerto style under the impact of continuo-homophony and remained essential only to the outermost voices. In the *allegro* movements the instrumental nature of the concerto style became particularly obvious in such features as rapid tone repetitions, fast scale passages, and the wide range of the themes. The rhythmic energy manifested by the mechanical and ceaselessly progressing beats was aptly described by North as the "fire and fury of the Italian style."

Bibliography

Most of the writing about tonality is not pertinent here since it is largely concerned with manifestations of tonality outside the period ruled by functional harmony. The first codification of the functional system of harmony appears in the theoretical writings of Jean-Philippe Rameau, beginning with his *Traité de l'harmonie réduite à ses principes naturels* (Paris, Ballard, 1722). The complete theoretical writings of Rameau are being reprinted in a facsimile of the original French edition by the American Institute of Musicology. To date five volumes of the series, apparently projected in six volumes, are available, including the harmonic treatise and the theoretical system as vols. 1 and 2, respectively. Relative to Rameau see also the article by J. Ferris, "The Evolution of Rameau's Harmonic Theories," *Journal of Music Theory*, 3 (1959).

Rameau's music has been edited by C. Saint-Saëns and published in an eighteen volume set, *Oeuvres complètes* (Paris, Durand, 1895-1913). Despite the title the set is not quite complete according to Rameau scholars.

15

THE Baroque era saw the establishment of many of the musical forms and media which were to be foremost in Western music during the next three centuries. Although their contemporary counterparts have changed from their Baroque ancestors, sometimes almost beyond recognition, opera, cantata, oratorio, sonata, symphony, overture, suite, and concerto all can trace their origin back to the turn of the seventeenth century. It is immediately obvious from a glance at the above list that some of those forms require voices for performance; it may not be quite so obvious, but it is nonetheless true, that *all* require instruments for performance. The seventeenth century was one which saw a growth in the development of instrumental music unprecedented in the history of music. Instruments no longer merely accompanied voices or dancing; they existed in church and concert performance for their own sake. Instrumental ensembles, originally created to accompany vocal music in church or opera, began to break away from their parent organizations and to experience an independent life. Ensembles increased in size, and frequently more than one player was required per part. Once this point was reached, the stage of the chamber ensemble had been passed and the orchestra was born. The orchestra could and did bring many aspects of style and musical form with it from the church and from opera, but it could not lead an independent concert existence on these alone. Such things as the sinfonia and ritornello were not intended to stand as independent forms, though their ideas could be retained and reworked into a new form. But a new form was needed for the new instrument that was the orchestra, and that new form was to be the concerto.

Baroque concertos were of three types, the concerto grosso, the solo concerto, and the orchestral or ripieno concerto, all of which experienced a period of great brilliance during the Late Baroque. By the mid-eighteenth century, however, further evolution had taken place so that the Classic versions of the concerto forms are not always immediately recognizable as the children of their Baroque parents. The concerto grosso and the orchestral concerto gave way to the newer sonata-symphony of the

German and Austrian composers, notably Franz Joseph Haydn. The solo concerto went forward in the form of the new piano concertos of Johann Christian Bach, youngest son of Johann Sebastian Bach, and on to the magnificent concertos of Mozart.

Arthur James Bramwell Hutchings is Professor of Music at the University of Exeter. His writings include *Church Music in the 19th Century* (New York, Oxford University Press, 1967), the section on the nineteenth century in vol. 3 of *The Pelican History of Music* (Harmondsworth, Middlesex, Penguin, 1968), and *The Baroque Concerto* (London, Faber & Faber, 1961; New York, Norton, 1965), as well as works on Schubert, Edmund Rubbra, and Delius.

The Origins of the Baroque Concerto

ARTHUR HUTCHINGS

However late or early the year to which different historians may assign the emergence of the concerto as a distinct genre, 1700 is a reasonably approximate year from which to trace the spread of concertos from Italy into the court and church orchestras of German-speaking States, and 1715—just after Roger had printed Corelli's Op. 6 and Vivaldi's Op. 3—a reasonably approximate year from which to observe such a rapid growth in the cultivation of concertos that the printers of Amsterdam and elsewhere issued band parts of hundreds of sets of concertos within a few decades, almost to the exclusion of other kinds of orchestral music. What they printed was no longer performed for aristocratic pleasure only. The concerto was the first orchestral form to be composed expressly for the most popular modern service of serious music—the orchestral concert; Londoners enjoyed public concerts before it was born; other European capitals were to establish regular public concerts during the years which saw the conquest of private court orchestras by the Italian concerto.

People who frequent concerts of purely instrumental music must either be attracted to sound as a moth to light and enjoy it in a kind of hypnosis or trance, or else their musical experience enables them to be satisfied with the forms and processes of music without help from words or dramatic action, such as dancing. In the early years of the concerto few commoners except the citizens of London had opportunity to gain such musical experience, but we should remember that it was available in many of the greater Italian and German churches. Cities as far apart as Bologna and Hamburg were famous as much for instrumental as for vocal music before 1700, yet Italians and Germans were slow to begin regular public concerts. When the San Cassiano Theatre first offered public opera at Venice in 1637 the popular demand for one kind of mu-

FROM Arthur Hutchings, *The Baroque Concerto* (New York, W. W. Norton & Company, Inc.), pp. 15-24. Copyright © 1961 by Arthur Hutchings. Reprinted by permission of W. W. Norton & Company, Inc., and Faber and Faber Limited. This selection is Chapter 1, "The Period and the Places," of Professor Hutching's book.

sic that had formerly been a princely pleasure was enormous; new opera houses were quickly opened for the general public in Venice and elsewhere; but only in London, Hamburg, Vienna, and perhaps one or two places concerning which I lack relevant information, did large numbers of citizens show themselves eager to enjoy the chamber music of the privileged until the eighteenth century was well advanced.

On returning to their estates, many of the princes and dukes who visited France during the grand epoch sought to recapture their enjoyment of the first famously disciplined orchestra—the royal band selected and trained by Lully to outshine the Twenty Four. They increased their own musical establishments, some of them to a larger complement of players than Lully's, sent their musicians to study the French methods, imported enough overtures and suites to provide an immediate French repertory, and expected their composers to add to it. At the beginning of the eighteenth century the largest orchestras in the royal, ducal or episcopal courts were those of Dresden, Stuttgart, Darmstadt, Vienna, Munich, Gotha, Grosswardein, Regensburg and Passau. Within a few years some hundred feudal rulers had augmented or bettered their orchestras, whether they had set up an opera theatre or not, by seeking leaders and trainers from Italy. During the century a small orchestra sometimes became a large and famous one when a highly musical employer succeeded to the throne, as at Stuttgart, Dresden, Hanover, Potsdam and Mannheim in turn.

Ensembles of few or many instruments in Italian courts and churches were more affected by "the French style" than some of our standard histories suggest, for the rhythms of many of Corelli's movements (even in church sonatas and concertos) were of French origin. Although the concerto came from Bologna and Rome, it was enriched when German musicians applied its principles and style of performance to the French overtures which they already knew how to compose. What they called an overture was a suite. Its opening was the composite slow-fast movement which we still call a French overture, after which there followed from three to as many as nine dance movements, the last of which might be a chaconne or a march, but was usually a gigue. Sometimes other movements than the first were quite long and ambitious, no longer the simple organisms that accompanied a ballet or divertissement.

Neither the concert-goer nor the discophile hears much of the early orchestral repertory in "the French style." The part of it that was imported from the ballets and operas of Lully, Campra, Destouches and other French composers became chamber music by the transfer; but the German court composers produced it specifically for concerts, for listening to an orchestra, and their workmanship was often superior to the French. The only works often heard in modern concerts to represent their efforts are the last and finest examples—Bach's suite in D with the trumpets and drums, his concerto-like suite in B minor for flute and strings, together with Handel's *Water Music* and *Fireworks Music*. When "the Italian style" shared programmes with "the French style" — in short when concertos joined overtures — music for instruments alone was still classified under a name that associated it with grand residences. It was chamber music unless it was played in church or theatre. Just as overtures, chaconnes and other dances had come first from the theatre, the Italian concertos had come from church sonatas and were used at High Mass. We speak of concerts and recitals, but in the seventeenth and eighteenth centuries music was named after the places in which it sounded — church, theatre, chamber — and according to that classification we do not hear church music when we listen to Bach's organ works in a concert hall, to theatre music when one of Handel's overtures is played in a cathedral, or to dance music when we play jazz records. Church sonatas became chamber music at sessions of the Bologna academies, in court music rooms or in London taverns. Within them, sober movements derived from sarabands, gavottes and other measures of the French suite would not openly be labelled with the names of the dances in a sonata or concerto *da chiesa*, yet such a sonata or concerto became chamber music in the Ottoboni Palace or the Queen of Sweden's music room. The rapid ascent of the concerto in the eighteenth century testifies not only to the number and quality of chamber concerts given by private orchestras maintained by aristocrats but also to the inauguration of regular public concerts, of music societies, academies and *collegia musica* in cities and universities which had rarely heard an ensemble of more than a few instruments.

We shall devote a chapter to the spread of concerts in various European countries and the conditions in which concertos were first performed. We are concerned here only to notice that the occurrence of a novel idea in Corelli's imagination was not alone responsible for the rise of the concerto grosso between 1680 and 1700. Concerti grossi had not suddenly grown after privileged visitors to the court of Louis XIV heard Lully's orchestra, nor did Englishmen compose a treasury of works on the scale of concertos for the English royal band. Purcell's overtures which include a trumpet (for instance the famous one in *The Indian Queen*) are not unlike the contemporary Bolognese trumpet concertos which they outshine, and of course there were listeners who enjoyed Purcell's overtures, chaconnes and dances as absolute music, just as there were English listeners to sonatas and string fantasias; but the fully orchestral works came within dramatic conceptions.

The time during which the concerto first appeared was not accidental; nor were the places associated with its emergence. The foremost Italian devotees of sonatas were members of the university and city of Bologna, ducal families who maintained chamber musicians, and the aristocracy of Rome, especially Cardinals Panfili and Ottoboni, and Queen Christina of Sweden.[1] Ottoboni's Academy of Arcadians, though enrolled for the avowed purpose of furthering the sciences and humane letters, especially poetry, was far more interested in music. Corelli lived and worked in the Ottoboni Palace but he had been taught in Bologna, and he called himself Bolognese on title-pages. He was thus associated with the city which, during the last quarter of the seventeenth century, produced more sonatas and instrumental works than any other in Europe. The immediate forebears of the concerto grosso were trio and violin sonatas rather than works called concertos—a name usually denoting an association of voices with instruments. Works for five-, six- or seven-stringed instruments with continuo, which might be called sonatas or concertos, were very often far more like canzonas and far less like the first concerti grossi than were the usual trio sonatas or sonatas for violin and continuo. The huge success of the concerto grosso was prepared by the cultivation of that kind of sonata which composers gradually omitted to designate as *da chiesa,* for it was not intended only for the church, and as it developed it owed to the suite its form of three or four distinct long movements instead of the many tempo changes of the canzona. The last characteristics of the older, canzona-like church sonata were the frequent slow opening, the counterpoint in an initial slow-fast movement, and the transformation into staid, dignified movements of dances which were openly named in chamber or court sonatas.

Although in Italy the orchestra had previously been associated with the theatre, the first concerti grossi did not come from the opera composers of Venice and Naples, but from Corelli and the musicians associated with Bologna—the university, the basilica of St. Petronio and the famous *Accademia Filarmonica.* An account of their origins and emergence can be misleading if it begins by tracing previous connotations of the word "concerto" and suggesting a direct chain of evolution. Misleading also is the application of *post hoc ergo propter hoc* to some notable feature of the concerto grosso. For instance, before Corelli's tutti-concertino pattern, the most remarkable contrasts of texture and density to be used consistently as part of a musical design were those between instrumental groups in the *symphoniae sacrae* and grand canzonas composed by Giovanni Gabrieli; but there is no more direct connexion between Gabrieli and Corelli than between Schütz and Bach. Even if we discover that Corelli heard or saw music by Gabrieli and Bach music by Schütz, we can surely say that the later masters would have composed as they did if the earlier ones had never existed. The grand instrumental

---

[1]Daughter of Gustavus Adolphus. In 1654 she became a Roman Catholic and abdicated in favour of her cousin Chas. X. She lived in Rome and was generous to the musicians whom she engaged for the splendid concerts given in her palace.

music at St. Mark's declined rapidly soon after Gabrieli's death. Its decadence continued through the middle years of the seventeenth century until Legrenzi was appointed director, while the music for string ensemble was ascendant at St. Petronio. Moreover the splendour of Bologna was of quite a different order from the splendour of Venice; it was less idiomatic, and to modern ears it sometimes sounds dry, suggestive of a proud academic and ecclesiastical community. Yet the Bolognese concerto was more directly beholden to the opera sinfonia of Venice than to any music associated with St. Mark's, for when the music of Bologna reached its zenith during the last decade of the century the most magnificent pieces heard in St. Petronio, and probably at sessions of the *Accademia Filarmonica*, were the *sinfoni con due trombe, concerti per trombe* and *sonate con trombe* by Torelli, Perti, Domenico Gabrielli[2] and Jacchini.

The kind of concerto that was destined to precede the classical symphony and to share its honour did not grow from previous large ensembles at all, except indirectly from Lully's string orchestra. Even under Legrenzi, who must have taught some of the concertists of the early eighteenth century, including Albinoni, large ensembles were often of mixed soloists—violins, viols, trombones, perhaps an oboe, often a bassoon, organs and instruments of the lute family. Concerti grossi were aggrandizements of the more integral sound of the trio sonata for violins and 'cello, which Corelli incorporated into his concertos by making it persistent in the fabric and exposed as a concertino. The nurseries which cultivated sonatas for nearly half a century produced in the concerto grosso what stood to the sonata as a standard rose stands to a bush, the leaves and flowers being similar. A new rose is widely grown only if thousands of amateur and professional gardeners share the first grower's ideal; they do not share his precise desire, for they lack his knowledge, imagination and laboratory, but their favour affects his experiments. During most of the seventeenth century no composers except those in England were deeply concerned with a wide general public if they had secured the favour of privileged employers or patrons in the church or aristocracy. The first exceptions were the Italian opera composers after 1637. Half a century later a considerable general public was ready to enjoy chamber music and to acclaim from Corelli onwards a series of increasingly marvellous violinists as enthusiastically as a former public had acclaimed opera singers.

London already enjoyed plenty of public concerts, and Londoners had only themselves or their incomes to blame if they knew little about sonatas; but their concerts rarely mustered an instrumental ensemble of

[2]Though also spelt "Gabrieli," this composer's name is best written as at St. Petronio, thus distinguishing him from the famous Venetians.

the size used in an Italian opera or in a concerto grosso, and their programmes were largely of songs interspersed with instrumental airs and
other solos. Not everybody who likes instrumental music in church or
playhouse can enjoy it for hours at a concert where it does not assist
other forms of expression, and the attitude implied by Fontenelle's "Sonate, que me veux-tu? " was by no means peculiar to France. The public for absolute music is always likely to be limited, and its taste depends upon its opportunities. Like the boy Verdi, it may form its first
judgements from the village band or church organ, and its later judgements of symphonies and concertos are then more than the acquired
gloss of fashionable education. There is, however, a wider concert public
which does not quickly take to music that is unemphatic and gently
coloured. It immediately loves the orchestra, the fine singer or virtuoso,
and perhaps the sound of a chorus with orchestra, but it acquires slowly
a taste for string quartets. Such listeners among the nobility and bur-
gessy swelled audiences for chamber music when it became orchestral.
During the second and third decade of the eighteenth century the presses
of Amsterdam, London and Paris outran those of Venice and Bologna in
the supply of printed parts of concertos.

Consideration of this wider audience may incline us to believe that
the title of the new concerto was no more accidental than the time and
place of its emergence. Corelli, Gregori, Valentini and Torelli—all the
early concertists except Dall'Abaco—called their works concerti grossi to
distinguish them from instrumental *concerti sacri* or *concerti ecclesias-
tici* and from *concerti da camera*, which might employ five or six instrumental parts but were not orchestral conceptions. The more parts,
the less orchestral the sound; for the sound most associated with the
orchestra in Italy was that of the ritornello to an opera aria, or of the
opera sinfonia and dance movements. The composers did not wish concerti grossi to produce the sound of single instruments except when, by
writing "solo" on the parts, they deliberately recalled the sonata during
concertino sections.

Albinoni, Vivaldi and the Marcellos—the immediate successors of
the Bolognese concertists—did not use Corelli's title even when they used
his outlay of instruments, and it was not generally favoured by the
German concertists who were inspired by Vivaldi and the Venetians. The
title and opus number of the finest baroque concertos, Handel's "Twelve
Concerti Grossi, Op. 6" seem to have been chosen as a tribute to Corelli
in the country which continued to honour him by verbal panegyric and
sedulous imitation for some fifty years after his death; yet Corelli's closest imitators in England, Geminiani who was his pupil and Avison who
was Geminiani's, called their publications "Six Concertos in Seven
Parts," not "Six Concerti Grossi." Plainly the adoption of the Corellian
model with its contrasts of tutti and concertino within the string texture

did not necessarily induce the eighteenth-century composer to adopt his title. On the other hand we know from Handel that concertos with no concertino sections could be called concerti grossi.

Because of a widespread mistake it is desirable to say again that Corelli and the others did not intend "Concerto Grosso" to designate a work with a concertino, but an *orchestral* conception, distinct from the *concerto a quattro* or *concerto a cinque* which we should call a string quartet or quintet with continuo. A concerto grosso for the church was more than a *sonata da chiesa* in many parts; a concerto grosso for the concert room was more than a suite of dances on too grand a scale to be called a *sonata da camera* or *trattenimento*.[3] It was the equivalent and rival of the sinfonia, the grand overture at the opening of a Venetian opera, or of the sinfonia that was heard on church or university high days at St. Petronio.

Hence the pendants to "Concerti Grossi" on title-pages, telling the buyer that he required more than one player to each violin part, that a double bass was desirable to complete the orchestral sonority although the organ and archlute served as fundament instruments, that many players could swell the ripieno but that none should double any part in the concertino. These works were not to be tackled indiscriminately by as many players as happened to attend in the organ gallery for High Mass or in the palace concert room after dinner. When the concertino sounded alone, the fine texture of a trio sonata emphasized the richer texture of those sections wherein it was no longer exposed. Corelli's design was a pattern of textures which differed from former concertos as an embossed fabric like brocade differs from a cloth of uniform thickness.

The habit of referring to the orchestral ensemble as the concerto grosso prevailed in parts of Germany and also in England, where professional pride, not stooping to the native "full" used by cathedral musicians, could have been satisfied with the single Italian word "ripieno" or "tutti." The ambiguity of "concerto grosso" may have prevented composers from using it as a title, but it has not prevented historians from referring to "the period of the concerto grosso" instead of "baroque concerto period" when they are dealing with composers from Corelli to Quantz. We loosely include among concerti grossi all Bach's Brandenburg Concertos and all his concertos for harpsichord and for violin. Bach, Handel and other late baroque composers still regarded the concerto as an essay in orchestral texture when part-writing took precedence during a fugue or a slow middle movement, and we shall notice how the concerto grosso outlived the baroque era.

The first concerti grossi crowned more than half a century of Italian devotion to violin playing that followed and reflected a former de-

[3]Bolognese and Venetian composers sometimes published suites of dances as *Trattamenti or Trattenimenti*, i.e. entertainments, diversions, or "courses."

votion to singing, for the sonatas and concertos played by the Vitalis, Torelli, Valentini, Corelli, Vivaldi, Geminiani, Veracini and others upon Amati's and Stradivari's instruments mark a golden age of the string ensemble that is comparable with the previous golden age of vocal ensemble. For Corelli and Vivaldi, as for Mozart, the violin was a wordless voice of super-human compass and range of expression, with clearer attack and greater agility than a human voice, and free from the strain of human fatigue. The second generation of concertists in Italy, notably the Venetians, introduced wind instruments. Their concertos are rarely like sinfonias for string and wind instruments; instead the oboe, flute or bassoon receives the affection elsewhere bestowed on the solo violin; but in Germany especially the technique and expression of wind instruments developed as the concerto developed, and the liberal inclusion of wind instruments into the ripieno prepared the larger court orchestras for the classical symphony.

The history of the baroque grosso may be somewhat crudely summarized thus:

1. *The Sonata Concerto*, emerging chiefly through a Bolognese-Roman school: Corelli, Torelli, Dall'Abaco, Albicastro and, in the next generation, Bonporti.
2. *The Suite Concerto* of the first German or Austrian School: Muffat, Aufschnaiter, Pez. (Certain composers classed under Nos. 4 and 5 below, e.g. Telemann and Handel, are partly "suite" concertists.)
3. *The Operatic or Dramatic Concerto* of the second Italian (Venetian) School, comprising the opera composers in Venice—Albinoni, Vivaldi, Alessandro Marcello, Benedetto Marcello. (Later followers: Tartini and, in France, Leclair.)
4. *The Kapellmeister Concerto* of the main German School. Chief composers: Pisendel, Heinichen, Fasch, Graupner, J. S. Bach, Telemann, Stölzel, Molter, Hurlebusch, Birkenstock, J. A. and K. H. Graun, Quantz, Hasse.
5. *The Public Concerto* of the English School. Chief composers: Geminiani, Avison, Handel, Stanley, Festing, Babell, Barsanti, St. Martini, Defesch and Hellendaal.
6. *The Symphonic Concerto*, including some of the later works by Vivaldi and by composers who were also symphonists, e.g. Locatelli and G. B. Sammartini.

Bibliography

The most complete source for further information on the Baroque concerto is the volume from which the preceding has been taken, *The Baroque Concerto* (London, Faber & Faber, 1961; New York, Norton, 1965). For related reading the following are recommended: three works by David Boyden, *The History of Violin Playing* (London, Oxford University Press, 1965), "The Violin and Its Technique in the Eighteenth Century," *The Musical Quarterly*, 36 (1950), and "When is a Concerto Not a Concerto?" *The Musical Quarterly*, 43 (1957); two works by Adam Carse, *The History of Orchestration* (London, Kegan Paul, 1925) for its chapter on seventeenth-century instruments, and *The Orchestra in the XVIIIth Century* (Cambridge, Heffer, 1940); Wilfred Mellers, *François Couperin and the French Classic Tradition* (London, Dennis Dobson, 1950); Ernst Hermann Meyer, "Form in the Instrumental Music of the Seventeenth Century," in *Proceedings of the Royal Music Association*, 65th session (1938-1939), pp. 45-56 (Leeds, Whitehead and Miller, 1939); William Newman, *The Sonata in the Baroque Era* (Chapel Hill, N.C., University of North Carolina Press, 1959); and two biographies by Marc Pincherle, *Corelli* (New York, Norton, 1956) and *Vivaldi* (New York, Norton, 1957).

Selected examples of music are contained in vol. 2 of the *Historical Anthology of Music* and in Hans Engel, ed., *Das Concerto Grosso* (Cologne, Arno Volk Verlag, 1962). Works by Italian composers may be found in Luigi Torchi, ed., *L'Arte Musicale in Italia;* works by German composers are contained in *Denkmäler deutscher Tonkunst, Denkmäler der Tonkunst in Bayern,* and *Denkmäler der Tonkunst in Österreich.* General indices to all these series may be found under "Editions, historical" in the *Harvard Dictionary of Music,* 2d ed. (1969). Corelli's works have been edited by J. Joachim and F. Chrysander in a five-volume edition, *Les Oeuvres de Arcangelo Corelli* (London, Augener, 1888-1891), and an edition of the works of Vivaldi is in progress, *Opere* (Milan, Ricordi, 1947-   ).

16

CERTAINLY no other musician has been the subject of as much research as has been Johann Sebastian Bach. Even a selected bibliography on Bach can become quite lengthy, and a complete bibliography would be not only of staggering proportions but also nearly impossible to assemble and keep up-to-date, so much is the writing that has been and is being done concerning Bach, his music, his family, and his times. One would think that, considering all the research which has been done on Bach, all the important material would have been discovered and interpreted and that the definitive picture of Bach might at last have been achieved. For many years this was considered to be so. The picture of Bach generally accepted was that given by Philipp Spitta a century ago when he set forth the rather mystical figure of the pious German cantor. This view may still be found not only in most of the historical works of a popular nature but also in some of those which make a pretense at scholarship, as well as in standard reference works. For example, *The Columbia Encyclopedia*, 3d. ed. (1963), states that Spitta's work is "classic" and that "most of his [Bach's] secular compositions resound with sturdy, pious morality." But current scholarship has begun to question the view of Spitta and to propose a new picture of Bach. In the introduction to J. A. Westrup's "The Historians and the Periods" (see p. 9) and in the article itself, it is emphasized that a definitive interpretation of music history is neither possible nor desirable. Views change from generation to generation, not only because new factual material comes to light, but because the old factual material is given a new interpretation filtered through the experiences of a new group of scholars. The following selection by Friedrich Blume is a good example of the proof and practical results of that theory. Professor Blume's new picture is, however, in no way intended to belittle either the intent or the scholarship of Spitta. There is no question here of whether the nineteenth century was incompetent, careless, and incorrect while the twentieth century is competent, careful, and correct. Spitta's work was indeed overwhelming in its scope and perhaps even "classic." But we of the twentieth century bring to the study of Bach new backgrounds and new experiences through which the factual material must be filtered; the result is a new picture. And in turn, those of the twenty-first century will doubtlessly bring forth still another new picture, superseding our own, which may then appear as one-sided as does Spitta's today.

Friedrich Blume, lecturer at the University of Berlin, has contributed many articles to encyclopedias and periodicals. He is perhaps best known, however, for his editorship of *Das Chorwerk* and especially for his general editorship of *Die Musik in Geschichte und Gegenwart,* the most comprehensive music encyclopedia ever assembled. Several of his entries in the latter have been translated into English and published under his name as *Renaissance and Baroque Music* (New York, Norton, 1967) and *Classic and Romantic Music* (New York, Norton, 1970). Both these volumes are essential reading on their subjects.

Outlines of a New Picture of Bach

FRIEDRICH BLUME

Translated by Stanley Godman

The picture which we have in our minds of the great masters of music is in a state of constant flux, and the ever-changing conception of Bach is a classical example of this process. From time to time new attitudes to history emerge and these lead to revaluations. The sources of the life and works, the original scores, letters, documents and records are subjected to fresh examination and a new generation is astonished to find itself eliciting quite different conclusions from historical materials that have not themselves undergone any change. Many a young historian on examining these sources has exclaimed: "Why has no one ever seen this before?" The answer is perfectly simple: the same facts were formerly seen in a different light. The corpus of source material that is available for the investigation of Bach's life, personality, work and environment has not changed in essentials since the time of Bitter and Spitta or since the time when the group of Bach-lovers led by Schumann, Mendelssohn and Jahn initiated the first complete edition of his works. Some items have been added, some have gone astray, but there has been no radical change. What have changed fundamentally are the methods of evaluating and interpreting the sources. And these new methods are themselves the symptoms of a different approach, a different awareness of history. Under their impact the old material brings forth new life.

The conception of Bach that prevailed until about the middle of the twentieth century and, so far as we can be said to have one at all, still prevails today among a majority of Bach-lovers, players and singers, is fundamentally the picture which Spitta painted about 80 years ago and which Albert Schweitzer, then barely 30 years old, touched up a generation later. Like the Bach scholars of the subsequent period, including Schering, Pirro, Terry and many others, right up to Arnold

FROM *Music and Letters*, 44 (1963), 214-227. Reprinted by permission of the author.

Schmitz, Friedrich Smend and others, Schweitzer did not violate the basic structure of the conception established by Spitta. He added one or two fresh colours, elaborated certain lines that had previously only been sketched in, and he made the picture somewhat more lively and full-blooded. He removed some of the superficial polish. Nevertheless, the face of Bach which Spitta had depicted somewhat over-smoothly and one-sidedly was still visible through all the additions, retouchings, renovations and alterations. And so it has been with Bach scholars from Schweitzer to our own time: while they have occasionally introduced fresh points of view and renewed and rejuvenated the picture by new interpretation of the sources — in particular, the sources of Bach's works, they have not been able or even tried to shake the foundations of the structure established by Spitta, that *monumentum aere perennius* which he left, after such mature research, to future generations.

Apart from one isolated attempt at a fundamental revision of the prevailing picture of Bach that was undertaken in the bicentenary year 1950 and which possibly was not based on adequate original research, it would be fair to say that until quite recently what Spitta bequeathed to us has remained the foundation of our conception of Bach. Renewed, supplemented and modified, enriched and surprisingly variegated, it has nevertheless been left basically intact, like an erratic boulder covered with lichens, mosses, colours and all the signs of weathering but still standing as firmly and unmoved as ever. In the last few years, however, a continually growing and disturbing change has been taking place, promoted by certain scholars in all quietness and modesty and with no undue haste. The effect of their slow but insistent pressure has been to question the ultimate stability and invulnerability of the hitherto immovable erratic boulder itself. Will it fall to pieces one day after all? Will it be forced to yield to a new organism altogether? That is the question, and it may not be inopportune to adumbrate a new picture of Bach at a Bach festival, though with all due reserve and caution. All it is possible to discern today are the mere outlines of a new picture, but the outlines are beginning to emerge from the mist with ever increasing clarity.

At the present time Bach research is marked by an absorption in textual investigation. This is both needful and useful. For a long time it was thought that the sources of Bach's works had been studied so thoroughly that there was no call for any further work on them. It was not thought that further study would yield more than a few minor details. Far into the twentieth century Spitta's work was considered conclusive and unsurpassable. The research of the last twelve years has shown that view to be mistaken. A completely fresh study of the sources in accordance with new methods has produced surprising, overwhelming and even revolutionary results. The erratic boulder is about to be burst asunder. It may be that a rather exaggerated dogmatism is prevalent at the moment: the belief that only that is true which results from the close textual investigation of the original sources and that whatever does not result from it cannot possibly be true. The climate of scholarship will change, however, and the textual scholars will not have the final word. The purely textual will be followed by a more interpretative phase. Only when we come to that stage will it be possible to draw from the latest researches the conclusions that are implicit in them, though they may not follow directly from the sources themselves. Historical knowledge does not derive exclusively from a slavish dependence on the sources: the sources have to be evaluated, interpreted, compared and blended, with all their contradictions, into a total picture. Only when this methodological process has run its course will the vague outlines of the newly emerging picture of Bach become completely clear and unmistakable. But that time will come and the outlines are already sufficiently evident for them to be defined at any rate approximately. And that is what I should like to attempt to do in this lecture.

In the nineteenth century Bach was sometimes evaluated in ways that did not ensue inevitably from the historical sources and which were not applied to Bach's contemporaries. How he came to be accorded this special interpretation I cannot explain in detail now. It happened between the appearance of Forkel's little book on Bach of 1802 and Carl Heinrich Bitter's book of 1865. Forkel's picture of Bach was still mainly that of the virtuoso and craftsman, of the instrumental player and instrumental composer; he deals hardly at all with Bach's church music. The Bach portrayed by Forkel is not at all the orthodox Lutheran, the preacher of the word of God, but rather a sort of national hero, a guardian of the true German spirit. Above all, and first and foremost, he is a musician. It was Bitter and then, far more emphatically, Spitta who turned Bach into the great Lutheran cantor, the retrospective champion of tradition, the orthodox preacher of the Bible and the chorale, who still prevails in the popular imagination today. It was these two scholars and their descendants who established the conception of Bach as supremely the church musician, and the ascendancy of the churchman over the musician. All manner of Romantic notions of Eisenach, the Wartburg, Luther, the tradition of the office of cantor, middle-class piety and so on have played their part in confirming the popular misconception. Bach did not, after all, come from the family of a church musician. His father was a municipal and court musician. There is nothing to suggest that as a boy Bach had anything more to do with church music than all the other Eisenach lads who had to sing in the church choir. There is certainly no question of his having had any ancestral connection with church music. The idea that he had an ancestral association with the organ is equally groundless. Apart from the picturesque anecdote of his stay with his Ohrdruf brother, nothing is known as to when or where Bach learnt to play the organ. No one knows where he acquired the knowledge of organ building for which he later came to be regarded with such awe and which he must already have possessed when he was still only eighteen (it was at that age that he was first invited, as an expert, to test an organ); no one knows when, where or from whom he learnt organ improvisation and organ composition.

All we know for certain is that he must have been a master of organ-playing and organ composition, in Weimar in 1703, and then in Arnstadt and Mühlhausen. But is it right to assume that he had any special fondness for the organ? The fact that he was a tremendous executant, virtuoso and technician, miles above all his contemporaries, predecessors and successors, does not necessarily mean that the organ was more to him than an instrument on which to develop his skill. Was Bach particularly attached to the organ? Hardly. His last official post as organist was the Mühlhausen appointment, which he gave up in 1708 when he was only twenty-three. In Weimar his duties were partly those of organist and partly those of the court musician. From 1716-17 he never had any further official connection with the organ whatever. He taught the organ, improvised, gave recitals, played for friends and important personages, tested and adjudicated on organs, but was never again a church organist. If Bach had felt a fundamental affinity with the organ he would certainly not have found it difficult to obtain one of the important organ posts of which there was still such an abundance in Germany. There is, however, no evidence that he ever made any effort to obtain such a post.

These are the kind of erroneous assumptions that have led, since Bitter and Spitta, to Bach being proclaimed the church musician, the great cantor, the *jongleur de Dieu,* and even the fifth Evangelist. When the sources are evaluated objectively it appears that Bach was no more a church musician than any of his few great and many smaller contemporaries. Telemann and Graupner composed far greater quantities of church music than Bach. As for his output of organ music, he was easily surpassed by Murschhauser, J. Kaspar Ferdinand Fischer, Vincent Lübeck, J. Gottfried Walther, and many others. Some of these, like Pachelbel, Buxtehude, Murschhauser, Zachow and others, were professional church musicians throughout or for the greater part of their lives. In 1708 Bach resolutely turned his back on the service of the church, with the declared intention of taking a court appointment. It was only with the greatest reluctance that he resumed the cantor's gown fifteen years later. Outward circumstances alone were responsible. How disappointed he was with Leipzig is attested clearly and beyond dispute by the letter to Erdmann of 1730. Did Bach have a special liking for church work? Was it a spiritual necessity for him? Hardly. There is at any rate no evidence that it was. Bach the supreme cantor, the creative servant of the Word of God, the staunch Lutheran, is a legend. It will have to be buried along with all the other traditional and beloved romantic illusions. All this has been known for a long time now. And if we have shrunk from drawing the obvious conclusions, a basic reason for this clinging to inherited ideas has lain above all in the ingrained picture of his Leipzig activities which, in spite of all Schering's corrections, still seemed to be dominated by Bach the church musician. Did he not, as Spitta taught us, rejoice the hearts of his congregations with his music for more than twenty years? With hundreds of cantatas, each one more beautiful than the last? And culminating in the group of about thirty so-called "late chorale cantatas"? Did he not also compose two or three deeply moving Passions, one of which has become one of the great confessional works of the Evangelical church? Did he not, in addition to a few short Masses, compose an overwhelming Mass in B minor which many have laboured indefatigably to interpret as a monument of the Evangelical-Lutheran faith? Were not the Passions accompanied by the three oratorios for Easter, Ascension (the so-called Cantata No. 11) and Christmas? Were there not also the ecclesiastical organ works, some of which Bach himself gathered together in Part III of his "Clavierübung" in 1739 and also in the six so-called Schübler chorale preludes of 1747, and finally in the "Eighteen Chorale Preludes" which were not published in his lifetime. What, compared with all these, were the few secular works, the first, second and fourth parts of the "Clavierübung," the keyboard concertos and a few other things which he produced in the 27 years in Leipzig? However his pre-Leipzig activities were judged, did not the works of the Leipzig period supply ample proof that Bach from 1723 onwards became aware of his deepest and most personal task, his innermost vocation, that of the great church musician?

How much of this picture will survive the results of recent Bach research? Very little, I am afraid. A landslide has taken place in the wake of the new chronology of the Leipzig vocal works established by Georg von Dadelsen and Alfred Dürr in recent years.[1] Bach's contribution to church music during his 27 years in Leipzig has now come to be seen quite differently. When he first took on the Leipzig post he produced one or two impressive works for the church ("St. John Passion,") "Magnificat"). Then, as if in a frenzy of creativity, for three years (from the first Sunday after Trinity in 1723 to Whitsun 1726) he supplied for every Sunday and church festival a cantata which was new to Leipzig (the fact that at moments of great pressure they were merely repetitions or rearrangements of earlier works is immaterial). What happened after 1726 is doubtful. Whether Bach also composed the fourth and fifth annual series of cantatas attributed to him by his son Philipp Emanuel and his pupil J. F. Agricola in their obituary notice, is debatable.[2] There is

---

[1]G. von Dadelsen, "Beiträge zur Chronologie der Werke J. S. Bachs" (Trossingen, 1958); A. Dürr, "Zur Chronologie der Leipziger Vokalwerke J. S. Bachs," in "Bach-Jahrbuch" 44 (Berlin, 1957), pp. 5-162.

[2]W. H. Scheide & A. Dürr in *Musikforschung*, xiv (1961) pp. 60 foll., 192 foll., 423 foll.

evidence of a small number of cantatas in the years subsequent to 1726 but they seem to have been mainly occasional works, of little import against the background of 24 years. Spitta's picture of the supreme cantor toiling away for years on end at the task of supplying his Leipzig congregations with cantatas has been destroyed. Bach's work as a composer of cantatas in Leipzig was confined to the first three (or possibly, first five) years of his appointment. What followed thereafter were merely incidental and occasional works. Quite apart from the fact that they consisted predominantly of adaptations of earlier works, the Passions and oratorios were, as Bach himself once said, an "onus," a task which he performed with considerable reluctance.

The prevailing picture of Bach has been further seriously upset by the results of recent research on his technique of adaptation, or "parody"[3]—the term used by musicologists to denote the adaptation of a secular vocal or instrumental work to a sacred text, the musical substance being either preserved intact or refashioned. It has long been known that there are very many "parodies" among the cantatas of Bach's early years in Leipzig. It is probable that there are many more than have so far been discovered. It is possible only under very exceptional circumstances to prove the existence of a parody. Bach had been a court musician for many years and had not thought of ever returning to the work of a church musician. Apart from the roughly 30 cantatas of the early years in Weimar (1714-16) he brought no supply with him. He now saw himself confronted with an overwhelming mass of church commitments. Nothing is more natural than that he should have gone back not only to his Weimar cantatas but also to secular and instrumental works of all kinds, re-arranging them in the form of arias, duets, choral movements, etc., to meet the requirements of his new office. There were probably far more of these re-arrangements or parodies than has so far been realized. The parody technique was applied to the oratorios and Masses as well as to the church cantatas. The "Easter Oratorio," as Smend demonstrated nearly 30 years ago, is entirely a parody of a secular pastoral cantata. The "Christmas Oratorio" is, apart from the recitative and chorales, an adaptation or parody of earlier secular works. The so-called "Ascension Cantata" is wholly or mostly a parody. The short Masses are probably without exception parodies, though the evidence is not quite complete. The Mass in B minor is full of parody movements; only the "Kyrie," parts of the "Gloria," of the "Credo" and the "Sanctus" was written as early as 1724). From the "Osanna" onwards the whole work is a parody.

Certainly the value and beauty of these works is not thereby diminished. But it does make a tremendous difference whether a work was

[3]In particular, F. Smend, "J. S. Bachs Kirchenkantaten," 5 & 6 (Berlin, 1948-9).

conceived from its own text or was merely re-written to fit the new text. Among the works other than cantatas the only great ones that remain are the "St. John Passion" and the "Magnificat." The "St. Matthew Passion" has long been a matter of dispute. It shares nine of its movements with the funeral cantata which Bach wrote for the funeral of Prince Leopold in March 1729; the chorale movement "O Mensch, bewein dein Sünde gross" is also of an earlier date. Ten years ago Friedrich Smend made a valiant effort to vindicate the complete originality of the "St. Matthew Passion" and to banish the funeral cantata among the parodies[4], but his arguments are not wholly convincing and it is not impossible that the intactness of the "St. Matthew Passion" may be broken. This all means, to say the least, that numerous works, oratorios, Masses, cantatas which we have grown deeply to cherish as professions of Christian faith, works on the basis of which the Classical-Romantic tradition has taught us to revere the great churchman, the mighty Christian herald, have *a limine* nothing in common with such values and sentiments and were not written with the intention of proclaiming the composer's Christian faith, still less from a heartfelt need to do so. The relationship between sacred and secular music was different then from what it is today, and what served for the flattering adulation of a prince was no less serviceable for the expression of Christian faith and worship. Seen from this historical point of view these works certainly forfeit none of their immediate impressiveness. The "St. Matthew Passion" will lose none of its depth of meaning and content if one day it should be proved to be a parody of the funeral music.

There are numerous cantatas where our sense of their religious quality is not in the slightest diminished by our knowledge that they are parodies, but which probably were so. The six Cöthen congratulatory cantatas were not by any means church music in the narrower sense, regardless of whether they were performed in church or in the throne room, and whether their texts are more religious or more secular in character. But the parodies of them have become genuine church music. They were not based on any heartfelt need or devout feeling. They were written in fulfilment of the duty of a court *Kapellmeister*. Graupner, Stölzel and other of Bach's contemporaries, in so far as they occupied the same office, fulfilled the same duty in precisely the same way.

Another picture that derives from Spitta is also deceptive: that of the ageing Bach harking back to some extent to his foundations in the chorale and the organ and, in the quietness of his study, writing the so-called "late organ chorale preludes," the stupendous "Eighteen," including "Komm, Gott Schöpfer, Heiliger Geist," "Schmücke dich, o liebe Seele," the variations on "O Lamm Gottes," etc., and culmi-

---

[4]F. Smend, "Bach in Köthen" (Berlin, 1952).

nating in the allegedly final "Vor Deinen Thron tret ich hiermit," which the composer, already blind, dictated to his son-in-law. We know that this picture is a false one. The ageing Bach collected and edited his early compositions and certainly rejected, completed, improved and possibly added one or the other piece. The third part of the "Clavierübung" of 1739, whose sequence of chorale preludes has given rise to the foolish appellation "Organ Mass," was probably a redaction. The sequence is easily explained by the traditional arrangement of the hymns in congregational hymn-books. Bach had not the remotest intention of producing a cyclic work. What could he or his contemporaries have done with a cycle in the form of a "German Organ Mass"? Nor can there be any question of his having returned in old age to the chorale or to the organ, as suggested by Schweitzer and Schering. The "late organ chorale preludes" are just as much a legend as the "late chorale cantatas." The only truth that remains is that of the ageing collector harvesting the essential proceeds of his life, the goldsmith giving the finishing touch to his work. The activity that occupied him in his final years was "esoterical," the ultimate perfecting, artistically and spiritually, of his life's work. Why should he have been interested in whether his contemporaries played these last works or not? They belonged to an age that was past and gone. It was already quite obvious that the new music of the time was to develop under completely different conditions and in a different soil.

About ten years ago much interest was aroused by two new methods of Bach interpretation which, without changing it fundamentally, have supplied valuable additions to the traditional picture of Bach. The rediscovery of the "doctrine of rhetorical figures" in the German musical theory of the seventeenth and eighteenth centuries has made us more familiar with Bach the rhetorician, and the discovery that a mystical, symbolistic theory of numbers survived right up to Bach's own time and found expression in his music has thrown more light on Bach the mathematician.[5] In recent years research on these matters has, in so far as they concern Bach, receded somewhat into the background, as compared with the textual research which I referred to at the beginning. Both methods of interpretation have doubtless contributed to the deepening and widening of our conception of Bach. The theory of rhetorical figures has shown that certain modes of expression in Bach's music which had already been recognized and understood as such have to be regarded as a king of teaching material on which there existed a methodical terminology. The theory of numbers has attempted to systematize earlier more occasional and isolated observations, but very soon reached a limit. Bach, brilliant master though he undoubtedly was of a kind of mathematical

---

[5]In particular A. Schmitz, "Die Bildlichkeit der wortgebundenen Musik Bachs," (Mainz, 1949); F. Smend, "J. S. Bach bei seinem Namen gerufen" (Kassel, 1950).

technique of composition, evidently made use of it only in selected cases. It is fair to say, therefore, that the two methods, while they have certainly deepened and extended our picture of Bach, have not changed it fundamentally.

The few indications of the results of recent research which I have been able to give will have shown that what is involved in the outlines of a new picture of Bach is not merely the gradual change that is constantly taking place in the process of history itself. What has happened here is the equivalent of an earthquake. Its centre is a new conception of history, and its epicentre the new chronology of the Leipzig choral works by Georg von Dadelsen and Alfred Dürr. This must now be regarded as fully established: a conference of specialists which met at Princeton University in the autumn of 1961 was unable to suggest any objections. Dürr had already established the chronology of the Weimar vocal works in 1951.[6] A new chronology of Bach's organ works is in process of development: the only thing that is certain is that many of them were written much earlier than was previously assumed—in particular, the third part of the "Clavierübung," the "Eighteen Choral Preludes," and of course the Schübler chorale preludes, which are merely organ arrangements of vocal movements, mostly from the cantatas of the year 1724-5. It was already known that most of the keyboard works and also the orchestral suites, the arrangements of the keyboard concertos, the violin concertos, the Brandenburg concertos and so on, originated partly in Cöthen, partly in Weimar and in any case before the Leipzig period and that only the seven keyboard partitas, possibly the Italian Concerto, and certainly the "Goldberg Variations" may be assigned with some assurance to the Leipzig period. The basically new valuation has been caused by the re-dating of the vocal works of the Leipzig period, and in particular of the church cantatas.

How then may we describe the outlines of a new picture of Bach, bearing in mind the earthquake-like effect of this recent research? The picture of the early years in Weimar, Arnstadt and Mühlhausen, that is, up to 1718, remains the same as before. They are the years in which Bach identified himself with the traditional Lutheran office of organist and was occasionally commissioned to write vocal works for the church, or for special events. It is for the most part impossible to do more than surmise what organ and keyboard works originated in this early period. The Mühlhausen letter of resignation makes it perfectly clear that Bach the church musician became Bach the court musician on moving to Weimar. Bach had in fact agreed on terms with the Weimar court in secret and confronted the Mühlhausen Council with a *fait accompli*. He did not find it difficult to choose between the traditional ecclesiastical office and the musical prospects of a secular court; he came down on the side which promised the musician the greater freedom of development.

[6]A. Dürr, "Studien über die frühen Kantaten Bachs" (Leipzig, 1951).

It is not quite clear what kind of tasks Bach undertook during the first five years in Weimar. He presumably played the organ in the Castle chapel and the harpsichord and violin in secular music-making at the the court. Certainly he was also engaged in teaching. In these years he probably composed the main body of his clavier and organ works — probably orchestral music too, though we have no knowledge of such. Very likely most of the concertos arranged for keyboard, Bach's own violin concertos, and possibly the sonatas for violin solo, and other chamber works, also belong to this period. In other words, Bach fulfilled precisely such duties as were imposed on a high court musician of the time. The gigantic quantity and the high quality of these works suggest that he fulfilled the duties with devotion and enthusiasm. Very characteristic was his reaction when in 1714 the Duke charged him to write "a new piece each month," i. e. cantatas for the Castle chapel services. As is proved by Dürr's chronology, Bach fulfilled the task conscientiously and punctiliously, composing his "piece" precisely once a month (with a few possible exceptions) and continuing to do so until the commission expired. There is no reason to suppose that he did not fulfil the ducal commission gladly and even maybe with enthusiasm: some movements of the Weimar cantatas are brimful of youthful warmth and energy. There is, however, no evidence whatever that he regarded the writing of cantatas as the be-all and end-all of his life or that he was particularly eager to write them. It was a court duty like any other. If instead the duke had commissioned him to compose ballets or serenades he would have fulfilled the commission with the same punctiliousness and technical skill.

Finally, in the much discussed Cöthen period from 1717 to 1723 Bach became the court director of music *par excellence*. Unfortunately even today we are not very well informed about the details of his activities. There is, however, nothing to suggest, as has been claimed repeatedly by Spitta and many subsequent biographers, that Bach regarded these years as a "golden cage" from which his heart yearned to escape to his true vocation of church musician. To these years it is possible to assign with probability or some measure of certainty a certain number of works, above all, keyboard works, suites, inventions, the 48 Preludes and Fugues, the Brandenburg concertos, probably the triple concerto in A minor, possibly one or other concerto arranged for keyboard. But no more. We have already mentioned the court congratulatory cantatas. The attempt to assign some of the organ works or even church cantatas to the Cöthen period is purely conjectural. Needless to say, these few works which we have mentioned did not absorb the whole of Bach's time. He was then at the zenith of his powers and no doubt composed infinitely more than has survived. A few overture and concerto movements of which there is no other evidence reappear in an arranged form in Leipzig church cantatas, where they are transformed into choral movements and arias with consummate skill. But the information they provide is small enough. In my view many more Leipzig cantata movements than has hitherto been realized are parodies of secular or instrumental works of the Cöthen period. The fact remains that, as Bach himself wrote in 1730, he felt that it was "not entirely agreeable to become a mere cantor after being a *Kapellmeister*" and that he had really intended to end his days as *Kapellmeister* to Prince Leopold. Becoming a cantor meant a descent in the social scale, and Bach felt no inner compulsion to make the change.

This does not of course alter the fact that during his first years in Leipzig he plunged with immense energy into the duties of his office in the church and in a quite inexplicable creative frenzy composed three, or possibly five, annual series of cantatas as well as a small number of motets, the "St. John Passion," the "Magnificat," and a few instrumental works. Nor does it alter the fact that these works were deeply informed with the spirit of Lutheran piety and abound in all kinds of profound symbolism—not to mention their technical skill. Bach thereby provided himself with the supply of church music which he needed for official purposes, and for the last 22 years, apart from isolated pieces written for special occasions, he composed nothing more in this field, contenting himself with repeating previous works. He was bitterly depressed by the narrowness of musical conditions in Leipzig and by his never-ending quarrels with the authorities and with his pupils. For years his energies were absorbed by the struggle for personal recognition. In his memorandum to the town council of 1730 he complained bitterly about the antiquated conditions in Leipzig, as compared with those prevailing in Dresden, with its brilliant court orchestra. The "St. Matthew Passion," of whose uncertain origins I have already spoken, was composed in 1729, then a few years later the "Christmas Oratorio" and the "Missa," that is, the first two movements of the Mass in B minor with which in 1733 Bach applied for the title of a "Royal Polish and Electoral Saxon Court Composer." All the quibbling in the world cannot alter the fact that the "Missa" was composed precisely for this purpose and therefore for the Catholic court service, that the "Sanctus" had been composed long before and that Bach at the very end of his life converted these movements partly by the addition of new compositions, partly by parodying earlier movements, into a complete Mass.[7] The work as a whole owes its existence to that tendency to collect and preserve that is the mark of Bach's last years.

From 1729 to 1740[8], when Bach was the conductor of the Collegium Musicum founded by Telemann, secular music-making evidently

[7]G. von Dadelsen, "Zum Problem der H-moll-Messe," in "Festbuch zum 35. Bachfest" (Stuttgart, 1958), pp. 77-83.

[8]According to recent research (W. Neumann in "Bach-Jahrbuch," 1960) Bach conducted the Collegium Musicum from 1729 to the summer of 1737, and again from 1739 to 1741 or 1744.

played a major part in his life. There were numerous public concerts. Bach took part in many academic ceremonials. In the period from 1727 to 1739 alone he composed and conducted at least fourteen and probably far more ceremonial pieces, serenades and the like. In all, Schering produced evidence of 53 festive occasions for which Bach may have written the music, only the smallest part of which has survived. In these years the office of cantor of St. Thomas's was overshadowed by that of town director of music. The cantor's resistance to the narrowness of the ecclesiastical régime grew deeper. He was accused of neglecting his official duties and was dubbed "incorrigible"—probably quite rightly so, from the standpoint of the authorities, since the fulfilment of his church duties was only an "onus," burden, to him, like the performing of the Passions.

The final decade of Bach's life was devoted to collecting and preserving and also to transmitting the tradition which he had received. The "Goldberg Variations" are a mixture of virtuosity and learning, unique of their kind in the whole history of music. The variations on "Vom Himmel hoch," the canons, the "Musical Offering," the "Art of Fugue" are works for teaching and the study; Bach himself was not interested in whether they were performed or were capable of being performed. In them he wished to continue a tradition of consummate contrapuntal skill, which he had inherited from the Roman school of the Palestrina period, by way of Berardi, Sweelinck, Scacchi, Theile, Werckmeister and G. B. Vitali. It was, as I have said, an "esoteric" activity, this disinterested transmission of a purely abstract theory. Of the same nature was his collecting and preserving of his own work, the compilation of the so-called Second Part of the "Well-Tempered Clavier," of the "Eighteen Chorale Preludes," and of the Mass in B minor. The "Musical Offering" is likewise probably at least to some extent a collection of existing pieces, enriched by various additions; and the "Art of Fugue" represents in an overwhelming document the consummation of the technical skill of centuries.

The outlines of a new picture of Bach are thus beginning to emerge from the results and insights of the latest research. Only the outlines— more than that I did not promise. It will be a good time yet before we shall have achieved a sharply defined, plastic and comprehensive new portrait of Bach. But the outlines are beginning to emerge. The overpainting of the Classical-Romantic nineteenth century is being removed and the portrait that appears underneath fits into Bach's own period better than the hitherto prevailing portrait. It is not so smooth, not so one-sided; like the Ulrich von Hutten portrayed by C. F. Meyer, Bach seems to be saying: "I am not a carefully thought-out book: I am a human being with all the conflicts and contradictions of a human being." The accents and emphases are being distributed more equitably: the organ and harpsichord virtuoso, the court musician supplying the musical needs of a secular court, the court *Kapellmeister* and composer, the cantor and schoolmaster, the church composer and church music director, the conductor in the coffee houses and public places of Leipzig, the teacher and the guardian of tradition: all these features are being given their due share. The picture must not be distorted by the works that happen to have survived: what has come down to us is merely a part of Bach's total output, and circumstances have brought it about that far more of the ecclesiastical part has survived than of the secular (this applies, incidentally, to many other composers of the period).

On the basis of this one-sided inheritance the enthusiasts inspired by Zelter and Mendelssohn laid the major emphasis on the church music and organ works, and Bitter and Spitta continued to build on these foundations. Thus there arose the one-sided and over-simplified conception that has dominated the Bach image to the present time. This conception is now being shaken, but the Bach we are beginning to see is certainly no less great than the previous one. At the same time he is more down-to-earth, more human, more tied to his own period. No hero resisting the stream of time, no reactionary sticking stubbornly to the past, no impeded mathematician, orator or theologian but a man bound up with his own age with every fibre of his being, a man who warmly welcomes the trends that point promisingly to the future, but who dutifully devotes all his powers to the traditional office of cantor when it devolves upon him: a man standing on the boundary between two epochs who is aware of the fact. And just as he serves the Lutheran office of cantor, so too he serves the bourgeois order and the showy life of a court; thus he serves the past by preserving it and gathering it in a final concentration of strength; thus he serves the future by blending with unique skill and sovereignty the new and the old. Those who see Bach as the mere guardian of tradition misinterpret him just as much as those who try to see him exclusively as the pioneer; and those who see in him only the churchman just as much as those who characterize him one-sidedly as the court *Kapellmeister;* and those who see him only as the learned musician in his study just as much as those who lower him to the level of the mere virtuoso, conductor and hack. He was all these things, and his greatness lies not least in the fact that he was able to combine them all in himself and to integrate them, from the power of his own spirit, in a work of absolutely unique quality.

Bibliography

It is not possible to give any sort of comprehensive bibliography on Bach in the space allotted here. For such a bibliography, though it is now twenty years out of date, see "Bach, Johann Sebastian;" in *Die Musik in Geschichte und Gegenwart*. A most useful work is that of Hans David and Arthur Mendel, *The Bach Reader* (New York, Norton, 1945; 2d ed. with supplement, 1966), which contains, in English translation, many of the documents that serve as source material for a biography of Bach. The works of Philipp Spitta, *Johann Sebastian Bach, His work and Influence on the Music of Germany, 1685-1750*, 2 vols. (London, Novello, 1885; New York, Dover, 1951), and Albert Schweitzer, *J. S. Bach*, 2 vols. (London, Black, 1938), give the old picture of Bach which Blume proposes to update. A criticism of Blume's article by Alfred Dürr, "Zum Wandel des Bach-Bildes," and a reply by Blume, "Antwort von Friedrich Blume," both may be found in *Musik und Kirche*, 32 (1962). Another article by Blume, "J. S. Bach's Youth," *The Musical Quarterly*, 54 (1968), adds more to the outlines of the new picture.

The complete works of Bach were edited by the Bach-Gesellschaft in the nineteenth century: Johann Sebastian Bach, *Werke*, 46 vols. (Leipzig, Breitkopf & Härtel, 1851-1900; Ann Arbor, Mich., J. W. Edwards, 1947). A new edition, *Neue Ausgabe sämtlicher Werke* (Kassel, Bärenreiter, 1954-   ), is now in progress. The thematic catalog of the works of Bach prepared by Wolfgang Schmieder, *Thematisch-systematisches Verzeichnis der musikalischen Werke von Johann Sebastian Bach* (Leipzig, Breitkopf & Härtel, 1950) referred to as BWV, is indispensable for any study of Bach's music. Another useful index to the works of Bach, arranged by melodic incipit, is that of May DeForest McAll, *Melodic Index to the Works of Johann Sebastian Bach* (New York, C. F. Peters, 1962). This is especially handy if one knows the first six notes of a Bach composition but not its name.

17

THE mid-eighteenth century marks the beginning of a period which provides a large part of the musical fare of many people today. Both musicians and nonmusicians, performers and listeners, draw heavily upon the music written between 1750 and the early 1900s, and some even confine their musical preferences almost entirely to this period.

The first segment of the period, that portion from the mid-eighteenth century to the early nineteenth, is usually referred to as the Classic period and by extension it has given its name to a modern cliché, "classical music." Sloppy speech and even sloppier thinking have rendered this term useless insofar as any precise musical meaning is concerned. It certainly cannot be said to refer exclusively to the music of the Classic period. Instead, as it is usually used it denotes any music considered to be art-music, which can cover a wide area depending on one's musical background or lack of same. If such background is minimal, the term "classical music" usually carries a connotation of music beyond one's understanding or personal taste, so that it is possible that some would apply the term to music ranging from Gregorian chant to Stravinsky.

The term Romanticism is almost as vague in its own way as Classicism. Not only is it applied to most of the music written during the nineteenth century, but the term is also conferred on any other music which seems to show characteristics of nineteenth-century music or to be akin to it in emotional content. References may be found citing certain fourteenth- or seventeenth-century compositions as Romantic, and the Romantic aspects of Bach, for example, are frequently discussed. Doubtless there are even some to whom any popular love ballad would qualify as Romantic music. To complicate matters further, the terms Classicism and Romanticism are also used to qualify one another, so that such concepts as Classical Romanticism and Romantic Classicism are not unheard of.

Classicism and Romanticism, or any term denoting a style or stylistic period, can be useful in discussing music, but only when the user and the reader or listener are in definite mutual understanding regarding their use. Too frequently they are used in a noncommunicative sense resulting in a situation where all concerned are deluded into thinking that their knowledge is specific when it is not, or else in one in which a lack of understanding exists for all and none has the courage to confess his confusion.

The following seeks to avoid such situations. Certainly some may not agree with the definitions of Classicism and Romanticism expressed therein; concurrence on Classic-Romantic terminology is far from unanimous. Nonetheless, the author reveals some thoughtful insights into those principles governing the music written between the mid-eighteenth and the early-twentieth centuries.

Hans Tischler is a faculty member of Indiana University School of Music. He has written a number of periodical contributions as well as several books, including *The Perceptive Music Listener* (Englewood Cliffs, N.J., Prentice-Hall, 1955) and *Practical Harmony* (Boston, Allyn & Bacon, 1964).

Classicism, Romanticism, and Music

HANS TISCHLER

Every music historian has had to deal with the questions "What are classicism and romanticism," and has had to give some answer. One leans toward a historical explanation, another will stress stylistic features, a third will make it a matter of attitudes; but each feels the insufficiency of his reply. The over-complexity of the problem forces us to give partial answers. This paper therefore proposes to discuss some fundamental approaches to the explanation of classicism and romanticism which are general and clear enough for questioners to grasp and retain, and to apply.

We start with an examination of the term "classic." Fundamentally this term refers to the most eminent artists and authors of Greco-Roman antiquity (and by transfer also to their works). In using the term, we may emphasize either the idea of "eminence" or the idea of "Greco-Roman antiquity," with the implication of a highly developed sensitivity to balance and clarity. In order to avoid confusion of these two meanings, we shall apply here the term "classic" to men of eminence and the term "classicist" to a penchant toward antiquity, balance, and clarity.

Thus men like Thomas Aquinas, Leonardo da Vinci, Shakespeare, Corneille, Rembrandt, or Goethe we shall call classics, because they were eminent and set standards for others. On the other hand, the *Renaissance*, because it harked back to antiquity and venerated balance and clarity, we shall call a classicist period. To state it differently: a classic creates models, a classicist accepts them.

The fact of this acceptance of models is crucial to an understanding of classicism, *i.e.* the classicist attitude. For classicism is basically an expression of satisfaction with one's environment. From this satisfaction flow a firm confidence in human possibilities and achievements, an ap-

FROM *The Music Review*, 14 (1953), 205-208. Reprinted by permission of W. Heffer & Sons Ltd.

preciation of secure, established facts and of clear presentation of thought, and therefore a fundamental optimism and rationalism together with a deliberate shutting-out from consciousness of anything undefinable or unaccountable—mystical doctrines, emotions, poverty, sickness, *etc.*

The contrast between a classicist and a classic, and yet the possibility of one person's being both, is illustrated in Mozart: in his acceptance of models from others and in his sensitivity to balance and clarity a classicist, but in creating out of these elements standards for those who followed a supreme classic.

The mention of Mozart, one of the Viennese classics of music, intimates that, in addition to the emergence of single classics and of classicist trends, there is a third phenomenon: the fact that certain generations in which classicism prevails also produce many men of genius. Such "classic eras" seem to follow two or three generations of artists who afterwards are looked upon as pioneers, precursors; they are, in turn, followed by two or more generations which accept their standards. Such a classic generation, because of its peculiar midway position, is able to strike a balance among all elements of an art. No longer engrossed in pioneering, it seizes upon models furnished by the precursors or by other periods, and with their aid creates an order and harmony to which later generations turn in the quest for fresh inspiration.

Classic eras in the various arts need not coincide, however, since they depend on two circumstances—a favourable historical situation and the genius to translate it into great art. One such classic generation occurred around 440 B.C. in Greece (excelling in drama, philosophy, sculpture, and architecture); others around 1250 in France (philosophy, architecture), 1500 in Italy (painting, sculpture, architecture, music), and 1590 in England (literature, music).

Similarly there arose during the latter part of the eighteenth century, and especially during the brief span about 1781-1803, a group of eminent masters in music and literature in Germany. The classic German poets gathered at Weimar around Goethe and Schiller, who in their creative works during those years were guided by the Hellenic idea of balance and repose. The musical classics, on the other hand, had their centre at Vienna, the home of Haydn, Mozart and Beethoven. Only with them did German music, for the first time in history, acquire preeminence in Europe. This supremacy it maintained, though not unchallenged, almost until the first World War.

The style of this particular classic era in music is the outgrowth of the *rococo* style. To the latter's features, however, it added a certain repose, an untroubled spirit of rest in the golden mean, a bright but mellow colour. There is neither overmuch seriousness nor overmuch hilarity: neither tragedy nor comedy go to extremes. A fine balance is brought about between melody and significant accompaniment, between expressive leading voice and light but masterly polyphony, between even *tempo* and metre and ever new rhythmic-melodic variants, or development.

This ideal balance was reached only rarely, and predominantly in Mozart's works; but even in them there are romantic traits: a preoccupation with human character in his operas, dramatic contrasts of volume, *tempo,* and instrumentation, a liking for surprise, a penchant for fairy tales in operas, *etc.* All these features emerged about fifty years before Mozart and they became central in the music of the succeeding century. The Viennese classics may thus well be called the central generation of the "classic-romantic" era, about 1740-1910 (for Italy and France about 1715-1910). What is usually termed the romantic era—roughly the nineteenth century—is truly but the second half of that period.

Now what is romanticism? Perhaps the most fruitful point of departure for an explanation is that, whereas classicism reflects a feeling of satisfaction, romanticism reflects a feeling of dissatisfaction with one's environment. Periods which are characterized by such dissatisfaction, such as the fourteenth and most of the sixteenth centuries, we shall call "romanticist," while we shall call artists of the nineteenth century more specifically "romantics."

Psychologically, dissatisfaction can express itself in three major ways, namely (1) in attempts at improvement, (2) in surrender to despair, and (3) in evasions and attempts to escape.

1. Attempts at improvement in politics take the form of revolutionary struggles, and in economics that of social reform movements. During the classic-romantic era these facets are well exemplified by the revolutions in North America (1776), France (1789), South America (1810), Poland and Italy, Roumania, Bulgaria, Greece, Ireland, Russia and Czechoslovakia, and on the other hand by the rise of the labour movement and of socialism. In graphic arts these attempts expressed themselves in such devastating satire as pervades Daumier's cartoons; and in literature in pamphleteering, propaganda, and art criticism. Music, however, unless associated with words, can hardly do anything positive about dissatisfaction, since it cannot translate feeling into action.

2. The second reaction, complete breakdown and despair, is, in the recent past, reflected by the great increase in nervous diseases and in suicides. Indeed, insanity claimed many important romantic artists, poets, philosophers and composers. As symbols of well-ordered procedures, works of art in general can hardly offer any analogies to such personal defeats.

3. The third adjustment, escape from unsatisfactory reality through vicarious satisfaction or relaxation, constitutes the chief means left for a distressed spirit to make life acceptable. It may be achieved by the flight from *(a)* the here, *(b)* the now, and *(c)* the crushing threat of immediate outside circumstance, and each provides materials for significant artistic expression.

(a) The flight from the here leads to distant places, like the countryside or the colourful Orient — in literature to pastoral poetry, travelogues, tales of Indians, Eskimoes, or of inner Africa. With an admixture of escape from the present the flight from the here reaches the past glories of India (as in the spread of Buddhism in the Occident), the Arabian Nights, the Crusades, or the afterlife in heaven. The religious revival, Catholic and Protestant alike, thus was an important facet of the romantic era.

(b) The second kind of goal, that of temporal flight, may, as we have seen, be the past or also the future. The search for the former will be directed toward traditions of family and nation. Nationalism and historicism are therefore two of the strongest traits of romanticism with a great influence on music. Flight into the future leads to idealism and Utopianism. Excepting a certain religious fervour, these activities can hardly influence music.

(c) The last avenue toward finding vicarious outlets for insufferable surroundings is the flight from them to a concentration on the inner adventure of self. It led, during the nineteenth century, to individualism, to expressionism, to impressionism, to withdrawal (solipsism, academicism, ivory-tower-ism, monasticism), and to the development of psychoanalysis.

Each of the escape mechanisms mentioned contributed to the music of the nineteenth century. *(a)* The flight to distant places opened the door to picturesque orientalism in opera and ballet, the interest in non-European instruments, such as Chinese blocks, gong, cymbals, triangle and marimba, and in non-European scales. *(b)* The retreat to the past brought the revival of Gregorian chant and the recovery and spiritual rediscovery of the music of earlier periods in general. It led to the emergence of national schools delving into, and employing much material from folklore. It stimulated research into folklore and interest in folk dances and folk opera. The desire to understand the work of art in its historical-social setting also springs from this source. *(c)* Individualism expressed itself in music as a search for special effects — sudden contrasts, certain characteristic chords or skips, highly differentiated orchestration, fragmentariness and surprise endings, contravention of accepted tonalities, *etc.* Emotionalism made itself felt especially in erratic and chromatic melodies and dissonant chords, which finally, in our century, led to the revision of the basic assumptions of classic and baroque music, *i.e.* of the keys, and the chords and cadences derived from them.

A word of caution seems necessary here. Classicism and romanticism are the two general attitudes — known by almost as many different names as there are authors who discuss this problem — between which the pendulum of artistic styles swings in a rather complex manner. Never, however, does this pendulum reach the extreme of complete realization of either; for this would spell death to art either in frozen formalism or in total dissolution. In all works of art and in all periods, therefore, we find both classicist and romanticist traits. When we classify a work or a period as classicist and another as romanticist we merely indicate the relative prominence of the particular traits. The analysis of these traits according to the principles discussed above, and the consequent understanding of their combination in any particular work of art or period is all the more valuable to us.

Bibliography

Bibliographies for Classicism and Romanticism are found following the selections "Music and Society in the Age of Enlightenment" (see p. 258) and "Romantic Principles" (see p. 308)

18

THE eighteenth century was one in which the ostentatious style of the Baroque gave way to the lighter and simpler style which is known as Classic. At the beginning of the century the works of Bach and Handel had yet to be written; by its end Mozart had come and gone. This transition from Baroque to Classic is one of the most complex in the history of music. Currents and cross-currents, influences and counterinfluences are numerous, and while much research has been done, much remains before a truly comprehensive understanding of the century may be achieved.

One of the most important forces behind the change in style was a social one, the emergence of a bourgeoisie or monied, nonaristocratic class as patrons of music. Not only did they constitute a new and sizable group of musical amateurs, but with the institution of public concerts they became a paying audience who had to be pleased if their financial support was to be retained. No longer were the church and the courts of the nobility the ones who determined the course of musical style; it was now the middle class who "called the tune" and it has remained so to this day.

This new source of musical patronage required music which would not be overly taxing on their abilities either as amateur performers or as listeners, and the resulting style was one that was simpler in melody, harmony, rhythm, and counterpoint. Yet, in spite of its simpler elements, it was possible to develop the Classic style to a high degree of artistic complexity, as Mozart did, but it must be remembered also that Mozart was a financial failure during the decade when he tried to survive as a freelance composer in Vienna. Melodies were less ornate and more lyric, possibly because of what is thought to be a greater influence of folksong, and melody came to dominate musical composition as never before. Harmonies, although still somewhat like those of the late Baroque in their tonal progressions, tended to move or change at a considerably slower rate of speed. The driving, motorlike rhythms of the Baroque were softened, and rhythm was subordinated to melody, setting it off in regular and predictable units, usually of four or eight measures. Counterpoint was deemphasized although not abandoned completely. Good counterpoint was still necessary between the melody and the bass, and frequently the inner parts might add a third and even a fourth contrapuntal line for a short time, but the counterpoint no longer began with the first measure and continued to the last.

The first trends toward the simpler style may be seen early in the century in France. France had never participated in the Baroque style to the extent that the Germanic countries and Italy had. A lighter style seemed more to the French taste, and they were the first to abandon the Baroque in favor of *le style galant,* sometimes also referred to as Rococo. This was still the style of an aristocracy, however, even though that aristocracy was beginning to find amusement in aping the manners of the lower classes. It remained for the German composers to adopt this style near the mid-point of the century and to develop it into the Classic style that came to be accepted not only as German but as pan-European. In their movement toward the final achievement of the Classic style, the German composers took two different, though not mutually exclusive, routes. One route stressed expressive and emotional qualities, as seen in the music of Carl Philipp Emanuel Bach, son of Johann Sebastian Bach. The second route, and the one which is more commonly known, stressed the formal possibilities of the style, as exemplified by the works of Mozart. By the close of the century the two trends were ready to unite in the music of Beethoven. The social reasons for the change in style from Baroque to Classic and the relationship of music to society during the Classic period are the subjects of the following selection.

Hugh Ottaway teaches and lectures, mainly in the West Midlands of England, broadcasts, and reviews for *The Musical Times.* Among his works are *Vaughan Williams* (London, Novello, 1966), *Sibelius* (London, Novello, 1968), and *William Walton* (London, Novello, scheduled to appear in 1972). He is a contributor to R. Simpson, ed., **The Symphony,* 2 vols. (Harmondsworth, Middlesex, Penguin, 1967), and to vol. 3 of Alec Robertson and Denis Stevens, eds., **The Pelican History of Music,* (Harmondsworth, Middlesex, Penguin, 1968). The following article was written as an introductory chapter to the section concerning late-eighteenth-century music in vol. 3 of *The Pelican History.* Many of the points raised are given considerable development by the author in succeeding chapters of that volume, to which the reader should refer.

Music and Society in the Age of Enlightenment

HUGH OTTAWAY

Mozart is a child of the Encyclopédie, Beethoven of the Revolution; their very greatness lay in the fact that they expressed the humanity of their own time, not the sentimental hankering after the emotions of the past.

EDWARD J. DENT

By 1750 the baroque state had passed its zenith. Absolute monarchy and feudal landlordism were to remain the dominant features of European society for many years to come, but the forces of change—bourgeois, rational, contemptuous of dogma—were already building up their pressure. This had much to do with the expansion of trade and the development of science. The scientific achievements of the seventeenth and early eighteenth centuries, culminating in the work of Newton, had given men renewed confidence in the power of independent thought. If human reason could "reconstruct" the universe, then equally it could remake society. While pleasure-loving aristocrats, the arbiters of taste and fashion, were delighting in the rococo, a new technique of criticism was being sharpened under their noses. One thinks first of Voltaire and the French *philosophes:* men like Montesquieu, imbued with the liberalism of Locke; Diderot and the Encyclopedists; Jean-Jacques Rousseau. . . . There are many differences here, but a desire for freedom and toleration, an awareness of human potentiality, and, with the striking exception of Rousseau, a passionate belief in reason as the key to enlightenment and progress—these were the all-pervading influences. In asserting the supremacy of "feeling" and of "nature," Rousseau released tremendous hidden energies; both the Revolution and romanticism were profoundly indebted to him.

FROM Hugh Ottaway, "Music and Society in the Age of Enlightenment," pp. 11-22 of vol. 3 of Alec Robertson and Denis Stevens, eds., *The Pelican History of Music* (Harmondsworth, Middlesex, Penguin Books Ltd.). Copyright 1968 by Penguin Books. Reprinted by permission of the publisher.

Whatever its contradictions and cross-currents — Voltaire *v.* Rousseau; reason *v.* feeling — the Enlightenment was a movement of immense optimism and promise. Significantly, its centre was France, the country in which autocracy had been most crushingly imposed and had conspicuously failed to justify its God-like pretensions. But the ideas of the Enlightment were not the possession of any one country; nor did they express themselves exclusively in literature. In one form or another, they coloured every aspect of eighteenth-century culture, not least the world of music.

Quite apart from their wider importance, Rousseau and Diderot, like d'Alembert and Grimm, have an immediate bearing on the history of music. When the Neapolitan *opera buffa* "hit" Paris in 1752, they were among its most polemical champions. They were quick to recognize that the *buffo* style, however slight, was human and alive and therefore capable of growth, whereas the French heroic opera *(tragédie lyrique),* even in the hands of so great a master as Rameau, represented a dying tradition, tied irrevocably to the forms and myths of autocracy. And so they acclaimed the "new music" based on naturalness, simplicity and reason — ideals to be reiterated again and again in the years ahead. Rousseau attacked Rameau in his *Lettre sur la musique française* (1753) — also in the *Encyclopédie* (1751-72), to which he was the principal contributor on music — and himself became an influential amateur composer. Grimm declared that one aria by Hasse or Buranello was more valuable than all Rameau's operas put together! It is easy to smile and say how wrong he was. At the time, he was right. The *Guerre des Bouffons* was a battle for the future, based on principle, and was not at all concerned with the niceties of historical judgement.

However clear-headed its protagonists, history is always richer and more original in its creations than anyone can foresee. Even the Encyclopedists had a limited appreciation of the way in which the Enlightenment would reveal itself musically. In particular, their theories effectively concealed from them the importance of instrumental and orchestral music. Grétry, who realized their ideals more persuasively than anyone — except the creator of *Le Nozze di Figaro!* — was first and last an operatic composer; he thought the new instrumental forms inadequate, even inept, *as means of communication* and believed that Haydn, too, would have written operas rather than symphonies if only he had met Diderot![1] Small wonder, then, that France, so fertile in ideas, contributed little to the rise of the sonata outlook. Compared with Mozart and Haydn, Grétry and Gossec are minor figures indeed. The sonata style was largely the

[1]Grétry would have known little or nothing of the operas Haydn did write. These were for his own productions at Esterház and did not travel like the symphonies, quartets, etc. Only very recently has a revival of interest in them taken place.

creation of Austrian, Czech and German musicians, and it developed in a milieu hitherto dominated by the highly artificial Italian opera of the courts. Just as we look to Paris for the mainstream of enlightened thought, so we turn to Mannheim and other German cities, and most of all Vienna, for a comparable ferment in the world of music.

Style Galant

Wherever artists challenged the baroque tradition, they stressed the importance of communication and simplicity. One thinks of Telemann advising his students to keep away from "the old fellows who believe in counterpoint rather than imagination." "Music," he argued, "ought not to be an effort, an occult science, a sort of black magic. . . . He who writes for the many does better work than he who writes for the few." Such views imply the existence of a new, middle-class public not content to participate vicariously in the culture of the courts. Meanwhile, aristocratic art was itself changing. The salon and the boudoir supplanted the opera-house, the painter the architect, as the essential expression of the late baroque. A private sensibility emerged from beneath the public grandeur, and strength of line became dissolved into rococo elegance. The old world had entered its autumnal phase: As Max Graf has splendidly put it, "the giant of the Baroque style had been transformed into an effeminate worldling with refined tastes and impotent longings."

Frequently, a single term is made to cover both these trends. The *style galant*, we are told, is characterized by melodic and formal elegance and a light, homophonic texture (melody and accompaniment) with a slow rate of chord change. Good enough. And then we find the term applied to music as diverse as Telemann's *Musique de Table*, a coloratura aria by Hasse or Graun, the opening movement of a Stamitz symphony, the lean, two-part texture of a sonata by C. P. E. Bach, an *affettuoso* movement from a Quantz trio sonata—and so on. If we compare the two extremes here, Hasse and Stamitz, we experience quite different worlds of feeling. With its elegant ornamentation and embellishment, Hasse's coloratura is pure rococo. This is indeed *galant* ("courtly"). In Stamitz, however, the "effeminate worldling" displays an unwonted masculinity: the homophonic texture is part of his music's assertiveness; it is a forceful, antibaroque gesture, matched by dynamic contrasts and instrumental fire.[2] Exceptionally, the term *style bourgeois* is used to mark this dis-

[2]For illustration, listen to the first movement from the Symphony in E flat (*La melodia Germanica*, No. 3) recorded on HLP 18. The second movement, too, is revealing; its sentiment is "domestic" rather than "courtly."

tinction, which is historically an important one. For although the *galant* and the *bourgeois* are aspects of the same cultural situation and share the same basically homophonic technique, their content is different; on the one hand a dissolution of the old "heroic" ideals, on the other a burgeoning of the new tonal drama of conflict and development. True, this distinction is immediately blurred in the pleasantries of polite social music, which doubtless explains why *"galant"* is so freely used. The vast quantity of social chatter which glutted the expanding music market of the 1760s and 1770s aimed at pleasing both the old and the new consumer. That this established a new "norm of expression" is shown again and again in contemporary musical journalism. One critic, writing in 1787, complained that Mozart's string quartets (the six dedicated to Haydn) did not "unanimously please," whereas the music of Kozeluch was "welcomed everywhere." Kozeluch, a prominent market name, is now "unanimously" forgotten.

It is to the *style bourgeois* that the great classical works of the last two decades of the century are indebted for their dramatic boldness. Classicism marks the climax of the anti-baroque movement.

"Good Taste": A Popular Fallacy

The new universal language of the so-called *style galant* forms the background to the achievement of C. P. E. Bach, Gluck, Haydn, Mozart and many lesser men.

From time to time one still meets with the assumption that, however great their individuality, the composers of the pre-revolutionary era, even Haydn and Mozart, worked within the well-defined limits of "good taste." The remedy for this is to read what their contemporaries had to say. "Good taste" is frequently the invention of the next generation. When Frederick the Great of Prussia resisted the music of the pre-classical symphonists, he did so precisely in the name of good taste, by which he meant the style of Hasse, Graun and Quantz. What he thought of Haydn and Mozart—if, indeed, he ever allowed their music to sully his ears—remains obscure. However, the views of others are well known.

At least from the time of *Figaro* (1786), Mozart was generally regarded as an over-rich, extravagant composer, of "more genius than taste"; his music was "too strongly spiced" and "overloaded with instruments." *Don Giovanni* was denounced for its "exaggerated, debauching contrasts." *Die Zauberflöte* was said "to make war on good taste and sane reason in a spectacle that dishonours the poetry of our age." These were the judgements of contemporary critics, the guardians of "taste." It was only when belaboured by the revolutionary Beethoven that they began to use Mozart as a model of propriety, and for this they "re-created" him in their own chosen image. Even that was not the end. "After he was dead people began to make him into a romantic. *The Marriage of Figaro* was almost a revolutionary manifesto; later generations, especially where the opera was patronized by a court and aristocracy, interpreted it as a piece of Dresden china prettiness."[3]

On the whole, Haydn got away with it far more lightly. There were many warmly appreciative notices. But one cannot escape the conclusion that he was also considered more lightly: "the most original humour and the most vivacious and most pleasant wit"—this is the aspect of his work most frequently commented on, both ways. Some were agreeably amused, for Haydn was "naturally playful and alluring"; others dismissed him as altogether frivolous. His apparent whimsicality, not good taste, is the predominant impression. (It must be stressed that these were the reactions of critics, not of the new musical public.)

Haydn was the great creative innovator of the second half of the century—"one of the great men against their time," Einstein calls him—and in a curious, negative way this seems to have told to his advantage. From the critics' point of view, he was always something of an outsider; his music was *expected* to behave unconventionally, unpredictably. But Mozart was an insider, aristocratically trained, a brilliant exponent of the courtly graces who had unaccountably "gone wrong." His later music was fraught with a strange, enigmatic passion, subversive of good order; and as everybody knew, it was the music of a man who had rebelled against his patron. At least to the composer Naumann, Mozart was "a musical *sans-culotte.*"

Classicism

Perhaps this blanket term, as difficult to define as its supposed opposite, Romanticism, is largely responsible for the fallacy of "good taste." For it does imply a certain composure, control and restraint. "Passions," wrote Mozart, "whether violent or not, should never be expressed when they reach an unpleasant stage; and music, even in the most terrible situations, should never offend the ear, but should charm it and always remain music." This is one aspect of eighteenth-century classicism, and it explains how lesser artists could hope to mask their mediocrity with a show of good manners. Hence the hollow conventionality of the minor music of this period.

[3]Edward J. Dent, *Opera* (Penguin Books, 1945).

We must distinguish between form and formality, the truly classical and the merely "classicist." Only in this way can we hope to see classicism as a positive and not a negative. When Tovey remarks on "all that variety of colour and rhythm and continual increase of breadth which is one of the most unapproachable powers of the true classics," he is directing us to a vital creative process, full of energy and life: the process creates the form, not vice versa.[4] It is a pity we have to generalize about classical "forms," as if they were moulds for casting or plans to be fulfilled; for as soon as they become such, formality has taken over, and this is as true for us as listeners as it is for a composer. Ideally, we should concern ourselves only with the form each movement reveals—the particular way in which themes, rhythms, keys, etc. interact and are held in equilibrium. In the classical style this sense of equilibrium is repeatedly threatened and disrupted, however subtly, but always renewed, re-established. This is Tovey's "continual increase of breadth."

Another necessary distinction is that between the classical outlook of the 1780s and 1790s, of which the German scholar Winckelmann was the foremost prophet, and the heavier, more doctrinaire classicism of the beginning of the century. Winckelmann's "noble simplicity and tranquil greatness" was liberal in intention, largely Hellenic in inspiration, and consciously opposed to the rococo and baroque. Humane and enlightened, this Hellenic revival had as its aim, not art for art's sake, but rather the triumph of art over the sorrows and imperfections of life. In music, probably the clearest and most helpful illustration is Mozart's G minor Symphony (K.550): Schumann was right in hearing this as "Grecian lightness and grace," though he seems to have missed the suffering which Mozart's imagination had encompassed and subdued.

Finally, a further point of historical perspective. It is often assumed that, if the Enlightenment was predominantly classical, the Revolution must have been romantic. It ought to be clear from Beethoven that this won't do at all; but Beethoven invariably has the force of a special case, and so conclusions go undrawn. The root of the trouble lies in a fondness for categories considered more or less in isolation: not surprisingly, the categories lose their meaning and become mere labels. When Beethoven revolutionized eighteenth-century music, he vastly expanded the classical forms and gave them a content that was highly charged with the romantic virtue of enthusiasm; like most major artists of the Revolution, he remained fundamentally classical in outlook, though his music repeatedly modifies our conception of the term. The Revolution certainly cleared the way for romanticism but practised it only marginally.[5]

[4]Tovey is still unsurpassed for his insight into "the true classics": see his well-known *Essays in Musical Analysis*, and his little-known *Beethoven* (O.U.P., 1944).

[5]For a wider discussion of this situation, see Arnold Hauser, *The Social His-*

Composer and Patron

In the Age of Enlightenment the forward-looking composer had greater problems than the writer. The writer had only to outwit the censorship: despite a struggle with church and state, the *Encyclopédie* appeared in print; by substituting *Freude* ("joy") for *Freiheit* ("freedom"), Schiller could publish his celebrated *Ode* (1785) and nobody was long deceived.[6] Music, however, is not fully realized until it is performed. And while the means of music-making were largely controlled by the courts and the aristocracy, aristocratic patronage was virtually indispensable. Only gradually, with the growing importance of the middle classes, did public concerts beome a prominent feature of musical life. In this and in the publishing of music, London and Paris led the way. Beethoven made a living of sorts, in Vienna, by selling and performing his own music. Mozart conspicuously failed to do so. Haydn served a princely family until he was nearly sixty and then, free at last, took the plunge into a completely different world, that of Salomon's London concerts.[7]

Times were changing, yet the terms of patronage remained much the same. To their patrons many musicians were liveried servants, superior artisans, in standing comparable with cooks and valets. Mozart, we know, found his status quite intolerable. Haydn was a great deal better placed, and more equable in temperament, but shortly before his unexpected release he described himself as "a slave," "a poor wretch," "constantly harassed with much work and all too little leisure." With the decline of the aristocracy, the role of such an artist became increasingly equivocal. He had still to meet his patron's demands, and this could mean a more personal control than that imposed by any censorship; at the same time, he was an innovator, developing in music an outlook that was fundamentally liberal and middle-class.

This does not mean that the great composers of the Enlightenment — Beethoven's predecessors — were revolutionaries anxious to proclaim the Year One. They were not. To some extent the courtly milieu could represent for them the continuity of civilization, within which the forces of reason and enlightenment would prevail. Haydn's Austrian Hymn was

---

tory of Art, Vol. 3 (Routledge Paperbacks, 1962), especially Chapter 5, "Revolution and Art."

[6]On the other hand, a composer of instrumental music, however revolutionary, could hardly be sentenced to ten years' imprisonment for "criminal outspokenness," as the poet Schubart was, in Württemberg.

[7]Eighteenth-century London was the first great music market, which makes the feebleness of English-born composers all the more remarkable. Apart from Thomas Augustine Arne (1710-78), a *galant* composer of talent, and the younger Thomas Linley (1756-78), hardly one is worth mentioning.

both a patriotic gesture and an expression of esteem for the Habsburg monarchy. Nevertheless, as Wilfrid Mellers has remarked, it is at least symbolical that three of the most noted composers of *opera buffa*—Piccinni, Paisiello and Cimarosa—spent part of their lives in prison for political reasons. *Opera buffa* was "comic" entertainment, and because it was comic the tensions in society could be given expression; there was a good deal of veiled satire—and, with the aid of "ad-libbing," not so veiled. It is very significant that virtually all the greatest operas from the end of the period—*Le Nozze di Figaro, Don Giovanni, Die Zauberflöte,* even *Fidelio*—are in the so-called comic or popular tradition. *Fidelio* is in the form of a *Singspiel*, the German popular opera, but the form is revolutionized by the subject and its treatment: we can actually point to the moment when it ceases to be a *Singspiel* in any recognizable sense— Leonore's great recitative and aria *"Abscheulicher! wo eilst du hin!."* In this moment heroic opera is reborn. Far from belonging to a mythological Golden Age, like the heroines of *opera seria*, Leonore is Beethoven's own ideal of womanhood, precisely in the year 1805. And Beethoven, we remember, treated his patrons as equals, or, if they let him down, as scoundrels. These two facts are intimately related, and each should be interpreted in the light of Beethoven's belief that music is "a higher revelation than the whole of wisdom and the whole of philosophy."

A New Aesthetic Principle

We have seen something of the impact made by *opera buffa* on minds seeking a new, liberal culture. The early symphony stands in much the same relation to *opera buffa* as does the baroque *concerto grosso* to *opera seria*; it is a projection, in terms of instruments alone, of cultural values established in the theatre. What has come to be thought of as the language of "pure" music was hammered out as a means of expression in which the absence of words and action gave an opportunity, not to be "abstract" in the modern sense, avoiding human content, but to embody new forms of content in music possessing its own inner drama. The sonata style represents a change in aesthetic principle among the most far-reaching in musical history; for it introduces a dynamic view of musical structure, and in particular a dynamic approach to tonality.

The long-term effects of key-change are so important in the music of this period that their technical basis is well worth understanding. The task implied is less formidable than is sometimes supposed, though it is, in the main, beyond the scope of the present survey.[8]

[8]For a thorough treatment of this and related matters the reader should turn to *Harmony for the Listener,* by Robert L. Jacobs (O.U.P., 1958), an excellent book which shirks nothing yet assumes only the merest rudiments.

A BRIEF backward glance at harmonic development may be useful. What the textbooks call the "harmonic revolution" of *c*. 1600, associated with Monteverdi and the rise of opera, was a late achievement of Renaissance humanism. This revolution had much to do with the realization of personal emotion by a solo singer in a grand, heroic context; the changing harmonies added depth to the expressive qualities of the vocal line. This does not mean, however, that composers suddenly ceased to think polyphonically. Neither does it mean that harmony, as such, was a new resource. The so-called revolution was three parts evolution, the remaining one part being the attitude to harmony rather than harmony itself. By 1600, however, the exuberance of the humanist movement was being disciplined and controlled by the Counter-Reformation and the rise of the great autocracies. In music this was to lead to a reaffirmation of linear thinking, but within the unequivocal framework of the major-minor key-system. The great "monolithic" forms, the fugue and the passacaglia, are its most highly organized expressions—and its sternest disciplines. Discipline, as understood according to the "doctrine of temperaments and affections," was the foundation of baroque expression, and it lay in the close adherence to a single mood or emotion throughout the length of a musical movement. There was scope for all manner of invention and embellishment, but ideally nothing was permitted to disturb, and therefore weaken, the "affection." This is the root of the intensity and concentration of the great baroque structures. But the "affective" concept was fundamentally non-dramatic, statuesque, a face which is immediately evident in the formal and expressive character of the *da capo* aria. Hence the long-term use of key-change was limited and of a purely spatial (architectural) significance; it did not involve tonal conflict. Hence, too, the impersonal, monolithic character of baroque music and of baroque art in general, itself a reflection autocracy.

When, after the religious and dynastic struggles of the seventeenth century, the courts of Europe staged a revival of Renaissance splendour in the manner of Versailles, a new humanism was already waiting in the wings. The sonata, with techniques of conflict and development among its conscious resources, was the characteristic new creation, the form in which a hopeful, expanding view of the world opposed itself to the feudal and clerical dogmas of the old order. It was historically inevitable that the music of the Enlightenment, however else it might develop, would break away from the unitary, "affective" principle, replacing it with thematic contrasts and tonal drama.

Bibliography

The most extensive work in English on the music of the Classic period is vol. 5 of *The Oxford History of Music* (2d ed.; London, Oxford University Press, 1931). It is especially noteworthy because of its stress on the historical importance of C. P. E. Bach. Reinhard G. Pauly, *Music in the Classic Period* (Englewood Cliffs, N.J., Prentice-Hall, 1965), is a good introduction to its subject, and Friedrich Blume, *Classic and Romantic Music* (New York, Norton, 1970), is essential reading. Charles Rosen, *The Classical Style: Haydn, Mozart, Beethoven* (New York, Viking, 1971) is limited mostly to the composers mentioned in its title but contains a chapter devoted to the origins of the Classic style. Adam Carse, *The Orchestra in the XVIIIth Century* (Cambridge, Heffer, 1940), contains a chapter on the working conditions of musicians of the time and traces the development of the orchestra. Written almost seventy years ago, the essay of Romain Rolland, "The Origins of the Eighteenth-century 'Classic' Style," is again available in English in *Romain Rolland's Essays on Music* (New York, Dover, 1959). Periodical articles of interest are: Walter Dahms, "The 'Gallant' Style of Music," *The Musical Quarterly*, 11 (1925); Ruth Halle Rowen, "Some 18th-century Classifications of Musical Style," *The Musical Quarterly*, 33 (1947); and Curt Sachs, "Romantic Classicist or Classic?" *Musical America*, 76, no. 2 (1956).

A representative sampling of eighteenth-century music is contained in vol. 2 of the *Historical Anthology of Music*. Selected works of the Germanic composers may be found in the series *Denkmäler deutscher Tonkunst, Denkmäler der Tonkunst in Bayern, Denkmäler der Tonkunst in Österreich,* and *Das Erbe deutscher Musik*. General indices to all these collections may be found under "Editions, historical" in the *Harvard Dictionary of Music*, 2d ed. (1969). New editions of the works of both Haydn and Mozart are currently in progress by the Haydn Institute in Cologne and by Bärenreiter in Kassel.

19

A RT forms combining music and the theater are probably as old as both. It is generally accepted that ancient Greek drama used music, although many of the details are not and may never be known. Music also played a part in the liturgical drama of the medieval church in several of the dramatic forms of the Renaissance. These, however, are examples of the use of music *in* drama, not of a *union* of music and drama. Only when music and drama are united, when the entire text of the drama (or at least a large part of it) is set to music is opera considered to result.

Opera is sometimes regarded as a Baroque form, at least in essence, and in one sense this is correct. The first opera of which we have music dates from *ca.* 1600, and the Baroque saw the rapid development of opera from its earliest stage into what could be considered a new musical form. The idea of opera, however, seems more Renaissance than Baroque. Those responsible for the first operas were men of the Renaissance, and their work was the result of thought developed during the sixteenth century rather than new thought representing a break with the Renaissance.

The first operas were little more than intoned speech. Rhythms and inflexions of the vocal lines were attempts at duplication, albeit stylized, of natural speech patterns. Little if any thought was given to creating a new musical form, and purely musical pieces—those imposing musical form and logic upon the text—were not prevalent. Quickly, however, music came to dominate as more and more operas incorporated principles of musical form, resulting, by the turn of the eighteenth century, in the establishment in Italy of the number opera with recitatives, in which the early techniques of imitation of speech patterns survived, alternating with arias or ensemble numbers which were based on abstract musical principles and essentially ignored the recitative idea. The number opera existed almost exclusively until the music dramas of Wagner, and its influence still survives in operatic construction.

Until the nineteenth century, opera was a rather progressive musical medium—not surprisingly. After all, its creators considered themselves to be advanced thinkers living in an advanced time, and their recitative-type operas were a radical departure from polyphonic music. Also, at least one of opera's musical antecedents, the madrigal, was in its day certainly far from a conservative musical form (see "The Musical Form of the Madrigal," p. 149). Thus opera sometimes led the way musically: public performances of opera were established before public concerts of instrumental music, and, in fact, overtures to operas were some of the first compositions to be played in public concerts; opera used certain orchestral instruments (the trombone and the English horn for example) before they became common in symphonic music; and opera influenced some forms of vocal music as well (for example, the oratorios of Handel and certain of the cantatas of J. S. Bach that are inconceivable without first there having been opera).

Since Wagner the influence of opera upon the general musical scene has declined. While the Wagnerian strain of opera survived in the works of Richard Strauss, the century since Wagner has also seen the use of many new techniques in opera as well as the revival of old ones. Serialism has been applied to opera in the works of Berg and in Schönberg's unfinished "Moses and Aaron"; the strict number opera has been revived in such operas as Stravinsky's *The Rake's Progress;* jazz has appeared in a number of operas, among them Krenek's *Jonny spielt auf;* the Broadway musical theater has produced works which, if not quite true opera, certainly have strong operatic overtones; even rock music has spawned a work with operatic pretensions, *Jesus Christ, Superstar.*

Because of the large number of people involved, operatic production has become more and more expensive. Although such "grand operas" as Poulenc's *Les Dialogues des Carmélites* (a successful example) and Barber's *Anthony and Cleopatra* (an unsuccessful one) continue to appear, a smaller type of opera—the so-called chamber opera, involving fewer instrumentalists and singers and less lavish staging—has gained considerable popularity in recent years, especially among university and civic groups having more limited financial and musical resources. Such groups, unhampered by the restriction of taste imposed by the monied supporters of the public opera houses, have, in fact, come to be among the leaders in the production of new operas and in the advancement of new operatic techniques.

The following article concentrates on only one small portion of operatic history. Its purpose is to give the author's view of how and why opera was in the forefront in the eighteenth century; of how eighteenth-century operatic and nonoperatic music may have been interrelated; and especially of how opera may have contributed to the development of the sonata-principle (see page 275). But in passing the author also

260

gives an idea of some of the fundamental qualities of Italian opera, not only in its eighteenth-century manifestations but in its seventeenth-century beginnings as well.

Biographical information about Edward J. Dent can be found following the introduction to "The Musical Form of the Madrigal" (page 149).

Italian Opera in the Eighteenth Century, and Its Influence on the Music of the Classical Period

EDWARD J. DENT

There are few episodes in the history of music which have been treated with such scornful neglect as has been meted out to that period of Italian opera which began with Alessandro Scarlatti and ended, according to most historians, with the reforms of Gluck. The *Oxford History of Music,* in spite of the fact that it consecrates two of its six volumes to the eighteenth century, leaves it almost unmentioned. Impartiality is generally supposed to be one of the first qualities which a historian must possess; but it must be remembered that the historian, like the painter or the map-maker, has to represent the world which he sees as he sees it from his particular point of view. Distortion is the inevitable consequence of the laws of perspective, and the historian who sets impartiality before himself as an ideal can only achieve it by viewing his subject, not from one standpoint, but from a circle of points. Whatever point the historian takes, something will have to be foreshortened, something will be left inaccessible to the eye, and the writer who attempts to make the circuit of his subject in this way will probably be censured for both tediousness and inconsistency. The learned authors of the *Oxford History* are in no way to be blamed because they are not impartial. They made no concealment of the fact that they viewed the eighteenth century from a standpoint that was exclusively German. It was the standpoint of their generation: Wagner and Brahms once accepted by the leaders of musical thought in this country, it was hardly possible to avoid accepting as a general principle of musical criticism the supposition that whatever was German was good, and whatever was Italian was bad.

FROM *Sammelbände der Internationalen Musikgesellschaft,* 14 (1912-1913), 500-509. Reprinted by permission of Breitkopf & Härtel, Wiesbaden, and the Trustees for the Estate of Edward J. Dent.

To that they added the subsidiary principles that as a general rule sacred music was superior to secular and instrumental music to vocal, exception being made only for polyphonic choral writing, solo singing of a strictly declamatory type, and of course German *Lieder*.

These principles once established, it was only natural that eighteenth century Italian opera should be regarded as the concentrated expression of all that was most evil in the art of music. The period under review was the period of Bach and Handel. Bach never wrote operas at all; Handel's formed only the least important part of his output, and if lesser men than Handel wrote operas, it was not reasonable to suppose that they should have been any better than his.

Let us shift our position, and see if it is not possible to view the period in a different aspect. Let us call to mind the fact that the three greatest men of the period, J. S. Bach, Handel and Domenico Scarlatti, were almost negligible quantities as far as the general musical life of Europe was concerned. Bach was buried alive in the provincial towns of Central Germany; Handel had made his home with the mad English, and Domenico Scarlatti was settled permanently in Spain. There is not the least difficulty in obtaining a general idea of the Italian outlook on the music of the period, since our own Dr. Burney in his *General History of Music,* his German and Italian tour, and his life of Metastasio has left us copious record of the cultivated opinion of his day. There is no need to sneer at Burney for being a mere follower of fashion. His literary productions and his friendship with Johnson are sufficient guarantee of general culture; the Diary of his Travels and his History of Music show him to have been a serious researcher and a careful critic, although it is only natural that modern investigation should have disproved many of his statements. Burney's critical opinions may not be in accordance with those of the late nineteenth century, but he certainly represents the most broadminded and intelligent type of appreciation to be found in his day.

Nothing could be more misleading than to judge Italian opera by the criticisms passed on the London opera performances by Addison, Lord Chesterfield and other writers, whose knowledge of music was of the slightest, and who were only too willing to take the Philistine point of view, common enough in our own day, that a drama in which people sing instead of speaking is from the very outset ridiculous. If Italian opera as performed in London often reached a low artistic level, the fault lay, not with the operatic form itself, but with those who insisted on presenting opera in Italian to audiences who did not understand that language. There is really no reason why the performances in London should receive any more consideration than those in St. Petersburg: Italian opera was composed primarily for Italian audiences, and we must endeavour to consider it from an Italian point of view.

It may be well briefly to summarize the history of Italian opera during the previous century. The first originators of the operatic movement, Peri, Caccini and their circle, were literary rather than musical, judged at least in relation to the generations which preceded and followed them. They had aimed at the simplest and most direct expression of words, unencumbered by the rhythmical complications of the polyphonic style. But it must be borne in mind that the Florentine group even at their most austerely declamatory moments regarded the human voice as their principal means of expression. They were making the attempt to restore the drama to those primitive conditions in which speech and song were one and the same thing. Their poets provided them with a language that was almost music itself, as Symonds says of Tasso's *Aminta,* acted in 1572:

> This pastoral drama offered something ravishingly new, something which interpreted and gave a vocal utterance to tastes and sentiments that ruled the age. Poetry melted into music. Emotion exhaled itself in sensuous harmony. The art of the next two centuries, the supreme art of song, of words subservient to musical expression, had been indicated. This explains the sudden extraordinary success of the "Aminta." It was nothing less than the discovery of a new realm, the revelation of a specific faculty which made its author master of the heart of Italy. The very lack of concentrated passion lent it power. Its suffusion of emotion in a shimmering atmosphere toned with voluptuous melody, seemed to invite the lutes and viols, the mellow tenors, and the trained soprano voices of the dawning age of melody.

It was possibly a mistaken ideal in some ways—poetry trying its hardest to be music, and music trying to be speech; but the really important thing for us to notice is, that whether the result were speech or song, it was the human voice, and not the instruments, that produced it. The instruments are there, one may say, only to prevent the singer from lapsing completely into speech; and even in the *Nuove Musiche* of Caccini, which are definitely lyrical and musical, with many passages that strike the modern reader as startling in a harmonic sense, the main burden of the musical expression is none the less borne by the voice, and the strange harmonies are to be explained not as single points of emotional colour, but as the result of a continuous line of melody supported by occasional chords.

Monteverdi has generally been held up to admiration for his wealth of orchestral colour and his bold treatment of harmonic dissonances. A close study of the *Orfeo,* and better still of *L'incoronazione di Poppea,* shows us that even in spite of his large orchestra and his numerous instrumental interludes, it is the singing voice which dominates the drama. The timbre of particular groups of instruments may be used to intensify particular situations, bold successions of chords may enhance the effect of sudden mental changes on the part of the charac-

264

ters represented; but Monteverdi never loses sight of their supreme importance, and the more complicated his accompaniment becomes, the more is it necessary to interpret his voice part as pure singing, in order to preserve a just aesthetic balance. The practice of modern composers, to give the main intellectual interest to the orchestra and to let the voice declaim any notes that can be managed to fit in, was entirely foreign to Monteverdi's mind.

The rest of the seventeenth century shows us a development of technique rather than a change of ideals. There was a gradual tendency to make opera appeal more and more to popular audiences, instead of reserving it for the entertainment of the aristocracy. It became, as modern audiences would say, "more dramatic." There was more action taking place on the stage: there was less beauty of literary language, and more of a story that could be grasped as a succession of events. Instead of taking a story such as the myth of Orpheus, which everybody knew, the dramatist aimed rather at surprising his audience with the unravelling of a plot which was not familiar to them beforehand. But this unfamiliarity did not last long: one opera imitated another, and the general scheme of seventeenth century musical drama was soon reducible to a fairly constant formula. The fact was, and the fact remains, that a series of surprises is not really suited to musical interpretation. It is a disturbing factor in the steady development of the music; and the musician has so much difficulty already in maintaining his hold on our minds with any continuity that it is often ruinous to the music to let the audience be distracted by externals which do not belong to the musical atmosphere.

It was perhaps for this very reason that the opera of the late seventeenth century became more and more discontinuous. With a story such as that of Orpheus, the poet had no need to be always giving us information about facts. He could take most of the facts for granted and concentrate himself on pure poetry; and as a natural result, the musician was never hampered by the necessity of setting those uninteresting statements of plain facts to music. It was the increased amount of time that had now to be given to mere explanations which forced Cavalli, Cesti, Legrenzi and the rest into the expedient of formal recitative. The balance could only be restored by the over-development of the aria.

Alessandro Scarlatti has often been censured for having stereotyped the Da Capo aria as the one and only form in which operatic emotions could be expressed. One might as well censure Beethoven for writing in sonata form instead of in those of the passacaglia, toccata and fugue. Whether Scarlatti is to be held responsible for the change it is difficult to say with certainty. He may very possibly have followed the example set by men of less lasting fame; at any rate the change can be followed without difficulty in his own works. A careful study of his operas and cantatas leads to the conclusion that so far from merely taking the line of least resistance in abandoning the varied forms employed by Cavalli, Stradella, and by himself in his earlier years, he acted in the best interest of musical development along the lines which at that particular moment were the most important. The little airs in binary form and on ground basses are often exquisite examples of neat and elegant construction, but they do not give much scope for dramatic expression. Forms which depend on the precise balance of a number of short phrases in different keys do not lend themselves to treatment on a large scale: they either lose the symmetry which is their principal charm, or else they retain their symmetry and give an uncomfortable sense of stiffness to the poetical expression. Moreover, the more complicated of these small forms — which we may perhaps compare with such poetical forms as the triolet and the roundel — often demanded a second stanza of verse to make their construction clear to an audience, and it will readily be understood that this exaggerated emphasis on formal construction was a hindrance to dramatic expression. The Da Capo form, which Scarlatti selected as the one and only type, was not perhaps the best possible of all forms for his purpose, but it was a step in the right direction, and probably the best that he could find at the moment. It was left for Mozart and his contemporaries to remove the blemish of the Da Capo, and to perfect the structure of the developed binary aria.

It is not until after the close of Scarlatti's artistic career that we come to that crowning achievement of Italian *opera seria* — the dramas of Metastasio. Scarlatti had been associated principally with Silvio Stampiglia, an Arcadian of the school of Marino, and in his last years, with Apostolo Zeno, a poet still respected in the history of Italian literature, but harsh in diction and over-learned in style. This criticism is indeed almost exactly the equivalent of that which was passed on the music of Scarlatti himself, strange as it may seem to us nowadays. Scarlatti, it must be pointed out, was really a composer of chamber music rather than a dramatist, and his audiences complained that his arias were too severe and intellectual for the theatre.

In these days, when few English people aspire to any acquaintance with Italian literature beyond a few hackneyed extracts from the most difficult of all Italian poets, the name of Metastasio is almost unknown. To Italians he is still one of the great classical poets, and it suffices to say that Carducci wrote of him in terms of the sincerest admiration. The remarkable thing about Metastasio is that his literary fame rests entirely on the librettos which he wrote for operas and oratorios. There are some thirty dramas which he composed with no other object in view than to be set to music. They were not written to be acted and afterwards turned into operas; they were designed for music, and designed with the consciousness that they were not complete until they were set to music and sung. Their beauties were recognized from the very first, and from

1723 to almost the end of the century they were set not once only but over and over again by innumerable composers: some, such as Hasse, even set the same drama twice over themselves.

It is difficult for us moderns to realize the effect which this must have had upon composers, singers and audiences. Whatever Metastasio's merits may be as compared with Ariosto or Carducci, he was unquestionably the greatest Italian poet of his day, the greatest perhaps that Italy had seen since the death of Tasso more than a hundred years before. His style was vigorous and direct in the extreme, carefully designed to make an instantaneous impression on the hearer, and to remain fixed in his memory. By the middle of the eighteenth century the average opera-goer—and that probably meant the greater part of the Italian people, at any rate in the towns—must have known most of Metastasio's dramas by heart, must have known them far more intimately than the average English play-goer knows *Hamlet* or the *Merchant of Venice*. And not only did he know the dramas but he must have known a good deal of the music to which Leo, Pergolesi, Vinci, Rinaldo di Capua and others had set them. Italian opera had indeed arrived once more at something like the conditions which were so favourable to its early development; stories which everybody knew by heart, expressed in noble and dignified language, which gave the fullest scope to the interpretative skill of composers and singers.

That the system broke down was not by any means due to the so-called reforms of Gluck. Gluck's innovations took effect only in France and Germany, where there was already developing a considerable prejudice against opera in Italian. No; Metastasio's dramas lost their hold over the Italian public because their ideal was too lofty for audiences which demanded amusement rather than edification. The seventeenth century had in characteristic fashion mingled tragedy and buffoonery; Metastasio having eliminated the comic element from his dramas (although I may point out that Metastasio had a very considerable sense of humour, as may be seen in his letters) the comic spirit had to find its outlet elsewhere. Naples had taken the lead quite early in the century with a school of comic opera in the local dialect, a school so short-lived that even Scarlatti only took up with the movement when it was in its decadence; it was rescued by the genius of the Venetian Goldoni, who in collaboration with Galuppi and other composers produced an enormous number of really amusing comic operas. It is however the inevitable fate of all really comic opera to degenerate under the evil influence of popularity into sentimental opera, since the public likes to have its feelings agreeably stirred at the least possible expense either of emotion or intelligence. When the time arrived for Mozart to write his masterpieces, *opera seria* had come practically to an end outside Italy itself, and Vienna only wanted to listen to musical comedy. In Italy the tradition remained, and has remained more or less continuously down to the present day; moreover, just as Italian opera fertilized German instrumental music in the days of Metastasio, so it continued to do so in the days of Cherubini, Rossini and Bellini, as long in fact as German music maintained the classical tradition. One might indeed say with some truth that the classical tradition is nothing more or less than the Italian tradition.

This brings us back to a more detailed consideration of the conventional aria and its artistic significance. Between 1720 and 1730 a marked change came over the form. If we look at almost any aria of Scarlatti's middle period, we shall find that the first part of it divides into two sections, the first modulating to the dominant, and the second returning to the tonic. The second section, after which the first is repeated, generally deals with the same thematic material, and modulates to remoter keys. Already by 1702 Scarlatti had (in his cantatas at any rate) arrived at subdividing the two halves of his first section in such a way as to present two definite themes—a first theme in the tonic, a second in the dominant, then the first theme in the dominant followed by the second theme in the tonic. This scheme makes itself gradually more and more conspicuous in the later operas; but it is only very rarely indeed that Scarlatti tries to make the two themes strikingly different in emotional content. Such treatment is reserved for arias in which the poet has laid great emphasis on the conflicting nature of the emotions to which the character on the stage is supposed to be a prey. In these cases, Scarlatti is sometimes startlingly effective in the invention of short phrases which contrast in character in the most vivid manner possible. His successors adopted a rather different plan. Their arias aim less at being intensely dramatic than at being broadly musical.

It is probably that the change was due to some extent to the influence of such singers as Farinelli, Vittoria Tesi and a few others who came into prominence at that time, and who seem to have achieved a standard of executive ability markedly superior to that of the previous generation. We need only refer to the pages of Burney to convince ourselves that Farinelli at any rate was no mere virtuoso but an artist of the first rank, and a man of exceptional dignity of character. Under this influence the aria was gradually more and more extended. In the first part of the aria, the two themes become clearly contrasted, and definitely separated, so as to give the singer an opportunity of exhibiting his powers in contrasted styles, generally in a broad sustained melody to begin with, followed by passages of brilliant *coloratura* as a second theme. The instrumental *ritornello* is expanded at the same time, and by entering after the first definite close in the dominant gives the singer a moment's repose, and adds to the general constructive effect of the composition. As long as this system remained in the hands of great composers such as Hasse and Jommelli, and great singers such as Farinelli, there was no lowering of artistic standards. Historians have often reprinted the alleged rules which regulated the composition of operas: the lists of arias — *aria di portamento, aria d'agilità, aria d'imitazione, aria di mezzo carattere* etc., and have held up to ridicule the system by which each scene, that is each entry of a character, invariably terminated with an aria, after which the character left the stage. These rules, it need hardly be said, were like all rules of musical composition, merely the deductions of theorists from the practice of the great composers. In all the arts, as in commerce, there are trade names for certain things, there are certain more or less regular categories into which those who are not men of genius find it convenient to classify them. There is no reason why the so-called rules of the Italian opera should affect our judgment any more than the rules which according to instruction-book have regulated the construction of fugues and sonatas. It so happened that at this particular epoch composers were preoccupied in the main with questions of what we call *form*, a preoccupation which lasted from the days of Scarlatti to those of Beethoven. At other times other problems have come into the foreground, just as in painting there was a period when all artists were obsessed with problems of perspective. It was only natural that having found certain obviously satisfactory forms they should insist upon them until their main outlines were so familiar to audiences that the composers could try all sorts of experiments in varying their inner details with a view to poetical expression.

For it was undoubtedly emotional expression at which the Italian composers were aiming. Indeed it was perhaps the weakness of their system that they sacrificed almost everything else to it. If every scene ended with an aria, it was because the actor was on the stage for that purpose. He was there to express himself vocally, and if he left the stage without an aria, he was for practical purposes a *persona muta*.

So intent were the Italians on the expression of individual personality in an aria that it was a long time before they could even reconcile themselves to duets or ensembles. They were moreover content, while a character was singing his aria, to ignore completely all other factors in the drama; one might say they had put themselves so completely into the personality of the singer of the moment that they could see nothing except what he was supposed to be seeing himself.

It will easily be understood that so imaginative a frame of mind was not possible among audiences to whom Italian was a foreign language, and that, just as there were few poets who reached Metastasio's literary level, there were few composers able to set his tragedies in a worthy style, and few singers able to give a worthy interpretation of them. A letter of Metastasio's quoted by Burney shows what his feelings were towards the maltreatment of his dramas by indifferent audiences and performers.

Metastasio, writing to an Abbé at Saluzzo about 1760–70,

"Thanks him and the ladies and gentlemen of Saluzzo for defending his poor dramas from the injuries which they daily suffer in all the theatres of Europe, from those ignorant and vain local heroes and heroines, who having substituted the imitation of flageolets and nightingales to human affections, render the Italian style a national disgrace, in the opinion of those countries which have been obliged to us for all their knowledge of the art."

"This alludes," says Burney, "to the abridging and changing the scenes and airs of his dramas, to humour the caprice of singers, who disregard character, place, and propriety not only in *Pasticcio* operas, but in every other, where no scruple is made to introduce an *Aria d'abilità* or *di bravura* which has been applauded in a former drama, without the least attention to the preceding recitative, or business of the scene. These airs taken out of their original niche, when translated in the book of the opera, continue to incline the good people of England to imagine the words of an opera to be *all nonsense;* and that even the musical dramas of Metastasio are as absurd and subject to ridicule, as those which Addison had described with so much pleasantry in the Spectator."

The aria remained fairly constant, whether in serious, comic or sentimental opera, to the end of the century. As the first part became more and more developed, the second part lost its importance; as new means of expression were found for the voice, and ornaments became more and more conventional, so that there was no dramatic effect to be expected any longer from the repetition of the first section after the da capo, the second section fell out altogether, and we see from the arias in Mozart's *Idomeneo* that a more wonderful and more passionate style of expression had been evolved out of structural necessities. The transposition of the two themes from tonic and dominant into dominant and tonic respectively necessitated a reconsideration of their position with regard to the singer's compass; and even in Vinci's day this had led to modifications of melody, which were developed by Mozart in a very striking way.

It will already have become clear, I hope, that this steady development of the operatic aria had a considerable influence on the development of the sonata and symphony, which took place for the most part in Germany, and which is naturally associated with the names of Emanuel Bach, Haydn, Mozart and Beethoven. We must however be careful to remember that the sonata was not suddenly invented by Emanuel Bach out of nothing. Recent research has demonstrated that there were Italian writers of clavier sonatas before Bach, and not merely sonatas of the undifferentiated, mainly contrapuntal type which we associate with the idiom of John Sebastian Bach or Handel, but sonatas which show at once their close affinity with those of Haydn and Mozart. This point has been elucidated by the labours of Fausto Torrefranca, the results of whose researches on the sonatas of Galuppi and Platti are to be found in recent numbers of the *Rivista Musicale Italiana*[1].

It has been the frequent tendency of musical historians to suppose that the development of any particular forms, *e.g.*, the sonata, the symphony, the overture, can be traced without any reference to other branches of music. This principle is often misleading, and we shall often do better to regard the actual form as a thing common to all kinds of music at any given period, and the technique of the particular instrument or group of instruments as an entirely separate matter. If we wish to consider the developments of musical form which ultimately led to the classical sonata, we must make a careful study of Italian operas and chamber-cantatas in the later seventeenth and early eighteenth centuries, and we may profitably study the operas of Lully and Purcell in addition. There are a variety of aspects under which the problem may be considered. During the earlier period the most interesting phenomenon is the interrelation of form and tonality. Thus in the period represented conveniently for us by the Fitzwilliam Virginal Book we see that a strong sense of modality as opposed to modern tonality goes with employment of forms which we may represent by the formula A_1 A_2 B_1 B_2 or even A_1 A_2 B_1 B_2 C_1 C_2. The really important change which took place in the course of the seventeenth century was the introduction of the principle of alternation, which led to the adoption of the scheme A_1 B_2 A_2 B_1. Until this principle was firmly established, composers, vocal and instrumental, had at their disposal a relatively large number of different forms, but none that admitted of organization on a large scale. It is obvious that such forms as A A B B, A A B B C C etc. are only practicable when the single sections A, B, C etc. are extremely small and concise. The only sound method of organization lies in the employment of a scheme based on the variation-idea — either ordinary variations (instrumental) or the type of vocal variations common in Luigi Rossi (two or three stanzas set to more or less different melodies on the same bass), or finally the ground-bass, passacaglia, chaconne etc. The principle of alternation once established in Scarlatti's day, the "centipede" type of construction—the stringing together of small consecutive segments—became almost entirely obsolete, and though the chaconne survived up to the early days of Mozart, it underwent considerable modifications of structure in the direction of the modern symphony. The form ABA was soon expanded under Scarlatti by making $A = a_1$ b_2 a_2 b_1 and by making B a thematic development of material drawn from A.

But this development of the form is almost exclusively vocal. Ales-

[1] F. Torrefranca, La creazione della Sonata dramatica moderna, *Rivista Musicale Italiana* xvii., 309. Poeti minori del clavicembalo, ib. xvii., 763. Le sonate per cembalo del Buranello, ib. xviii., 276, 497, xix., 108.

sandro Scarlatti's harpsichord pieces and symphonies dating from 1715 or later are structurally far in arrear of the chamber-cantatas which he composed some ten or fifteen years earlier. The fact was that in all this period it was the singers who took the intellectual lead in music, and the instrumentalists who followed humbly in their wake. With the appearance of Domenico Scarlatti, Giovanni Platti and Galuppi a new influence begins gradually to make itself felt, an influence still more apparent in the clavier sonatas of the Germans. The publication of Domenico Scarlatti's complete works for the harpsichord[2] has enabled us to obtain a new insight into the methods of this most original of composers. Among the 500 and more pieces printed by Longo there are scattered some dozen sonatas which were originally composed for violin and *continuo*.[3] What first caused them to be noticed was their difference from the others in form. They are not single movements in the developed binary form familiar to all students of Domenico Scarlatti, but groups of short movements, generally either dances, slow airs or contrapuntal movements, not showing much advance on the sonatas of Corelli. It is possible of course that they may be early works, although they are to be found in a volume dated 1742 which includes harpsichord pieces of a very advanced nature. It is impossible at present to make any attempt to group Domenico Scarlatti's harpsichord sonatas in any sort of chronological order; but it is fairly easy to pick out examples here and there which from their style alone can be attributed either to an early or a late period. Their form however does not vary much, in spite of harmonic audacities, and we may safely assume that the developed binary form had been established by him almost at the outset of his career.

It will be obvious from what has been said above that this form was derived from the opera and the chamber-cantata. Moreover, a study of the thematic material employed will show that Scarlatti was indebted to the opera for his actual ideas just as the pianoforte works of Weber and Chopin are indebted to the operas of Rossini and Bellini. Modern musicians have been inclined to regard Scarlatti simply as a virtuoso; but a more careful study of his works will show that there is often a strong sense of vocal melody underlying his scales and arpeggios. His use of the direction *cantabile* is very significant.

In spite of the fact that the Italians took the lead in the composition of clavier-sonatas, it must be admitted that with certain outstanding exceptions the Italian sonatas are inferior in actual musical value to those of the Germans. The reason for this seems to be that the Italians had no great need to write harpsichord sonatas when their singers were expressing their ideas for them in so much more vivid a manner. Most

[2]Edited by Alessandro Longo (Ricordi).
[3]This discovery was made by Donald Francis Tovey, and confirmed by the late Joseph Joachim. An investigation of the MSS. at Venice further corroborated this.

of their harpsichord sonatas were in fact published outside Italy, in Nuremberg, Amsterdam or London. They probably found more admirers in the countries dependent on those remote publishing centres than they did in the land of their origin. And the avidity with which their German imitators took up the style and developed it shows us clearly what the point of view of these admirers was. What the Germans were aiming at in their harpsichord sonatas was the reproduction for ordinary domestic consumption of those wonderful Italian arias which every Italian could hear in the theatre as often as he liked, but which only rarely came the way of the average music lover north of the Alps. And so the strange phenomenon becomes apparent that the sonatas of C. P. E. Bach are more dramatic, more melodious, more emotional than those of Galuppi or Platti.

If C. P. E. Bach was saturated with Italian influences, they were equally strong on Haydn, the pupil of Porpora, and still stronger on Mozart. The influence of Jommelli on the Mannheim school of symphonists is now generally admitted; but I do not know whether musicians have begun to realize that it is hardly possible to interpret Mozart and the rest adequately without having some familiarity with Italian vocal music. Torrefranca seizes the characteristic point when he speaks of *la sonata dramatica moderna;* the word *dramatica* is what exactly indicates the difference between the music of C. P. E. Bach and that of his father. The modern sonata was dramatic, because it was based on the Italian aria, and the Italian aria did not become capable of inspiring the sonata until the contemporaries of Domenico Scarlatti, the generation of Leo, Vinci, Pergolesi etc. had extended the aria-form by breaking up its continuous melodic phrases into emotional fragments which lent themselves to thematic development. It was this emotionalism that the Germans sought to reproduce—the ever recurring phenomenon of the union of romantic Faust and classic Helen, the German infatuation with Italian beauty and the strange transformation of it into an unfamiliar medium.

Bibliography

Donald J. Grout's *A Short History of Opera,* 2 vols. (New York, Columbia University Press, 1965, 2nd ed.), is the most thorough general survey of opera available in English. Grout is also the author of the entry on opera in the *Harvard Dictionary of Music.* Both these sources have extensive bibliographies. The *Concise Oxford Dictionary of Opera* (London, Oxford University Press, 1964) and Alfred Lowenberg's *Annals of Opera, 1597-1940,* 2 vols. (Geneva, Societas Bibliographica, 1955,

2nd ed.), are useful for information about characters, plots, first performances, singers, conductors, and others involved in opera production. The articles by Edward Dent, "Problems of Modern Opera," in *Music Today* (London, Dennis Dobson, 1949); and by Harvey Chusid, "Can Opera Survive in Its Gilded Plumage?" in *Opera Canada*, 12, no. 2 (Summer 1971), deal with problems of modern opera, as does the entire issue of *World Theatre*, 17, no. 3-4 (1968), containing such provocative articles as that by Pierre Boulez, "Opera Houses? Blow Them Up!"

A few excerpts of pre-Mozartian opera are contained in the *Historical Anthology of Music*, vol. 2, and in *Die Geschichte der Musik in Beispielen*. Further examples of early opera can be found in the following series: *L'Arte musicale in Italia*, vol. 6; *I classici della musica italiana*, vol. 24; *Chefs-d'oeuvre de l'opéra français*, 40 vols.; *Denkmäler deutscher Tonkunst*, vols. 32, 33; and *Denkmäler der Tonkunst in Bayern*, vols. 25, 29. General indices to these and other historical series can be found under "Editions, historical" in the *Harvard Dictionary of Music*, 2nd ed. (1969). Many popular operas written since the mid-eighteenth century are easily obtainable in piano-vocal scores from publishers such as G. Schirmer.

20

THE sonata was the reigning form of the Classic period. Not only was there a veritable deluge of sonatas, especially by those composers under the Austro-German sphere of influence, but the sonata was often present even when its name did not appear on the title page of a musical composition. Symphony became a sonata for orchestra; concerto, a sonata for solo instrument or instruments with orchestra; string quartet, a sonata for four string instruments (or three instruments if the title were trio, five if it were quintet, etc.). Opera also participated in the sonata, at least in its overtures, which frequently were in the form of sonata movements. Even the field of vocal music was invaded by the sonata, as may be seen in a work such as Mozart's motet for accompanied solo voice, "Exultate jubilate," with its familiar concluding "Alleluia."

Sonata, however, had not always been as the late eighteenth-century composers shaped it. Between an early piece such as the "Sonata pian e forte" of Giovanni Gabrieli, or the "Sonata sopra Sancta Maria" from the 1610 vespers of Monteverdi, and a nineteenth-century sonata such as the Sonata in B minor of Franz Liszt lies a period of development and transformation so extraordinary that the early examples of sonata do not in the slightest resemble the late ones. Early Baroque examples of sonata varied in form and content, but they soon came to have one element in common, a change of tempo from one selection to the next resulting finally in a succession of movements. By the late seventeenth century the sonata had become a group of movements, usually from three to six, alternating between slow and fast. The prevalent, though not exclusive, type was the trio sonata, as much a texture as it was a form, requiring two solo instruments and a bass instrument as well as a fourth performer who reinforced the bass line and filled in a harmonic accompaniment on a keyboard instrument.

The Baroque sonata, organized according to a principle of continuous melodic expansion, was gradually transformed during the eighteenth century into the Classic sonata, organized not by expanding but rather by opposing themes and key relationships. The form that emerged from this late eighteenth-century sonata lent itself well to analysis by dissection, making it so easy to analyze that a false concept of sonata form has been and is still being perpetuated. The neat analyses and catalogues of sonatas compiled by writers of textbooks on musical form caused generations of students to think that a sterile and rigid formalism was the ideal of the Classic composers. This lack of teaching still continues, unfortunately, causing hundreds of students to argue among themselves about which beat of which measure announces the recapitulation of some apparently irregular sonata, an argument that is the musical equivalent of that of how many angels might stand on the head of a pin. Such a presentation of the sonata-principle misses the point entirely, as is pointed out in the following selection. The late eighteenth-century sonata was a logical expression of the musical thoughts of its composers. There was no textbook example; no two sonatas are exactly alike. Composers wrote as their thoughts dictated, and there was no consideration of breaking rules, intentionally or unintentionally, because there were no rules in the textbook sense.

The composition of sonatas has declined considerably during the twentieth century. Although the composers of the Neoclassic group (especially Hindemith) writing between the two World Wars continued to produce sonatas, many composers active since 1945 do not appear to be as attracted to that form. Some, it is true, continue to write music containing certain elements of the sonata — opposition of tonal centers and development of thematic material — but these two items alone do not constitute a sonata in the eighteenth- and nineteenth-century sense. Thus, while compositions bearing the title "sonata" or using some ideas related to the sonata-principle will possibly continue to appear, it seems likely that the late twentieth-century sonata may, like the Baroque sonata of the seventeenth century, be rather loosely related to the Classic-Romantic sonata.

Philip Barford is Senior Lecturer in Music at the Institute of Extension Studies, University of Liverpool. His writings include *The Keyboard Music of C. P. E. Bach* (London, Barrie & Rockliff, 1965) and numerous periodical contributions, especially to *The Music Review*.

276

The Sonata-Principle

PHILIP T. BARFORD

Musical history becomes coherent only when the historian defines a number of basic standpoints from which to view it. To a considerable extent, the history of music in the eighteenth century is correlative with the development of the sonata-principle—an inclusive and synthetic mode of musical thought not sufficiently explained by the traditional account of sonata-form or of the conventional structure of the sonata as a whole. The following discussion of the essential spirit of the sonata style is an attempt to define a critical vantage-point from which instrumental music in the eighteenth century and the achievements of Beethoven can best be studied.

The word "form" may be understood in different ways. For example, we may say of an instrumental movement that it is "in sonata-form," meaning that certain general principles of musical structure are expressed in it. On the other hand, a piece of music is a unique form, a living work of art with an individual value and characteristics which cannot be accounted for by the abstract concept by which we classify it. The abstract concept "sonata-form" is related to a particular movement "in sonata-form" as shadow to substance. One has a purely ideal existence. The other is a vital reality appealing not only to the intellect but also to the emotions and the imagination.

What gives a sonata-form movement vitality then, is not the fact that it is in sonata-form, but the particular value of the material in the movement and the individual scheme of its arrangement. The composer's main task is to arrange his material in such a way that a thread of continuity animates a whole work, and satisfies the listener's desire for intellectual coherence and imaginative stimulation. In a critical examination of movements in sonata-form, the important question is whether there

FROM *The Music Review*, 13 (1952), 255-263. Reprinted by permission of W. Heffer & Sons Ltd.

really is a dynamic continuity between all the different parts, or whether the relationship between them is arbitrary and unconvincing. In a satisfying sonata-form movement, the impulsion from theme to theme is vital and compelling, adventurous yet logical, and it guides our listening in such a way that we are made powerfully aware of the unity of form expressed in the relationship between all these different things.

In a weak sonata-form movement there may be an arbitrary continuity achieved simply by arranging different fragments according to a certain general plan; but there will not be a real impulsion from each to each. There may be a surface unity, realized by observing the abstract concept of sonata-form; but there will be no significant wholeness. Whether a sonata-form movement is convincing or otherwise seems to depend upon the composer's initial approach to composition. The great sonata-composer usually refrained from composition until his material had crystallized and arranged itself in his mind with some regard for the individual organic whole in which it was to be built. This certainly appears to have been Mozart's method. But in some of the earlier piano sonatas of Clementi, inspiration seems to have been limited by the skeletal conception of sonata-form as a sort of pastry-mould. In fact, the essential difference between a weak and a good sonata-form movement is amply illustrated in the works of Clementi. Compare, for instance, the first movement of the Sonata in B flat which Clementi played before the Emperor Joseph II in competition with Mozart, with the first movement of the G minor programme Sonata *"Didone abbandonata."* The material of the B flat movement is limpid, and docile in its observance of the abstract sonata-form scheme. The G minor movement is also strictly formal; but in this case the formalism is subsidiary to a higher principle of organization. Both convey an impression of formal unity; but the unity of the latter is truly organic.[1]

Both composition and listening demand an insight into the unified multi-dimensional structure of a work. A thorough understanding of a movement is therefore characterized by a constant reference from any particular melody or modulation to the whole formal structure of which these are parts, and then from a gradually deepening knowledge of this structure in its wholeness back again to the parts. Because of this cross-reference between the parts and the whole it is very necessary to understand how the parts express the whole—how, for example, the unity of a good sonata-form movement is felt in a continuous stream of sound made up of so many bits and pieces. There are, of course, many modes of musical thought contributing to a satisfying wholeness of design.

The most obvious mode is melody. If we consider any familiar tune,

[1] I have developed this point in an article on Clementi. See "Formalism in Clementi's Pianoforte Sonatas," *Monthly Musical Record,* October and November, 1952.

or, better still, make one up for ourselves, we find that the pitch and rhythmic function of each note seem to be determined. During composition, they are determined by some ideal of the melody as a whole. When we contemplate the melody in its final form, each note seems to be determined absolutely by its context.

It is well known that Beethoven used to hammer melodic fragments for a long time before their shape finally satisfied him. In this hammering process, Beethoven was not simply relying upon his feeling for melodic fitness. In a very real sense he was trying to discover the *nisus* of the basic fragments with which he began. There was an interaction between his poetic "feeling" of the melody, and his critical contemplation of it as an object with an existence and inner logic of its own. The important point is that his melodic sensibility, motivated by a regard for wholeness, operated selectively upon alternatives suggested by the original idea.

In the composition of melodies there is, I suggest, a constant reference from the initial notes to some ideal of the whole melody conceived as an object, except in those cases when the composer's melodic faculty is prompted by a spontaneous lyrical impulse. In the harmonic mode of musical thought, there is a similar relationship between parts, as they evolve, and a feeling of wholeness and unity which harmonic movement expresses. Harmonic movement proceeds by alternations of what is relatively dissonant and consonant. Any chord which the ear apprehends as a dissonance occasions a desire for its resolution. Thus, even before the resolution occurs, the mind's ear conceives the dissonance in relation to a future resolution; and so the particular series of chords constituting discord and resolution is felt ultimately as an organic unity.

Much the same can be said of rhythm, a vitalizing factor intimately bound up with melody and harmony. Each unit in a series of rhythmic impulsions is imaginatively referred to our apprehension of the series as a whole.

Two other modes of musical thought assume importance in specialized styles of composition. Both are creative impulses in which unity is achieved in and through opposition between contrasted elements.

The first of these is counterpoint. In composing fugal textures, Bach's ideal was the harmonic reconciliation, within a dynamic whole, of melodic lines possessing the highest possible degree of melodic individuality. Of course, linear opposition of this kind is generally present in good composition, since the effectiveness of any harmonic progression depends upon the opposition between the linear constituents of each chord. Unless there is a feeling of melodic independence in the two outer parts at least, it is difficult to fill the space between them with completely satisfying harmony. Polytonality carries the principle of linear opposition to a more extreme degree.

The idea of opposition is taken into the sonata-principle, which gives it a special significance, and which includes the other modes of musical thought to which I have referred.

The realization of unity through opposition appears in various forms. The logic of sonata-form, and of the sonata as a whole, is based upon the interplay of contrasting musical ideas. This is a logic arising directly from experience, to which the abstract formal concepts traditionally associated with the sonata-style do justice. But in the eighteenth century these concepts tended to develop independently of the immediacy of the composer's creative impulse. Hence it was possible for Clementi and others to "pour" notes into formal moulds, in much the same way that a B.Mus. student composes sonatas according to rule. In the sonatas of the late eighteenth century there is thus a deeper kind of opposition going beyond the use of contrasting material. This is between developed formal conceptions (by this time crystallized into conventions) and dynamically contrasted material which demands an increasingly powerful part in the determination of its modes of expression. In the great sonatas of the Viennese school there is not only an opposition between the contrasted sections of a work as they evolve within a prior wholeness of conception which disciplines their evolution. There is also an interaction between this organic wholeness of conception, and the conventional avenues of formal expression. It will be useful to discuss these two kinds of opposition before attempting a comprehensive definition of the sonata-principle.

It seems obvious that the masters of the sonata understood musical form in more than its temporal aspect. The construction of a piece in sonata-form involved a constant reference to an ideal of the finished movement conceived as a whole—as a sort of non-temporal actuality conditioning its temporal presentation. In precisely the same way that a melody is composed in relation to an exploratory feeling for its final shape, so the contrasting sections of a sonata-form movement are arranged with a constant reference to the scheme of the whole—not just the abstract conception of sonata-form, but "this particular" sonata-form movement. Its highest perfection is achieved when varied content is fused within a single vital conception appealing to the contemplative intellect. In fact, the sonata-principle contains the most developed musical expression of the Greek principle of unity in variety in the history of music.[2]

It will be helpful at this point to turn to a literary source. Coleridge made a celebrated distinction between Fancy and Imagination.[3] He conceived the imagination as a faculty which struggles to idealize and to unify images with a concern for some central conception which

[2]A discussion of this principle in its more general aspects may be found in Bosanquet's *History of Aesthetic*, Chap. III.

[3]An admirable appreciation of this distinction is contained in Basil Willey's *Nineteenth Century Studies*, Chap. I (iii).

it is desired to convey. The imagination is thus the characteristic energy of the true poet, and a poem is more than a mere association of images. A good poem is a fusion of different elements within a form which is satisfying in its essential unity and directness of appeal. It orders our mental images with a dynamic oneness of purpose.

This dynamic, integrating power of the mind is distinct from merely fanciful association. Fancy does no more than juxtapose different images, and fanciful association does not appeal in virtue of any singleness of aesthetic purpose. Fanciful association may amuse and entertain; but there will be no central principle of construction, no dominating inspiration. A fanciful verse then, lacking the unifying drive of the imagination, will be ultimately unsatisfying, no matter how regular the metre, or how neat and shapely the arrangement of words. An irregular and outwardly formless piece of blank verse may convey a far more satisfying impression if it is fed by a single stream of imaginative vitality.

Obviously this conception has a special application to the sonata. The "tonal imagery" which the composer works into a prescribed formal scheme must be integrated by an individual wholeness of conception. Many eighteenth-century sonata-form movements are composed of material which is fancifully associated rather than imaginatively fused. There is no vital antithesis in them, no impetus of organic impulsion from phrase to phrase. Formally, they are insipid.

The historical development of the sonata-style then, is far more than the evolution of formal methods of arranging material. This may be said equally of sonata-form and the whole sonata scheme. After all, and it is salutary to remember this simple truth, we can only discover what a sonata is by studying sonatas. As soon as we turn to the great sonata composers we find that their characteristic musical problem was not how to pour out a stream of music which obeyed the abstract rules of sonata-form, or some conventional three or four movement pattern, but how to reconcile an intellectual formal concept with emotionally varied material, how to achieve an organic unity in variety within prescribed formal limits. This problem, which demanded a perfect marriage of the ratiocinative intellect and the Coleridgean imagination, was not always solved.

In the sonatas of C. P. E. Bach, J. C. Bach and the Viennese composers, one fact immediately commands attention: the term "sonata" is used to cover a universe of contrasting musical ideas. It stands for a principle of unity giving purpose and significant coherence to the fruits of musical imaginations liberated from traditional polyphonic techniques, stimulated by the lyric and dramatic expressionism of opera, and already touched by the incipient spirit of romanticism. Many of the themes, and even whole movements which C. P. E. Bach and J. C. Bach worked into their sonatas are shot through with romantic feeling, even though they may exist side by side with a kind of musical thought which is the very antithesis of romanticism. In one Sonata, for example, Philip Emmanuel follows a scampering Scarlatti-like *allegro* in E flat with an expressive slow movement in B flat minor, very suggestive of early Beethoven. This, in turn, is followed by an *allegretto* in F in the monotonous rococo style sometimes imitated by Haydn in his less inspired moments.[4] A more interesting juxtaposition occurs in a Sonata by J. C. Bach, where a romantic *andante* in C minor leads into a self-consciously strict fugue.[5] Both examples contain fine music; but they reveal an attempt to blend subjective feeling and objective formalism which is not wholly successful.

Any good musical theme may be said to have significance—that is an intrinsic life of its own, and latent formal implications. Thus, a Bach fugue subject is intrinsically appealing; and at the same time it invites contrapuntal treatment. This twofold life of a theme owes much, if not everything to the composer's emotional vitality—a point which is well brought out when we consider what happens in the performance of any kind of music. Both the singer and the instrumentalist identify themselves with what they interpret. In a sense they lend their own vitality to the object they are recreating. They have to if they are to achieve a sensitive performance. The latent energy of the composer's own vitality is re-expressed through the performer, and it is surely not true, as C. E. M. Joad suggests, that the best player of Bach fugues has a soul as dry and withered as a pea in an old pod.

The suggestion that every melody expresses the subjective vitality of the composer does not contradict a traditional distinction between classical and romantic music—between music in which the formal and patternistic element is uppermost, and music which is predominantly subjective in tone. All good themes have a vital subjective element. But in some this subjectivity is merely *implicit,* and subordinate to the objective demands of form. In others, it is *explicit,* and when this is so the tendency is generally towards drama, lyricism, romanticism and impressionism. In the *Art of Fugue* for example, Bach's emotional vitality is implicit—that is disciplined and transcended by a creative will to order. In Beethoven's sonatas, it is often explicit; but I submit that the last quartets and sonatas, for all their super-abundant expressionism, approximate to the condition of the *Art of Fugue.* The poetic vision, the heartfelt emotional utterance—the whole subjective burden is subordinate to an intuitive but none the less profoundly intellectual grasp of principles of tonal order hitherto undreamed of, and, significantly, not accounted for by the traditional intellectual framework of the sonata.

The history of the sonata from the sons of Bach onwards is the history of a mode of musical thought in which the subjective element becomes ever more explicit, and the objective demands of form more

---

[4]C. P. E. Bach. *Sechs Sonaten.* Vol. II No. 5. Schott Edn. No. 2354.
[5]J. C. Bach. *Zehn Klavier-Sonaten.* Vol. II No. 9. Peters Edn. No. 3831 G.

imperative. And so, although the abstract sonata-form scheme reached a clearer definition in the eighteenth century, the prevailing tone of much of the material subjected to formal treatment is often self-consciously expressive, and on many occasions frankly romantic. For a time, formalism seemed to be absolute in its own right, witness the arid stretches of Alberti-bass, and conventional scraps of Italianate melody and passage-work often to be found in the sonatas of Christian Bach, Haydn and Mozart. However, in the better sonatas of the sons of Bach, and in those of Clementi, Dussek, Haydn and Mozart, strict formalism frames many a profound thought. And as Beethoven acquired ever greater powers of musical insight, the subjective dynamism of the material demanded a new approach to the framework which C. P. E. Bach was the first to associate regularly with explicit subjective expression.

The greatness of Haydn, Mozart and Beethoven owes much to the way they objectified and unified the dynamic emotional elements with which they worked. In their greatest works they reconciled two opposing ideals—objective formal adequacy and truth of subjective feeling. Objectivity is the mainstay of the classical ideal; but absolute objectivity in music, as some modern composers have shown, is unattainable. Nevertheless, the abstract concept of sonata-form, and the basic idea of associating different movements in a single composition, are products of essentially objective and classical thinking lending a powerfully objective tone to the unity of contrasted material which is the essence of a good sonata, quartet or symphony in the eighteenth century.

The sonata-principle then, is neither the abstract principle of sonata-form, nor the concrete principle of unity in variety animating any individual sonata or sonata movement. It is the higher synthesis comprehending both, a principle or musical thought observing an objective formal ideal but deriving its wealth of content from the universe of human experience. The immediacy of contrasted musical ideas arising directly from the composer's significant experience is unified by the synthetic power of his imaginative insight. The resulting "world" is ordered by a vigorous formal discipline which thrusts it into objectivity. The classical composer thus dissociates himself from his music in a way that the romantic composer does not. The impersonality of purely formal musical thought gives universality to the often intense expressionism of the material. This fact underlies a paradox often to be discerned in discussions of Beethoven's late-period works. On the one hand, it is said, the last quartets are abstract, rarefied, the very absolute of "absolute music"; and on the other, so personal, so communicative of subjective feeling. The resolution of this paradox lies in the listener's ability to grasp an experience unique in its quality of integration, which combines the extremes of independent musical thought and the profoundest communications of the human spirit.

There is a very striking parallel here with the philosophy of Hegel which, interestingly enough, was developed during the life of Beethoven who gave it a most significant expression and justification, unknown, of course, to himself.[6]

The keynote of Hegel is the dialectic—the movement of thesis and antithesis to a higher synthesis, the reconciliation of opposites in a transcendent whole which is more than a merely subjective affection of mind. Now in the same way that there is an opposition in music between form, abstractly considered, and subjective tension concretely expressed in sound—an opposition completely overcome in the magnificent synthesis of Beethoven's last quartets, so there is an element of opposition in Hegel's own conception of the dialectic. In the *Phenomenology*, Hegel appears to conceive the dialectic as a living movement of experience—what one commentator has described as a "logic of passion." In the *Logic*, he is more concerned with the movement of opposites in its abstract formal aspects. In this abstract shape the dialectic seems unreal, and is largely discredited today. What is living in Hegel's philosophy becomes apparent when we reconcile the more emotional and subjective aspect of the dialectic with its objective logical form—when we actually experience the synthesis of disparate and contrasting elements within a significant whole, and see this as a perfectly rational activity, a formal idealization accomplished by the imagination.

We have to do just this in unlocking the secrets of Beethoven's last works. We are presented with an amazing variety of material, juxtaposed in an apparently fragmentary and conflicting manner, and much of it has an extreme subjective burden. But the real greatness of the last quartets and sonatas lies in the intensity of their logical integration.

Ideally considered from the standpoint of the sonata-principle, the orientation of musical thought in the eighteenth century was towards the end which Beethoven achieved, the knitting together of strands of thought which are variously emphasized in the works of his predecessors. The sonata-principle is implied, but not always successfully expressed in the works of C. P. E. Bach who set the stage for important musical developments. C. P. E. Bach is generally credited with being the father of sonata-form. I think it is truer to say that his most significant contribution to music is the consistent association of the sonata-form scheme (already in the air) with music embodying the flexible expressiveness of *Empfindsamkeit*. In the keyboard sonatas different elements can be found side by side, but they are seldom reconciled. We can observe these, at least: an element of patterned figuration not un-

---

[6]Beethoven: b. 1770, d. 1827. Hegel: b. 1770, d. 1831.

Hegel's authoritative writings were published as follows:—*Die Phänomenologie des Geistes*, 1807: *Wissenschaft der Logik*, 1812-16: *Encyclopädie der philosophischen Wissenschaften im Grundrisse*, 1817 (2nd ed. 1827; 3rd ed. 1830): *Grundlinien der Philosophie des Rechts*, 1820.

connected, perhaps, with the art of J. S. Bach and D. Scarlatti;[7] a somewhat self-conscious intellectualism, leading to formal experimentation and hence to the sonata-form idea and the association of movements on a ground plan owing much to the Italian overture;[8] the use of thematic contrast which sometimes rises to the level of dramatic antithesis, but more often to a fragmentary style not unified by an overall rhythmic flow; and a vein of "sentimental rhetoric" (Tovey), often tedious, but sometimes achieving great depths of romantic feeling, especially in the slow movements.

These characteristics demanded the unifying power of the sonata-principle, which C. P. E. Bach lacked the creative insight and the technique to apply. Hence, although his taste for formal experimentation gave rise to "veränderten Reprisen," and stimulating oppositions of tonality and theme, his intellectual insight and flexible expressionism do not always come into a completely successful relationship.

Bach passed on to Haydn a structural technique which Haydn, in the piano sonatas at any rate, did not always master. Many Bach sonata movements consist of a number of short phrases idly—we might say fancifully—juxtaposed, and not imaginatively fused into a significant unity. Some of Haydn's have the same weakness. Compare the *allegretto* finale of the Bach Sonata already mentioned (see note 4) with the first movement of the fourth Haydn Sonata in Augener's selection of twenty-three. But Haydn extended and emphasized the function of thematic contrast and development, and proved himself a better disciple of C. P. E. Bach in this respect. In the sonata-form movements of his quartets and symphonies, Haydn achieves a mastery over diverse material presented in the exposition by an intensification of contrapuntal texture in the development. Moreover, the contrasting movements of a symphony or quartet are much more closely integrated than the different movements of a Bach sonata. The same is largely true of Mozart. But it is important to note that Bach presented material contrasted in mood and tonality within a single composition, even though he could not always unify it. In Beethoven's sonatas, the element of contrast is increased, and there is a corresponding emphasis upon development, both before the reprise and in *coda* sections. The logical end of this chain of musical thought is the conception of whole works wherein the different movements have much the same kind of relationship to one another as the contrasting material within a single sonata-form movement. This end is achieved in Beethoven's last sonatas and quartets—notably the Sonata *opus* 110 and the C sharp minor Quartet.

[7]See the collection of keyboard pieces: *Sonaten und Stücke*, Peters Edn. 4188. Nos. 2, 5, 7 and 8 are especially interesting in this respect.

[8]H. Prunières, in his *Nouvelle Histoire de la Musique*, refers in passing to a purely intellectual streak in C. P. E. Bach. The designation of the sonatas published in 1761-2-3 is also significant: "Sechs Sonaten für Clavier mit veränderten Reprisen."

Another closely related development is particularly noticeable in J. C. Bach and Mozart. This is the achievement of balance and unity through a rhythmic flow which tends to "smooth out" oppositions of tonality and theme. Rococo ornamentation which in some cases weakens the rhythmic structure of C. P. E. Bach's melodic lines[9] is less pronounced in the sonatas of his younger brother, which perpetuate the idea of thematic contrast, but also introduce an Italian verve and simplicity of texture. Whether or not it is true that "Form is Rhythm Writ Large," it is certainly true that Christian's melodic faculty enabled him to compose long sections of music with a smooth rhythmic impetus. Mozart, of course, who acknowledged a debt to Christian Bach, had this gift in a supreme degree. All his great music has a poise and balance—no matter how varied the material it contains—deriving directly from the rhythmic impetus which reconciles the ear immediately to the most striking melodic and harmonic contrasts.

Both these tendencies taken together—the idea of contrast intensified and overcome in development, and the subjection of contrasting elements to an overall rhythmic discipline—combined to establish a body of formal conventions, a set of ideas about what a sonata must be, and what rules ought to be observed by the symphonist. Towards the end of the eighteenth century, these conventions re-presented, but in a more advanced shape, the original conflict between the intellectual, formalizing element of musical thought and the subjective impulse expressing itself in the principle of unity in variety, a conflict which first appeared in C. P. E. Bach. Thus, even after Mozart and Haydn had successfully assimilated the abstract logic of musical form, objectively considered, to the living musical material with which they were inspired, Beethoven quickly discovered a new antithesis between what he wanted to say and the accepted means of saying it. And so he subjected the accepted formal ideas to modification and development. The important point, however, is that he preserved the ideal of classical objectivity which these ideas represented (except in one or two special cases), and submerged the subjectivity of his experience in an art of universal significance.

In egarding Beethoven as a composer who welded together different strands of eighteenth century musical thought, I do not of course wish to perpetuate the crude error of seeing in Haydn, Mozart and the sons of Bach mere preludes to grand opera. I submit, however, that the essential modes of musical thought which find their own diverse and characteristic expressions in eighteenth-century music, do reach a transcendent synthesis in the sonata-principle as Beethoven conceived it, and as I have tried to define it.

[9]Though his rhythmic sensibility is liberated in many a beautiful slow movement.

Bibliography

The three volumes by William Newman, *The Sonata in the Baroque Era, The Sonata in the Classic Era,* and *The Sonata since Beethoven* (Chapel Hill, N.C., University of North Carolina Press, 1959, 1963, 1969), are encyclopedic in scope and essential to any study of the sonata. Each volume contains an extensive bibliography including both writings about sonatas and editions of sonatas. Analyses of selected sonatas that show great insight into the nature of sonata construction may be found in Donald Tovey, *Essays in Musical Analysis,* 7 vols. (London, Oxford University Press, 1936–1944).

The sonatas of C. P. E. Bach, J. C. Bach, Haydn, Mozart, Clementi, Beethoven, and others are easily available in a number of modern editions, as are anthologies of sonatas by eighteenth-century composers. William Newman, ed., *Thirteen Keyboard Sonatas of the 18th and 19th Centuries* (Chapel Hill, N.C., University of North Carolina Press, 1947), contains works by lesser composers that are not so easily obtainable.

21

BEETHOVEN stands paradoxically at the turn of the nineteenth century. Works devoted to eighteenth-century Classicism must consider him as a conclusion of their subject, yet works on nineteenth-century Romanticism cannot begin without him. Beethoven created no new forms or media; he took the sonata, the orchestra, the string quartet, and other instrumental and vocal combinations that his predecessors had used and adapted them to express his own thoughts. But the nature and content of these thoughts and the ways in which he used the forms of his musical heritage were so individual that the results appear many times to be new and even revolutionary.

Not only did Beethoven push the sonata to its limits in content of ideas, and the orchestra to its limits in conveying these ideas, he also championed a new relationship of the creative artist to society. Throughout his life he maintained the position of a composer who was free of any sort of patronage which might be dictatorial to his art. Composers had of course worked independently before. Handel had survived successfully in London, Mozart somewhat less so in Vienna. But for Beethoven the issue was not so simple as wishing to be free to operate as an independent businessman; it was a profound moral issue. It was the duty of society, he maintained defiantly, to support him so that he might create music not for entertainment, but music for the moral improvement of man. With Beethoven we see the establishment of the concept of the artist as a man free to create, purely as his genius dictates, for the good of all mankind.

The literary and social background of this new concept of the artist is the subject of the following selection. Beethoven's attitudes were not unique to him, though certainly none before had expressed them as intensely as he. They were attitudes which had come at a time ready for them. Had it appeared at an earlier time, Beethoven's unique genius might not have survived.

Wilfrid Dunwell is a professor and examiner at Trinity College of Music, London, and a lecturer in music at London University. His works include *Evolution of 20th Century Harmony* (London, Novello, 1960), *Pianoforte Accompaniment Writing* (London, A. Hammond, 1950), and *Music and the European Mind* (London, Herbert Jenkins, 1962, Cranbury, N. J., A. S. Barnes, 1962).

The Age of Goethe and Beethoven

WILFRID DUNWELL

Beethoven (1770-1827) inherited the musical language and forms of Haydn, Mozart, and their prolific contemporaries. Although he brought a new power and a new emotional charge into music, the sonata remained for him, as it was for them, the normal medium of expression. Like his predecessors too, Beethoven was first and foremost a pure musician. This in spite of the fact that for a large number of people he speaks more eloquently than any other composer in directly human terms, conveying the emotion of moods of every kind. He did this with an intensity of personal feeling which was unprecedented in instrumental music, but he did not depend, for the direction of his thought, on the external stimulus of literary or pictorial images. In his single-minded pursuit of his own art he remained a classical composer, and so, in essentials, did his younger contemporary Schubert (1797-1828). They showed no departure from the traditional attitude of the professional musician, making music simply through inner compulsion, and unconsciously revealing their character in the process. But a new note nevertheless is unmistakable in their work. In addition to the expression of personal character (which indeed had been evident enough in the work of Haydn and Mozart), a new attitude to art becomes apparent, and a new relationship with society. This was induced by influences which had long been taking shape but which had not yet made an impact on that earlier generation.

The ideal of liberty was foremost among these influences, a natural tendency to react against hardened institutions both in life and thought. The storming of the Bastille by the Paris mob in 1789, and the collapse of clerical and aristocratic privileges in France, seemed to all Europe to promise a new age of freedom. How elusive that ideal was to be soon

FROM Wilfrid Dunwell, *Music and the European Mind* (Cranbury, N.J., A. S. Barnes, 1962), pp. 163-171. Reprinted by permission of A. S. Barnes and Company, Inc., and Barrie & Jenkins Ltd.

became apparent. The first results of revolution were a barbarous reign of terror and expansionist military ambition, provoking rigid conservative reaction throughout Europe after 1815, and a further half-century of alternation between monarchic and democratic pretensions. There was to be no short cut to a state of social equilibrium. But as far as political institutions can contribute to liberty, a stage of development was reached before the close of the 10th century, when parliamentary government had become established in all of Europe outside Russia. If human fellow-feeling demands at least a sharing of the basic necessities of life, we are bound to consider this stage to be an advance in social organization from one in which the populace went hungry for bread. But the mere attainment of parliamentary government is not the end of the quest for liberty. During the last two hundred years the problem has been restated in various ways, in terms of Nationalism, Socialism, Individualism, and a proliferation of -isms in the present century; for its solution we can only rely on the power of human genius to adapt itself to the challenges of life. On this note we can turn from the political to the literary search for freedom as it appeared in the 18th century.

The formalism of the French style, with its pseudo-Classical discipline, dominated much of the artistic life of Europe. England provided a healthy exception with a broadly-based literature, which ranged from the urbanity of Pope's polished couplets to the visions of Blake and his moments of high poetic beauty. The writings of Addison, Swift, Johnson, Gibbon, Hume, Goldsmith, and Sheridan are among the greatest treasures of our language. Each name recalls a fresh activity of mind, and in the newly emerging prose novel, Richardson, Fielding, and Sterne were developing still another medium for the study of human motives and conduct. Character and manners were the subject of drama in other parts of Europe. Molière's example had given the stimulus, and it bore fruit both in a new Danish literature, with the plays of Holberg (1684-1754), and in a refreshing of the older traditions of Spain, where Moratín (1760-1828) achieved both comedy and psychological insight which place him high among the century's dramatists. In Italy, Metastasio (1698-1782) was the central figure, both through his own literary and dramatic skill and through the predominance of opera, to which he contributed so many libretti. Along with him stand Gozzi and Goldoni, who lifted the old farce to the level of true comedy. The former, with a love of fantasy and fairy-tale combined with irony, remains in our contemporary memory as the author of *The Loves of the Three Oranges* and *Turandot*.

But the new creative force which broke through the crust of tradition was found in Germany, still not a nation, but a loose assembly of separate states united only by a subtle sense of ancient kinship. The German-speaking peoples had already shown in architecture and music the extent of their revitalization; in the mid-century they were on the eve of their greatest period of literature. Since the Thirty Years' War, the French style had appeared to present the only worthy model in literary as well as social convention, a situation that could not permanently satisfy the native genius. This external authority lay heavily on Gottsched, Professor of Poetry at Leipzig, who worked during the second quarter of the century to bring some unity into the German language itself and to raise the level of the theatre above vulgar farce and fantastic tragedy. While improving taste, he looked no further than the French dramatists for guidance. But his efforts to be a German Boileau provoked a controversy from which fruitful ideas emerged. Two Swiss professors, Bodmer and Breitinger, pleaded for imagination rather than regularity of form, and in pointing to Milton as an example, they turned the German mind towards English sources which henceforward proved to be singularly liberating and inspiring. Enthusiasm for Milton was one of the sources of inspiration for Klopstock (1724-1803). As the first of the new German poets he claims more attention than his intrinsic qualities would warrant, at any rate for the modern reader. In his grandiose epic *Der Messias*, whose twenty cantos appeared at intervals from 1748 to 1773, he used a new metre, the hexameter, and in his *Odes* exalting the ancient Germanic tradition he showed a rough vigour in varied rhymeless forms. If only in this metrical freedom, he broke the monopoly of the French Alexandrine, and gave a suggestion of the flexibility which Goethe was to consummate in his lyrics. Already we can see in Klopstock three of the influences which were to form the new literature: example and stimulus from England, consciousness of German national character, and a spirit of rebellion against the constraints of convention. England's influence was especially helpful in this latter respect. Her dramatists had shown that a play can have coherence as a living organism without depending on prescribed formulas, and they, and the contemporary novelists, showed how limitless is the scope for observation outside the elevated circles of heroic and mythological personages. Wieland (1733-1813) brought Shakespeare within reach by his translations, and his interest in the English novelists led to his *Agathon*, the first of a distinctively German genre, the psychological and pedagogic novel.

More powerful both in mind and influence was Lessing (1729-81), in whose critical writings and plays aspiration became solid achievement. Shakespeare held the foremost place in his thought about drama, exemplifying Aristotle's dictum that tragedy should "purge the emotions through pity and fear," not, as with Corneille, through the severity of its moral lessons. Lessing's own plays of middle-class life seem closer to the modern world, in theme and social atmosphere, than to the courts where at that very time music was adopting its classical form. The value Lessing set on folk-song recalls the gulf which was felt to exist between the conventions of aristocratic society and the truth of simple nature. But although he applied his art to the illumination of ordinary life, Lessing did more than anyone else to make clear the artist's function. In all his work as a journalist and critic he sought to clarify the thought of his generation. He gave a consciousness of the artist's function in society which was to be a distinctive feature of the new phase of mental activity, appearing first in German literature, and then in art generally with the 19th century.

The sense of the dignity of the artist, even of the superiority of his vision, is strongly present in Beethoven; it is one of the traits which separate him from his musical predecessors. In a letter from Bettina von Arnim to Goethe, these are some of the statements imputed to him: "Music is a higher revelation than all wisdom and philosophy," "Music is the one incorporeal entrance into the higher world of knowledge which comprehends mankind but which mankind cannot comprehend." Confident assertions of this kind show how the artist's relation to society was changing. Lessing provided much of the intellectual basis of this attitude; Herder gave it emotional impetus.

Herder (1744-1803) is notable not for any permanent value in his own writing, but for his influence, especially on Goethe. Like Rousseau, he looked to nature for inspiration which the Enlightenment failed to give to ardent souls. But in place of abstract notions concerning the blissful state of uncivilized man, he substituted an evolutionary view, that every age achieves artistic expression suited to its character, and that each reveals some fresh aspect of truth. The poet, in every age, was a heaven-sent genius, and he who would be a poet now must seek his inspiration in communion with the highest minds of the past. In this belief, Herder praised the creative genius of Homer and Shakespeare; he collected ballads and folk-songs of all nations, published in 1778-9 as *Stimmen der Völker in Liedern;* and he succumbed to the glamour of the Middle Ages. A group of lyrical poets, Claudius, Hölty, Bürger, responded to this stimulus in verse which received many musical settings in the following century. But more startling was an outburst of drama in a phase called *Sturm und Drang* (from the title of a play by von Klinger). The main figures of this episode of storm and stress—the angry young men of the 1770's—gave a liberal interpretation to Herder's protest against narrow convention. They were the opponents of all convention, social, moral, political, or literary. Nothing less than Shakespearian grandeur and passion would serve to conquer a new age in which the world should belong to the strong in will. The world has forgotten those ardent spirits, Lenz, von Klinger, Schubart, Leisewitz, and Müller, but it remembers one whose genius was fired during this glow of aspiration.

The mind of Johann Wolfgang Goethe (1749-1832) was all-embracing; he gathered up all the diverse strands of thought and literary expression of his age. In his universality, in his insight into human character, in his use of every medium of expression, from those which embrace the whole human scene to the lyrics of passionate individual experience, he is of the stature of the greatest of any age. But his copious writings do not form a homogeneous whole; they do not come to a focus in the same way as those of Dante, Cervantes, or Shakespeare, who seemed to bring to a white-hot centre the spirit of their respective ages. Goethe reflected the mind of his time, or rather he raised its thought to a far higher power, but the strands which ran through the 18th century were so sharply defined that they could not blend into a unity. This was inevitable, for at the time when the new German literature was coming into being, there seemed to be no new way of creation which did not involve at the same time criticism and destruction. And when assertion was made, it was in the name of individuals, not of a corporate mind. The dichotomy which existed in France, the apparently irreconcilable claims of reason and the heart, reappeared at every point in the literature of Germany. It revealed itself in Apollonian natures on the one hand—in Lessing and Winckelmann, with their strong Classical predilections; and Dionysiac ones on the other—in Herder and the dramatists of *Sturm und Drang.*

In the astonishing mind of Goethe, both attitudes are to be found. He grew up in the rationalist tradition of Leipzig, and he was always a fervent admirer of Greek civilization. But his creative powers were liberated when Herder fired him with enthusiasm for the directly human qualities in art. He experienced his own *Sturm und Drang,* a phase in which he explored the theme of personal individuality: first, in its assertive aspect, with *Götz von Berlichingen* (1773), a play which set rebellious genius against the institutions of society; next, in its passive aspect, with an analysis of morbidity in the novel *Werther* (1774), which anticipated one of the moods of the Romantics. More directly personal were the supreme lyrics which sprang from his own passionate experiences, and in the same glow of feeling and imagination he was working at *Faust* and completed the scenes of Gretchen's betrayal. The Italian visit of 1786-8, however, contributed the sense of proportion so essential to his insatiable nature, but far more important was its contribution to the harmony of his mind, to the balance of intellect and emotion which characterized the work of his maturity.

Goethe's is one of the greatest minds of Europe, and one of the most unusual. Supreme artist as he was in parts of his work, we do not think of him exclusively as poet, dramatist, or novelist, absorbed in art alone and unconsciously communicating the spirit of an age. In this, he differs from Beethoven and Schubert, the two great contemporaries of his later years; and from Schiller too (1759-1805), essentially a dramatist and poet. We think of Goethe as "the sage of Weimar," probing the mysteries and the unsolved problems of life. His conversations and letters, fortunately so fully recorded, are an essential part of his mind. In his inquiring attitude, his concern with man's place in the universe in social and physical as well as spiritual matters, he is of the modern world; but he transcends the purely scientific and the purely philosophical approach through the power of his poetic imagination. He had little respect for metaphysics, as appears in Mephistopheles' ironic comments to the Student in *Faust,* or in Eckermann's report of a conversation with Hegel: "I am certain that many a dialectic disease would find a wholesome remedy in the study of nature." With Goethe we stand at the cross-roads. He is in the succession of men of the highest genius who speak the language of art, but in thought he belongs to an age which can accept neither religious dogma nor Renaissance assertion of individuality as ultimate certainties.

Attempts to capture truth in a net of logic were resumed in a series of formidable philosophical systems which began with Kant's *Critique of Pure Reason* (1781), and his *Metaphysic of Morals* (1785). To explain how the human mind can comprehend the material world, Kant assumes the existence of "things in themselves," and also the presence of faculties in our mind by which we can synthesize the materials presented to our senses. These faculties — "forms of intuition" about space and time, "categories of thought" about attributes and qualities, cause and effect — are implanted in our minds; they are transcendental, not derived from experience. Our knowledge can only be of the appearance of things as interpreted by these presumably God-given faculties. A new note which Kant introduced into his moral philosophy is interesting through its relation to the broader mind of the age. Again, this involves assumptions, of God's existence, of man's free-will, and of immortality. Man, for his part, is subject to the "categorical affirmative," a conception of moral duty as a law of nature. A rational being conforms to such law by his will, not for self-interest. He has the consolation of knowing that although virtue does not necessarily bring happiness on earth, God correlates virtue with happiness, and the hereafter exists so that man can reap his eventual reward. . . .

Kant's system can be left to the mercies of his brother philosophers. His theory of knowledge was soon abandoned. But the tone of his moral philosophy, with its call for the harmonization of man's will with an ideal moral law, is in keeping with the new temper of mind which we have seen already in Goethe, and which we associate especially with Beethoven. We must guard, as always, against the assumption that a composer sets out in an instrumental work to express any particular mood or thought. Beethoven, however, gives us strong clues to his general sympathies when choosing and setting words: in the theme of liberty and heroism in *Fidelio,* in the title *Eroica* for his Third Symphony, and in the setting of Schiller's *Ode to Joy* in the Choral Symphony. And apart from his music, his own views on the great issues of life are known: he believed in no personal God, but he was convinced of the reality of a spiritual power immanent in nature, and he had a sense of mission to communicate the uplifting power of his belief through his art. It is obviously absurd to suppose that such thought can be translated literally into musical sound; but it is not absurd to suggest that the states of mind and the emotions which the composer himself experienced should emerge unconsciously in his phraseology, his rhythms, his buildings of climaxes, and his alternation of tension and repose. By the time Beethoven began to compose, instrumental music had become a language so rich in associations that a composer who had command of its resources was using a medium in which he could scarcely avoid self-revelation. If he was a Dussek, he uttered platitudes; if a Beethoven, the quality and the orientation of his mind were inevitably apparent in his music.

Beethoven appeared at a time when all conditions were favourable to his genius and temperament. Serious by nature, and strengthened in character by early responsibilities, he grew to maturity in the noblest phase of German literature and moral philosophic thought. Assertively individual, he lived at a time when the ideal of liberty inspired both thought and action. Urgent in feeling and powerful in mind, he inherited a musical language which was already highly expressive, but capable of flexible expansion to meet his urgent demands. Unlike the poets and dramatists who had had to free themselves from an alien convention, Beethoven found in the sonata a living organism, not a stereotyped form. As a medium for conveying thought and feeling it is a musical counterpart to the drama, but not being restricted to direct representation and the physical limitations of the stage, it allows the composer to range over the whole realm of the spirit. The sonata has its own principles of artistic organization, and can communicate the highest aesthetic satisfaction through the endless scope it gives for securing formal order in sound. One part of Beethoven's greatness lies in his unsurpassed command of it as a purely artistic medium. The other lies in his assumption of the liberty to use it in expressing every human feeling. It is natural to crave for liberty, though so often the ideal remains an abstraction. But at some moments in history, the conception has become a reality, in strange and unexpected ways. Ancient Athens found expression of her genius when freed from the Persian menace; ordinary humanity was given spiritual release from formal religion by Jesus of Nazareth; Giotto freed the art of painting from subservience to external abstractions; Monteverdi set music on a new road by breaking with a convention which was not appropriate for his expressive purposes. Beethoven in his turn brought a new freedom, not by discarding an artistic convention, but by bringing within its scope a new range of human experiences. Michelangelo offers the closest parallel in art, employing Renaissance forms, but displaying a titanic energy which made new developments imperative to successors who did not possess his reserves of power. Beethoven had the same masterful energy; none fought more heroic battles of the spirit than he. They were his own personal struggles, of deeply individual import even in his setting of the Mass. They might, as in the Third and Fifth Symphonies, show man seeking reconciliation with the external forces of the world; or they might represent, as in the last string quartets, the search for peace within his own soul. Besides these strenuous moods, all those others are to be found that spring from a generous nature, and from the positive spirit of a man who, though afflicted by deafness during most of his working life, turned a courageous face to the world.

Summary

German literature in the second half of the 18th century records the successive stages, in criticism, constructive thought, and imaginative creation, by which Europe passed from the acceptance of absolutism to assertion of individualism in things of the mind. All aspects of this process of transition are visible in Goethe, through whose breadth and sanity as well as artistic genius the transformation took place with a tranquillity which contrasted with contemporary political stresses. In Beethoven the assertion of individualism was complete, but it was expressed in terms of a highly organized musical form which prevented a descent into mere subjectivism. Beethoven, in this respect, stood at the end of an era in which music still had universal significance, while at the same time he was the most powerful figure among many whose musical activities were beginning to show the pattern of a new individualistic age.

Bibliography

The standard biography of Beethoven, though now a century old, is that of Alexander Wheelock Thayer, *The Life of Beethoven*. It is available in a revised edition by Elliot Forbes in two volumes (Princeton, N.J., Princeton University Press, 1964). Emily Anderson has translated and edited *The Letters of Beethoven*, 3 vols. (New York, St. Martin, 1961) as well as a one-volume abridgement, *Selected Letters of Beethoven* (New York, St. Martin, 1967). The last work of Donald

Tovey, *Beethoven* (London, Oxford University Press, 1944), contains some very perceptive analyses of the composer's work. In commemoration of the bicentennial of Beethoven's birth, the *Journal of the American Musicological Society*, 23, no. 3 (Fall, 1970), and *The Musical Quarterly*, 56, no. 4 (Oct., 1970), devoted entire issues to Beethoven. Paul Henry Lang's introduction to *The Musical Quarterly* issue is especially recommended.

Beethoven's music is available in a complete edition, *Ludwig van Beethovens Werke*, 25 series (Leipzig, Breitkopf & Härtel, 1864–1890). The thematic index by George Kinsky and Hans Halm, *Das Werk Beethoven* (Munich, G. Henle, 1955) is helpful in using this set. A new edition of the complete works, *Beethoven Werke*, is in progress (Munich, G. Henle, 1961–   ). The compositions of Beethoven are available separately and in collections in a number of standard editions, such as G. Schirmer, Peters, and Kalmus.

22

MUCH of the music of the nineteenth century is usually grouped together under the label Romanticism. Yet, once these compositions have been gathered up for examination, even a brief look makes it clear that an inclusive definition or description of what makes these works Romantic is nearly impossible. Nineteenth-century music includes short, simple works for solo instruments; extended works for soloists, especially pianists and violinists, requiring dazzling virtuosity; works for small groups of instruments; gigantic symphonic works; intimate songs of only three minutes duration or less; operas running six hours in performance time; works which appear to be based strictly on formal techniques and models taken from earlier centuries; works which appear to be completely original in formal principles or organization. Yet in this apparent diversity and contradiction there may be some unity. The nineteenth century was one of great individualism, and individualism breeds contrasts. Contrasts were very much a part of Romanticism, yet contrasts can make definition difficult. It has been said that Romanticism in music is much easier to identify than it is to define. Paradoxically, it is this difficulty of definition, based on individualism, which helps define Romanticism.

The idea was once held that Romanticism broke with Classicism at its beginning and with Impressionism at its end. This led to difficulties in terminology because it soon became clear that Romantic traits and ideas existed before the nineteenth century and still exist. For example, this anthology of writings about music history rests on a Romantic idea, for it was Romanticism which gave birth to the discipline of historical musicology and to the belief that there was value in trying to understand the music of the past in order to understand better the music of the present. The theory of a Classic-Romantic opposition has now been abandoned. The period from the late eighteenth century to the early twentieth has come to be seen instead as a Classic-Romantic period in which both Classic and Romantic tendencies existed side by side in constantly shifting balance, frequently even within the works of a single composer. This broader view of Romanticism is the subject of the following selection

John Culshaw is head of music programs for the British Broadcasting Corporation Television. His writings include *Rachmaninoff, the Man and His Music* (New York, Oxford University Press, 1949), *Ring Resounding* (New York, Viking, 1967), and *A Century of Music* (New York, Roy Publishers, 1952).

Romantic Principles

JOHN CULSHAW

The Spirit of Music pervades all Nature
E. T. A. HOFFMANN

Romanticism, as a philosophy, encourages the utmost artistic freedom; and since this is a somewhat vague concept, we must not be surprised to find a number of apparent contradictions within the romantic era. Equally, we must not expect to find an adequate, simple definition of the word. For it is the case that many so-called romantic principles are implicit in the works of other periods.

The term, however, is useful; for if it is possible to isolate certain musical and philosophical considerations which were predominant a hundred years ago they may be regarded as the basis of romanticism. What is important is to remember that for music to possess a romantic-nature, or for a composer to be considered a romantic, it is not necessary for either to have been conceived in the mid-nineteenth century.

There is a tendency, particularly prevalent in the more formal history books, to divide music into a series of hermetically sealed periods, each possessing its own musical style and philosophy. To some extent this may foster a false sense of historicism in the reader who, on hearing a piece of music, may be tempted to judge it according to its date, or according to how much it was ahead or behind the *avant garde* of its period. The disconcerting effects of such an attitude must be very apparent to those who, having finally sealed Bruckner and Mahler as the last two specimens within the romantic casket, promptly opened another — labelled "impressionist" — which seemed to contain the negation of everything that had been called romantic. But now, in perspective, it has been realised that the neatly labelled caskets are not so strongly different

FROM John Culshaw, *A Century of Music* (New York, Roy Publishers, Inc., 1952), pp. 15-21. Reprinted by permission of Roy Publishers, Inc., and Dennis Dobson.

303

from each other as at first they seemed, while some of them have burst their sides and released a stream of composers rushing madly here and there in search of their spiritual homes. Stravinsky, in particular, has proved specially obstinate in his determination to travel only on a tourist ticket, by which he is able to wander from period to period composing in a series of by no means mutually exclusive styles.

There is, in fact, no thesis-antithesis relation between classicism and romanticism, or romanticism and impressionism; the differences arise through a change of outlook towards a stable ideal of expression, and the style of any creative musician is conditioned mainly by the music he has heard and to some extent by the literature, art and philosophy of his time. By the most popular definition, we learn that the romantics encouraged the most intimate types of expression in music, laying stress on emotional qualities and showing a certain indifference to the classical perfection of form. Like most generalities this statement is to a certain degree true, and to a larger degree useless. It is dangerous in its implication that composers of the classical period wrote music largely to indicate their craftsmanship in the creation of a coherent musical structure. Similarly, it implies that romantic composers were pioneers in discarding traditional features of form whenever the latter came into conflict with what they desired to express; by such a standard, Mozart was far more romantic than Brahms. It is clear that the nature of Mozart's musical ideas demanded that they should find expression within the very flexible bounds of a form whose general outline was stable, but whose details varied according to the material. Many of the greatest moments in Mozart's music conform with no formal "regulation," though they fit within a formal pattern; the fusion of two themes in the last few bars of the first movement of the K 516 String Quintet is not a formal device but a means of emotional expression which resolves the nature of the movement.

We must accept, therefore, that the form of most music is conditioned by its content, not the content by the form. With this realisation, the pseudo-problems of romanticism lose much of their terror, and it is no longer necessary to waste pages of discussion in assessing the relative merits of, for example, Liszt and Mozart. There is nothing more absurd than the assumption that formal structures admirably suitable for composers of the classical era are necessarily superior to those evolved by the romanticists. It may indeed be the case that one's personal preference is for the classicists, and such a preference may tempt one to censure the romantic for failing to achieve something he never attempted. No formal difference can indicate the whole story; if this were so, the symphonies of Brahms would be pale imitations of an already perfect original; but, as we shall see, Brahms was a romantic whose musical thinking led him into more or less conventional formal paths. Just as the musical thoughts of Delius occurred in a free, rhapsodic manner which is as strong and as important a characteristic as their somewhat unstable harmony, so the ideas conceived by Brahms found their expression in what we have learnt to call classical form. The fundamental importance of this relation between content and form may clearly be gathered by examining those works — such as Chopin's Piano Concertos — where the form is an external device; instead of a natural and simultaneous growth of music through form, the music is poured into a formal strait-jacket, within which its struggles for freedom are all too apparent.

Perhaps the most clearly apparent difference between the romantic approach to music and that of other periods lies in the relationship between the composer and society. It is a legitimate generalisation to say that before 1800 the position of the composer was not conducive to wide experiments in music; in general, the utilitarian principle applied, in so far as composers wrote music on commission, and with a specific audience or patron in mind. Originally, the Church had been the most powerful patron, and the most narrowly definitive in its requirements. Later, the rise of the aristocratic patron gave the court composer a somewhat wider degree of freedom and, within limits, the opportunity to indulge in experimental works if he so desired. Even Mozart who, in his later years, became a "free artist," rarely, if ever, composed simply for the sake of composition; the necessity of a commission remained. On first acquaintance, such an attitude may seem strangely mechanistic, but one cannot judge the psychology and creative background of the eighteenth century by the standards of the twentieth. The music of Mozart and Haydn is obviously more than occasional, "utility" music; we have to recognise that the presence of a patron — whether it was the Church, aristocracy or concert audience — was a factor which the composer both accepted and expected. The presence of a commission was a spur that roused the imagination, and was generally at that time an inseparable complement of musical creation.

By the beginning of the nineteenth century the patronage of the aristocracy was waning, although even Beethoven, despite his rugged individuality and reputation for furthering the "emancipation of the composer" was not beyond accepting occasional commissions if they were good enough. Yet the tendency of the time was based on the newly discovered freedom of the individual and, no less than any other human beings, composers began to exercise their freedom to create what they wanted without the "burden" of a special commission. The romantic composer's creed was emphatically "art for art's sake" — which as a principle stands midway between the earlier "art for God's sake" and the later "art for the sake of the broad masses."

At the same time, the composer became obsessed with the nature of artistic creation, both in his own field and in those of literature and the visual arts. This interest in other fields, a profound romantic strain, was eventually to lead — as did many romantic ideals — to disintegration in an orgy of excess. Schumann's interest in the novels of E. T. A. Hoffmann is characteristic of the romantic absorption in literature and is an early indication of a trend which, in the later, less sensitive romantics, led to an all-pervading desire for a fusion of the arts, such as that imagined by Scriabin in his last years.

The considerable independence of the artist and his growing self-consciousness led him naturally to abhor the patronage of earlier periods. But the romantic composer, and indeed the whole romantic principle, abounds with inconsistencies which are nowhere more obvious than in the composer's somewhat precarious relationship with his society. On the one hand the artistic freedom, the "art for art's sake" ideal, clearly implied the composer's indifference towards his audience; the act of creation itself was the reward, and was the secret enjoyed only by the creative artist, whatever his sphere. The preoccupation with "the music of the future," the desire to experiment both in terms of sound and with the formal qualities of music are all distinctive romantic tendencies,[1] and closely related to the composer's attitude — somewhat uncompromising, as it appears — towards his public. But it is equally characteristic that most romantic composers developed a secret love of mysticism (especially in connection with the act of creation) which in itself prevented them from thinking very clearly and from realising that their philosophy embraced a number of conflicting ideals. Thus the exercise of artistic freedom mingled with rather patronising approaches to the masses — the ideal of composing for mankind, the cult of the universal. Yet here at least is one profound difference between the romanticists and the early "utilitarian" classicists. Both Liszt and Berlioz proclaimed a vision of the universal to be expressed in Church music; and later, until the inevitable reaction came with *Parsifal*, Wagner held a similar ideal for his music-dramas. Similarly, the deliberate rejection of past formalities went hand in hand with a determined cultivation of "lost masterpieces"; the chosen romantics felt it their duty to rescue from oblivion those works which the public had, for various reasons, ignored. We may be thankful for their work in this respect, though in praising, for example, the work of Mendelssohn on behalf of Bach, we tend to forget that not all propagandists had such vision and taste, and that many of the works so rescued have subsequently retired again to the oblivion which is their just environment.

The cultivation of a broader outlook naturally led the romantic composer towards literary associations within his music, not only in the thriving *lieder* but also in the "new" programme music. Here we may

[1]These, as we shall see, are related also to the romantic phenomenon of the virtuoso-composer.

find the typically romantic ideal of poetic expression—the idea that the essence of a poem or a picture may be intensified, or at least suggested, through the medium of music. Again, this idea is not exclusively a romantic invention, though the outlook of the romantics was more pretentious than that of the composers who had previously attempted programme works. One has only to hear Vivaldi's set of violin concertos known as *The Seasons* to realise that programme music in the widest sense existed long before Liszt or even Beethoven, and although Vivaldi peppered his score with literal allusions (in the "winter" episode one passage is meant to suggest, and is labelled, "the chattering of teeth") the fact remains that, abstracting from these allusions, the work manages to express something of the atmosphere of the seasons it depicts.

In time, the romantic vogue for programme music led to a new philosophy in which all music—whatever its period—came to be regarded as programme music, since it expressed some kind of thought; doubtless the romantics thought that they had discovered something new and profound, and some of them went so far as to attempt to explain this profundity through the written word. Yet all they had done was to broaden the application, and thus weaken the sense, of the word "programme." Their motive was probably a subconscious awareness of the limitations of their own programme music, and a desire to align it with the "abstract" masterpieces of the classical era by means of some unifying principle.

The elements of romanticism in music are therefore diverse; they lie equally within the bounds of a thirteen-bar Prelude by Chopin and a fourteen-hour opera cycle by Wagner; they lie equally within the cultivation of specifically national flavours and the pursuit of an intensely personal, sub-national, style. They foster a determination to avoid the principles of classicism, while admitting a deep envy of classical composers and a tendency to revert to classical ideals—as in the case of Berlioz and Schumann in their later years. The only worthwhile unifying principle that we may discover in the period is the overwhelming self-consciousness of the artist: his outlook as a crusader—an outlook which pervades romantic music and which is also to be found in the writings of Berlioz, Schumann, Wagner and Liszt, to mention only four. The motive for this crusade varies according to the composer, but the desire is uniform. It is not a bad thing, though its overall implications are more important than its purely musical manifestations; Schumann's "battle" with the Philistines does not now make our enjoyment of *Carnaval* any more intense, though it gives us some insight into the workings of his mind. Of only one thing can we be quite certain—the age of romanticism did not cease with the arrival of the twentieth century. Its roots survive, and will continue to survive as long as musical creation remains the prerogative of the individual.

Bibliography

The literature on Romanticism in music is so extensive that only a few general works can be listed here. Friedrich Blume, *Classic and Romantic Music* (New York, Norton, 1970), is essential reading. Other general surveys of nineteenth-century music are: Alfred Einstein, *Music in the Romantic Era* (New York, Norton, 1947); Rey M. Longyear, *Nineteenth-century Romanticism in Music* (Englewood Cliffs, N.J., Prentice-Hall, 1969); and Gerald Abraham, *A Hundred Years of Music* (3d ed., Chicago, Aldine, 1964). Jacques Barzun, *Berlioz and the Romantic Century*, 2 vols. (Boston, Little, Brown, 1950) contains much information on Romanticism in general as well as on Berlioz specifically. An abridged edition was issued under a different title, *Berlioz and His Century* (New York, Meridian, 1956). Selected articles on Romanticism include: E. J. Dent, "The Romantic Spirit in Music" in *Proceedings of the Royal Music Association*, 59th session (1932–1933); Paul Henry Lang, "Liszt and the Romantic Movement," *The Musical Quarterly*, 22 (1936); D. C. Parker, "Reflections on Romanticism," *The Musical Quarterly*, 4 (1918); Leon Plantinga, "Schumann's View of 'Romantic'," *The Musical Quarterly*, 52 (1966); and Arnold Salop, "Intensity as a Distinction between Classical and Romantic Music," *Journal of Aesthetics and Art Criticism*, 23, no. 3 (Spring, 1965).

Much of the music by such Romantic composers as Chopin, Schumann, Liszt, Mendelssohn, Berlioz, Wagner, Brahms, and many others is easily available in one or several modern editions, such as Peters, Kalmus, and G. Schirmer. A small anthology containing selected piano compositions, songs, and vocal part-music, which includes works by composers less well known than those named above, has been edited by Kurt Stephenson, *Romanticism in Music* (Cologne, Arno Volk Verlag, 1961). This is vol. 21 in the series *Anthology of Music*, distributed in the United States by Leeds Music Corp.

23

AT the mention of the word "symphony" the image that is most apt first to come to mind is that of the nineteenth-century symphony. With the exception of certain late eighteenth-century symphonies, notably the last works of Mozart and Haydn, it is usually a nineteenth-century symphony that appears today as one of the major items on a standard orchestral program. These symphonies are works usually in four movements (or sometimes three or five), requiring the forces of a medium-size to large orchestra. They are conceived as complete and independent works intended to be played at public concerts, and they have no connection with other musical forms or media. Yet this has not always been true, for the first symphonies were born of the opera.

Symphonies, or sinfonias, frequently appeared as introductory movements (one can hardly call them overtures yet) and as interludes in early seventeenth-century operas. The first examples were very short, but by the early eighteenth century the *sinfonia avanti l'opera* (symphony before the opera) had become standardized, at least in Italy, as a three-movement work of rather extended proportions. The establishment of public concerts about the turn of the eighteenth century caused the sinfonia sometimes to be detached from its opera and played in concert for lack of other concert fare. This of course quickly led to the composition of similar works, also titled "sinfonia," works intended as concert pieces with no connection whatever with an opera. Thus the concert symphony was born.

Early eighteenth-century forms other than those connected with opera also influenced the symphony, forms such as the Baroque concerto and the trio sonata, so that after 1700 the symphony was no longer purely an offspring of opera. By the mid-eighteenth century the symphony had taken over the sonata form, and after this the symphony can no longer be considered separately from the sonata because the symphony had become a sonata for orchestra.

At one time the mid and late eighteenth-century symphony was considered to be the invention of Franz Joseph Haydn. Then the works of other composers of the so-called Mannheim School, centered around Mannheim, Germany, came to light, and they were permitted to share Haydn's fame. Later research has revealed that there were in fact many, many other composers, such as C. P. E. Bach, whose work was too long overlooked, who contributed so greatly to the sonata-symphony that it can no longer be viewed as the invention of only a few composers or groups.

The following selection traces the way in which the nineteenth-century symphony evolved from the works of Haydn, Mozart, and especially Beethoven, and how it progressed or declined, depending upon one's point of view. Certainly the twentieth century has seen a decline of the symphony in quantity, caused by some of the same factors that have led to a decline of the sonata (see "The Sonata-Principle," page 277). Furthermore, the nineteenth-century orchestra, which sometimes numbered a hundred performers or more, is becoming less and less feasible economically as a medium for performing symphonies. It is quite possible that those of two centuries hence will regard the symphony as one of those defunct forms which flowered so brilliantly in the Classic-Romantic era.

Biographical information about Paul Henry Lang can be found at the end of the introduction to "Musical Thought of the Baroque: The Doctrine of Temperaments and Affections" (page 192).

The Symphony in the Nineteenth Century

PAUL HENRY LANG

The home of the symphony was Vienna; yet we should consider the designation "Viennese school" more generic than geographic. Histories of music tend to treat Salzburg, Prague, and Eszterháza as suburbs of Vienna, although they were musical centers removed from the capital and as varied as the ingredients of the Viennese symphony. Among the composers who contributed to the development of the Classical symphony there were a number of non-Germans—Austria was a polyglot empire of Germans, Slavs, Hungarians, and Italians—and what lured them to the capital city was a court and many aristocratic sponsors generous toward music. It would be useful to remark that of all members of the Viennese school, Schubert was the only native son; all the others came from elsewhere. Since among these musicians there were many Czechs who arrived in Vienna as mature and established musicians, "Austro-Bohemian school" would be perhaps a more accurate designation than "Viennese school"; but since the latter term is firmly embedded in musical historiography, and since Vienna became the symbol for the great era that stretches from Johann Josef Fux to Anton Bruckner (and once more from Mahler to Webern), we had better retain the term. While at first, and after a preliminary impulse in Italy, the Classical symphony was indeed created and practiced mainly in Austria, the symphonic idea gradually diffused to the north of Germany, to France, and later to Russia, Finland, and Scandinavia.

As the new century, the nineteenth, opens, all of Europe speaks, or attempts to speak, the language of Vienna. Haydn and Mozart had woven the fabric of music seemingly for eternity. In the Germanic countries the continuation was natural; Haydn was as highly appreciated in Leipzig, Amsterdam, and London as he was in Vienna, and it is indicative

FROM Paul Henry Lang, ed., *The Symphony, 1800-1900,* A Norton Music Anthology (New York, W. W. Norton & Company, Inc.), pp. viii-xiv. Copyright © 1969 by W. W. Norton & Company, Inc. Reprinted by permission of the publisher.

of the universal familiarity with the idiom that piratical publishers produced spurious Haydn quartets and symphonies in quantity. As we advance into the nineteenth century we notice that while Viennese Classicism had a strong Latin, notably Italian, vein, the Romantic symphony, especially in the latter part of the period, became almost exclusively German in spirit and tone. Debussy considered Brahms the most German composer of them all. In the Latin countries symphony and quartet remained largely foreign imports. Not that the Classical style was rejected or unknown; it made its appearance in the theater, in church music, and in the conservatory, but it was not practiced as the principal style in instrumental music. To the Italians and, to a lesser degree, the French, the lyric theater was the very manifestation of life, natural and autochthonous, and most of their composers exerted their energies in working for the opera house and the church, church music having been for a long time closely related to dramatic music. In the century of Romanticism, then, the bulk of the symphonic literature as well as its outstanding representatives will still be German, just as the bulk of the operatic literature and its outstanding representatives will still be Italian. (Wagner is an exception that does not alter the general situation.) To be sure, here and there one finds a distinguished "foreign" master who could speak the Viennese language to perfection, like Cherubini. This mysterious, puritanical conservative, residing in Paris, whom Haydn and Beethoven admired and Berlioz detested, was a true Classic, but he wrote only one symphony; all his magnificent craftsmanship and cool Beethovenian ardor went into the making of operas and large-scale church music. We might also mention an example from the other camp, Saverio Mercadante, called "The Italian Beethoven," whose *Sinfonia fantastica* preceded Berlioz; but he too became famous as an opera composer and left no mark on the history of the symphony.

As the nineteenth century dawned, the symphony, the favorite genre of orchestral music since the latter part of the previous century, had reached such heights as were felt to be unsurpassable. The original mixture of Italian opera derivatives, the German suite, the concerto, the divertimento, and other ingredients had coalesced, mainly under the wise and immensely imaginative Haydn, into a genre and idiom based on the art of development and exploitation of thematic material carried out within a constructive framework that we call the sonata form. The Germans were used to this sort of thing, if in a different medium: fugue and the art of variation; but formerly they operated with themes, whereas the eighteenth-century symphonic procedure favored fractions of themes, mere motifs. A theme has a physiognomy of its own, a motif is only a fragment of a musical idea; a theme is a self-sufficient musical entity, a motif offers only potentialities which can, through elaboration, become the support of a tremendous musical edifice. Perhaps the incarnation of the symphonic ideal, of motivic architecture and logic as well as of overwhelming expressive force, is the first movement of Beethoven's Fifth Symphony; it is built on a little motif of four notes, three of which are repeated. No full-blooded Romantic composer would even look at such an insignificant subject—insignificant in isolation; yet the Classical composers deliberately sought just this sort of material. It did not matter where the original idea came from, as indeed almost all symphonic allegro themes in the eighteenth-century and far into the Beethovenian era came from the public domain; all that mattered was what would happen to it. In this art of elaborating a small particle or snatch of a musical idea, the eighteenth-century composers were infinitely ingenious, the particles assuming all shades of expression, from the humorous to the profound, from the brilliant to the noble. Contrary to the Romantic concept of "invention," which demanded original and unmistakably personal themes, the eighteenth century understood by "invention" the art of elaboration, combination, and permutation of any given subject. Only in opera, and in the slow movements of instrumental works, was melody as an entity preferred; in a symphonic allegro an independent, significant theme would hobble the composer's imagination, because a well-shaped melody cannot be splintered and dissected—such a procedure would ruin it. Motivic-thematic elaboration carries with it a certain melodic frugality. The Classical symphonists were not interested primarily in the sensuous quality of music, but in its possibilities of manipulation; it was not the beauty of the "invention" that mattered to them, but the characteristic melodic-rhythmic profile, the springiness, the many possible "meanings" of the motif in different contexts, the constructive use of the given material. This was the age of witty conversation, the challenge, the quick repartee—and the symphony, played in aristocratic residences rather than in concert halls, conversed with equal wit in the realm of music. The mature eighteenth-century symphony is difficult to grasp, though its elegance and sprightliness always delight and fall easily on the ear, because the incessant sparkle of the thematic convolutions requires the listener's active mental participation. Even today this is difficult to the layman, and it was found difficult by the Romantic composers, too, who eventually had to abandon it and create their own principles of construction and cohesion. The contrapuntal finesse in the late symphonies of Haydn and Mozart, the imitations, the dramatic juxtaposition of the particles obtained by "exploding" the symphonic subject, are so sophisticated that the more knowledgeable and historically informed composers, like Brahms, hesitated to enter the particular preserves of the Classical composer—i.e., the quartet and symphony.

The formal scheme of the Classical symphonic ideal was the so-called "sonata form," usually associated with the opening allegro, but often appearing in the finale (frequently combined with the rondo) and at times in the slow movement. A good deal of misconception is attached to this constructional scheme, and one frequently encounters the remark that such-and-such a movement is composed in "strict" sonata form. But there was nothing "strict" about the sonata form. In fact, the eighteenth-century composer had not even heard the term, which was coined in the nineteenth century; he followed certain *principles*, not a pattern. The basic concept was to present the idea or ideas to be elaborated in a first section, which our theorists call "exposition," develop this material in the middle or "development" section, then prepare and execute a "recapitulation" or "reprise" in such a manner as to reconcile the warring, antithetic tonalities by restoring the unequivocal supremacy of the main key. Within these general principles the composer was absolutely free; there were no "rules" because the statute books were all written in the nineteenth century, and if Haydn could see them he would have a hearty laugh. Thus, a composer could use a "second" or "subsidiary" theme, or perhaps a whole theme group, but he could also base the entire movement on a single theme. The transition to the subsidiary theme may contain material that later acquires more importance than the principal subject; Haydn often uses a second theme only to ignore it in the elaboration of the exposition — indeed, he may even ignore his principal subject and barrel along magnificently with a little snippet taken from the final cadence in the exposition. This freedom of the sonata form, as opposed to the restrictions we have since read into it, is shown in a variety of ways. For example, the exposition of an allegro movement may present a thematic group we designate ABC, but of this group only A is developed, whereas the reprise ignores A, begins with B, and ends with C; then the coda gives A a generous workout. As a matter of fact, the coda, the postlude in the sonata form, constantly gains in importance. In the last movement of Beethoven's Eighth Symphony, one of his longest movements, and a work in which, as in the Fourth Symphony, he lovingly returns to the eighteenth century, the coda is only a few measures shorter than all the rest of the movement and has a little coda of its own. The overriding principle was not a formal pattern but the logic and continuity of thematic elaboration; whatever was selected for elaboration had to be pursued until all possibilities were exhausted.

There was a certain pattern in the relationship of development to exposition, but even in the eighteenth century it was not binding. Haydn might compose a development section twice the size of the exposition; Mozart might do the same, though he was just as ready to write a large and highly developed exposition and a development that was one third of its size. With Beethoven's Third Symphony (the *Eroica)* and with the Romantic symphonists, the development section expands, though, once more, Schumann and Dvořák were willing to reverse the proportions. Then again, in the second movement of Mendelssohn's Third Symphony ("Scottish'') the development is shorter than the exposition and the reprise shorter than the development, but the coda nicely restores symmetry and balance. The exact opposite is true in the fourth movement of Schumann's Second Symphony, where the reprise is almost twice as long as the exposition and the coda twice the size of the reprise. All this goes to show that we should beware of categorical ''rules''; they exist only in textbooks written after the fact. To reiterate, the sonata was a ''free'' rather than a ''strict'' form, its disposition entirely determined by the composer's will, imagination, and sense of tonal balance; only the principles of thematic development and tonal stress and resolution were binding.

The sonata principle was retained by the ''pure'' symphony of the nineteenth century, but it was enlarged and extended, often to all four movements. Furthermore, a relationship between the individual movements, the so-called cyclic principle, was established, which may encompass two or even all movements. Simple quotation from preceding movements, however, does not necessarily amount to cyclic construction. The oft-cited example in the finale of Beethoven's Ninth Symphony, where the composer quotes bits from the previous movements, is not of a structural nature; these are only reminiscences that are not organically connected, unlike the case of his Fifth Symphony, where the scherzo and the finale are inseparably entwined. We shall see imaginative and vitally important structural connections between movements in the symphonies of Schumann, Brahms, and Dvořák, and in Bruckner's Eighth Symphony all four movements are united in a mighty contrapuntal apotheosis.

This brings us to an important change in the hierarchy of the movements. In the eighteenth century the first allegro was usually the weightiest movement, but later the finale began to gain in status, to become in Brahms's First and Fourth and in all of Bruckner's symphonies the culmination of the work. The hymnic finale, even in purely instrumental form, is palpably descended from Beethoven's Ninth, though some of his earlier symphonies also contributed to the idea, as the Third, the Fifth, and the Sixth rise to dithyrambic heights in their final movements. The ultimate in the cyclic idea is to be found in Beethoven's last quartets, where the principle transcends the boundaries of the individual work to embrace several of the quartets.

To the eighteenth-century composer, the material dictated not only form and substance, but also their external manifestations, such as the choice and employment of instruments. The Classical composer of symphonies did not orchestrate, he composed for orchestra; that is, the ideas and their realizations came in their full and finished orchestral garb requiring very few adjustments. In his operas Mozart used a far more varied and elaborate orchestral idiom than in his symphonies, and in many a divertimento the winds were given virtuoso tasks that we never encounter in the symphonies. The reason for this was that the terse and dynamic Classical symphony used the weight of the orchestra, especially brasses and drums, not for effect but for delineation of the form and for emphatically nailing down the tonalities. To be sure, there was also color in this orchestra and (especially in Beethoven) many imaginative orchestral turns, but these remained secondary in importance until the late Romantic symphony, and even then were more conspicuous in the French and Russian works than in the German ones.

In the meantime the orchestra underwent considerable change, but since as usual the development took place in the opera pit, the German symphony was unaffected by it, beyond a modest degree, almost to the time of Richard Strauss. The new, "noisy" apparatus, inaugurated by Lesueur, Simon Mayr (an expatriate Bavarian residing in Bergamo), and Gasparo Spontini (an expatriate Italian lording it over Paris, and later Berlin), strongly affected the French, notably Berlioz, as well as Meyerbeer, Liszt, and, to a certain degree, Wagner; but none of these composers was a true symphonist. Perhaps the greatest change influencing the sound of the orchestra in the post-Beethovenian era was the invention of the valves for horn and trumpet. The Classical symphonists, limited to the very restricted number of "natural" tones, tailored their use of these instruments to their capabilities. The horns furnished the glue that bound strings to woodwinds, their octaves, fifths, and thirds gently blending the two choirs; then in the rousing tuttis they united with the trumpets in proclamative assertion. But not both instruments could play all the chromatic tones within their entire compass, inviting a new way of writing for them. (Just the same, it is entirely false and unnecessary to "correct" brass parts in older works, as Mahler and other conductors were wont to do; the eighteenth-century composer knew the limitations and composed accordingly.)

Still, though enlarged to keep pace with the changing style and with the requirements of the larger concert halls, the nineteenth-century German symphony orchestra remained basically unchanged. Beginning with Schumann the standard Romantic symphony orchestra consisted of pairs of woodwinds, four horns, two trumpets, three trombones, a pair of timpani, and strings, to which Brahms occasionally added a contrabassoon or a bass tuba. Except for the tuba, this orchestra was identical to Beethoven's in the Ninth Symphony half a century earlier. This is surprising if we realize that by the time Brahms composed his First Symphony, Berlioz and Wagner used triple or even quadruple winds, English horn, bass clarinet, up to eight horns, harps, two pairs of timpani, and assorted other percussion. In the symphony, at least in the central European symphony, but also in Tchaikovsky, all this was absent. Dvořák would use the English horn for a solo, and Bruckner raised the number of the horns to eight, but on the whole these were exceptions, and the late Beethovenian orchestra remained the norm. Nevertheless, the use of wind instruments and especially the relationship between the individual choirs underwent some changes, if for no other reason than the liberation of horns and trumpets. The winds still reinforce and articulate, but they also live their own lives. Yet despite the modernized orchestra, the improved wind instruments, and the enriched color scheme, the mainstream of the symphony still, to a large extent, observed the old Classical condition that orchestral effects must not intrude upon the construction. This is what Berlioz no longer understood; but then he no longer composed symphonies in the original sense.

Bibliography

Literature in English concerning the nineteenth-century symphony is scarce, and an extensive treatment of the subject does not exist. Some information may be found in Ralph Hill, ed., *The Symphony* (Harmondsworth, Middlesex, Penguin, 1949), and in Robert Simpson, ed., *The Symphony*, 2 vols. (Harmondsworth, Middlesex, Penguin, 1966-1967). H. C. Robbins Landon, *The Symphonies of Joseph Haydn* (London, Universal Edition & Rockliff, 1955), and its *Supplement to The Symphonies of Joseph Haydn* (London, Barrie & Rockliff, 1961), is a model for works of its type and a valuable study of the symphony in the late eighteenth century. Many of the titles listed in the bibliographies following "Music and Society in the Age of Enlightenment," "The Sonata-Principle," and "Romantic Principles" (see pages 258, 287, and 308) deal in part with the symphony and should be consulted, especially the analyses by Tovey. Works in languages other than English may be found in the bibliographies following "Symphony" in the *Harvard Dictionary of Music* and "Symphonie" in *Die Musik in Geschichte and Gegenwart.*

A selection of nineteenth-century symphonies has been assembled by Professor Lang and printed in score in *The Symphony, 1800-1900* (New York, Norton, 1969). Many symphonies by these and other composers are available in complete score in inexpensive pocket-size editions from publishers such as Kalmus. A selection of symphonic movements, not limited to the nineteenth century, has been edited by Lothar Hoffman-Erbrecht, *The Symphony* (Cologne, Arno Volk Verlag, 1967), as vol. 29 of the *Anthology of Music*, distributed in the United States by Leeds Music Corp.

24

RICHARD WAGNER was a controversial man during his lifetime, and he remains so a century later. It is unlikely that a greater ego than his has ever existed in the field of music. Taking his mandate from Beethoven, or so he thought, his goal was to integrate music into a form of artwork that would lift man up and help him to become master of life as was intended for him. Wagner's philosophy denied any entertainment value in art and recognized only moral and spiritual values. Art was a religion, and he was the high priest; art was to lead man into a new promised land, and he was the new Moses, though he would no doubt be enraged at being compared with this Biblical Hebrew.

To accomplish his ends Wagner fashioned a new form of opera, known as music drama, into which music was theoretically equally integrated with the other arts. He was his own poet and librettist, his own director, and his own conductor. He designed and had built a special theater at Bayreuth where the faithful might come to worship. He enlarged the opera orchestra, had new instruments designed for it, and made new demands on both performer and listener. By all this he became one of the major influences in the history of the opera, and almost certainly most if not all opera since has been affected by his work in some way, either positively or negatively.

The subject of the following selection, however, is not the work of Wagner but the aftermath of Wagner, for there was an aftermath not only musically but aesthetically. In the twenty years that have passed since the selection was written the fever of the Wagner cult has eased considerably, so that the musical influence of Wagner on the operatic public is not what it once was. But the most lasting influence from Wagner may not be a musical one but rather a philosophical one. Debussy is reported to have remarked that "Wagner is a beautiful sunset which has been mistaken for a dawn." Insofar as certain technical aspects of musical composition are concerned—harmony, melody, counterpoint, use of chromaticism, orchestration—this possibly apocryphal statement may be true. Insofar as Wagner's influence on the role of music as a part of mass culture is concerned, it appears that the sun has not yet set.

Jacques Barzun, cultural historian and critic, is University Professor at Columbia University. Among his many works are *Berlioz and the Romantic Century*, 2 vols. (Boston, Little, Brown, 1950), *Classic, Romantic and Modern* (Boston, Little, Brown, 1961), and **Darwin, Marx, Wagner: Critique of a Heritage* (Boston, Little, Brown, 1947).

After Wagner: What Is Art?

JACQUES BARZUN

*I wish to see Wagner uprooted, however clever he may be, and I
don't doubt he is: but he is an anti-artistic, and don't doubt it.*
— WILLIAM MORRIS

The Nietzschean view of art was doubtless too difficult for the public to
extract from his contradictory and allusive sentences. It was much simpler for the "well-informed" to echo here and there an isolated outburst
against morality or a hymn to reckless strength, and to unite Nietzsche
with Wagner and Ibsen as the prophets of the new life. On the other
side, the defenders of a purely imaginary "established order" condemned
all three, with Tolstoy, Dostoevski, and "those Russians," likewise as
symbols of degeneration.[1] The century that ended to the tune of Natural
Selection, Socialism, and Anglo-Saxon Supremacy did not distinguish dis-
harmony among the parts, it merely sensed it somewhere in the orchestral
mass.

And although this chaos of tendencies was felt as marking the end of a
period, the impression that remained with the majority was one of cultural
accomplishment. It was typified equally well by the carrying of the White
Man's Burden and by Wagner. Conquering all difficulties, an artist had tri-
umphed and had been declared a great man: the age could not be so materialistic in the bad sense as some had charged. The public, rather, was flat-

---

[1]Two books published at the turn of the century give the temper of the moment: Max Nordau's *Degeneration* and H. S. Chamberlain's *Foundations of the
Nineteenth Century*. Though the thesis of each is incoherent, these two works are not
the "obviously crazy" productions they have been called. Their success at the time
shows how little obvious their folly actually was to readers familiar with Galton, Lom-
broso, Karl Pearson, and other scientific "authorities."

FROM Jacques Barzun, *Darwin, Marx, Wagner: Critique of a Heritage* (Boston, Little,
Brown and Company), pp. 335-347. Copyright 1941 by Jacques Barzun. Reprinted by
permission of the publisher.

tered by the thought that it had known enough to choose him and to learn about art at his capable hands.

With Wagner the "life of art" became a recognized substitute for life itself. Not only was Nietzsche not understood, but thoroughly lucid writers like George Bernard Shaw and Romain Rolland[2] were unable to depict the relation of art to society and religion, or to vindicate art from the charges of a Nordau, without being interpreted as saying that culture was exclusively the reading and making of books, the talking about pictures and concerts. Similarly, the social function of art was simply the depicting of industrial horrors in documented novels. The essentially Wagnerian confusion of art with both reality and unreality could not be disentangled, for the question of what was real and what was not could not be solved intelligently in an era which saw only Matter and non-Matter as the criteria of real and unreal. In any case, art had won the place that Wagner hoped it would win: that of absolute dominance, at least in the speech of the educated. Art for art's sake, which was a mild and redundant ideal, gave way to life for art's sake.

But this unlikely esthetic awakening of all Europe was so self-conscious that it was hard to distinguish it from the general faith in moral mechanisms that filled the spas and hydropathic establishments, the "new thought" studios and theosophic chapels. The few who kept their heads vainly raised their voices in behalf of simplicity and a direct use of the good things in life, which happen to include art. In the year of Wagner's death, for example, the English critic Edmund Gurney advanced the idea that the public had the right to look at pictures and listen to music that interested it, and no duty to endure any other. It already seemed a paradox to say: "Most students of the *Oper und Drama* must have admired, as in a dream, the earnest minuteness with which every sort of conscious reference, theoretic and practical, is read into the past history of opera and its public; the only point of view omitted being that which recognizes in the genus opera-goer . . . a wholesale indifference to theory, and a quite unpractical habit of enjoying what it may and enduring what it must."

Gurney went on to analyze with an accuracy we can appreciate today the advantage which Wagner's artistic practices gave him as weaver of spells over musical and unmusical alike.[3] "Wagner professes to 'cast off Beethoven's shackles' and to 'cast himself fearlessly in the sea of music' where . . . sinking, he finds himself naturally in the variegated home of invertebrate strains. . . ." To us as listeners this means: "*our* enforced flurry, *our* active impotence. But their creator is wise in his generation. Give the public from a couple to a score of firm bars they

[2]His long novel, *Jean Christophe*, which educated a whole generation to music and social thought, remained popular on the Continent until the World War.

[3]"Wagner and Wagnerism" in *The Nineteenth Century*, March 1883. Reprinted the same year in *Topics of the Times*, ed. T. M. Coan, 158, 169.

can seize and feel reliance in, and keep their eyes employed; and on these terms their ears will be quite content to stray about . . . for the next quarter or half hour. . . ." The critic rightly deplores Wagner's success in "making the expressiveness itself mechanical and independent of any impressiveness whatever." Finally, Gurney put his finger on the secret of the great nonmusical appeal of the new art. It is the "prosaic fallacy that the essence of music is vague namable expressiveness, instead of definite unnamable expressiveness."[4]

The word "prosaic" tells the story. Wagnerism made art a demagogic approximation to a dimly sensed truth, a form of free public education, an adjunct of the newspaper press. It confused giving art to the people with making the people think they could learn its meaning in a few easy lessons, and promised outsiders that they could *hereinstudieren* themselves into the elite. It was the confusion of vulgarity with popularity; and in so saying it is necessary to redefine vulgarity, for in this same period the word acquired a new meaning. Originally it meant what belongs to the crowd and is liked by it; the crowd being the common people, rough and untutored. It is this sort of vulgarity that salts Shakespeare's plays or Hogarth's scenes, and is seldom absent from great art. But with the advent of industrial city dwelling, popular crudity was lost. What had been rough became falsely polished, pretentious, apish, and cheap. The common people of former ages had made folk songs and folk tales and had sung them themselves; the new plebs had cheap songs and cheap tales made for them by hacks in imitation of the high-class product. A new vulgarity, known by its falseness and pride, henceforth permeated culture.

As regards Wagner's share in purveying a superior brand of it, it is significant that in his later musical output, which was designed particularly for the lay public, there is not a folk tune or the reminiscence of one, not a vulgar passage in the primary sense of the word. He speaks to a theater-bred audience, even when he poetizes nature, and he is at his worst when he tries to give sailors or apprentices a catch to sing. The dignity of the theater will perhaps not allow it, but the genteel substitute for commonness is vulgar in the secondary sense.

It was the smelling out of this vulgarity that made William Morris turn against Wagner so early. As a socialist and a man who was trying to reintroduce art into a mechanical society, Morris might have been expected to sympathize with the innovator whom Francis Hueffer depicted in such attractive terms. But the reading of the *Ring* was conclusive. Morris knew the original legend just as he knew the Venusberg story, and he felt that Wagner's handling was not only an alteration but a perversion of these ancient poems. The poet may always take liberties, since recapturing in modern speech the simple realism of the early versions is impossible, but to transform the human drama into a farrago of wandering discussions,

[4]*Ibid.*, 190.

the characters into wooden symbols of doubtful integrity—that was to be an anti-artist.

Nor was Morris altogether alone in his feeling. The materialist poet John Davidson, who had begun as a Wagnerian, soon decided he must write new ballads on the themes of the legends that Wagner had spoiled. He must as it were disinfect them. More violently still, the American critic John Jay Chapman, who felt so much at home in Germany and was so well disposed towards a new dramatic art, could find no simple explanation of his intense disgust at Wagner. But of the sharpness of the sensation he did not doubt: "The essential lack in Wagner is after all a want of sanitary plumbing. No amount of sentiment or passion can wholly make up for this. One feels all the time that the connection with the main is fraudulent. I should be grateful to you or anyone else who will tell me . . . why I am against him body and soul, sleeping and waking, and think him a bad man and a bad influence."[5] Henry Adams's objection, like Ruskin's, was on grounds of literary form. Neither could feel any sympathy—much less enthusiasm—for a system that merged all distinctions of dramatic structure, even that of moods. Like the Bernard Shaw of later years, they grew tired of losing themselves in the bottomless sea of harmony, and for his part Adams was only willing to drink it "in short gulps."[6]

THE fiercest attack, though the most easily discounted, came from Tolstoy. He also had gone through a transvaluation of all values and had emerged as a primitive Christian and an apostle of peasant simplicity. He did not merely wish to destroy modern art, he replaced it under his own hand with a truly popular folk literature; he did not merely announce his renunciation of the world, he lived its precepts as a cobbler with only one shirt. Meantime he defied Europe and scorned its new treasures in a pamphlet, *What Is Art?* containing a chapter on Wagner which became at once famous. The description of *Siegfried* was only too true: "When I arrived, an actor in jersey and tights was seated in front of an object intended to represent an anvil; his hair and beard were false; his hands, white and manicured, had nothing of the workman's; the carefree air, the bulging stomach, and the absence of muscle betrayed the actor. With an incredible hammer he struck, as no one ever struck, a sword that was no less fanciful. It was easy to see he was a dwarf because he bent the knee as he walked. He shouted for a long time, his mouth strangely open. . . ."[7]

The rest of Tolstoy's analysis of the *Ring* derides the monotony and pettiness of the human motives it presents and the inartistic pretense it

[5]To Owen Wister, Jan. 7, 1895. See also in M. A. de Wolfe Howe's valuable life and letters of Chapman a later comment, p. 271.

[6]*Letters*, ed. Ford, ii, 335.

[7]*What Is Art?*, ch. xiii.

makes at an illusion which it does not produce. Its further pretension to being a moral and a popular art Tolstoy exposes without mercy, showing it to be instead a boring and insidious product of overcivilized, artificial exclusivism. These objections would of course apply to most operas, certainly to all operas produced with an eye to stage realism. How great art could be achieved in unaffected simplicity in the midst of a contrary-minded civilization Tolstoy showed in his later tales and his *Four Reading Books* for children, but he did not touch again upon opera or dramatic music.

It was nevertheless from Russia that the purely musical emancipation from Wagnerism was preparing. The European recognition of Moussorgsky, Balakireff, Borodin, and Rimsky-Korsakov marked the return to simplicity and folk inspiration, to the use of musical rather than scenic devices in dramatic music. It was from these men, whose works had accumulated during the Wagnerian sweep, that the French Impressionist school of Debussy and Ravel gained the strength and knowledge to pierce through the wall of interwoven leitmotifs. The Russians had found keeping their independence a hard fight; what had saved them artistically was their devotion to native music and legends and the example of their two masters, Glinka and Berlioz.

As early as 1868, the Imperial Music Director Vladimir Stassoff was writing to the dying Berlioz in Paris how his immediate circle felt: "We do not think that Wagner is a prophet of the future. We think rather that he has made music regress from its status in Weber; though the prestige of a German name, the word "future" attached to his music, the show of scenery and costume, will no doubt produce an effect on a public little developed musically."[8] From Glinka's orchestration and use of folk tunes, from the lessons contained in the scores which Berlioz left with the Russians when he visited them twice during his career, the Russian "five" and their pupils fashioned their own ideal of lightness and clarity and discovered a preference for melody and nuance over harmonic and orchestral massiveness. Opera regained its rights and dramatic effects returned to Mozart's and Weber's practice over Wagner's head.

The French School, working in the midst of a flourishing Wagnerism, found its own emancipation still more difficult. Its style became a sort of negative offprint of the Wagnerian—discontinuous, all nuance and slight construction, with harmonies as sensuous as the Wagnerian but more sparse. It was also wedded to literature, not only for its inspiration but for its interpretation: the scores are marked with precise or poetic tags. In the opera, it hardly dared compete with the man who had captured the place of Meyerbeer. Yet the one attempt by Debussy suffered from the same affliction of making the music subserve the words, whence "the mad-

[8]October 5/17, 1868. Reprinted in *Revue Musicale*, May 1930.

dening repetitions in Wagner's operas, [akin to] the maddening repetitions in *Pelleas.*"[9]

Music was thus left "weak and exhausted by the fierce Wagnerian domination and hag-ridden by the alien and equally pernicious influences of literature and the plastic arts."[10] Artistic questions, wrongly put and confusingly answered, were left in a chaotic state; legitimate efforts to expand musical or other means of expression were misjudged, great personalities of earlier periods were misrepresented, and critical perspective on all past art was foreshortened until a reaction in the form of surrealist parody was inevitable. Erik Satie's telling Debussy after a performance of a piece marked "Dawn—Noon—Afternoon" that he liked especially the little bit around half-past eleven is the fitting dissolution in laughter of the mechanical conception of meaning in art.

FORWARD-LOOKING critics and their readers may agree that Wagner is an end, a monument that shortly turned into an attractive ruin, and provided fine fragments for the museum. They may say that he is farther away from us than Mozart or Berlioz,[11] and they may begin to do justice to Weber, Verdi, Meyerbeer, and Rossini. They may even rehabilitate the critic Hanslick.[12] But the world does not move like an army behind its vanguard; it straggles behind, rather, like the black guard. In the same way as we find parts of the world not yet ready for Darwin and not quite sure whether Marx is a living agitator, so the bulk of the listening public still finds Wagner at the threshold of the temple of culture. Commercial and educational needs still give Wagner the preponderance over every other composer. New interpretations of the *Ring* continue to appear. Wagner Dictionaries, with their usual hero-centering of history, find a sale, and opera houses the world over live mainly by Wagner. Among musicians, he is still presented as the only many-sided composer, among teachers and students it is still most convenient to utilize his well-indexed musical form for teaching and learning dramatic music. Conductors, finally, know that they can be sure of a certain kind of response by playing or recording anew the Ride, the Murmurs, the Good Friday, or the Love-Death.

On a more exalted plane the contributions of Wagnerism hold their own. Art is still entangled in precious theorizing and historical justification. It is held to be a product of evolution just as the artist is held to

[9]Constant Lambert, *Music Ho!*, London, 1933, 29.

[10]Cecil Gray, *History of Music*, 209.

[11]Paul Rosenfeld, *Musical Portraits*, 10, 87.

[12]On Verdi and Rossini, see the works of Francis Toye; on Weber, the Stebbins biography already cited; and *In Defence of Hanslick* by Stewart Deas, recently published in London. N. Slonimsky's *Music Since 1900* also contains valuable indications of old and new attitudes in chronological order.

be a product of his times, and the world makes demands in consequence. The artist must defend himself in print and show how others are wrong, for all artists are presumably seeking "solutions" to contemporary problems. At any one time only one solution is valid, hence only one artist has "the answer." The artist is made into a kind of research scientist and sociologist combined. He must have opinions, not only for his private use, but for his public work, and through it he must exert an influence upon all matters of social concern. To avoid frivolity, art must teach, alter the course of history, and regenerate mankind. It deals, in short, with the conduct of the will, the improvement of the State, and the purification of the soul. This *Schwärmerei* of the French Revolution, carried on by Wagner, has become a more or less explicit assumption throughout t the world of art, and a positive command in that part of it which is Marxist.

Again, critics who find in myths the explanation of the power and meaning of art find in Wagner the chief of their band. For him and them, all myths are related, are one myth; and that one is a symbol of human life which successive works of art play variations on. The genetic fallacy glories here in its fullest reduction of the complex to the oversimple. But the newer names of Freud and Thomas Mann give it the color of authority, supported by the traditional scholarship of the evolutionary century.[13] In music, proper, evolutionism has flourished particularly in Wagnerian studies, whence it has spread to the past and present of the art. As W.D. Allen has shown, there have been two main schools, a Darwin-Wagner school, largely French, and a Spencerian, largely Anglo-American, whose musicology has strengthened our belief that art grows and improves, not logically but biologically.[14] The language of much of our criticism betrays this faith and our judgments take on the deceptive coloring: "Weber," says Mr. Dennis Arundell, "'never produced a prize bloom, nor perfected a single species . . .'" implying, it would seem, that the artist's task is set, competitive, horticultural.[15]

A kindred form of evolutionary thinking affirms that melodies "grow" from root tones, chords, or simple musical figures. This in turn leads to the notion that composers express observations of fact and laws of nature by their choice of musical ideas. Thus the heaviness of gold at the bottom of the Rhine has been found "expressed" in the repeated chord that underlies the long opening of *Das Rheingold*. The most elaborate treatment of music (chiefly Wagnerian) on these principles is to be read in F. W. Robinson's *Aural Harmony* (New York, 1936), where we are told that "the

[13]In her latest essay, Dorothy Sayers assails this fallacy, using, as it happens, the *Tristan* legend and its reduction by scholarship to a marriage-by-capture story. *Begin Here,* London, 1940, 105-06.

[14]*Philosophies of Music History,* N. Y., 1939, 269 ff.

[15]*Heritage of Music,* ii, 134.

major triad, being found in Nature, is natural; the minor triad, being man-made, is less natural. . . ." From this it is said to follow that certain chords are fitted to express static and others dynamic feelings, and this in turn enables us to find "God-like and human love" simultaneously expressed in the first chord of *Tristan* or stability insured in the Valhalla motif. The great masters are supposed to have recognized these "natural laws," and we in turn need no longer find Wagner's harmony "enigmatic" so soon as we learn this type of analysis.[16]

Again, Wagner's personal preoccupation with revolution remains a criterion with which we judge his contemporaries or prod our own. It does not seem to matter that his was a pitiful example of incoherence and self-seeking, nor that after having been touted as a revolutionist, he should now appear as a dangerous forerunner of fascism.[17] Like the Russian censors of Shostakovich, modern critics are ready to believe that art grows directly out of political ideas and that bars of music carry political meanings. And for the same reason, again in the spirit of Wagner, nationalists and would-be nationalists try to impart a quality of the soil to their music or their painting, in the naïve belief that the topic's the thing. The error does not consist in choosing American subjects for symphonic poems, but in supposing that the choice of such subjects will *ipso facto* create a piece of American music. On this point, the example of the Russian school, rather than Wagner's, is worth remembering. They refused no outside help or inspiration, quite the contrary, but they assimilated what they learned and utilized what their native tradition offered. Their subject matter could be Arab or Spanish, their music was their own because they were at one within themselves, their minds unencumbered with tendentious ought's and don't's.

The belief in a direct linkage between art and its source makes also for the fallacy of art-as-illustration. This is perhaps the most dangerous legacy of Wagnerism, the hardest to combat in a world supersaturated with mechanistic ideas. Whether in Salvador Dali's setting for the *Tann-häuser* Bacchanale—indeed in all ballets made from music not designed for the purpose—or in more ambitious attempts to "educate the masses" by combining skillful film sequences with music from the masters, the Wagnerian error of pictorial duplication goes on unabated. It is a danger not to music alone, though that is bad enough; it imperils the very idea of art, which by its nature can never enter into a one-to-one relation with anything else.

[16]On this theory the very "dynamic" opening of Beethoven's Third Symphony ought to be as restful as Valhalla. In Mr. Robinson's book see especially Part I, pp. 23-4, 26-7; Part II, 6, 11, 100, 105, 175.

[17]See Henri Malherbe's recent book on Wagner as revolutionist, Peter Viereck's articles in *Common Sense* (1940) showing him as a fascist, and the correspondence in the *Nation* (fall of 1940) on the same subject.

Art is always precise but never systematic, consequently its "interpretation" can never come from formal "notes" or explanations in another medium. Art has to do with the real world, of which it is a concrete extension; it has to do with morality and social life, of which it is, in Matthew Arnold's phrase, a criticism; hence its language cannot be learned bookishly, apart from the experiences which both art and life afford. It certainly cannot be learned by gluing in parallel strips the symbols of a less familiar art with those of another, more familiar. Neither music and pictures nor music and words, nor pictures and words nor words and words, will together teach the meaning of the arts. Interpretation may at times be necessary, but it can only fill the role of a dictionary — a help over a single difficulty now and then. As well try to translate *Hamlet* into Dutch by setting down the equivalent of each word as it comes as try to understand the Pastoral Symphony from "equivalents" of whatever kind — poetic, technical, or visual.[18]

To attempt it is to repeat the error of mechanistic materialism, the effort to understand one definite sensory experience through another. It is, within limits, legitimate in science; but its error even there is that the medium of translation distorts. It lets through only so much as is common to both experiences, the unique part of each being lost when looked at through the lens of the other. Mozart can "portray" the Don Juan of literature, but the music and the words do not possess one and the same contents. Each art takes from life a separate aspect suited to itself, and though a play could tell us what the Don thought of the Lutheran Church, no music could possibly convey the same information. In compensation, however, three bars of recitative tell us something that could never be put into words. There is, in short, no pinning down of any subject, object, or idea so that it can be fixed, carried about, and combined with kindred expressions from other arts, as in the system with which Wagner captured and ruled the willing imaginations of his age.

Bibliography

The standard biography of Wagner is that of Ernest Newman, *The Life of Richard Wagner*, 4 vols. (New York, Knopf, 1933-1946). A more recent work is that of Chappell White, *An Introduction to the

---

[18]In Schweitzer's classic work on Bach, composers are divided into "poetic" (Beethoven and Wagner) and "pictorial" (Bach, Berlioz, and Schubert). This seems an unfortunate terminology to describe the difference between the use of "atmosphere" and the use of melodic line to achieve what is in both cases nonpictorial. No one has ever seen music, though things can be shown while music is playing so as to link the two through habit.

Life and Works of Richard Wagner (Englewood Cliffs, N.J., Prentice-Hall, 1967). Wagner's autobiography, *My Life* (New York, Tudor, 1936) is available in English translation, as are his *Prose Works,* 8 vols. (London, 1892–1899). An excerpt, in English translation, from *Das Kunstwerk der Zukunft* (*The Artwork of the Future*) is reprinted in Oliver Strunk, ed., *Source Readings in Music History* (New York, Norton, 1950).

A complete edition of the works of Wagner has never been assembled. His operas are available separately either in orchestral score or in piano-vocal score from a number of publishers, such as G. Schirmer.

25

AFTER Wagner, Romanticism in music seemed to be disintegrating. Several trends could be discerned, some nationalistic, some still Romantic, and some apparently anti-Romantic. Two of the most important of these, German Expressionism and French Impressionism, and their basic differences of approach are the subjects of the following selection.

Expressionism was of Wagnerian parentage. In the early twentieth century a group of composers centering around Arnold Schönberg and Alban Berg were writing music with an ambiguous tonality and even without tonality. Such pantonal or atonal compositions had their origin in the chromatic harmonies of Wagner, of which they were considered to be a logical outgrowth.

Impressionism, on the other hand, was at first thought to be a reaction against Romanticism. Arising in France and typified in the work of Claude Debussy, Impressionism was anti-German. Its subtle harmonies, its emphasis on color, and its general understatement, all so non-Wagnerian, must thus be anti-Romantic, or so it was thought. But this view of Impressionism is no longer held. It is true that twentieth-century music owes much to the compositions of Debussy, one of the most original and creative composers of all time, but the movement of Impressionism in general is not the beginning of a new era. Rather it is viewed as one of the last vestiges of Romanticism and of the Classic-Romantic period, a period which began with the sonata in the mid eighteenth century.

The reader should be warned that the term Expressionism is used in the following selection in a broader sense than usual. Normally Expressionism refers to the group of composers that includes Schönberg and his disciples, and specifically to those of their compositions written during the second and third decades of the twentieth century. The author of the following, however, appears to include under Expressionism any composer who seeks to express himself emotionally or dramatically through music which does not abandon the basic formal organizational principles of the past. Such a definition could be taken to include composers who are not normally considered members of the Expressionist group.

Adolfo Salazar (1890-1958) was a Spanish composer and musicologist who spent his last years as a writer and teacher in Mexico City. Of his many writings in Spanish, only one, *La Música Moderna* (Buenos Aires, 1944), appears to have been translated into English, as *Music in Our Time*, Isabel Pope, trans. (New York, Norton, 1946).

Post-Romanticism:
Impressionism and Expressionism

ADOLFO SALAZAR

Translated by Isabel Pope

Debussyism was not the work of Debussy alone but a traditionally logical stage of modern evolution.

CHARLES KOECHLIN

At the musical high tide of the new century we can distinguish two vital streams which characterized and determined the future course of music; two currents, springing from distant sources which, as the nineteenth century unfolded, became ever more clearly defined. In the ordinary language of the day the one is called expressionistic, for in it predominates the artistic impulse of the romantic composer who gives to the inherited structure of earlier musical forms an emotional and dramatic content. The other is termed impressionistic, for in it those purely sonorous qualities of color and chord values (by which is understood the *chord* as an independent entity rather than as related to and generating others) stand out from the musical fabric through the composer's primary interest in harmonic combinations. To sum up more concisely, one may say that those composers who are moved by considerations of *expression* in the dramatic human sense, those who write symphonic poems are formalists (in the stricter terminology of the musical critic), while those composers who seek an *impression*, in the purely musical and aesthetic sense, are harmonists.

Both tendencies necessarily possess points of contact. The exploitation of the expressive values of harmony is one of the considerations

FROM Adolfo Salazar, *Music in Our Time: Trends in Music Since the Romantic Era,* translated from the Spanish by Isabel Pope (New York, W. W. Norton & Company, Inc.), pp. 143-150. Copyright 1946 by W. W. Norton & Company, Inc. Reprinted by permission of the publisher.

which impel the formalist composer from within, urging him toward a constant development of the elements of form. Vice versa, the impressionist finds himself continually confronted with problems of form in the effort to give coherence to his experiments in the domain of pure harmony. Nevertheless, the urge toward form (though the forms may change or be entirely new) predominates in the one since he is moved primarily by emotional experiences just as was the romantic composer, while the other is moved by entirely new aesthetic criteria. The latter seeks to exploit the qualities inherent in musical sound, both in their essence and in combination.

We shall see, in fact, that it is this impulse which dictates the experiments of the harmonist or, in popular parlance, the impressionist. Before going further, however, it is necessary to resolve an apparent paradox. If the musical impressionist is guided by sensations of an aesthetic order which awaken in him purely musical reactions (the desire for new harmonies, etc.) how does it happen that impressionistic music, certainly in the beginning, was linked with evocations, more or less concrete, of an extrinsic or literary nature which lie within the field of the emotions? Does that which distinguishes the expressionist from the impressionist composer consist simply in a change in the object which awakens the emotion? Can it be that, while the one is inspired by heroism, tragic love, religious mysticism, the ominous presentiment of death, the other responds to the mystery of nature, the murmur of the woods, the tranquillity of night or perhaps the friendliness of majesty of mountains or the sea, of the fertile plain or the desert? No, the difference is far more profound.

In fact, each moves in contrary orbits. The first case, that of the composer who seeks in music the translation of his emotions, resembles the poet who seeks in the vocabulary of his language words and phrases best suited to express his inner sentiment and who sometimes is obliged to rediscover forgotten words or to invent new ones. When Wagner played on his piano for the first time the chord:

the seed from which *Tristan und Isolde* sprang like a gigantic flower, did he realize the possibility of creating a vast dramatic work from the emotional potentialities hidden in this chord or, on the contrary, did he find that this chord summed up the dramatic impulse which burned within him? Did the chord bring *Tristan* into being or did *Tristan* find musical expression in the chord? We may accept the second alternative. Wagner, then, proceeds like the poet described above. The discoveries of his harmonic idiom are rather a consequence of his desire for expression than the result of the compulsion of sonorous material in search of translation in artistic terms. He himself fought long and hard to make the musical world understand the essential humanness and pathos of his music, its emotional essence in search of a form, its drive which inspired his followers, the creators of the symphonic poem.

The impressionists pursue a contrary path. Beginning with Chopin himself, as the best example, it is the chance discoveries of the keyboard that acquire prime importance. Yet this chance is only relative. The explorer of new worlds is guided by a certain intuition as he equips his caravels. He does not know with scientific certainty what he is going to discover but he knows that he is going to discover something. Chopin did not let his fingers play over the keyboard in a thoughtless or arbitrary fashion. At first his fingers were guided by a fully mastered traditional and classical technique to which his ear responded. But these systematic combinations of sound arrive at last at limits where the average musician halts while Chopin, inspired by the spirit of adventure, risks going forward. Step by step he advances, little by little, always treading with care. This prudence is not calculated but results simply from the necessity of maintaining contact with the realm of the intelligible, while advancing just a degree beyond the point hitherto understood and accepted by the crowd. Now he requests still another step forward which the more advanced minds readily grant. Even if slower spirits cannot follow as yet, it will not be long before the universal frontier of music has advanced to a new line which the restless soul of the musician constantly seeks to extend.

On his voyage of discovery the composer has found a new flower, a rare gem he cannot classify according to the terminology of the science in which he has been trained. These chords, these novel combinations of tone that he hears for the first time with such keen delight, can they be assimilated to his earlier experiences? Can the composer, indeed, classify these new musical sensations in the conventional romantic repertory as of heroic, amorous, pathetic, or pastoral inspiration? Obviously not. All that is outworn. It belongs alike to the repertory of the old-fashioned poets and to the music of their day.

Now while the composer pursues his discoveries on the responsive keyboard, other artists, painters, and poets are seeking similar values in their respective domains in literary or plastic forms. The musician feels himself closely drawn by the common will which impels his brother artists. For example, a painter will put on his canvas a mixture of delicious colors not representing anything concrete, although they are inevitably reminiscent of some form: a flower, a cathedral, an apple or a bottle, a locomotive, or perhaps a rosy nymph bathing in the tremulous light which filters through the leaves.

Similarly, the piece of music which our musician composes of these new ingredients does not have a well-defined form. He experiences something[1] which may be compared to the delight aroused in us by the combination of colors to which the painter gives such titles as water lilies, nymphs, or twilight. Or, again, they may correspond to the vague, sweet resonances with which the contemporary poet evokes a landscape. Is it really *this* the musician wished to translate in sound? And how translate that which has never yet been clearly expressed?

Does it not happen rather that these colors, these verses awaken in the composer a like impression—certain corresponding sensations? To new sensations of sonority must correspond a new order of plastic or verbal sensations. In order to clarify his process of thought for the listener, somewhat disconcerted by this new aesthetic approach, the composer seeks the aid of the painter or the poet in giving realization to these new sonorous elements. He says that his piece of music is something *like* those "magnolias at twilight" or *like* those "perfumes in moonlight,"— titles which, without malice, we all understand to be mere excuses.

There is one poet, however, who is wholly explicit:

In Nature's temple living pillars rise,
   And words are murmured none have understood,
   And man must wander through a tangled wood
Of symbols watching him with friendly eyes.

As long-drawn echoes heard far-off and dim
   Mingle to one deep sound and fade away;
   Vast as the night and brilliant as the day,
Color and sound and perfume speak to him.

Some perfumes are as fragrant as a child,
   Sweet as the sound of hautboys, meadow-green;
Others, corrupted, rich, exultant, wild,

Have all the expansion of things infinite:
   As amber, incense, musk, and benzoin,
Which sing the sense's and the soul's delight.[2]

Charles Baudelaire gives the title "Correspondances" to this poem in which, at the midpoint of the century, the new aesthetic philosophy already stands declared. (*Les Fleurs du Mal*, in which these verses ap-

[1]"Our observant spirit finds itself confronted with a form for which it possesses no intellectual equivalent, from which it must extract the unknown." Marcel Proust, *Le Côté de Guer-Mantes*, I, 45.
[2]Translation by F. P. Sturm.

peared, was published in 1861 but it includes works dating from 1845.) We observe, first of all, that Baudelaire still uses the classic form of the sonnet; his meter is the traditional Alexandrine; his rhymes are regular; his prosody impeccable. Yet the content must have been disconcerting, must have seemed anarchical, even dangerous, to his contemporaries. Perfumes, sweet as hautboys, are green, corrupt, even triumphant. He speaks of echoes melting in the distance in a "profound and shadowy unity"—a unity that is mysterious yet clear as are "confused words" for he is dealing above all with symbols, a word to be remembered. To sum up, he speaks of a correspondence of sensations which appeal equally to the spirit and to the senses and in which perfumes, sounds and colors respond to each other by virtue of that "vicariousness of the senses" or that act by which, in the phrase of Friedrich Nietzsche, two or three decades later, certain senses momentarily change places with each other.

This correspondence between aesthetic sensations is not, however, a discovery of Baudelaire. Strictly speaking it is, indeed, an old problem of romanticism but only as a correspondence between music and poetry. In the early years of German romanticism, Tieck asked: "What, were we not to think in chords, compose music with words and thoughts?" As a result, Tieck endowed his Teutonic idiom with grace and lightness. He employed assonance and alliteration with an onomatopoeic insistence only surpassed by Richard Wagner beginning with the scene of Siegfried's forge and continuing to the death of Isolde.[3] Tieck further wrote directions for his verses such as: "chord in A minor," "arpeggiando," "dolce," and "forte," which imply more than a simple prosodic indication for the benefit of the reader or reciter.

John Field may wish to indicate by Nocturne simply a piece to be played in the night. But, when Chopin calls his pieces nocturnes and Schumann his pages *Nachtstuecke*, they both see in these words something more than music in the night; the titles contain an allusion to their source of inspiration. The relationship between the emotional sensations aroused by different arts, such as those of color and of sound (an interchange which is called synesthesia), interested Berlioz for the "color" which he discovered in each tonality or musical scale and his idea of modulation is to be compared with the art of mixing color tones on the palette.

---

[3]*"Hoho! Hahei! Blase, Balg."* Alliteration and onomatopoeia are a basic element in Wagner. Recall, for example, *"Weia! Weia! Weia! Wagalaweia!"* of the Rhine maidens; *"Hojotoho"* of the Valkyries; *"Hehe! Hehe! Hieher! Hieher!"* of Alberich; *"Heda! Hedo!"* of Donner. Verses of another type are
  Brünhilde: *"Nicht Gut, nicht Gold,*
            Noch göttliche Pracht;
            Nicht Haus, nicht Hof,
            Noch Herrischer Prunk, . . ."
  Sieglinde: *"Was im Busen ich barg, was ich bin*
            hell wie der Tag taucht'es mir auf . . ."

The orchestrator, likewise, was to follow a similar process the moment he felt that each instrument had a characteristic color: green for the pastoral oboe, heaven's blue for the flute, vibrant red for trumpets and trombones. These elemental synestheses are equivalent to the classical ethos of the Greek modes. After the correspondences of Baudelaire, the more advanced heirs of his symbolist aesthetics, like Jean Arthur Rimbaud, find definite color in the vowels: *"A noir, E blanc, I rouge, U vert, O bleu—"* Poets like René Ghil went so far as to codify this sensorial or sensual vicariousness in a system according to which each sound in the French language, or each vowel at least, could find a translation in the timbres of different orchestral instruments. Thus the sound "ou," according to Ghil, has the color of flutes; the French "u," a sound lost since the Greeks, finds its counterpart in the timbre of the treble flute; the sounds "eu" and "o" correspond to trumpets and trombones, and so on.

In Hugo's verse, better than in Tieck's, it is possible to find syllabic motives that act as musical cells. For example:

On *était dans le* mois *ou la nature est douce* . . .
Une immen*se* bonté tom*bait du fir*mament . . .

The syllabic motifs in *m, n* may be compared to the motif *l* which mingles deliciously with the vowels in:

*C'etait l'heure tranqui*lle *ou les lions vont boire.*

There is something more here than mere classical alliteration which, nevertheless, also responds to the imitative phenomenon on which synesthesia is based. A step further and Claude Debussy will translate effectively into musical tones the song of the brook as it tumbles over its rocky bed:

Le ron — lis sourd des cail - loux

In romantic music, the invitation to synesthesia occurs on different levels: from *(a)* the employment of allusive values which we already recognize (as the pastoral in the Scene in the Fields from the *Symphonie Fantastique); (b)* then to new motives, yet ones belonging to the same category as the first (the use of the supernatural from Weber to Berlioz and Liszt); and, *(c)* to a plasticity in the characteristic motive suggested ordinarily by the gesture (as in Carnaval, by Schumann); *(d)* finally, to new sensations produced by definite musical means—such as the use of unusual chords or by the liberal use of chords little employed in the technique of the preceding period; the linking of harmonies not hitherto recognized as related; licenses of various kinds from exceptional chord resolutions or non-resolutions to free appoggiaturas; vagueness of tonality which comes with chromaticism; hints of a mingling of tonalities which result in the use of arabesques stretched delicately on a harmonic basis foreign to their essential tonality.

We have seen that all this occurs in Chopin and is extended by the pianistic development of the romantic period. We are now, therefore, in the presence of a definitely new phenomenon. Thus, both Chopin and Debussy compose nocturnes. Liszt and Ravel allude to valleys echoing to distant bells whose sounds dissolve in the mist while the harmonies of Chopin and Debussy vanish in the half-light of the dying day. Between them, the phenomenon differs only in degree but it departs radically from that of its classical predecessors. From the romanticism of the first to the impressionism of the others there is the almost imperceptible development of sonorous subtleties which depend for their full appreciation on the listener's musical culture and refinement of taste. Paul Bekker justly says that "the excessive gradation of all essentially romantic qualities leads to their decay." Thus, in fact, one may speak of the decadence of Debussy's music as well as that of the poetic production of more than half a century, from Baudelaire to Mallarmé. Already with Verlaine this "excessive gradation" becomes consciously defined. "No more color, only shading," he says in his *Art Poétique* which, in setting forth the new aesthetics of impressionism in painting and of symbolism in poetry, is the final manifestation of romanticism.

Now a new element—the musical quality—appears in the pictorial and poetic arts, just as music had earlier borrowed poetical and pictorial qualities from her sister arts. "Music before all else," says Verlaine, translating in verse what Walter Pater[4] expressed in philosophical terms when he said "all art aspires unceasingly to become music"; this is certainly true in this period when one could say, to the astonishment of the Encyclopedists of the eighteenth century (could they have heard), that "the Gothic is frozen music, a visible music," just as it would be equally possible to reverse the figure saying, "music is a liquid architecture, an architecture that can be heard."

This dissolution, the melting of the outlines of things in an iridescent mist through subtle chromatic changes as delicately tinted as mother of pearl, this dissolving of the normal harmonic pulsation of the tonic-dominant of classical music and, finally, this relaxing of rhythmic tension is typical of the new impressionistic aesthetics in music.

Similarly, prosody itself will soon dissolve in the atmosphere of pure

[4]"All art constantly aspired toward the condition of music;" and again: "But although each art has thus its own specific order of impressions and an untranslatable charm, while a just apprehension of the ultimate differences of the arts is the beginning of aesthetic criticism; yet it is noticeable that, in its special mode of handling its given material, each art may be observed to pass into the condition of some other art,

lyricism as did tonality and form before Debussy.[5] The time for Mallarmé is ripe. In a little-known sonnet of Verlaine, the alliteration possesses a musical quality which can only be described as Debussylike. In it, the poet achieves the quintessence in words, the reduction of language to pure sound values whose poetic images are intelligible only through intuition. This, which we may call—how illogically yet how truly —the abstract image, constitutes the whole poetic art of Stéphane Mallarmé. Verlaine's sonnet to Parsifal begins thus:

> Parsifal a vaincu les Filles, leur gentil
> Babil et la luxure amusante—et sa pente
> Vers la chair de garçon vierge que celà tente
> D'aimer les seins légers et ce gentil babil. . . .

Abstract image! Toward that abstraction, no longer plastic but musical, all impressionism tends. It is useless and misleading now to speak of the external object as the motive. Claude Monet may paint the shadowy façade of the cathedral at Chartres, showing it in a mist of evanescent colors—light refracted into its primary colors which "melt" in the transparent atmosphere or, again, he may depict the unsubstantial water lilies in his garden. Yet the painter's interest is no longer in a special object as a pictorial motive but rather in the manner in which the light plays on its surface. In the art of poetry, likewise, we find ourselves very far from the simple use of the syllabic patterns which served to support the poetic idea in Hugo. Alliteration, the interplay of the sonorities of language, reach a higher plane which dominates the aesthetic will of Verlaine in the sonnet to Parsifal, as later with Mallarmé. What will be the source of inspiration for the impressionists in music? Will they be content with naïve musical descriptions of romantic landscapes or dancing nymphs? Obviously not. If light for its own sake, if the sonorous interplay of vowels and consonants attract the painter and the poet at this moment in European art, it is evident their contemporaries in music will concern themselves with pure music, with its essential and intrinsic elements. Above all, they will seek independent harmonic sensations for their own sake, for their essential worth, not simply for their function in tonal relationships.

---

by what German critics term an *Andersstreben*—a partial alienation from its own limitations, through which the arts are able, not indeed to supply the place of each other, but reciprocally to lend each other new forces." Walter Pater, "The School of Giorgione," *Studies in the History of the Renaissance*.

[5]"In comparison with the pure dream, the unanalyzed impression, a definite, a positive art is blasphemous. Here, everything has the needful clarity and the delicious obscurity of harmony." Charles Baudelaire, *Le Spleen de Paris* (1860).

Bibliography

There is little in English dealing with the general areas of Impressionism and Expressionism in music. One must approach these through the leading representatives of the movements, Debussy for Impressionism and Schönberg for Expressionism. Debussy is treated in some detail by William Austin in *Music in the Twentieth Century* (New York, Norton, 1966). For a biography of Debussy see Edward Lockspeiser, *Debussy*, 2 vols. (New York, Macmillan, 1962-1965). Debussy's essays were translated into English as *Monsieur Croche, the Dilettante Hater* and have been reprinted in **Three Classics in the Aesthetic of Music* (New York, Dover, 1962).

Schönberg is discussed by Dika Newlin in *Bruckner, Mahler, Schönberg* (New York, King's Crown, 1947) and by George Perle in *Serial Composition and Atonality, an Introduction to the Music of Schönberg, Berg and Webern* (Berkeley, Calif., University of California Press, 1962). Schönberg's *Theory of Harmony* (New York, Philosophical Library, 1948) has been translated into English, but also abridged, by Robert D. W. Adams. Schönberg's essays, *Style and Idea* (New York, Philosophical Library, 1950), are also available. An historical survey of the transition from tonality to atonality which took place during the period of Viennese Expressionism may be found in Anton Webern, *The Path to the New Music* (Bryn Mawr, Pa., Theodore Presser, 1963).

Examples of Impressionism may be found in the compositions of Debussy and in some of the early works of Ravel, both published by Durand, Paris. Expressionism is exemplified by the music of Schönberg and Berg written during the second and third decades of this century. These compositions are published by Universal Edition, Vienna.

26

TWENTIETH-century music has experienced a growth of techniques and approaches—some experimental, some reactionary—unmatched by any other century. While there has been, of course, music based on the heritage of past centuries, there has also been other music which sought to provide new ways, or sometimes merely to avoid old ones, of expressing contemporary thought. This has had the effect of giving the music of our century an appearance of disorder and confusion that it may not deserve.

The remaining contributions to this anthology are rather specialized; each deals with a specific and frequently technical aspect of twentieth-century music. But an article was needed to bridge the gap between late Romanticism and the music of the mid-twentieth century, and also survey the first two-thirds of the century while attempting to place in perspective the apparent confusion and disorder of trends. Such an article should, the editor thought, not only be fresh and undated in viewpoint but also be designed specifically for the place it would occupy here—in short, a reprinted article would not do, a new one must be written. Kurt Stone's "The Why and How of Our New Music" was, therefore, written for this anthology at the editor's request and appears in print for the first time. In it the author outlines some of the twentieth-century musical trends, pointing out the reasons that produced them, in a manner so direct and readable that no further introduction is needed.

Kurt Stone is Consulting Music Editor for Charles Scribner's Sons and also director of the project of the Index of New Musical Notation, currently underway at the Library and Museum of the Performing Arts, The New York Public Library at Lincoln Center. Formerly he was Editor-in-Chief of Associated Music Publishers and Director of Publications at Alexander Broude, Inc. He has lectured and written on contemporary music, contributing to such periodicals as *The Musical Quarterly* and *Perspectives of New Music*. Through his work in publishing he has been closely connected with contemporary music and musicians and has gained an intimate and practical knowledge of the current musical scene.

The Why and How of Our New Music

KURT STONE

Compared with the normal fluctuations of human history, the twentieth century will most probably be known for its particularly violent erosion of traditional axioms and creeds in all fields of human life and endeavor. Our entire spiritual and physical environment has become increasingly unstable, especially since World War II. Everything is questioned as to its validity, reexamined in light of ever-changing new contexts, and the changes are often so drastic, so continuous, and so rapid, that concepts such as "eternal truth," "constant value," "foreseeable future," and "Establishment" have all come to be utterly incompatible with present realities.

Not that this incompatibility has actually liquidated and removed all tradition, or even shunted it to a siding. Quite the contrary: traditional ways are still with us, clinging militantly to their inherited position of dominance, fighting off novel approaches. What makes them seem so exhausted and unsatisfactory to many of us, what causes them to be so inappropriate and irrelevant, is not their intrinsic qualities (which are not questioned) but their inability to reflect our present environment, to respond to the concerns of today's world.

There are those among us who object to such views, saying that there have always been generational conflicts, and that they have always faded into the great current of human history. Our present struggle, however, is unusually profound and bitter, its geographical range wider than at any previous time, and its pervading impact and diversity all but total. Equally unprecedented, and more alarming yet, is the fact that in many vital areas man seems to have become the almost powerless victim of his own creations—a sorcerer's apprentice with no master in sight. As a result, our era's struggle and search for new solutions, new constants, has grown much more complex than those of earlier times, more agonizing, and more persistent. In fact, no one knows how and when it will end, if ever, nor what the world will be like if and when

Copyright ©1972 by Kurt Stone.

it does settle down to a more serene flow of events and ideas. All we know at this stage is that present realities *force* us to leave behind the ways of the past in favor of a search for more compatible responses to our environment.

THE arts—*all* manifestations of artistic activity—naturally are part of these developments. Here too, established norms were found to be in need of new vitality, of new approaches, and during the first half of the twentieth century attempts were made toward rejuvenation and extension of traditional practices. It soon became apparent, however, that far more basic steps were needed if the arts were to meet the awesome challenges of our era and survive. Our very esthetics had to be scrutinized, not merely styles and fashions, but the prime elements of all established forms of artistic expression. They had to be singled out, isolated, stripped of all connotations, examined for their intrinsic qualities and potential usefulness, and newly manipulated and combined, or else discarded.

The painters were relatively early in recognizing the dilemma; the poets followed a little later; film makers became embroiled a decade or so ago; and in music this tortuous process began as a *general* trend after World War II. It was, and still is, a colossal disturbance, equal in magnitude only to two previous comparable musical eruptions, the first being the spectacular change from monophony (plainchant) to polyphony around the year A.D. 1000, and the second, somewhat less striking, the emergence around 1600 of functional harmony as the driving force behind all musical continuity, form, and expression.

HAVING sketched the *general* situation, let me now narrow our examination to what happened *musically* immediately before our era's great upheaval, so that we may understand why these eruptions and realignments *had* to occur.

At the turn of the century Western music had reached an unprecedented degree of harmonic complexity and technical refinement, particularly of orchestration, just as composers had become immensely skillful in mastering these complexities. However, the gigantic structures of late Romanticism—the symphonies of Mahler, the tone poems of Richard Strauss, Schoenberg's *Gurrelieder*—could not be developed further without danger of crumbling from overweight or, conversely, from lack of substance. The emotional steamheat of the era's chromaticism had already begun to turn harmonic progressions formerly considered daring into clichés of empty emoting and gesturing. Even the new language of Impressionism with its hypersensitive subtleties could not easily be extended without the risk of turning into sickly-sweet artificiality. The end of the road seemed to have been reached; new approaches, new substances, fresh air were needed desperately.

345

This early search for rejuvenation took two directions:

1. expansion of the traditional harmonic language through inclusion into the chordal vocabulary of *all* possible pitch combinations of the chromatic scale, regardless of their degree of dissonance and apparent harmonic ambiguity.[1] This trend neither resembled the emotional spicing-up of traditional chords with chromatic alterations and nonchord tones, nor the Impressionistic feature of neutralizing the chords' harmonic characteristics in favor of color values, texture, and atmosphere;

2. revival of the more abstract, less subjectively emotional forms and the leaner textures of the Baroque and early Classical eras: chiefly the suite, the sinfonia, certain contrapuntal structures, variations, and the number opera.

In addition, attempts were made to derive new life from the popular music of the day, and the traditional elixir—folk material—was broadened to include imagined as well as genuine Oriental and African elements.

A development actually more profound and propitious, and as it turned out, more enduring than any of the foregoing took place in the realm of rhythm. Rhythm had been subservient to harmony ever since its emergence; it had never before had comparable exposure and prominence. The appearance of dissonant harmony and the corresponding weakening of harmony's power over the other musical ingredients loosened the chains that used to stifle rhythmic independence.

This emerging rhythmic emancipation proceeded along two different paths: one of them based predominantly on intuitive creativity; the other on more consciously deliberate structuring.

The towering representative of the first trend was Igor Stravinsky, who with his uniquely imaginative genius burst the confines of rhythmic periodicity and metric regularity (pulse) with a force that was as overwhelming as it was unprecedented. After the *Sacre*, rhythm never again was the same.

Less instinctive, and thus more easily defined theoretically, was the

[1] Paul Hindemith was the only significant composer to have worked out a comprehensive analysis, codification, and teaching method of this new dissonant harmony. In his book *The Craft of Musical Composition*, first published in Germany in 1937, intervals are classified on a sliding scale, first according to their degree of dissonance, then according to their tonality and harmonic value (from tonal explicitness to ambiguity). Thereafter, chords of three or more tones are similarly examined and ordered according to the intervals they contain. The qualities of these intervals and their respective positions within a chord determine the chord's root, harmonic value, and degree of dissonance. Melodic phenomena are understood in the traditional way, i.e., as successions of chord tones interspersed (usually) with nonchord tones, only that the chords themselves are of course of the new, dissonant vocabulary. The harmonically strongest chord-tone formations in the melodic line determine its tonality. (Needless to say, this very rough and oversimplified description only skims the surface of Hindemith's theory.)

346

work of Olivier Messiaen. His rhythmic and metric modes and their highly complex and sophisticated manipulations have had, and continue to have, a decisive influence on much of the music of our century.

Several exciting decades of what seemed then to be the new music were the result of these activities, and many fine works by imaginative and accomplished composers were written (and continue to be performed with great success). But in the end, the assumed panacea turned out for the most part to have been a mere palliative, incapable of getting to the roots of the problem: the inseparable and still all-powerful hierarchy of melody, harmony, and rhythm, which continued, essentially unshaken and stubborn, to govern and subordinate all other musical components, no matter whether the new music was called Expressionism, Neo-Classicism, Dissonant Style, Absolute Polyphony, or whatever.

When the traditions of painting began to fail to provide suitable raw material for the painters' needs, the basic elements of the art — colors, shapes, materials — were explored, divorced from all representational implications. Similarly in music, individual sounds — sounds of any kind whatever — now were singled out for examination and experimentation, divorced from their harmonic implications, and their timbral and articulative characteristics were investigated. Timbral manipulations and combinations of all sorts were tried out, by themselves and in different contexts, and a host of methods were devised for organizing and governing such manipulations.

Historically this new approach toward the basic components of music (although then usually confined to pitches) had of course begun a good deal earlier with Schoenberg's (and also Hauer's) experiments to compose with "twelve equidistant tones related only to one another." Instead of the relatively intuitive invention of a composition's thematic material, typical of the nineteenth century and earlier, Schoenberg planfully constructed his thematic raw material by way of organizing twelve-tone rows, i.e., pitch successions whose maximum interest was "guaranteed" because no pitch could recur (generally speaking) before all other eleven pitches of the chromatic scale had been sounded. One such tone-row usually was sufficient to act as the sole structural raw material for the pitch and interval content of an entire composition, because a row lends itself to a large number of manipulations and metamorphoses. For example, each row may appear in any of four basic shapes: original form, inversion, retrograde, and retrograde inversion. Furthermore, the row's twelve tones may be divided into structurally related segments of $6+6$, $4+4+4$, or $3+3+3+3$, and each of these row segments may, in turn, appear in any or all of the four basic shapes mentioned. In addition, each row or row segment, in any of the four shapes, may be transposed to each and any of the twelve steps of the chromatic scale, and the individual pitches of each row-form may be transposed up or down one or more octaves, as the composer chooses. Finally, any number of such row-forms or segments may be sounded simultaneously with other such "sets," or be telescoped into chords.

The intervals from pitch to pitch also can be manipulated, primarily by multiplication, so that a row beginning, say, with intervals comprising 2, 3, and 7 half-tone steps, respectively, might be transformed into 4, 6, and 14 (2 base 12).

With this method of composing, the traditional hierarchy seemed at last to have been utterly destroyed, since pitch organization and manipulation based on Schoenberg's row concept is fundamentally different from traditional methods and esthetics. For example, twelve-tone rows are deliberately devoid of all harmonic functions in the traditional sense.

And yet, although Schoenberg opened up a completely new world of pitch uses, the elements that are *not* directly governed by his method —the melodic gestures, rhythmic patterns, dynamic rhetoric, instrumental ensembles, etc.—although they are often drawn in to support certain aspects of his pitch structures, retain a pronounced and somewhat incongruous ring of high-pitched, Viennese late Romanticism. No doubt it is for this reason that the music of Schoenberg (and that of his great disciple Alban Berg, though rarely that of Anton Webern) is more often classified as Expressionism than as *new* music, i.e., it is more often linked to the past than to the present.

All this, however, in no way detracts from the fact that Schoenberg's role as innovator was tremendous, as is proved—if proof be necessary—by the fact that composers everywhere, throughout the Western world and even in Japan and other non-Western places, have adopted his structural concepts and procedures more and more over the years, and developed them further.

Foremost among his American followers is Milton Babbitt, one of whose chief contributions consists of having recognized certain procedures occasionally employed by Schoenberg as being capable of further elaboration, and for having systematized them. These particular properties of twelve-tone music Babbitt calls "combinatoriality."[2]

After World War II composers began to apply Schoenberg's row technique to *all* musical elements, resulting in both complete intellectual control over all compositional ingredients and a radical departure from all traditional holdovers. In music of this nature—music of "total organization" or "total serialism"—not only are pitches governed by preconceived structural schemes, but the succession of durations (sounds as well as silences), timbres (instruments), textural densities, dynamics, articulations, and whatever other elements enter into the composition, are subjected to similar and often interrelated organizational manipula-

[2]See Milton Babbitt, "Some Aspects of Twelve-Tone Composition," on page 359.

tions. Moreover, the Schoenbergian insistence on twelve pitches per series gradually gave way to other forms of prime sets: sets that include unpitched sounds; and sets having fewer or more than twelve pitch elements (microtones). Among the foremost pioneers of such totally organized works are Pierre Boulez and, in his early works, Karlheinz Stockhausen.

Listeners to music of this nature are of course handicapped in several ways, chief among them a natural tendency to search for familiar phenomena (which are no longer present in such music) while missing those that *are* operative. In other words the listeners' dilemma is primarily one of focus.

For performers the greatest difficulty lies in playing the new rhythms and in staying together in an ensemble. While in traditional music an ensemble is governed by a metric pulse common to all and intrinsic to the music's rhythmic flow, such pulses are foreign to music whose durations are serially derived. Since, however, some form of common metric denominator is essential for synchronized ensemble playing, composers must construe and superimpose a pulse. The performers, in trying to reconcile this regular but artificial pulse with the irregular rhythmic progressions of the music proper are often too absorbed by this discrepancy to be able to involve themselves in the expressive content of the music they are performing. As a result, electronic realizations of such complex scores are often more successful than live performances.

PARTLY as a direct reaction to the procedural rigidity of total serialism with its attendant (though self-imposed) curbs on the composer's "free will" and the performers' creative involvement, a counter-trend of musical activity emerged, exhibiting the extreme opposite approach: *music of chance* or *aleatory music*. This trend seeks, through conceptual ambiguity and other means, to achieve the greatest possible creative participation of the performers and occasionally even the audience. It accomplishes these aims chiefly through notational vagueness: instead of indicating exact pitches and durations and supplying a host of auxiliary signs and verbal instructions for increased interpretative precision, composers of aleatory music provide the performer with "implicit graphics" of infinite variety and many degrees of indeterminacy, and with more or less ambiguous verbal directives. The interpretation and performance of such scores thus depends to a large extent, and at times completely, on the creative imagination and technical skill of the performers.

Naturally, there are different kinds of vagueness, ranging from short, improvisatory passages within otherwise predetermined and predictable scores, via all sorts of choices from among more or less exactly notated passages, to freely interpretative reactions to graphics, game rules, prepared or chance-derived sounds and noises, extra-musical occurrences, etc., and finally to the utter interpretative freedom offered by pieces such as John Cage's *0' 00"*, to be performed in any way by anyone, or his famous *4' 33"*, a piece asking for 4 minutes and 33 seconds of silence, so that the silence and whatever stray sounds might enter it become audible.

In short, aleatory music endeavors to bring about:

1. the greatest possible creative participation by everyone involved: composer, performer (including conductor, tape manipulator, etc.), and listener;

2. uniqueness and unpredictability, since no two performances must or can ever be the same;

3. spontaneity, since such music, to be truly aleatory, can only be rehearsed in very broad outline, if at all, while the execution of the details must always be created anew at each performance.[3]

In recent years, predictable music and music of chance, although seemingly irreconcilable, have come to a state of "peaceful coexistence." Thus we find strictly composed sections *alternating* with aleatory ones (for example, Earle Brown's *Hodograph I*); *simultaneous* occurrences of strict and aleatory music (for example, George Crumb's *Night Music I*); strictly composed musical "events" performed in *free succession* (for example, Henry Cowell's *Mosaic Quartet*—a rather early manifestation); again explicit "events" now played not only in free succession but also in unpredictable *manners of performance* (for example, Karlheinz Stockhausen's *Klavierstück 11*), to list only a few manifestations.

Some of these last-mentioned procedures have gained sufficient acceptance to amount almost to a new "common practice" and are generally referred to as *controlled chance*—a marriage of discipline and freedom.

The interpretative freedom in aleatory music has not been confined to purely musical elements but has branched out to include phenomena once considered to be beyond the realm of music proper. Often such manifestations reverse traditional roles. For example, while music used to provide the accompaniment to motion pictures, a motion picture now might represent the accompaniment to a piece of music. And so we enter the bewildering field of *multi-media,* where music may be coupled with almost anything: lighting effects, slides, film, theatrical effects and actions, chance noises and happenings, and of course audience and general environmental participation.

In almost all of these chance pieces and happenings the listener (or witness) is likely to be even more mystified than he is when confronted

[3]See Anthony Cross, "The Significance of Aleatoricism in Twentieth-Century Music," on page 389, and Eric Salzman, "The Revolution in Music," on page 453.

with total serialism, because aleatory music and its offshoots consist largely of instant interpretations of unconventional or even unique graphics and other stimuli, as well as a profusion of game rules and directives. With no score to follow and no knowledge of the verbal instructions, an audience has absolutely no way to understand what is happening or why. A listener therefore can do little more than immerse himself in the sounds and events, revel in the succession of surprises, and leave it at that. But to many listeners it is most unsatisfactory to be outsiders deprived of all information concerning the reasons for all the goings-on.

WHILE the serialists, from Schoenberg on, have been and are still concerned with a *single germinal idea* permeating an entire composition and being developed in an *ordered succession* of highly controlled events and manipulations, and while the aleatory composers operate with an *indefinite number of ideas* in deliberately *unpredictable successions* and executions, a third trend, prophetically introduced by Charles Ives, aims at combining a *multitude of contrasting ideas* and their developments in *simultaneous occurrence* within a single composition.

The technique of combining independent melodies is of course not new: we find it in quodlibets, in fugues, and in more complex textures such as the prelude to Wagner's *Die Meistersinger* or in Hindemith's *Sinfonia Serena*. All of these, however, were planned carefully to result in harmonious blends. Ives, by contrast, would have none of such harmoniousness; he aimed at lusty friction. No "participant" in the musical melee should lose any of his own, strong, and outspoken individuality. Thus, in *Central Park in the Dark*, two orchestras, one onstage, the other off, play different pieces at the same time, regardless of the consequences. In the second movement of Ives's *Fourth Symphony*, one section of the orchestra speeds away from the rest of the players in a chaos-provoking accelerando; and in the fourth movement of the same work, a percussion group "marches" through the music with its own beat, independent of and unaffected by any of the goings-on in the orchestra that surrounds it. In addition to such large-scale "confrontations," Ives's music abounds with jarring and fighting details: polymetrics, polyharmonies, sudden invasions by seemingly irrelevant material, and everywhere, from piccolo to double bass, quotations of hymns and pop tunes, seriousness and sarcasm, religion and blasphemy, strident dissonances and harmonic trivia, all moving on at the same time.

Ives's often somewhat awkward pioneer work has been greatly refined and expanded in recent years by Elliott Carter. Carter's music is neither serial nor aleatory, yet it too is meticulously controlled. One of its most discussed features (though not necessarily the most important) is now generally called "metrical modulation." What this means is that accents that first appear as syncopations within one metric context, grow in prominence until they outrank the prevailing pulse and thus "modulate" into a new metric context in which *they* are the regular beats—soon to be contradicted by a new set of syncopations. . . . An early and rather easily perceived example is the last movement of Carter's *Sonata for Flute, Oboe, Cello, and Harpsichord* of 1952. Often such metric manipulations occur simultaneously in different voices, so that each voice acts according to its own, separate metric/rhythmic character.

A feature referred to less often, but likewise an extension of Ives's simultaneity approach, concerns pitches. In Carter's *Second String Quartet,* for example, each of the four instruments not only has its own rhythmic and expressive character and its own predominant playing technique (pizzicato, arpeggios, sustained double stops, etc.), but also its own vocabulary of intervals. Thus, if a melodic phrase goes from instrument to instrument, its *overall* contour of up and down motion remains unchanged, but differs in *detail* for each instrument according to the respective instrument's "personal" reservoir of intervals: a wide skip may be a major seventh in one instrument and a minor sixth in another (stepwise motion is the same in all instruments).

Concerning what was referred to above as "large-scale confrontations," here too Carter's music exhibits many different manifestations, the most daring of which, to date, occurs in his *Concerto for Orchestra* (1970) whose four movements proceed simultaneously (literally!) but are structured and orchestrated in such a way as to remain recognizable (although in varying degrees of clarity) throughout the work. They are not only identifiable by their different pitch ranges and instrumentation, but also by a number of other aspects. Thus, one movement performs a continuous controlled accelerando, beginning slowly in its lowest pitch register and ending fast and high. Another movement soon becomes recognizable for its nervous and fragmented character: it keeps entering and dropping out of the total texture. And so forth.

As is obvious even from this very superficial characterization of Carter's music, the Ives-Carter trend goes its own way, combining at the same time (more inadvertently than deliberately) the disciplined complexity so typical of the serialists, with the freely imaginative, humanly dramatic inventiveness of the (ideal) aleatory musicians. (However, Carter's music is completely composer-controlled; there are no chance elements.)

It is obvious from what has been described above that this kind of music is immensely involved. Yet it can be perceived and enjoyed *by ear* if listened to with attention and patience.[4]

[4]See Elliott Carter, "Shop Talk by an American Composer," on page 411.

It is perhaps a moot question whether electronic music should be considered a separate trend—a new compositional approach—or simply the product of a new performance medium. Electronic music operates with pitches, timbres, durations, and intensities, as does nonelectronic music. A good deal of electronic music includes unpitched as well as essentially extramusical sounds and "aural events" *(musique concrète)*. However, this too is found in today's live music. Electronic music does provide an unprecedented variety of timbres and pitches within a single instrument. It also excels in spatial effects through the use of multiple speakers. Perhaps most importantly, it makes possible the most exact (though icy cold and clinical) performances imaginable, a very valuable feature when one is dealing with the extreme complexity of much serial music.

Composers of electronic music are in the unique position of being able to produce definitive, composer-directed and controlled realizations of their own works. They may accomplish this intuitively, through experimentation, or through careful planning, measurements, and calculations carried out with or without the aid of computers.

Electronic devices also may function as auxiliary instruments. Through them one can amplify and alter live sounds, superimpose sounds (live or electronic) upon sounds, filter them, distort them, and do all sorts of other things to them. Furthermore, electronic devices need not necessarily be manipulated deliberately and planfully, but can be activated by chance occurrences of many kinds: inadvertent physical acts, lights, noises, and so on. Even so, manipulating or otherwise activating electronic devices still means little more than playing an instrument.

The "inhumanity" of electronic music has given rise in recent years to juxtapositions of electronic and live (human) sounds, resulting in a number of fascinating compositions, such as the *Synchronisms* by Mario Davidovsky.

No matter how great the wish to classify electronic music, *one* indisputable fact remains: electronics have become a main force and an integral part of our environment.[5]

The trends outlined above do not, of course, provide complete coverage of today's musical "scene." For example, popular music, and particularly the world of rock, has not been dealt with at all. But even confining the discussion to the field of today's "serious," "advanced" music cannot possibly result in completeness because of the immense diversity of trends that come and go or exist side by side. Yet in spite of their many and often radical differences, these trends have one aspect

[5]See Ernst Krenek, "What Electronic Music Is and How It Is Made," on page 373, and Gerald Warfield, "Electronic Music: Synthesizers and Computers," on page 383.

in common: all, or at least most, of our advanced contemporary compositions set their own problems, offer their own solutions, and thus generate their own forms. Each composition is a unique manifestation, a law unto itself. We no longer have a common musical language in the traditional sense. We only have a certain similarity of very broad and general concepts.

This aspect of singularity is entirely new to Western music; it represents a profound break with all our traditional concepts, and it *must* be understood before any of this music can be sensibly approached and grasped.

Naturally, a monumental upset such as this does not pass by quickly; its problems are too fundamental to permit quick solutions. Experimentation has been in progress for decades, yet we are still far from being sure of any answers to our quest. We do not know if today's experiments, or tomorrow's, or yesterday's, will lead to music's future. We do not even know if there *is* to be a future for music. Ours is a difficult time for making prognoses.

Bibliography

A third of the history of music of the twentieth century, obviously, has yet to be experienced, much less recorded, and some of the recent past events must wait for a more objective analysis possible only with the passing of time. Therefore, works devoted to a general study of twentieth-century music are few in number and too frequently concentrate on listing the accomplishments of specific individuals rather than attempting to trace the development and historical significance of trends and ideas. William Austin's *Music in the Twentieth Century* (New York, Norton, 1966) is an important study but limited primarily to the period prior to 1945. Another recent work is Eric Salzman's *Twentieth-Century Music: an Introduction* (Englewood Cliffs, N.J., Prentice-Hall, 1967), which deals with ideas, not men, and covers the century up to the mid-1960s. Much of the significant writing on twentieth-century music is and will continue to be found in periodicals such as *Perspectives of New Music, Journal of Music Theory, The Score, Die Reihe, Source, Melos*, and perhaps even new periodicals yet to be born. Past, current, and future issues of these, as well as the music sections of newspapers such as *The New York Times*, should be consulted for critical and frequently perceptive articles.

A number of modern composers have recorded their views and philosophies toward music, both their own music and that of others, thus giving valuable insights into contemporary musical thought. Some of these volumes are: John Cage, *Silence: Lectures and Writings* (Middletown, Conn., Wesleyan University Press, 1961); E. Schwartz and B. Childs, eds., *Contemporary Composers on Contemporary Music* (New York, Holt, Rinehart & Winston, 1967); Paul Hindemith, *A Composer's World* (Cambridge, Harvard University Press, 1952); and Igor Stravinsky, *Poetics of Music* (New York, Random House, 1956).

Additional suggestions for books and representative music of the twentieth century may be found in the remaining bibliographies in this anthology.

27

THROUGHOUT the Romantic era composers strove to expand the limits of the traditional tonal and harmonic system that had become established during the late seventeenth century. New harmonic relationships were continually sought, sometimes producing chromatic harmonies that gave an unclear tonality. All this resulted, early in the twentieth century, in compositions intentionally lacking a tonal center, as may be seen in the works of a young composer of the time, Arnold Schönberg.

Schönberg's goal, gradually formulated, was to create music in which individual pitches existed as independent units rather than units dependent upon or even demanding resolutions to other pitches in order to have identity or function. This meant that no single pitch was to dominate as a tonal center to which other pitches would be attracted for resolution. Schönberg wished such music to be described as pantonal, that is, as embracing all tonalities equally; unfortunately the negative term, atonal, is the one that won general usage, and for the sake of convenience it will no doubt remain.

According to Schönberg's theories, tonal centers were to be avoided, thus also those elements that establish tonal centers such as triadic harmonies, octaves, fifths, and bland consonances. Gradually he devised a method of using pitch, the twelve-tone or dodecaphonic method, which served to organize it in such a way as to avoid anything reminiscent of traditional harmonies and tonal centers. By this method the composer organizes the twelve pitches of the chromatic scale into a series (hence the term "serial technique") from which the melodic and harmonic material of the composition is then derived; a new series is established for each composition. A description of the uses and possibilities of twelve-tone technique is too complicated to permit even a simple explanation here. The reader should consult under "Serial," "Twelve-tone," and "Dodecaphonic" in the standard music dictionaries and encyclopedias for an introduction to the subject.

Serial music has attracted many followers and, although it has at times been pronounced a musical dead-end, there is presently no indication that it is about to expire. There are probably few composers today who have not been affected in some way by serial techniques, although there are perhaps many who may have used these techniques only sporadically or possibly even unconsciously.

Since 1945 the younger generation of serial composers has concentrated on using serialization more for creating new means of musical expression than for avoiding old ones. Serialization has been extended to include non-pitch elements such as rhythm and timbre, resulting in compositions that are described as being totally organized.

The following selection discusses two devices, combinatoriality and derivation, used in the organization of pitch in certain types of twelve-tone music, and concludes with a few remarks about the serialization of non-pitch elements. All this is not with the intent of trying to tell the reader all there is to know about twelve-tone music within the space of ten pages, an impossibility too frequently attempted. Instead it is an attempt to make the reader aware of the enormous possibilities that the twelve-tone method affords the composer and of the complexities that are a part of serial music.

Milton Babbitt, a well-known American composer of serial and electronic music, is Professor of Music at Princeton University. Among his most significant compositions are his *Composition for 12 Instruments* (1948), *Vision and Prayer* for voice and electronic tape (1961), *Philomel* for the same media (1964), and *Relata II* for orchestra (1968). He is a member of the editorial board of *Perspectives of New Music* and has made numerous periodical contributions concerning serial and electronic music.

Most of the footnotes to the following article were written by Mr. Babbitt in answer to specific queries addressed to him after publication of the article. They are included in the hope that they will help the reader to grasp more clearly some of the more difficult concepts in this important study. The addenda, printed for the first time, were prepared in September, 1971, by Gerald Warfield in consultation with Mr. Babbitt. Mr. Warfield, a former student and colleague of Mr. Babbitt, is also a contributor to this anthology in his own right (see "Electronic Music: Synthesizers and Computers," on page 383).

Some Aspects of Twelve-Tone Composition

MILTON BABBITT

To disdain an alliance with those journalist critics, official composers, and custodians of musical patronage who regard the mere presence of "twelve tones" as sufficient evidence of a fall from musical grace, or, on the other hand, with that smaller group—created, perhaps, by understandable reaction—which regards the same phenomenon as a necessary and sufficient condition for the presence of profound musical virtues, is to deny oneself the possibility of making any convenient summary of American twelve-tone music. For American twelve-tone composers, in word and musical deed, display a diversity of "idioms," "styles," compositional attitudes and accomplishments that almost seems calculated to resist that segregation by identification which many of their enemies, and some of their friends, would impose upon them. If this extreme diversity is, to some degree, a reflection of that multiformity which characterizes all aspects of American cultural life, it is also symptomatic of the relative isolation in which each composer pursues his own work and determines his own direction. The interaction of ideas and influences that probably would be produced by a wide knowledge and intimate understanding of each other's work can scarcely exist when this body of music goes largely unpublished, unrecorded, and unperformed by the larger orchestras or by the widely known and travelled chamber music groups. In this respect, it must be added, twelve-tone music suffers only slightly more than other "difficult," "advanced" music—to the extent that the label itself supplies a basis for automatic rejection; for the American "music lover's" conservatism, a conservatism of ignorance rather than of considered choice, is nurtured and fostered by performers, concert managers, and Boards of Directors, for their own comfort, convenience, and profit.

Finding oneself a member of a minority within a minority may pro-

FROM *The Score*, no. 12 (June, 1955), 53-61. Reprinted by permission of the American Society of Music Arrangers.

vide solace for but few composers; observing "unintelligible" music from abroad being treated with respect and awe while comparable American music produces only anger and resentment may result in nothing more substantial than righteous indignation, while the realization that, if one's own music is performed infrequently if at all, the last three works of Webern are yet to be heard in New York, provides chilly comfort. Nevertheless, the number of twelve-tone composers here, as elsewhere, continues to increase.

The strategic date in the pre-war development of twelve-tone composition in the United States was that on which Schoenberg arrived here in 1933. Prior to that time, only the compositions of Adolph Weiss — Schoenberg's first official American student in Germany — and the *Dichotomy* of Wallingford Riegger had directed any attention to the American manifestations of twelve-tone composition, and Weiss soon became less associated with composition and more with performance, while *Dichotomy* remained a relatively singular work in Riegger's output until about 1943, when he became more closely identified with twelve-tone music.

Schoenberg's residence in the United States affected the musical climate not only because of his mere physical presence, or his activity as a teacher, but also, and primarily, because of the increased interest in, and performance of his music that resulted. The arrival of Ernst Krenek, five years later, added another figure who, through his writing and teaching as well as his music, directed attention to twelve-tone composition. Before the outbreak of the war, a number of young American composers — including George Perle, Ben Weber, and the present writer — were identified with the "twelve-tone school."

Since the war, the music of such composers as Erich Itor Kahn, Kurt List, Jacques Monod, Julius Schloss, and Edward Steuermann — whose careers had begun in Europe — have been relatively widely heard, while among the "natives," Robert Erickson, Richard Maxfield, Dika Newlin, George Rochberg, and Keith Robinson are but a few of those whose music is evidence of the creative interest in twelve-tone composition among the younger composers.

In addition, there are those composers — including the most widely known — who have indicated their awareness of and interest in twelve-tone composition, either in an isolated work, or by frequently employing certain techniques that are associated generally with twelve-tone music.

The above list of composers is neither complete nor presumed to be representative or selective. As has been indicated, no one can be in a position to possess adequate enough and accurate enough information to compile a comprehensive list. Very likely there are composers often performed and exerting real musical influence whose music is unknown beyond a specific locality.

For this, and other obvious reasons, the present article, rather than including the customary descriptive catalogue—consisting of the names of composers whose music is of necessity scarcely known to the readers of the article, attached to adjectival paragraphs and four-bar musical quotations that possess meaning only to the extent that they are misleading—will concern itself with a brief presentation of the sources and nature of one significant phase of twelve-tone activity in the United States that should be of particular interest to non-American readers for its obvious relation—in intent, if not in inception and method—to a widespread and more highly publicized development on the Continent.

The first explicit steps in the direction of a "totally organized" twelve-tone music were taken here some fifteen years ago, motivated positively by the desire for a completely autonomous conception of the twelve-tone system, and for works in which all components, in all dimensions, would be determined by the relations and operations of the system. Negatively, there was the motivation by reaction against the transference to twelve-tone composition of criteria belonging to triadic music.[1] The specific bases, discussed below, for achieving a total twelve-tone work, were arrived at by the end of the war, and when, a short time later, there were reports of a group of young French, Italian and German composers who apparently shared like aims, their work was eagerly awaited. However, their music and technical writings eventually revealed so very different an attitude toward the means, and even so very different means, that the apparent agreement with regard to ends lost its entire significance. The most striking points of divergence can be summarized in terms of the following apparent attributes of the music and the theory associated with it. Mathematics—or, more correctly, arithmetic—is used, not as a means of characterizing or discovering general systematic, pre-compositional relationships [see addendum 1, page 369], but as a compositional device, resulting in the most liberal sort of "programme music," whose course is determined by a numerical, rather than by a narrative or descriptive, "programme." The alleged "total organization" is achieved by applying dissimilar, essentially unrelated criteria of organization to each of the components, criteria often derived from outside the system, so that—for example—the rhythm is independent

---

[1] e.g., that of consonance and dissonance, carried over from a domain where the structure of the triad is the criterion of intervallic stability to a domain where the triad has no such prior function, and where—thus—criteria of consonance and dissonance, if the terms have any meaning whatsoever, must be determined by principles relevant to twelve-tone phenomena. The same applies to the transference of the external "forms" of triadic music to twelve-tone contexts, resulting in a divorce of these "forms" from their essential tonal motivations; this, at best, leads to a merely thematic formalism, and if one is seeking mere formalisms, there are certainly more ingenious ones than "sonata-form," "rondo-form," etc., for all that they might not possess this purely verbal identification with the hallowed past.

of and thus separable from the pitch structure; this is described and justified as a "polyphony" of components, though polyphony is customarily understood to involve, among many other things, a principle of organized simultaneity, while here the mere fact of simultaneity is termed "polyphony." The most crucial problems of twelve-tone music are resolved by being defined out of existence; harmonic structure in all dimensions is proclaimed to be irrelevant, unnecessary, and perhaps, undesirable in any event; so, a principle, or non-principle, of harmony by fortuity reigns. Finally, the music of the past—and virtually all of that of the present, as well—is repudiated for what it is not, rather than examined—if not celebrated—for what it is; admittedly, this is a convenient method for evading confrontation by a multitude of challenging possibles, including—perhaps—even a few necessaries. This latter represents a particularly significant point of divergence from the development to be considered here, which has its specific origins in the investigation of the implications of techniques of the "classics" of twelve-tone music. Indeed, it is a principle that underlies the bulk of Schoenberg's work (namely, combinatoriality),[2] and another, superficially unrelated, principle occupying a similar position in the music of Webern (derivation), that have each been generalized and extended far beyond their immediate functions, finally to the point where, in their most generalized form, they are found to be profoundly interrelated, and in these interrelationships new properties and potentialities of the individual principles are revealed.[3]

Quite naturally, it was the "early American" works of Schoenberg that were the most influential. As an example of a typically suggestive, but by no means unusual, passage, consider the opening measures of the third movement of the *Fourth Quartet*. Even a cursory examination reveals a number of significant techniques of local continuity and association: the exploitation of ordered adjacencies (the repeated adjacencies C-B of bar 619 and G♭ -F of bar 617 cross-associate with the opening two notes of the movement and the G♭ -F of the first violin in bar 621 to effect the closure of a structural unit [see addendum 2, page 369]: the three-note adjacency C-B-G of 619 also registrationally duplicates the first three notes of the movement), delinearization (the dyads of the first violin line of 620-1 are distributed among the three instruments that immediately follow [see addendum 3, page 369]), intervallic preparation and association (the simultaneously stated fourths of 619, 620 and 621 prepare the predefined fourth of the cello and viola in 623; the repeated C-B states with regard to the G in 619 the intervallic succession continued by the relation of the D♯ -E to the B in the same measure), mo-

[2]See footnote 6.

[3]Much of the remainder of this article is a highly condensed version of certain sections from the author's *The Function of Set Structure in the Twelve-Tone System* (1946).

362

tivic progression (the joining of forms of the set in 618 gives rise to the motive stated in the prime set itself by the last three notes, and the third, fourth, and fifth notes; the distribution of the elements of the inverted set between second violin and viola in 623 results in a three-note motive in the second violin which is the retrograde inversion of notes five, six, and seven of the simultaneously stated prime, at precisely the same total pitch level, and at the same time, the resultant viola line reveals two 16th-note groups of four notes each which symmetrically permute the minor second and major third), functional "orchestration" (the six-note unit of the first violin in 620-1 combines with the six-note unit of 622-3 to form a set), etc. But of far greater systematic significance, and far more susceptible to extension, is the familiar Schoenbergian principle of constructing a set in which linear continuity can be effected between sets related by the operation of retrograde inversion, by equating the total, unordered[4] content of corresponding hexachords [see addendum 4, page 369] at a specific transpositional level [see addendum 5, pages 369-370]. Such a set created by this ordering of hexachords supplies the basis of progressions in bars 616 to 619, and, in general, such "secondary set" construction supplies a basis of progression beyond mere set succession [see addendum 6, page 370]. A necessary corollary of this structural characteristic is that corresponding hexachords of inversionally related forms of the set, at the specific transpositional interval, possess no notes in common, and therefore span the total chromatic, thus creating an "aggregate."[5] In bar 623, successive aggregates are formed by the simultaneous statements of the prime form in the cello and the inverted form in the viola and second violin.

In almost all of his twelve-tone works (indeed, in all of his twelve-tone works of this period) Schoenberg employed a "semi-combinatorial set"[6] of the type just described; in his later works, his increased pre-

---

[4]i.e., the total pitch content, without considering the order.

[5]"Secondary set" and "aggregate" are necessary terms to define elements that arise compositionally, but are not pre-defined systematically. A secondary set (for example, that defined by the second hexachord of the prime set and the first hexachord of the inversion at the required transposition) is, indeed, in the strictest sense, a set, since it states a total ordering of the twelve tones (see addendum 7, page 370); however, it is not necessarily equivalent to a derived set (see addendum 8, page 370), nor is it ever one of the fundamental forms of the set. Of course, it can be thought of as a linear juxtaposition of parts of primary forms of the set (see addendum 9, page 370). An aggregate can be thought of as a simultaneous statement of such parts (see addendum 10, page 370), but in essence it is very different, since it is not a set, inasmuch as it is not totally ordered, because only the elements within the component parts are ordered, but not the relationship between or among the parts themselves (see addendum 11, page 370).

[6]"Semi-combinatoriality" indicates the property of creating such secondary sets, or aggregates, between a specific pair of forms (in the case of hexachordal semi-combinatoriality); "all-combinatoriality" denotes the possibility of constructing such secon-

occupation with the hexachord as an independent unit led to his using it often without regard to fixed ordering, but merely with regard to total content. Strangely, he never used the other two types of semi-combinatorial sets: that which gives rise to secondary set relationships between inversionally related forms of the set [see addendum 13, page 370], and thus, aggregates between retrograde inversionally related forms, or that which gives rise to secondary set relationships between retrograde related forms, and thus aggregates between prime related forms. (Obviously, any set creates aggregates between retrograde related forms, and secondary sets between prime related forms.)

The structural significance of such sets suggests a generalization to the construction of sets in which secondary set and, thus, aggregate structures obtain between any two forms of the set. There are six such "all-combinatorial" source sets, here indicated arbitrarily as beginning on the note C, for purposes of easy comparison:

(1) C-C♯-D-D♯-E-F / F♯-G-G♯-A-A♯-B
(2) C-D-D♯-E-F-G / F♯-G♯-A-A♯-B-C♯
(3) C-D-E-F-G-A / F♯-G♯-A♯-B-C♯-D♯
(4) C-C♯-D-F♯-G-G♯ / D♯-E-F-A-A♯-B
(5) C-C♯-E-F-G♯-A / D-D♯-F♯-G-A♯-B
(6) C-D-E-F♯-G♯-A♯ / C♯-D♯-F-G-A-B

It must be emphasized that these are "source sets,"[7] and that any ordering, to effect a specific compositional set, may be imposed on either hexachord without affecting the combinatorial properties. Among these six source sets, beyond many other secondary bases of similarity and dissimilarity, the first three sets possess the common property of creating combinatorial relationships at one and only one transpositional interval; they are thus termed "first order" sets [see addendum 14, page 370]. Set (4) possesses two such interval levels, and is termed "second order"; set (5), of "third order," possesses three such levels; set (6), of "fourth order," possesses six such levels. There is an inverse relationship between the multiplicity of these functional transpositions and the intervallic content within the hexachord. Thus, first order sets exclude one interval, second order sets exclude two, third order sets exclude three, and fourth order sets exclude six [see addendum 15, page 371]. As a re-

---

dary sets or aggregates among any pairs of forms of the sets, at one or more transpositional levels. "Combinatoriality" is the generic term including both the others (see addendum 12, page 370).

[7]"Source set" denotes a set considered only in terms of the content of its hexachords, and whose combinatorial characteristics are independent of the ordering imposed on this content.

sult, all-interval sets, for example, can be constructed only from first order sets; even so, there is basically only one independent all-interval set that can be constructed from each first order source set. (This excludes such sets as that of the first movement of Berg's *Lyric Suite*, which uses the elements of set (3), though not combinatorially. This set is a derived set, as defined below, since the two hexachords are related by retrogression.)

It is of interest to note that Schoenberg employed set (5) in his *Suite*, op. 29, but only as if it were merely semi-combinatorial; however, in his last, unfinished work, *The First Psalm*, he used the same source set, but the "set table" indicates his awareness of the total combinatorial resources of the set.

In addition to the value of such sets in effecting an interrelation of the "vertical" and "horizontal" far beyond mere identity, in generating fixed units of harmonic progression within which the components can in turn generate associative and variable relationships, and in determining transpositional levels, there is a far more fundamental aspect, in that a hierarchy of relationships exists among these sets as determinants of regions, an hierarchical domain closely analogous to the "circle of fifths," and defined similarly by considering the minimum number and the nature of the pitch alterations necessary to reproduce source sets at various transpositional levels. For example, in set (1), the transposition of note C by a tritone — the excluded interval — or the similar transposition of the symmetrically related note F, reproduces the set structure a half step lower in the latter case, or a half step higher in the former case, with maximum association of content to the original set. Thus, any degree of motion away from the pitch norm is measurable. Also, the motion from the region whose structure is defined by one such source set to that defined by another source set is achieved and measured in precisely the same manner. For example, the transposition of the note C♯ in set (1) by a tritone results in set (2); likewise, the symmetrically related E, when so transposed, results in set (2). These properties suggest that whether the source sets are used as specific compositional sets or not, they possess properties of so general a nature as to warrant their presence as implicit structural entities.

An investigation of the six all-combinatorial source tetrachords reveals a hierarchical universe analogous to that of the hexachord. There are four such tetrachords of first order, one of second, and one of third order [see addendum 16, page 371]. An understanding of their implications, and of those of the analogous trichordal units, together with the interrelationships among all types of combinatoriality, though fruitful enough in itself, leads one inevitably to a consideration of the technique of derivation.

Although this technique has often been used independently, it is only when considered in relation to combinatoriality that its extraordinary properties are fully revealed. Consider the set, so characteristic of Webern, that is used in his *Concerto for Nine Instruments*. It is presented in four three-note units: B-Bb-D, Eb-G-F♯, G♯-E-F, C-C♯-A; the first "prime" three-note unit is followed by its retrograde inversion, its retrograde, and its inversion. Though Webern uses this set as his total set, it is obviously possible to apply this technique to a three-note unit of any set, and thus—by the operations applied to the total set—generate a derived set.[8] Any three-note unit—with the exception of the "diminished triad"—can generate such a set,[9] and, in terms of the total content of hexachords, three independent sets can be generated. Of these, at least one is all-combinatorial. Of the twelve permutationally independent three-note units that exist, two generate one all-combinatorial set each, seven generate two, and two generate three (indeed, one of these latter two can generate four, though obviously not within the trichordal permutation of a single derived set). For example, the set of the Webern Concerto, though not so utilized,[10] is a representation of source set (5); by interchanging the second and fourth units, we have a representation of source set (1). The eleven three-note units are individually unique with regard to the combinatoriality of the source sets represented by their derived sets, so that a given three-note unit of a set is a unique means of effecting change of both functional and structural areas. Consider a set constructed from source set (1), with the following initial hexachord: C-Eb-D-E-C♯-F. The first three notes can generate derived sets of combinatoriality defined by source sets (1) and (2). Considering the first possibility, if we choose as the transpositional level for the three-note unit that defined by its pitch level in the original set, we derive the following initial hexachord: C-Eb-D-Db-Bb-B, which is a transposition of the original combinatorial structure; on the other hand, the original three-note unit, if transposed to D-F-E, could have generated a hexachord at the same pitch level as that of the original set; this, in turn, establishes a new transpositional level for the original hexachord, beginning on D. The original three-note unit also can generate the hexachord: C-Eb-D-G-E-F, and thereby establish the combinatorial region defined by source set (2).

In this manner, the functional and structural implications of a compositional set can be determined by the derivational interrelationships

---

[8]A derived set is *not* a new set in the composition. It can be thought of, also, as resulting from the juxtaposition of segments from the fundamental forms.

[9]For example, the triad C E G, A F D, C♯ A♯ F♯, G♯ B D♯. (Observe that this is also an all-combinatorial set.)

[10]Webern does not exploit the combinatorial properties of this set; he does not create progression through secondary sets or aggregates, nor does he determine his transpositions in terms of such properties.

of such units, in relation to the original set, and to each other, as defined hierarchically by the total domain of source sets.

As there are combinatorial trichords, tetrachords, and hexachords, so are there three-note generators, four-note generators, and six-note generators;[11] the extraordinary interrelationships that exist within and among the domains so defined emphasize the essential significance of the inherent structure of the set, and the unique compositional stage represented by the fact of the set, as the element with regard to which the generalized operations of the system achieve meaning, and from which the progressive levels of the composition, from detail to totality, can derive.

The twelve-tone structuralization of non-pitch components can be understood only in terms of a rigorously correct definition of the nature of the operations associated with the system. In characterizing the prime set, it is necessary to associate with each note the ordered number couple—order number, pitch number, measured from the first note as origin—required to define it completely with regard to the set [see addendum 17, page 371]. Then, as transposition is revealed to be mere addition of a constant to the pitch number, inversion—in the twelve-tone sense—is revealed to be complementation mod. 12 of the pitch number. (In other words, pitch number 4 becomes pitch number 8, etc.; naturally, interval numbers are also complemented.) Likewise, retrogression is complementation of the order number, and retrograde inversion is complementation of both order and pitch numbers. Any set of durations—whether the durations be defined in terms of attack, pitch, timbre, dynamics, or register—can be, like the pitch set, uniquely permuted by the operations of addition and complementation, with the modulus most logically determined by a factor or a multiple of the metric unit.[12] Thus, the rhythmic component, for example, can be structured in precisely the same way, by the identical operations, as the pitch component; rhythmic inversion, retrogression, and retrograde inversion are uniquely defined, and combinatoriality, derivation, and related properties are analogously applicable to the durational set. The result can be a structuring of all the durational and other non-pitch components,[13] determined by the opera-

---

[11]i.e., 3, 4 or 6-note units which serve to generate derived sets.

[12]"Set of durations" means specifically a "set" in the sense of twelve-tone set. By durations defined in terms of attack, is meant the time that elapses between actual attacks, measured in terms of a fixed unit of durational reference. Likewise, timbral duration is defined by the duration of a certain timbre or, conceivably, of related timbres. The same with registrational durations.

[13]The question of structuralizing non-pitch elements is certainly a very complicated one. If, for example, a rhythmic set is constructed with combinatorial characteristics, then secondary set structure, aggregate structure, derived set structure can all be arrived at in precisely the same manner as with pitches. The specific use of these means would depend upon the pitch structure of the composition.

The "form" would arise out of the specific implications of the set itself, in terms

tions of the system and uniquely analogous to the specific structuring of the pitch components of the individual work, and thus, utterly non-separable.

Even this extremely incomplete presentation should indicate the possibility of twelve-tone music, organized linearly, harmonically in the small and in the large, rhythmically—indeed, in all dimensions—in terms of the essential assumptions of the system.

Certainly, the resources indicated here do not constitute a guarantee of musical coherence, but they should guarantee the possibility of coherence. Above all, it is hoped that they serve to give at least some indication of the extraordinary breadth and depth of the twelve-tone system.

---

of its total content, the content of the derived sets which its generators give rise to, the transpositional levels to which the derived sets lead, etc.

Naturally, this does not mean to say that a given set uniquely implies a given composition, but rather that a given set defines, in these terms, certain general possibilities which are uniquely associated with this set.

Addenda

by GERALD WARFIELD (1971)

1. "Pre-compositional relationships" are not relationships calculated by the composer before beginning to compose but are instead relationships resulting from operations within whatever musical system is being employed. For example, in twelve-tone music there will be for each set (twelve-tone row) a specific transpositional level of its inversion which exchanges the order position of any two pitch classes of the prime form of any set. (E.g., if the prime form began C,D,A, the inversion on D would maintain the first two pitch classes as adjacencies but reverse their order positions, D,C,F.) Precompositional relationships exist within the twelve-tone system (and in any musical system) whether a composer elects to display them consciously or not.

2. In the prime form of the set (see addendum 18 for terminology) that Schoenberg used for the *Fourth Quartet* (C,B,G,A♭,E♭,D♭,D,B♭,G♭, F,E,A), C and B (and later in the set also G♭ and F) appear as adjacencies. In RI$_8$ (A♭,D♭,*C,B,G,D*♯,E,D,A,B♭,*G♭,F)* those same dyads again appear as adjacencies, although in different order positions. This precompositional relationship is prominently displayed in the first eight measures of the piece.

3. In measure 620 and 621 the first violin presents the last six notes of RI$_8$ (E,D,A,B♭,G♭,F). A transposition of the retrograde (R$_9$) immediately follows, the first hexachord of which contains those *same* notes, this time broken up into dyads and presented simultaneously (viola, E,D; 2nd violin, A,B♭; 'cello, F,G♭). For further discussion of the *Fourth Quartet* see Babbitt's "Set Structure as a Compositional Determinant" in the *Journal of Music Theory*, 5, no. 2 (April, 1961) 72-94.

4. A hexachord is a collection of six notes or pitch classes. The term is usually used in reference to the first or last six pitch classes in a set (i.e., the first hexachord and the second hexachord).

5. By "linear continuity" is meant the formation of secondary sets. In the *Fourth Quartet*, when P$_0$ is followed by RI$_8$ (the pitches are given in Addendum 2) the second hexachord of P$_0$ and the first hexachord of RI$_8$ (in measures 616 to 619), having no pitch classes in common, thus together form a complete twelve-tone set. This set is not, however, the basic set of the piece on which operations (e.g., R,I, RI) are effected, hence the term "secondary" set. It follows, of course, that the first hexa-

chords of both these forms (P_0 and RI_8) have exactly the same pitch content irrespective of ordering, as do also the second hexachords.

6. For example, relationships of the type displayed in Addenda 2 and 3 or larger-scale relationships such as those between nonadjacent notes.

7. This is easiest to see if one thinks of the sets stated linearly, first the prime form and then the inversion. The secondary set is therefore a result of the juncture of those two sets.

8. See footnote 8 on page 366.

9. If P_0 is followed immediately by another P_0 then the last hexachord of the first set and the first hexachord of the second set form a secondary set. This is, of course, a trivial example of secondary set formation.

10. If, as in Addendum 7, the prime and the inversion are capable of forming secondary set structures, then their simultaneous statements would result in corresponding hexachords having the same pitch class content (irrespective of the ordering within each of these hexachords). However, if the *retrograde* inversion were used in place of the inversion, the corresponding hexachords would display all twelve pitch classes. These are aggregates: vertical-type constructions, whereas secondary sets are of a linear type.

11. For instance, the intervals created *between* the notes in the corresponding order positions of the two sets.

12. It is perhaps helpful to consider the general shape of the hexachords when trying to get a mental picture of the properties of combinatoriality. A hexachord containing the notes C-C♯-D-D♯-E-F♯ is a solid chromatic cluster broken only by the whole-step interval between E and F♯ (F is missing between E and F♯). Obviously, the shape of a hexachord utilizing the remainder of the chromatic pitches would be exactly the same as the first hexachord except upside-down (the half-step vacancy appearing at the other end). A set made up of two hexachords of the types just mentioned is semi-combinatorial and displays RI combinatoriality in the formation of aggregates. In addition, a hexachord whose pattern is symmetrical within itself, such as C-D-D♯-E-F-G, is obviously more flexible in that it can display a combinatorial relationship with more forms of the set. An all-combinatorial set must display this intervalic symmetry. Note the shapes of the six all-combinatorial source hexachords given in the following paragraph of the text.

13. That is, between the *prime* and one or more inversional form of the set.

14. For example, if source set #1 were ordered D♯-C-E-F-D-C♯/B-A-F♯-A♯-G♯-G, then a secondary set could be formed with the retro-

grade inversion *only* at RI_1, and, correspondingly, the inversional level for aggregates could only be I_5. A secondary set with the inversion could *only* be at I_{11}, and thus the retrograde inversion aggregate level could *only* be RI_7.

15. This is taking into consideration every interval between every note within the hexachord.

16. First order (1) C-C♯-D-D♯, (2) C-D-D♯-F, (3) C-D-F-G, (4) C-C♯-D-F♯; second order (5) C-C♯-F♯-G; third order (6) C-C♯-F♯-A.

17. The Schoenberg set given in Addendum 2 would be represented 0,0; 1,11;2,7;3,8;4,3; etc.

18. Additional Terminology.

A *pitch class* is a collection of pitches in which the fundamental frequency of each pitch is a whole number multiple of every other pitch within the class. In other words, the pitch class C would be made up of all C's. This is a useful concept generally, and, indeed, a necessary one in twelve-tone music in that the notes of the basic set and its transformations do not designate the register in which the notes are to appear. The ordering of the twelve pitch classes most basic to a piece of twelve-tone music is known as the *prime* form of the *set* (twelve-tone row) abbreviated P. The standard transformations are inversion (I), retrograde (R), and retrograde inversion (RI). A numerical subscript indicates the beginning note. The first note of the prime is always zero no matter what pitch class it is. Zero is used instead of 1 for the sake of the correspondence between the order number and the pitch number in the representation of the set (and its transformations) as a series of ordered number pairs. (See Addendum 17 and the corresponding section of the text.) P_{11} means the prime form of the set eleven half steps above whatever zero represents. Note that R_0 means the retrograde beginning on whatever note P_0 begins on; it is not just P_0 backwards. For a more exhaustive treatment of this aspect of twelve-tone music see Babbitt's "Twelve-Tone Invariants as Compositional Determinants" in *The Musical Quarterly*, 46, no. 2 (April, 1960), 246–259.

Bibliography

Some of the bibliography relating to twelve-tone music has already been mentioned in the bibliography following "Post-Romanticism: Impressionism and Expressionism" (see page 341). A bibliography of twelve-tone music has been prepared by Ann Phillips Basart, *Serial Music: A Classified Bibliography of Writings on Twelve-tone and Electronic Music*

(Berkeley, Calif., University of California Press, 1961). This lists every major article and book on the subject written prior to 1960 but is of course now considerably out of date. It can be updated by a study of the articles and reviews printed in issues of *Perspectives of New Music, Journal of Music Theory,* and *The Score* that have appeared since then. The issues of *Perspectives* are especially valuable. George Perle's *Serial Composition and Atonality* (Berkeley, Calif., University of California Press, 1962) remains one of the most lucid introductions to twelve-tone music and treats the subject from Schönberg to Babbitt.

A listing of even the major composers using serial techniques is impossible here. Some are mentioned in the above selection; other names are given in the entry on "Serial Music" in the *Harvard Dictionary of Music,* 2d ed. (1969). Many of the works of Schönberg, Berg, and Webern are published in Vienna by Universal Edition. Publishers vary for other composers.

28

THE invention of the vacuum tube has made it possible to produce music electronically. Not only has electronic amplification, and also distortion, been applied to tone originating by conventional means but new instruments producing sounds by purely electronic means have appeared. Early electronic efforts were not intended to create a new kind of music. Instruments such as the Theramin, the Ondes Martenot, and the instruments of the Hammond company all had as their purpose the production of conventional music and in some cases the instruments themselves were built in imitation of instruments already existing. Only the means of production were new. It was not until the arrival of the tape recorder in the 1940s that a new kind of electronic music was to appear in quantity. The tape recorder brought new possibilities of sound through such techniques as montage, splicing, and running tape backwards, and composers were quick to put these to use in assembling and recording not only sounds produced conventionally *(musique concrète)* but also sounds produced electronically.

Electronic music has brought with it certain implications for the music profession which are not always immediately obvious but which are nonetheless of great importance. The composer now has total control over his composition. He can record nuances of pitch, rhythm, dynamics, and timbre that he could never expect from a performer and he can be assured that these effects will always be present at each hearing of his composition since they are permanently stored on tape. Composition and performance have become one action and the composition can never be subject to even the slightest change by the interpretation of a performer because the performer has been eliminated. This brings to its ultimate culmination a movement toward composer control that began centuries ago with the invention of notation. Not only has the performer been eliminated but also the music publisher, since there is now nothing to publish. The need for printed scores meant to serve performers no longer exists. Finally, the role of the public concert has changed. Concerts previously have existed to enable the public to hear new composers, new composition, new performers, and new performances. Electronic music, by eliminating the latter two, enables anyone with the necessary tape and playback equipment to hear the composition *exactly* as he would have heard it in public concert; there is no longer a need to attend concerts to hear music under new conditions because there can be no new conditions.

Another aspect of electronic music should be mentioned: the combination of electronic music with live, non-electronic music. Many compositions are being written in which the tape recorder is only one inflexible unit of an otherwise flexible and live performance. Such compositions combine the sounds and possibilities of live performance with those of the electronic world, eliminating neither, and it is possibly here that some of the most fascinating prospects for electronic music lie.

The following is concerned with a definition of electronic music and a description of some of its early stages of development; tools of electronic music developed since the mid-1950s are treated in "Electronic Music: Synthesizers and Computers" (see page 383).

Ernst Krenek is one of the best-known living composers. His prolific compositional output includes music for many vocal and instrumental media. He has held teaching positions at Vassar College and at Hamline University where he was at one time Dean of Fine Arts, and he is also the author of several books and articles.

What Electronic Music Is and How It Is Made

ERNST KRENEK

Translated by Margaret Shenfield and Geoffrey Skelton

In my experience, most people, when they hear the words "electronic music," think either of the breathy whine of the old-fashioned cinema organ or the sound effects which accompany the Mars rocket's landing on the forbidden planet in space films. The more advanced parties who already know of the twelve-tone technique and regard it as an intellectual perversion of nature, consider the efforts of electronic music to be the final, devilish degradation of the most spiritual of all arts, ground under the heel of mathematics and mechanics. As usual all the people who express these decided views have one quality in common: they do not know what they are talking about. This essay is an attempt to help them, so that they at least know what they are fighting.

Electronic music is made up of sounds that are not made by a man directly causing a substance to vibrate, but by electric impulses in vacuum tubes. Anybody who finds this "mechanised" way of producing tone questionable, might bear in mind that the time-honoured organ is based on a similar (though not electric) principle. The organist does not blow his doubtless emotion-laden breath straight into the pipes, but presses down a key which operates a valve which lets a purely mechanically stored stream of air into the pipe. If the player wants to modify the timbre and volume of the tone so produced, he has to work other mechanical devices through which the size of the air-stream entering the pipe can be regulated or the stream can be introduced into a pre-ar-

FROM Ernst Krenek, *Exploring Music,* trans. Margaret Shenfield and Geoffrey Skelton (London, Calder and Boyars Ltd., 1966), pp. 211-220. Reprinted by permission of the publisher.

ranged combination of pipes. Clearly, then the organist only influences the sound indirectly via mechanical devices.

En passant it may be mentioned that electronic music differs from *musique concrète*, with which it has often been confused, in that it is fundamentally made up of electronically produced sounds. *Musique concrète*, as developed by a group in Paris, is essentially a montage of existing acoustic phenomena—bells, railway noises, fragments of human speech, animal noises and the like. These elements are recorded with a microphone, distorted by manipulating the tapes and put together in startling patterns. The effects are often provocative and sometimes interesting in the same way as the shock effects of Dada were interesting and, like Dada works, amusing for a short time. But these experiments have little in common with music as an art aiming at the organisation of tones.

Tone produced in a vacuum tube differs from all the tone produced by known musical instruments in having no overtones. If the layman says that in listening to a trumpet, say, he is not aware of any overtones but only the single note, he is right in so far as these overtones cannot be distinguished as individual sound-phenomena. Nevertheless they appear very clearly in the sense that it is they which give the trumpet its characteristic sound. If the same note were to be played with another group of overtones in the foreground everybody would say: "That is a violin." Given another "spectrum" of overtones the connoisseur will immediately recognise his favourite tenor and the fact that he is singing "ah." (When he sings "oo" the spectrum changes slightly.) Every way of producing sound known hitherto has had such a spectrum, because they were all based on causing some material to vibrate, and the different materials have different combinations of overtones. But electronically-produced tone has none. This can easily be demonstrated with the aid of an apparatus that makes the vibration-patterns of sound visible. While all conventional tones show complicated and irregular curves, electronic tone produces the symmetrical sine-curve familiar from geometry. Hence it is known as sinusoidal tone. Sinusoidal tone is the basic material of all music, and indeed of all acoustical phenomena in general —the atom of audible matter, so to speak. Everything we hear is made up of a mixture of sinus tones which combine in innumerable gradations of pitch and volume to form the billions of constellations of the audible cosmos. Only electronic tone-production has made it possible to isolate this atom from its complicated connections and allow us to hear it on its own. The far-reaching and revolutionary consequence of this is that we are now in a position to be able to make this atom enter into new combinations with other atoms—combinations not to be found in the existing world of sounds, which is dependent on the material make-up of vibrating bodies.

Our basic instrument is the frequency-generator, an iron box about the size of a small suitcase. With it we can produce sinusoidal tones of every number of vibrations within the limits of audibility and even outside them. Practically speaking, the lower limit of pure sinusoidal tone may be taken as 55 Hertz (i.e. 55 vibrations per second), which is three octaves below tuning A. Even lower notes can be heard, but only when overtones vibrate with them (as for example in the bottom octave on the piano). For musical purposes 5,000 H is a sufficiently high top limit. Many people can perceive notes up to 11,000 H, but in this stratosphere pitch can no longer be clearly distinguished—everything is just "very high."

The note an octave above our lowest note (55 H) has twice as many vibrations, 110. If we go up from this keynote in the conventional note-system, there are twelve different notes before we reach the A above. As we can register each vibration-number on the frequency-generator we have 55 different notes at our disposal between the lowest note and the one an octave above it. While we hear the notes as rising in a straight line, so that for example all octaves seem to cover acoustical areas of the same size, despite their absolute pitch, the vibration-numbers rise in a much steeper curve, so that the number of each note is twice as great as that of the one an octave below. Thus if our first octave goes from 55 to 110, the second goes from 110 to 220 and so on. Again, while previously we could only divide this second octave into twelve notes, we now have 110 different notes. Of course neither 110 nor even 55 notes in an octave can be distinguished so easily that they can be used in the kind of melody-structures we made with twelve notes. But it is easy to estimate what undreamed-of possibilities this opens up in the way of creating new sound-spectra by mixing so many separate notes.

By the way, these possibilities have long been known and the various instruments known under the collective name of "electric organs" —the regrettably christened "novachords" and "orgatrons" and even "cla-violines"—are all based on this principle. But they got in the way of the development of real electronic music because their inventors were not interested in a new world of sounds but only in imitating the old one synthetically. The electronic instrument was only worth the money if its tone could not be distinguished from a real violin, trumpet or what have you, and it tried to justify itself by pointing out that you only needed to press a button to get seven different timbres, thus enabling the instrument's owner to economise on the wages of six musicians. This has nothing to do with electronic music.

To sum up the acoustical aspects: we know that we can produce thousands of musical atoms, or sinusoidal tones, within the limits of audibility. What are we doing with these tones? One cannot play on a frequency-generator as on a piano because it only produces one note at a time; nor is it like a flute, because after each note the dials have to be re-set to produce the next frequency. In order to make music out of this basic material, the notes must first be captured in some way.

This is where we call on the second technical innovation essential for true electronic music: tape-recording. That vacuum tubes produce notes has long been known, as aforesaid. But before a method of recording these sounds had been found, the tubes had to be built into an apparatus like an organ with a keyboard if it was to be played. The limitations of this arrangement are obvious: exactly as with the traditional organ one has to be content with a certain number of predetermined combinations, and there are severe technical restrictions on the changes from one combination to another that one can make during performance.

But now the notes and sounds we produce are recorded straight on tape. There is no microphone, as when a violinist, say, records something; the electric impulses of the frequency-generator go directly to the input of the tape-recorder. The tape, then, is the place where the music we want to make is gradually stored as we get it from our sound-sources. But the tape is also the means by which our music becomes audible. The music is "performed" by playing the tape. So the tape represents both the composition and the performance. That is, composition and performance are identical. What we record on the tape is the music. It does not need later "performance" by musicians—in fact, it cannot have it, for it does not exist off the tape. And this tape is really a magic device. Even after ample experience it is impossible to estimate just what one can do with this modest half-inch-wide strip of dull-looking brown material to produce sound effects that could not be achieved in any other way.

First, the sound composed of the frequency-generator's sinusoidal tones can be manipulated in many ways. For example, the volume of each note of a sound can be gradated most delicately and precisely, and a series of changing sound-patterns can be produced by this alone. With devices that work like filters, and so, reasonably enough, are called filters, certain frequency-areas can be brought out while others disappear into the background, so that the sound gains luminosity or sinks into darkness. If the tape on which the sound is recorded is cut obliquely, smooth insertions can be made, whereas rectangular cuts give hard, percussive attacks. If a sound that begins like this is quickly faded out (that is, the input-unit is quickly switched off) one gets a percussive note; if more slowly faded out, the note dies away more gently. A really three-dimensional echo can be obtained by using the echo-chamber, an ordinary empty room in which the sound is emitted by a loudspeaker and recaptured together with the room's reverberations, by a microphone opposite. This "signal" returns immediately (at the speed of light) to the studio and we can put in more or less echo. We can start the sound "dry" and then gradually add more and more echo. We can filter the echo so that, say, the lower notes gradually fall out of the echoing sound and finally only the high ones sound as an echo. We can cut the "dry" beginning of the sound out of the tape, or wipe it off, so that only the echo (of nothing, so to speak) remains floating in space. And we can run the tape backwards so that we get an increasing echo, starting from nothing, which suddenly breaks off. By arranging the feedback in a certain way we can make the sound shake at regular intervals. We can play this result three octaves higher on a machine for the purpose. At this pitch the sound becomes thin and cutting and the slow shaking goes eight times as fast, producing an effect of aggressive vehemence. Many, many more things could be added to the list of what one can do with a simple sinusoidal note by manipulating the recording machine. It may be of interest that very costly equipment is by no means necessary. All the phenomena I have described come only from an extremely intelligent, inventive use of standard machinery which, as far as I know has only been elaborated in the electronic studio of the West German Radio in Cologne.

The layman has already heard many of these effects behind the aforementioned space-ship in the cinema or on television. They are improvised by technicians experimenting with the brown tape in the still watches of the night. It needs the composer to discover how this enormous mass of sound material can be turned to account in presenting musical ideas. In this lies the real importance of the great precision with which musical time-relationships can be regulated by means of tape. It must be remembered that modern music, particularly the music developed on the basis of atonal expressionism, is very complicated rhythmically. In other words, the segments of time between the single events of a musical passage are irregular in length and often distinguished only by very minute differences. Although it is crucially important to the musical idea for these time-relationships to be absolutely accurate, they give performers, particularly ensembles, a great deal of difficulty. The rehearsal work necessary is often out of all proportion to the result, which in the final analysis depends on the unforeseeable nervous condition of the performers at the moment of performance, and so is threatened by considerable uncertainty factors.

Producing the music on tape disposes of all these difficulties at one blow. The duration of a note or any other musical unit is expressed by the length of the bit of tape on which it is recorded. This length depends in its turn on the speed at which the tape goes through the recording apparatus. So far the best results in electronic recordings have been obtained with the maximum speed on normal machines—76 cm. per second: a note that lasts one second takes up 76 cm. of tape. Of course the tape can be cut accurately to a millimetre. But even if we content ourselves with distances of one centimetre, time-differences of one-seventysixth of a second can be accurately presented. This is a much smaller difference than the human ear can perceive. It has been proved experimentally that when, for example, a sequence of four notes whizzes past above a certain speed limit the ear can no longer distinguish the order in which the notes come. Normally time-differences of, say, one-twentieth of a second are enough to produce considerable effect, musically speaking. It would be arrogant, cruel, and, in any case, hopeless to suggest to a group of musicians that one should begin at the beginning of a second, the second three-twentieths, the third twelve-twentieths and the fourth seventeen-twentieths later, while the first perhaps plays another note ten-twentieths after his first.

With the aid of tape the problem can be solved without fear and trembling. The second note must go past the recording head 12 cm. after the first, the third 48 cm., and the fourth 68 cm. after, while the first player's second note is recorded 40 cm. after zero. It is child's play to measure off these distances, cut the tape into the correct lengths and stick the pieces together in the right order.

The problem becomes more difficult with musical processes progressing simultaneously. After all, music does not consist merely of a sequence of single notes. With simultaneous processes the musical progress must be split into horizontal layers which must be organised so that the maximum number of successive elements in the complex are got into each layer without "overlapping." For one layer, but only one, can be recorded on a single tape without difficulty. The next layer goes on another tape, and so on. After all the layers have been recorded they have to be synchronised: each tape is so placed in its own machine that when all the machines begin to play simultaneously the tapes all play at the moment required for the composition. All the machines are connected to a recording machine which records the total result on a new tape. If this *sounds* complicated it is much more so in reality. The ingenuity and inventiveness of the technicians who carry out these synchronisation-processes cannot be too much admired. Without reliable and, to a certain extent, manageable synchronisation-systems, electronic music would have to remain no more than a dream.

As I have said, the precision of this machinery is attractive above all because it makes it possible to "perform" limitless irregularities. So the total determinacy of machines serves to create a symbol of complete freedom. This is not to be confused with the "agogic nuances" which make a human performer's playing appear to be "living." (The new science of communications, cybernetics, to whose thought-processes electronic musicians rightly feel attracted, calls these irregularities "aleatoric elements"—from the Latin *alea*, dice, because they are really only statistically determinable chance-results.) When, in an "inspired" performance of sixteen bars of Beethoven, no two bars are exactly the same length, although the composer has not indicated any differences, the hearer is not conscious of the differences: if he was, the performance would not be "inspired" but distorted. The listener is principally conscious of the dominant regularity of the structure and feels it to be "living" because of the imperceptible variations. The structures of new music are irregular *a priori,* so that the intrusion of aleatoric elements, above a certain point, can easily make them unrecognisable.

Total mastery of great complexity is a perfectly legitimate art-ideal. It principally attracts those composers who are concerned to "generalise" the serial principle derived from the later twelve-tone technique. Not only the sequence of intervals between the notes of the basic pattern but the time-sequence of the events (the rhythm), their relative volume and every aspect of the musical organism is governed by a pre-selected system of measurements and proportions. This system is called a "row" in the broadest sense of the word. (There is more medievalism in this concept than many of its supporters would admit.) If the measurements selected are not trivial—if they are, the whole exercise is not worth the trouble—there emerge results so complex that only electronic performance can guarantee that they will be faultlessly carried out. With the strange and wonderful dialectic that runs through this, as through all human endeavours, this knife-edge accuracy often sounds like the triumph of the aleatorical. This is, of course, due to its complexity. The same dialectic makes the machine, apparently a totally rationalised medium, the ideal field for real compositorial improvisation. A musician who improvises at the piano is not composing, but using certain fabric-making procedures which have emerged from experience in order to pursue a musical idea for a while in a playful, non-obligatory way. (Beethoven who, it is recorded, was an exciting improviser, worked for years on a phrase when he was composing.)

Now the electronic musician can work as directly on his material as the painter or sculptor. You cannot say to the brass in a rehearsal: "Please try to play that a little later—say about half a second." But it is very easy to shift a tape in the synchronisation so that the note arrives 32 or 38 or 42 cm. later. The aleatoric element is no longer the function of an individual "re-creating" the music, but the direct expression of its creator's imagination. At some point on the far horizon the lines of freely chosen assumption and assumptionless free choice meet.

A tangled prospect? We are still at the very beginning of it all.

Bibliography

Although electronic music is still a new area, a considerable bibliography has already accumulated. Over 1500 items have been compiled by Lowell M. Cross in *A Bibliography of Electronic Music* (Toronto, University of Toronto Press, 1967), and obviously many more have been written since 1967. Issue no. 1 of *Die Reihe* (1955), translated into English under the same title (Bryn Mawr, Pa., Theodore Presser, 1958), is devoted exclusively to electronic music and contains articles by Boulez, Klebe, Krenek, Pousseur, and Stockhausen. Many of the significant recent articles on electronic music are contained in *Perspectives of New Music;* issues from vol. 1 (1962) forward should be consulted. Brian Fennelly's article, "A Descriptive Language for the Analysis of Electronic Music," in *Perspectives,* 6 (Fall–Winter, 1967), is especially interesting since it deals with the problem of analysis of electronic music, which must be done aurally because there is no printed score. A thesis concerning the future of electronic music and its relation to other serious music as well as to jazz and pop music is proposed by Placide Gaboury in "Electronic Music: The Rift between the Artist and Public" in the *Journal of Aesthetics and Art Criticism,* 28, no. 3 (Spring, 1970). Karlheinz Stockhausen's "The Origins of Electronic Music" in *The Musical Times,* 112 (July, 1971), contributes information by one of the earliest pioneers of the medium.

Electronic music can be studied only by recordings. Some composers who have been active in electronic music are: K. Stockhausen, G. Ligety, L. Berio, H. Pousseur, V. Ussachevsky, and M. Babbitt. For additional names see the entry on "Electronic Music" in the *Harvard Dictionary of Music,* 2d ed. (1969). Current recordings of music by these composers and others are listed in the *Schwann Record and Tape Guide,* issued monthly.

29

THE early stages of electronic music are discussed in the preceding selection, "What Electronic Music Is and How It Is Made" (see page 373); however, many new things have happened in electronic music in the few years since that was written. The necessity for some of the cumbersome techniques of montage and splicing has been partially eliminated by the invention of electronic synthesizers permitting the composer to create and record on tape a number of effects simultaneously. But there are still limitations and a completed composition may require not only a combination of several synthesizer processes but also certain manual operations. The first synthesizers, such as those of RCA, were so bulky and expensive that commercial production was not feasible. Smaller and more economical synthesizers of a somewhat similar type are now available, so that it is possible for any school or college sufficiently interested to own one.

Synthesizers, however, are not a panacea to solve all the problems of electronic music, as is emphasized in the following selection. While synthesizers do afford new possibilities, there is danger of overestimating their potentialities; furthermore, they may not offer as much promise for composers of electronic music as computers, nor may they be as economical since a computer is more likely already to be part of a school's equipment. The following, written expressly for this anthology and printed here for the first time, gives a general description of the operations of synthesizers and computers in the realization of electronic music as well as the author's views on their respective merits and hazards.

Gerald Warfield, a young American composer, has taught composition and theory at Princeton University where he was also manager of the Princeton branch of the Columbia-Princeton Electronic Music Center. While at Princeton he prepared a manual on the computer synthesis of sound for the use of students there. Presently he is working on the Index of New Musical Notation, a project currently underway at the Library and Museum of the Performing Arts, The New York Public Library at Lincoln Center, and having as its aim the standardization of new forms of musical notation. Mr. Warfield's textbook on tonal theory is soon to be published by David McKay, New York.

Electronic Music: Synthesizers and Computers

GERALD WARFIELD

Since the beginnings of electronic music in the United States (at Columbia University in the early part of 1952) both private and university owned electronic music studios have become almost commonplace in this country, and, as one would expect, a great number of changes have occurred, due to general technological advances as well as to work done specifically in the field of sound synthesis. With respect to methods of sound generation, there are, at present, four types of electronic music: (1) *musique concrète*, (2) manual tape studio music, (3) synthesizer music, and (4) computer music. Only the first two types were in existence when Krenek wrote the preceding article, and the distinction he makes between them is still a basic differentiation in electronic music. It is interesting to note that many composers evidently agree, at least in part, with his aversion to *musique concrète*. Today, if the technique is used at all, it is usually in the manipulation of a single element within a composition. For instance, a piece might contain a voice part which has been transformed electronically (a *musique concrète* technique) while the other sound elements of the piece are generated entirely electronically (as in Stockhausen's *Gesang der Jünglinge).*

At its inception it was thought that electronic music would give the composer absolute freedom in the selection of sonic material, but the mere presence of "new" sounds hardly constitutes freedom. Some components of the average studio, ring modulators and multipliers, for example, are capable of generating, within limits, very complicated sounds. However, if one has a preconceived notion of *exactly* what these sounds should be, there are often insurmountable difficulties because such units do not give independent control over *all* components of the sound. A

Copyright ©1972 by Gerald Warfield.

complex sound has a large number of partials, each with an independent shape (envelope). The number of re-recordings necessary to construct such a sound in an electronic studio would result in a noise and distortion level on the tape so high that it would render the sound all but useless, even if one could synchronize all the components efficiently enough in the first place. And all of this would be necessary for the production of a *single* tone: a very inefficient and time consuming process.

The attitude of many composers, however, has been to accept these limitations: the easily produced sounds constitute the pool of resources from which he selects as he makes a sort-of acoustical collage. There is certainly nothing wrong with this approach. (Listen to, for example Mario Davidovsky's *Synchronism #1.)* It is in some ways similar to the situation of the composer writing for an instrumental medium: there is a specific relationship between his conception of the piece and the sound material available. However, if more control over the electronic material is desired, clearly it is necessary to have ways to synchronize and effect many operations simultaneously. It is this problem which leads us to the topic of synthesizers.

Early synthesizers, such as the Mark I and Mark II, both made by RCA, attempted to imitate the sounds of natural instruments (hence the name synthesizer). The present contribution of synthesizers, however, is to increase the efficiency of the tape studio by making it possible to interconnect and control many different types of apparatus both simultaneously and sequentially.

Most of the operations of these devices are based on voltage control, which means using an outside voltage source to control, or "drive" a unit. For example, instead of turning a knob manually to set the frequency on a wave generator, it is set precisely by the relative power of a voltage—the stronger the voltage, the higher the frequency. One might utilize a rapid stream of differing voltages, thereby causing the oscillator to yield a correspondingly rapid series of varied frequencies. Consider the following diagram of a process characteristic of the synthesizer.

The sequencer (the long rectangular box) has a series of knobs by which one can set relative voltages. The pulse generator on the left sends pulses to the sequencer causing the output from the sequencer to change from stage to stage, in order left to right. Thus if one wants an ascending string of notes, each knob is set a little higher than the last. The resulting string of different voltages outputted by the sequencer (this is the control voltage) goes to the wave generator, causing it to produce a string of frequencies corresponding to the relative power of each voltage. These "notes" then go to an attack and decay generator which modifies them by shaping each with an attack and decay. Such a set-up is very flexible in that many different arrangements of the equipment are pos-

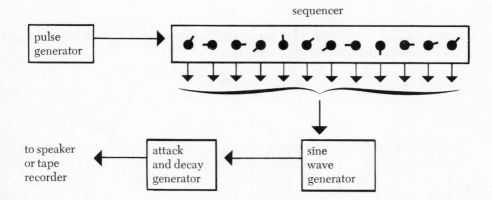

sequencer

pulse generator

to speaker or tape recorder

attack and decay generator

sine wave generator

sible (using filters, wave multipliers, keyboards, among other things), and additional controls can usually be introduced at every point.

Most studios today have a synthesizer of some kind, and the techniques of the manual tape studio augment the resources of the synthesizer. The synthesizer has its dangers, however, because it is often not recognized for what it is, i.e., simply an extension of a conventional electronic music studio having inherent in it the same problems as conventional studios. Also, unfortunately, the synthesizer gives the impression that it can "make" music automatically because the recent manufacturers of such devices have emphasized, in their design of synthesizers, the generation of long series of notes rather than the control of the individual components that make up a single sound event. Without sufficient control of these components a string of notes from a sequencer can be very uninteresting, not because of the lack of variety, but because structural elements of a composition cannot utilize parameters which are not sufficiently controlled. Discriminating use of a synthesizer can yield extraordinary results (listen to, for example, Milton Babbitt's *Philomel*), but its "automatic" aspects must be kept carefully under control.

The computer synthesis of sound brings about a totally new concept in the generation of electronic music. However, it should be emphasized that the computer does *not*, in the context in which we are speaking, compose; it is a performance device. A computer can, of course, be programmed to generate a series of random numbers or even possibly a Mozart-type sonata. Our discussion, however, is limited to the computer as a medium of performance. (Listen to, for example, J. K. Randall's *Mudgett.*)

Rather than attempting to build up sounds with preexisting generators, the computer simply calculates (or plots) the final wave form for each sound desired. The composer has only to supply the necessary specifications for each sound. The computer then represents these sounds with a series of numbers that stand for successive instantaneous amplitudes such as in the following example.

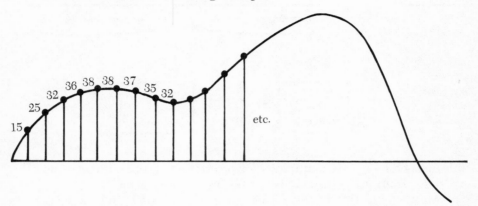

No matter how complicated a sound, it can be represented by a single-line function or wave form corresponding to the atmospheric density at any given moment. (After all, the tympanum of the ear drum can only be at one place at one moment.) A digital-to-analog (number-to-sound) converter then converts these numbers into a continuous wave form.

The whole process is roughly as follows. The composer first composes the piece. He then sets up a computer program that is capable of accomplishing anything needed during the course of the piece (glissandi, white noise, nonharmonic partials, etc.). Next he punches computer cards, usually one card per note of the piece, telling the computer when to play the note, how loud, the frequency, timbre, and any other pertinent information. The computer calculates the numbers representing the wave forms and the results are then converted into sound and recorded.

It is in the impeccable precision of the computer that the future of electronic music lies. Although some of its aspects are still in the developmental stage, suffice it to say the most important contribution of computers to electronic music is the availability, as a compositional resource, of precise control over more variables within the aural domain than ever before possible.

Bibliography

Bibliographical suggestions for electronic music are given following the preceding selection, "What Electronic Music Is and How It Is Made" (see page 383). A collection of essays dealing with the uses of computers in musical composition, analysis, and information storage has been compiled and edited by Harry B. Lincoln, The Computer and Music (Ithaca, N.Y., Cornell University Press, 1970).

30

ALEATORY music appears to stand in direct opposition to the composer control of electronic music. With aleatoricism (from the Latin *alea*, meaning dice, hence chance or uncertainty) the composer deliberately renounces control over the shape of his composition, either by giving control to the whim of the performer or else by letting the shape be determined literally by casting dice or by some other form of chance. If aleatoricism is to be present in performance, the composer may (1) fix the length and order of the sections of the composition but permit the performer to determine rhythm, dynamics, and/or notes within the sections; (2) fix the musical material within sections but allow the performer to determine the order of sections and even to omit some; (3) combine the first two approaches. On the other hand, the composer may deny the performer any aleatory rights, but instead put the composition together himself by a method or methods of chance. Obviously, the possibilities of aleatoricism are vast, especially in ensemble music where a number of players are involved, some or all of whom may have aleatory rights, at once or at different times.

Aleatoricism in music is not new. Examples of it from earlier centuries may be found, but these are usually musical games or jokes. It appeared in twentieth century music, however, as a serious and significant approach to composition. The following selection, rather than describing the most recent manifestations of aleatory music, attempts to place aleatoricism within a historical context, maintaining that it is a logical outgrowth of the music of composers as different from one another as Schönberg, Stravinsky, and Bartok. The author's conclusion, with which some readers will no doubt disagree, is that aleatoricism is a temporary stage in the modern composer's search for a logical form to express his musical ideas.

Anthony Cross is an English musician and scholar. He has contributed to *The Musical Times* and *The Music Review*.

The Significance of Aleatoricism
in Twentieth-Century Music

ANTHONY CROSS

The present century has seen many revolutionary innovations in the technique of composition, and criticism has generally been directed at the fact that these have resulted either in a high degree of disorder (atonality), or in the imposition of an order which is imperceptible to the ear (twelve-note technique).[1] Music which abandons tonality, it is often said, has lost all syntax, can no longer be considered a language and therefore cannot communicate the rich variety of expression found in tonal music. At best one can hope for sensual and beautiful sounds which are however condemned to remaining essentially decorative. Such criticism, applied to the music of an earlier generation of composers such as Schönberg, Berg and Webern, would hardly be taken seriously today. The music of Schönberg and Berg retains strong enough links with the nineteenth century to guarantee communication, and with familiarity, the musical personalities of these composers are much more varied than was once thought. As recent analysis has shown,[2] the music of Webern too (particularly the later works) possesses clearly perceptible shape and form, ensured by the adaptation of traditional contrapuntal techniques, and a serially derived motivic technique. In recent years, however, the old criticism of incomprehensibility has been raised again, particularly with the introduction of so-called aleatory techniques, or chance, into the process of composition. It is assumed, with apparently invincible logic, that to leave the formal evolution of the music to chance amounts to a renunciation of responsibility on the part of the composer and is

[1] Much analytical terminology (e.g., atonality, arhythmic, athematic) faithfully reflects this view which regards new music merely as the negation of tonal music.

[2] See, for example, Boulez' analyses in *Penser la Musique Aujourd'hui*, Mainz, 1963.

FROM *The Music Review*, 29 (1968), 305-322. Reprinted by permission of W. Heffer & Sons Ltd.

an admission that the music can have no significant form. It is certainly true that many composers have used the element of chance quite deliberately, just to avoid the creation of significant form and an ordered syntax in the traditional sense. In his Lecture on Indeterminacy,[3] John Cage, writing of indeterminate pieces by Wolff, Feldman and others, states that this music is not meant to be understood and evaluated; the pieces are not objects in this sense but "processes essentially purposeless," where "sounds are just sounds." The element of chance in this music is often entirely fortuitous and completely outside the composer's control as is shown by the following anecdote recounted by Cage:

> One day when the windows were open Christian Wolff played one of his pieces at the piano. Sounds of traffic, boat-horns, were heard not only during the silences of the music, but, being louder, were more easily heard than the piano sounds themselves. Afterwards someone asked Christian Wolff to play the piece again with the window closed. Christian Wolff said he'd be glad to, but that it wasn't really necessary, since the sounds of the environment were in no sense an interruption of those of the music.[3]

It is clear that the usual critical notions, concerning the composer's responsibility for his own work and the necessity to create an ordered structure comparable with the logic of tonal music, are irrelevant in face of this radically new conception of the very nature of music.

Pierre Boulez, on the other hand, in his article *Alea*[4] clearly rejects such a view when he writes:

> La forme la plus élémentaire de la transmutation du hasard se situerait dans l'adoption d'une philosophie teinté d'orientalisme qui masquerait une faiblesse fondamentale dans la technique de la composition; . . . je qualiferais volontiers cette expérience—si tant est que c'en soit une, l'individu ne se sentant pas responsable pour son oeuvre . . .—je qualiferais donc cette expérience de hasard par inadvertance.

The matter is clarified when Boulez differentiates between pure chance, where the composer has little or no control over the form, and non-determinate choice, where the function of chance would be strictly limited:

> The work must provide a certain number of possible routes . . . with chance playing a shunting role at the last moment. As people have pointed out to me, this notion of shunting does not belong to the category of pure chance, but in that of non-determinate choice and this difference is fundamental; in a construction that is as ramified as compositions being written today there could not possibly be total indeterminacy.[5]

[3] John Cage, Lecture on Indeterminacy, *Die Reihe*, no. 5.
[4] P. Boulez, "Alea" in *Relevés d'Apprenti* (collected essays), Paris, 1966.
[5] P. Boulez, "Sonate que me veux-tu?," *Perspectives of New Music*, Spring, 1963.

Here, Boulez is writing of his third piano Sonata, but good examples of this conception of non-determinate choice can also be found in other works. Example 1 shows the degree of choice available to the conductor in the closing pages of *Don (Pli selon Pli)*, which consist of a sequence of sections, presented antiphonally by contrasting groups of instruments, the ordering of which is variable in a number of prescribed combinations, the two groups coming together only for the final section.

Ex. 1

(Letters do not refer to musical relationships.)

Edward Lockspeiser has criticized the use of chance in *Pli selon Pli* in the following terms:

> ... I think there is a fallacy in Boulez' conception of 'aleatoric' music. . . . Which notes shall be played, which developments shall be used? The composer does not know, the interpreter does not know. Therefore a decision must be reached by chance. Any decision will be valid resulting from nothing more than a metaphorical casting of dice.[6]

Lockspeiser is obviously unwilling to differentiate between pure chance and non-determinate choice for it is obvious that in this work composer and performer do in fact know "which notes shall be played, which developments shall be used." It is merely that there is some freedom in the ordering of sections already fully realized by the composer, and in which the element of chance plays no part.

Nevertheless, it is true that Boulez' methods in recent works cannot be fully understood in such simple terms; in this article we shall attempt firstly to discover the significance of Boulez' preoccupation with chance, secondly to consider briefly music by other composers in similar terms, and thirdly to trace the origins of this preoccupation with chance.

Example 2 is taken from Boulez' recent purely instrumental work *Eclat*. Whereas in the example from *Don*, considered above, chance intervened only in the relationship of fully composed sections, here, chance occurs at a much lower level of organization; the musical events the ordering of which is variable are now only single chords or brief arabesque-like figures, and not only the ordering of these events but their duration and dynamic intensity are also left to the momentary

[6]E. Lockspeiser, "Mallarme and Music," *Musical Times*, March, 1966.

Ex.2

choice of the performer. The element of chance therefore enters into the very constitution of the musical material itself, and brings the music close to the ideal of John Cage where "sounds are just sounds" with no language-structure to detract from their purity. On the technical level indeed, Ex. 2 can be described only negatively; it is completely athematic with no attempt at motivic organization, arhythmic in that there is no sense of pulsation or phrasing but only a highly irregular and unpredictable sequence of events, and finally the relationship between the dimensions (parameters) may be described as negative in character. Freedom of choice in the field of rhythm and dynamics means that the dimensions are necessarily conceived separately. The significance of this may be understood if a comparison is made with tonal music. Here the dimensions are considered inseparable because conceived together from the start, and their individual significance may be said to derive only from the totality they go to make up. The nature of their interaction is best understood as resulting in varying degrees of tension and relaxation. This is not the place to embark on a complete account of a highly complex problem, but Ex. 3 is a clear instance of the way in which dissonance and tension in the dimensions of pitch and rhythm (duple metre momentarily displaces triple metre), together with dynamics and texture, complement one another. However, this kind of tension-flow is entirely absent from Boulez' aleatoric music in *Eclat* (Ex. 2), above all because of the lack of rhythmic pulsation and any sense of cumulative harmonic

Ex.3 Allegro

tension so that the separate dimensions are merely added together as it were, rather than indissolubly fused into a higher unity. The music's general character is well summed up in the performing direction "vague et flottant." It is also apparent that the traditionally subsidiary dimension of timbre is invested with new significance brought about by the lack of significant organization in the primary dimensions of pitch and rhythm. In this respect of course, *Eclat* is continuing and extending a strong tendency in twentieth-century music.

The level of formal organization at which chance intervenes is clearly of great importance as may be seen by comparing Exs. 2 and 4. In Ex.

4, taken from the closing pages of *Don* (the aleatoric organization of which is shown in Ex. 1), the music possesses a clear, almost traditional melodic construction (the influence of Messiaen is perhaps discernible here), easily perceptible though irregular pulsation, and regularity of dynamic intensity. All these features ensure that, in contrast with Ex. 2, the music possesses perceptible shape and form.

Aleatoricism therefore is most significant when employed at the lowest level of organization since it implies the ousting of all techniques of organization comparable however remotely with traditional practice. Introduced at a higher level however *(i.e.,* in the relationship of completely composed sections which may vary in length from a few seconds duration to a complete movement[7]), aleatoricism has no necessary implications for the general character of the musical material.

In both cases discussed above chance intervenes in the horizontal aspect of form, but it may also occur in the vertical relationship of structures whereby two or more superimposed layers may evolve more or less independently of one another. Several instances may be found in *Don;* for example, see figure 11 where the third harp is directed to play independently of the conductor and the other instrumentalists. In a situation like this the effect of chance relationships on the character of the music *(i.e.,* the degree of organization which is actually perceptible) will depend on factors peculiar to each case: the character of each layer considered separately, and the density of the resulting texture; the greater the density of texture the more difficult it will be to hear through, and thus the less organization perceptible to the listener.

[7]See Boulez, third piano Sonata where chance sometimes intervenes on both levels of organization simultaneously.

At first sight it would appear difficult to reconcile Boulez' use of chance in *Eclat* with his demand that the composer must be entirely responsible for the resulting form—even though in this piece the music never reaches the degree of indeterminacy sometimes found in the music of Cage and others where the notation often provides no more than the vaguest indication to the performer. However, if we examine the form of *Eclat* as a whole, the real significance of this use of chance becomes clearer. The long section of aleatory writing from which Ex. 2 was taken, is flanked by sections markedly contrasting in character in that they are highly organized, giving the work therefore a tripartite form. We have space only for a description of the most important features.

A. Piano Solo (Score, pp.1-4). A perceptible structure is ensured by intervallic relationships springing from the harmonies of the opening phrase: dissonant semitonal chord clusters are contrasted with more consonant intervallic groupings (whole tones and thirds). We find in addition an interrelationship between certain dimensions: *accelerando* and *ritenuto* are respectively combined with *crescendo* and *diminuendo* (Ex. 5). Note also in this passage the progressive widening of intervals

Ex. 5

from the whole tone to the major ninth, and the motivic development, both these factors contributing to the high degree of organization. Despite the rhythmically free, almost improvisatory character of the rather Debussyan piano writing, the music's character is remote from the indeterminate writing discussed earlier; the sequence of events impresses the listener as being necessary and inevitable.

B. A brief extract from the long middle section has already been discussed (Ex. 2). Its general character, as we saw, is one of amorphousness caused by the frequent intervention of chance in the constitution of the musical material itself. The musical material is of considerable variety (trills, brief arabesques and single notes or chords). Such contrasts enable the composer to create a broad ternary shape within this section as a whole. Some motives are also occasionally reminiscent of the introductory piano solo. Nevertheless, the overall character is one of discontinuity and unpredictability. There is little or no continuous logic in the course of events.

C. (Score, pp. 23-26). The final section falls easily into two paragraphs separated by a brief and violent interjection reminiscent of the material of B. Whereas in section A intervallic and motivic organization ensured a feeling of logical progression, in C it is the presence of rhythmic pulsation (regular in C_1, irregular in C_2), contrasting with the arhythmic character of B, which is chiefly responsible for the feeling of coherence. The more uniform level of dynamic intensity also adds to this effect.

In his article *Alea*,[4] Boulez explains the significance of such contrasts between highly organized "directed" structures, and episodes where chance plays an important part in the very constitution of the material:

> Si nous voulons intégrer le hasard à la notion de structure elle-même dans un ensemble orienté, alors nous devons faire appel à des différenciations plus subtiles et introduire des notions comme celle de structure définie ou indéfinie, structure amorphe ou directionelle, structure divergente ou convergente. Il est indéniable que ce développement de la chance dans la composition créera un univers nettement plus différencié qu'auparavant et marquera un développement plus aigu d'une perception renouvellé de la forme. Dans un ensemble dirigé, ces divers structures doivent être obligatoirement controlées par un 'phrasé' général, comporter nécessairement un sigle initial et un signe final. . . .

There exist, then, two basic types of writing, the one highly organized ("structure définie, directionelle") depending on such procedures as rhythmic pulsation, motivic, harmonic or intervallic relationships, the other with little or no perceptible organization ("structure indéfinie, amorphe")—athematic and arhythmic. Their opposition provides a means of creating contrast necessary for the perceptible articulation of form. At the same time, the boundary between these two types of writing is not precisely defined and one can envisage a continuum from one extreme to the other permitting much greater subtlety than might at first be apparent. This may be seen particularly in *Don*, whereas in *Eclat* the contrasts are much more clear-cut.

It would be a mistake to think of the tripartite closed form of *Eclat* as a new standard form—the long awaited replacement of sonata form[8]—but there is no doubt that in this short piece Boulez has achieved a comparable kind of formal articulation in that the internal character of a particular section, its movement, defines the function of that section in the form as a whole. In Sonata form, for example, the contrast of the middle-section or development, is achieved to a considerable degree by means of a more unstable tonal organization (harmonic movement from dominant to dominant), compared with the strongly established tonal centres of exposition and recapitulation. In *Eclat* the improvisatory piano solo possesses unmistakably the character of an introduction and

[8]Contrast, for instance, the open forms of the third piano Sonata.

the more rhythmic final section rounds the work off with a feeling of inevitability that is very traditional, variety and contrast being provided by the middle-section with its unpredictable yet basically static textures. *Eclat* seems to be the musical example for the following description of a formal plan given in *Alea:*

> Partant d'un sigle initial, principiel, aboutissant à un signe exhaustif, conclusif, la composition arrive à mettre en jeu ce que nous recherchions au départ de notre démarche: un 'parcours' problématique, fonction du temps—un certain nombre d'événements aléatoires inscrits dans une durée mobile—ayant toutefois une logique de développement, un sens global dirigé—des césures pouvant s'y intercaler, césures de silences ou plateformes sonores—parcours allant d'un commencement à une fin. Nous avons respecté le 'fine' de l'oeuvre occidentale, son cycle fermé, mais nous avons introduit la 'chance' de l'oeuvre orientale, son déroulement ouvert.

Having established that the use of chance is most significant when used at the lowest level of organization, other questions impose themselves. What is the function of chance employed at the higher level of organization when the musical material itself is not affected and may well be highly organized in character? (Ex. 4). Is the difference between various realizations really significant? No doubt in the closing antiphonal passage of *Don* a listener would probably be aware at least of differences between various performances; but for all that such differences would hardly amount to a radically new experience of the work: one would simply hear a different arrangement of the antiphony. For that matter the same question may be asked concerning the aleatory music in *Eclat* with even more justice, for here, changes from one performance to another would hardly be noticeable. It could be argued that the use of chance in this piece is a symptom of disorder rather than a cause. This in fact is borne out by the historical development, for the amorphous writing of *Eclat* is already realized, in essentials, in the same composer's earlier *Structures I* (1952), where, of course, aleatoricism as such plays no part (Ex. 6). Here we find the same negative technical features: athematicism, absence of rhythmic pulsation (even though the music is notated metrically the pulse is imperceptible), and it was in totally serialized works like *Structures* that the independence of the dimensions was first theoretically established as a principle of composition. In *Structures* therefore, as in the overtly aleatoric passages of *Eclat*, the music's evolution is not felt in the listener's experience to pursue a logical and inevitable course. In both cases there is nothing to replace the logic of tonal harmonic progression and cadential functions. Because there are no *decisive* events, because what happens at a particular point in the music's evolution has no effect on what comes later (or is heard to be the result of what has happened earlier), the music's pro-

gress is felt literally to be a matter of chance. This identity between the seemingly opposed ideas of strict, total serialization and aleatoricism has since been recognized by the composer:

> Au moment où toutes les organisations sont synchronisées je n'ai aucune liberté de choix, je peux choisir une des possibilités offertes, ou ne pas choisir du tout et les laisser comme *devant être choisies:* je retrouve la probabilité mais elle régit les structures de l'extérieur. Constations que rigueur et automatisme dans la rencontre des structures aboutissent au même résultat esthétique que liberté et choix. Cela nous conduit dir-ectement à l'emploi des formes polyvalentes et à l'intervention de la pro-babilité.[9]

In *Structures I* and in similar works written by other composers at about the same time[10] amorphous textures are not used as an ele-ment of contrast in an effort to articulate form as in *Eclat*. As Ligeti has shown,[11] the primitive sectional form of *Structures Ia* is articulated by the purely external features of polyphonic density and dynamics rather than by the internal characteristics of the music as in *Eclat*.

In a sense, therefore, aleatoricism is the logical outcome of an ear-lier tendency (found in works like *Structures),* to avoid all traditional symmetry and continuity. At the same time this use of chance, giving the performer a choice in the realization of the music, has little or no significance for the listener. Just because such passages are formless in

[9]P. Boulez, *Penser la Musique Aujourd'hui,* p. 123.
[10]E.g., Nono's *Incontri,* 1955, Messiaen's *Mode de Valeurs....*
[11]G. Ligeti, "Decision and Automatism in Structure Ia," *Die Reihe,* no. 4.

their very nature, changes from one performance to another have no significance, even when perceptible. While it seems likely that in future composers will continue to make use of varying degrees of perceptible organization as a means of formal articulation, comparable with Boulez' methods in *Eclat*, it is doubtful if the performer will be presented with a choice in the realization of these amorphous "structures." This development can indeed already be seen in a work like Gilbert Amy's *Triade*,[12] so called because of the distribution of the orchestra into three groups. A detailed analysis of this work would have to begin by taking account of the two contrasted types of writing (directed and amorphous) which are presented in alternation—Amy avoids the closed tripartite form of *Eclat*. Other subtleties of formal organization (the function of timbre and the relationship between sections), would then be considered on this basis. Amy creates the necessary contrasts primarily by rhythmic means, rather than by relying as well on the presence or absence of motivic and intervallic organization. In the case of the amorphous textures, which are very similar in style, in the character of the material and the timbres used, to those of *Eclat*, the composer does not allow the conductor any freedom of choice in the ordering of events. These sections are marked *senza tempo*, and the notation is like that used by Boulez, the conductor being asked simply to give an indication ("signe") to the players; the composer warns: "Les durées comprises entre deux signes ne sont nullement isochrones." Any suggestion of metrical rhythm therefore is to be avoided, and as in *Eclat* the listener's chief impression is one of discontinuity and unpredictability. The passages notated metrically are in fact distinguished by their more continuous rhythmic activity rather than by a clear sense of pulsation as such. More homogeneous in character they are also frequently individually characterized by timbre: predominantly high strings, arco or pizzicato. Nevertheless, the impression of two contrasted types of writing is maintained quite unambiguously and Boulez' terminology, directed as opposed to amorphous writing, is highly appropriate to describe the formal contrasts of the music.

We have so far considered Boulez' development from *Structures I* (the title of which we now see is somewhat less than appropriate), as far as *Eclat*, without mentioning this composer's most famous work. *Le Marteau sans Maître* was written immediately after *Structures* and even a cursory examination of the score reveals that this is a transitional work. The writing reveals much greater definition and contrast than *Structures* (a clear sense of rhythmic pulsation is often established), but the composer never employs the fundamental contrasts found in *Eclat*. When compared with the subtlety and vagueness of formal relationships in an instrumental movement like *Commentaire III de Bourreaux de*

---

[12]G. Amy, *Triade*, Heugel, Paris, 1967.

Solitude, Boulez' later works reveal a considerable simplification leading to greater clarity of form.

However, the method of analysis outlined above, based on discovering contrasted types of writing, is often appropriate to works written before *Structures I*, though the principle is never exploited in the interests of formal articulation as fully as in *Eclat*. Examples 7 *(a)* and *(b)* are both taken from the last movement of Boulez' piano Sonata no. 1. In

Ex. 7(a)

Ex. 7 *(a)* continual quaver movement ensures at least a basic rhythmic coherence (despite constant assymmetry in the combination of motives), and there are also obvious, perceptible motivic relationships. In Ex. 7 *(b)*, however, the rhythmic organization and wide-ranging "voices" clearly foreshadow the amorphous textures of *Structures*.

Ex. 7(b)

This method of analysis could also be extended occasionally to other works of this period. One example from the cantata *Le Soleil des Eaux*, settings of Boulez' favourite poet René Char, is especially worth considering in these terms. In the first movement, the soprano's monody is continually interrupted by short orchestral interludes, inspired by the text which has just been sung; the interlude beginning at figure 6 (miniature score), comments on the words, "Les herbes des champs qui se plissent." This evocation of the grass of the meadows is frequent in Char's poetry. "A la fois appui et abri l'herbe est substance mère dont la densité aérienne sait recouvrir — campagnol, taupe, orvet, grillon — tout

400

un peuple naif et désarmé.''[13] This quality of *densité aérienne* is admirably conveyed in the orchestral interlude by the creation of what we may term a sound-mass: the density of texture is such that individual motives, though apparent from a study of the score, are in practice inaudible and any sense of rhythmic pulsation, or indeed any feeling of organization as such, is obscured, resulting thereby in the same kind of amorphous effect described earlier.

The employment of such dense textures has in fact become a characteristic sound of much new music; countless examples spring to mind: Stravinsky's *Huxley Variations,* Ligeti's *Atmosphères,* Messiaen's *Chronochromie.* This technique may be employed largely for its poetic effect as in Ligeti's *Atmosphères,* and in the Boulez example discussed above, or with more subtlety, as another means of articulating form, comparable with Boulez' methods in *Eclat.*

In *Eclat* as we saw, strong contrasts were obtained, depending on the degree of organization perceptible in the music. Also, there existed the possibility of continual movement from one extreme to the other. The sound-mass is another way of achieving the same results: at one extreme the amorphous effect created by a dense superimposition of motives where musical sound becomes virtually noise and where, since the details of the music are inaudible as such, the actual superimposition of events could virtually be left to chance as far as the listener is concerned; at the other extreme, transparent textures where every pitch and rhythm can be heard individually. The same contrast between what Boulez termed "directed," and non-directed or amorphous writing, is obtained. As we suggested earlier, what is important is that formal contrasts should be based not merely on superficial external form-articulating dimensions such as timbre, dynamics and tempo, but on the internal character of the writing; it is a contrast which is best described in terms of *movement,* amorphous writing giving a static effect, especially when created by density (or a sense of unpredictability and discontinuity also leading to stasis as in *Eclat* where everything can be heard), directed writing suggesting, conversely, a strong sense of movement comparable with harmonic and rhythmic movement in tonal music. Such unequivocal contrasts of movement are one of the most significant developments in new music and permit us to suggest that there has come into existence a new *language* of music which will enable composers to create significant form comparable in that respect with the symphonic structures of the past.

In this article we have space only to indicate in general terms how fruitful such a method of analysis would be.

Considering Stockhausen's career as a whole, one cannot help no-

[13]Jean-Pierre Richard, René Char in *Onze Etudes sur la Poésie Moderne,* Paris, 1964.

ticing an evolution similar in some respects to that of Boulez in that successive instrumental works which appear to be strictly comparable in their aims *(Kontrapunkte, Zeitmasse* and *Gruppen)* reveal progressively greater and greater clarity and variety in the means of articulating form.

In *Zeitmasse,* as in *Eclat,* the employment of chance is an important factor in creating stronger, more perceptible contrasts of movement than exist, for example, in the earlier *Kontrapunkte.* Chance intervenes, however, not in the horizontal succession of events—their precise rhythmic duration and sequence—as in *Eclat,* but in the vertical dimension. Variable tempi are superimposed: one player, for instance, being directed to play strictly in tempo while another may be asked to play as fast or as slow as possible; furthermore, these possibilities may be combined with *accelerando* and *ritenuto.* As Ligeti has pointed out however,[14] these contrasting tempi effectively cancel one another out, especially when all five instruments are playing together. The absence of clear pulsation in any individual part and the frequently elaborate character of the writing also contribute to this, and the result is an amorphous texture where the listener can hardly perceive any clear organization due to the very complexity of the relationships. Such textures are contrasted with passages where all instruments are co-ordinated in tempo, even to the extent, at times, of playing in rhythmic unison (see after bar 137). The section beginning at bar 105 is a good example of this directed writing where a sense of pulsation, albeit highly irregular, can often be felt, giving way in bar 154 to an amorphous texture of the type described above.

The form of *Zeitmasse,* considered in these terms is far from relying simply on block contrasts between clearly opposed types of texture and movement. Stockhausen makes use of considerable variety in between the two extremes (amorphous textures on the one hand, passages in rhythmic unison on the other). For example, the free writing beginning at bar 154 never reaches the degree of amorphousness found after bar 29. Such contrasts of movement are, of course, not the only means of articulating form in this work,[15] but without doubt such methods of creating contrast in the *internal* character of the writing enable the composer to achieve considerable sophistication of form.

Although works like *Zeitmasse* or *Gruppen* show many quite new features of formal organization, above all, of course, in the nature of the

---

[14]"As a result of the high degree of permeability, the various sequences of events tend to melt into one another, and their original variety is resolved into a high unity; the various different interfering tempi become simply relationships of density, and the virtual space that is the result mercilessly gobbles up any individual "time-measures." "Metamorphoses of Musical Form" by György Ligeti in *Die Reihe,* no. 7.

[15]G. Marcus, "Stockhausen's *Zeitmasse,*" *Music Review,* May, 1968.

musical material itself, the large-scale aspect of form is not always as remote from traditional practice as might be thought. The well-rounded, closed form of *Eclat*, as we saw, evoked traditional ternary form, and more important, the basis of tonally organized form, where the harmonic and rhythmic character of a particular section defines its place in the form as a whole. Something of this traditional approach to form is also found in *Zeitmasse*. A particularly clear instance is the unique passage, beginning at bar 337 where the music possesses for a time easily perceptible regularity of pulsation. As in the final section of *Eclat* the composer's aim seems to be to create (in relation to what has gone before), a sense of repose, thus heralding the approaching conclusion of the work: a procedure quite comparable with the pedal points and regularity of rhythm and phraseology used for the same purpose in tonal music.

In *Gruppen*, too, the overall form (especially the placing of the main climax, score, p. 108, and its careful preparation) is strongly reminiscent of traditional practice in that on repeated hearings it acquires a feeling of inevitability. Relative density of texture plays an important part in articulating the form, particularly at the climax. The main climax is preceded by a lesser, preparatory climax (the echoing brass crescendi, fig. 119), and the leading-up in both cases is achieved, through a combination of accelerando and crescendo, by means of very transparent textures, chiefly trumpets and trombones with piano after fig. 118, chiefly percussion after fig. 121. The music in both cases has a strongly directed onward-moving character created by the clearly perceptible pulse-rhythms as well as tempo and dynamics. The main climax is contrasted with this preparation by its extremely dense and amorphous textures where musical sound borders on noise. Here, too, then, the internal character of the music defines its function in the form, and the climax is a fitting culmination and release of the tension and energy "contained" in the preparation.

The works of Stockhausen considered above share an almost traditional concern with the inevitability of the formal process. Chance plays a very restricted role in *Zeitmasse;* as in *Eclat* chaos is only apparent and, paradoxically, becomes a means of creating greater formal coherence. In *Gruppen* chance as such plays no part at all except in so far as it is *virtually* present in the amorphous sound-masses which are such a feature of the work.

In more recent works, however, Stockhausen would appear to have renounced such a concern with form in this sense. This is apparent especially in his conception of "moment form," where concern with the overall formal shape is sacrificed to the momentary and instantaneous musical event. In the short piece *Refrain*, for piano, celesta and vibraphone (each instrumentalist also playing percussion instruments), Stockhausen apparently makes no attempt to create a significant form comparable with *Zeitmasse* and *Gruppen,* and the music is therefore closer to the essentially decorative style of composers like Cage and Feldman with their emphasis on sound for its own sake to the exclusion of all else. Chance as such plays only a limited part in *Refrain.* Music is notated on a plastic strip which may be placed in various positions over the printed score; as the composer writes, "the trills, short melismas, bass notes and glissandi/clusters written on the strip occur six times as a refrain and 'disturb' the context." To that extent there is a clearly perceptible form suggested by the title. One could however make the same criticism as of other aleatoric works. Since the refrains may interrupt the amorphous textures of the music at a number of points, they can have no real significance in relation to the context which they disturb. Why not simply write the refrains permanently into the score, since there is no essential difference between any one realization and any other? In this piece Stockhausen has abandoned all the means of articulating significant form found in earlier works: the contrast between the refrains and the context they "disturb" is of a different order and on a much more superficial level. Above all, the absence of perceptible pulsation throughout makes it impossible to create the strong contrasts in the internal character of the writing necessary for the creation of significant form. It is true that there is considerable variety in the musical material, and the work is full of delicate and imaginative sounds, but essentially *Refrain* is a regression when considered in the same terms as works like *Zeitmasse* and *Gruppen.*

The evolution of Messiaen's music since the war may also be considered in similar terms. The famous *Mode de Valeurs et d'Intensités* antedates *Structures* by about three years, and was one of the first works in which the principle of total serialization was realized. Although there are differences in procedure, a common impression of formlessness is created in both works, and their historical significance is likely to be immeasurably greater than their purely musical importance. In later works Messiaen has tended to rely on rather primitive formal principles, chiefly the mosaic-like juxtaposition of self-enclosed sections. A typical example illustrating both the limitations and virtues of this composer's music is the piano piece *Canteyodjaya* (1953). Here we find occasional contrasts between amorphous textures, similar to those of the *Mode de Valeurs et d'Intensités,* and strongly rhythmic passages deriving ultimately from *Le Sacre.* The rondo-like repetition of the opening idea and the occasional use of refrains is an attempt to give a degree of coherence to the overall form, but in reality a patchwork effect is the chief impression: one feels that the actual ordering of these self-enclosed sections is basically a matter of indifference since Messiaen makes no attempt to compose transitions or to articulate individual sections according to their function in the form as a whole. As a result, the course of the music lacks any feeling of inevitability. Thus *Canteyodjaya* anticipates the later use of aleatoricism on both levels of organization: its amorphous textures, like those of *Structures,* being a forerunner of the aleatory techniques used in *Eclat,* its virtual use of chance in the relationship of individual sections anticipating Boulez' methods in the closing pages of *Don.*

The evolution of musical techniques and styles does not proceed with logical regularity, and coincidence between all aspects of structure. The musical language will often for some time be, so to speak, pregnant with later transformations and it is important to differentiate between a new development which is still at an incubatory stage, and the same feature used as a principle in its own right.[16] This explains the difference between, say, Boulez' purely descriptive use of the sound-mass in *Le Soleil des Eaux* and Stockhausen's more functional use of the same technique in *Gruppen;* or between Messiaen's primitive opposition of contrasting types of writing in *Canteyodjaya* and Boulez' more highly developed awareness of the possibilities in a work like *Eclat.*

The historical period we have so far considered has been from about 1950 down to the present, but the possibilities which we have seen gradually clarified during this period can in fact be traced back a good deal further into the past. Do we not find a similar opposition between highly organized, directed writing and more amorphous textures in the slow movement of Bartok's third piano Concerto? In fact, all Bartok's examples of *Night Music* constitute a remarkable anticipation of later developments, with their emphasis on sound for its own sake, and an acute awareness of timbre, even though, of course, the freedom of organization of the later music which permitted the introduction of chance into the very constitution of the musical material is still far from being fully realized. Similar contrasts may also be found in Berg's *Lyric Suite.* H. F. Redlich writes of the *tenebroso* sections in the fifth movement as follows: "The *flautando* harmonies of these episodes, drawn like an inverted pedal point through the obscurities of their *amorphous* musical landscape, are among Berg's boldest experiments in rarefied sonorities"[17] (my italics). Schönberg's Five Orchestral Pieces, *op.* 16, show similar features, notably in the relationship of *Farben* to the other four pieces.

There is, however, a more important anticipation of the later developments which we must take note of. The first fifteen years of this century, as is now well recognized, saw a marked tendency to abandon tra-

[16]This may appear to lend support to the views of those who claim to discover serial technique in Mozart—an embryonic foreshadowing of later events. Mozart's language however is not transitional but a language in a state of maturity and equilibrium, and there would seem to be no need to discover procedures which are analytically redundant even though their existence cannot of course be disproved.

[17]H. F. Redlich, *Alban Berg,* London.

ditional forms of organization: principally functional tonality, but as Webern in particular saw, this in turn logically entailed the abandonment of related forms of organization (i.e., in instrumentation, rhythm and form). Before new forms of organization were discovered, tonal organization had been largely abandoned, and the result of this hiatus may be seen above all in the instrumental miniatures written by Schönberg, Berg and Webern. Webern's evolution down to the Cello Pieces, op. 11, is evidence of great singlemindedness of purpose in the gradual but inexorable discarding of tonal organization. This may be seen if a comparison is made between the two sets of Orchestral Pieces, op. 6 and op. 10. In op. 6 essentially tonal thematic organization is still only in the process of being dissolved; in op. 10 the process is almost complete. A consideration of the general character of Webern's instrumental miniatures (op. 9, 10 and 11) reveals in fact a remarkable anticipation of the position later reached in works like Structures I. Parts which continually cross (which can, therefore, no longer be regarded as "voices") continue a process initiated in the wide-ranging melodies of Wagner and Strauss and completed forty years later in the polyphonic web of Structures. Similarly, the idea of a principal part(s) with accompanying texture which depends on functional tonal relationships or at least the preservation of typical quasi-tonal figuration, is largely abandoned. More important, the music proceeds with an absence of motive relationships which cannot be described as "continual variation" since nothing remains the same. There is also a marked tendency to obscure the sense of pulsation by means of irregular division of the pulse, ties over the bar-line, and frequent fluctuations of tempo. Pulsation is far more difficult to hear than appears to be the case from reading the score. All these features imply a radically new conception of the musical material which can only be fully understood by reference to the later concept of athematic groups. It must be admitted that despite Webern's mastery in handling such difficult material, the separate formal elements or groups, are often felt to be interchangeable. To all intents and purposes, therefore, the music is practically aleatory even though, of course, the composer has finalized the ordering of events. The brevity of these pieces is witness to Webern's awareness of the problems posed by his new "language"; the means of contrast, of significant articulation of form (in Boulez' terms, the evolution from a "sigle initial" to a "signe exhaustif") are practically nonexistent. The absence of continuous, unambiguous pulsation and of motivic or harmonic relationships makes it very difficult for the composer to create a form which in retrospect the listener can feel has followed a necessary course. The music at any given point has no implications for its later development and no relationship to what has gone before. For the same reasons it is difficult for the music to carry any meaningful structural significance at a particular stage in its evolution.

Subsequent works reveal Webern's various attempts to escape from what he evidently regarded as a *cul-de-sac*. In the Songs, *op.* 12 (1915-17), he retreats from the extreme position reached in *op.* 11 (1914), and appears to be adopting a solution common to many twentieth-century composers: the conscious revival of earlier forms and styles. The Songs, *op.* 12, with their clear melodic shaping and tonal phraseology revive the German *lied* tradition. Subsequent vocal works reveal Webern's attempts to find an original solution to the problem of formal articulation through the employment of canon and serial technique. But it is only in later instrumental works such as the Saxophone Quartet, *op.* 22, and the Concerto, *op.* 24 (1934), that Webern realized a unique application of Schönberg's method enabling him to create audibly significant forms without at the same time relying directly on traditional procedures as Schönberg did. The Concerto, *op.* 24, is probably the most analysed of all twentieth-century compositions. Its first movement especially reveals with great clarity Webern's considerable achievement in avoiding any suggestion of formal indeterminacy. Different areas of the composition are articulated by a serial motivic organization which is clearly perceptible, and the function of each section is defined according to its position in the form as a whole. A comparison may be made with sonata form, though Webern makes no literal use of traditional tonal procedures. Thus the middle-section or development — which may be subdivided into a lyrical passage for violin, clarinet and piano, and a more violent "tutti" section — is characterized by a more varied serial organization compared with the limitations of exposition and recapitulation where only 3-note motives are used. The initial exposition of the row and the coda-like summing up of the closing bars are likewise unambiguously characterized.

The significance of Webern's solution has not been altogether lost on later composers even though there has been a marked tendency to revert to more athematic writing; this is true, for instance, of the music of Stockhausen and Berio. There are, however, instances, particularly in the music of Boulez (piano Sonatas 1 and 2, Flute Sonatina) where a type of motivic organization similar to Webern's is to be found. The actual serial derivation is not always easy to show in these later works, but in any case, what counts is the perceptible result of serial processes and not the processes themselves.

The development we noted in Webern's music from an atonal language, still largely traditional in structure, to the indeterminate pieces, is also found in the music of Schönberg and, to some extent, of Berg. It is in their music, written in the language of free atonality rather than in the 12-note technique, that this tendency to indeterminacy occurs. However, generally speaking, neither composer reaches the extreme position found in Webern's short instrumental pieces. This emerges clearly if we compare Schönberg's most celebrated essay in miniaturization, the Six Little Piano Pieces, *op.* 19, with Webern's *op.* 11 — both sets dating from 1914. In the former we still find traditional methods of thematic construction, though on a very small scale, rather than a specifically new conception of the musical material. Schönberg's traditionalism is further borne out by the part-writing and easily perceptible pulse rhythms. Only the enigmatic final piece employs a technique comparable with Webern's method of assembling musical events, as opposed to traditional motivic-thematic writing which Schönberg is usually reluctant to abandon altogether. Nevertheless, the ordering of the musical ideas—thematic or athematic—is often still felt to be a matter of indifference, due to the lack of tonal organization which would provide a thread of continuous logic. Berg's Clarinet Pieces, *op.* 5 (1917), are comparable in this respect with Schönberg's Little Piano Pieces.

In many ways, Schönberg's earlier set of three Orchestral Pieces (1910)[18] represents his most extreme position. The second piece in particular, with its more thorough-going athematicism and greater rhythmic flexibility comes close to the style of Webern's Orchestral Pieces, *op.* 10. In the published works of this period one can only point to isolated examples where, due to athematicism and rhythmic ambiguity, there are strong suggestions of formal indeterminacy.

There is one fact especially worth noting. All these earlier composers, after having approached to the brink of formal indeterminacy later withdrew into some form of reconciliation with the past. This is even noticeable momentarily in Webern's development as we saw, though he was the only composer who went on to discover and exploit radically new means of organization.

In this respect, of course, one thinks immediately of Stravinsky. There is no need to stress his withdrawal into neo-classicism after the violent eruption of revolutionary techniques in works like *Le Sacre*. *Le Sacre* is interesting however not only on account of its rhythmic innovations but also in respect of its form.

The musical language of *Le Sacre* is still tonal and to that extent may appear to be the very opposite of the atonal language of the Viennese. Structurally, however, the modal, pentatonic and whole-tone tonality is remote from major-minor tonality. The precise functions of the latter are considerable eroded in *Le Sacre* where the very idea of harmonic progression is largely negated. Tonal identity of a very general kind persists, but even the tonic function is often either missing or seriously weakened.[19] One could even say that the harmonic language of *Le Sacre* is less traditional than that of the Viennese where, despite

[18]Unpublished and the last piece unfinished. A facsimile of the MS. is reproduced in Rufer's Schönberg Catalogue.

[19]The frequent absence of a tonic in folk-music is now generally accepted; see Constantin Brailou's essay "Sur une melodie russe" in *Musique Russe II*, Paris, 1954.

atonality, a suggestion of tonal harmonic progression is often maintained. T. W. Adorno has made the penetrating remark that Stravinsky's method of extending his melodies by a kind of circular development, or permutation of a limited store of notes within a static harmonic field, seems to give the effect of resulting merely from "a throw of the dice." Still, this is hardly comparable with the later employment of aleatoricism. On the other hand, the undermining of tonal functions often leads to indeterminacy of structure at higher levels of formal organization. This is particularly noticeable where Stravinsky uses strongly contrasting ideas (as in *Jeux des Cités Rivales*, figures 57 to 61). The result is a mosaic-like structure, also found in other works of this period, where the different pieces of the pattern are to some extent, interchangeable. (If Stravinsky had left the MS. of *Le Sacre* in the same state as Bartok left his Viola Concerto, it is doubtful, in movements like this, whether anyone could guarantee a correct assembly of the jig-saw.) Also, the uniformly static harmonies and, in some movements, the constant irregularity of rhythm, effectively prevent the functional articulation of form.

Occasionally in *Le Sacre* we also find that the vertical co-ordination of separate layers is felt to be a matter of chance. This is particularly noticeable at fig. 86 where several layers of static harmonies, pedals and *ostinati* evolve quite independently of one another. Here the absence of perceptible organization is quite comparable with its effect in later works, and the amorphous character of this passage is all the more noticeable because the flanking sections, beginning respectively at figs. 79 and 89, are more traditionally shaped and therefore strongly directed in character. Another radically new technique found here and there in *Le Sacre* is the accumulation of in themselves insignificant motivic particles into a dense texture or sound-mass. At the climax of the opening movement this technique is so highly developed as to be directly comparable with later examples[20] already discussed, where the very density of texture prevents the listener from perceiving any significant organization.

In covering a wide historical perspective we have necessarily had to restrict ourselves to giving brief analytical comments, rather than analysis in depth. Nevertheless, it should have emerged that aleatoricism is no mere abberration on the part of a handful of composers who have deliberately cut themselves off from tradition. The preoccupation with chance on the part of composers like Stockhausen and particularly Boulez, pinpoints the chief problem faced by composers of the so-called post-Webern school: with the abandonment of tonality, of all pre-existing language, how is the composer to achieve the meaningful articulation of form? Even if, as we have suggested, the literal use of chance turns out to be only a temporary phenomenon, at least it will have enabled these

[20]Compare with *Gruppen*.

composers to conceptualize their problem in the clearest possible way. In retrospect, as we can see, it has been a problem faced by many twentieth-century composers who have attempted a radical renewal of the musical language.

Bibliography

Many significant articles on aleatory music have appeared and will no doubt continue to appear in *Perspectives of New Music, The Score,* and *Die Reihe.* See especially Pierre Boulez, "Alea," *Perspectives,* 3 (Fall-Winter, 1964); and Roger Reynolds, "Indeterminacy: Some Considerations," *Perspectives,* 4 (Fall-Winter, 1965). An interesting thesis is proposed by Robert Charles Clark in "Total Control and Chance in Musics: a Philosophical Analysis," *Journal of Aesthetics and Art Criticism,* 28, no. 3 (Spring, 1970), which, after considering some differences between Cage and Stockhausen, concludes that total control and chance music both end in the same result.

One of the most active composers of aleatory music is John Cage. His aleatory works should be studied as well as those of such other composers as Morton Feldman, Yannis Xenakis, Karlheinz Stockhausen, Earle Brown, Luciano Berio, Silvano Bussotti, Henri Pousseur, Mauricio Kagel, and Cornelius Cardew. Representative works of many of these composers are published by Universal Edition; the works of Cage and Feldman are published by C. F. Peters; Xenakis' music is published by Boosey & Hawkes; and Brown's works are published by Associated Music Publishers. *Source,* a semi-annual, presents a wide variety of scores of the latest aleatory music as well as pertinent writings about it.

31

THE four previous selections have each dealt with one of three major approaches to contemporary music: serialism, electronic music, and aleatoricism. There is, however, at least one more approach to modern music, one which is completely original and independent from the three already mentioned. This fourth approach is presently without a label, and since this may be one of its many virtues, albeit a minor one, I shall not disturb this delightful state by assigning it a pigeonhole. This fourth style is characterized by originality; problems which arise are given logical, musical, and often unique resolutions. There is much counterpoint, both melodic and rhythmic, and the whole is often characterized by what has been described as "simultaneous contrasting levels of musical activity." Early manifestations may be found in the music of Charles Ives; the most outstanding modern exponent is Elliott Carter. In refining some of the techniques of Ives and developing some of his own, all the while retaining his own individuality, Carter has written music that has won great praise among professional musicians, although recognition by the musical public has not been so rapid, perhaps because of the demands Carter makes on the listener. In the following selection the composer speaks for himself in explaining some of the aspects of his style.

Elliott Cook Carter is one of America's most outstanding modern composers. Among his most significant works are his *String Quartet No. 1* (1951), *Variations for Orchestra* (1955), *Double Concerto for Harpsichord and Piano* (1961), *Piano Concerto* (1965), and *Concerto for Orchestra* (1970). His teaching career has included appointments at Yale, Columbia, M.I.T., and the Juilliard School. In addition to composing and teaching he has written a number of articles on contemporary music.

Shop Talk by an American Composer

ELLIOTT CARTER

When I agreed to discuss the rhythmic procedures I use in my music, I had forgotten, for the moment, the serious doubts I have about just such kinds of discussion when carried on by the composer himself. That a composer can write music that is thought to be of some interest is, of course, no guarantee that he can talk illuminatingly about it. It is especially hard for him to be articulate because inevitably his compositions are the result of innumerable choices — many unconscious, many conscious, some quickly made, others after long deliberation, all mostly forgotten when they have served their purpose. At some time or other, this sorting and combining of notes finally becomes a composition. By that time many of its conceptions and techniques have become almost a matter of habit for the composer and he is only dimly aware of the choices that first caused him to adopt them. Finally, in an effort to judge the work as an entity, as another might listen to it, he tries to forget his intentions and listen with fresh ears. What he is aiming at, after all, is a whole in which all the technical workings are interdependent and combine to produce the kind of artistic experience that gives a work its validity and in so doing makes all its procedures relevant. There is no short-cut to achieving this final artistic relevance. No technique is of much intrinsic value; its importance for the composer and his listeners lies only in the particular use made of it to further the artistic qualities and character of an actual work. If in discussing his works, therefore, he points out a procedure, he is bound to feel that he is drawing attention to something of secondary importance and by dwelling on it misleading others into thinking of it as primary. Schoenberg expressed such doubts in essays on his use of the twelve-tone method. And he was right, for certainly the twelve-tone aspect of his works accounts for only a part of their interest, perhaps not the most impor-

FROM *The Musical Quarterly*, 46 (1960), 189-201. Reprinted by permission.

tant part. For from Opus 25 to his last works the number of different kinds of compositions he wrote illustrates the very broad range of expression and conception and the wide variety of musical techniques that can incorporate the system and yet be distinguished from it.

In any discussion of specifically contemporary procedures, there are a few serious risks involved that must be constantly borne in mind. The first is the danger of rapid and wide dissemination of oversimplified formulas that shortens their life. It is obvious that one technical fad after another has swept over 20th-century music as the music of each of its leading composers has come to be intimately known. Each fad lasted a few years, only to be discarded by the succeeding generation of composers, then by the music profession, and finally by certain parts of the interested public. So that through over-use many of the striking features of the best works lost freshness, it was hard for those close to music to listen to these works for a time, and many of the better works disappeared from the repertory without a trace. Such a formula as the Impressionists' parallel ninth chords, for instance, wore itself out in the tedious arrangements of popular music current until recently. Each of the trends of our recent past—primitivism, machinism, neo-Classicism, *Gebrauchsmusik,* the styles of Bartók and Berg and now those of Schoenberg and Webern—has left and will leave in its trail numbers of really gifted composers whose music, skillful and effective as it is, is suffocated, at least for a time, by its similarity to other music of the same type. Of course, ultimately this faddishness is trivial, but its mercurial changes today have made the life of many a composer a great trial, more even than in the time of Rossini, who is now generally thought to have been one of the first outstanding composers to have given up composing because he could not change with the times.

The tendency to fad has been greatly encouraged by the promulgation of systems, particularly harmonic systems. Many recent composers following Schoenberg, Hindemith, and Messiaen have gained renown by circulating descriptions of their systems even in places where their music was not known. This kind of intellectual publicity can lead to a dead end even more quickly than the older fads derived from the actual sound of music in styles the composer did not even bother to explain.

The popularity of modern harmonic systems is, unfortunately, easy to understand. Textbooks led music students to think of harmony as a well-ordered routine, and when they found it to be less and less so in the years from Wagner to the present, they were much troubled—and still are—by the gap between what they learn and what they hear in modern music. For mature composers, lack of system is usually not much of a problem since they write, as they probably always have, what sounds right to them. This "rightness" has come, I suppose, from a developed sensitivity and experience that take time to acquire. When modern systems of harmony that were orderly and easy to explain appeared they filled an important pedagogical need for the inexperienced.

The very ease with which any of these systems can be used has its obvious dangers, as I have said. With the help of these and other shortcuts a vast amount of music is being written today, far more than can ever be played, than can ever be judged or widely known. At the same time there seems to be little corresponding development of discrimination, or even of ability or desire to listen to new music, little expansion of opportunities for performance, at least in this country. The struggle to be performed and to be recognized makes it very hard for one not to become, even against one's will, some kind of system-monger, particularly if one uses certain procedures that are considered effective. For among students there is today a hunger for new formulas, and they constitute an interested public.

Obviously the only way to withstand the disturbing prospect of being swept away by a change in fad is to plunge into the even more disturbing situation of trying to be an individual and finding one's own way, as most of us have tried to do, not bothering too much about what is or will be sanctioned at any given moment by the profession and the public. We may then have to lead our lives producing works "too soon" for their time as Webern did, if they are not really "too late" since, if professional, they presuppose an attentive public which seems to be getting rarer. We are caught in a development dictated by convictions impossible to change with the fads.

All this is to say that I do not consider my rhythmic procedures a trick or a formula. I do not even feel that they are an integral part of my musical personality, especially in the way I used them in my First String Quartet (1951), which delves elaborately into polyrhythms. As I have suggested, all aspects of a composition are closely bound together, and for this reason I cannot give an orderly exposition of any without bringing in a large perspective of ideas. So I do not know where to begin, and I need your help in directing this discussion to regions that will be interesting and useful to you. Almost anything I might say, I suppose, preferably on musical subjects, might be considered relevant to the subject you have so kindly invited me to discuss here.

Question: In the program notes of your Variations for Orchestra which you wrote for the Louisville performance, you described your method of variation as being a method of transformation, which you compared to the transformation from one life-stage to another of some marine animals. What did you mean by this?

Answer: As musicians you are all familiar with the problems of program notes. Technical discussions baffle the greater part of the audience and the few who do understand are apt to feel that the composer is a calculating monster, particularly since musical terms are ponderous, not always very definite in meaning and too often give the impression of complexity when describing something very obvious to the ear. If I had described the augmentations, diminutions, retrograde inversions as they occur, this would have been positively bewildering to the public and would not have helped it to listen—certainly not the first time. So I tried to find a comparison that would help the listener to grasp my general approach. Serious music must appeal in different ways. Its main appeal, however, emerges from the quality of the musical material or ideas and perhaps even more from their use in significant continuities, but does not always depend on grasping the logic of the latter on first hearing. There has to be something left for the second time, if there ever is a second time.

As in all my works, I conceived this one as a large, unified musical action or gesture. In it, definition and contrast of character decrease during the first variations, arriving at a point of neutrality in the central variation, then increase again to the finale, which comprises many different speeds and characters. This work was thought of as a series of character studies in various states of interaction with each other both within each variation and between one and the next. Activity, development, type of emphasis, clearness or vagueness of definition, I hoped would also contribute to characterization. Form, rhythmic and development processes as well as texture and thematic material differ in each one for this reason.

The characteristic effort of the serious composer, as I see it, is not so much in the invention of musical ideas in themselves, as in the invention of interesting ideas that will also fill certain compositional requirements and allow for imaginative continuations. Serious music appeals to a longer span of attention and to a more highly developed auditory memory than do the more popular kinds of music. In making this appeal, it uses many contrasts, coherences, and contexts that give it a wide scope of expression, great emotional power and variety, direction, uniqueness, and a fascination of design with many shadings and qualities far beyond the range of popular or folk music. Every moment must count somehow, as must every detail. For a composer it is not always easy to find a passage that fits the particular situation and moment at which it appears in the composition, that carries to a further point some ideas previously stated, that has the appropriate expressive quality motivated by what has been heard and yet is a passage that sounds fresh and alive.

As far as I am concerned, I am always interested in a composer's phrases and their shape and content, the way he joins them, the type of articulation he uses, as well as the general drift or continuity of a large section, and the construction of a whole work. The small details of harmony, rhythm, and texture fall naturally into place when one has interesting conceptions of these larger shapes.

Q: What do you mean by metric modulation?

A: If you listen to or look at any part of the first or last movement of my First String Quartet, you will find that there is a constant change of pulse. This is caused by an overlapping of speeds. Say, one part in triplets will enter against another part in quintuplets and the quintuplets will fade into the background and the triplets will establish a new speed that will become the springboard for another such operation. The structure of such speeds is correlated throughout the work and gives the impression of varying rates of flux and change of material and character, qualities I seek in my recent works. The wish to accomplish this in the domain of heavily emphasized contrapuntal contrasts led me to work out the plan of metric modulation described by Richard Goldman.[1]

Q: Why are the contrapuntal lines in your quartet so much alike, using equal note-values?

A: You cannot have listened to the work very carefully or looked at the score. Of the nine notes in the first four measures, there are seven different lengths, the longest 18 times the shortest. There are, it is true, a few places near the beginning in which several contrapuntal parts each of equal note-values are combined, but in complete polyrhythmic contrast emphasized by intervallic, bowing, and expressive contrasts. In these I was particularly anxious to present to the listener the idea of polyrhythmic textures in its most definite form, for even this quality of texture develops during the work, leading, in the second movement, to a four-part fragmented canon in continuous sixteenths and, in later movements, to lines of much notational irregularity. But even if the values were more frequently equal than they are, as for instance in the polyrhythmic, posthumous Études of Chopin, I cannot see that this would be a real objection, as you imply. Many a fine work has dealt in continuous streams of equal note-values.

Q: Does your music have any harmonic plan?

A: A chord, a vertical group of pitches either simultaneously sounded or arpeggiated, like a motif, is a combination to be more or less clearly remembered and related to previous and future chords heard in the same work. Whether the composer is conscious of it or not, a field of operation with its principles of motion and of interaction is stated or suggested at the beginning of any work. The field may be tonal, employ traditional harmony, or it may be unrelated to traditional har-

[1]Richard Goldman, "The Music of Elliott Carter," in *The Musical Quarterly*, XLIII (1957), 151.

mony, as my music seems to be nowadays, in which case I feel it imperative to establish clearly, near the beginning, the principles upon which the composition moves. Once this field of operation is established, its possibilities are explored, interesting new aspects of it are revealed, patterns of action of contrasting types emerge as the work goes along. A work whose world is not clearly defined loses a great deal of possible power and interest, one whose world is too narrow and restricted runs the risk of being thin, although if the world is unusual enough this narrowness can produce a kind of hallucinatory quality—one that I do not concern myself with in my own works. This extension of the traditional methods of coherence can rarely be attained nowadays solely by intuition, I think, because of the vast number of musical means, new and old, that we know. Some composers, it is true, insulate themselves from new musical experiences in an effort not to be distracted. Others, whose curiosity and interest prompt them to follow what is going on, feeling, perhaps, as Charles Ives did, that "eclecticism is part of his duty—sorting potatoes means a better crop next year,"[2] have to make a number of conscious choices and establish the frame in which to work before they can compose at all.

In my First String Quartet, I did use a "key" four-note chord, one of the two four-note groups, that joins all the two-note intervals into pairs, thus allowing for the total range of interval qualities that still can be referred back to a basic chord-sound. This chord is not used at every moment in the work but occurs frequently enough, especially in important places, to function, I hope, as a formative factor. It is presented in various kinds of part-writing and interval combination, the number of notes is increased and diminished in it, in ways familiar to all of you. The chord, here in its closest position, showing its content of intervals of a diminished fifth and less, is also used both in many intervallic inversions and in total inversion:

Ex. 1

Here is an example of its use in counterpoint that occurs in measure 477 of the last movement, where the quality of the chord is strongly dwelt on—each vertical combination except the last being made up of it:

Q: Did you try to shape the free writing found in your quartet into formal patterns?

[2]Charles Ives, *Essays Before a Sonata*, New York, 1920, p. 94.

Ex. 2

A: Since I consider form an integral part of serious music, I certainly did. Strange as it may seem, the intention of composing a work that depended so much on change of movement and polyrhythmic texture involved me not only in special questions of clarity and audibility that one does not usually have to face, but in special problems of form also. One of the solutions I tried, to keep this rather free-sounding technique from seeming haphazard and thus lose its connection with the progress of the work and the attentive listener's ear, was to establish thematic patterns made up of components of different ideas that could be separated. This feature emerges in the last movement, many of whose motifs are disintegrated to produce polyrhythms (Ex. 3). This is only one of the many ways I tried, hoping to give the impression of that combination of freedom and control that I greatly admire in many works of art.

Ex. 3

Q: *Do you use the twelve-tone system?*

A: Some critics have said that I do, but since I have never analyzed my works from this point of view, I cannot say. I assume that if I am not conscious of it, I do not. Naturally out of interest and out of professional responsibility I have studied the important works of the type and admire many of them a great deal. I have found that it is apparently inapplicable to what I am trying to do, and is more of a hindrance than a help. Its nature is often misunderstood, it is a building material and not the building, and it allows, I think, for certain greater freedoms than were possible using traditional harmony with its very strict rules of part-writing, just as reinforced concrete allows for certain construction patterns impossible with stone. I must also say that having known many of these works all of my adult life, I hope the recent fad will not cause them to seem commonplace too soon. The results of total serialization are more recalcitrant to musical handling, I think.

Q: *Do you mean to say that your rhythmic method is not a product of serialization?*

A: It is not. But it is true that, like all music, mine goes from one thing to another—the pattern on which serialization is based—but my choices of where to start and where to go are controlled by a general plan of action that directs both the continuity and the expression. Single details, chords, rhythmic patterns, motifs, textures, registers follow each other in a way that combines them into clearly perceivable larger patterns and then patterns of these patterns, and to me this cannot be easily accomplished with total serialization, at least the kind I study my way through in European articles these days. Perhaps another more useful and not so arbitrary kind of serialization could be devised. The present one resembles the turning of a kaleidoscope and usually produces not much more—or less—interesting results. Indeed it can be fascinating to listen to the total repertory of pitches, note-values, timbres, registers, and dynamics being touched upon in rapid succession and from a point of view we are unaccustomed to. But the cumulative effect of this is self-defeating since neither the attention nor the memory is appealed to. For who can decipher, by ear, the complexities of total serialization in most works of the sort? On the other hand, those in which this process can be followed are too obvious to be of any interest.

Q: What is your attitude about performance difficulty?

A: I realize with brutal clarity that orchestral music requiring a lot of rehearsal can, by the nature of American musical life, find very few, if any, performances. This is not true of difficult music for soloists or small standardized instrumental groups, for obvious reasons. Our orchestral musicians are trained to play in the demanding scores of Strauss, Mahler, Debussy, Ravel, and early Stravinsky. One might imagine that one of the obligations of a present-day composer would be to use the skills of these excellently trained musicians to their full, lest their abilities deteriorate for want of use; that the challenge of good, effective yet technically advanced scores would be helpful in raising them, as it did in the past. But this does not seem to be a consideration here, and, as you and I know, new works that make an immediate effect with a minimum of effort and time are favored. The real effort goes into the standard repertory, where it is more widely appreciated. Therefore, a composer who wishes to write orchestral music and get it played here has to tailor his work to these practical conditions, whether his ideas are suitable to such exploitation or not. Those who find that they can do nothing of interest under these conditions either give up writing orchestral music or, if they cannot, hope for European performances of their works. For these reasons, the scores of our composers often show a lack of practical experience that reveals itself in conventionality and timidity. How can a man be adventurous, under the circumstances that obtain here? Any casual look at the European scores written since the war will show how far in advance of us even beginners are there in this respect. As in many other things, we may be willing to accept the final, accomplished results of European training and experimental efforts but we cannot afford and are impatient with the step-by-step experience needed to produce them.

Naturally, music that is both difficult and yet practical to play is not easy to write, and it may even be difficult to listen to. It does not make for a comfortable life to have this as one's mode of expression. There is an undoubted beauty in reducing things to their essentials or to their simplest form if something is gained thereby. When a composer cannot find an interesting and satisfying way of writing easy music, he is at least free, here, to use the level of difficulty he needs to set forth his ideas completely—even if this results in no performances. But I see no reason for being just difficult. Whenever difficult passages seem imperative in my works, I try to make them especially rewarding once they are played correctly.

For I regard my scores as scenarios, auditory scenarios, for performers to act out with their instruments, dramatizing the players as individuals and participants in the ensemble. To me the special teamwork of ensemble playing is very wonderful and moving, and this feeling is always an important expressive consideration in my chamber music.

Q: Have you ever thought of composing electronic music?

A: Naturally, I have often been intrigued with the idea of electronic music and have visited the Milan electronic studio several times to find out what is being done. I must say that almost all I have heard seems to me to be in a primary stage, and has not resolved some fundamental problems of matching and comparison of sounds that would raise it above the physical scariness that makes this music useful for television science fiction and horror programs. As far as composing it myself is concerned, you can imagine that since I am very enmeshed in the human aspect of musical performance, I would find it hard to think in terms of the impersonal sound patterns of electronic music. Certainly, impatience at not being able to hear my works in performance and impatience at the inaccuracies of some performances have occasionally made me wish that I could have a machine that would perform my music correctly and without all the trouble and possible disappointments associated with live performances.

Q: What do you think of Charles Ives now?

A: My opinions about Charles Ives as a composer have changed many times since I first came to know him during my high-school years in 1924-25, but my admiration for him as a man never has. No one who knew him can ever forget his remarkable enthusiasm, his wit, his serious concern and love for music, and his many truly noble qualities

Shop Talk by an American Composer

which one came to notice gradually because they appeared casually,
without a trace of pompousness, pretention, or "showing off." Attracted
to him by a youthful enthusiasm for contemporary music, I first admired, and still do, the few advanced scores privately available in those
days, the *Concord Sonata,* the *Three Places in New England,* and
some of the *114 Songs.* However, after I had completed strict musical studies here and abroad, I saw these works in a different light.
Misgivings arose which I expressed with considerable regret in several
articles in *Modern Music* after the first performance of the *Concord
Sonata* in New York in 1939. My doubts were of two kinds. First,
there seemed to be very large amounts of undifferentiated confusion,
especially in the orchestral works, during which many conflicting things
happen at once without apparent concern either for the total effect
or for the distinguishability of various levels. Yet in each score such as
the *Robert Browning Overture,* the *Fourth of July,* and the second
and fourth movements of the Fourth Symphony where this confusion is
most frequent, it is the more puzzling because side by side with it is
a number of passages of great beauty and originality. Even more disturbing to me then was his frequent reliance on musical quotations for
their literary effect. In spite of these doubts, I continued for many
years to help bring Ives's music before the public since he would do
nothing for himself, rescuing, among other things, *The Unanswered
Question* and *Central Park in the Dark* from the photostat volumes of
his work he had left with the American Music Center. I arranged for
first performances of these at a Ditson Fund Concert at Columbia University in, I think, 1949.

What interests me now is his vigorous presentation in music and
essays of the conflict between the composer with vision and original
ideas, the musical profession, and the American public. It is the living
out of this conflict, made poignant by his strong convictions, the anger
it produced, the various actions and attitudes it led him to, the retreat
into a subjective world, and, unfortunately, the terrible toll of energy
and health it took, that makes of Ives an artist really characteristic
of America, not unlike Melville. Without the dimension of this struggle
and the quality it gave his scores, his *Emersons* and *Hallowe'ens*
would be of superficial and transitory interest.

His rage, which explodes between the waves of his transcendental
visions in prose as it does in the scribbled comments in the margin of
his musical manuscripts, reveals troubled concern over the problems of
the American composer and his relations with the public. The music
profession is castigated in one place as being more hide-bound, more
materialistic, petty, bigotted, and unprincipled than the business world.
The latter, his refuge from the bleak, meager life of the conventional
American musician of his time, he respected and identified himself with

enough to adopt an American business man's view of the artistic profession, one that was especially characteristic of that time of wealthy
art-collectors. Making of the artist an anti-business man, Ives saw him
as a prophet living in the pure, transcendent world of the spirit, above
the mundane matters of money, practicality, and artistic experience.
The 19th-century American dream of art and high culture, which
Henry James liked to project against the sordid European background
from which it came, was the source, as Aaron Copland and Wilfrid
Mellers have pointed out, of Ives's greatest misfortune. In gradually retiring into this dream, he cut himself off from music's reality. Too
many of his scores, consequently, were never brought to the precision
of presentation and scoring necessary to be completely communicative
to the listener—or so it seems now. One could say that Ives was unable
completely to digest his experience as an American and make it into a
unified and meaningful musical expression. The effort of remodeling the
musical vocabulary to meet his own personal vision, almost without
encouragement or help, was too great, and too often he had to let hymn
tunes and patriotic songs stand for his experience without comment.

As I have said, Ives's life vividly presents the special conflicts inherent in the American composer's situation. Today, even more than in
his time, the division between the musician's professional code of ethics,
his traditional standards of skill and imagination established at another
time in another place, and the present standards of behavior respected,
sanctioned, and rewarded by the society that surrounds us, is very pronounced. The familiar training of a composer giving him knowledge
and skill in the accumulation of musical techniques, past and present,
and the development of skill in notating them, presupposes trained copyists and performers who can grasp what he means and respect his notations. It also presupposes critics and, if not a large public, at least an
influential élite that will be able to perceive the sense of the composer's efforts and skill, value them and enable him to develop them further, by giving them careful consideration. When one or more of the
links in this chain is not sufficiently developed or non-existent, as is
often the case here today, the composer has a bitter fight just to keep
his skill, let alone develop it.

This misfortune can be laid to the general lack of unanimity about
and concern for the profession of composing on the part of the mass
musical public that plays such an influential financial role in America.
By training, the composer learns to write for a musically educated public that is also an influential élite, which does not exist and may never exist here. He cannot help but feel that he will be heard by a large
majority of listeners and even performers that disagree with him, if they
have any opinions at all, on the most fundamental issues of his art.
Questions of style, system, consonance, dissonance, themes, non-themes,

being original or an imitator, which imply some agreement on fundamentals, are not the stumbling blocks. A professional composer has today, as Ives certainly had, the training to be "communicative," "melodious," "expressive," qualities considered to have a wide appeal, just as he is now trained to use advanced techniques that will be appreciated by only a few professionals. How shall he decide? He is free, here, to do what he likes, of course, but it does not take him long to realize that whatever he chooses to do, radical or conservative, his music will further divide into small sub-groups the handful of people who will listen to contemporary music at all. Not one of these small sub-groups has the power or the interest to convince the large public by publicity or other means of the validity of its opinions, as happens in the other arts here. While diversity of opinion is much to be welcomed, where so little support exists such decimation of interest, one hesitates regretfully to conclude, can lead to cancelling of efforts and ultimately to their negation.

Even America's panacea, publicity, seems strangely useless in this field. Good reviews do not, often, lead to further performances, but they do help to sell more recordings. One might have thought that Ives, now so much discussed and publicly admired, would be often heard. That a number of his recordings have been discontinued, that only a few of his easiest pieces are heard while some of his more remarkable works are still unplayed or scarcely known, is surely an indication of how confused and desperate is the relation between the composer, the profession, publicity, and the musical public.

Bibliography

The music of Elliott Carter is the subject of at least two articles in *The Musical Quarterly*. Richard F. Goldman's "The Music of Elliott Carter," 43 (1957), is of course limited by date. Kurt Stone's remarks in "Current Chronicle," 55 (1969), bring things up to date by discussing the *Second String Quartet*, the *Double Concerto for Harpsichord and Piano with Two Chamber Orchestras*, and particularly the *Piano Concerto*, all written since 1957. The most recent work to appear about Carter is Allen Edwards's *Flawed Words and Stubborn Sounds—A Conversation with Elliott Carter*, (New York, Norton, 1972). Two of Carter's articles on Ives are contained in *Modern Music*: "The Case of Mr. Ives," 16 (1939); and "Ives Today: His Vision and Challenge," 21 (1944). Other articles on Ives include those of Wilfrid H. Mellers, "Music in the Melting Pot: Ives and the Music of the Americas," *Scrutiny*, 7 (1939);

Kurt Stone, "Ives's Fourth Symphony: a Review," *The Musical Quarterly*, 52 (1966); and Dennis Marshall, "Charles Ives Quotations: Manner or Substance?" *Perspectives of New Music*, 6 (Spring-Summer, 1968). Henry and Sidney Cowell have written Ives's biography, *Charles Ives and His Music* (New York, Oxford University Press, 1955; rev. ed., 1969). Two other items by Cowell, both written at a time when Ives's music was very much out of style, are "Charles Ives," in *Modern Music*, 10 (1932); and "Charles E. Ives," in *American Composers on American Music* (Stanford, Calif., Stanford University Press, 1933). Ives's own writings, edited by Howard Boatwright, are collected in *Essays before a Sonata and Other Writings* (New York, Norton, 1961).

Much of the music of Elliott Carter is published by Associated Music Publishers, New York. Information about the compositions of Ives, both published and unpublished, has been collected by Dominique-René DeLerma in *Charles Edward Ives: A Bibliography of His Music* (Kent, Ohio, Kent State University Press, 1970).

32

SOMEWHERE near the beginning of the nineteenth century, musical life in the United States developed a split personality. Previously there had been no clear distinction between popular and art music. A concert could easily include both, apparently with no danger of embarrassing either performers or audience. After the turn of the nineteenth century, however, a cleavage appeared between popular and serious music and musicians; for some reason the two were no longer compatible in the same concert.[1] Part of the trouble was very likely due to an equal amount of snobbery on both sides. The split between the two camps was deplored by all, but each camp thought the ideal solution to be the capitulation of the other. Proponents of popular music came to maintain that their art was serious and worthy of greater respect; lovers of serious music dreamed of the utopian day when their music would be truly popular, i.e., universally accepted by the people as its preferred music.

The author of the following thinks that the long-established barriers between popular and art music now show signs of giving way, and that some of the credit is due to jazz. How this may be true, how and why jazz is American, and other aspects of the musical and social history of jazz are his subject.

Sidney Walter Finkelstein has written a number of books on music and other subjects. Among his works are *Jazz: a People's Music* (New York, Citadel, 1948); *How Music Expresses Ideas* (London, Lawrence & Wishart, 1952); *Sense and Nonsense of MacLuhan* (New York, International Publishers, 1968); and *Composer and Nation: the Folk Heritage of Music* (New York, International Publishers, 1960).

---

[1]For a discussion of this cleavage see H. Wiley Hitchcock, *Music in the United States: A Historical Introduction* (Englewood Cliffs, N.J., Prentice-Hall, 1969), chs. 3-6.

Jazz as Folk and Art Music

SIDNEY FINKELSTEIN

The most widespread American influence on twentieth century world music is that of jazz. A creation of the American Negro people, it has become an American national art, with Negro and white performing in friendly collaboration. And it has been both studied and enthusiastically performed in countries like England, France, Italy, Sweden, Germany, Australia and Japan.

Jazz may be described as a music of African tribal roots which has gone through a rapid "hot-house" development in a country the most advanced in the world in industrial production and one that has made the commercial production of popular music into a major industry. Jazz has grown as an organic part of this music-manufacturing industry, constantly feeding ideas into it, and yet at the same time has been in constant opposition to its standardized procedures. It exhibits the perfect taste of a people often with little or no professional musical education, when they create music as a communal emotional expression, for at its best it has a plastic economy and purity in the handling of melody, rhythm and tone color foreign to commercial popular music and comparable to art music.

Its history reveals many lessons which throw new light upon all music; the absorption by folk music of material from the most varied sources, including art music, and their transformation into a new homogeneous art; the rise in folk music of a natural, improvised polyphony; the influence of the human voice upon instrumental style inspiring the development of fresh, expressive instrumental timbres. Its secret of growth is based on a principle actually very old in music and rooted in folk art, but appearing strikingly fresh and vital in twentieth century America and Europe; improvisation, not simply as a display of

FROM Sidney Finkelstein, *Composer and Nation: The Folk Heritage of Music* (New York, International Publishers, Inc.), pp. 301-322. Copyright © 1960 by International Publishers Co., Inc. Reprinted by permission of the publisher.

individual technique, but as a collective and social act, and as a form of immediate communication between performer and listener. For this reason, while an integral part of American commercial popular music, jazz has played the role within this music of a rebel, raising a banner of freedom. To musicians employed in the business of manufactured popular musical entertainment, with its dehumanized division of labor and apportionment of specialized tasks, it has opened up a creative path, restoring the unity of musical inventor and performer, like a humanization of music making.

The first forms of jazz were the ragtime and blues heard among the Negro people in the 1890's and the first decade of the twentieth century. This music differed from the anonymous, group music of slavery in that it was a solo music, reflecting the hard-won ability of Negro people, after the end of slavery, to move from place to place and to assert their individuality as entertainers. Some of these musicians, coming from the most poverty-stricken and depressed areas of life in the Southern states, became legendary figures in the Negro communities.

Ragtime was the more "educated" music. Its creators were pianists, many of whom had gotten some rudimentary musical instruction. A factor in its rise was the fact that in this period cheap upright and player pianos could be found almost anywhere they went. Ragtime embraced a wide area of music, from popular airs of the period, Spanish tangos, and quadrilles, to operatic airs such as were commonly found in easy instruction books for the piano. Thus one of these inspired ragtime pianist-composers, Ferdinand "Jelly-Roll" Morton, in his recordings made with Alan Lomax for the Library of Congress in 1938, has shown how in the early years of the century a French gavotte and the *"Miserere"* from Verdi's *Il Trovatore* were transmuted into ragtime pieces. The first prolific ragtime composer, Scott Joplin, had ambitions to write operas dealing with Negro life, aimed at "educating" his people, and had he been able to break out of the trap which kept such musicians from mastering the heritage or from being taken seriously as musicians, he might have become a truly notable figure.

Ragtime pieces were generally in two-part form, the second part contrasting to the first like the "trio" of a Sousa march, and this form moved into the "verse" and "chorus" of the typical 32-bar jazz popular song. Its special characteristic was its complex, continuous opposition of two rhythms. The bass line, for example, will accent each second beat of a four-beat measure, while the melody line will accent every third beat, thus creating a syncopated alternation of accents on strong and weak beats. This constant "catching up" of the rhythm could have been heard in some of the more joyous or "jubilee" spirituals, like "On My Journey to Mount Zion," or "I Want to Be Ready, Walking into Jerusalem Just Like John." It could have been heard in the slave dance known as the "cakewalk," and in minstrel music. In other words, it was a renewed flowering of a musical style that had been preserved by the Negro people, perhaps from Africa. But within every such flowering, enabling old materials to be transmuted into something new, lay a new content. And the special expressive content of ragtime was its wit; a kind of ironic, playful musical laughter, full of rhythmic stops and starts, of shocks and surprises.

A tradition of such satire, masked by buffoonery, had existed in the cakewalk. Thus an old Negro entertainer, Shephard N. Edmonds, as quoted by Rudi Blesh and Harriet Janis, describes the cakewalk: "The slaves, both young and old, would dress up in hand-me-down finery to do a high-kicking, prancing walk-around. They did a take-off on the high manners of the white folks in the 'big house,' but their masters, who gathered round to watch the fun, missed the point."[1] The wit of ragtime, like all folk wit, is a semi-secret language, understood only by those possessing the key. The key is the ability to grasp what is unsaid, through what is said. This rests on a familiarity with the aspect of life, or music, which is being thrown into high relief by being thus artfully distorted or stood on its head.

Because of the kind of hard-boiled defiance and independence latent in ragtime, it was often heard—and this would also be true of the blues and jazz—in places that put no premium on respectability: saloons and houses of prostitution. Then after being derided, it was suddenly "discovered" by the commercial music industry, hard-pressed for new ideas. Fortunes were made by white imitators and followers, on musical ideas learned from Negro musicians. And the music was often at the same time misunderstood and vulgarized, its surface characteristics heavily stressed while the subtle humor slipped through the imitator's fingers. This process would be repeated throughout the entire history of jazz.

THE origin of the blues is still cloudy. A great number of very different folk and popular songs are known as "blues," like "Careless Love," "St. James Infirmary," "It Takes a Worried Man to Sing a Worried Song," "When the Sun Goes Down," and "How Long, How Long," the only connection among them being a balladeer sadness. But within this general body of song there is a unique form that is more specifically the "blues:" a Negro creation. It is not a fixed song so much as song material, malleable, and capable of infinite variations and melodic sprouts, which remain at the same time unmistakeably "blues." It speaks of an African current flowering into a new form of folk art, indigenous to the American land. Suggesting African roots is the irregular scale, which may embrace from three to seven notes. In

[1]Harriet Janis and Rudi Blesh, *They All Played Ragtime*, Knopf, N. Y., 1950, p. 96.

428

its simplest form, it is anchored about a tonic note, a "dominant" five tones higher, and an intermediate note dangling between the major and a minor third. Thus it falls outside the major-minor pattern, and in the seven-note form, this character is emphasized by flatting the seventh note. The melody is highly speech-inflected or *parlando-rubato,* with the singer often making a strong expressive use of the "blue note" flattened third and seventh, along with slurs from one note to another, to emphasize certain climactic words.

Yet—and this is a basic difference from African music—the blues are an architecturally rounded song form, for all their looseness. The song unit consists of three "statements," each within four bars of music. The first is built of descending, lamenting phrases; the second repeats the first, but with greater tension; the third is a rounding out. This reflects as well the "dialectic" of the word stanza, which consists of three lines, the first challenging or arousing the interest of the listener, the second line repeating the first, and the third rounding out the thought.

Other African seeds flowered in the blues texture. One is African polyphony, which the blues developed in a manner that can be compared to the "trio-sonata" texture of baroque music. There is a melody line, that of the singer, which continues for two and a half bars, and then an "obligato," antiphonal line, or answer, rises from the accompanying instrument, such as guitar or piano, to fill out the four bar statement. And third is the bass line, which provides the underlying 4/4 rhythm and also the "blues chords." There is no such free three-part polyphony in other American folk song. Also unique is the interplay of rhythms, the *parlando-rubato* melody contrasting to, subtly anticipating or lagging behind, the basic beat.

An integral part of the blues is the special wit and humour, rising out of the contrast between statement and answer, between the unflagging beat and the speech-inflected freedom of melodic accents. The difference in this respect between blues and ragtime is that in ragtime the wit is uppermost, providing the sparkling surface; in the blues, it is the lamenting song that takes over, while the wit becomes a constant brake or check on the outpouring of feeling. It is as if the expression of misery had always to be wrapped up in a note of irony or defiant refusal to succumb. As Willis L. James' powerful Negro work song says, "Don't pity me down!"

How and when did this blues form arise? It is not found in African music. It is not heard in other music of the Americas created or deeply influenced by Negro people, such as that of Cuba, Haiti or Brazil. It is not heard among the spirituals, although some spirituals suggest the blues, like the descending, sad phrases of "Sometimes I feel like a motherless child, a long way from home," or the three line stanzas, with the second lines repeating the first, of "He Never Said a Mumberlin' Word," the great "Crucifixion" spiritual which Roland

Hayes points out as definitely African in origin.[2] Field calls, "shouts," and "hollers" are suggested as an origin of the blues with their descending phrases and slurred notes, but they also are not exactly the blues. However the fact that blues singers are called frequently "blues shouters," and many blues are called "moans," indicates what the music itself confirms; the close connection of the blues to a cry of the human voice.

In music and words the blues reflect the conditions arising in the last decades of the nineteenth century, when after the terrible onslaught against the Negro people which followed their achievement of freedom from slavery, many became homeless wanderers. Thus E. Franklin Frazier writes, "Among the million Negroes who deserted the rural communities of the South, there were thousands of men and women who cut themselves loose from family and friends and sought work and adventure as solitary wanderers from place to place. Some of the men had their first glimpse of the world beyond the plantation or farm when they worked in sawmills, turpentine camps, or on the roads."[3] The music, of self accompanied solo song, is that of a wanderer. The words tell of events that happened in one place or another, and a frequent theme is that of the railroad, symbolic of travel and swiftness of movement. A blues line like "Well, I'm going to buy me a little railroad of my own" expresses, as Russell Ames points out,[4] the resentment of discrimination on the railroads.

W. C. Handy, in his autobiography, *Father of the Blues*, describes the brutality with which these wanderers were treated in St. Louis. "I slept on a vacant lot at twelfth and Morgan streets, a lot I shared with a hundred of others in similar circumstances. I slept on the cobblestones of the levee of the Mississippi. My companions were perhaps a thousand men of both races. . . . Two popular songs grew out of the brutality of the police in those days, *Brady He's Dead and Gone* and *Looking for the Bully*. Policemen carried nightsticks about a yard long. They had a way of hurling these at the feet of fleeing vagrants in such a way as to trip up the fugitives. One frequently heard of legs broken in this way."[5]

Handy was the first to write down and publish blues songs, in 1909, but as he recounts, the form itself of the blues existed long before. He was himself a somewhat educated musician, with an upbringing close to the middle class, and the music known to the most exploited,

[2]Roland Hayes, *My Songs*, Little, Brown, Boston, 1948, p. 121.

[3]E. Franklin Frazier, *The Negro Family in the United States*, Dryden Press, N. Y., 1951, p. 210.

[4]Russell Ames, *The Story of American Folk Song*, Grosset & Dunlap, N. Y., 1955, p. 254.

[5]W. C. Handy, *Father of the Blues*, Macmillan, N. Y., 1947, pp. 27-28.

vagrant and laboring Negroes came to him as a strange surprise. "A lean, loose-jointed Negro had commenced plunking a guitar beside me while I slept. . . . The singer repeated the line three times, accompanying himself on the guitar with the weirdest music I had ever heard.[6] . . . The primitive Southern Negro as he sang was sure to bear down on the third and seventh tones of the scale, slurring between major and minor. Whether it was in the cotton fields of the Delta or on the levee up St. Louis way it was always the same . . . I had never heard this slur used by a more sophisticated Negro, or by any white man."[7]

It is not sufficient to say that the blues simply "arose" among the Negro people. What stamps a work as "folk" is that it expresses the communal mind and becomes part of communal life, not that it is collectively created, and in folk art there have always been inspired individual creators, whose work came to be absorbed in the common heritage. The likelihood is that the unique, rounded and yet germinating form of the twelve-bar blues was created out of familiar material by such a genius, and was then taken up by one singer after another, the others finding in its very malleability an apt form for anything they wanted to say in words and music.

As for the period, it would seem to be the beginning of the 1890's. Among Negro folksingers, the earliest blues is reputed to be a song called "Joe Turner Blues," and the singer "Big Bill" Broonzy recounts the legend about "Joe Turner;" that he was a mysterious figure who, during the great catastrophes of 1891-92, would bring help to poor people, Negro and white.[8] Such catastrophes, like river floods, high winds and tidal waves, always wreaked their greatest devastation on the Negro and poor white population, who lived in flimsy shacks near the waterfront or in the lowlands. At the same time "relief" and assistance customarily went first to the houses of the wealthy. The blues could have risen at a time of such devastation. And certainly there are many such flood stories among the blues, one of the most beautiful being Bessie Smith's "Backwater Blues."

Among the blues composers and singers were Negro women. Women have always played a strong, leading role in Negro life. Under slavery, with families broken up, the fathers traded away, children often knew only one parent, the mother. Two of the great heroes both in the Underground Railroad escapes and in the fight for the right to vote after the Civil War, were Harriet Tubman and Sojourner Truth. In the renewed oppressiveness of the late nineteenth century, a double burden fell on the women, often deserted by men who were themselves desper-

[6]*Ibid.*, pp. 74-76.
[7]*Ibid.*, p. 120.
[8]*Big Bill Broonzy—His Story* (Interview with Studs Turkel). Recorded, Chicago, 1956; Folkways Record 3586, N. Y.

ate, and this shattered love relation is expressed in countless blues, from the woman's viewpoint. Her indignation is often fierce. Frazier quotes a Negro woman, "I tried nineteen years to make a husband out of him but he was the most no 'count man God ever made. Since I seen I could make no husband out of him I left him." With little change, this could become the words of a blues.

Typical is Bessie Smith's "Lost Your Head Blues." It starts, "I was with you, baby, when you didn't have a dime." Then it tells bitterly the man's changed attitude when he had some money, and goes on to a declaration of independence. "I'm gonna leave, baby, ain't gonna say goodby, but I'll write you and tell you the reason why." Following is a lament over the price of independence, a "moan." "Days are lonesome, nights are so long, I'm a good gal but I've just been treated wrong." This of course comes from the 1920's, when the blues, having inspired the development of jazz and in turn influenced by jazz, became in the hands of great popular artists like Bessie Smith something approaching a fine art form. Thus "Lost Your Head Blues" has not merely rounded stanzas but a cumulative development, reaching a climax in the cry of the woman against double oppression.

JAZZ proper rose in New Orleans in the early years of the twentieth century. To the Negro people at the time, there was a sharp demarcation between "gospel songs," which were sung in churches; "blues," which were a profane or secular music, of the countryside and labor camps; "ragtime," which was a virtuoso piano music heard in cities like Sedalia, Memphis and St. Louis, often in red-light districts; and "jazz," which was a "Creole," or New Orleans music. Each had its own style.

The word "Creole" spoke not only of Creole folk songs but of the French influences in New Orleans, including French folk songs, reels, gavottes and quadrilles which were played by Negro musicians at balls for the white "masters," and also the opera house for which New Orleans had been musically renowned. There were also street parades, and the Negro fraternal lodges had their own bands. It was from band music that jazz took its basic instrumentation, of clarinet, trumpet, trombone, and tuba, only the latter being later replaced by a plucked string bass.

Much early jazz was a march music, which at the same time could be turned into dance music, like the "one-step." It embraced the popular marches known from Civil War times, and the inspired marches of John Philip Sousa (1854-1932). Sousa, son of a Portuguese father and Bavarian mother, had been a variety hall musician before he became the leader of the United States Marine Band. He knew and respected Negro music, and in turn influenced it. The Sousa strain can be heard for example, in one of the classics of early jazz, the new Orleans marching tune "High Society."

Yet what made jazz unique was that even when it most closely resembled the march, it combined with this the characteristics of both ragtime and blues. From ragtime came the dazzling free rhythmic solos of the "melody" instruments against the underlying beat, giving the whole performance a feeling of exuberance and individual life contrasting to the mechanical pattern of the military march. Thus ragtime pieces became marches, and marches became "rags." These ragtime solos could also embody blues phrases and "blue notes." The blues also became transformed from a vocal to an instrumental music, using the band instrumentation but with a free, interweaving three-voice polyphony or antiphonal "statement and answer," the instruments such as clarinet, trumpet and trombone taking on deeply expressive vocal inflections. Slow blues played as dances were "slow drags;" fast blues were "stomps." The blues could infiltrate music of the most varied origins such as the march, Creole songs, Spanish dances, popular ballads, with a variation on the melody taking on typical blues phrases, rhythms, and slurred "blue notes." Typical of blues style was the "break," a sudden, expressive rhythmic gap, with a blues phrase rising in answer; and the "riff," or blues phrase repeated in *ostinato* style, with melodic solos above. The blues became the expressive heart of the jazz improvisation, preserved as an unbroken thread throughout all the subsequent changes of jazz band form and instrumentation. As to the folk blues singer, so on a higher level to the instrumentalists in collective improvisation, the blues provided the infinitely flexible material through which the soloist could speak his heart.

Shortly before the first world war, small band jazz, known as "Dixieland," using a New Orleans band instrumentation with added piano, providing a music of marches, one-steps, ragtime songs with blues phrases and intonations, began to be heard about the country. It was at this time that the first "shock" works were being heard in European music, like Stravinsky's *Rite of Spring.* But it was in the postwar, "jazz age" 1920's that jazz captured the major part of American popular music, with much of it in the process, becoming commercially hardened and vulgarized.

A complex period was opened up by the first world war. There was a vast increase in production and profit-making, born out of the war industry. The United States had changed from a debtor to a creditor country, and instead of being a field for foreign investment was seeking investment abroad. To the great mass of citizens, there was the uneasy feeling that the country was now a world power, and its diplomacy was at variance with its proud democratic heritage. The masters of wealth did not have any greater ease of mind. The appearance of

433

socialism in Russia, beating back all attempts of the great powers to strangle it, was a spectre arousing hysteria. The 1920's opened with the Palmer raids, jailing and deporting hundreds of people on the basis of the principle that disloyalty to the interests of trusts, banks and monopolies was disloyalty to America. Open violence was used against the workers seeking to bring trade unions into the great mushrooming industries like meat-packing, auto, oil, steel and rubber. A tidal wave of jingoism arose, aimed at the immigrant families who made up the great mass of the working people in the factories, and at the Negro people. The Ku Klux Klan, discovering mysterious sources of funds, anti-Negro, anti-labor, anti-Semitic and anti-Catholic, became a power North as well as South. Large-scale hypocrisy entered American life as never before with the constitutional amendment prohibiting alcoholic liquor. It made millions of citizens into law-breakers, and fostered gangsterism as a grotesque underworld form of large-scale financial enterprise, corrupting political parties, police and courts.

The music produced in this era reflected the unease of mind of the people. A band of young American composers found the "liberation" they had been seeking in the bleak, sardonic primitivism and motor energy of *avant-garde* European music, producing music equally percussive, dissonant, hiding its lonely nostalgia under a hard-boiled surface, like Aaron Copland's *Piano Variations*. And the same moods, without the same craftsmanship, were found in the popular commercial jazz, with its blatant instrumentation and pounding rhythm, lacking in the warmth, wit, sensitivity and folk spirit of the music as the Negro people had produced it. The hard-boiled surface of the Negro jazz style was copied, without its inner pathos. And it was this side of jazz that was taken up by European composers, as another primitivism, part of their bleak, ironic portrayal of an inhuman civilization. It was used thus by Shostakovich in his *Lady Macbeth of Mtsensk*, Gliere in *The Red Poppy*, Stravinsky in *L'Histoire du Soldat*, Milhaud in *Le Creation du Monde*, Weill in *The Three-penny Opera*, Krenek in *Jonny spielt auf*.

Yet some work of quality appeared amidst the flood produced by the popular music industry. Its wild growth reflected the prosperity of the 1920's. No other country was able to make so prolific a use of the new inventions such as radio and the phonograph, exploiting the vast market of people hungry for musical entertainment. Nor could the industry rest on its old stock in trade of sentimental ballads, European style waltzes and operettas, like those of Victor Herbert, or Irish, Negro and Italian dialect songs. Both its growth, and the interest in new rhythms like the tango or fox-trot, made the search for fresh talent imperative, and amidst the host of commercial hack workers composers genuinely gifted in melody were discovered like W. C. Handy, Irving

Berlin, Hoagy Carmichael, George Gershwin, Vincent Youmans, Jerome Kern, Thomas "Fats" Waller, Richard Rodgers and Cole Porter. The victory of the new music over the old was seen in the ingratiating scores that appeared for the Broadway musical comedies; Vincent Youmans' *No, No Nanette* (1924) with songs like "I Want to be Happy" and "Tea for Two;" Richard Rodgers' *A Connecticut Yankee* (1927) with "Thou Swell" and "My Heart Stood Still;" Jerome Kern's *Show Boat* (1927) with "Old Man River," "Why do I Love you?" and "Can't Help Lovin' that Man;" George Gershwin's *Girl Crazy* (1930) with "Embraceable You" and "I've Got Rhythm."

Music like this represents the song-producing industry, or "tin pan alley" of the 1920's, at its best. There is something sad as well as captivating about both these songs and the shows from which they come. The texts are the most prosaic doggerel and mindless dramas ever set to music, reflecting the perpetual terror of the commercial producer at the thought of ever taking an honest, open look at real life, even through the spectacles of comedy. *Show Boat* was a slight exception in its feeling, if a sentimental one, for the American scene, and its sympathetic, if patronizing, portrayal of a Negro. The part was made famous first by Jules Bledsoe and then by Paul Robeson. The music lives in its sweetness of melody, but this lacking any inspiration towards musical adventure from the text, falls into a conventional mold. Meaningless are the harmony and instrumentation. The older literature of operetta, had suffered, like the Broadway musical show of the 1920's, from a lack of real musical character-creation, being content to offer a string of tunes. But compared to these Broadway shows of the 1920's, the works of Johann Strauss, Milloecker, Offenbach, Gilbert and Sullivan, Victor Herbert, are masterpieces of musical craftsmanship. Tin-pan-alley music at its best is a broken and half-realized art.

Of all the popular and musical show composers who appeared in this period, George Gershwin (1898-1937) had the most fresh and distinctive style, with least of the "old world" about it. It took its substance from Negro ragtime and blues, but transformed this into something unique to Gershwin. His rhythms, lilting and syncopated, were sophisticated and "hot-house" in comparison to the open air feeling of marching jazz, but were witty and captivating. His melodies lacked the heartbreak and lurking, sardonic laughter of the blues, but were nevertheless wry, jaunty, tender and sweet. And it was he who with many song hits behind him, took the step into serious musical composition, producing such works as the *Rhapsody in Blue* (1924), *Piano Concerto in F* (1925), and *An American in Paris* (1928). They have a solid place in American musical history. For all their structural crudities, they live, sing and hold together. They indicate that the material of American popular music, including jazz, can be used successfully for greater musical and artistic ends. Their themes are typical of the best Gershwin songs, and he has transmuted them into genuinely symphonic material. These works confirm the truth that for a writer of good symphonic music, it is a great help to be able to write a good song.

The 1920's also saw a lusty growth of creative jazz, almost unnoticed by and independent of tin-pan-alley, and mirroring the changed conditions among the Negro people. The demand for labor by the mushrooming war industries had served to break down some jim-crow restrictions, and more than a half-million Negroes left the South for cities like Chicago, New York, Detroit and Philadelphia. There were racism and segregation to be faced, taking violent form as in the race riots whipped up by real-estate interests in Chicago. Yet in Chicago the Negro communities played a militant role in union organization. A Negro, Oscar De Priest, was elected to Congress.

Musicians had moved North as well, and the jazz that developed in cities like Chicago was a flowering of seeds born in the South: an amalgamation of New Orleans marches and ragtime pieces, with that fluid, poignant, sardonic blues improvisation at their heart, and worked up through performance after performance into instrumental pieces, sensitive in instrumentation, many-voiced in texture. It is a remarkable music, with the odor of folk earth on it, but advanced beyond any folk music and moving to the level of a small-form art music in its knowing, skillful and collective working out. It is a music, born of folk art, but growing under twentieth century conditions, its roots in the South, but its finished form reflecting the greater freedom and independence of both the musicians in the Northern cities, and the Negro communities for whom they played. And the phonograph record industry played an unintentional role in helping this music grow, for it discovered a flourishing market among the Negro communities for the recordings of artists like Bessie Smith, Joe "King" Oliver, Louis Armstrong, Ferdinand Morton, and the groups about them. However weird and even barbarous the industry thought this music to be, referring to the recordings as "race records," it was willing to exploit this profitable market, especially as, since the musicians were Negro, most of them could be paid very little.

One of the reasons for the perfection of style of this music, in contrast to the commercial jazz, was that to the white performers, music was simply a way of making a living; to the Negro, it was a form of national group expression, its common language of the blues permitting both a collective improvisation and a direct communication to the listeners. Yet, despite the barriers of racism and segregation, which not only poured scorn on this "race" music but also forbade white musicians to play alongside of Negro, an increasing number of young white musicians, like Leon "Bix" Beiderbecke, Jack Teagarden and Benny

Goodman, began to study and play in this style, valuing its freedom of expression, and its breakdown of the barrier between performer and creator.

In 1927, Nicola Sacco and Bartolemeo Vanzetti were executed by the State of Massachusetts allegedly for robbery and murder, although the evidence showed they were obviously innocent. Their real offense was that they were, to use the refined words of the trial judge, "those anarchistic bastards." Their execution disclosed again a basic truth of American life: the existence, side by side with the great tradition of pride in and defense of democracy, of a tradition of brutal, selfish, wealth-inspired anti-labor violence proclaiming itself as "Americanism." The movement in defense of Sacco and Vanzetti enlisted some of the finest minds in American life, and indicated that even in the midst of the "jazz age," the democratic battle was gathering intensity. Then in 1929 the stock market collapse brought an abrupt end to the "jazz age" itself. In the five years following, the face of United States political and cultural life was transformed. The struggles of the unemployed for relief and jobs, the unstoppable movement of the workers in the great monopolized industries for the right to form unions, the angry defense by the farmers of their land against the mortgage-holding banks, brought deep democratic currents to the surface. These linked up with the world-wide horror of working people and all democratic people against fascism. With people of every national background, including Negro and white, discovering that they had common problems and needed one another, with gigantic battles of ideas breaking through in the political arena itself, a host of myths and stereotypes began to melt away. The history of the country was re-examined, and temporarily forgotten truths of its democratic heritage restored.

One product of the "proletarian thirties" was the first systematic collection and study of American folk music, aided by the operations of the work relief projects in the arts and by the Library of Congress. Another was the heavy blow given to cultural racism. Demolished was the racist approach to Negro music which described creative jazz as "jungle sounds" while ignoring its sensitivity, wit and pathos, and which ignored the earthy realism of the blues to transform them into an erotic performance for white slumming audiences. The folk roots of jazz and the blues were recognized. Jazz itself reached a new height of controlled and polished form, with Negro musicians in the leadership, such as the splendid bands grouped about Edward Kennedy "Duke" Ellington and William "Count" Basie.

Two trends arose, mutually influencing each other; that of a large-band music, and that of a "chamber music" of from three to seven players. Both of them explored the inexhaustible ore of the blues and also improvisationally reshaped popular tin-pan-alley songs in terms of the blues style and idiom, creating a finely organized music in which melody, harmony and instrumental timbre made one integral texture. Different from the instrumentation of the "New Orleans-Chicago" jazz of the twenties was the expanded role of the saxophone, both as a solo instrument and as a choir, in interplay against the brass choirs, and the elaboration of the "rhythm section," of piano, bass, guitar and drums, playing a sensitive harmonic and melodic as well as percussive role. The developed jazz band was an instrumental body of extraordinary sensitivity.

Also discovered in this decade were the riches of blues piano improvisation, by self-taught folk composers like Jimmy Yancey, Meade Lux Lewis and Pete Johnson. The best of the music thus produced, like the best of the rags, marches, blues compositions and "stomps" of the 1920's, although not written down, existing only on records, collectively makes up one of the most unique and vital bodies of music yet produced in the United States. As before, the new ideas, largely coming from Negro musicians, were adopted by the commercial music industry, stereotyped and vulgarized. Large and small band music, partly composed, partly improvised, was commercially known as "swing." Blues piano music was known as "boogie-woogie." But there grew as well an open recognition by white musicians of their debt to the Negro. Benny Goodman's band, which won enormous popularity, gave composer credit (something new for tin-pan-alley) to the Negro classic arrangements of blues, rags and stomps that he included in his repertory. Goodman and Artie Shaw broke a long-standing unwritten racist law by including Negro musicians side by side with white in their bands, although this aroused fury in many parts of the country, and the racist practises they fought are still today far from eliminated from the music industry.

The democratic currents which showed themselves in the jazz of the 'thirties were also felt by the Broadway musical theatre. *Of Thee I Sing*, with music by George Gershwin and text by George S. Kaufman, Morris Ryskind and Ira Gershwin, was the most brilliant and intelligent satire yet to emerge from the New York musical stage.

Gershwin's *Porgy and Bess* was a further step towards an opera touching with some seriousness on the life of the Negro people. It did little justice to its subject, substituting for invidious stereotypes the patronizing ones common to white people who declare themselves "friends of the Negro" but show a total ignorance of their real life and mind. The story is melodramatic and the characterizations are childish. The inanities, for example, of the mock-spiritual, "It Ain't Necessarily So," are a sharp contrast to the dignity and poetic imagination of the great treatments of Biblical legend in the spirituals created

438

by the Negro people themselves. Missing from the music-drama was the central factor of Negro life in the United States: the struggle for liberation, and the character of the oppression the people suffered. The situation could probably not have been much remedied at the time by having a Negro write the text. Negro people in popular cultural life still worked in an atmosphere of constant defensiveness, always aware of the manifold forms of prejudice and misunderstanding, using wit and even a mask of buffoonery as a protection, unwilling to speak openly. And to this day, there is no area of the American theatre, musical or otherwise, in which the Negro people can develop an art wholly shaped to their own satisfaction, without the hampering censorship brought by the presence of white agents, producers, managers, collaborators, critics and audiences. Yet *Porgy and Bess* showed the strength that could come from a move in the direction of the actualities of American life. And it was adorned by the Gershwin stream of melody, which consciously tapped Negro sources.

In 1936 came Marc Blitzstein's *The Cradle Will Rock,* in which a well-equipped composer used the idiom of jazz and popular ballad in the deliberately sardonic style of Kurt Weill's *The Three-penny Opera.* Its text, attacking the labor-baiting, strike-breaking and fascist-minded forces in American life, was too strong for acceptance by either the Federal theatre project, for which it had been written, or the Broadway commercial stage. But it was a popular-sponsored success.

Thus, just as "new" had supplanted "old" in the 1920's, with the jazz strains replacing the European-style operetta, so in the 1930's and early 1940's "new" again supplanted "old." The musical show in which an inane plot served as a vehicle for comedians, tap dancers, singers of "hit" tunes and a display of chorus girl pulchritude, was replaced by a more realistic approach to life and to musical form. The triumph of the new may be seen in the character of the shows that continued to win favor such as *Oklahoma, Carousel* and *South Pacific* by Rogers and Hammerstein, Cole Porter's *Kiss Me Kate,* and Kurt Weill's *Street Scene.*

Among "art composers" most dedicated to the purity and integrity of their style, a desire appeared to be "understood" and to find some contact with an audience by drawing upon folk music and finding themes in the American scene. Four composers may be cited as typical; William Grant Still (*b.* 1895), Virgil Thomson (*b.* 1896), Roy Harris (*b.* 1898) and Aaron Copland (*b.* 1900). No monumental achievements appeared; a sign not of the futility of the approach, but of the immensity of the problem. There was little searching critical discussion in musical circles of the way in which music achieves true national expression, or of the use of folk material other than the superficial process of quoting actual folk tunes.

In the *Afro-American Symphony* and the opera, *The Troubled Island,* William Grant Still tackled projects directly in the great tradition of a Dvorak and Mussorgsky. But while he produced works using Negro folk material with great dignity, warmth and beauty, lacking in them was the richness of texture and psychological depth necessary for greatness. Not enough of the knowledge contained in the heritage of past music was brought to bear upon the problems of the present. Thomson, in the cinema score, *The Plough that Broke the Plains* and the operas, *Four Saints in Three Acts* and *The Mother of Us All,* tended to use folk music in light, almost playful style, reminiscent of Poulenc and Milhaud in France. It is an art circumscribed by an abhorrence of the classic tradition, seeing it as too "pompous," and an equal abhorrence of the romantic traditon, as too self-revelatory. Its emotional life is limited to whimsicality, light tenderness and wit. Yet what it does display, if not depth, is the genuine love of the composer for his material.

Harris, in works like the *Third Symphony* and *Folk Song Symphony,* moved to the other extreme of a deep subjectivity, saturating himself in folk song but letting its melodic contours and sense of the outer world be drowned in a diffuse modal harmony and a brooding inner life. Nor does his polyphonic texture add real strength, for it has no links with the outer world of human movement and social activity. The moving yet unrealized quality of his work is a tragedy, for more than most American composers, he feels folk music as a creative and germinating material.

Copland's music remained restricted to a narrow emotional life, which had little room for the great drama taking place in American life outside of him. He moved between a nostalgic sadness and an outburst of hard motor energy and excitement. He fashioned a perfect musical style for this emotional life, one that was lean, economical and with his distinctive signature. Never is there a platitude in his work. Every sound is used lovingly. But the works in which folk themes entered, like *Appalachian Spring, Billy the Kid, Rodeo* and *A Lincoln Portrait,* failed to break this restrictive emotional framework. The folk tunes he used were beautiful. But they were handled with a Stravinskian aloofness, given a polished and clean-cut setting, expertly varied, and yet never used as a malleable material for human portraiture.

Yet, in this period of the 1930's and early 1940's, American music came closer to providing a richly democratic, if still incomplete, national expression. This achievement was the collective contribution of the best of jazz, of the best of the popular musical plays, of the folk-inspired "art" music, and of the rediscovery of the treasures of American folk music.

THE "Cold War" of the late 1940's and 1950's with its brandishing of hydrogen bombs, its McCarthyite witch-hunts, its steps so inimical to the interests of the American people as the rebuilding of the great German trusts, cartels and armament industry which had brought Hitler's fascism into being, the support of Latin American dictators like Jiménez in Venezuela and of fascist governments like that of Franco in Spain, has had a chilling effect on trends towards a democratic national expression. Many composers have withdrawn into a shell.

And yet, there is a groundswell in the direction of a musical art in which the American people can recognize their own presence, and it shows itself in a move towards the breakdown of the barrier between "art" and "popular" music. Other than in jazz, the greatest activity in this direction has been in music for the theatre. The following works of recent years can be cited, none of them achieving the stature of a great American opera, but together adding up to an impressive movement. One is Marc Blitzstein's *Regina,* with its fine social-critical drama, adapted from Lillian Hellman's *The Little Foxes,* and its frequently affecting musical setting, despite its lack of deep musical characterization. Another is Earl Robinson's *Sandhog,* with a libretto by Waldo Salt, embracing a warm approach to the working people of the land, and possessing genuinely lovely melody. There are Douglas Moore's *The Ballad of Baby Doe,* with a libretto by John LaTouche, and Carlisle Floyd's *Susannah,* which turn to the American scene and make an engaging use of folk strains. Notable is Robert Kurka's *The Good Soldier Schweik,* with a libretto based by Lewis Allen on Jaroslav Hasek's great novel. It is distinguished by its bold anti-war satire and its brilliantly witty score, with fine lyrical touches. There is Gian-Carlo Menotti's *Maria Golovin,* with its seriousness of plot and fine craftsmanship in setting text and stage action to music. A product of the Broadway theatre is Leonard Bernstein's *West Side Story,* composed to a book by Arthur Laurents, with its plea to end racism, and its strong, effective score, if somewhat too driving, hard and primitivist in its handling of jazz and popular musical motifs.

A potent influence upon American musical life has been the movement rising among all the world's peoples for a permanent end to war, which shows itself also in a deep interest by each nation in the life of others, and in an exchange of culture to an extent greater than ever before. And the United States music which still most fascinates other countries is that of jazz.

In jazz, there have been fresh developments since the end of the Second World War, with again Negro musicians leading the way, like John "Dizzy" Gillespie, Thelonius Monk, Charlie Parker, Errol Garner, Charles Mingus, and John Lewis and his Modern Jazz Quartet. It has moved to a knowing exploration of harmony, rapid modulation

SIDNEY FINKELSTEIN

through the circle of keys, dissonance, the interplay of two keys at once, and the utmost refinement of timbres. With Gillespie, it expresses a derisive wit aimed at the platitudes of commercial popular music, and there is a similar, if more impish, commentary in Thelonius Monk. Parker, drawing upon the blues for a touching, speech-inflected music, expressed a lonely and sometimes anguished emotional life. With Mingus there is also an explosion of lonely, bitter feelings. Garner combines an airy wit with a sweet lyricism.

With the Modern Jazz Quartet, the collective improvisation of jazz approaches a refinement of sound, mood and texture like that of impressionist composition. About them there have risen a flock of lesser talents, including also empty virtuosi, imitators and commercial vulgarizers. As always in jazz, only a comparative few have something to say of value. But a notable aspect of this "progressive" or "modern" jazz is that it has won a devoted popular audience, eagerly following its trials and errors, unintimidated by its experimental laboratory; a quite different situation from the classical concert hall, where the announcement of a "new" American work is likely to drive an audience away with its prospect of mystification or boredom.

Modern jazz, to its creators, represents the final, conclusive answer to the charge that jazz is an amateur, unlettered music and the product of inspired ignorance. But the freedom it proclaims is only that of the musician asserting his own integrity in the face of a musical world, still run by the market place and inimical to human values. It is also weak in form. Those who speak learnedly of the "form" achieved by modern jazz are making the same mistake as that of theoreticians of "art" music. They substitute a refinement of techniques and of textures, a succession of "moments," for genuinely strong art form, with its cumulative, developmental emotional experiences and sweep of life. And it is hardly possible for the jazz creators to take up such broader problems because of the conditions under which jazz operates, with talents bartered and sold like commodities, with unending threat of unemployment, and with a constant pressure for "novelties" to keep a musician's name before the public whether or not he has evolved some fresh musical ideas. There is no leisure but that brought by the lack of a job, no arena or forum in which a musician thinking seriously about life can work out the tools to create new forms of breadth and significance. There is no opportunity to range over the real heritage of music. Even the most inspired jazz musicians have little chance for growth.

The career of a jazz musician tends to follow an almost iron-clad pattern. He feels that he has something vital of his own to say. He develops a style, a "musical speech," in which he says it. He has a struggle for recognition. He is recognized, and perhaps even lionized,

442

with articles written about him, and he may discover his name mentioned in books. Disciples and imitators appear. Then a few years pass, new names push his to the background, and although the books on jazz may describe him as a "genius," he has all he can do to keep his head above water. For the truth is that although talent is an individual gift, the conditions for growth are laid down by society.

Jazz has its limitations even as a "national expression" of the American Negro people, as seen by the fact that they have developed other powerful forms of musical expression. There is the living stream of music heard in the Negro churches, the "gospel" singing of women like Mahalia Jackson, Rosetta Tharpe and Marie Knight, the striving of composers like William Grant Still or Ulysses Kay to master the "learned" heritage of music, the communication of the human core of the tradition of song which a Roland Hayes, Marian Anderson and Paul Robeson bring to the concert hall.

Jazz is a special product of the American Negro people within the artistic shambles of the commercial music industry, and in a society in which they are denied basic freedoms. It embodies a defiance of surrounding hostile and oppressive forces, with its growth, forms and textures shaped by a pathos and bitterness wrapped in a protective clothing of wit. If it has found so wide an acceptance among other peoples, who also collaborate in its creation, this is because they also feel the need for the freedom implied in its defiant expression. It is not a "music of the future" which will supplant the traditional musical heritage, as some of its historians claim. It is a valid, moving expression of its times. Its importance, aside from the body of genuine music it has by now already provided, is that it says something central to American life that no other American music, "art" or "popular," has said. It is that the strength of American music lies in its ability to speak for human freedom, that the demand of the Negro people for freedom strikes a response in the heart of other peoples, and that so long as the Negro people are not free socially, politically and culturally, no American people are free socially, politically and culturally. If the American people have not yet in sufficient numbers demanded the eradication of racism from American life, the influence of jazz has nevertheless been to make a host of people conscious of the corrosion in social and cultural life brought by this undemocracy and inhumanity.

To this jazz adds the reiteration of other truths about music. One is that music is a democratic art, not an art of an "elite," and that there are vast creative powers latent among the masses of people. Another is that music can flower in the most miraculous way from a handful of folk motifs, granted that the musician himself has something real and heartfelt to say in response to life. The growth of jazz, with its flock of performers and its audiences, also indicates the deep hunger for music on the part of the American people. This hunger is revealed as well in the vast sales of "classical" music through longplaying records, and the number of young people who take up "art" music despite the forbidding conditions of making a living through their musical talent. All these trends point to the coming breakdown of the artificial barrier between "popular" and "art" music.

What kind of music will we have when racism will be considered an incomprehensible relic of barbarous times? When the great heritage of centuries of musical art, along with the treasures of folk music, become a widespread popular possession? When music, like all the arts, will be considered a necessity of life, part of the development of the "whole man," without regard to its need to show a market-place profit or to be an exclusively professional career? When an all-over concept of music of integrity, serving a multitude of uses from dance and song to an expression of the deepest psychological portraiture and most sweeping drama, will replace the meaningless compartmentalization into "folk," "art," "popular," and "classical?"

Jazz will be part of it, as will symphonies, chamber music, tragic music drama, musical comedy, and popular song, all of them linked to one another in an honest portrayal of American life. It is in the direction of such a music that the United States will make its great world contribution, granted the elimination of racism, the ability to turn the immense productive forces of our land to the ending of starvation and poverty, the ability to turn the achievements of science from weapons of destruction to tools for the conquest of nature, and the opportunity of all peoples to progress peacefully with each helping the other. These are not dreams. They are today's unfinished business. They are the set of keys that will unlock the full creative resources of the nation.

Bibliography

The bibliography for jazz is quite large; the following represents only a relatively small selection of the material available. There are two bibliographies of jazz, both somewhat out of date: Alan P. Merriam, *A Bibliography of Jazz* (Philadelphia, American Folklore Society, 1954); and Robert George Reisner, *The Literature of Jazz: A Selective Bibliography* (New York, The New York Public Library, 1959). Additional reference works are: Robert S. Gold, *A Jazz Lexicon* (New York, Knopf, 1964); and Leonard Feather, *The Encyclopedia of Jazz*, rev. ed. (New York, Horizon, 1960), with its supplement, *The Encyclopedia of Jazz in the Sixties* (New York, Horizon, 1966), which include biographical material on jazz musicians. Books on the history of jazz and the blues include: Rudi Blesh, *Shining Trumpets: A History of Jazz*, 2d ed. (New York, Knopf, 1958); André Hodeir, *Jazz: Its Evolution and Essence* (New York, Grove, 1956); Charles Keil, *Urban Blues* (Chicago, University of Chicago Press, 1966); Paul Oliver, *Blues Fell This Morning: The Meaning of the Blues* (New York, Horizon, 1960); and Gunther Schuller, *Early Jazz, Its Roots and Musical Development* (New York, Oxford University Press, 1968). Nat Hentoff and Albert J. McCarthy, eds., *Jazz* (New York, Rinehart, 1959), and LeRoi Jones, *Black Music* (New York, Morrow, 1970), are anthologies of writings about selected topics and personalities of jazz. The Macmillan Company publishes *The Macmillan Jazz Masters Series* under the editorship of Martin Williams. Titles include: *Jazz Masters of the Twenties, Jazz Masters of the Swing Era, Jazz Masters of the Forties, Jazz Masters of the Fifties,* and *Jazz Masters of New Orleans.* A number of periodicals are devoted partially or entirely to jazz: in the United States, *Down Beat, Jazz and Pop,* and *Jazz Report;* in Canada, *Coda;* in the United Kingdom, *Jazz Journal, Jazz Monthly,* and *Jazz Times.* For jazz periodicals of other countries consult the music section of *Ulrich's International Periodicals Directory.*

Jazz is more a performer's art than a composer's; thus it can best be studied in performance, both live and recorded. For jazz recordings currently available consult the Jazz and Pop section of any recent issue of the *Schwann Record and Tape Guide.*

33

POPULAR music in the United States has been far from monolithic. Its many versions have included minstrel songs, operetta, Broadway ballads, ragtime, blues, jazz, folk, country and western, and most recently, rock and roll. Born in the 1950's, rock was an unpromising infant, was many times pronounced dying, and is now a teenage giant whose influence is being felt not only in popular music but throughout all areas of music. It has entered the concert hall sponsored by such scholarly groups as the Pro Musica Antiqua; the musical theatre with *Hair*, the second-longest-running show currently on Broadway; and the church, as exemplified by some of the recent vesper services organized by Alec Wyton, Organist and Master of the Choristers at the Cathedral of St. John the Divine in New York. For example, "The Age of Aquarius," the hit tune from *Hair*, has been used as the theme for an improvised postlude on the Cathedral organ at Sunday vespers.

If jazz began the removal of the barrier between popular and art music, rock has now also taken up the work. But the interchange has been reciprocal. Not only has the musical world been affected by rock, but rock has become serious both in its lyrics and in some of its techniques which it seems to have taken from art music. Some of the aspects of rock, its distinctive characteristics, and how it is changing music and also being changed is the subject of the following selection.

Arnold Shaw, author, lecturer, composer, and performer, has worked successfully in both popular and serious music. He has lectured at Juilliard and at the New School and has worked in music publishing. He has edited much of the music and writings of Joseph Schillinger, as well as having written his own books, of which the most recent are *The World of Soul* (New York, Cowles, 1970) and *The Rock Revolution* (London, Crowell-Collier, 1969). The following article is the introductory chapter to the latter book, in which the how and why of the nineteen points set forth here by Mr. Shaw are greatly developed.

Points about Rock

ARNOLD SHAW

The phrase Rock Revolution may sound like a metaphor or hyperbole. It is neither a figure of speech nor a rhetorical exaggeration. It quite literally characterizes what has happened to American music in the 1960s—a complete upending of the pop music scene.

When it first manifested itself in the mid-50s, rock was dismissed as an aberration and an abomination. At one end of the spectrum, Pablo Casals termed it "poison put to sound" while, at the other, Frank Sinatra damned it as "a rancid-smelling aphrodisiac." Repeated prophecies of its early demise, however, proved futile cries of frustration, as a St. Louis radio station demonstrated when it smashed stacks of rock 'n' roll disks over the air. Before the Presley rockabilly movement subsided, there was a rising tide of Negro rhythm-and-blues. Then came Bob Dylan and folk rock. Beatlemania took England and Europe by storm and proceeded to inundate American teenagers. Today, we have soul, raga rock, psychedelic rock and an influx of exotic instruments, electronic sounds and magnetic-tape music that is rattling the rafters of the entire music world, art as well as pop.

The year of Dylan's embrace of the electric guitar and the Big Beat, 1965, was the year in which the teenage rebellion matured into full-scale musical revolution. By then it was clear that the old days of so-called good music were not coming back. The era of the Big Bands, the Big Ballads and the Big Baritones was gone, along with crewcuts. Rock was not just a passing fad, but the sonic expression of the Now, the Turned-On, the Hair Generation. Literature had the antinovel and antihero. The stage had its Theater of the Absurd. In painting, there were mixed media, op, pop and ob art. And in pop, it was rock.

FROM Arnold Shaw, *The Rock Revolution* (London, Crowell-Collier Press, Collier-Macmillan Ltd.), pp. 1-6. Copyright ©1969 by Arnold Shaw. Reprinted by permission of The Macmillan Company.

The main features of the overthrow of the older generation's popular music culture may be listed as follows:

1. The guitar and other plucked, picked and strummed string instruments have superseded bowed instruments (violin), blown instruments (reeds and brass) and the piano as vocal accompaniment.

2. Control of pop has been taken out of the hands of major record companies, staff Artist and Repertoire (A & R) executives and Broadway-Hollywood publishing companies. The choice and character of material are now dictated by under-thirty artist-writers and independent record producers, and no major record company is today without a "house hippie," a hirsute A & R man in search of rock artists.

3. Established song forms, like the 32-bar chorus-cum-bridge, have given way to new forms characterized by odd-numbered formations, shifting meters, radical stanza patterns and changing time signatures.

4. The traditional division of labor among performer, writer and record producer has broken down. Instrumentalists sing and singers play instruments. Originators of material tend to account for the total product. "The medium is the message," and the record *is* the song.

5. Just as blues singers treated their voices as musical instruments, and balladeers of the 1940s handled the microphone as if it were an instrument, rock artists have made the recording studio their instrument and the amplifier their tool.

6. We are in the midst of an electrical explosion of sound. Magnetic tape and electronics have made the 1960s an era of echo chambers, variable speeds, and aleatory (chance) and programmed (computer) composition. New procedures include manipulation of texture as a developmental technique, "wall-of-sound" density and total enveloping sound. Philosophical as well as esthetic concepts underlie these developments: a concern with sensory overload as a means of liberating the self, expanding consciousness and rediscovering the world.

7. New subject matter includes an exploration of the cosmos of strange experiences, from the psychedelic expansion of the mind back into the world of medievalism and beyond time into transcendental meditation. We are in an era of meaningful lyrics, protesting, probing and poetic.

8. But we are also in a period when sound itself, as in jazz but in a more complex way, frequently is theme and content. If the folk orientation of rock emphasizes *meaning*, the psychedelic stresses tone color, texture, density and volume.

9. The record is being transformed into a miniature theater of playlets with music. The integrated suite, the extended pop song and unstructured music are becoming commonplace. *Continuity* becomes a compelling concern as more and more rock albums are for listening, not dancing.

10. Superalbums represent a new driving force, with outrageous sums of money being lavished not only on recording but on packaging.

11. Rock groups are concerned not merely with uniqueness of sound, long a requirement of singing and instrumental success, but with total image. Hair styles, wardrobe, LP covers and liners, and even the styling of promotion matter are no longer left to professionals but are the subject of personal and group expression.

12. The era of the raucous disk jockey is in a transitional stage. FM and progressive radio stations are receptive to recordings that by-pass traditional restrictions on time, treatment, outlook and even language.

13. The discotheque, a melange of vibrating colors, blinding images and deafening sound, has superseded the night club, cocktail lounge and jazz club as after-hour pads for teenagers.

14. For the first time in the history of popular music, we are developing canons of criticism. Just as there has long been a phalanx of concert and jazz critics, we now have an under-thirty group of reviewers whose work appears regularly in rock publications like *Crawdaddy, Rolling Stone, Cheetah* and *Eye* and is beginning to find space in *The New Yorker, Esquire, Life, Vogue* and other over-thirty periodicals.

15. Rock has brought a renascence of the bardic tradition. Like the medieval troubadours, Celtic bards and epic Homers, Leonard Cohen, Bob Dylan, Paul Simon and John Lennon are poets, singing rather than reciting or just printing their verses.

16. Rock is a collage, capable of absorbing the most diverse styles and influences: folk, blues, bluegrass, jazz, soul, country-and-western (c&w), rhythm-and-blues (r&b), motion picture themes, Broadway show tunes, Indian ragas, baroque, tape, computer and chance music. There is an increasing crossover between popular songwriting and serious composition.

17. In the outlook of the under-thirty generation, as reflected in rock, romanticism is dead. Realism, naturalism, mysticism and activism are the new acceptable and conflicting ideologies. Young people appear restless, tough, alienated, hostile, defiant, aggressive, frustrated—looking to the East rather than the West, more concerned with black than white, and vacillating between the put-down and the put-on, the hippie withdrawal from society and the yippie assault on it.

18. Rock is reaching an audience once impervious to and snobbish about pop music and rock 'n' roll. Whereas the college crowd once went for jazz, folk and symphony, it is now buying rock records and supporting rock groups.

19. The traditional tension between generations has grown to a point where the gap is almost like that between classes in a revolution-

ary era. The teeny-boppers, flower children, hippies and yippies all represent something more than mere rebellion against over-thirty values. Condemning the supermaterialism, duplicity and hypocrisy of the older generation, they are raising the banners of a new ideology embodying communal sharing, nonviolence, plain talk and equality. This is the first song culture, not only *for* under-thirty but *of* and *by* under-thirty.

How all this happened and *why* are among the questions I propose to answer. We also want to learn *who* made the revolution, details of their contribution, the varied manifestations of change, and the present direction and possible future of the insurrection. In short, I am concerned with the sociology and psychology as well as esthetics of what *Life* has called "the most popular music of all time."

In *Billboard's* year-end survey published early in 1968, the Artist of the Year was a forty-seven-year-old sitar player whose records never made pop bestseller charts. The curious choice of Ravi Shankar was sound recognition of his tremendous impact on teenage musicians and listeners. It was also an index to the vast expansion of outlook and content that pop and rock have undergone. In the classical field, traditionally separated from popular music by a deep moat of snobbery, record companies have also begun breaking out of their cramped confines. Suddenly, their new releases include large samples of modern European and American music, with increasing stress on electronic and avant-garde composers. "Without the Beatles," one company executive conceded, "we would have had no success with *Silver Apples*, an electronic work." And another stated, "There is no longer a fixed division between pop and classical." In other words, something of a revolution is beginning to develop in the classical field. Is it too much to suggest that the open-minded attitude of rock musicians and listeners is beginning to carry over into so-called serious music?

Having been patronized and reviled during much of its frenetic existence, American popular music is today being accorded the status and recognition of an art form. This, too, is a major, if not revolutionary, change that rock has effected.

Bibliography

Some of the more recent books on rock are: Carl Belz, *The Story of Rock* (New York, Oxford University Press, 1969); Nik Cohn, *Rock from the Beginning* (New York, Stein & Day, 1969); Jonathan Eisen, ed., *The Age of Rock* (New York, Random House, 1969), which is an anthology of writings on rock; Charlie Gillett, *The Sound of the City* (New York, Outerbridge & Dienstfrey, 1970); H. Kandy Rohde, ed., *The Gold of Rock and Roll 1955-1967* (New York, Arbor House, 1970), which includes weekly lists of the top ten rock recordings for the years 1955-1967 inclusive; and Lillian Roxon, *Rock Encyclopedia* (New York, Grossett & Dunlap, 1969). Lillian Roxon has observed that one of the greatest problems in writing about rock is that rock won't hold still long enough to have its picture taken. Writing on rock dates quickly because of the rapid changes to which rock is subject; the most up-to-date material is to be found in periodicals. Both *Down Beat* and *Jazz and Pop* include coverage of rock; *Crawdaddy* and *Rolling Stone* appear to be devoted exclusively to rock. Many perceptive articles on rock appear in non-trade magazines, such as *The Saturday Review, The New Yorker, Esquire,* and *Vogue.* The reader should consult the entries for "Rock Groups" and "Rock Music" in the *Reader's Guide to Periodical Literature* for these articles.

Current rock recordings are listed in the *Schwann Record and Tape Guide.* Current rock hits are usually available in sheet music at most music stores. Some rock hits fade quickly, however, and many of the older ones may be out of print.

34

FOR centuries some fundamentals have remained constant in music. The composer set down his musical ideas and frequently developed and varied them, all according to a musical logic accepted throughout Western civilization. Completed, the composition required that copies be written or printed in notation conventionally understood if it were ever to be perceived by anyone other than the composer; only through the distribution of such copies could the composition receive recognition. Once the copy reached a performer, either the composer himself or another, the composition could be transferred into the world of sound by performance, but a performance heard only by those performing and by such others as happened to be within hearing. This was the process necessary for the composer to convey his ideas to the public. The steps from composer to listener were so many that they necessitated a music profession—performers, teachers, concert managers, instrument makers, publishers, printers, copyists, salesmen—all those who function and earn their living in the world of music.

Music no longer conforms to the process just stated; although the points outlined above have not been entirely negated, not a single one is now essential for music to pass from the composer's mind to the listener's. A change has taken place in music, a change possibly as great as any which has ever occurred. The realization that things can never again be as they were is growing in all areas of music, except possibly education, and even there the truth must become evident soon. Students can no longer accept an education that trains them in an eighteenth- and nineteenth-century approach to music, else they will surely perish economically upon entry into the professional world.

An era is ending, one that goes back at least to the beginning of the Renaissance and perhaps even further; but a new era is beginning, one that can be just as thrilling, as challenging, and as difficult for those who are willing to accept it instead of mourning over bygone times. A revolution in music has come, and its weapon is the apparent-

ly harmless phonograph recording. How the phonograph has revolutionized music, some of the consequences of the revolution, and the changes
that are going to be necessary are the subjects of the following selection.

Eric Salzman, composer, author, critic, and teacher, is a contributing
editor to *Stereo Review,* and a program director for radio station WBAI
in New York. He has taught at Hunter College and has been a regular
music reviewer for both *The New York Times* and the now-defunct *New
York Herald-Tribune.* Virgil Thomson has pronounced him "the best
critic in America for contemporary and far-out music." He is author of
Twentieth-Century Music: An Introduction (Englewood Cliffs, N.J.,
Prentice-Hall, 1967) and of many periodical contributions on the contemporary musical scene.

The Revolution in Music

ERIC SALZMAN

In spite of the cliché about its universality, music has always been the most social of the arts—the most tied down to its time and place and the most susceptible to technological change. For example, the madrigal was the product of the new intellectual and humanist leisure class at the Renaissance courts, and it vanished as soon as the conditions which brought it about had disappeared. Opera, founded by and for an intellectual aristocracy and sustained by the absolutist monarchies of *le grand siècle*, evolved into middle-class entertainment. These changes are reflected in the switch from mythological subject matter *(Orfeo)* to pseudo-history *(Giulio Cesare)* to bourgeois comedy *(The Barber of Seville)*, and in the evolution of style represented by the humanist and innovative Monteverdi, the eclectic and learned Handel, and the melodic and popular Rossini. The poetry of Chopin and the virtuosity of Liszt are inconceivable without the technology to manufacture and reproduce a complex piece of machinery like the piano and the rise of a monied middle class to patronize the instrument and the salons and public concerts where it reigned supreme. Nor is it a coincidence that Viennese expressionism, "atonality," and dodecophonism appear in the city of Freud at the moment of the maximum technical refinement of traditional musical means and the advent of social anxiety, alienation, and crisis as dominant categories of experience.

Such examples could be multiplied indefinitely. But the purpose here is not to sketch the as-yet unwritten social history of music; it is merely to open a perspective for understanding the development of new music and musical life today. For contemporary music is no less responsive to the conditions of contemporary society and technology. Indeed, these conditions are altering musical life and musical experience in revolutionary ways. We can begin with the basic and most sweeping

FROM *New American Review,* no. 6 (Spring 1969), 76-96. Reprinted by permission of the author.

change: that the central means of musical communication is no longer the live performance but the recording.

Recorded music is, first of all, omnipresent today. In a (sometimes vain) attempt to cover up both the din and the void of contemporary existence, music pours out of transistor radios, out of elevator, factory, and department-store loudspeakers, out of jet plane headphones, restaurant walls, and open windows. But it would be a mistake to think of the ubiquitousness of recorded music only in terms of Muzak or the latest pop-rock. As Paul Goodman has noted, even the dropout owns a record-player—the one artifact of the technology that he thinks worth preserving. Records have made the new FM as well as the old AM radio possible. Many young people who have never been to a concert (and wouldn't dream of going) own large and varied record collections and have more musical sophistication (of a kind, to be sure) than most of the subscription public of the New York Philharmonic. There has been, above all, an incalculable increase in the sheer amount and variety of musical experience that is easily and inexpensively available.

RECORDINGS widen the range of musical experience in every direction. Through recordings we have far more of the past available to us than at any previous time in musical history. Contrary to popular belief, music has been, until recently, an art virtually without a past. Nothing dies faster than yesterday's music. The complete output of many a famous composer, of entire performing traditions, vanished in a generation or less. The handful of older classics that survived or were revived were reedited, bowdlerized, or otherwise distorted. The attempt to give music a past began at the end of the nineteenth century with the foundations of modern musicology, but it is only in the last decade or two that this work has borne fruit. Literally hundreds of works and dozens of composers—whole epochs, such as the Renaissance, and non-Western traditions, such as the Indian—have entered contemporary consciousness through recordings. Ravi Shankar, Vivaldi, John Cage, early ragtime, Gagaku, medieval chant, Varèse, Balinese gamelan, Dufay, Schoenberg, African drumming, Josquin, late Beethoven quartets, electronic music, rhythm and blues, Monteverdi, Mahler, Carl Nielsen, Charles Ives . . . the list could be (and is being) extended indefinitely. Most of this was unknown, forgotten, or esoteric a mere decade ago. Today, along with all kinds of pop, folk, jazz, and rock, along with Montevani, Muzak, background music, and the classical repertory, it has all become part of the shared common experience. Any day's FM radio in one of the larger cities transmits a more varied repertoire than the symphony orchestras of the United States produce in a year. If the myth of universality is now becoming a reality, this is almost entirely the result of recording technology which, by preserving performance and by diffusing the world's musics quickly and cheaply, has given the art for the first time a past, multiple presents, and a possible future.

THIS multiplicity and diversity of musical experience is the most central change that recording has wrought, but it is by no means the only one. For example, the only general writing about music of any wide interest in the United States today is to be found in the record magazines, one of which recently absorbed (as an insert!) the last remaining general music magazine. These record magazines and FM radio are the principal sources of information for an informed and responsive audience that barely overlaps the traditional "musical public." This explains why an off-season concert by a provincial European artist known for his popular-price recordings will outdraw all but a handful of the great romantic virtuosi. Although public performance still carries residual prestige, the concert world is rapidly becoming an adjunct to the recording industry. Many established performers regard live appearances in major cities as an effective way of embellishing their reputations as recording artists. Others use recordings as publicity leaders for their live tours. Meanwhile, record companies are becoming the behind-the-scenes powers in the music business, dictating the selection of conductors, soloists, and even repertoire. Who plays and what is played Saturday night can be recorded Monday morning if a record company is interested. Recording sessions and recording contracts pay deficits and augment salaries. The rest of the syllogism is easily supplied.

RECORDINGS have also influenced the interests and performing style of the present generation of musicians. The vogue of early music invaded the concert hall from the recording studio. Similarly, the contemporary taste for accurate, clear, and unmannered performance derives from the priorities of the recording medium. The extension of this style into live performance is undoubtedly an error, but it is a revealing one. (Most musicians and critics would be astonished by the notion that different media might require different interpretations of the same work.) The prevailing aural image today is that of "canned" sound; the LP generation actually prefers the resonance that engineers love to introduce, as well as the subtle, inevitable biases of loudspeaker systems, and is often disappointed by the imperfections and lack of "presence," or richness, of most live performance. Modern concert halls are built to sound like hi-fi sets, and pop music is based entirely on electronically amplified sound.

Recordings are often cited by tradition-oriented musicians as the reason for the decline of live music. There is, as we have seen, some basis in fact for this charge. However, the dominance of recorded music does not justify the further charge that the recording culture has fostered a passive involvement with music. On the contrary, there is good reason to believe that one of its principal effects has been to encourage and improve active participation. Amateur chamber music performance today enjoys a popularity and technical proficiency never remotely equaled in the legendary old-world salons. Pop music today is almost entirely in the hands of "amateurs." Young performers today can sight-read difficult music by Schoenberg or Boulez that their elders could barely cope with; I have heard Princeton high school students give accurate and musical performances of the Webern cantatas, which only a few years ago were considered to be all but impossible to perform.

Thanks to recordings, the transmission of musical culture and professional practice through the inadequate system of notation, the uncertain master-pupil relationship, and the occasional live performance is becoming largely a thing of the past. Instead of visual cues, learning routines, and uncertain recollections, recordings present the thing itself in an unvarying, repeatable form. Even though American music students are not particularly noted for their discipline, and even though the old regime of Czerny and Hanon is practically dead, the general level of technique has never been higher; Americans lead the world in these matters. After half a century during which performers fell further and further behind the demands of new music there has been a sudden and dramatic breakthrough in only a few years. The reason for this is that when music can be adequately conceptualized, trained fingers will eventually follow along. Recordings offer conceptual models in actual sound, and the impact on performance has been enormous.

Because the recording can provide the experience in its proper form, *as sound*, it has also virtually replaced the expensive printed score as the primary means of disseminating a work or an interpretation. New works are often recorded directly from manuscript. (Occasionally the success of a new work in recorded form is used to justify publishing a study score!) Formerly pianists published "editions" of their interpretations of the classics to reach a larger audience and to pass on information and insight. These, too, are being supplanted by recorded versions. In general, the record has shifted the musician's focus of interest from the printed score and brought it back to the sound experience itself.

With this change, the whole notion of what constitutes a musical work of art has altered. The tendency of the nineteenth and early twentieth century, which brought to perfection a strict, complex system of notational devices, was to circumscribe the musical work more and more as an object: hence the mystique that still surrounds the "score." The primacy of recorded music has put the emphasis back where it belongs—on the performance, on the listening experience, on the fact of realization in time. Much of the new pop music, as well as most electronic composition, cannot be reduced to a score in any meaningful way; existing notations are used merely to remind performers of the way it goes or else for copyright purposes (records cannot be copyrighted).

THE end result of the recording process is an endlessly repeatable fixed performance. By a kind of reverse effect, however, recording has also stimulated interest in the nonfixed (open-form, improvised) live performance. Improved recording techniques, the introduction of stereo, and a general revival of interest in acoustical problems have helped to suggest new dimensions for musical discourse, notably the use of the space of a performance as an integral part of the musical conception. Furthermore, some aspects of musical experience which had been inadequately provided for in traditional notation and which had always been considered "external" and of purely secondary importance—texture, timbre, accent, dynamic—have become major points of interest.

All of this has been aided and abetted by the technology itself. Tape editing and mixing eliminates error and also introduces all kinds of simple technical possibilities. Any known sound may be recorded and juxtaposed or mixed with any other known sounds. Environmental sounds (the so-called *musique concrète)* as well as musical material in the old sense may be spliced or mixed together in untouched form, or altered and transformed through a variety of tape and electronic techniques. Electronic music proper includes the wide-open range of "synthesized" sound produced by various kinds of signal generators. The input of the system is no longer taken from physical sound but is produced directly by special equipment which offers the composer direct and refined control as well as a huge range of possibilities, many of them obtainable by no other means. The composer of electronic music builds up his piece on tape, working directly with the material and shaping it just as a visual artist works directly on and with his material. The original exists only as a master tape, which may then be copied—like prints or casts—or put on a disk.

Formerly, a good deal was made of the distinction between "pure" electronic music and *musique concrète;* nowadays, however, the media are quite generally mixed. Similarly, the distinctions between live and electronic works are less and less clear-cut. Electronic musical instruments (incapable of the wide range of the synthesizers but designed to be played in real time like traditional instruments) include the electronic organ, the theremin, the *ondes martenot,* the electric piano and harpsichord. Formerly considered hybrid or bastard types, they have recently been accepted as legitimate. Electronically assisted sound, long a commonplace in pop music (milked voices, electric guitar, etc.), is now used elsewhere—surreptitiously by "classical" singers who wish to boost small voices, openly by composers who want to oppose live and amplified sounds, control dynamic and timbre, and project sound into the space of the hall. Such sound pickups can also be altered electronically on the spot—the rock guitarist's "fuzz" tone is a good example—as well as mixed and projected in various ways that are only beginning to be explored.

ALL of which is to say that the impact of electronic technology on musical culture is evident on all sides; yet there has been little recognition that a revolution even exists. The dependent relationship of live to recorded music, the growth of a new audience brought up on recorded music, and the changing role of music in contemporary life are matters of only the most superficial concern to the business-as-usual music business. The older musical world lumbers on: as in most other areas of our lives, we are trying to manage late twentieth-century developments with nineteenth-century institutions. Foundations put huge sums of money into "worthy" musical causes, often with the avowed aim of sustaining the older institutions or creating new ones on the model of the old—and often thwarting genuine new growth in the process. Elaborate facilities, modeled on Lincoln Center, are established, and then there is a desperate search for content, for something to put inside. Conservatories and schools of music prepare thousands of talented students for careers that simply do not exist. Composers write hundreds of worthy works for no possible audience and no meaningful purpose. The solo recital is in trouble but no one quite knows why. Jazz musicians, ousted from the clubs and dance halls by rock amateurs, cannot understand why they cannot do their thing and make a living. After having spent a small fortune on a New York debut recital (even hiring a publicity agent), young performers discover that they cannot draw an audience without papering the house and cannot cash in on their reviews.

In a certain sense, much of what passes for official musical "culture" is a vast deception: there is a thin and artificially supported veneer of live "classical" subscription culture at the top, a huge industry of music education and management at the bottom, and the bitter "real" world of pop and show biz in between. Recording is regarded as a kind of spurious offshoot, resented, misunderstood, and tolerated because it is so wildly successful, but seldom understood as a positive, innovative force. New music, the real source of vitality in any musical culture, remains in a curious limbo—despised by the critics, ignored by the intelligentsia, misguidedly supported in its weakest aspects by the foundations and the academy, raided for ideas by pop groups, jazzmen, arrangers, and background-music composers, and surviving in its own underground subculture and through recordings.

Rock is the music of the hour. A number of critics and journalists and even some classically trained musicians regard it as the wave of the future. But there is no reason to think that the vitality and success of rock make other forms of contemporary expression invalid, or that rock is somehow above or beyond the forces that have pushed and shaped other forms of contemporary expression. On the contrary, we see that within a period of only a few years, rock has undergone the same cycle of growth, popular appeal, intellectual acceptance, commercialization, neoclassicism, and avant-gardism that jazz and nonjazz underwent earlier. Experimental rock flourished briefly, and has now been apparently submerged in a wave of nostalgia and neoclassicism. But it will return just as surely as avant-garde music bounced back after the nostalgic, populist thirties and forties, or as experimental jazz picked up the motifs of progressive jazz after they were supposedly dead and buried. There is no essential difference today between experimental rock, the new jazz, and all the rest of the avant-garde—only between traditionalists, sentimentalists, neoclassicists, minimalists, and maximalists in every field.

THE reason for this merging of contemporary modes is that the nature and the "quality" of musical experience have irrevocably altered. Up until a decade or so ago, most musical culture was "mainstream;" only limited kinds of shared musical experience were widely accepted or even available. This is no longer true. As has been suggested, music finally has a real past as well as a diversity of present tenses. In theory and, increasingly, in reality, the entire musical expression of the human race that has been handed down to us is now part of the common fund of experience, indeed part of the buzzing, blooming aural confusion of contemporary life. These seemingly limitless invasions of aural information and experience in perpetual transmission through technology quickly become incorporated into the general consciousnes. At the same time, through a kind of electronic version of the Heisenberg principle, technology alters every experience it transmits—whether intentionally through the conscious use of electronics or merely through the fact that electronics so often intervene now between the sound and our perception of it. This multiplicity of nonverbal, transformed aural experience—information over-load if you will—inevitably produces new kinds of sensibility and new modes of perception.

The "musical public," educated in and by another kind of musical culture, opposes the expression of this consciousness. Perhaps they are right to do so: our traditional musical institutions were created by another age for another kind of experience, and should perhaps be protected as museums for traditional art. However, just as the old mode of musical communication is no longer the only (or even the dominant) one, so its musical public is no longer *the* music public. Technology

ERIC SALZMAN

has created a multiplicity of publics; the myth of a single "serious" audience is no longer tenable. The members of a later generation, not
brought up on the traditional forms, have other modes of taste and
awareness. If they know the traditional forms, they know them through
a different medium and in another way—not as a unique tradition but
as part of a larger conditioning. The LP generation *hears* differently—
more comprehensively, without much concern for the old priorities of
order and progression. The new generation is aurally oriented, and music (especially in its nonlinear manifestations) is its art. Similarly, the
myths of developing styles and schools, of historical necessity, of some
single, necessary mentality in modern art—all notions held over from
the old dialectical view of cultural history—are no longer serviceable.
The old dualisms are dead; there is no avant-garde any more. All
styles, all schools—all *possible* styles and schools—exist simultaneously;
or, which is much the same thing, the notion of school and style is
dead. "Modern music" is dead . . . long live modern music!

WE can take it for granted that new art will respond to this diversity
in diverse ways. No doubt much new music—even some that passes
for "avant-garde"—represents a continuation of older modes of thought.
It is in the nature of things nowadays that various kinds of music
will coexist and even be newly created. Instead of the single river of
culture that seemed to dominate Western Europe after the Renaissance,
we have many smaller streams, combining, separating, and recombining,
appearing and disappearing, ebbing and flowing at different rates of
speed—rapids, eddies, backwaters, and all.

One response has been to retreat from the aural over-load I have
been describing into a pure art world. This is not only the position
of the so-called conservatives, like Menotti, Barber, or Britten, but also of the minimalists, who consciously reduce the art work to a single
unitary experience in order to give it definition, to keep it free of
extraneous material, and, perhaps, to add a kind of probing, scientific
aura. Mini-art carries the single experience to its ultimate possible conclusions, or derives all the ramifications of some single premise. Although
the term "minimal" has been mostly applied to certain recent works
of visual art, it can characterize a broad tendency of new musical developments since World War II—curiously enough, of both the ultrara-
tional, total-control "serialists" and the antirational, anticontrol composers of aleatory, or chance, music. The basic tenet of serialism—whose
leading figure has been Milton Babbitt—is maximum variety with maximum unity achieved through the total permutations of a short, single
set of elements. But most so-called aleatory music structures a situation
in which only certain choices—whether "musical," gestural, or both—
are possible and these must be chosen randomly (one choice being as

462

good as another) or in obsessively repetitious cycles. Serial and aleatory music, then, express a parallel reduction of content. Bits of experience are sustained or repeated over and over in various phased cycles whose effect is "mathematical" or "psychedelic"—"head" music either way.

A good deal of mini-music has a lineage that traces directly back to John Cage—mainly through the work of Morton Feldman, whose long-drawn-out soft sounds set at the very edge of perceptibility have had great influence. But Cage's work, much of it indubitably "mini," escapes such easy classification, and its long-range significance probably lies elsewhere. His famous *4′ 33″* of silence, at first blush the very model of an extreme mini-music, really has to do with the idea that art and life should be identical—Cage wanted his audience to hear the accidental, "natural" sounds of the environment. The notion that a musical experience is simply a matter of opening your ears—anywhere, anytime—and *really* listening takes us very far from the purity and escapism of minimal art.

Cage's insistence on discrediting the old distinction between art and life (which has, ironically, led to his own personality and life being described as his greatest work of art) brings us close to the elimination of art altogether; not surprisingly, Cage has become a kind of culture hero to the anti-Culture radicals. For many young (and not-so-young) people, the old notion of High Art and Kultur is a false value which they reject along with the rest of bourgeois culture. The Happenings—many of whose organizers had studied with Cage at The New School—were, in part, a stage along the way. A further and more decisive step has been the replacement of art by some kind of activism— street theater, "guerrilla theater," actual social protest or disruption. The Yippies have been quite explicit about the use of imaginative put-on and disruption as a kind of anti-Art art form. This is more than commitment in art; it is the transformation of art into something else. At another extreme, drug culture—while it lasted—was also a kind of art-substitute: every man his own artist. Such energies are now often directed toward the ideal of a community in which there are no specialists such as artists and everyone participates in all activities including the production of music, which generally plays an important role in the communal life. (Hence the interest in tribal cultures such as that of the Balinese, who have no word for art; asked why, a Balinese sage replied, "We have no 'art'; we just do the best we can.")

The communitarianism of the Hippies, Diggers, Provos, *et el.*, has deeper roots in American culture than most people care to realize. Along with religious sects such as the Shakers, Amish, Moravians, and Mormons, the social landscape of the nineteenth century was dotted with utopian communities bred by native American radicalism. Some of this influence can be found in the work and thought of Charles

463

ERIC SALZMAN

Ives, who spent the last thirty years of his life working on a "Universal Symphony" which everyone who wanted to could perform and even contribute a part. Similarly, the work of Harry Partch in building musical instruments and creating a community of young performers—not necessarily professional musicians—is influential in the communal movement. There are today a number of groups of "non-artists" (or ex-artists) working together in cooperatives without regard for the old distinctions of form or medium. Most of these brethren disdain the cult of "art": they usually refer to their groups as "media workshops" and their products are not individually signed. Their work is technologically oriented and mainly environmental-visual—light shows, electronic sculpture, and the like. What is essential to recognize here is the growing reaction against the restricted Romantic notion of art and the art work, notions that none of the earlier pioneers of twentieth-century art—with the exception of Duchamp and perhaps Ives and Varèse—succeeded in throwing off.

Given all this, the fascination with rock and related forms of pop is easy to understand. Rock is non-High Art; it is back-to-nature matured under the impact of technology; it is, in its recent forms, very much a cooperative activity, and it is participatory, not just because anyone can do it but because it invites and is performed in situations that encourage physical reaction—not dancing in the old sense but free physical expression. Rock is improvisatory, creative within an easily graspable framework, and expressive of the moment. By borrowing the light show and media mix from the Happenings and environments of the late fifties and early sixties, it has achieved a total environmental form. It even aspires to universality both in its worldwide impact and in its attempts to use, absorb, and transform all kinds of other musics. White rock (as distinct from the black modes from which it derives) is in fact a consciously synthetic *art* which has borrowed and sometimes absorbed elements from such diverse sources as rhythm and blues, country music, folk music, Indian music, jazz, baroque music, Beethoven, and even tape and electronic music.

Attempts like that of the Vanilla Fudge to recreate the history of music with a rock beat, or of the Beatles and the Mothers of Invention to redo the history of American pop music, or of several other groups to merge the divergent streams of jazz and rock are astonishing examples—disastrous in some cases, fascinating in others—of an intuition which I believe is fast becoming the most basic characteristic of the new sensibility—the acceptance of all modes of experience: *Nihil humananum alienum est.*

THIS, in my view, is the most important and basic thing we can learn from Cage and his work and, interestingly enough, it leads us in

464

exactly the opposite direction from mini-art. Earlier precedents can be found in the work of Ives and Varèse—which is why their music is still a vital influence where the impact of the European modernists has faded. In this light, some of the anti-Art attitudes become comprehensible since the Romantic notions of art and culture are limiting and exclusive. Some commentators have claimed that rock "liberates" the musics or musical "styles" that it uses or absorbs by giving them a new and "meaningful" context. But the actual process is just the reverse: the loosening up of big beat music by infiltration. The new rock has already succeeded in making a younger audience responsive to nonrock. Ravi Shankar and Indian music are obvious examples, but there is a whole new audience for other kinds of nonpop as well. It is all but impossible to explain to most of the older generation in this country what it is that a contemporary nonpop composer actually does, but it is only necessary to say to a member of the younger generation, "Oh, I write electronic music." I have played tape music in rock emporiums in the East and West with considerable success, and records of electronic music are becoming popular among the younger audience. Interestingly enough, the term "electronic music" is not restrictive to them at all but has come to refer to any new music, whether actually electronic or not.

There is a kind of prescience in this open-ended view of things. The old distinctions between the categories and genres and even the Art-versus-anti-Art question of the media workshops become secondary once the real issues of new musical expression and the state of the culture that must be expressed are understood. We are in a situation which is entirely new in the history of music: *anything is possible.* This is not merely a statement of libertarian aesthetics but of an overwhelming practical, technical problem. Any sound that exists can be recorded and is therefore potential raw material. The limitations are no longer those of a performer's vocal chords or fingers but the limitations of perception. All levels of control or noncontrol are available. The composer-performer-audience relationship is necessarily redefined by each new work or each experience. There is no *a priori* reason why any type of sound or aspect of sound (for example, pitch or "melody" in the traditional sense) should be dominant over other types or aspects (for example, noise or tone color), although a particular work may make it so. Sound may be used for its own value as the experience itself (whatever that means), but it may also appear as imagery—i.e., as allusions to the sounds of the real world or to other music, much in the manner of visual images.

But this is not a roundabout way of saying "anything goes." I have been outlining a rather precise set of conditions with certain specific implications. To say "anything is possible" is the beginning of an attempt to understand certain conditions of contemporary auditory experience which must be mastered, interpreted, and put to meaningful use. Nor is this only an issue of "technique." To use McLuhan's image, our auditory nerve has been suddenly extended around the world, and we are receiving impulses from all corners of the global village. The entire musical expression of mankind—as it has been handed on and as it continues to develop—is available to us along with all the known and unknown sounds of the visible and invisible world. This is not mysticism but simple fact.

In the face of it, the concept of the art work and its function needs to be genuinely redefined. The romantic notion of "style"—of the art work as an artifact, historically determined but reflecting the individuality of its creator, expressive of its time but hopefully ahead of it—dies hard. Indeed, in this sense, most modern art is only the last phase of romanticism, with its search for individuality and historical necessity. Creative artists are still sometimes thought to choose or find "their style" from among the many possibilities available. The original ones are those who invent "new styles"; there is much learned discussion about borrowings and influences. But all this suddenly seems irrelevant. All styles—all possible styles, one is tempted to say—are now perpetually present, continuously, terrifyingly available. The old linear forms based on process and directionality—the musical equivalents of narrative—are, if not superseded now, only one set of possibilities among many.

THE pressing task, therefore, is not that of accepting or rejecting traditional (or any other) modes and media, or, as in earlier modern art, of handling some new fund of materials and processes. The pressing task is to create a new context for different kinds of experiences. We are not merely talking about new forms but about a new totality of possible forms; not merely about technical processes but about a *maximum* of experience which includes process and nonprocess; not about polemical prescriptions for avant-garde art but about a condition of contemporary life which becomes a condition of its artistic expression.

Originality and individuality will continue to take care of themselves; they will result naturally from the operations of an original mind on complex cultural material. Or from a collaboration of such minds. The necessity for collaboration has always been the fatal flaw of the romantic notion of individuality: Wagner could write the words, compose the music, direct the stage and the orchestra, even design the scenery and the theater itself; but not even Wagner could play all the instruments and take all the roles. Nor could he be his own audience. The whole complex apparatus of nineteenth-century music education and appreciation, with its goal of producing the trained, specialized virtuoso listener as well as performer, was doomed to failure. Its *reductio ad absurdum* is the piece of modern music designed to be heard only by Ph.D. candidates. Similarly, minimal art can be considered the last phase of the old notions of individuality and style carried to their extremes.

Once these ideas are discarded or at least recognized to be limited, many other kinds of musical forms and meanings suggest themselves, particularly in the areas of art-as-environment, art-as-activity, art-as-theater. The ordinary notion of performance may be extended through the mixing of styles and modes of performance, through electronic amplification and transformation as well as sound synthesis. Electronically synthesized sound and sound recorded from the real world may be put together with plain, amplified, or recorded "musical" sounds and this whole body of materials, activities, and experiences can be projected and mixed with visual elements. Familiar and unfamiliar experiences may appear in new and surprising forms and juxtapositions. Qualities of experience—which may be described in terms such as strictness and freedom, fixed detail and improvisation, motion and stasis, high and low tension, complexity and simplicity, confusion and clarity, sound and silence, abstract sound and language, dramatic and abstract form, image and process, live and recorded, extremes of register, dynamic, density, and spatial directionality and so forth—must not be misunderstood as new dualisms replacing old ones but as continuums of experience which are at once raw material and subject matter. The range of possibility is represented by a slice of it—a cross-grain cut so to speak—which is organized by the very act of mediation between contradictions and extremes. The conditions under which this takes place must be established and reestablished freshly and uniquely by each work and even at each performance.

Interestingly enough, the experience of working in this way—maximal instead of minimal—suggests that the typical modern-art idea that a perceptive experience may be valid for its own sake is not adequate. The fact that *any* perceptive experience is possible suggests that merely using any *one* for its own sake is not in itself quite enough. One wants to know how such experience might be recapitulated, focused, heightened, interrelated, and communicated throughout the range of human capacities. Curiously, one comes back by a very involved route to an obvious, old bit of wisdom: it's not merely what you do that counts but how you do it.

The fact that it is possible to go up to and beyond the boundaries of perception makes the exploration of those boundaries a viable subject matter. The best new music is expressive in the sense that it is an art that is again "about something"—the complex nature of contemporary experience and perception. Ranges of perception, conflicting information, modes of communication, and "informational overload" are explored through a particular set of premises growing out of an increasingly enlarged and shared fund of knowledge and experience. Music has always been in some sense a metaphor for the way people relate to one another and to their environment, but in the new music this becomes an explicit and even dramatic subject matter.

THE problem of illustrating maximal music is not an easy one, especially since the few contemporary works which have penetrated the general consciousness are not especially *a propos*. I may be criticized for using my own work as a relevant example of the foregoing discussion, or for producing the foregoing as a justification for my own work. Both comments have their point. It is always difficult to measure the extent to which one's creative work follows from one's general views and, conversely, the extent to which these views derive from one's own work.

Foxes and Hedgehogs (Verses and Cantos) was written in 1964-67 and first performed on November 30, 1967, at the Hunter College "New Images of Sound" series in New York. The form is called "music theater" — a term that is meant to stand in contradistinction to both conventional opera and the musical. It deals with multidimensional, multilayer situations, and the extension of live performance through technology, all expressed in a musical-dramatic form. The dramatic elements of the work are derived from the musical experience — the opposite of the old procedure in which the music follows a preexisting text or plot. The texts come from John Ashbery's *Europe,* a poem which is in itself closer to certain forms of contemporary nonverbal art than to traditional poetic form. *Europe* is an extraordinarily rich arrangement of nonlinear language which functions not merely as sounds or patterns on a page but also as highly charged conveyors of meaning and nonmeaning — from the most banal to the most picturesque, from the verbal cliché to the most complex and obscure sequences of images. Meaning operates not as narrative or as lyrical evocation, but as a series of cross-cuts through an immense variety of verbal experiences and images. The expressive unit may be a single charged word or a verse-paragraph of 150 words of flat-footed exposition. This complex of verbal cues and metaphors, images of confusion and contradiction, and states of recognition, suggested a musical form in which layers of memory and expectation, familiarity and strangeness, consistency and confusion, inevitability and randomness, conscious recall and irrational association would appear as giant counterpoints — one could almost say counterpoints of states of consciousness or even ways of life.

Foxes and Hedgehogs, however, is not a "setting" of the text in the usual sense. It strives toward a parallel form based on "layers" of experience of which the text is one: at times on the surface, at others submerged by its new environment; at times a primary factor, at others a peripheral one; at times clarified in ways that could never be achieved on the printed page, at others ripped apart, jumbled, and destroyed.

These texts are conveyed principally by four solo singers, one of whom doubles as a narrator. There is a pit band, with a conductor in formal dress, performing the ritualistic functions of a theater or opera orchestra. A second group of players—something like a jazz combo—are participants in the action. They warm up on the stage and have their exits and entrances, their dialogues and arias, just like the vocalists. All of the live sound is at times picked up by microphones and amplified to various degrees. By this means, single strands can be picked out of a complex texture, live sound can be boosted and altered in various ways and projected into, and from, different parts of the hall. There is also tape material which ranges from the unaltered, pre-recorded sound of the live performers to collage. Sound that is heard first live comes back afterward as a kind of echo from the back of the hall. Other musics are heard first in recorded form or in simultaneous live and tape versions, or in one or the other form only. Thus live sound is transformed and projected out into the hall and then, in a kind of image-versus-reality confrontation, projected back from the hall toward the stage. Techniques of traditional-modern music appear in conflict with elements of pop and jazz, simple lyric song alternates with nonverbal vocal activity of every description, changing textures and densities of vocal and instrumental sound interact with tape and electronic projections. Instrumentalists shout and speak as well as produce a wide array of tones and noises, many of them well beyond the classical techniques of their instruments. The act of performance itself is sometimes highly structured through precise notation, sometimes loose and improvisatory, permitting a flexible unfolding of simultaneous and sequential events, and an interaction (or lack of it) among the performers and between the performers and the aural images of their activities as projected out and back electronically. The work, however, has a general form that moves from strictness to freedom, beginning with complex, structured instrumental material and verbal inarticulateness and ending with a wide-ranging collage of verbal and vocal sounds and of tape and live fragments. The climax is a giant collision of a live structured improvisation and a rock collage on tape pouring out of every loudspeaker.

In *Foxes and Hedgehogs*, nothing is given up; there are no acts of penance, no renunciations. We are talking about an art that is inclusive, not exclusive. There are no *a priori* judgments or precodified rules of form. There are no fixed goals because this is an art of transformations—transformations which take place in every domain and throughout the range of perception. Transformations are ways of experiencing and acting, and of relating action to experience—i.e., of knowing. They can themselves extend the quality of experience, of the way we perceive and the way we relate our perceptions—i.e., the way we know.

No doubt something is lost in the process; it could hardly be otherwise. Certainly there are dangers and pitfalls—the dangers of "anything goes," of overfacility, of confusion and incoherence, of gimmickry, of a new multi-media escapism. But at least they are the real and relevant dangers and can be faced as such. The problem is to understand the nature of the technological and cultural change and try to find out how something creative might come out of it.

WE are not, it seems to me, at the end of art but at the beginning of a new kind of artistic experience. It might still be possible to create something for old forms in a new way—it should not be necessary to discard any means, even the most traditional. But the overriding issue is the search for new forms—and the new social and cultural institutions that must be created to go with them. I have said little about this latter question, but it is not a separate one. Our Lincoln Centers are not prepared or equipped to deal with this problem; neither are our symphony orchestras, nor our opera houses, nor our concert institutions, nor the foundations, nor the critics, nor the mass media, nor even the record companies. I am not certain what forms these new institutions will take, or to what extent they will have to come as part of a general change in the structure of our society. They will surely have to make meaningful use of the incredible array of performing and creative talent that this country now wastes—like some unconserved natural resource. It will be necessary to rethink the problem of creation-performance-audience, the role of live music and the role of technology, the question of active and passive participation. It will be essential to discard the notion of the art work as consumer goods and to redefine the relationship of music—and of all sorts—to society. In all this, creative expression will have to play the leading role. Whether the highest forms of such expression can come into being without the needed institutions, or whether (as has happened in the past) they can help create these institutions, remains to be seen. I prefer to be optimistic and to get back to work.

Bibliography

Changes taking place in twentieth-century music are treated in Ralph Alan Dale, "The Future of Music: An Investigation into the Evolution of Forms." *Journal of Aesthetics and Art Criticism*, 26, no. 4 (Summer, 1968); Richard F. French, "The Dilemma of the Music Publishing industry," in Paul Henry Lang, ed., *One Hundred Years of Music in America (New York, Schirmer, 1961); Wolf-Eberhard von* Lewinski, "Where Do We Go from Here? A European View," *The Musical Quarterly*, 55 (April, 1969); Leonard B. Meyer, *Music, the Arts and Ideas* (Chicago, University of Chicago Press, 1967), which contains a valuable bibliography; Kurt Stone, "Problems and Methods of Notation," *Perspectives of New Music*, 1, no.2 (Spring, 1963); and Edgar Wind, "The Mechanization of Art," in *Art and Anarchy*, (New York, Knopf, 1963), reprinted in Vol. 2 of *Readings in Art History*, Harold Spencer, ed. (New York, Scribners, 1969). Articles will no doubt continue to appear in future issues of such periodicals as *Perspectives of New Music* and the *Journal of Aesthetics and Art Criticism*.